160°

Sandwich
Islands
Mission
A.B.C.F.M. 1820)

Hawaii

The dates refer to the arrival of missionaries/teachers or, in exceptional cases, to the
independent adoption of Christianity.

A.B.C.F.M.	American Board of Commissioners for Foreign Missions
H.E.A.	Hawaiian Evangelical Association
L.M.S.	London Missionary Society
W.M.M.S.	Wesleyan Methodist Missionary Society succeeded by Australasian Wesleyan Methodist Missionary Society in 1855.

0°

L
Y
N
E
S
I
A

Rakahanga
(1849)

Tongareva (1854)

Manihiki (1849)

Marquesas
Islands

Manihi

Takaroa

Tuamotu

Society
Islands

Faaite

Anaa
(1821)

Archipelago

Cook
Islands

20°

Rurutu (1821)

Rimatara (1822)   Tubuai (1822)

Mangareva (1832)

Austral
Islands

Raivavae (1822)

Pitcairn

Rapa (1825)

160°   140°

Messengers of Grace

Rev. Thomas Haweis
chaplain to the Countess of Huntingdon and
'Father' of the South Sea Mission

NIEL GUNSON

Messengers of Grace

EVANGELICAL MISSIONARIES IN
THE SOUTH SEAS
1797-1860

1978

Melbourne
OXFORD UNIVERSITY PRESS
Oxford   Wellington   New York

Oxford University Press

OXFORD   LONDON   GLASGOW

NEW YORK   TORONTO   MELBOURNE   WELLINGTON

IBADAN   NAIROBI   DAR ES SALAAM   LUSAKA   CAPE TOWN

KUALA LUMPUR   SINGAPORE   JAKARTA   HONG KONG   TOKYO

DELHI   BOMBAY   CALCUTTA   MADRAS   KARACHI

First published 1978

NATIONAL LIBRARY OF AUSTRALIA CATALOGUING IN
PUBLICATION DATA

Gunson, Walter Niel.
   Messengers of grace.

   Index.
   Bibliography.
   ISBN 0 19 550517 4.

   1. Protestant churches — Missions.   2. Missions —
   Oceanica — History.   I. Title.

226.023099   *BV3670.G93x*

This book has been published with the
assistance of the Research School of
Pacific Studies and the Republic of
Nauru Fund of the Australian National
University.

TYPESET BY DUDLEY KING PTY LTD, MELBOURNE
PRINTED AND BOUND AT GRIFFIN PRESS LIMITED, ADELAIDE
PUBLISHED BY OXFORD UNIVERSITY PRESS, 7 BOWEN CRES., MELBOURNE

PRINTED IN AUSTRALIA

Contents

APPENDICES

List of Illustrations

MAPS

Glossary

RELIGIOUS LABELS

ANTINOMIAN   Person believing that justification by faith abrogates the moral law; used as term of denigration for one who justifies moral lapse by claiming that God has withheld grace.

ARMINIAN   General follower of Jacobus Arminius (1560-1609) whose view of predestination emphasized the role of free will in the attainment of grace, a view adopted by the Wesleyans and also by some Anglicans and Dissenters.

CALVINIST   General follower of John Calvin (1509-1564), believing in both predestination to grace and damnation.

moderate Calvinist: follower of Calvin with a liberal view of predestination as outlined by a school of early nineteenth century commentators.

hyper-Calvinist: follower of Calvin with an extreme view of predestination; a subscriber to the 'five points' of the Synod of Dort.

CHURCHMAN   Supporter of the Anglican establishment.

CONNEXION   Preachers and societies attached to a particular Methodist leader, originally as members of the Church of England, e.g. Wesleyan Connexion, Countess of Huntingdon's Connexion, Tabernacle Connexion.

DISSENTER   Person dissenting from the principles of the Church establishment in England and penalized by the Test Acts until 1828; commonly called a Nonconformist. Early Methodists regarded themselves as Churchmen but members of the various Connexions became Dissenters by law.

EVANGELICAL   Person subscribing to the doctrines of the Evangelical Revival (whether Churchman, Dissenter or Methodist) more generally used of the Calvinists; and name of a party in the Church of England.

METHODIST   Follower of a Methodist leader, viz. Wesley, Whitefield, Howell Harris and the Countess of Huntingdon; but generally applied to the Wesleyans in the nineteenth century.

PURITAN   Person who stood for reform of the Church of England in the sixteenth and seventeenth centuries and, by extension, a clergyman ejected from an English living in 1662 or his Presbyterian/ Independent follower. 'Puritan' was coterminous with 'seceder' in Evangelical literature.

WESLEYAN   Follower of John Wesley; Methodist subscribing to Arminian doctrine.

POLYNESIAN TERMS

BURE ATUA — Tahitian expression recorded by the missionaries for Christian converts or 'praying people'.

LOTU — Noun and verb, used principally in Tonga, Samoa and Fiji, and later widely used in Melanesia, to denote religion, or to adopt religion, usually the Christian religion.
lotu Tahiti: LMS teaching.
lotu Tonga: Wesleyan Methodism.
lotu Pope: Roman Catholicism.

MANA — A term used in Polynesia to denote an energy or force present in matter (especially persons) to a greater or lesser degree synonymous with power; that which gives prestige; the same term in Melanesia refers to a similar power external to persons which can be manipulated by propitiation of the ancestors or spirits.

MARAE — Polynesian site for religious and political assemblage; in Tahiti always an elevated stone structure; frequently translated as temple.

TAPU — Noun and verb, used in Polynesia in relation to restrictions on human activities or contact with 'sacred' objects where *mana* was involved.

TUTAE AURI — Tahitian expression adopted by the missionaries meaning 'excretion (from) iron' or 'iron (like) excreta', used to describe the young people who threw off the restraints of mission teaching.

Preface

MESSENGERS OF GRACE is a study of the first three generations of Protestant missionaries to penetrate the South Seas. The text closely follows my doctoral thesis submitted to the Australian National University, though a certain amount of interpolation, excision and rearrangement was necessary for publication. While the work is essentially intended to provide students of Pacific and missionary history with an analytical account of the first successful missionaries in the Pacific islands, the story should also interest those who make no claim to specialist knowledge.

The work of missionaries has an important place in the history of the South Seas. Missions have played a significant role in directing much of the current thinking of the South Sea islanders, and the traditions of Christian teaching have become as fully a part of the ideological background as the traditions of their own culture. Although the degree to which Christianity has affected the traditional ways of life varies from group to group, and from island to island, the total effect of Christianity has been to minimize the sanctions of the past, even if at times it has failed to exalt the spiritual authority of Christ.

The historian is not necessarily concerned with the moral problem of the 'rightness' of missionaries being sent to non-Christian countries. He is more concerned with the success or failure of the missionaries to do what they set out to do, and with their management of the problems arising from their contact with other peoples and other ways of life. He must, before all, record change. The change that had taken place before 1860, in eastern Polynesia, was in most cases only half a change — a new culture had been grafted on to the old; indeed in some instances it appeared that the old ways had merely been re-oriented. It is the purpose of this study to show something of the mentality of the missionaries who sought to change the social systems of the South Seas.

Two general points should be made about the role of the Evangelical missionary. The first is the development of a new mentality in the countries from which the missionaries came and in the islands. We see in the sub-culture created by the mission families the growth of a spirit similar to that Evangelical zeal which took the missionaries to the field. This spirit, reinjected into the culture of the countries from which the missionaries came, has served as a powerful stimulus to progress. A number of

1

distinguished and influential people in England, Australia and the United States, including administrators, educators and artists, derive immediately from the mission families.

Second, the impact of the Evangelical missionaries often provided the quickest way to self-assertion by the native peoples. In the world of culture conflict, which is in a sense the world of Evangelical religion, the islander was given a plank to support himself in the tide of new concepts. Wherever that plank was grasped, the islander's potential for self-assertion was increased.

The missionaries examined in this study are described as 'Evangelical'. Mission historians, such as Gustav Warneck, have previously used the term 'Evangelical' to distinguish Protestant missionaries from Catholic ones. In a broad sense, ecclesiastical writers frequently distinguish between evangelicals and conservatives when outlining the history of a particular denomination. However I have used the term in its more strictly theological sense, as applied to Anglicans and Dissenters alike.* The missionary movements with which this study is concerned stemmed from the Evangelical or 'Methodist' movement of the eighteenth century. The great missionary societies were the direct outcome of the preaching of the revivalists Whitefield and Wesley. There were also certain definite doctrinal and methodistical characteristics associated with Evangelicalism. First and foremost there was the preaching of the atonement, the doctrine of the cross; there was an emphasis on the eternal peril of the soul; and there was an emphasis on the propagation of the Bible. Likewise the missionaries were Evangelicals in that their sentiments were those which were promulgated from Exeter Hall, meeting place of the great philanthropic and reform societies, and which played such an important role in the shaping of British home and colonial policy during the nineteenth century.

The term 'Puritan' has been purposely avoided, as it was resented by the Evangelicals of the Church of England and by the various Methodist 'connexions' who themselves defined the Puritan as being essentially a dissenter from the Church of England. However, in most respects, Evangelical doctrine is essentially Puritan doctrine. The Reverend S. C. Damon used the

---

*On this point see Reynolds, 1953, pp. 1-4; A. S. Wood, 1957, pp. 12-14. I have ignored the more restrictive theological use of the word, current at the beginning of the nineteenth century, as a synonym for 'Calvinist'. Wesleyan missionary candidates were excluded by the LMS because they were not 'Evangelical'.

term 'Puritan' to cover all the Protestant missions in the Pacific in his time, but he admitted that he was stretching the term.[1]

In my preliminary investigations into the background and motivation of Protestant missionaries in the Pacific, carried out mainly from published sources at the University of Melbourne in 1954,[2] it became necessary not only to investigate the doctrinal evolution of Calvinism but also to explore the complex history of the Calvinistic Methodists. Despite their very considerable impact on English church life, the Calvinistic Methodists are still neglected by serious social historians. While Wesleyan Methodism in the eighteenth century has a voluminous and critical literature the equally significant Calvinist wing of the Revival must be studied from fragmented sources. Although much of this doctrinal background material has been omitted here, it is essential to emphasize the interaction of social and doctrinal forces if only to counterbalance the purely theological interpretations of much current missiological writing. Fortunately, some of the leading writers on missions are aware of the limitations of such interpretations. Dr Stephen Neill, formerly Professor of Missions in the University of Hamburg, has demonstrated the need to divest mission history of its ethnocentricity[3] while Dr Max Warren, in his Cambridge lectures, has paid me the compliment of citing my findings on the social origins of the missionaries.[4] By making plain the interaction of social, economic and doctrinal factors it has been possible for the missiologist, as well as the historian, to make useful generalizations.

This book does not claim to be a history of the various missions in the Pacific. Detail of a purely chronological and descriptive kind must be gleaned from the standard histories of the various societies, bearing in mind that so much of what passes for history is written specifically as religious propaganda.* Because of the restricted purpose of the author the reader can be deceived into drawing false conclusions simply because all has not been said. The Tahitian missionary historian, Davies, was well aware that

---

*Richard Lovett's first volume of *The History of the London Missionary Society 1795-1895* (London, 1899) followed earlier official histories by William Ellis, George Cousins and Silvester Horne. *The History of the Wesleyan Methodist Missionary Society* by G. G. Findlay and W. W. Holdsworth (London, 1921) similarly replaced the works of William Moister and others, though the Australasian story can also be learnt from James Colwell's *A Century in the Pacific* (Sydney, 1914). These works are supplemented by the many published biographies, memoirs and journals of individual missionaries.

some missionary narratives gave false impressions and he was determined to abide by more historical rules in his own writing. In a letter to the Reverend William Orme, whose writings in defence of the South Sea missions were a little too roseate, he denounced the propagandist authors:

> The doctrine of 'pious fraud' is hateful, let its abettors be who they may — nothing but truth will stand its ground at a future day. There is a way of stating things so as not to be false in itself, yet calculated to convey false impressions, to such as are inacquainted with all the circumstances.[5]

There has also been a tendency amongst missionary societies to single out a few individuals whom they have decked up in great glory, not satisfied only in making them saints or martyrs, but in publishing many popular accounts of them and in endeavouring to perpetuate their memory in ships and institutions. On the other hand, men of learned societies, anthropologists, historians and purely secular writers, have tended to eulogize certain missionaries whom they have believed to be apostles of a different light, of scientific methods and of learned curiosity. Hero-worship has a legitimate function in the inspiration of men, but the historian must be careful to place the heroes in their right perspective and to separate them from their mythology.

The unravelling of historical fact from the biased accounts of sectarian propaganda is not, of course, such a great problem when primary documentation for the period is both considerable and available. Besides the extensive body of missionary literature there are many general works which record the impressions of voyagers, travellers, officials and other observers. Most of those who came in contact with the missionaries either wrote glowing reports of their work or denounced them. Some were more carefully critical. The very existence of this wide coverage of published material ranging from pious appraisal to savage criticism means that most popular views of the missionaries and their contribution reflect one of these extremes. This study is an attempt to place the missionaries in historical perspective by returning almost exclusively to the original sources, the letters and diaries of the missionaries; I have tended to draw very little on the extensive published primary material. Much of the documentation has a vitality of its own which not only makes the historical enquiry real and satisfactory for us, but enables the scholar to obtain clearer insight into the character of the writer.

Consequently I have let the missionaries speak for themselves whenever possible.

There have been other problems of selection. With such a vast amount of material it has been necessary to take representative samples rather than concentrate on any one chronological sequence. Although a great number of islands were exposed to missionary influence before 1860, most of the problems related to missionary attitudes were common to the whole period. Some problems on which there is a body of controversial material, such as the non-acceptance of polygamy or of nativist reactions to Christianity, have been omitted. They are problems which require a degree of psychological or anthropological analysis outside the scope of this study. If at times the Tahitian mission seems to figure largely in the narrative, it must be borne in mind that this was the principal mission for the first thirty years, and that its history has a greater variety than that of the other fields. New Zealand and Hawaii, although both scenes of Evangelical missionary activity, have not been examined in any great detail, except for the purpose of comparison.

Considering what has previously been written about the Reverend J. M. Orsmond of Tahiti,[6] especially as his own Society cast doubts on his statements, perhaps some sort of defence or apology or even caution should be made for having frequently quoted his writings. Even his more devoted colleagues recognized that Orsmond's behaviour was often 'eccentric and imprudent', at times he appears to have suffered from mental ill-health, and his emotions often got the better of his judgement, yet despite all this he was a much misunderstood man, and his actions, even when not in line with those of his brethren, were consistent with the ideals he professed on becoming a missionary. Indeed, some of his most unexpected statements are corroborated by the more prosaic of the missionaries.

It would be impossible to express adequately my acknowledgements to everyone who has helped, particularly the many descendants of missionaries with whom I have had either personal contact or correspondence. Those who gave of their time or supplied manuscripts include Mrs Elma C. Andrews of Auckland, Mrs D. L. Riley of Canberra, Mr L. Lawry Waterhouse and Dr C. M. Churchward of Sydney (Waterhouse); Mrs M. A. Carnachan of Auckland, Mr Percy R. Henry (Henry and Orsmond); Mrs Dorothy Walton of Queensland (Crook); Mr Arthur E. Cadden, Miss Eleanor Cadden of Melbourne, Miss Gertrude Storey

(Bicknell); Miss Elsie M. Pratt of Sydney (Bicknell and Pratt); Mrs Clare Hall of Sydney (Hassall); Miss Etela Williams of Sydney (Williams); Miss Sadie Creagh and Mrs Dorothy S. Maynard of Sydney (Buzacott and Creagh). I am also indebted to Mr Hugh Williams of Hitchcock and Williams Ltd for allowing me to see a short history of the Hardie and Hitchcock families written by Mrs Ida Oswald.

My thanks to librarians and research officers are also given generously. Miss Mary Walker of the American Board of Commissioners for Foreign Missions and Miss Berenice Judd of the Hawaiian Mission Children's Society were informative correspondents. Miss Irene Fletcher, Librarian and Archivist of the Congregational Council for World Mission, has given me the benefit of her extensive knowledge of the LMS archives and has shown me many kindnesses. Her great interest in my work has given me encouragement and she has never failed to pass on news of discoveries and developments. I am grateful to the Reverend C. F. Gribble of Sydney for allowing me to use the Methodist Church collection housed at the Mitchell Library, and the Reverend Norman Cocks for allowing me to read Charter's journal and other manuscripts. The Reverend D.W. Farr, former acting Warden of Camden College, New South Wales, also came to my assistance with some additional papers once in the possession of the Reverend L. E. Threlkeld. While I am grateful for these personal contacts, I must also extend my thanks to the institutions they represent for permitting me to quote from their records. In this context I would also like to thank the trustees of the Mitchell Library and the National Library of Australia. Mrs Pauline Fanning of the National Library and Miss Margaret McDonald, formerly of the Mitchell Library, were particularly helpful when this book was being written.

The Australian National University made possible my visit to Fiji and the Gilbert and Ellice Islands in 1957. The experience gained on this trip was invaluable. The Congregational Council for World Mission (then LMS) generously allowed me to travel on the *John Williams VI* and I received much help and co-operation from the various missionaries throughout the islands and stations visited. My year in London was made possible by the generosity of the British Council. A field trip to the Society Islands and Hawaii (to attend the 10th Pacific Science Congress) in 1961 was of considerable importance in my understanding of the missionary situation. For this visit I owe thanks to Professor Gordon Greenwood and the University of Queensland.

A very personal debt of gratitude is felt towards those scholars in other places who have been working on various aspects of South Seas history bearing on this subject. The late Mr R. A. Derrick of Suva, Dr G. L. Lockley of Brisbane and Dr Allan Tippett have given me assistance at various times. Father Patrick O'Reilly, Dr Bengt Danielsson, Dr Aarne Koskinen and Professor G. S. Parsonson have shared with me their knowledge of sources. In Tahiti Mr Ralph Gardner White translated many documents which have given me a better understanding of the Tahitian viewpoint, and M. Henri Jacquier placed the archives of the Musée de Papeete at my service. Professor Gavan Daws, Mrs Judith Binney and Dr John Owens have shared with me their understanding of the environment of the missionary's dilemma. Dr Roland Oliver helped me in many ways during my postgraduate year at the School of Oriental and African Studies, London.

Lastly I must thank my colleagues over the years at the Australian National University. My debt to them is obvious. Dr Dorothy Shineberg first directed my thoughts to the exciting field of missions. Professor Derek Freeman, the late Mr R. P. Gilson, Professor H. E. Maude and Dr C. W. Newbury all contributed by discussion or indicated valuable sources. In more recent years I have had the benefit of discussing missionary themes with Professor R. G. Crocombe, Professor Gregory Dening, Dr David Hilliard, Mr Robert Langdon, Dr Hugh Laracy and Dr Sione Lātūkefu. Dr Walter Phillips and Professor Ian Breward suggested some useful amendments; Mrs Jennifer Terrell and Mrs Barbara Hau'ofa helped in reading the manuscript and I am grateful for their useful criticism. To Mrs Norah Forster my thanks are due for bibliographical assistance. I owe a great deal to the judgement, experience and invaluable criticism of the late Professor J. W. Davidson. A number of typists helped with drafts and correspondence over the years, particularly Mrs Anvida Lamberts. I much appreciate their expert work. Mr Hans Gunther was responsible for the excellent maps.

Niel Gunson
Australian National University

Prologue

Delightful scenes! ye southern isles!
Where yet a fruitful Eden smiles,
  And plenty flows around!
Your shores no beasts of prey infest,
Nor pois'nous creatures e'er molest,
  As if *un-curst* the ground!

Strange! that your *Swine* should not desire
To roll, like ours, in filthy mire,
  But choose a cleanlier rest!
But yet — unhappy still the place!
Immers'd in sin, a sensual race,
  Man wallows there — a beast!

All-hail! the gen'rous plan of love
(The spark descended from above
  That wak'd the sacred fire.)
'Tis yours, ye messengers of grace,
Who flew to help a ruin'd race,
  To raise them *from the Mire!*

IOTA, 'On reading that Hogs at Otaheite have not the custom of wallowing in the Mire', *Evangelical Magazine,* April 1801, p.176.

The Spread of Missionary Settlement: a chronological survey

UNTIL Magellan had crossed the Pacific in 1521, the islands of the great South Sea were unknown to the Christian world. Even St Thomas, the 'Apostle to the Indies', and his disciples had not gone beyond the Malabar coast. Then, with the dawning of the great age of Spanish and Portuguese exploration and exploitation, new apostles sought to extend the labours of St Thomas, entering the Pacific at first by way of the Indies, and also by way of the newly discovered Americas. These men were mostly Jesuits and Franciscans, who confined their attention to the South American coast and to those archipelagos contiguous to the Asian coast, particularly the Philippines and the Indies, where the Spanish and Portuguese had commercial interests. Spanish missionary activity did not extend beyond the Carolines and only one attempt was made to evangelize any of the islands farther eastward during the long history of Spanish contact, when two Spanish priests were settled in the district of Taiarapu in Tahiti in 1774, but they made no progress and abandoned their mission in 1775.[1]

The Dutch were as transient in their contact with the islands as the Spaniards, though their missionaries in the Indies nearly reached the Pacific in their eastward expansion, and already in the eighteenth century, before the principal Evangelical missionary societies had been formed in England or the Netherlands, these men were labouring in close proximity to the great island of New Guinea. In 1838 the Reverend John Williams of the London Missionary Society paid a tribute to a missionary of the Dutch Reformed Church who, seventy years before, had been 'eminently successful in his Missionary efforts in the Arafura Sea'.[2] The population of Kisar, near Timor, was then entirely Christian, and a large portion of the Aru islanders were Christian, having native pastors, school teachers and the Bible in Malay in Roman character. The Dutch missionaries, however, never penetrated the South Seas.

It was left to the discoveries and rediscoveries of the English voyagers of the eighteenth century, such as Wallis and Cook, to stimulate the interest of English Christians. At first only a humanistic and scientific curiosity was aroused, though Evangelical readers of Cook interpreted his statement on the likeli-

11

hood of settlement as a kind of challenge, believing that he implied that Christians were not sufficiently disinterested to labour
in such remote islands.[3] It was also typical of the rationalism of
the age that the view prevailed that the 'noble savage' was
sufficient unto himself, and would be spoilt by any kind of
change. It was only in the newly stimulated Evangelical circles,
both within and without the established Church of England, that
any concern was shown for the 'perishing heathen'.

Prominent amongst the Evangelicals interested in the South
Seas was the Reverend Thomas Haweis, chaplain to the Countess
of Huntingdon. A man of considerable influence, Haweis made
several attempts to establish missionaries in the islands.[4] A plan
to send a party with Bligh in 1791 was thwarted by the refusal of
the Bishop of London to ordain two of the missionaries — they
were not university men — notwithstanding the influence of
Wilberforce and the Reverend William Romaine. Another party
was quickly recruited but, according to Henry Bicknell, who
later went out in the *Duff* in 1796, the ship sailed without them.

The founding in 1795 of the Missionary Society (from 1818
officially known by its sub-title, the London Missionary Society)
in which Dr Haweis took a prominent part, gave him the opportunity he had always wished for, and it was largely his own personal influence and his liberal financial support that persuaded
the directors to establish their first mission in the South Seas. A
ship was purchased, the *Duff*, which, as to crew and company,
was far more saintly than the *Mayflower*. It took a complement
of thirty missionaries, several of whom were married, and four of
whom had received regular ordination, and established three
missions in 1797 at Matavai in Tahiti, at Tongatapu, and at
Tahuata in the Marquesas. The Tongan and Marquesan missions were short-lived, terminating in 1800 and 1799 respectively,
but the Tahitian mission, though temporarily abandoned in
1808, survived to become the nucleus of the LMS in the South
Seas, and between 1817 and 1822 European missionaries were
also established at Huahine, Raiatea, Borabora and Tahaa in the
Leeward Islands. Thus began the first sustained Christian missionary activity in the South Sea islands.

In New Zealand a similar Evangelical mission was established
by the Church Missionary Society at the Bay of Islands in 1814,
under the immediate direction of the Reverend Samuel Marsden.
Although Marsden has received his due in most things, his
biographers have not always acknowledged that it was his direction and policies which most influenced the Church, London
and Wesleyan Missionary Societies in the South Seas until 1826.

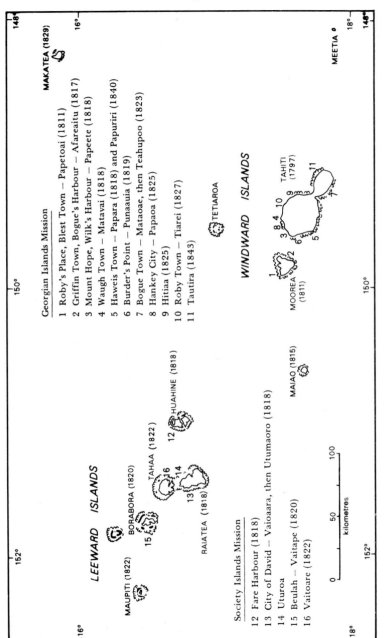

Georgian Islands Mission

1 Roby's Place, Blest Town — Papetoai (1811)
2 Griffin Town, Bogue's Harbour — Afareaitu (1817)
3 Mount Hope, Wilk's Harbour — Papeete (1818)
4 Waugh Town — Matavai (1818)
5 Haweis Town — Papara (1818) and Papuriri (1840)
6 Burder's Point — Punaauia (1819)
7 Bogue Town — Mataoae, then Teahupoo (1823)
8 Hankey City — Papaoa (1825)
9 Hitiaa (1825)
10 Roby Town — Tiarei (1827)
11 Tautira (1843)

Society Islands Mission

12 Fare Harbour (1818)
13 City of David — Vaioaara, then Utumaoro (1818)
14 Uturoa
15 Beulah — Vaitape (1820)
16 Vaitoare (1822)

Map 1 Society Islands (Georgian and Society Islands missions)

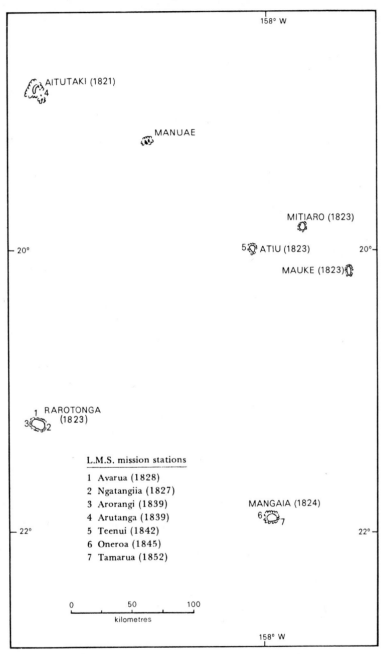

Map 2   Cook Islands (Hervey Islands mission)

As a director of the LMS he was principally responsible for the resumption of the Tahitian mission in 1811, and his work as agent of the society, though often thankless, was invaluable. It was Marsden also who first really divided the South Seas into Evangelical compartments. Had there not been his disinterested zeal at the outset, sectarian differences might have been emphasized and party quarrels taken earlier into the South Seas. Marsden himself took part in the opening of the Wesleyan mission in New Zealand during the years 1819 and 1822.

The LMS did not resume the Tongan mission, although one of the first missionaries, William Shelley, who served for some time in the Tahitian mission, never abandoned the idea of returning to Tonga himself. In 1807 he visited several of the islands, making observations on the suitability of establishing missions. In 1808 he sailed to England in order to obtain assistance in carrying out his plans. Marsden was also in England at the time, but both men were unable to influence the directors who, in Marsden's own words, 'for want of local knowledge and practical experience, were not able to appreciate the value of Mr. Shelley's communications to them'.[5]

Although Shelley was disappointed he visited the islands again in 1813, and decided to draw up all his observations for publication. On his final visit to Tonga Shelley left a European with the people to prepare for his return with his family, but he died shortly afterwards in 1815, and the European was brought back to Port Jackson.[6] But if Shelley was not able to return permanently to Tonga, his widow continued to advocate the resumption of the Tongan mission, and the arrival of the first Wesleyan missionary to Tonga (Reverend Walter Lawry) in 1822 was part of a continuous movement rather than an isolated attempt to found a new mission. Mrs Lawry herself was the daughter of Rowland Hassall, an old *Duff* missionary. Lawry, however, was forced to abandon the Tongan mission, owing to his own health and difficulties with the committee at home. Although supported by the committee, his effort was in many ways a private venture.

With the successful establishment of Protestant Christianity in Tahiti and the Society Islands the work of expansion in the direction of Tonga was taken over by agents from the young churches. As early as 1822 native missionaries from the church of Borabora were sent to Vava'u in the Tongan group. In 1826 Tahitian missionaries were sent to Lakeba in the Lau islands of the Fijian group, but they were detained at Tongatapu, and had begun an effective ministry there when the Wesleyan mis-

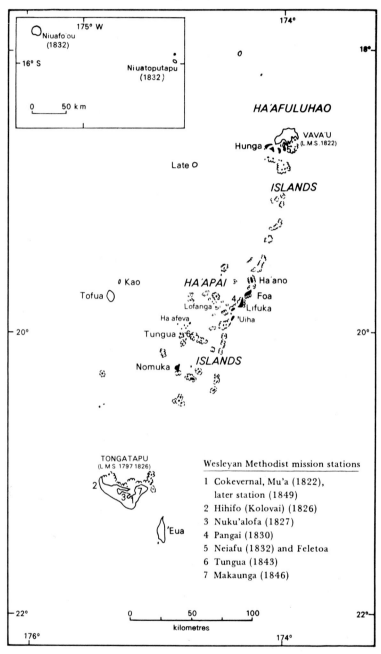

Map 3   Tonga (Friendly Islands mission)

sionaries recommenced their labours in 1826.* European missionaries settled at the Ha'apai and Vava'u islands in 1830 and in 1832. Teachers from these groups were almost immediately sent to Niuatoputapu, Niuafo'ou and Uvea (Wallis). At Uvea a civil war and the establishment of a strong Catholic mission resulted in the death of the Tongan teacher and the withdrawal of the Wesleyans.

In 1835 the Wesleyans extended their labours to Lakeba, which had first been entered by three Tahitian teachers in 1830. These teachers had been forced to leave Lakeba about 1832, but had been quite successful at Oneata, where they continued to labour until their deaths. Rotuma was also taken over from LMS native agents.

The Wesleyans also entered Samoa. This, unlike the entrance into most groups, began as a 'follow-up' movement, some influential Samoan families having embraced Christianity, both at Tonga and by means of Tongans living in Samoa. The first Wesleyan missionary, the Reverend Peter Turner, arrived from Tonga in 1835. As early as 1830 LMS native agents had been brought to Samoa. After the arrival of a large group of LMS missionaries in 1836 a bitter controversy about which mission should remain arose between the two societies. Although the Wesleyan missionaries reluctantly withdrew, the followers of the *lotu Tonga,* as the Wesleyan worship was called, refused to unite with the LMS. In this they were largely influenced by Samoan politics, the 'imperialistic' policy of the Tongan king, the self-interest of Tongan teachers, and perhaps the encouragement given by some of the Wesleyan missionaries in Tonga. The committee of the Australasian Wesleyan Methodist Missionary Society,† who took over the South Sea Missions in 1855, regarded the continued existence of a Wesleyan cause in Samoa since the late 1820s as sufficient reason for resuming the mission, and notwithstanding the various agreements between the two London societies the Australasian Conference sent a missionary (Reverend Martin Dyson) who arrived in Samoa in 1857.

Another early Evangelical missionary society to commence

*Although the Tongans appeared anxious to learn the 'rules' of Christianity, the inability of the Tahitian teachers to communicate in Tongan — although they had the help of Tongan chiefs who had lived in Tahiti and Tahitians living in Tonga — meant that they could do little more than introduce the outward form of worship and prohibit the more obvious pagan practices.

†This society was established by the Australasian Wesleyan Methodist Conference. The executive committee or 'Sydney board' consisted of the members of the general committee of the Society resident in New South Wales. See Rigg, 1863, pp. 181 ff.

work in the South Seas was the American Board of Commissioners for Foreign Missions. In 1820 a mission was established at the Hawaiian Islands. In the years immediately following, this mission was assisted by the Reverend William Ellis from the Society Islands mission and a band of Society Islands teachers. The ABCFM confined most of its labours to islands north of the line, but during 1833 and 1834 this society attempted to establish a mission in the northern Marquesas. It was not until 1851 that they turned their attention to the great ocean of islands known as Micronesia. Stations were commenced at Kusaie and Ponape in the Caroline Islands in 1852, at Ebon in the Marshall group in 1855, and at Abaiang in the northern Gilberts in 1857. In Hawaii a local missionary society was formed which reopened the Marquesan mission in 1853, and also sent ordained Hawaiians and catechists to Micronesia. The only European connected with the Marquesan venture was James Bicknell (afterwards ordained), a great-nephew of that Henry Bicknell who was to have come with Bligh.

There is little doubt that LMS native agents played an important role in the establishment of the Wesleyan missions at Tonga, Fiji and Rotuma, and of the American mission in Hawaii. Between 1820 and 1830 many other groups were opened up by these agents. Native teachers were early sent from the Society Islands churches to the Australs and the Tuamotus (Anaa and Rurutu, 1821; Raivavae, Tubuai and Rimatara, 1822; Rapa, 1825; Makatea, 1829; Mangareva, 1832). No LMS missionary resided on these islands before Lind went to Rurutu in 1852 and remained until 1855, although two German missionaries, belonging to Gossner's Society, spent several months on the same island earlier in 1852. However periodic visitations were made by senior missionaries to baptize converts and supervise the work of the teachers.

Native teachers went to Maiaoiti (Tupuaemanu) and to Maupiti in 1822. The Cook Islands were also evangelized from the Society Islands by native teachers (Aitutaki, 1821; Rarotonga, Mauke, Mitiaro and Atiu, 1823; Mangaia, 1824). European missionaries soon followed, the first arriving at Rarotonga in 1827. In 1825 the first native teachers were sent to the Marquesas, but they made little impression. They were still being sent when European missionaries from Tahiti arrived in 1834 to supplement the efforts of the Americans in the north. In 1841 this second mission was abandoned and no more attempts were made until the work was reopened by the Hawaiian Missionary Society, an offshoot of the ABCFM.

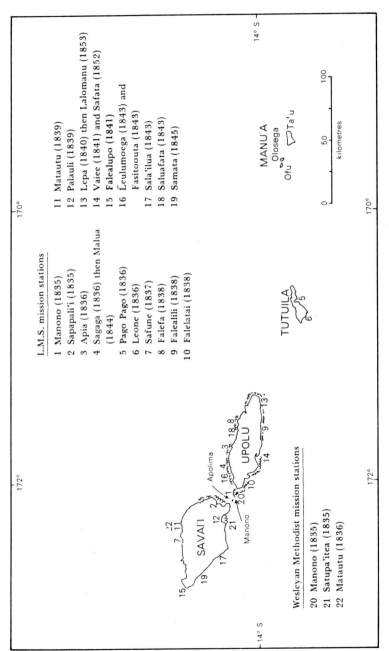

Map 4 Samoa (Navigator Islands or Samoa missions)

L.M.S. mission stations

1 Manono (1835)
2 Sapapali'i (1835)
3 Apia (1836)
4 Sagaga (1836) then Malua (1844)
5 Pago Pago (1836)
6 Leone (1836)
7 Safune (1837)
8 Falefa (1838)
9 Falealili (1838)
10 Falelatai (1838)

11 Matautu (1839)
12 Palauli (1839)
13 Lepa (1840) then Lalomanu (1853)
14 Vaiee (1841) and Safata (1852)
15 Falealupo (1841)
16 Leulumoega (1843) and Fasitoouta (1843)
17 Sala'ilua (1843)
18 Saluafata (1843)
19 Samata (1845)

Wesleyan Methodist mission stations

20 Manono (1835)
21 Satupa'itea (1835)
22 Matautu (1836)

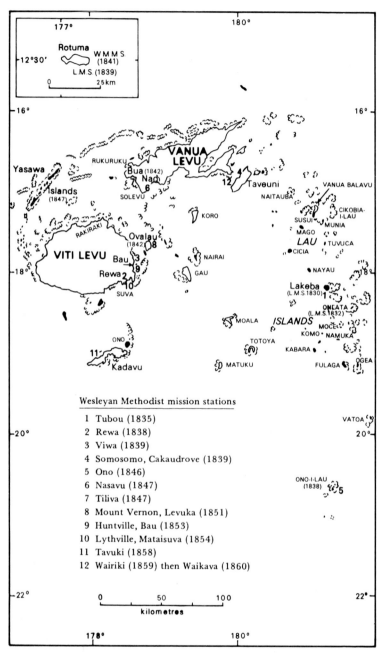

Map 5   Fiji (Feejee Islands or Fiji mission)

A new age of missionary pioneering began when the Reverend John Williams, the LMS missionary who had first taken teachers to Samoa, sailed westward to the 'dark' islands of Melanesia, and to his death. As early as 1839 teachers from amongst the Samoan converts of the LMS were sent to the southern Melanesian islands, then known as 'Western Polynesia'. They were joined in this pioneering work by Rarotongan teachers. Samoan missionaries also laboured (from 1839 to 1845) at Rotuma, which the Wesleyan Missionary Society occupied in 1841. The various islands of the southern New Hebrides group were entered in fairly quick succession (Tana, 1839; Eromanga and Aniwa, 1840; Aneityum and Futuna, 1841; Efate, 1845). However several attempts had to be made on some of them before missionaries could be permanently settled. For two years (1842-43) European missionaries actually resided on Tana, but the mission was not permanently established until 1854. Samoan and Rarotongan missionaries also pioneered the mainland of New Caledonia (1841-45), the Isle of Pines and the Loyalty Islands (Mare, 1841; Lifu, 1845; Tika, 1852; Uea, 1857), but the mission at New Caledonia was not resumed. There were no European missionaries resident in the Loyalty Islands until 1854.

During his visit to England (1834-38) John Williams appealed to the Presbyterian Churches for missionary support. He visited Scotland in October and November 1835, and stimulated interest in the South Seas as a mission field.[7] Judging by the reception accorded him by the United Secession Church, he believed that it would be possible for that body to support a mission to New Caledonia. He conferred with several ministers, and it was on the understanding that he should place native teachers on New Caledonia that £300 was placed at his disposal. However when the first independent Presbyterian missionary* arrived (Reverend John Geddie, sent by the Church of Nova Scotia) he was placed at Aneityum in the New Hebrides.

From 1840 onwards the Samoan mission of the LMS was anxious to see the 'Westward Islands' occupied by European missionaries. The Presbyterians were the first to respond to the encouragement of the Samoan mission and occupied the southern New Hebrides. On the other hand, New Caledonia and the Loyalty Islands, which had been the proposed 'site' for the Presbyterian mission, were for a time without a sponsor. The Samoan brethren attempted to interest the Church Missionary Society, as a kindred Evangelical body. The CMS does not appear to have reciprocated, and the LMS, rather than expose

---

*There were already Presbyterians amongst the LMS missionaries.

the ground which the Samoan missionaries had prepared to the 'Puseyite errors' of the Melanesian Mission, decided to retain the Loyalty Islands. This was facilitated by the decision of the Australian Congregational Churches (through the New South Wales auxiliary of the LMS) to support two missionaries.

It is interesting that the LMS missionaries at Samoa took such a definite stand against any missionary schemes which might be supervised directly by Bishop Selwyn of New Zealand, for whom they had a high personal regard, and with whom they corresponded in the most amicable way. Selwyn himself employed the greatest tact and diplomacy in dealing with them, and his counsel to the Reverend W. Nihill, whom he left on Mare because of his health, is a memorial to his good sense and his desire not to offend the religious susceptibilities of his Evangelical brethren on what was virtually their own territory. 'Even if the island were already ceded to us', he wrote, 'some discretion and tenderness would be necessary in altering the form of worship to which the native converts have been accustomed'.[8]

At meetings of the LMS missionaries in Apia between 1848 and 1852 resolutions were passed that the New Caledonian group should only be handed over to missionaries who were under the 'exclusive control' of the directors of the CMS, and Bishop Selwyn figured in the transaction simply as President of the Central Board of the CMS in New Zealand.[9] Although for a number of years Bishops Selwyn and Patteson visited most of the westward islands, they turned their attention more to the northern islands of the New Hebrides and to the Solomon Islands, where they eventually settled missionaries.

The island of Niue (Savage Island) was also evangelized from Samoa. Several abortive attempts were made, but nothing was effected until the settlement of a native teacher in 1846.

Although the islands to westward had attracted the attention of the Cook Islands mission, opportunities were taken quite early to send missionaries to the coral atolls immediately to the north. In 1849 a successful beginning was made at Manihiki and Rakahanga, and in 1854 and 1857 openings were secured at Tongareva (Penrhyn) and Pukapuka. An attempt was also made to land a Samoan teacher in the Tokelaus in 1858, but this group was not successfully entered till 1861. During the following decade mission work commenced in the Ellice Islands and the southern Gilberts, and to westward the great island of New Guinea was entered from the Polynesian side, so that it alone remained, a great pagan land situated between the old Dutch

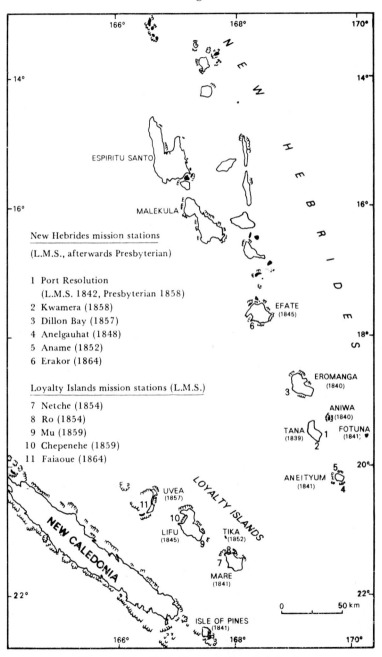

Map 6   New Hebrides and New Caledonia
(Western Polynesia and New Hebrides missions)

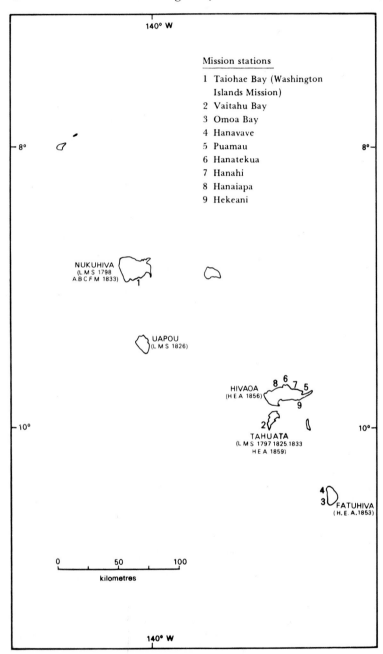

Map 7   Marquesas Islands
(Marquesas and Washington Islands missions)

Protestant influence and the new-awakened Protestantism which had so quickly crossed so many reefs.

Of the German Evangelical missionary societies, Gossner's Society* was the only one which sent representatives to the islands, although missionaries from the North German Missionary Society went to New Zealand. Gossner had agents in western New Guinea and the Chathams, but his missionaries to the Australs abandoned their station after only a few months' residence. However two of Gossner's former students were successful agents of the LMS.

In the pre-1860 period there was one major political event which disturbed the progress of Evangelical religion in the South Seas, and which, to the missionaries of that period, seemed to loom over them like a great tidal wave. This was the advent of the French, independent of, yet closely identified with, the missionary enterprise of the Catholic Propaganda. The major ecclesiastical effect of the French protectorate which was established at Tahiti was the 'establishment' of the Protestant religion. During the initial stages of the process, the LMS missionaries were recognized as pastors of the national church. However they were opposed to any connexion between Church and State, and maintained that the church members, not the governor or the chiefs, had the right to appoint pastors. In 1852 a majority of the missionaries resigned over this issue of conscience. Only two elderly missionaries, Davies and Darling, retained their stations. The Reverend William Howe continued as minister of the English church and as agent of the LMS at Papeete. The resignation of the missionaries virtually put an end to the effective labours of the LMS in Tahiti, and the French administration encouraged the appointment of Tahitian pastors rather than Europeans. Nevertheless Howe's ministry served as an important link between the LMS and the Société des Missions Evangéliques in Paris, which finally accepted the superintendence of the Protestant churches of Tahiti. Although Howe was one of those who sacrificed his Society's mission for his own particular ecclesiastical principles,† his consistency, and his courageous

*Johannes Evangelista Gossner (1773-1858), pastor of the Bethlehem Church in Berlin and a former director of the Berlin Missionary Society, founded his own society (*Gossnersche Missionsgesellschaft*) in 1836 on the principle that missionaries should be self-supporting. His agents, some of whom formed communities of pious artisans supervised by ordained men, worked independently or with the LMS or Presbyterian missions.

†Although these principles do not appear to be in exact harmony with the 'fundamental principle' of the LMS, it should be remembered that at this period these views would have been held by most of the supporters of the Society (Congregationalists), and that the missionaries themselves argued that Congregational principles had been adopted by the Tahitian Church.

stand against French governmental and Catholic episcopal intimidation, earned him wide respect, and was one of the principal factors in sustaining the Protestant Church at Tahiti.

The result of the French establishment of a national church was that distinct missionary societies were no longer recognized, and that disconnected missionaries were employed by the government to superintend the official church. Both Orsmond and Simpson (two missionaries dismissed by the LMS) were employed as successive 'directors' of the national church. Orsmond ordained pastors and superseded the LMS in every way. However, Howe and his colleagues had little esteem for an establishment which excluded the rights of Dissenters, and much of Howe's ministry was occupied with a struggle for religious freedom. Such questions as this did not arise in any of the other groups in this period, for the indigenous governments conformed to missionary standards.

Roman Catholic missionary activity recommenced almost thirty years after Protestantism had entered the South Seas. Proselytism was directed towards converts to Protestantism as much as to pagans. The Congrégation des Sacrés-Coeurs de Jésus et de Marie (SS CC), or Picpus Fathers, began their labours in Hawaii in 1827, where they came into conflict with the indigenous government and the American missionaries. They wished to establish themselves at Tahiti, and with this end in view began a mission at Mangareva in 1834. However it was not until 1841 that priests were permanently settled at Tahiti. Comparatively little headway was made by them, although under the protectorate, and after the resignation of the LMS missionaries, the priests and an order of Sisters were put in charge of many of the district schools. Catholicism advanced more successfully in the neighbouring islands of the Tuamotus, where priests were first established in 1849. As early as 1838 the Picpus Fathers entered the Marquesas, where they made some limited progress.

The other principal Catholic order in the South Seas in this period was the Société de Marie (SM). Just as Mangareva was established as the centre of Picpus influence, so Wallis (Uvea) became the centre of Marist influence. Both Wallis and Futuna were first entered in 1837. In 1838 a Catholic mission was established at Hokianga in New Zealand. The remaining groups of the Central Pacific were entered in quick succession (Tonga, 1842; Fiji, 1844; Samoa, 1845; Solomons, 1845; New Hebrides, 1848; Tokelaus, 1852). In the islands where Evangelical influence was firmly established the Marists made only isolated advances. In Wallis and Futuna, as at Mangareva, they were able to establish themselves in the semi-theocratic manner of the earlier Evangelicals. However they experienced considerable reverses in the more western Melanesian islands, particularly in the Solomons. A number of missionaries were killed, and in 1847 the Marists withdrew from the Solomons. A third society, the Istituto delle Missioni Estere di Milano (Foreign Missions of Milan), took over the work of the Vicariate of Melanesia and Micronesia in 1852. They continued the work begun by the Marists at Woodlark and Umboi near New Guinea, but the mission was withdrawn in 1855.

Another non-Evangelical organization, the Church of Jesus Christ of Latter Day Saints (Mormon Church), entered the South Seas in 1844, before that Church had been established at Salt Lake City. A Society Islands mission was established, complete with a high priest as president. Although the Mormons were unsuccessful at Tahiti, Raiatea and Borabora, they were able to establish themselves effectively at Tubuai and in the Tuamotus. Serious difficulties arose after the establishment of French authority in those islands, and the Mormons were obliged to leave. Some years later the Josephite or Reorganite Church (a breakaway Mormon group) attempted work in the same area.

Despite the presence of the Mormons and, especially, the Roman Catholic Church, the South Seas of the pre-1860 period was, apart from Mangareva and Wallis-Futuna, essentially Protestant and Evangelical. The islands of the South Seas experienced in full the extension work of the Evangelical Revival. Revival was not simply a quickening of an old faith, but 'true conversion', the 'rebirth of the new man', and to effect this spiritual rebirth was the principal object of all Evangelical missionaries. Their mission or vocation was to convince all men (in whatever state, all equally condemned) of their innate depravity, of their need for a saviour or mediation with God, and finally of belief in the atonement and the consequent salvation of believers.

After 1860 revivalism still played an important part in the Pacific mission field, but in Polynesia proper a new era of Christianity was dawning. In most of the groups European governmental influence was being felt, and the almost theocratic power of chiefs and missionaries was on the wane and no longer of such significance. New doctrine and new ideas were making themselves apparent. Moreover revivalism had achieved its great object: the destruction of the 'old man'. Strong churches had been built up in the islands, and the missionaries were now pre-occupied with combating secular influence. It is true that Melanesia was only in the first phases of Christianization and therefore less adaptable to revival techniques, but the missionary enterprise of 'Western Polynesia' was an outlet for the Evangelical activity of the missionaries and the Polynesian churches, just as Polynesia had attracted the Evangelicals from the beginning of the modern missionary era.

The American Board sent no more missionaries to the Hawaiian Islands after 1854. In 1855 the Australasian Conference undertook the direction of the Wesleyan missions in Tonga and Fiji. By 1860 the missionaries in Fiji had ceased to be the sole representatives of law and order, a British consul having been appointed in 1858, and already the British government was being reluctantly forced to consider the question of annexing Fiji. In 1862 the Protestant cause in Tahiti, which had been all but abandoned in 1852 by the LMS was taken up by the Paris society. In the period immediately after 1860, missionary history in the South Seas was dominated by the great figures of Shirley Baker, George Brown, James Chalmers and W.G. Lawes. A new missionary era had dawned, and the commencement of missions in eastern New Guinea fulfilled, at least in geographical terms, the dreams of the first missionaries.

This was the pattern of missionary activity in the South Seas, a gradual and quickening expansion from small but enthusiastic beginnings, predominantly Protestant, and revolutionary in its effect upon the culture and transformation of the island peoples. Before we can analyse the impact of these missionaries and study the influence of their ideas it is necessary to examine their social and doctrinal background, to probe the theological thought which conditioned their actions, and to delineate the economic and social environment which nurtured and shaped these ideas.

PART ONE

The Missionary in the Making

The Gospel when preached by Missionaries holding Arminian sentiments has been made equally instrumental in raising the degraded Heathen, and bringing them to the saving knowledge of the true God, as when administered by the followers of Calvin. And the divine sanction with which the labours of each have been thus honoured has afforded demonstration that, notwithstanding their differences of opinion on some points, both hold the great and vital and saving doctrines of the Gospel.

Wesleyan Methodist Magazine (1834), p. 201

1

A Set of Tinkers

AT THE END of the eighteenth century and at the beginning of the
modern mission era the social positions of the missionary and
his South Sea subject were the reverse of what they would become
by the mid nineteenth century. As far as polite society was
concerned, unless perhaps in the salon of a Countess of Huntingdon or a Lady Anne Erskine, the missionary was thought of as a
kind of tinker, who, as the Reverend Sydney Smith described
him, could not look a gentleman in the face. This view was
emphasized by those most opposed to missions. Jorgen Jorgensen,
the Danish adventurer, said that no great discernment was
required to see that the missionaries at Tahiti were 'selected
from the dregs of the people'. 'They are deficient in address, and
their behaviour is timid without being respectful. They look
somewhat like humble petitioners at a gentleman's door, and it is
easy to observe that they are men of no education, nor have ever
conversed with any but the lowest classes of society.'[1] Similarly,
Thomas Elley, the British vice consul at Tahiti (1826-27), is
said to have represented the missionaries to the Tahitians as 'a
Set of Tinkers having no bread to eat in England'.[2]

On the other hand, although somewhat of a curiosity, the
South Sea islander was regarded as the epitome of the natural
man, a 'noble savage' and fit companion for a king. The celebrated Omai was a lion in English society, and was received as a
house guest in homes where many of the missionary candidates
would have eaten with the servants.

With few exceptions the bulk of the Evangelical missionaries
to the South Seas belonged to the lower middle classes. Even if
their origins were sometimes very humble, they were quickly
drawn into the middle classes, because they began to acquire
skills and began to save, and because they cultivated middle-class
attitudes. They were not content to remain labourers. Techni-
cally, the best word with class connotations to describe the missionaries is a word which has now lost its nineteenth-century
meaning, the word 'mechanic'. The early nineteenth century
was very much the age of the mechanic class, the latest addition

to the lower ranks of the middle classes. It was from the 'godly mechanics' that most Evangelical missionaries were drawn.

Several of the poems of the Sheffield poet, Ebenezer Elliott, illustrate the life of the industrious mechanic extremely well.

> You seek the home of taste, and find
> The proud mechanic there,
> Rich as a King, and less a slave,
> Throned in his elbow-chair:
> Or on his sofa reading Locke,
> Beside his open door:
> Why start?— why envy worth like his
> The carpet on his floor?[3]

In this verse, and indeed in the scant literature which we possess on the domestic life of the mechanic class, we see very clearly the results of a desire to 'better oneself'. The goal of respectability, so long the prerogative of the middle classes of the seventeenth and eighteenth centuries, was postulated as an ideal for those who had been less fortunate in their birth but who had the character to rise above their origins. In one sense the Evangelical Revival was responsible for this social emancipation of the lower classes. Evangelical religion had a greater appeal to the labouring man and simple artisan than had the Puritan 'revival' to the 'lower orders'.

Thus, at the beginning of the nineteenth century we find a social class of humble origin which was already distinguishing itself from those who had not made the move upwards in the social hierarchy. 'Respectability' became a much more important distinguishing mark than wealth, and a certain measure of independence was aimed at. Throughout the first half of the century the education and enlargement of the mechanic class was nurtured by the establishment of various social institutions such as school societies, tract societies and mechanics' institutes. These aimed not only at teaching mechanics the rudiments of education but at giving them the benefits of higher learning. Lectures given at mechanics' institutes were often comprehensive and of high standard. Popular magazines which disseminated scientific and polite knowledge did much to form the character of the new class. Special handbooks to polite behaviour were written, such as Mrs Ellis's* series on 'the Women of England'. Because this section of society was so close to its origins, it appears to have been particularly class-conscious.

---

*Sarah Stickney, Quaker poetess and second wife of the missionary and director William Ellis.

In another verse of 'The Home of Taste', Ebenezer Elliott laments:

> Oh lift the workman's heart and mind
> Above low sensual sin:
> Give him a home: the home of taste:
> *Outbid* the house of gin!

Elliott was primarily a social poet, a Radical who was not given to uttering devotional piety, and hence his evidence is of considerable value. It shows that the genius of the mechanic class was not wholly Evangelical. It was this desire to 'outbid the house of gin', to escape from the shackles of social bondage, which gave so much zeal and vigorous character to the new class. We see this same drive translated into the doctrine of reparation, the attempt by the Calvinist missionary to atone for the past, for the period of 'hopelessness' before his conversion (see page 49). Often this period of being enslaved to nature was painted in lurid colours because of the intensity of the mental conflict experienced by the convert. Greater force is given to this doctrine when placed in the social context.

The social doctrine of reparation was closely akin to the religious doctrine and, no doubt, the two were often simultaneous reactions. The mechanic resented his past subservience to all forms of tyranny symbolized by King Gin, one of the greatest of the social evils of the eighteenth century. His reaction, always with an eye to economy, tended to be one of abstinence; and self-discipline became a test of membership of the new class. The great teetotal movement of the 1830s was one of the characteristic features of this era.[4]

The emphasis of the Revivalists on the right use of time and on stewardship was naturally compatible with the attempt to move into another social scale. Men accepted their social vocation very much as a task imposed by a higher religious discipline. If a man was a steady, industrious worker he might be regarded as one favoured in the sight of the Lord, and his outward well-being, provided he had faith, would show that he had attained the perseverance of the saints. Religion, in being applied to business life, had come to make rules for it. The effect of this doctrine of the calling on the missionaries was not only to confirm them in their own vocation but to give them a more exalted opinion of the dignity of labour and the rightness of trade. It gave them the feeling that material prosperity would be both conducive to good living and a proof of spiritual progress.

Intimately connected with the idea of the particular calling was the idea of the particular account, the belief that each man must answer for himself how he has carried out his work and how he has used his talents. The doctrine of personal responsibility was one of the social views most prevalent amongst Dissenters, and was also one of the leading social features of the Revival. Men were concerned about the right use of money and also the right use of time. Idleness was one of the greatest moral evils to those who held the stewardship view.

To the Evangelical the business of life is the salvation of the soul. It has been pointed out that salvation involves 'God's service in perfect obedience to His Will, and of this industrial and commercial concerns are a part.'[5] The pursuit of industry and trade was thus sanctified. All aspired to that middle station of life — 'the upper station of low life' which Robinson Crusoe's father had found 'by long experience, was the best state in the world, the most suited to human happiness.' The social views of the Evangelical shopkeeper were of an utilitarian nature: a man's worth was in his 'usefulness', an institution's worth was in its 'usefulness'. Henry Brooke, the Methodist mystic, was but one exponent of this view. 'Nothing is truly estimable', he said in his eulogy of the merchant, the manufacturer and the tiller, 'save in proportion to its utility'.[6] The utilitarianism of Bentham and Mill was aligned with the social teaching which the Evangelicals discerned in the scriptures. Like the Puritans and Pietists of previous eras, they tended to make the best of two worlds, endeavouring to separate themselves from the 'wasteful' uses of their surplus wealth. Wealth was reinvested or went to charitable causes.

The Evangelicals were thus encouraged to mould their environment according to their own convictions. Rarely could any society withstand the onslaught of their social ethic, which had all the force of a class struggle. It had no mean influence in encouraging missionary activity, exemplified in the desire to convert one's associates and to reform one's trade. A story is told of John Hall, the father-in-law of the Reverend Charles Tucker of Tonga, in this connexion.[7] When Hall's father told him that he was to be apprenticed to a glazier he protested that the trade was 'not respectable'. His father's reply to this was that it was for him to *make* the trade respectable. Hall believed himself to have achieved this when he could speak of his firm's 'various branches of extended business and its great prosperity'.

The psychology of the new mechanic was a factor in shaping the attitudes of the Evangelical missionaries. The mechanic class had, like the Puritans, 'separated' itself from among its brethren.

It was an artificial class in that it was distinguished largely by its way of life and not by economic differences. It existed as a kind of 'better half' to its neighbours, and in some degree of conscious contrast. Like most intermediary classes it required a lower class which acted alternately as recruiting ground and place of contrast. This *need* for a lower class was part of the psychology of Evangelical missionaries who substituted the 'poor heathen' for the 'lower orders'.

It is an interesting commentary on their social origins that a number of tales have been fostered in their families which endeavour to conceal their derivation from the new mechanic class. There is no evidence to support the claim that Crook, the 'gentleman's servant', was the son of a French émigré count. The story was not circulated during Crook's lifetime, and Crook is an old Devonshire name. The Waterhouse family, so prominent in Wesleyan missions, maintained that they were originally French and were called 'de Waterhouse'.[8] Family tradition also affirms that Orsmond, a carpenter, was the son of a French priest and a Spanish countess (they eloped and came to England), but this was no more authentic than the Crook tradition.[9] One finds it difficult to believe that such distinguished parents would confer the second name of 'Muggridge' on the son of their strange union. Furthermore, the legends surrounding Orsmond's second wife, Isabella Nelson, suggest a romantic attempt to cover up convict origins. Instead of being proud of the emancipist Isaac Nelson, who was one of the first school teachers in New South Wales, some past member of the family created the vague figure of Isaac Nelson, Surveyor-General of New South Wales (there was none by that name) and his wife, Lady Sarah Stanley, daughter of an Earl of Derby.

The social origins of the missionaries themselves reveal the various stages of the rise in the social scale by way of the mechanic class. The LMS engaged 108 recognized missionaries in the South Seas up to and including the year 1860 (see Appendix IV). Only two of these came out and did not remain. In addition to these men there were almost as many wives, who usually regarded themselves as being missionaries, together with their adult children, who often helped their parents until they obtained positions for themselves or were sent to England or Australia. Likewise there were a number of expatriate Europeans who did voluntary mission work connected with this Society.

Of the 108 missionaries, over seventy were ordained as pastors and used the designation 'Reverend'. These included sixty-four men (one a surgeon) who were sent out ordained; two mechanic missionaries, two printers and one 'assistant missionary' who were ordained in the islands; and several mechanic missionaries who regarded their original charge as being equivalent to ordination, and consequently assumed pastoral duties and the designation 'Reverend' when churches had been formed under their auspices. 'As to our designation or ordination, for the words are of the same import', wrote William Henry, 'I consider it one of the most solemn that ever took place since the days of the Apostles'.[10] Most of the remaining missionaries were regarded as mechanic missionaries, three were described as missionary artisans, one was a surgeon, another was a printer and two were teachers. There was also an 'assistant missionary' who was not ordained. The ordained men were sent out for the express purpose of instructing the people amongst whom they were to live in the principles of Christianity. The mechanic missionaries were also expected to instruct the people in their own particular skills. Some critics have felt that the occupations of some of the first mechanic missionaries were quite out of place in the South Seas. What, for instance, was the purpose served in sending out a tailor or a hatter? But this was not really the case. These men were hand-picked because of their basic Christian experience and zeal. Although as mechanics they each possessed individual skills, it was assumed that these skills were fairly readily acquired. It was also assumed that these mechanics would benefit from one another's experience. Furthermore, the 'godly mechanics' of the LMS went out on a different footing from those whom Marsden employed as mechanics in the service of the CMS or those whom the LMS sent out expressly as missionary artisans. These 'godly mechanics' were expected to teach and act as catechists, and it was from these men that the pastors of the first Tahitian churches were drawn. On the other hand, most of the mechanics employed by Marsden had specific trades to teach to the Maoris.[11] Although some of these men were catechists, they were intended originally to 'civilize' the Maoris, on the assumption that civilization would facilitate the introduction of Christianity. The LMS believed rather that evangelization was the most important thing, and that civilization would inevitably follow in its wake. Thus, missionary artisans *as such* were not sent out until after the nominal Christianization of Tahiti and the other Society Islands.

It was the large Calvinistic Methodist party among the directors which virtually insisted on the engagement of 'godly mechanics' as missionaries. The Reverend Rowland Hill and an influential minority believed that 'the best education for missionaries was NONE AT ALL', and that 'the next best was that which consists in teaching them to make wheel-barrows and plant turnips'.[12] Haweis himself observed:

> A plain man, — with a good natural understanding, — well read in the Bible, — full of faith, and of the Holy Ghost, — though he comes from the forge or the shop, would, I own, in my view, as a missionary to the heathen, be infinitely preferable to all the learning of the schools; and would possess, in the skill and labour of his hands, advantages which barren science would never compensate.[13]

However in his 'Memoir' he observed: 'We hope to obtain some, who are not destitute of letters, and education, but the greater number we expect from the inferior classes of life'.[14] For him 'vital godliness' was the first qualification. It was believed that, given grace, a man could be miraculously filled with a sufficient knowledge of God.

The critics of this system were not confined to the 'Presbyterian' academicians. Some of the Anglican Evangelicals interested in the Society looked with considerable suspicion on an enterprise which was predominantly artisan in character. Melvill Horne, for instance, disapproved of the large proportion of 'pious Mechanics' to ministers in the Tahitian mission in 1796 and urged against 'a new levy of irregular troops'. His social views are clearly revealed in a letter to the Reverend Samuel Greatheed.

> Allowing for those exceptions which are to be found to almost every general rule, I have remarked a strong line of characteristic difference between the Xtian Laity & their Ministers. The same wch. exists between regulars & a militia, or in animals between War Horses, Hunters & Racers & inferior breeds. Where J. Xt calls a man to the Ministry, he gives to the man the *heart of a Minister* — something of the zeal & authority, the disinterestedness & courage, the affection & patience, the willingness to spend & be spent in the work wch. is so strongly exemplified in St. Paul, & wch. we seldom find in a similar degree in the laity. . . . I fear M^r. Haweis & other Directors of weight among you seem too much disposed to rest the cause on inferior characters. Surely, the work calls, I do not say for learning, but for large minds, clear heads, souls enflamed with ardent love to the cause of Xt & of Souls & who esteem it their peculiar calling, to lay down their lives for the gospel. Are such minds, heads, hearts often to be found among men engaged in low mechanic Arts?[15]

Zachary Macaulay likewise implied criticism of the social origins of those missionaries who were prevented from reaching Tahiti by the capture of the *Duff* on its second voyage.[16] These included several ordained ministers of humble origin, some India House porters and a former footman to Wilberforce. The wife of one minister had been 'a Potgirl to an ale house' but became a bunting weaver after marriage. Most were regarded as 'ignorant', 'conceited' and 'proud'. One wife was described as 'vulgar low bred and indelicate'. Of those missionaries who eventually reached Tahiti most were described as 'silly and ignorant'. Youl was labelled 'ignorant conceited and assuming'. In evaluating Macaulay's assessment, one must take into account that he was obviously incensed by reports that many of the missionaries were 'violent' in their politics and actually wore the French cockade, and that both he and Horne attributed the failure of the 'Fowlah Mission' to the 'utter unfitness' of the mechanic missionaries.

It has been generally assumed that the first missionaries sent to the South Seas by the LMS were of an 'inferior' type to those later sent out. This opinion was based largely on the fact that the majority of them were not ordained and had not received any particular missionary training, and was strengthened by the comments of the Reverend Samuel Marsden who had cause to criticize several of the less worthy missionaries (see page 65). However it would appear that the first missionaries came from the same cross-section of the lower middle and mechanic classes from which a large proportion of missionaries or their parents were drawn throughout the period. Nor does it appear that the missionaries of either the Wesleyan or Church Societies differed very greatly from those of the LMS in class composition. Unlike the missionaries of the later-formed Melanesian Mission, most of the Church missionaries were men of comparatively humble origin. Family connexions between members of the LMS and the CMS were not uncommon in the early years.[17]

The first missionaries of the *Duff* and the *Royal Admiral* suffer by comparison with the later brethren because they did not have the advantages of a course of missionary study and because the Society sent them out in special clothing which robbed them of the status to which they aspired. One of them wrote angrily to the directors in 1801:

> You have actually denied us the things which are necessary for maintaining respectability and insuring success. . . . What has a greater tendancy to refine, and make a people engaging in their manners (a thing so necessary in a missionary) than polite company and was it to be expected, that we would find admission into any such, when no better dressed than common Seamen. Your own Missionaries paid money out of their own Pockets, to the Taylors, and had their Clothes better than you allowed, but Mr. Scott and I knew nothing of this measure, nor of its necessity till we were at Sea. We were kept in a genteel Manner, in every respect when in

Scotland, and we did not expect to be much beworsted when under your Care.[18]

It should also be remembered that the first missionaries were less carefully selected and were wholly unfamiliar with the task before them. Most of them were extremely young. Certainly a few of them were not very good hands at writing or spelling, but at least they could write well enough to be understood, and there were men like them even after the establishment of a Missionary Seminary.

It is quite clear that from the commencement of the Tahitian mission the ordained missionaries were not regarded as having any ecclesiastical control over the others.* Nevertheless the ordained men seem to have had better opportunities to study than the others. The Reverend Thomas Lewis was a pastor in the Countess of Huntingdon's Connexion; the other three ordained men received what might be termed 'Evangelical' ordination, in that they were ordained at a ceremony in which ministers of the various Evangelical denominations took part.[19] According to W.P. Crook, the four ordained brethren were

> appointed to preside during our voyage round three fourths of the globe, for the sake of order. But when we arrived in the islands we felt ourselves perfectly authorized to preach the gospel to the natives, to form our converts into churches, to preside in those churches and to administer the seals of the covenant.[20]

Kelso and Harris were similarly ordained in the islands to minister to the other missionaries at Tonga and the Marquesas. It is interesting that when Bicknell was in England (1809-10) Dr Haweis recommended to the Reverend Matthew Wilks that he should be ordained, 'as he would thereby be rendered more respectable in the eyes of his brethren; and the ordination appeared to be the more necessary, as there is now only one ordained Missionary remaining in the South Sea Mission.'[21] Wilks, however, put his 'decided negative' to this recommendation. This is an interesting comment on the subject of ordination, and we may assume that those who were ordained belonged to a more intellectual or clerical section of the middle class. Men like Bicknell and Nott were representative of the more humble classes. Their letters betray a very rudimentary knowledge of

---

*The Reverend John Jefferson was actually excommunicated on board the *Duff* for expressing Arminian opinions, and his principal accuser was a mechanic missionary. Despite this incident, Jefferson possessed qualities of leadership which determined his position as the principal figure in the mission until his death. He was also more experienced than the others, having been pastor of Fowey Chapel in Cornwall.

writing and spelling, although Nott, who was much younger, made great strides in self-education. Bicknell, who was a member of the Countess of Huntingdon's Connexion, was a house carpenter, sawyer and wheelwright. Nott was a Congregationalist from Birmingham and had been a bricklayer.

William Pascoe Crook, who arrived at Tahiti in 1816 on his second missionary venture, presents an interesting example of the social rise of a missionary candidate. Although attempts have been made to suggest that Crook was not a 'gentleman's servant', but rather 'the servant of the Lord',[22] there is no evidence that he was otherwise employed. In some accounts Crook is listed as a tin-worker, but he appears to have been apprenticed to learn this trade after joining the LMS.[23] He had already spent two very adventurous years in the South Seas as the pioneer missionary of the Marquesas. In 1799 he returned to London and for two years was engaged in preaching for the London Itinerant Society. By profession of faith he was a Calvinistic Methodist, but like the majority of that Connexion in England[24] he early adopted the principles of Congregational church government. Crook arrived in Sydney via Port Phillip in 1803. Instead of proceeding to Tahiti, he engaged in missionary work amongst the settlers, and even served as colonial chaplain for a short period. He and his wife ran a boarding school for three years. By means of his varied experience, his contacts with the leading Evangelical clergy and his own study, Crook attained a respectable position in society. When he returned to the islands in 1816 he was also equipped with some surgical knowledge.

One of the few non-mechanic occupations of this early period was that of Lancelot Edward Threlkeld. After serving an apprenticeship during his youth he became an actor with the Royal Circus and later with the Royalty Theatre.[25] He also went into business. After his conversion he became an itinerant preacher.

John Gyles, who came to Tahiti as an 'agriculturist' in 1818, was the first of the non-preaching missionaries to arrive. He was sent out expressly to instruct the Tahitians in growing various trade crops. He was not particularly suited to missionary work, as he had been a plantation manager in the West Indies and had been used to the management of slaves. Gyles' social status is less easy to define, but he did not altogether fit in with the other missionaries. Of the two 'missionary artisans' who arrived in 1821, Elijah Armitage is another typical example of the social aspirations of the mechanic class. Armitage's father, Elkanah Armitage, had risen considerably in the cotton manufacturing business. He had been a convert from Unitarianism to Calvinism and his family became prominent Congregationalists in Manchester. One of Elijah Armitage's brothers, Sir Elkanah Armitage, became Mayor of Manchester in 1848.[26]

After the nominal conversion of Tahiti it had been the policy of the Society to ordain all its missionaries except those expressly sent out as 'missionary artisans'. When John Rodgerson applied he was very deficient in general knowledge and was recommended as a 'mechanic' only. He made application to a shipbuilder at Whitehaven in order to acquire some knowledge of boat construction. Notwithstanding the recommendation, Rodgerson eventually received ordination. Another candidate who was 'extremely deficient in all points of learning' was the brass-founder, George Pritchard. It is usually assumed from his pretensions that Pritchard, who afterwards became British consul at Tahiti, belonged to a less humble section of society. Although he was brought up in the established Church, Pritchard was converted under the ministry of John Angell James of Birmingham. Another candidate of humble origin, recommended as a 'very suitable Mechanic Missionary', was the blacksmith, William Mills. When Mills retired from missionary work he became a chemist in Sydney, again illustrating the social transformation of the mechanic class.

A definite change in the composition of the LMS missionaries can be seen for the first time in those who came out in 1838-39. Some of these men belonged to what might be called the 'greater middle class'. Joseph Johnston, who was a 'Normal Schoolmaster', was the son of a business proprietor. Thomas Joseph was supported by his parents whilst training to be a teacher. Charles Stevens had been the foreman of a firm of hatters in Bristol. William Howe, who arrived in 1839, had been an infant school teacher before becoming pastor of a Congregational church. Although the differences were often largely a matter of education and opportunities, it is revealing that the older missionaries referred to the newer ones as 'gentlemen missionaries'. Some of the new missionaries came from families which had risen rapidly to respectability. William Gill, who had become manager in a retail leather-cutter's business, was the son of a tanner and currier who became a cabinet-maker and upholsterer. Robert Thomson, the only non-Congregationalist among the party, who came out with Williams in 1838, was nearest in origin to the earlier missionaries. A member of the Presbyterian United Secession Church at Dundee, Thomson was a joiner who had received some architectural training. Both clever and cantankerous, Thomson was ill-at-ease with his 'gentlemen' companions.

The missionaries who arrived in 1842 were the first group who were exclusively non-mechanics. McKean and Jesson had both been Congregational ministers; Krause, a Prussian, had received a medical and theological education in Berlin. Most of the missionaries who came out between 1840 and 1860 were clerks or skilled tradesmen. William Wyatt Gill graduated B.A. at the University of London. W. A. Lind was a copperplate engraver, which was his father's trade. Yet even in this period the mechanics were well represented. Law (1852) was a roll turner at a large ironworks near Rotherham. John Jones (1854), who had been brought up in a Calvinistic Methodist atmosphere (the chapel became Congregational), followed his father's trade as a shoemaker, and Samuel McFarlane, also a Congregationalist (1859), was a 'mechanic' employed in a railway machine shop at £1.9.0. per week.

The Presbyterian missionaries to the New Hebrides had similar backgrounds to those of the LMS. Those who came from the United Presbyterian Church of Nova Scotia very often had farming origins. However John Geddie (the first of these distinctly Presbyterian missionaries) who arrived in 1848 after a time as minister of the Secession Church on Prince Edward Island, was the son of a clockmaker. Those who had been members of the Reformed Presbyterian Church had mostly been apprenticed to trades. Paton was the son of a stocking manufacturer. The Scottish missionaries, in the main, came from less prosperous families than their American brethren.

In the New World, Evangelical Dissent was more intimately connected with economic prosperity. Most of the missionaries of the American Board, like those from Nova Scotia, were drawn from mercantile and farming stock. Most of them, like the LMS missionaries, were Congregationalists. W.P. Alexander, a pioneer missionary to the Marquesas, was a Presbyterian. He belonged to a slave-owning family which had prospered in the farming lands of Kentucky. Although the actual social standing and worldly prosperity of all the missionaries from the American States and Nova Scotia appear to have been higher than those of the English and Scottish missionaries, their social values were similar, and the differences were not so obvious in the islands. James Bicknell, who was the only European missionary in the Marquesas mission of 1853, came nearest in type to the old class of mechanic missionaries. Born in the missionary environment of Tahiti, he had learnt the trade of carpenter in New South

Wales. Bicknell was subsequently ordained, and was a pastor in Hawaii for many years.

The Wesleyan missionaries provide more obvious contrasts with those of the LMS. The WMMS was exclusively under the direction of the Wesleyan Conference, whereas the LMS and CMS were autonomous bodies which existed independently of the churches which supported them. Between 1822 and 1860 sixty-five missionaries laboured in connexion with the WMMS in the South Seas, excluding New Zealand (see Appendix IV). Most of these men were ordained. Of the three school teachers or 'training masters' sent out, one was afterwards ordained, as was one of the two printers connected with the mission.

At the beginning of the Tongan mission lay mechanic missionaries were appointed, after the manner of the CMS in New Zealand. Ordained mechanics followed: John Thomas had pursued his father's trade as a blacksmith; Peter Turner, the son of a cotton-spinner, had begun as a piecer in a cotton factory, but became a silk-weaver. Apart from the lay agents, all the missionaries were married. A few of them were classed as 'assistant missionaries'.

With respect to social background, the most obvious difference between the missionaries of the WMMS and the LMS is that the Wesleyans tended to come from the same recruiting ground as their regular ministers, whereas the Congregational and Presbyterian ministers tended to come from more established and mercantile families. Thus some of the Wesleyan missionaries appear to have belonged to the upper ranks of the social hierarchy within Methodism. The functions of missionary and settled minister were less distinguishable in the 'world parish' conception of the Wesleyan Methodists than in the other denominations.

Another noticeable difference between the composition of the two Societies is that a higher proportion of the Wesleyan missionaries appear to have come from rural districts, whilst more of the LMS missionaries were drawn from urban congregations. Walter Lawry, Nathaniel Turner and James Calvert were farmers' sons. Hunt's father had been an overseer or bailiff on a farm and he himself had been put to farm work. Thomas Adams was also brought up on a farm in Cornwall where his father was a tenant-farmer. Although of comparatively humble origin, Thomas Adams and his brothers, who were noted astronomers, all achieved some eminence.[27] It is significant that his brother John, when Senior Wrangler at Cambridge, tried to persuade him to 'prepare for college, with a view to his ministry in the established church'.[28]

Although many of the wives of LMS missionaries came from New South Wales, all the accredited missionaries were recruited in London. The Wesleyans, however, had very close relations with the colonial churches. The first lay mechanics were from New South Wales. George Lilly was a soldier's son and was engaged as a carpenter. Charles Tindall was a blacksmith. Thomas Wright, the 'agriculturist', was a ticket-of-leave convict. Thomas Bambridge had also been transported, but after his pardon (he had previously 'given evidence of his conversion') he was engaged as a carpenter.

The quality and social standing of the colonial Wesleyans varied considerably. John Von Mangerhoussen Weiss, who was engaged as an 'assistant missionary', had been Superintendent of Government Boats at Sydney. On the other hand, John Watsford, the first Australian-born missionary, who went to Fiji in 1844, was the son of a coachman who had been transported.[29] There was a tendency to look down upon the colonial missionaries, an attitude encouraged by the failure of several of those appointed in New South Wales to adapt themselves to the island conditions. However these deficiencies were not general. Watsford, the son of a convict father, was one of the most active and efficient missionaries in Fiji. Lawry, in particular, was prejudiced against 'Colonial young men' and made no secret about it. Joseph Waterhouse, on the other hand, believed that the colonial missionaries such as himself and his brother were as efficient as, if not superior to, their English brethren. '*We are not behind any of the pure English missionaries*', he wrote in 1852. 'Take Mr. Hunt away and perhaps we are, certainly we *shall* be, *superior*: Come along, Samuel, join our number, Feejee wants *colonial-British* energy . . . Feejee is mine and Sam's.'[30] No doubt the feeling that it was necessary to prove themselves gave additional force to the Australian missionaries.

Surprisingly enough, very few of the Evangelical missionaries were connected with clerical or missionary families. Only two sons of LMS missionaries engaged in the work. Samuel Wilson did valuable pioneering in Samoa until his forced retirement owing to moral lapse. John Barff was engaged as a 'missionary labourer' or 'assistant missionary' after he had completed his schooling in England, but was not ordained until 1841. W. E. Henry assisted his father for some years but showed no inclination to become a missionary. In fact, most of the sons of the LMS missionaries showed a decided antipathy to the work, and many of them openly opposed the principles for which their parents stood. The son of one of the old missionaries was seriously considering returning as a missionary in 1852, but when Buzacott mentioned it to the missionaries at Tahiti 'an opinion was expressed that no one *bearing that name* would do to labour in the South Seas. Their characters had been so notorious for licentious conduct that even this same . . . had seduced a respectable native girl by whom he had two children . . .'.[31] Most of those who did repent and who showed a definite interest in the work would have had difficulty in being accepted as ministers because they had invariably 'sown their wild oats' in public. George Platt, junior, who had been a thorn in the side of Charter in the Raiatea mission, gave considerable voluntary assistance to Chisholm in the same mission, and Isaac Henry did much preaching at Tahiti. J. C. Williams also engaged in various teaching duties. Quite a number of missionary daughters married missionaries.

Naturally those born in the islands who showed an inclination for missionary work were more likely to understand the problems confronting a Christian teacher in the islands than their parents. John Barff, in the Society Islands, Dr Luther Halsey Gulick and Hiram Bingham, junior, in Micronesia (both sons of pioneer missionaries to Hawaii) and James Bicknell in the Marquesas were all particularly efficient missionaries. These men, however, held fast to the traditional teaching and way of life of their parents.

Amongst the LMS missionaries who had clerical and missionary connexions were Samuel Ella and Thomas Slatyer. Ella, who went to Samoa as mission printer in 1848 and afterwards entered the ministry, was the nephew of the Reverend Benjamin Bailey, a missionary to south India. Slatyer's elder brother (William) was a missionary in the West Indies, and he himself was married to the daughter of a Baptist minister. Both Ella and Slatyer convey the impression of being more 'gentle born' than their colleagues. Amongst the Wesleyans were men with similar backgrounds. William Fletcher, a graduate of London University, was the son of a missionary to the West Indies. Fletcher's family played a prominent role in colonial Wesleyanism. His sister was the wife of the Reverend John Polglase of Fiji. One of his brothers, the Reverend J. H. Fletcher, was a prominent figure in New Zealand Methodism. The Waterhouse family was another 'mission dynasty'. Joseph and Samuel Waterhouse of Fiji were both sons of the Reverend John Waterhouse, the first General Superintendent of Wesleyan missions in the South Seas. John Waterhouse was an influential figure in English Methodism. His wife was the daughter of a shipbuilder, and the family lived in very comfortable circumstances.

Quite a number of missionaries' wives were born in the manse. Mrs Macdonald of Samoa and Mrs Stevens of Tahiti were both daughters of the Reverend Ezekiel Blomfield, author of several popular Evangelical works. Two of their sisters were married to CMS missionaries in New Zealand.[32] James Watkin of Tonga was married to the niece of the Reverend Joseph Entwisle, one of the most eminent Methodist preachers of his day. William Wilson was likewise married to a daughter of the Reverend Peter McOwan, another prominent Methodist. It is not uncommon to find that missionaries' wives were members of closely-knit mission families. Mrs A. W. Murray (née Cobden) was the sister of Mrs William Reeve and Mrs George Mundy, missionaries in south India. Mrs Buzacott and Mrs Hardie were the sisters of George Hitchcock, in whose drapery warehouse at St Paul's Churchyard the YMCA was founded. Another sister was married to the Reverend James Sewell of south India. Other members of the Hitchcock family were equally prominent in Evangelical movements. A family of comparatively humble origin, they rose quite rapidly in the commercial world during the first half of the century.

The Evangelical missionaries to the South Seas were not derived from all classes of society but rather from the lower middle and mechanic classes. A number of them were carpenters, and they regarded their vocation very much as a personal call from the 'Master Carpenter'. The rural background of many of the Wesleyans is conspicuous, and there is also a noticeable representation of Yorkshire and Cornish Methodists. The Wesleyans and the American missionaries tended to have influential clerical and mercantile connexions. Most of the missionaries, however, whatever their experience or their training, took with them into the field the New Mechanic's consciousness of his social position, his desire to better himself, and his dependence on, and obligations to, the less fortunate.

2

Doubly Called

THE KEY TO the understanding of most missionary activity is revivalism. To understand revivalism in the terms of the missionaries who went to the South Seas it is necessary to clarify the distinction between the doctrines of the Wesleyans and of the Calvinistic Evangelicals. The essential religious experience of revival, and of Evangelical conversion generally, is the 'new birth', being born again in the spirit. As Monsignor Knox phrased it, this experience meant to Wesley 'that you were then and there conscious of Christ having died for your sins, and of yourself as then and there accepted in Him; but nothing proved you would not have fallen away from that faith in six months' time'. For Whitefield, on the other hand (Knox declared) the experience 'gave you the conviction that you were irrevocably sealed for heaven'.[1]

Thus, although both schools of Revival thought taught the doctrine of the atonement as the principal doctrine of Christianity, and although the essentials of their faith were the same, each placed a different emphasis on the Christian life. Wesleyans, in preaching the doctrine of 'entire sanctification', urged holiness of life above all other things. We find repeatedly in Wesleyan journals the renewal of the original experience of conversion. Soul-searching was much more exacting and there would appear to have been more recognized stages of faith and holiness. Calvinists, in preaching the allied but slightly different doctrine of 'the perseverance of the saints', stressed entire dependence on the gift of grace. Wesleyan critics suspected that such a belief was the natural beginning of Antinomianism; people convinced that they were saved would pay less heed to the practice of the holy life. Certainly Antinomianism was more usually the outcome of a misapplied Calvinist belief, but on the other hand backsliding was a more common feature of the Wesleyan movement. In other words, in making provision for backsliding Wesleyanism was less fair, psychologically, to weak characters. The faith of a Calvinist often enabled a man to overcome his former weaknesses through sheer belief in his salvation.

Whereas the Wesleyan or Arminian stressed 'love to God' and 'love to souls' as the principal motives for missionary activity, the Calvinist was often moved by the pressures of his own inner conflicts. While the Wesleyan was perhaps more concerned in promoting 'revival', the Calvinist was eager to create a 'new society' as visible evidence of redemption from guilt and sin. Holy zeal was characteristic of both parties but the subtle pressures of the Calvinist conscience could give to motivation something of the fever of neurotic compulsion. This force was not always as obvious as the emotionalism of the Wesleyan revival but it was equally if not more powerful, and of a more lasting character. Whereas revival emotionalism often gave way to despondency and reflective inaction, it was out of a state of despair, of spiritual desolation, that the Calvinist took his secret strength.

It was not simply love of the 'perishing heathen' which led men to the South Seas. It was love of God, the glorification of God.* This may seem too remote a cause of missionary activity. But together with the desire to glorify God exists the equally compelling concern for the individual soul. The missionaries who went out to convert the heathen were as much concerned with their own souls as with those of their coloured brethren. They had all asked at one time of their life: 'What shall I do to be saved?'

The missionary vocation was a pilgrimage in perseverance. Christian must confront trial and temptation, he must pass through the valley of the shadow of death, he must come through unscathed. The only physical relief was death, but death took on a new significance.

> You ought [said Pentycross to the missionaries], after living for so glorious a purpose, to conclude it will not be your lot to die the common death of all men . . . The soil of the South-sea Islands may require your ashes to impregnate it with the most abundant salt of salvation.[2]

One of the qualifications demanded by the directors of the Missionary Society was holy zeal. As Dr Bogue expressed it in his sermon before the Society in 1795:

> A missionary must be a burning and a shining light. The rays of divine knowledge must shine forth brightly from his mind, and the fire of divine zeal burn with a pure flame in his heart.[3]

*Positive Christian motivation has possibly been over-emphasized by the missiological writers. For their analyses see Van Den Berg, 1956 and Warren, 1965, pp. 36-55. Warren, however, acknowledges the desire to make reparation for the slave trade.

Belief in the divine commission necessitated some action on the part of the believer, but the force of the enthusiasm was inevitably linked with the experience of conversion. The Calvinist Evangelical regarded himself as a brand plucked from the burning and his enthusiasm for converting others was usually charged with an excessive sense of guilt.

We must not undervalue the positive side of the experience. The great missionary enthusiasm of the Evangelical Revival *was* a positive force. 'Expect great things from God. Attempt great things for God' — these were Carey's great missionary texts. This holy zeal dominated the whole conception of the missionary's vocation.[4] Nor must we forget that the doctrine of the calling contributed zeal and energy to the social life of the Calvinist citizen. But it does not wholly explain the zeal so characteristic of the Evangelical Calvinist. To explain this zeal we must evoke a negative doctrine, the doctrine of reparation.

The force of this doctrine depended on two things; experience in conversion, and a sense of vocational failure, frustration or trial. It was a specifically personal doctrine and emphasized a highly developed sense of sin, or guilt. The Calvinist who believed in the doctrine of the atonement should not have been gloomy and should not have had doubts, but an awareness of sin or a consciousness of backsliding inevitably led to his doubting his perseverance as one of the saints, and the Calvinist, like Job, was sorely tried. These Calvinists tended to believe in a special doctrine of works, not mere good works but a personal effort to exalt the glory of God in an attempt to retrieve the evil of one's past conduct or present imperfections.

> Even if Christ did not expressly require it — if he were even to give us a dispensation from it — would our sense of obligation, our agony of solicitude to retrieve the past, allow us to accept it? If tears could wash away the evil of the past, could we do less than wish that our head were a fountain of waters, that we might weep night and day? But tears cannot; to remove its guilt there must be blood of infinite value; and to counteract its depraving influence, a spirit of almighty power; while all that we can do — and surely we shall not plead for doing less — is to be the devoted unintermitting channel for the communication of both to the world.[5]

Three things gave emphasis to the doctrine of reparation. The first of these was the idea of man as the natural enemy of God. This doctrine gave the title to one of Jonathan Edwards' sermons, the thesis being that man in his natural state is corrupt and must inevitably perish. This was linked with the doctrine of reprobation. Those who held this theological position were directly opposed to the thesis popularly ascribed to Rousseau, for the 'noble savage' was a contradiction in terms. Some moderate Calvinists were satisfied that a savage could be saved by the light of nature when judged according to that light, but the majority preached the doctrine of salvation by revelation alone.

The second thing connected with the experience of conversion was the fear of hell. Hell was a very real place to the Calvinist convert. In 1766 a poem entitled *The Methodist* was published in which Whitefield's sermons were thus exhibited:

> He knows his *Master's** realm so well,   *The Devil
> His sermons are a map of hell,
> An *Ollio* made of conflagration,
> Of *gulphs* of brimstone, and *damnation*,
> *Eternal torments, furnace, worm,*
> Hell-fire, a *whirlwind,* and a *storm.*[6]

One finds justification for this on reading such a sermon as *The Eternity of Hell Torments.* 'The duration of sufferings inflicted on the wicked in the future state' was a subject afterwards discussed by Tahitians at their 'conversational' meetings.[7]

The third thing connected with conversion was the sense of guilt arising from previous excess and carnal temptation. Again and again the converted men expressed their unworthiness. This was often accompanied by fear of immediate physical punishment, just as sailing on the Sabbath was an open invitation to destruction.[8]

In examining the lives of the missionaries we find an accentuation of the consciousness of guilt at the time of conversion.[9] This sense of guilt often seemed to be completely out of proportion to the conduct of the believer. The neophyte underwent days of agony and doubt, was reduced to tears of penitence and finally of gratitude and devotion. This experience of conversion demanded an outlet in vital activity. Most accounts highlight the worldly sins before conversion, and the language used often suggests gross depravity. John Williams confessed that before he heard the Reverend Timothy East preach he was very wicked, though 'not outwardly immoral'.[10] It appears from most of the accounts, however, that very few of the South Seas missionaries could have confessed to 'outward immorality'. Not only did most of them deny the commission of any vice, but if they had been guilty of any gross lapse they probably would have followed Vanderkemp's example and confessed to it to show the extent of the divine power or grace.[11] Most of the 'wickedness' referred to consisted of the 'vices of childhood': disregard for the Sabbath, lying and swearing.[12] More sophisticated sins are mentioned by Samuel McFarlane. 'Before God drew me to Himself by the cords of His Love I had a strong passion for the ballroom, the billiard table, and such fruitless and destructive pleasures'.[13]

The majority of the LMS missionaries confessed to an 'awful state' at some time during their adolescence.[14] William Harbutt testified to 'deep agonizing convictions'. The presence and fear of death also played an important part in the 'awakening' experience. One of the most dramatic of these is the account left by Joseph Moore. Whilst articled to his employer, who conducted a boarding school, he 'imbibed lax principles and gave [himself] to the pernicious reading of novels'.

> *Tom Jones* and other works, of this description, were put into my hand, under the fair pretence of giving me a 'knowledge of the World'. My leisure time in fact was entirely consumed in novels and plays which had a most injurious effect on my mind. They produced in my corrupt heart determinations, the most hostile to seriousness, and filled my mind with the most impure thoughts. I was on the verge of destruction.[15]

His employer was then taken seriously ill, and thinking himself about to die he admonished Moore 'never again to peruse the fascinating works he had recommended'. The plays and novels were duly burnt, and Moore endeavoured to find out more about religion. He thus describes his state of mind. 'Frequently I have had such tormenting fears of eternal punishment as to quit my bed in the night season and pray for forgiveness.' Lind, also a novel-reader, had a similar experience. During his mental disquiet he had a dream that he died and went to hell.[16]

A few candidates testified to the doctrine of 'man's natural enmity'. 'Soon as reason dawned', said William Law, 'I took up the arms of rebellion against God'.[17] He said that there was never a period when he did not feel that God was striving with him; he had even attempted to persuade himself that there was no God.

The importance of the conversion experience in missionary motivation and character formation cannot be overemphasized, especially as it was also the key factor in revivalism. There were two distinct stages. There was an awakening to the perils of the unregenerate soul; and then there was the experience of 'rebirth'. All Evangelicals believed that a man could only be 'born again in the spirit' through faith in the salvation of the soul through the atonement of Jesus Christ, the mediator between God and man.

A good proportion of the Evangelical missionaries had comparatively 'quiet' conversions, but these men had usually been nurtured in churches and homes already impregnated with Evangelical thought, and it was less difficult for them to adjust their emotions to the religious doctrine which they accepted. It was not uncommon for children in Evangelical homes to be 'converted' at a very early age.

It is important to appreciate the intensity of the initial religious experience of the various missionaries when considering their actions, their attitudes, and their effectiveness. Evangelical thought placed a peculiar emphasis on the saving merits of faith, and it is easy to see that many of the missionaries were not as fearsomely wicked before their conversions as they tended to paint themselves. All that concerned them was their original disobedience and the terrible wrath and retributive justice of an offended God.

One of the more dramatic conversions was that of the Reverend Charles Wilson, who had been brought up by 'godly parents' in Aberdeen. When he removed to London in 1788, he was 'led captive by Satan living in the indulgence of corrupt desires and inclinations through the force of custom still attended to hear the gospel preachers, but felt nothing of its power till the year 1794'.[18] Wilson had become interested in astrology, and after having studied the practice for two years 'was come to some proficiency in pretending to fortel future events in regard to particular persons'. He apparently believed in his own prognostications, and when he cast his own horoscope he was filled with terror on learning that he was about to die. Whilst thinking about death he was 'awakened to see that [he] was a condemned sinner by the Son of God'. He 'saw hell ready to receive [his] condemned soul'. He tried to remember what he had heard from the pulpit, and his mental suffering was great. 'But the time which I fixed upon for my Death was now come.' When he told his minister, the Reverend Alexander Waugh, what a sinner he was, he found no comfort in the stories of Manasseh, Paul and Magdalene. And then — to him it seemed to be a particular interposition of divine providence — he found relief in the text of a sermon, 'The King of Israel is merciful. . . . He will save thy life'. Charles Wilson did not die, and the effect of the sermon was to ensure his dedication to Christian service.

Charles Barff, a devoted and tolerant missionary, had a less dramatic conversion. At the age of six or seven, Barff says,

> when attending the flocks or herds of cattle in the fields my meditations were sweet on the wonderful works of God. My prayers

altho' mixed with ignorance were attended (I trust) by the Holy
Influence of the Spirit of God yet unable to withdraw the temptations
to which I was exposed I often trembled within while I laughed
with the wicked at folley.[19]

At the age of nineteen, Barff went to live in London, but he soon
found 'that Satan had his agents in London'. Undaunted by
these he attended Surrey Chapel, and sat 'under the droppings
of the word with delight'. Although he appears to have been
obsessed with 'doubts and fears', these were little more than
misgivings about his ability to serve as a minister or a missionary.

David Darling observed that he could not state the exact time
of his conversion, but he was able to relate circumstances which
would convince the directors that he had been 'turned from
darkness to light'.[20] Sermons very frequently influenced the
hearer. Charles Pitman, who would have joined his 'vicious and
wicked companions' but for the restrictions and displeasure of
his father, was influenced strongly by a sermon preached by the
Reverend J. Hyatt at Tottenham Court Chapel.[21] However, for
a time he was 'still in bondage, thro' a dread and fear that all
was a deception', and his soul was not 'liberated' until he
attended the ministry of the Reverend J. Hunt of Chichester.
John Williams was another who was largely affected by one
sermon.

Books of a devotional character were often instrumental in
securing Evangelical conversions. Perhaps no book made such an
impression on the lives of prospective Evangelicals of all denominations as Hervey's *Theron and Aspasia*. This work, written
in the form of a philosophical dialogue (a very popular medium
during the eighteenth century), set out the claims of the
Evangelical system with particular emphasis on the Calvinist
doctrines. Another influential work was Doddridge's *Rise and
Progress of Religion in the Soul*.[22] One book which particularly
influenced many of the missionary candidates was *The Anxious
Inquirer* by James of Birmingham. James wrote a series of
manuals which dealt with all stages of Christian experience.
A student of revivals, he used the revival techniques to convince
the 'inquirer' of the necessity of becoming a Christian. George
Spencer tells how, when he became 'deeply convinced of the
importance of eternal things', he determined to read this book.
Although he was employed in his father's office until 10 or 10.30
every evening, he would come home and read portions of *The
Anxious Inquirer* until it was finished. On discovering that he
was 'ruined and undone', he passed through a state of anxiety

for four or five weeks, until a 'great change' was wrought in him.[23]

Wesleyan conversions followed a similar pattern, although they frequently contained more mystical elements. Calvinist missionaries, convinced of their election in this world as well as in the world to come, seemed to be sustained by their initial religious experience. On the other hand the Wesleyan missionaries were much more given to self-examination, and they seemed to require constant renewals of the outpouring of the Holy Spirit. Revivalism came more frequently to the Wesleyan camp. Whereas 'Are you saved?' seemed to be the watchword of the Calvinists, 'Are you right with God?' seemed to be that of the Wesleyans.

The conversion of Peter Turner is particularly interesting because his account of this experience survives for us in some detail.[24] The son of a poor factory worker, Turner attended Chapel and Sabbath School, although there was no form of religion maintained at home. His father drank heavily. His mother had been servant to a 'pious lady who kept a young ladies' school'. Turner records that in 1817 'the Holy Spirit worked gently on [his] mind, and showed [him] that [he] needed a Saviour. The desire to obtain salvation became intense'. Whilst seeking he attended as many services as he could. One day he went to a class meeting, but felt out of place amongst so many well-dressed persons, and decided that the class was 'too respectable' for him. He hero-worshipped the class leader, Joseph Pearson, recording that he had 'a great love and reverence for my leader, and thought him very handsome and very good. I loved the ground he walked upon'. Beset by all sorts of doubts and temptations, Turner waited for some experience to *convince* him of his salvation. He read the accounts of the remarkable conversions of Silas Todd and Colonel Gardiner. 'I used to look up when in the fields [,] praying and expecting to see the clouds open and the Saviour to appear to my view, and fully satisfy my soul'.

Turner became familiar with the different levels of experience when listening to the testimonies of the others who attended class meetings and 'love-feasts'. Some would give accounts of their 'justification'; others of their 'sanctification'. 'I had the fear, the slavish fear of God in my heart, but nothing of love.' On removing to Macclesfield, Turner's experience did not give him the satisfaction that he desired. He gave up going to class meetings, and indulged in 'courtship after school on the Sabbath'. This 'blunted the moral sensibilities of the soul, and

1 Rev. Henry Nott mechanic missionary, principal translator of the Bible into Tahitian and adviser to King Pomare II

2 Rev. J. F. Cover first Protestant missionary to preach in Tahiti

3 Rowland Hassall mechanic missionary, became a prosperous settler in New South Wales

4 James Hayward mechanic missionary, in Tahiti, afterwards colporteur in New South Wales

5 Rev. Thomas Heath
missionary in Samoa and
visitor to the other LMS
stations after the death of
John Williams

6 Rev. George Pritchard
missionary, afterwards
British consul at Papeete
and Apia

7 Rev. Aaron Buzacott
pioneer missionary in the
Cook Islands and principal
translator of the Bible into
Rarotongan

8 Rev. William Ellis
missionary in the Society
Islands and Hawaii, later
author of *Polynesian
Researches*, and Foreign
Secretary of the LMS

opened the door to many evils'. For several years he continued to sin 'against light and knowledge'. The state of his mind is revealed in his account of a thunderstorm. He went into an out-house, and was dreadfully afraid lest he should be 'struck down by the vengeance of an offended God'. Although he made vows and promises he still was afraid to make an open profession of faith. Subject to Calvinist influence, he was also afraid that he was 'not one of the elect, but reprobated by God, and should ultimately be lost'.

Turner then rejoined the Wesleyans and again attended class meetings. It was in this environment that he had his initial experience at a Friday evening prayer-meeting. All 'sense of sorrow and condemnation and dread of God' was removed from his mind. He was filled with 'peace, joy and hope'. He was advised to hold fast the grace given as 'God would witness to the reality of the work wrought in the heart'. That night the experience continued. 'God was very gracious to my soul, he gave me the full assurance of my pardon! . . . I rose very early to seek him whom my soul loved.' He was 'unspeakably happy', and remained in this state of mind till the following Tuesday.

After the experience Turner began a pilgrimage in pursuit of holiness. Two years later he was still doubting his own religious integrity, and again required a 'sense of pardon'. Again and again entries in his diary convey his keen desire for the full sanctification of his soul, 'the point on which my soul is fixed'.

Turner analysed his experience in theological terms. This is important to remember, as he became one of the leading re-vivalists in the South Seas. It would seem that his technique was based both on a close examination of other revivalists and on his own experience. Turner knew the spiritual anatomy of man so well that he could place his fingers on all the nerve spots.

Turner's account of his later experience of entire sanctification is also worthy of notice as it shows how his emotions were wrought to a revivalistic fervour. On 6 September 1828 he records: 'I cried for divine assistance and for power to believe in the all-cleansing blood of Jesus'. He felt

> an increasing deadness to the world, and that [his] inward depravity was being washed away and that God [was] destroying all [his] idols and giving [him] a clean heart. This was the negative part of sanc-tification taking away all evil, destroying all evil — emptying the vessel, preparing the heart.

On the Tuesday he felt his faith becoming stronger, 'more simple and unmixed by doubt and unbelief'. Wednesday was 'a day of conflict with the enemy'. The big moment came on Thursday. 'I was favoured with three remarkable manifestations of the presence of God when in my closet. There seemed but a thin vail [sic] which came between me and God.' He was filled with speechless awe, and could no longer doubt the blessing of sanctification. This was the grand climax. Succeeding entries show, however, that Turner still had moments of doubt and despair when Satan 'raised many clouds' around him to 'dim his evidence and darken his path'. Nevertheless, he was 'truly converted to God'.

Most of the other Wesleyan accounts have not been preserved in such great detail. The conversion of John Hunt was somewhat similar. Hunt's boyhood resembled that of most other Evangelicals. When afraid of 'dogs, gipsies, thunder and lightning or even a shower of rain', he had recourse to prayer 'as sure means of deliverance from every evil'. 'Though much tempted to be brave and swear and lie, and break the Sabbath like other boys, I never could fully enter into the spirit of wickedness till I was fourteen or fifteen years of age'.[25] Hunt was affected by reading the Book of Revelation. Later he became interested in the preaching of the Wesleyans. On one occasion he attended a prayer meeting. The preacher, John Smith of Lincoln Circuit, prayed 'Send us more power', upon which Hunt knelt down and said 'Amen', with some degree of feeling. 'Immediately a most overwhelming influence came upon me, so that I cried aloud for mercy for the sake of Christ, while I was in a minute as completely bathed with tears and perspiration as if I had been thrown into a river.'[26]

When asked if he believed that God was satisfied with the atonement of his son, and for his sake forgave him, Hunt could not answer, 'but cried to God for help', and was thereby 'enabled to trust in the sufficient atonement of Christ on [his] personal account'. At that moment he 'felt the pardoning love of God'. Hunt himself became one of the leading exponents of the Methodist doctrine of holiness. His *Letters on Entire Sanctification* (London, 1853) was later used as a textbook by theological students.[27] Many years later, whilst walking in his garden in Fiji, Hunt was meditating on the goodness of God when he too claimed a mystical experience.

> I at once had a peculiarly delightful view of the love of God. It seemed to be as free as a sunbeam, and I almost felt as if I could see a stream of mercy come from heaven like a stream of light and fall upon my breast. . . . I remember something like it in John Howe's Life, only he had the feelings in a dream, and also something like it in Brainard's life.[28]

A similar mystical experience was documented by another influential missionary in Fiji, Dr R. B. Lyth. 'I did arise and go to
my Father being sweetly drawn by love. I looked unto God and
was saved. . . . I wept before the God of love.'[29] Familiar with
Evangelical doctrine from his childhood, Lyth admitted that
there had always been within him a 'continual struggle between
light and darkness'. In a powerfully drawn account of his conversion, he built up the contrast between his unregenerate state
and his transformation. Lyth's conversion is particularly interesting because it was followed almost immediately by a 'backsliding' into sin. 'After this glorious manifestation', he wrote,
'I again grieved God's good spirit — but was restored after a long
night of bondage'. This tendency to backslide gave special impetus to the doctrine of reparation.

John Watsford's conversion was equally dramatic.[30] He felt
'the witness of the Holy Spirit' to be so clear and distinct that at
the time he believed God really spoke to him in pardoning his
sins. Most of the Wesleyans could name a day as their spiritual
birthday, even those who were converted while very young. It
was also usual for many of them to speak of their spiritual
fathers, those ministers who had been instrumental in bringing
them to God.[31]

Most Evangelicals found a precedent for their experience in
the account of the conversion of St Paul. As a boy Thomas Baker
had been 'led captive by the Devil at his will'.[32] At the age of
fourteen his alleged vices had perhaps a greater variety than
most. He indulged in Sabbath-breaking, deriding the outdoor
preacher, night walking, smoking, frequenting the Ale House,
gambling, swearing and fighting. Several events caused him
spiritual uneasiness. On one occasion, when breaking the Sabbath, 'the two spirits were struggling for the mastery, and it
seemed as though I could not speak without swearing, truly my
mouth was full of bitterness . . .'. He then began the usual course
of seeking and attended class meetings. And then, on 1 December
1849, as he was walking on the Morpeth road at midday, the
ascent of a little hill on the way brought to mind what he had
read in Bunyan's *Pilgrim's Progress* concerning the Hill of
Difficulty: 'At once the simplicity of faith appeared to my mind,
I ventured, was saved, then and there in the middle of the road.
I felt great peace through believing, and went down the road
rejoicing, clapping my hands'. Something of the nature of the
spiritual life after conversion is contained in these words of
Baker's: 'Sometimes I have been on the mountain and sometimes

in the valley, but yet I bless the Lord for what I am. Glory to
God, I am out of hell'.[33]

Conversion, revivalistic in nature, directed the whole personality of the missionary and was the moment most cherished
throughout all the years of varied experience in the South Seas,
or wherever else he chose to live.

Each missionary underwent a second type of conversion, the
conversion to the missionary vocation, as distinct from the mere
desire to extend his personal experience to others. This decision
to be a missionary was not unlike the experience of the 'call' to
the ministry. The motivation varied considerably. Very often
there were subsidiary motives, such as economic or psychological
ones, which played an important part in the decision.

The missionary societies only accepted obedience to Christ's
commission,[34] the desire to save the heathen, and the glorification
of God as the real motives for entering this service. All personal
considerations had to be subsidiary to these. The LMS was particularly careful on this issue. In the Society's *Questions for
Candidates* (1836), item 12 reads: 'As there is too much reason
to fear that some persons have become Missionaries under the
influence of improper principles, you are desired seriously and
sincerely to state what are the MOTIVES by which you are actuated
in offering yourself as a Missionary to the Heathen'. Very few
candidates specified those subsidiary motives which had influenced them. We have to look for these in the background and
personality of each missionary. Some of the first contingent on
the *Duff* were regarded as having acted under the influence of
'improper principles'. Because of their subsequent defection from
the Society and from Evangelical principles of behaviour, it
was assumed that such missionaries as Cock and Main had been
little more than adventurers attracted by the descriptions of the
Tahitian Paradise.

Although it is said that a man cannot live by bread alone, he
cannot live without bread. In a period of unemployment or
economic distress one would expect to find men desiring to
leave the country in search of economic security. In the case of
godly men, there would also be some mental security in the
belief that God would provide. As Elijah was fed in the wilderness, so would the messenger of salvation be cared for in the
uttermost parts of the earth, and what could be read in books
suggested that these uttermost parts were lands flowing with
milk and honey.

Certainly there was economic distress amongst various sections of the mechanic class in England during the French Revolutionary period and the Napoleonic wars. One reads of 'Evangelical aid' to distressed weavers.[35] Nor were there many opportunities for advancement in the weaving business. The Reverend George Burder of Coventry abridged and revised a booklet entitled *The Weaver's Pocket-book, or Weaving spiritualized* for the benefit of his 'poor neighbours'. Rowland Hassall, one of the *Duff* missionaries, belonged to Burder's church and came from this environment. It is interesting that Hassall never returned to Tahiti after quitting, principally because he was far too prosperous in his settled state at Parramatta. All records of him show him as a man of influence and property.

The letters of Hassall's English relations reflect the conditions in England. In March 1800 Thomas Hancox, Hassall's brother-in-law, was out of work.[36] In the winter he lost nine weeks' work. Business was very bad and he thought of beginning a new trade. His wife was to sell new and old clothes. Burder, writing to his former church member, painted an equally gloomy picture.

> The Wickedness of man has raised wheat to the enormous price of a Guinea a bushel, Barley and Oats, tho' very fine and plentiful are also very dear. . . . Never was in our days so much want and misery among the poor. . . . The trade in Coventry is worse than ever. Little work to do. . . . Bread so dear, that very many are half-starved. At least and I do fear more than a few have really died for want.[37]

There were riots, and a 'Famine Guard' to keep people quiet, 'or the farmers would soon be roughly handled'.

The charge that the missionaries were in the islands because they had 'no bread to eat in England' was certainly an exaggeration and could only have had meaning at the beginning of the century. In the later period in answering the twelfth question most of the candidates asserted that they were holding down good positions, and many of them were about to receive an increase in salary or some sort of promotion. It is doubtful whether any of the missionaries expected less arduous employment than at home, but it is highly probable that many of them were attracted by the measure of independence and freedom of action which would be theirs. There was, and still is, a certain romantic attraction about missionary labour, and a spirit of adventure fostered in reading travel accounts and the histories of earlier missions appears to have influenced their decisions. Missionary enterprise also appealed to the misanthropic individual, the man who found it difficult to get on with others of his own caste. The social misfit was attracted by a career in which he was able to build his own 'new world'.

Perhaps no books influenced Evangelical Christians to enter the mission field more than the biographies and journals of David Brainerd. Brainerd's journals were re-edited, abridged, rewritten and amplified. Missionaries of the CMS, LMS and WMMS all testified to the influence of these works.[38] Other missionary heroes were John Eliot and C. F. Schwartz.[39] As the nineteenth century progressed more recent missionaries were added to the list of the great, names which strongly influenced those who were still in the Sabbath school: Henry Martyn,[40] William Carey, Vanderkemp and the Judsons of Burma.

One of the most powerful influences was that of the personalities of some of the leading mission propagandists of the period. Silver-voiced preachers could often create a picture of the missionary life which would powerfully attract the young listener. The giants of this art were some of the missionaries who had already served in distant fields. Some of these men were 'idolized' by the young and impressionable. Many of them not only possessed strength of personality but were also gifted with a commanding presence. Paragons of moral virtue and physical beauty, they appeared like angels commissioned to call the young convert to the mission field. The Reverend Richard Knill, missionary to India and Russia, was perhaps the greatest of these. About six feet in height, well-proportioned, with a fair complexion and blue eyes, Knill possessed a voice which, according to one of his contemporaries, was

> very powerful and melodious, and went easily to the furthest limits of an assembly. It was used without apparent art, and seemed to follow the mental impulse. From the loudest pitch he descended, without harsh abruptness, to the quiet, confidential tone of conversation, in which, generally, he introduced his anecdotes.[41]

The missionaries Barnden, Buzacott, Charter, Howe, Pratt, Stair, Stevens, Slatyer and Johnston were all influenced by Knill's preaching.[42] Buzacott was so affected 'that sleep departed from him until he was brought to a resolution to surrender himself to Christ's service among the heathen'.[43]

John Williams had a similar magnetic appeal, especially after the publication of his *Missionary Enterprises*. The Reverend Dr John Campbell's sketch of Williams' character is perhaps one of the best verbal portraits of any of the missionaries which we possess.[44] This sketch is particularly frank and blunt. 'On nearly all subjects, except that of Missions', wrote Campbell, 'his views were narrow and superficial'. Notwithstanding these limitations, Campbell, who heard Williams preach, testified to his ability to gain a far wider audience than a more gifted and intellectual 'missionary' such as Dr Philip of Cape Town. The imaginative picture which Williams painted of the 'isles of the sea' was ever afterwards a sore point with some of the missionaries who believed themselves deluded by his accounts. The letters of the missionaries who arrived in the Society Islands in 1838 are filled with complaints.[45] Even the older missionaries were forced to comment. Platt wrote to his former colleague, William Ellis:

> What wicked men *you officers* must be to deceive simple young people, and trepan them (for it cannot *be us* who have done it) into a service to which their hearts have no sympathy. You make them believe they are going to heaven. But when they arrive, instead of heaven, they find black men and fiends, and barbarized Missionaries and even the devil himself not cast out. . . . Alas poor Williams! It appears he was the arch deceiver. . . . O that we could soon behold his like in the work; And as fully devoted.[46]

Amongst those missionaries who acknowledged the influence of Williams were John Barff, George Gill, Moore, Pratt, Thomson and Slatyer.[47]

Missionaries frequently delivered sermons at the annual meetings of the local auxiliary missionary societies. Although their London sermons were much more publicized, their greatest influence was possibly exerted at these provincial meetings. A great fervour of devotion was always aroused, especially when the heroes of the occasion were about to depart.[48]

The missionary vocation was not infrequently regarded as the Evangelical alternative to entering the army. To be a 'soldier for Christ' had very real meaning for many of them, largely because of the intensity of their own personal struggles. Richard Knill joined the militia. He afterwards delivered tracts to a garrison, and whilst in India he induced a large number of officers to attend his chapel. Many of the missionaries were the sons or grandsons of men who had served in the army.

John Hunt of the Wesleyan Society was early charmed with the heroic life. He thus wrote of his early 'day-dreams':

> Many a time I have enlisted as a common soldier, by virtue and valour I have passed through the different grades of preferments, until at length by the good hand of Providence, which always attended me, I have found myself at the head of a victorious army, conquering wherever I made an attack, and enriching myself with

the spoils of nations, and I generally ended my career of glory by returning home to the bosom of my Father's family and spending the remaining years of my life in supporting my parents and friends.[49]

This of course was written when Hunt was already a missionary, and he doubtless meant the reader to compare his real missionary career with his childhood ambitions. But this heroic concept of the missionary's career was quite a significant motivating force.

Many of the missionaries denied being 'carried away' by speeches and emotional gatherings. Thus William Law accounts for his zeal:

> These wishes were not originated when a returned missionary was received with deafening applause; or when some modern Apollos electrified an assembly, with flashes of eloquence and wisdom. In the silent depths of my own spirit, with little aid from external circumstances, those ideas were evolved, and those feelings aroused, which have continued to haunt me from that time to the present.[50]

A lottery-like use of the Bible was also instrumental in directing the thought to missions. William Law tells how he asked the question, 'Lord, what wilt thou have me do?' He took up his Bible, and was convinced by his reading that he should follow the example of Jesus and St Paul. William Howe's experience was similar.[51] One evening he was sitting with his Bible before him, thinking about the heathen. When he opened his Bible his eye caught the question, 'Who will go for us . . . ?' He immediately knelt in prayer saying, 'Here am I, send me'. The means usually adopted to test the reality of the 'call' was to pray earnestly that the desire should be weakened or strengthened according to God's will in the matter.[52]

The Wesleyans became missionaries for similar reasons. With them there was a greater degree of duty and obligation to the Church involved. Wesley had said that the world was his parish, and accordingly his followers were expected to labour in foreign lands. The Wesleyans were influenced by most of the missionary works which influenced the other Evangelical missionaries. One work which was particularly Wesleyan in character was an emotional appeal written by the Reverend James Watkin of Tonga entitled *Pity Poor Feejee*. The effect of this work was not restricted to Wesleyans, however, as it was widely read. Even a German missionary in New Zealand, J. F. H. Wohlers (1811-85), had been influenced by a German translation.[53] Lawry was influenced by reading the life of Dr Coke which 'in a measure rekindled that Missionary flame' which he had felt burning within him for so long.[54] 'My views of my call to the Missionary work', he wrote two years later, '. . . are the same now as they used to be when I was ploughing the sod or reaping down the corn'.[55]

One of the main determining forces in the 'conversion' to missionary work was the belief of the Evangelical convert in the sanctity of labour. Missionary labour was often viewed as another form of mechanic employment. The missionary had to use his hands. He was a practical man, and he was not to abandon the trades he had learnt. Rather he was to add a few more to his present skills. Law, in describing his strenuous Sabbath day's programme at Rawmarsh, said that he was early convinced that 'labour worship' was the best, by which he meant itineration and village preaching.[56] This kind of idea was linked with the practical work of the week, with mechanic-class utilitarianism and with the idea that physical strength was one of the most important talents entrusted to man's stewardship.

3

A Smattering of Many Things

THROUGHOUT the great era of Evangelical expansion, one of the problems which called forth serious debate was the necessary educational qualifications of missionaries. The first 'godly mechanics' who engaged in the service of the LMS possessed the rudiments of learning, being able to instruct in Sabbath schools. To dispel the myth that *all* the missionaries on board the *Duff* were barely literate, it is only necessary to mention William Henry who had received tuition from Walker of Dublin*, and James Puckey, a carpenter and joiner by trade, who possessed a tolerable knowledge of navigation, and was 'qualified to keep the journal of a ship'. He was 'acquainted with Geography, Architecture and Drawing, and brought with him some specimens of his ability, such as Charts, Maps, and Plans'. He had superintended an evening school in Falmouth, and also instructed children and youths in reading, writing and arithmetic. His pastor recommended him as a schoolmaster.

One of the most interesting contrasts between Evangelical religion and traditional Puritanism is seen in the education controversy. The Calvinistic Methodist directors of the LMS, like their Wesleyan counterparts, placed much more emphasis on qualifications in zeal and piety. The Puritan tradition, on the other hand, emphasized the value of learning, and it was the Independent and Presbyterian directors who urged the need for a systematized education of missionaries. This was one of the issues behind the clash of personalities of the Methodistic and monarchical Dr Haweis and the Dissenting and republican Dr Bogue. It should also be remembered that Bogue disapproved of the South Seas mission so fondly cherished by Haweis.

Until the institution for missionary students, under Dr Bogue, was opened at Gosport, near Portsmouth, in 1801, most theological and general educational training was conducted by individual

*The Reverend John Walker, a Fellow of Trinity College, Dublin, was a director of the LMS for Ireland and probably gave Henry some private tuition in his rooms, which would account for the family tradition that Henry was educated at Trinity College although his name is not to be found in the *Alumni Dublinenses 1593-1860*.

clergymen, usually directors living in the country or the provincial cities. Rev. William Roby of Manchester was one of these.[2] This system of private tuition appears to have been successful; moreover it continued to be an important feature of missionary education even after institutional training was introduced. The more backward candidates usually spent a year or two with a pious clergyman, living in his house and preaching in the villages. Haweis believed that little more training than this was necessary for missionaries. No doubt he would have sent these 'godly mechanics' out as laymen to act as catechists and to support themselves and the mission by applying their skills.

During the early years of the Society the views of the 'Methodist party' seemed to predominate. For instance, at the first meeting of the directors in October 1795 one of the Rules for the Examination of Missionaries stated, 'It is not necessary that every missionary should be a learned man; but he must possess a competent measure of that kind of knowledge which the object of the mission requires'.[3]

Thus it was that the first missionaries were mostly experiential Christians with little knowledge of the metaphysical side of theology. Most of their training was received on board the ship *Duff*, which has been described as a 'floating college in which the thirty missionaries on board laboured to prepare themselves for their great task'.[4] Marsden was one of the first to criticize the system. He argued that the missionary should be well-informed, 'not taken from the dregs of the common people, but possessed of some education, and liberal sentiments. He should rather be of a lively active turn of mind than gloomy and heavy. A gloomy ignorant clown will be disgusting even to savages, and excite their contempt'.[5] Marsden went on to say that some of the missionaries who had come to New South Wales were 'the opposite character to the above. They are totally ignorant of mankind, they possess no education, they are clowns in their manners'.

Some of these early missionaries did have the ability to improve themselves. Nott, for instance, developed into a first-rate Tahitian scholar, as did the bilingual John Davies.[6] However, the orthography and sentence structure of a number of the early letters reveal the inadequate training of these teachers of men.

Dr Bogue, Dr Waugh, Joseph Hardcastle and Alers Hankey were among the first to insist on educational training. At a meeting of directors, 12 May 1797, Bogue read a paper recommending the institution of seminaries for the special training of missionary students. This movement resulted in the formation of a committee, and the appointment of Bogue as Missionary Tutor in

August 1800. The Report on Missionary Training, drawn up by the Committee in May 1800, suggested that the two leading objects of the training should be 'the communication of knowledge, and the formation or rather strengthening of good dispositions'.[7] 'With respect to the former', the committee declared, '. . . as our design is not to form mathematicians, philosophers, or even linguists, it would be unwise to appropriate a great portion of their limited term to these inquiries'. All their studies were to be directed towards the attainment of scriptural knowledge which was the 'desirable qualification' for a Christian missionary. 'Their whole education must be missionary, and therefore conducted on a plan dissimilar from other seminaries, and even from those where the Christian ministry in this country is the object.'

The Report also advised that no missionary should be sent until a year after his acceptance, and that 'they should carry with them some acquaintance with agriculture, or those branches of mechanics which admit of an useful application in uncivilized countries'. The Report acknowledged that more knowledgeable men should be sent out and also advised that they should 'all acquire a knowledge of surgery and the medical art'.

Certainly the missionaries could not all be brought to the same standard of education, but every attempt was made to develop the intellectual capacities of those who had received few opportunities. Most of them desired to better themselves, and were willing to 'grind' in order to obtain the necessary respectability. Not a few made rapid progress. David Darling wrote in 1816:

> I would very much wish to go, to some place of instruction, as I have got, some money in the Bank, that I would wish to spend upon my self, in getting Instruction. . . . I was oblidged to you, for your advice concerning the improvement, necessary to be made by me in the English language, I am making all the progress I can. I have got Scotts Pronouncing Dictionary and Murray Grammar. . . .[8]

Darling made good progress, and was ordained in the following year. George Barnden was another candidate who sought further instruction. In 1834 he wrote that he had been early called to 'active labour for the bread that perisheth', and that he had not had 'time or apertunaty of cultivating [his] mental so as to fitt [him] for this important work'.[9] Most of the other candidates had received what they called 'a plain English education'. A few had received some classical education either privately or at a grammar school.

The Mission Seminary at Gosport, conducted by the Reverend

Dr David Bogue (1750-1825), was run in conjunction with the Congregational Academy which he had opened at Gosport in 1789 for training Independent ministers.[10] Bogue (who was assisted by his son, David, a qualified classical teacher) regarded the office of tutor as 'the most important of all offices', and his practical interest in the theory of education is reflected in the pages of the *History of Dissenters,* which he wrote in conjunction with the Reverend J. Bennett. Bogue agreed in every point with those who drew up the Report of 1800. The first place in the instructions was to be given to Biblical studies. Many of the missionaries had time for nothing else, being unable to attend the usual three-year course at the Academy which besides Latin, Greek and Hebrew,[11] consisted of 120 lectures on theology, 30 lectures on the Old Testament, 30 lectures on the New Testament, 20 lectures on the 'Evidence of Christianity', 16 lectures on Jewish antiquities, 40 lectures on 'the pastoral office', 28 lectures on ecclesiastical history, four lectures on 'Dispensations prior to the Christian era', eleven lectures on 'the different periods of the Church also prior to that time', and ten lectures to students entering the Seminary. There were also five lectures on 'Universal Grammar', five lectures on logic, 35 lectures on rhetoric and 30 lectures on geography and astronomy.[12]

The course at Gosport was defective in several respects. Many of the candidates were not sufficiently advanced to comprehend the logic of Calvinist theology.[13] Their opportunities had been meagre, and their theological knowledge was limited to the simplified theology of the Sabbath schoolroom, the sermon and the prayer meeting. Those who had received a course of private tuition outside the Seminary were at a decided advantage. The principal means of instruction appears to have been the taking of notes in full.[14] Bogue also intended that the authors he referred to should be read, but the vast range of his course left little time for supplementary reading, nor were students encouraged to form differing opinions from his own on theological matters.[15] The Seminary was in many ways a factory for turning Evangelicals of various shades and opinions into orthodox moderate Calvinists and orthodox Congregationalists. The rarefied intellectual atmosphere which had distinguished many of the older Dissenting academies was not to be found there.

The value and some of the deficiencies of the education received at Gosport have been recorded by one of its most celebrated pupils, John Angell James. His picture of the establishment reveals the inadequacies of the system.

My literary advantages at Gosport were of a most slender kind. The fact is, Dr. Bogue, though possessing a great mind and noble heart, was not a great scholar, mathematician, or metaphysician. His forte was theology; that is, the systematic theology of the Puritan school; the theology of Owen, Bates, Charnock, Howe, and Baxter, together with the foreign divines, Turretin, Witsius, Pictet, and Jonathan Edwards. . . . But his theology was almost exclusively dogmatic. Of hermeneutics we heard little, of exegesis, nothing. His lectures were drawn up in the form of a syllabus, somewhat resembling Doddridge's, but far less systematic and philosophical. They resembled the skeletons of sermons, with heads and particulars, divisions and sub-divisions, and references to books, which we were required to read. . . . By this method we certainly acquired a great deal of acquaintance with old divinity, and a relish for the writers and their works of bygone times. . . . The labour of copying out the lectures was a drudgery, which we were compelled to do before we could read upon them.

I remember that when I entered the college the class were in the middle of the system of divinity, and the first lectures I had to copy, to read upon, and to study, were on *The Freedom of the Will;* and one of the first books I had to read was Jonathan Edwards' celebrated treatise on this profound question. To those who are acquainted with that extraordinary piece of theological logic, it will be no surprise that to a youth just leaving the counter, with no previous habits of study, who had gone through no process of mental training, such a volume should prove a most vexatious and discouraging commencement.[16]

Besides the theological lectures, students attended a course of missionary lectures, prepared by Bogue, which they also had to transcribe. This course of twenty-six lectures covered the whole theory of missions as then understood. The first lecture was on 'the Office and Qualifications of a Missionary'. Three lectures were devoted to preaching and the remainder to the other departments of missionary activity. The intention of these lectures was not to lay down strict rules of procedure, but to fulfil the second object mentioned in the Report of 1800, the 'strengthening of good dispositions'. Lecture 16, for instance, was devoted to 'the Behaviour of Missionaries to each other'. Some lectures, such as those devoted to catechizing, 'Writing and Publishing Books', and 'Setting up Schools', and the 'Conduct and Doctrine of Missionaries respecting Civil Government', did make the *duty* of the missionaries to their Society clear, but it seems doubtful whether a lecture devoted to the 'History of Missions before Christ' (with a subsection on the antediluvian world) gave any practical guidance to the missionaries. Bogue's missionary lectures were also restricted in that he could only draw on a limited range of practical missionary experience.*

Although Calvinism and respectability distinguished the students at Gosport[17], Bogue's missionary enthusiasm permeated the atmosphere of the Institution. Every month he would read aloud to the students letters received from various missionaries abroad.[18]

That perhaps too great an emphasis was placed on 'respectability' and academic qualifications at the Seminary is suggested by the early deportment of one of its most distinguished graduates in the South Seas, John Muggridge Orsmond, afterwards Polynesian scholar and linguist. The various social rules for students suggest very clearly that Bogue emphasized the 'apartness' of ministerial candidates and sought to eradicate all traces of rough speech and manner, impressing them with the dignity of their office.† Orsmond was the first missionary to go to the South Seas who had completed the full ministerial course at Gosport and the only one to have had all his theological training under Bogue. Sent to the South Seas somewhat against his own wishes, he consoled himself with the fact that he was a 'classical scholar' who would spend most of his time translating the Scriptures after he had acquired the language. He irritated his less qualified brethren by insisting that he alone had the right to wear an academic gown. In Sydney his host, Dr Redfern, and his family were subjected to readings of Bogue's 'Lectures on Rhetoric', a refinement calculated to impress upon them his own dignity. In the islands he provoked the antipathy of the old missionaries by confining himself to language studies and even watching them labouring on his own house, himself dressed in morning gown, with gloves on his hands. We are told, however, that he participated in the manual crafts of his early apprenticeship on learning that the Tahitians understood him to be incompetent or, as he found to his dismay, *'e taata maua'*, a 'clodpate'.[19]

Most of the missionary candidates received a brief course of

---

*Most of his references were thus confined to the Danish missionaries to Malabar; the American missionaries Eliot, Mayhew and Brainerd; the Moravians; and the Roman Catholics.

†In his lectures for 'Students on entering the Seminary', Bogue laid down different rules for behaviour 'to Christians in respectful stations of society' and 'to Poorer Christians'— the latter included 'Not too much familiarity' and 'Not too much time with them in visits'. Students were further warned to 'Throw off all vulgarisms and provincialisms' and 'Guard against loud and boisterous speaking'. Courtship and close friendships were discouraged. See Bogue's Lectures (copied by J. Lowndes), vol. 8, pp. 509ff, 518-519 in New College, London.

theological training at Gosport, but some of them were given extra tuition. The practical part of the training course, such as the acquisition of particular or specialist mechanical skills, usually meant that the candidate attended classes at a London academy for a time. Thus William Ellis, after he was accepted in December 1814, entered Gosport to prepare for the ministry; yet, wrote his son, 'little more than four months were allowed for this preparatory work'.[20] Ellis then spent six intensive months in London where he learnt all the processes of printing and bookbinding, and where he attended lectures on medicine and surgery, besides actual practice at St Bartholomew's Hospital. At the same time he was given some tuition in Greek by the distinguished theologian, Dr Pye Smith at Homerton Academy in London.* Until he began his course Ellis had received very little formal education, but he had taught himself a lot by avid reading.†

Not all the candidates took to learning easily, and some had to be prepared before entering Gosport. In January 1820 George Pritchard entered the home of the Reverend John Chalmers of Stafford, who conducted a boarding school. Chalmers praised Pritchard for his preaching talents, his industriousness, and for rising early, but in all points of learning he found him 'extremely deficient'.[21] 'To many words with which one would naturally conceive he would be familiar he either affixes no ideas, or ideas so foreign to their meaning as to be quite ludicrous'. He appears to have been so slow that 'many a youth could learn with ease in one day what costs him hard labour for three days'. Chalmers taught Pritchard English grammar, Latin, writing and arithmetic. However when the time came for Pritchard to enter Gosport Chalmers was not happy about his pupil's progress. 'I humbly conceive however that unless a development of talents take place

*Rev. John Pye Smith, D.D., LL.D., was the professor of theology at Homerton (see p. 73) for forty-five years. A man of unusual learning, a prominent preacher and a director of the LMS, Pye Smith was one of the earliest among the Dissenters to recognize the value of the theological contributions of German scholars (see R. Steel, A. W. Murray of Samoa, p. 44 — ML). He was also one of the first to attempt a reconciliation between modern science and the doctrine of divine revelation.

†Charles Pitman was similarly placed when he entered Gosport (see Pitman, 18 August 1820 — CQ). Charles Barff, who went out shortly afterwards, does not appear to have attended Gosport although he was required to study Bogue's lectures and to attend at Homerton. That the training received by these men was quite often very limited might be gathered from a letter written by Barff in 1816 on his way to the islands. 'I am going to write Mr. Bogue's Lectures on Theology, Phylosophy, etc. I hope to be a greek and hebrew scolar and write those lectures' (Barff to Hill, 29 February 1816 — SSM, 100.)

at Gosport it would be much better to send him forth as a Catechist than as a preacher especially as I understand the Directors intend henceforth to divide their Missionaries into these two Classes'.[22] It is not a little surprising to find that nine years later Pritchard was principal of a seminary at Papeete for the training of Tahitian missionaries.

On the other hand, there was the odd missionary at Gosport who had already received an education for the ministry. One such was Thomas Jones, educated at Llanfyllin Academy in Montgomeryshire,[23] who wrote to the directors, on the advice of Bogue, in January 1821, requesting 'a Grammar, a Vocabulary, a Testament, or any Book or Books' that might assist him in learning the Tahitian language.[24]

The Seminary was annually visited by a deputation from the Society who gave a report.[25] The students were examined in Greek, Latin and Hebrew as well as in theology and the examiners placed emphasis on the correctness of doctrinal views.

When Dr Bogue died in 1825 the temporary superintendence of the Gosport Seminary was undertaken by Dr Ebenezer Henderson. In 1826 the students at Gosport were transferred to premises at Hoxton in London which had formerly been a Dissenting academy, and which later became the Wesleyan Mission College.[26] Dr Henderson accepted the post of resident theological tutor. As John Angell James observed in the opening sermon, 'the gift of tongues is gone, and grammars and lexicons supply its place'.[27] More attention was paid to the acquisition of native tongues.* In 1830 the directors resolved to discontinue their own college, mainly because of the expense and the increased facilities for educating missionaries at the various Evangelical colleges and seminaries.

After 1830 the character of missionary education changed, and there was much greater variety in the educational backgrounds and training of the LMS missionaries for the South Seas. The principal academies which the missionaries attended on the recommendation of the directors were Homerton, Highbury (formerly the Independent Academy at Hoxton), Newport Pagnell (Northamptonshire) and Rowell (Bedfordshire). The largest single group of missionaries appears to have been the educationally backward who were trained at Turvey in Bedfordshire. Although Turvey was not an academy, in a very real sense it replaced Gosport and Hoxton, in that so many of the candi-

---

*Students were, nevertheless, examined in Greek, classics, Hebrew, Biblical literature, theology and mental philosophy (see, for example, *Missionary Register* 1827, p. 514; 1829, p. 440; 1830, p. 388).

dates for the South Seas attended there for some months, whether they went to one of the colleges or not. Situated only four miles from Olney, Turvey maintained the Evangelical tradition associated in that district with Cowper and Newton.[28] The Reverend Richard Cecil, who took charge of the students, was minister of the local Congregational Church. Cecil had the confidence of the directors of the LMS and they appear to have been chiefly guided by his judgement in receiving or rejecting candidates for missionary training.[29] As most of those who attended Turvey had received only a slender primary education, Cecil's work was very similar to that of the country clergymen who prepared candidates for the larger academies. Occasionally a candidate who had received very few opportunities made such rapid progress that he was sent to an academy.

On the other hand, some candidates made very little progress. John Rodgerson, for instance, eventually had to receive private tuition from another clergyman. Cecil believed that his talents were 'rather below than above mediocrity', and recommended him as a 'mechanic, who might preach occasionally'. Rodgerson displayed 'a natural want of life and elasticity', and there was nothing to counterbalance this 'want of animation'.[30] The comments of the Reverend Archibald Jack of Whitehaven, who took over Rodgerson's training, also provide an interesting commentary on Turvey. Jack observed that

> a habit of reading seems never to have been contracted before he became the subject of serious impressions and from that time, till a short space before his application to the Society, he had read but little else than the religious periodicals of the day — and of these not the most likely to enlarge the mind. Hence the meagreness of his general knowledge. I question if ever he read a volume of history in his life. His acquaintance with Theology, when he went to Turvey was I knew chiefly of a practical kind; and I had hoped that he might have gained a greater acquaintance with the Science during his studies there than I find he has.[31]

Jack criticized the system at Turvey, implying that too exclusive a place was given to the Latin and Greek languages. 'Yet I think it a desideratum in Mr. Cecil's plan that he does not require of the students exercises in composition to a greater extent than he does.' Rodgerson spent two hours each day with Jack reading history, geography, English composition and theology. Jack also undertook to familiarize Rodgerson with the Tahitian grammar. Despite all this extra tuition Rodgerson never overcame his initial backwardness, and his character as a missionary was not

particularly attractive. He lacked tact, was arbitrary in his dealings with island peoples, and was slow to adapt himself to new
conditions. This was particularly obvious in the Marquesas.

In contrast to Rodgerson, Robert Thomson was a candidate
who had also received little education, but whose powers of
perseverance enabled him to become an efficient missionary.
When he applied in 1836, Thomson said that he had been
practising writing, arithmetic and mensuration and had been
reading English grammar, ancient and modern geography and
Latin, but admitted that, from 'want of application', he never
was a good scholar.[32] Thomson, however, had a natural brilli-
ance. One of his workmates wrote that he had often been 'put
to the blush' at Thomson's 'supperior style of Essay writting',[33]
and doubtless the young joiner did impress his fellow mechanics
with his 'learning'. Thomson's stay at Turvey was short and he
seemed to benefit most from preaching experience. Unfortunately
he was 'conscious even to a painful degree' that he was inferior
to his colleagues 'both in talent and extent of education'. It had
been suggested that Thomson should go out to the Marquesas
before being ordained, but he opposed this because he had heard
enough to convince him that he was regarded by some of
his brethren as being considerably their inferior, and it had
occasioned a 'little unpleasant feeling'.[34]

Those candidates who did not go to Turvey might be gathered
into two groups, those who were already at academies when they
applied, and those who were sent to academies by the LMS.
During the eighteenth century the Dissenting academies had held
a very important place in the history of English education.[35]
Indeed, the principal academies had been regarded, even by some
leading Churchmen, as offering at least as good an education as
Oxford and Cambridge.

Homerton Academy was the more intellectual successor to
Gosport and Hoxton. A Congregational establishment, Homerton
had originally been founded by the King's Head Society at New-
ington Green about 1732. This academy had a varied career,
but unlike some of its kind it had been consistent in its
adherence to Calvinist doctrine.[36] Great importance was also
placed on the value of the classics. The normal course for
ministerial training at Homerton was four years. Examinations
were held in natural philosophy, the 'Philosophy of Mind',
rhetoric, ecclesiastical history, biblical criticism and divinity.[37]
The intelletual life of Homerton centred around Dr John Pye
Smith, known to theological scholars for his understanding of
the new school of German criticism, but to the LMS directors

for his ability to discern and develop the talents of bright candidates who had received very little primary education.[38]

Another training place for missionary candidates was Cheshunt College. The followers of Whitefield were not as oblivious of the practical uses of ministerial education as their Wesleyan brethren. A college for the training of ministers had been founded by the Countess of Huntingdon at Trevecca. Eventually this establishment developed into Cheshunt College.[39] A three-year course was given free of charge to Calvinist candidates for the ministry of any Protestant denomination. Although Latin, Greek and Hebrew were taught, it is quite clear from the reports that preaching practice was the central feature of the course. The old Dissenting academies had placed considerable emphasis on occupational training, but Cheshunt outdid them all. The whole course was directed towards the cultivation of the art of preaching. It was not part of the curriculum to broaden the mental horizons. In 1838 Cheshunt became a training place for missionaries. It was regarded as a kind of 'finishing school' for those candidates who had received a good education elsewhere.[40]

In the late 1840s and 1850s the Academy at Bedford became the missionary seminary for the South Seas. The tutors at Bedford,[48] like those at Turvey, were concerned with 'raw, uncultivated' recruits. Law and McFarlane both belonged to that class. Similarly John Jones was given some instruction at Cotton End Academy, near Bedford, after receiving some tuition from the Reverend W. Legge of Fakenham.[42]

The other class of missionary candidates who applied to the LMS after 1830 were those students who were already in theological colleges. Instead of removing to a 'missionary seminary' they completed their various courses. Hackney college was perhaps the most influential of these other academies, and trained as many missionaries for the South Seas as Homerton.* The missionaries trained at Hackney included Bullen, Powell, George Gill, Lind and Spencer. A report written by the Reverend John Jefferson, after Bullen had completed his final year in 1838, is of interest as it is one of the few available examination reports for a South Seas missionary.

*Hackney had been founded by Rev. John Eyre, minister of an Episcopal chapel at Homerton, a founder of the LMS and joint editor of the *Evangelical Magazine*. His original aim had been to provide a 'short and economical course of instruction, to prepare itinerants to preach Christ to the poor', hence the official title of the foundation, 'Hackney Theological Seminary, and Society for the Propagation of the Gospel, usually called the Village Itinerancy, or Evangelical Association for the Propagation of the Gospel'.

Mr Bullen fully sustained the high character of which he gave early promise. He read in *Latin,* ex Andria Terentii, — in *Greek* from the Crito of Plato, and the Oedipus Tyrannus of Sophocles; in *Hebrew,* the third chapter of Job; and in *Syriac* from the second chapter of John. He read also a portion of the Epistle to the Romans, and furnished an analysis of the epistle. He stated also, at considerable length, and with great accuracy, the evidence for the Authenticity and Inspiration of the Pentateuch, with special reference to the miracles, and to some of the popular objections of infidels; and was prepared to give a general view of the Old Testament Revelation, as developed [in the] character of the Great Deliverer promised to man, and of the New Testament Revelation as exhibiting his person and claims; the whole investigation having been pursued as the basis of a system of theological truth deduced immediately from the Scriptures themselves.[43]

The other academies at which missionaries to the South Seas were trained included Wymondley, the 'Presbyterian College' at Caermarthen, Airedale College, Blackburn Independent Academy, Western College and Highbury.* In Scotland missionary candidates attended the Theological Academy conducted by the Reverend Greville Ewing and Dr Ralph Wardlaw at Glasgow.[44] As at Cheshunt, the emphasis was on preaching but the students were encouraged to attend the University of Glasgow. Thomas McKean, for instance, took his A.M. degree while others attended language classes.[45]

The only missionary previously ordained for parish work who did not attend a theological college was the Reverend William Howe. He informed the directors that his education had been 'strictly of a private nature'.[46] The Bible had been his principal study and he appeared to be very proficient in Hebrew and Greek. He had read the Bible and the Septuagint in Hebrew and made a practice of reading the Greek Testament in conjunction with different commentaries. He had studied several critical works and adopted the methods laid down in Campbell's *Systematic Theology.* Besides theology, he had studied 'mental philosophy', natural history and astronomy.

Although private tuition and theological courses played the

---

*Highbury College, formerly Hoxton Independent Academy, was directed by Dr Ebenezer Henderson, who had been the missionary Tutor (see above, p. 71). For more detail concerning the course at Highbury see Jesson, 30 April 1840 — CQ. Amongst Henderson's students were Loxton, Jesson and William Wyatt Gill. Wyatt Gill, who was also a graduate of London University, afterwards became one of the foremost scholars of Polynesian culture. He completed his theological training at New College, which was formed in 1850 when Homerton College (Mile End), Coward College and Highbury College (Hoxton Academy) merged.

major role in the training of the South Seas missionaries, some applicants attended the mechanics' institutes. The desire of the mechanic class for knowledge, and the desire to disseminate it, led to the formation of societies and institutions for the purpose of giving instruction in scientific and cultural subjects.[47] These institutions became a powerful influence in nineteenth-century life, and many of the missionaries received instruction which greatly supplemented their theological or specialized courses. Mills, who had received only 'an ordinary education', attended popular lectures given in Glasgow on natural philosophy, chemistry and anatomy.[48] With this grounding he was enabled to attend classes in anatomy, chemistry and the theory and practice of medicine. As a result he became a useful medical missionary. Mills had a thirst for education which is some ways typified the age and the class. He believed implicitly that a missionary should be well educated.[49]

The educational qualifications of the Presbyterian missionaries were similar to those of the LMS missionaries. All the Presbyterian missionaries, except the catechist Archibald, were ordained ministers before entering the field, and consequently they had taken theological courses.[50]

The American Board missionaries were also well trained, mainly owing to the close association between the missionary movement and the colleges. The American Puritans had always placed a high value on education, and although Whitefield and others had done much to stimulate their Evangelical zeal, there had been no great infusion of Methodist principles. The same revival in New England during the last decade of the eighteenth century which gave rise to several societies in the eastern States for disseminating missionary intelligence was responsible for the founding of Williams, Bowdoin, Union and Middlebury Colleges.[51]

In the island of Moorea next to Tahiti there was an institution which also contributed to the education of South Seas missionaries. This was the South Sea Academy which was opened in March 1824. Although there were only three male missionaries born in the South Seas who attended this academy,[52] a number of missionaries' wives were educated there. J. M. Orsmond was the first master of the 'academy' and was succeeded by Alexander Simpson in 1831. In 1839 Simpson resigned when Howe agreed to take over the institution. Howe shortly afterwards withdrew, and no successor was appointed. Thenceforward the children of the missionaries were sent to England. Neither Simpson nor Orsmond had received any training as school teachers, and their methods are an interesting revelation of the general teaching practice of the missionaries. Orsmond was in many ways a talented man, but his educational system consisted mainly in requiring his pupils to commit large sections of textbook knowledge to memory. Thus at an examination held in 1826 the fourteen-year-old Samuel Wilson, son of the missionary Charles Wilson and himself afterwards a pioneer missionary to Samoa, repeated the following impressive list:

> The epistle to the Hebrews; and also the Epistle of James; thirty-one hymns; fifty-one pages of Ayliffe's Catechism on Divine Revelation; the whole of the Missionary hymns; Murray's Grammar to the end of Syntax; ten chapters of Pinnock's Catechism on Geography; twenty-two chapters of ditto on Chronology; the whole of the Assembly's Catechism with the proofs; twenty-nine pages of a Catechism on the Arts and Sciences; seven chapters of Pinnock's Catechism on Rhetoric.[53]

No doubt this method of teaching reflects the effect of Bogue's course at Gosport. A writer in the *South-Asian Register* shrewdly observed that 'making boys learn off by heart as a task, sublime or interesting passages, is the way to pall the pleasure of them, or lessen their interest in after life'.[54]

Evidently this was not the case with Samuel Wilson. In the same year he felt that God had begun 'the work of Grace in the soul'.[55] At the end of 1826 Wilson was sent to Sydney, where he lived in the family of the Reverend Dr J. D. Lang. During the next two years he 'acquired a sufficient knowledge of the Latin, Greek and French languages to enable him to read the Holy Scriptures in each of these languages with fluency'. In 1829 he was appointed teacher of the Caledonian school in Sydney.[56] In 1831 he was doing pastoral work. Crook observed that there was a certain manner about him 'in consequence of his being brought up at Tahiti' which was noticed by all discerning persons.[57] All European boys from Tahiti, Crook believed, would 'appear halfwitted when brought to a civilized country'. Wilson continued his studies and attended a course of lectures on natural philosophy and chemistry delivered by the Reverend John Mac-Garvie, the Presbyterian chaplain at Portland Head.[58] In 1832 he returned to Tahiti, where he continued to study Euclid and algebra. He also received some assistance from George Pritchard and copied out the outlines of Bogue's theological lectures. A year after his return he wrote to the LMS directors saying that it would be more advantageous to him to 'acquire a knowledge of the Tahitian Dialect' and acquaint himself a little with 'the

manners and customs of the people, ignorance of which would
be unpleasant to [him] when in the company of friends in
England'. Wilson had spent so much time out of Tahiti that he
had possibly absorbed less Tahitian culture than any of the
other missionaries' sons. His desire to know more of island
customs was in part stimulated by Dr Lang,[59] but is was also
something which came independently of education, and was
eventually to lead to his fall (see page 154).

John Barff was at the Academy under Simpson, and when
admitted could only speak Tahitian. While there he learnt some
Latin, but 'was unable to proceed for want of suitable books'.[60]
In 1834 he was taken to England where he was further educated
at Silcoates School, and was taught Greek and Latin. After returning to the islands in 1839 he assisted Pritchard at Papeete where
he was 'acceptable as a Preacher, both in English and Tahitian'.[61]
In 1841 he was at Huahine and continued his studies with his
father. In June of that year they had gone through part of the
New Testament in Greek and the first book of the Aeneid in
Latin, and had reached the eightieth of Bogue's lectures, 'reading
appropriate works'.[62] At this stage John Barff had achieved a
proficiency in the Tahitian language 'not to be obtained by any
but those born here'. In 1842, on offering himself to the mission,
the Tahitian Committee required him to submit an exegesis on
Job, ix, 2, and an exposition from the original of 2 Corinthians,
iv, 3-4, besides an essay on 'the duration of future punishments'.[63]
Barff was ordained in 1844, and his training, combined with
his great knowledge of Tahitian, rendered him a very capable
translator.

James Bicknell was also at the Academy under Simpson, after
which he was sent to New South Wales where he was apprenticed
to a carpenter. Bicknell was the only missionary associated with
the American missions who did not receive a regular theological
training, and this was because he joined on a voluntary basis as
a lay helper. His knowledge of island customs and his missionary
zeal made him in many ways the unofficial leader of the
Marquesas mission. He returned to Hawaii and there received
ordination.

The majority of the Calvinist missionaries who went to the
South Seas received an intensive course of theological training
which included instruction in the original languages of the
Bible. Other training was incidental to this. But they all were
impressed with the importance of education, and the desire to
be better educated was about as keen as the desire to impart the
'saving truths' to the islanders.

The Methodist Revival, however, tended to emphasize the importance of preaching, and to disregard theological and classical learning. Orthodox Churchmen and learned Dissenters shared in the spirit of the Revival, but they were often concerned by the unlettered character of a vast number of the evangelists.[64]

Many of Wesley's followers were very ill-educated, receiving no more instruction than that obtained from dame schools, and perhaps from personal tuition. Throughout Methodism there appeared to be a certain suspicion of higher education, especially of the classics and polite learning, and a fear that such subjects would detract from a pristine holiness and zeal. Even the academic training given at Trevecca by the Calvinistic Methodists emphasized the role of preaching and placed less emphasis on non-scriptural subjects. Indeed amongst the Wesleyans men appeared to be educated according to their station in life.

This aspect of Methodism, especially of the Wesleyan Connexion, was a social phenomenon rather than the policy of its leaders, and as the majority of Wesley's followers in the early nineteenth century became better educated through the means of Sabbath schools, mechanics' institutes, and the dissemination of popular educational literature, the old distrust was gradually broken down. There had always been a number of Wesleyan leaders who endeavoured to raise the standards of education of the local preachers. Wesley himself had planned to establish a 'Seminary for Labourers'.[65] The great scholars of the Wesleyan movement were also firm advocates for better training. In 1806 Dr Adam Clarke appealed for 'some kind of seminary for educating such workmen as need not be ashamed'.

Only for the children of Wesleyan preachers was there any real attempt to provide a classical education, no doubt in the hope that sons would follow their fathers in the ministry, though Kingswood School, founded by Wesley in 1746, had been started as a model boarding school on Christian principles to set it apart from the 'pagan' schools of the day.[66] While many of its scholars afterwards entered the Wesleyan ministry, very few volunteered for missionary service. Those who went to the islands, with the exception of Thomas Jaggar, missionary in Fiji, belonged essentially to influential middle-class clerical families.*

*E.g. William Fletcher, Joseph Waterhouse (pp. 45-6 above). Fletcher's missionary father, conscious of his social position, sent his son to the Methodist college at Taunton to study for London University and 'qualify himself to take a good position as a teacher in schools of the higher class' (Fletcher, 1892, p. 19). After obtaining his B.A., Fletcher became a master at Lincoln Grammar School. He then joined the staff at the Wesleyan College and Seminary at Auckland and was headmaster of that institution when he joined the Fijian mission.

However, from the 1840s a number of missionary sons were sent from the islands to Kingswood, Woodhouse Grove, Taunton and other Methodist schools.

Until 1834 the training given to Wesleyan missionaries was comparatively limited. Thomas and Hutchinson of the Tongan mission were men of few opportunities, and it was only by arduous application that Thomas was able to develop into a competent missionary. As a boy Thomas had been taught to read and write, but throughout his missionary life he was conscious of lack of education. 'I have been engaged today chiefly in my study', wrote Thomas in 1827.

> Had I possessed more information, and a more competent ability for this great work before I left home, then I might have spent more time in the study of the language than I can now . . . What a raw, weak, uncultivated wretch was I when I left old England![67]

Whilst he was a local preacher he had studied the Bible, Wesley's works, and some of the writings of Doddridge. Thomas continued to read in theology, and he and Hutchinson requested some standard reference works to take to Tonga.[68] A story told by John Watsford throws some light on the educational limitations of John Thomas. On one occasion, when Watsford was talking with Hazlewood about grammar, they said that they thought John Wesley's grammars were all too brief, and were unfit for learners. 'Mr Thomas was at us in a moment, and came down on us very severely. That two mere boys should dare to criticise the work of that great man was almost as bad as the unpardonable sin.'[69]

Because these early missionaries had received scarcely any training their preaching was often crude and not always acceptable amongst Europeans of their own persuasion. The Reverend Joseph Orton, for instance, criticized James Watkin of Tonga for 'dictatorial freedoms with his audience', and expressions which were in many instances 'decidedly coarse and unbefitting the pulpit'.[70]

Peter Turner is typical of the early missionaries whose education extended to little more than learning the three Rs and reading theological works recommended by their seniors. Amongst the less fortunate of the missionaries of the LMS and the majority of Wesleyans, self-culture played an important part, in fact many of them mastered an amazing amount of knowledge even if they did not secure academic polish. Turner's first training was at a Sabbath school, although his mother, who was a 'superior reader', possibly helped him.[71] He afterwards attended a young men's class in a Wesleyan Sabbath school in Macclesfield. The standard of this institution might be gauged from the fact that the reader had 'no learning' and could not write although he could read. When on trial as a local preacher, Turner greatly lamented his lack of 'literary qualifications'.[72] His only books at this stage were the Bible, Wesley's *Notes on the New Testament,* a small edition *of Pilgrim's Progress,* 'an old magazine' [Methodist?] and Baxter's *Saints Rest.* He lamented that 'more was not done for such as [himself] by the preachers in the Circuit'.

Turner was in some ways more fortunate than others, as he attended a Saturday evening class conducted by the local Independent minister (Dunkerly of Macclesfield). Soon after this he was given some private tuition by a Wesleyan minister but although this groundwork in grammar and theology was usually quite thorough, it tended to give men such as Turner a sense of inferiority.

Throughout his life Turner kept a list of all the books he read. Most of these works were concerned with theology or religious biography, although he did read some novels.[73] He records that he found 'nothing poluting to the mind' in *David Copperfield,* but he considered that the *Christmas Books* were 'not worth anybody's time reading'. Such 'foolish stuff' and Disraeli's *Vivian Grey* were 'only fit for waste paper'. This restricted vision and narrow outlook was typical of those who had fought hard to gain the literary advantages which they possessed. Their goal had been to understand the scriptures better in order to be able to preach better, and literature was only commendable when it served or assisted this purpose.

Walter Lawry, the first of the Wesleyan missionaries to Tonga, possibly made the greatest advances in self-improvement. In November 1815, at the age of twenty-two, he wrote that he had begun to study grammar, geography, and Greek, 'according to [his] wish'.[74] He was confident that he would become proficient in these subjects because he 'loved' them. Lawry's letters and journals display talents and knowledge equal, if not superior, to those of his LMS contemporaries. Most of his reading, however, appears to have been of a devotional nature.[75] Another early missionary who was better educated than most was John Weiss. Although when he volunteered for missionary work Weiss had forgotten most of the Latin and French he had learnt at school, he had passed the examination of the Royal Naval College, as a candidate for a lieutenancy, and understood navigation and astronomy. His theological reading had been confined to the basic works of Methodism.[76] The District Meeting reported that he possessed 'most of the qualities which the others lacked'.

> His *youth* and *superior education* fitted him for an expeditious acquirement of the language; . . . his *thorough knowledge of Navigation* both in theory and practice, and his *readiness in the use of the pen,* were acquirements of which the Mission was utterly destitute . . .[77]

Only two Wesleyan missionaries who left England before 1834 received an education comparable to that of the academic training of the LMS missionaries. These were David Cargill and Dr Richard Burdsall Lyth. Cargill, an M.A. of King's College, Aberdeen, equipped with a classical education, was fitted for translation work. Somewhat self-opinionated, he was not particularly popular with his less-educated brethren. Cargill's journal, written on the voyage out, mentioned the theological works he was then reading.[78] These included discourses by Dr Chalmers 'on the Christian Revelation viewed in connexion with Modern Astronomy', and James' *Family Monitor,* 'a work of incomparable worth, and which next to the Bible should be carefully perused by everyone who wishes to enjoy domestic felicity'. Despite his background and training, Cargill's reading does not appear to have been greatly different from that of his colleagues.

The need for better training was most obvious in the various mission fields. One writer in the *Methodist Magazine* denied an assertion that the Wesleyan missionaries compared favourably with the 'Dissenting Ministers, with all their academical training'.

> Can a man study with advantage the grammar of another language, when he has not thoroughly studied that of his own? . . . 'But have not our Missionaries made equal progress in the different languages with the progress made by Missionaries belonging to other Societies?' I answer, *They have not.*[79]

At the Wesleyan Conference of 1833 a committee was appointed to draw up plans for an institution to provide two or three years of instruction for candidates for the ministry. As might be expected, there was considerable opposition to overcome, and advocates of better training had to show that it was neither an innovation nor contrary to the teachings of Wesley.[80] The committee met in October 1833 and drew up a plan which was discussed and approved at the Conference of 1834.[81] Provision was made for an institution to be established in London so that the students could attend lectures by 'eminent Professors in several important branches of useful knowledge'. It was also desirable that missionary candidates should be 'within reach of those instructions which are adapted to their peculiar work and prospects, and which they can receive only from Missionary Secretaries'. The Reverend Jabez Bunting was appointed the first President of the Institution.* The Reverend Joseph Entwisle was appointed first Governor and acted as class leader of the students, whilst the Reverend John Hannah was appointed theological tutor. Hannah was undoubtedly the most influential tutor at the Institution. Perhaps the most conspicuous thing about his course was its strict conformity to established Wesleyan forms, adhering as it did rigidly to methods used by Wesley and Watson.[82] Thus his division of Christian theology into four parts — Evidences, Doctrines, Duties, and Institutions — was based on the plan adopted by Watson in his *Theological Institutes*. [It was a plan, moreover, which had received the 'official approbation of the Wesleyan Conference'.][83] In other respects the course was very little different from that given in the Dissenting academies. Lectures were given, and the students were expected to consult the references. Calvert records that he transcribed theological lectures from seven lecture-books.[84] Hannah was most emphatic about the peculiar nature of theology as a subject for learned study. With all the non-Calvinist's distrust of speculation and the treatment of theology as a science, Hannah cautioned his prospective students to 'remember that the Christian system is concerned with the heart of man; and that, while it instructs the mind, it especially seeks to restore him to the favour, the image, and the communion of his God'.[85] In emphasizing a Christocentric theology he warned that both Calvinist doctrine and Wesleyan revivalism led to Antinomianism.

The Wesleyan Theological Institution was opened at Hoxton in the very buildings formerly occupied by the LMS as a missionary college, and classes commenced at the end of 1834.[86] The Reverend Samuel Jones, a graduate of Trinity College, Dublin, was shortly afterwards appointed classical and mathematical tutor. Amongst the first students at Hoxton were two of the early missionaries to Fiji, John Hunt and James Calvert. The effect of the training was very marked on Hunt, and he was one

*Jabez Bunting (1779-1858) was then senior secretary of the WMMS. He dominated Methodist affairs during the first forty years of the nineteenth century. Not only was the theological institute established, but his district missionary meetings in the Leeds circuit in 1813 had led to the formation of the Missionary Society itself. As the 'Pope of Methodism' he was largely responsible for Wesleyan developments, including the use of the designation 'Reverend' (1818) and the revival of the practice of ordination by laying-on of hands (1836), which helped to give Methodism separate status as a Church.

of the few missionaries of any of the Evangelical societies in the
South Seas whose religious inclinations were directed to theology.
As early as May 1835 he reported on his progress to Hannah
Summers, a young Methodist convert from Newton-upon-Trent,
whom he afterwards married.

> I have lately had my views of the greatness and Goodness of God
> much enlarged and of course my views of myself corrected by the
> study of the Evidences of Christianity, the Being and perfections of
> God and some facts of Natural Philosophy and Astronomy. I shall
> be able I hope to teach you a little about those sublime subjects If
> I live to come to Newton again and in after life if by the will of
> God we should be brought together. . . . I hope to have another year
> in the Institution. I have learned but little I have had so many
> things to learn. I have got a smattering of a many things. Grammar.
> Geography Astronomy Chemistry Logic Greek Latin and Divinity
> and myself my own ignorance and weakness.[87]

Hunt in fact had two more years at Hoxton. He paid most
attention to experiential religion and already in December 1835
he was preaching on the subject of 'entire sanctification', which
state of grace he did not claim as his own until after November
1836.[88]

Hoxton was vacated at Michaelmas, 1842, and Richmond
Theological Hall was opened in September 1843.* An intimate
picture of life at Richmond is given by the Reverend Samuel
Wray in his account of the early life of the Reverend W. O.
Simpson, a missionary to India. There was the closed circle of
the students of the third year whose power it was 'to admit or to
taboo, to promote to honour, or to keep back from honour'. An
annual soirée was held just before the long vacation in honour
of these men before they went to their stations. 'There was some
feasting — liberal, but strictly temperate, much pleasant conversation, speech-making, singing of hymns, and prayer.' The
theological tutor at Richmond was the Reverend Thomas Jackson who, like Hannah, insisted on the pre-eminence of theological studies over classics and mathematics.[89] The reading room
was furnished with 'the foremost reviews, magazines, and newspapers of the time', but few students could spare time from their
studies to make use of the extensive library.

Amongst those who received their theological training at Richmond were William Wilson and Royce of Fiji, and Vercoe of

---

*It was opened as the 'southern branch' of the Wesleyan Theological
Institution; a 'northern branch' had been opened at Didsbury, Manchester,
in September 1842. Richmond became exclusively a missionary college in
1863 when it was purchased by the Wesleyan Missionary Society.

Tonga. Even after the establishment of Hoxton and Richmond distrust of secular learning remained characteristic of provincial Methodism. One student believed that the course at Richmond was 'too theoretical' and that little was done to 'equip the soul'. He complained of the number of classes, the variety of subjects and the shortness of time, reckoning that a man with a defective memory had little chance of succeeding. It was the personal influence of the instructors which seemed to have the most lasting effect on the students.[90]

Jesse Carey is representative of the missionaries who did not receive any theological training after the establishment of Hoxton and Richmond. Until the age of twelve Carey attended the National school at Stockwell (1839-44), after which he transferred to the British and Foreign school at Brixton Hill. He also attended the Wesleyan Sunday school. During the years 1845-47 he missed a considerable amount of schooling owing to an injured foot. He then went to night classes conducted by his former schoolmaster.[91] He next received lessons in Latin from the master of a private school in exchange for attending to the schoolroom. He also visited a chemist twice a week in order to study Latin contractions as used by chemists and medical men. After this he spent some time connected with Sunday school and 'ragged school' work. Whilst out of employment and doing voluntary teaching, Carey continued his studies at home until he migrated to Australia. He was possibly better equipped than others placed in similar circumstances; he possessed the natural ability for self-culture (and a talent for versification).

Similarly missionaries recruited in the colonies went to the islands without any theological training. John Watsford had attended The King's School, Parramatta. Thomas Baker received some assistance from his minister, especially in the study of English grammar. His educational deficiencies appear to have delayed his acceptance as a missionary.[92] John Millard who, at twenty, possessed 'all the gravity of an aged Minister', was regarded by his circuit superintendent as a 'good English Scholar' who understood Latin and had some knowledge of Greek.[93] These men acquired their theological views by reading Wesley's Sermons and Notes.

About the same time that the Methodists began to take an interest in the education of their local preachers and missionaries, they also began to realize the importance of training their school teachers. Indeed, the matter seemed urgent to them because of the 'corrupt and anti-scriptural' policy of the British government which was to secularize education and make religion a mere subject in the schools instead of retaining it as the central feature. Believing that religious and secular education could not be separated, the Methodist Education Committee began, in 1839, to send their prospective teachers to the teacher-training institution or 'normal seminary' conducted by a successful educationalist, David Stow (1793-1864), at Glasgow. His first principle of teaching was that education must aim at the development of religious and moral character.[94] Amos of Tonga and Binner and Collis of Fiji had attended the Glasgow Normal Seminary, and went out expressly to introduce the Glasgow system to the islands. Although these men were well trained for their particular duty they appear to have been less knowledgeable in theology and the classics than the majority of their colleagues.

The contrast between the different types of missionary was not to be found in their religious views but in their attitudes to their work. However much time men such as Thomas and Peter Turner spent in quiet study, however much they laboured to 'improve' themselves, they could never acquire the confidence, or the conceit for that matter, of the man who had received some formal training. Often the less educated man made a more efficient missionary, in that he was less timid about using the axe to fell the old culture. Activated by something akin to the doctrine of reparation, he felt that he had to work harder in order to make up for his educational deficiencies. 'I might not know much about Greek and Latin, but I've won more souls for Christ' was very real in their thinking. Men such as this made good revivalists.

Although there was little difference between the class backgrounds of the LMS and Wesleyan missionaries, the standard of education and formal training was much lower amongst the Wesleyans, except for a few individuals who had received specialized training. Thus there was a balance. The Wesleyans, in an economic sense, tended to be more nearly middle-class. On the other hand, the LMS missionaries received educational advantages which gave them a superior status, in a social sense. The life of the Wesleyan missionary had less of the success story about it. The humble mechanic and the prosperous shopkeeper tended to keep their places in the social hierarchy. Not so with the LMS missionaries; there was a more democratic levelling, and the reason for this was that all were given an opportunity to receive higher education.

A further difference between the two groups of missionaries

9 Rev. John Williams
wide-ranging missionary and shipbuilder, killed in 1839 at Eromanga

10 Mary Williams
wife of John Williams and
mother of Consul J. C.
Williams

11 Eliza Pritchard
wife of George Pritchard
and mother of Consul
W. T. Pritchard

12 'Samoan with long hair as worn by dissipated characters'—a contemporaneous description

13 Rev. Peter Vi early Tongan convert and confidant of King George Tupou I

14 Papehia pioneer Raiatean missionary to the Cook Islands

was that the training of the Wesleyans was much more exclusively theological. The Wesleyan missionary was regarded as a minister or local preacher who had offered himself for foreign service in Wesley's world parish. There was nothing special about his dedication, he was not obliged to introduce the arts of civilization, and he tended to be conservative in his thinking.

4

Apprenticed to the Means of Grace

MOST, IF NOT ALL, of the Evangelical missionaries went to the islands with some home missionary experience. Many of the early missionaries of the LMS were field preachers. In the market place and village square they proclaimed Christ to the people and, like Wesley and Whitefield, were often stoned for it. Crook, Hayward, Youl and Warner were active members of the London Itinerant Society so closely associated with Hackney College (see page 74). Their work was in the direct tradition of the Revival. Threlkeld had accompanied an itinerant preacher in Devon, and had spoken to the villagers.[1] Rowland Hassall had been stoned at Welston.[2]

The directors of the LMS expected all candidates to have had some experience in religious teaching. The fifth question asked of candidates (see Appendix I) was:

> Have you been accustomed to engage in any social or public religious services — in prayer meetings — in the instruction of the young — in visiting the sick — in the distribution of tracts, or in any other effort for the spiritual good of others? — and if so, state the particulars.

Nearly every candidate answered that he had been a Sunday school teacher. Most answered that they had engaged in the other activities, and this was also true of the missionaries' wives. However there was some variety in the religious employments of the candidates.

The leaders of the Evangelical Revival had set the example of preaching to the poor. Much of this work was carried on by young laymen who were anxious to 'proclaim Christ to the world' but who did not have the qualifications to preach to church members. Barnden, for instance, spent a year speaking to adults in lodging houses and rooms 'where the gospel is preached to the poor'.[3] It was ever part of Evangelicals' thinking that the miserable poor and the 'poor heathen' were designed for the same philanthropy. A grass skirt became all too easily a beggar's rags.

Preaching in 'destitute' villages was an important feature of home missionary work, and young men, anxious to become preachers themselves, would often serve an 'apprenticeship' by accompanying an itinerant minister. This apprenticeship on more than one occasion was the commencement of a missionary career. Aaron Buzacott assisted the home missionary in his own district in Devonshire, visiting the villages by turns. He was then invited by the Reverend James Hardy, a home missionary in Herefordshire, to live with him as his assistant. According to his application to the directors, he frequently preached eight or nine times in a week.[4] It was Hardy who recommended Buzacott for the ministry. Students at the theological colleges were expected to engage in village preaching as part of their extra-curricular training. For several years William Harbutt walked from ten to twenty-five miles on a Saturday, preached on the Sabbath, and returned on the Monday, 'without experiencing any inconvenience'.[5] Even in the 1830s village preaching could be as dangerous and difficult as in the days of the earlier Methodist field preachers.[6]

Not all the missionary candidates had engaged in the more strenuous forms of home missionary work. Henry Gee, for instance, had never conducted a public religious service. His principal exertions had been to address the Sabbath school children, and to speak at public tea meetings and at the local Useful Knowledge Society.[7] When one considers Gee's later pathetic attempts to adjust himself to the rigour of missionary itineration in Samoa, one feels that he would have benefited considerably from the kind of training which Harbutt received.[8]

A considerable number of the missionary candidates were already either full-time colporteurs or paid agents of local home missionary societies when they applied.[9] Perhaps the most notable of these full-time evangelists was A. W. Murray of Kelso in Scotland. The Evangelical ministry in Kelso had organized a Town Mission and Murray was appointed its first agent. Kelso was a place of revivals, and Murray received his apprenticeship in the use of revival techniques whilst in this atmosphere of religious enthusiasm. The directors of the Kelso Town Missionary Association expressed their satisfaction with Murray as an evangelist.

> We can refer to particular instances in which the divine blessing seems evidently to have rested on his labours, where the proofs of substantial benefit having been conferred are decisive and unequivocal.[10]

This counted for something in an environment where a man's

missionary reputation rested on the number of souls he had saved which could be tallied off abacus-fashion. Like many of the missionaries, Murray had a particular attachment to youth work and was superintendent of a boys' Sabbath evening school connected with the Church of Scotland at Kelso.

Several of the missionaries had been settled pastors. Howe, Jesson and McKean were all Congregational ministers. During a pastorate of six years Jesson had been responsible for building two new chapels in villages adjacent to his own.[11] Another candidate, J. P. Sunderland, occasionally preached in the villages in connexion with his church, and for twelve months before entering college though not then ordained, he had acted as the pastor of a country church.[12]

Very few of the South Seas missionaries had any prior experience in foreign fields. Both Threlkeld and Krause spent a number of months in the Americas (in Brazil and Guatemala respectively) on their way to the South Seas, but much of this time was spent in working amongst Europeans, and their principal employment was the distribution of Protestant tracts. C. W. Schmidt, however, was one of Dr Gossner's missionaries, and came to Australia with other missionaries at the invitation of Dr Lang. His experiences from 1838 to 1844 in missionary work with the Aboriginals were not happy,[13] but it is quite probable that they helped him in Samoa. A little cynicism at the beginning of a missionary venture was a better guide than all the enthusiasm aroused in Exeter Hall. Certainly in Samoa Schmidt appears to have won the affection of his people.

Most of the Presbyterian missionaries in the New Hebrides had also had home missionary experience. Geddie had been a settled minister. G. N. Gordon had founded the City Mission in Halifax. Johnston had acted as a colporteur in Kansas and Nebraska. John G. Paton taught in a Free Church school, and even had a midday class of young women who came to study writing and arithmetic. He was appointed an agent of the Glasgow City Mission.[14] By the time he went to the South Seas he had had at least ten years experience of teaching and preaching.

Similarly most of the American Board missionaries had had some experience of Sabbath school teaching and preaching. In addition, Dr George Pierson served as a missionary to the Choctaw Indians before going to Micronesia, and B. G. Snow was a pastor in Pembroke, Lubeck, and Cooper, Maine, before becoming a missionary.

Among the Wesleyans, all the fully accredited missionaries had been local preachers. The average length of time that a man had been a local preacher before he offered for foreign service was three years. The career of John Thomas is typical of the untrained local preachers. As a young man he had engaged in various home missionary duties. He began a school for children on Sunday afternoons and earned the displeasure of the local rector who 'further insisted that he should at once give up his evil ways in visiting the sick and the ungodly in his parish'.[15] He also engaged in field preaching and his early efforts were opposed by 'a rabble shouting, cursing, and singing lewd songs, drumming on tin cans, and laughing uproariously'. When he became a local preacher, Thomas made many long journeys and conducted numerous services within the limits of his circuit.

The success of a local preacher depended very largely on his ability to draw large congregations. Most modelled themselves closely on the pattern set by John Wesley. Being for the most part untrained, their appeal was more to the emotions than to the intellect. Revival techniques were an essential feature of the Wesleyan system, and the efficient local preacher endeavoured to be a good revivalist. It was one way of showing to the world that he was possessed of grace. For example Walter Lawry was anxious to create his reputation as a revivalist during his Cornish ministry. Letters he wrote to his parents describe his apparent success. On one occasion he described a meeting at Redruth:

> They are heard from one end of the chapel to the other breaking out in ah, ah, ahs — and sometimes I have seen them literally *dance* under the pulpit — so that it is next to impossible to have a dry time.[16]

Lawry had additional experience in New South Wales* before going to Tonga.

Peter Turner had also earned a reputation as a revivalist in his English circuit. He became an exhorter and then a local preacher about two years before he obtained the 'blessing of entire sanctification'.[17] In the initial stages Turner had to overcome a great reluctance to preach. He was well aware of his lack of education and it became almost an obsession with him and no doubt influenced him to emphasize the importance of religious experience. He found that he could work on the emotions of other men, and whilst a local preacher in the Mac-

---

*There he delighted in one man's reference to him as prospective 'Bishop of Botany Bay', and in his characteristic egocentric style remarked, 'perhaps I am already the most popular Preacher in New Holland' (Lawry, 23 December 1818, Diary — ML.) That he afterwards became cynical about revivalism is not surprising when we take into account his comfortable respectability and his peculiar personality.

clesfield circuit he was having revivalistic success: 'While preaching this word, the people were much affected and wept much'.

Those missionaries who had been local preachers in the Australian colonies found it difficult in the islands to obtain recognition from the English-born missionaries whose tendency to look down on the colonials has already been mentioned (page 44). Most of the first missionaries appointed from the colonies were not given full status and went to the islands as 'assistant missionaries'. This arrangement was not a happy one, and invariably placed the assistant in an invidious position. Usually his qualifications were the same as those of the English appointments, the only difference being that his was not a home appointment. Under the direction of Thomas, the Tonga District Committee passed a resolution 'reprehending in severe and unjustifiable terms' the conduct of the New South Wales District in sending a man like Thomas Wellard.[18] Although Thomas's criticisms of Wellard may have had some validity, it seems quite clear that Thomas's opposition was at least partly due to his cantankerous disposition. Thomas regarded the actions of the New South Wales district committee as interference in his own domain, and resented the influence of the gentlemen ministers, Joseph Orton and his like, who had been critical of his own talents. Orton was quick to censure the Tongan resolution, and wrote to Watkin: 'You appear to have a decided objection to the class of "Assistant Missionaries", especially referring to their operations in the Islands.'[19] Notwithstanding, the New South Wales District continued to recommend local preachers as 'assistant missionaries'. Millard and Moore, who both came from New South Wales, were similarly regarded as being below standard. Joseph Waterhouse wrote thus to his sister:

> Mr Moore will never be more than an Asst. Missionary. Mr Lawry accuses the Sydney preachers of having deceived him with reference to Millard and Moore. He was told they were two men as suitable for the work as he could get, if he searched all England. Whereas, the only qualification Bro. Moore has, is his piety. Mr. Lawry says he would make a very poor local preacher. Moreover he was sent from Sydney without any examination, and can scarcely read Mr L. says! However, Brother Hazlewood . . . says 'we all take 100 per cent off what Mr. Lawry says, on any subject' so you must make the reduction.
>
> These failures make weight against Col.l. young men. So that they will not be prepossessed in *my* favour. Mr. L. says he will have nothing more to do with Colonial young men![20]

Events showed that Moore was just as efficient a missionary as those with English appointments. Apart from the exaggerated statements of Thomas and Lawry, there is little evidence that the colonial missionaries were 'very poor local preachers' and unsuited to missionary work. Calvert afterwards wrote to the Reverend Elijah Hoole in defence of the colonial missionaries:

> The men we have from the colonies are all we can desire. It is desirable that some should be supplied from England — yet those from the Colonies are not inferior. We are very sorry that you let the reflection on the men of the Colonies which Mr. Lawry wrote pass . . . I hope the stigma will be wiped.[21]

Besides Nathaniel Turner, who commenced his missionary career amongst the Maoris, and Moore, who spent a year amongst the Queensland Aboriginals, the only other Wesleyan who had received any experience in another mission field was Richard Amos. From 1843 to 1845 Amos was attached to the Wesleyan mission in Sierra Leone. He was then dismissed after returning 'under a serious charge of violence towards a Pagan Negro'.[22] When he entered the Tongan mission it was in the capacity of a schoolmaster.

The majority of Evangelical missionaries in the South Seas were thus men who had already experienced the techniques and hazards of missionary activity. If some of them had not already been confronted by hearers drawn from an alien culture, at least all of them had had considerable preaching or teaching experience. Even those who had not received any formal training had had experience in teaching others to read and write and to 'understand' the authorized version of the Bible. The value of itinerant preaching and the instruction of young children in the training of the missionary is difficult to assess, but it was possibly that part of their education which best fitted them for their vocation, and it certainly influenced their policies. We shall see that in the islands the importance placed on itineration and on the instruction of the young was very high. There was an eagerness to keep abreast with the latest teaching methods in England. The LMS missionaries were quick to introduce the Lancastrian system and the latest infant school methods. The Wesleyans adopted the Glasgow system which was introduced in Tonga and Fiji.

Although they could hardly be called 'raw and inexperienced', many of the missionaries were young. Very few men of middle age were sent to the South Seas and the majority were men in their twenties. Naturally, youth gave the missionaries some very desirable qualities. Many of them had inherited and developed robustness of body, stamina and powers of concentration. Hardie was described as being superior to the 'ordinary man' in health and strength, and McFarlane was described as a 'tall, robust, healthy young man' with a 'fine intelligent countenance'.[23] Peter Turner and Thomas West were big, well-built men, and Crawford of Fiji had a reputation for strength. These men were quite naturally accepted as chiefs by the island peoples.

On the other hand there were as many, if not more, who were of a sickly cast. The medical histories of these men make interesting reading and one learns much about the more controversial characters of the time. The energetic John Thomas of Tonga, for instance, had periods of ineffectualness. For some time during 1823, whilst he was still a local preacher, Thomas was 'altogether laid aside from work by extreme feebleness, loss of appetite, much drowsiness, and pain in the head, accompanied by stupor, which prevented his reading and made continuous thought impossible'.[24]

One feels with some of these men that they despised their own physical weakness, and entered the mission field with a concealed desire to prove themselves. One feels the importance which the missionaries themselves placed on stamina, when a brother of less forcible character was placed in their midst. If he could not stand up to the daily routine of the mission, he was despised and considered a handicap to everyone. Invariably he fell prey to victimization and had to leave the field. Pratt's contempt for Gee in Savai'i and Thomas's contempt for Wellard and Hill in Tonga are parallel examples of a subtle form of mental sadism. 'Had Mr. Gee become insane instead of Mrs. we should have been more prepared for it', wrote Pratt on learning of Mrs Gee's illness.[25] As far as he was concerned Gee was not a *man*. Murray complained of the way in which Pratt attacked Gee, and held him up to contempt, saying that Gee was 'by no means a man to be despised'.[26]

Missionary candidates had to satisfy their directors or committee that their faith was sound and that their intentions were honourable. LMS candidates had to fill in questionnaires and supply referees. They were also interviewed by the directors. Although the Wesleyan missionary candidates were all local preachers who had been recommended by their local district meetings, they were still required to go before a meeting of 'the Preachers of the London Districts for the Examination of Missionary Candidates'. At this meeting each candidate was required to give an account of his conversion and call to the ministry and to show that he understood Methodist doctrine and discipline. There was a set of questions similar to those on the LMS questionnaire. The Wesleyans placed particular importance on the ability of the candidate to preach a sermon. Interviews were often very exacting, and the timid candidate was at a disadvantage. When Pitman went up for his interview in 1820, his minister, John Hunt of Chichester, wrote jocularly: 'If Dr. Waugh should happen to be at the Head and Br. Platt at the Tail of the Table I should not wonder if he be struck dumb — I believe him however to be all stirling gold'.[27] When Aaron Buzacott, junior, applied to the directors in the hope that he would be sent to the South Seas (he was born in Tahiti and reared in Rarotonga), his application was rejected. He wrote a very full account of an interview he had with the directors which reveals both the nature of their procedure and requirements and the independent, self-confident attitude of the subject of their inquisition. A little of the interview may suffice by way of illustration:

> *Mr. Philip*: Perhaps our young friend has read some books that have perplexed his mind [;] there is a book by Morell.
> *A.B.*: I suppose you refer to the Philosophy of Religion.[28]
> *Mr. P.*: Yes — Have you read it?
> *A.B.*: The most of it.
> *Dr. Morison*: What do you think of it?
> *A.B.*: I do not think that it gives me sufficient data by which I may distinguish divine truth.
> *Mr. P.*: I am glad I have asked the question.
> *Dr. Morison*: Have you read any of Emerson's works[?]
> *A.B.*: Yes — I have read three or four of his Essays.
> *Dr. Morison*: What did you get out of them?
> *A.B.*: Only a few historical facts.
> *Dr. M.*: If you are in want of time to read on Theology — how is it you find time to read these trashy books?
> [Left unanswered][29]

When a missionary was selected there were many fields to which he could be sent. In this connexion, it is necessary to take into account the place of the South Seas in the plans and policies of the Evangelical missionary societies. For many years the Tahitian mission was regarded as one of the most interesting in the world. Its popular fascination was largely due to interest already aroused by Cook and Bligh. So glowing indeed were the reports given by the early voyagers of the virtues of the Polynesians that the Tahitian was regarded as a living representative of the 'noble savage'. The Evangelical clergy, however, were not convinced. When the directors of the LMS proposed a mission to the South Seas, they were not deceived about the 'natural innocence' of the Polynesians. There was enough in the pages of Cook to show that the standards and customs of the Tahitians were inconsistent with Evangelical conduct. Certainly Dr Haweis' glowing reports of Tahiti suggested the possibilities of a paradise,[30] but he was under no delusions. He had access to much oral knowledge communicated by captains and seamen, and he was familiar with the manuscript of James Morrison from which he derived most of his knowledge of Tahiti.* To Haweis, the Tahitians were as manifestly depraved as any other heathen race which was 'without God and without hope in the world'.

Although Haweis was able to rouse enthusiasm amongst the directors, and although he was able to obtain popular support for the missionary colonization of Tahiti, he was almost alone in genuine enthusiasm for this field. On the other hand, his colleague, Dr Bogue, was decidedly averse to the South Seas project. Although Haweis mixed in aristocratic circles, he showed in all his actions that he valued the soul of the simple man as highly as that of the greatest in the land; but like most Methodists he believed in 'station' and did not indulge in criticism of the social hierarchy. Bogue held much more radical egalitarian views, and yet one feels that he favoured the sort of intellectual aristocracy which Milton advocated. One also suspects that Bogue showed considerable preference for the soul of an educated person and saw little hope for those who did not belong to a superior civilization. His own missionary sympathies were definitely with the heathen of 'civilized' countries. He was principally interested in sending missionaries to India and China, and to the Catholic countries of Europe. Haweis, on the other hand, looked primarily to the South Seas and Africa.

Bogue also felt that the islands of the South Seas were insignificant compared with the vast continental countries. In his 'Lectures on Missions', he showed clearly that he did not regard the South Seas mission as of the first importance.[31] In listing the most important fields of labour, he did not include the South Seas. Furthermore, many of the directors held the view — it was held by Haweis — that because the Polynesians were comparatively uncivilized, the South Seas mission was more properly a field for artisans and the less intelligent or less scholarly

*Whether the manuscript given to Haweis at Portsmouth was by Morrison or another *Bounty* mutineer is not known. Haweis' articles on Tahitian religion in the *Evangelical Magazine*, however, appear to have been derived from Morrison's account.

volunteers. It is evident that the more scholarly, gifted and 'respectable' missionaries were sent to India and the Orient. The missionaries in Africa actually voiced their resentment against this discrimination, and George Barker of Theopolis wrote an angry counter-blast to Bogue's written statement that 'Africa is of little importance'.

Let the D[r]. tell me, in what part have missionaries been more useful. But I want to know what is so unimportant, wether the Missionaries or the stations we occupy, or the people to whom we preach and should be glad if someone, or the D[r]. himself would explain it. Perhaps the D[r]. has fallen in with the idea, that, Africans have no souls. . . . With regard to what the D[r]. says of our being plain men &c. What were all your Missionaries & many of the Directors themselves. Had we have had the same time at the D[rs]. Semenary as our brethren, we probably, some of us, might have shone as brilliantly as others. . . . Do the Directors consider their African missionaries totally void of feeling, or what idea have they of us?[32]

Certainly the argument that the missionaries sent to the East should be more carefully trained, and able to answer or refute the philosophical questions put to them, was a valid argument. On the other hand, the directors and their agents underestimated the intelligence of the Polynesians. Missionaries in the South Seas, and other European groups, have always had a tendency to treat the islanders as children, an attitude of mind easily cultivated by observation of certain characteristics less apparent in Western societies; but according to island tradition the Tahitians themselves looked upon the first LMS missionaries as 'a kind of children, or idiots, incapable of understanding the simplest facts of island politics or society'.[33]

There was a definite tendency to encourage men who had the requisite stamina and an abundance of zeal, but who were otherwise inadequate, to enter missionary service. Men who were unsuited to the home ministry were thought of as being quite adequate instructors of the 'ignorant heathen'. Missionary service was regarded as a kind of monitorial system in that the monitor was not much further advanced than his pupil. Many of the missionaries who came out on the *Duff* would not have been accepted into the home ministry. Jorgen Jorgensen savagely criticized the policy of the directors in sending out 'illiterate and ruined tradesmen' who took it upon themselves 'to explain to others what they [did] not comprehend themselves', and suggested that three or four learned professors from the universities of Oxford, Cambridge and Edinburgh should be sent out.[34]

Jorgensen, however, underestimated the qualities of the smaller
body of missionaries who remained after the various defections.
These missionaries themselves had come to realize that the Polynesians were quite a sophisticated people, and they resented the
appointment of missionaries whom they regarded as being below
their own standards. The most flagrant example of an unsuitable
missionary being sent out was the case of William Caw. Caw had
been a church member and skilled artisan when he applied, and
he evidently convinced the directors that had been called to
missionary work. The Tahitian missionary secretary wrote:

> We must acknowledge ourselves not a little surprized that a person
> of Mr Caw's advanced age, impediment of speech, and peculiarity of
> manners — should be thought a suitable character to be sent so many
> thousand miles to be an instructor of heathens of a dark and strange
> speech in the Christian religion and youth in the art of reading
> English. Certainly our honourable Directors must have formed very
> erroneous opinions of the office of a missionary or school-master
> among savages especially the light, giddy, sacastick, contemptuous
> inhabitants of Taheite, to whom Mr Caw is already an object of
> ridicule . . .[35]

Caw was a continual source of embarrassment. Domestic quarrels
resulted in his excommunication, and his preference for the
company of beachcombers induced him to separate himself from
the other missionaries; for many years he lived on unwanted by
either missionaries or natives, a pathetic and lonely figure.[36]

No one quite as unsuited as Caw was ever again sent to the
South Seas. Nevertheless the idea that the less talented could be
sent to the islands persisted.[37]

India certainly attracted the majority of the candidates and
several of them stated their preference for that field.[38] The considerable attention paid by Dr Bogue to Indian missions in
his lectures, possibly influenced his students, and perhaps his
tendency to emphasize the importance of large populations influenced the *expansive* policy of John Williams.[39]

Unless they had responded to a particular request for missionaries for a specified field, many of the students did not know
where they would be posted. In fact it was regarded as an
essential qualification by some of the directors that a missionary
should be prepared to go *anywhere*. This was certainly the
Methodist ideal. On the other hand, there were directors who
were fully aware of the shortcomings of this system, and believed
that every missionary should have some particular knowledge of
the field to which he would be sent. The students at Gosport,

for instance, knew much more about the Eastern fields than the South Seas. Consequently a missionary was at a considerable disadvantage when appointed to the South Seas after the completion of his course. James of Birmingham was one director to criticize this system: 'In my judgment a Missionary should be educated for a particular situation, and receive an education adapted to that situation'.[40]

Health considerations also played a large part in determining fields of labour for missionary candidates, and the climate of the South Seas was considered as a partial remedy for some ills. Whether this was always the medical case or not, the belief was popularly held. Thus Richard Knill, whose health had broken down in India, wrote from Madras:

> I trembled at the thought of being a *Cumberer* in the Lord's vineyard. I felt a wish to go to Otaheite, or any place which they thought more suited to my constitution. . . .[41]

Although the ministers of the Wesleyan Connexion tended to come from the same social groups as the Wesleyan missionaries, it would appear that some of the missionaries were recommended for the South Seas, not only because they were physically suited, having youth and zeal, but also because they were not eminently suited for home preaching. Hutchinson was deemed suitable for ministerial work in the colonies,[42] but it was not so with some of the other missionaries. The case of Thomas Wellard throws some light on this policy of sending out those who were sufficiently zealous, but who lacked English preaching powers. When he was rejected by the Tonga District Committee, Wellard had only been three months in the islands. Being of a somewhat submissive nature he acquiesced in the decision, although he was not even at the meeting which judged him incompetent. The committee made the following objections to Wellard:

> He does not possess the talents suitable for the work of the Lord in these Islands. . . . 1. His manners and embarassed mode of delivering his Message to remove which every effort made has proved unavailing both in the Colonies and in these Islands. 2. His extremely defensive mode of quoting the Scriptures ascribing to one Apostle or Prophet that what was spoken or written by another. 3. The extreme difficulty which he finds in pronouncing the Tonga language which should he ever acquire we think he will never be able to speak it so as to profit those who hear him.[43]

The committee said further that Wellard had been 'by no means an acceptable Local Preacher in the Circuit from which he came', and censured the New South Wales district meeting for recommending him.

Even though Wellard was rejected as being incompetent, many of the Wesleyan missionaries themselves believed that a man might be an effective missionary although he would not be acceptable in England or in the colonies. Thus, when Miller was appointed an 'Assistant Missionary' in 1841, it was 'with the distinct understanding that he shall have no claim to labour in the Colonies or in England'.[44] Similarly, Walter James Davis was sent out as a printer on the understanding that he could not enter the ministry in the islands. When he desired to leave the mission because of ill health, the Secretary of Conference wrote him an 'unkind and unfeeling letter' stating that in the opinion of the brethren, he would not 'meet the reasonable expectations of the people' as a preacher. 'Very probable', was his own comment, 'and no one is more sensible of his inability for the work than myself. I learn that men in every way my superiors cannot satisfy the itching ears of a Colonial congregation'.[45] Amos, in a letter to Rabone, commented on the 'terrible letter': 'Who could have written it? Surely this is not the way to treat anyone. To tell him he has not talent, and that he was taken out for the Islands . . .'.[46]

One reason for sending men out as missionaries, although they were unsuited to normal pastoral work, was because it was assumed that the standard of English preaching was of little importance in the field. Indeed, one finds many references in the narratives of voyagers to the South Seas alluding to the poor preaching abilities of Evangelical missionaries, although this was very often probably due to lack of practice in English.

Some of the Wesleyans were also directed to the South Seas for reasons of health. Unfortunately, some of the stations proved injurious to good health, and even those with sound constitutions succumbed to dysentery and various diseases. Medical knowledge was also limited, and many of the missionaries took risks with their health. For example, Crawford, who was regarded as the strongest man in the Fijian mission, did not change his clothes after getting wet through. His death from dysentery shortly afterwards was attributed by his colleagues to his carelessness in this respect.[47] Amongst all the Evangelical missionaries the sickness rate was very high, and ill health in the family was a constant anxiety to nearly every missionary, and more than other causes it was responsible for ending the effective careers of otherwise promising missionaries.

Wesleyan missionaries were also expected to be prepared to

go anywhere. Before the appointment was made, of course, they were consulted, but on numerous occasions missionaries who had definite preferences were not able to indulge them. A story was told amongst the missionaries that Hunt of Fiji believed that he had a 'loud call' to go to Africa. On mentioning his call to Jabez Bunting, the latter 'almost ridiculed it and thought that God gave none in the present day, a call to a particular locality or people'.[48]

Before the missionaries embarked for their destinations it was necessary to give them some idea of how they should behave in their new situation. A superior training in mathematics, languages and logic did not necessarily provide the missionary with any set rules of procedure. There was only one fundamental rule and that was to act consistently with scriptural practices. From the first voyage of the *Duff* onwards, it became customary for the directors of the LMS to write detailed instructions to each party of missionaries or each individual missionary.* These provided a specific guideline for personal conduct and ecclesiastical matters or dealt with specific problems. The Wesleyans, already bound by the 'Rules' and 'Minutes' of their societies, received even more detailed instructions (see Appendix II) augmented by annual circulars. In 1832 a compendium of these instructions was issued for the private use of missionaries as *Miscellaneous Regulations: being an Appendix to the General Instructions of the Wesleyan Missionary Committee.*

While these letters and instructions were important in the public and private lives of the missionaries, they ignored completely the problems arising from cultural difference. Those instructions which could be interpreted as dealing with native cultures were negative ones, such as the Wesleyan rule forbidding Society membership to polygamists. But no instructions existed which would help missionaries either to understand or to deal effectively with radically different cultures. Although a considerable amount was written about the theory of missions, most of it was in semi-philosophical vein, on the merits of civilizing.

Dr Bogue's 'Missionary Lectures', used by the LMS, could not seriously be regarded as a textbook laying down methods of procedure. It was simply an introduction to the subject and a guide which set forth the attitudes which should be held when

---

*See, for instance, the 'Instructions to the Missionaries appointed to proceed in the Royal Admiral to the Pacific Ocean', South Seas Odds, Box 2 — LMS. Duplicates of letters written to departing missionaries and thos: in the field are contained in the LMS Western Outgoing Letters.

facing problems. As Joseph Mullens, a later Secretary of the
LMS, remarked, the early directors left the missionaries 'large
discretion as to the best and most effective methods of carrying
out their high commission as messengers of the gospel'.[49] This
is an accurate account of the aim of Bogue's lectures.

In 1822 James Douglas of Cavers, an independent gentleman
who contributed the article on 'Missions' to the *Encyclopaedia
Britannica,* published his *Hints on Missions.* This work was read
widely by missionaries in the field, both LMS and Wesleyan.[50]
Douglas believed that Christianity should be propagated by
means of colonizing and 'the introduction of the arts'. He dis-
countenanced the method of simple preaching which up till that
time had received some support.

> Can we be surprised . . . if men of thought, but whose thoughts are
> confined to the present world, should despise missionaries, who,
> instead of reclaiming barbarians to civilized habits, have sunk down
> to the outward condition of the people to whom they are preaching?
> And certainly the accusation of indolence is naturally brought
> forward against missionaries, who will not make the moderate
> exertions requisite to procure the comforts of life for themselves and
> those around them. . . .[51]

These sentiments were shared by most of the missionaries at
that time.[52] The missionary was accepted as the chief promoter
of civilization, and colonization was regarded as the most efficient
means of effecting Christian civilization.[53]

Even in 1842 *Hints on Missions* was still seriously considered.
In that year Thomas Heath of the Samoan mission drew up a
paper entitled 'On certain defects and desiderata in the Polynesian Missions of the London Society', which showed that he
had been considerably influenced by Douglas. Amongst other
things he felt that the 'advantages of civilization' were not sufficiently appreciated, nor sufficiently 'thrown into the hands of the
natives', and that 'the standard of taste—moral—intellectual,
and *domestic*' wanted raising in all the islands. Heath also argued
for a college for islanders in New South Wales, as proposed by
Douglas, and also agreed with Douglas that pious colonists
should be encouraged to emigrate. Finally, and in this he was
also following Douglas, he argued for the greater dissemination
of missionary knowledge and theory. 'These missions as well as
others would be greatly aided by some central medium of communication, which should collect and transmit information from
and to all quarters of the world.'[54]

But, despite its considerable influence, *Hints on Missions* only dealt with general policy. What most missionaries desired was an authoritative handbook on day-to-day problems. John Williams put the case very clearly at the end of his 1832 Journal, which became the basis for his *Enterprises*.

> I have frequently thought that a standard work on Missions is much wanted, a work that should be admitted into all our Missionary seminaries and form a book of reference to the Missionary on critical and difficult subjects with which every Missionary will have to contend in a greater or less degree.[55]

Williams suggested that this work should embrace the various plans which had been adopted by the missionaries of various societies, and that it should draw attention to the difficulties which they had to contend with, and the measures used to overcome them. This work would be divided into two 'grand divisions' representing civilized and uncivilized countries, and would be documented from the experience of the Moravians, the Baptists, the Church, Wesleyan and London Missionary Societies. It is also interesting that Williams thought that an examination of the plans and methods adopted by the Jesuits amongst the South American Indians might be a fruitful study. He was inclined to think that they could be 'adopted with advantage in some uncivilized countries'. Williams also mentioned some of the works which he thought might be usefully studied, such as Jowet's *Researches,* Judson's *Letters and Life,* Dr Buchanan's *Researches,* Swan's *Letters on Missions,* and the works of Ward and Ellis. These works were written by missionaries from their own experiences. Consequently, Williams felt, one missionary's solution to a problem could not be taken as a general rule. There was need for more correlation and the gathering of new material. This he believed could only be done thoroughly and impartially by a minister at home.

A compendium of missionary experience was never written. However works like Williams' *Missionary Enterprises,* and those books which he himself had mentioned, were regarded as standard works on missionary procedure. Swan's *Letters on Missions* was very popular although it gave very few practical hints.[56] That most published works on missions were eagerly read and criticized is evidenced by the fact that strictures were occasionally passed on some of them in the minutes of local mission committees. Thus the Samoan brethren in 1844 passed the following resolution:

> That we record our deep regret occasioned by a passage in Campbell's Philosophy of Missions [pp. 250, 251 second edition] which among

other things upon which we might animadvert, asserts that all which remains to be done in the South Seas 'is a very plain unpoetic everyday sort of affair'. How could Dr Campbell send forth to the world such an assertion?[57]

During the first half of the nineteenth century, missionary theory was in an experimental stage. General works such as *Hints on Missions* and Swan's *Letters* were influential in so far as individual missionaries were guided by them, but no attempt was made to advocate set principles and methods in the mission colleges. Missionary practice was largely imitative, and the greatest theoretical influence throughout the period came from the published accounts of the labours of earlier missionaries.

PART TWO

The Missionary in the Field

A Missionary society achieves little good, except when
it can send forth an individual who wants no teaching
or training from the society, but who carries his commission and chief power in his own soul. We urge this,
for we feel that we are all in danger of sacrificing our
individuality and independence to our social connexions.

WILLIAM ELLERY CHANNING, 'Remarks on the
Formation of Associations' (1829), *Works*, I, p. 182.

5

Innocents Abroad

> John Williams: You know, my young friend that the
> Directors are not acquainted with the state of things and
> we are, and we must adapt our proceedings to circumstances.
> The Directors write excellent instructions, which look very
> well upon paper but they become a mere bagatelle when we
> get here.
>
> J. JOHNSTON, 15 DECEMBER 1843

IT WAS THE voyage out which helped to determine the missionary's final attitudes, severed him from his roots, and made him aware of his isolated vocation. This was even true of the first voyage of the *Duff*, which was a singularly piously manned ship. But it was in the later years, when convict ships and whaling vessels and even passenger ships were used, that the missionaries were more vigorously initiated into their new life. A note of typical apprehension and resignation was at once captured by John Thomas on the eve of his departure in 1825:

> I am now going to encounter new and untried difficulties, first at sea, a long sea voyage, with strange and possibly worldly and wicked people; and this is only preparatory to my taking up my abode amongst rude and barbarous tribes, far beyond the bounds of British protection, where I have to live, and labour, and suffer, and possibly die.[1]

Indeed, for many of the missionaries the voyage out was almost the *worst* experience of their missionary careers, especially from an emotional point of view. William Ellis and his colleagues had an unpleasant journey out on a government transport ship.[2] Not only was mutiny constantly feared, but the missionaries suffered from the 'rude and unmanly conduct' of the commander. Mrs Ellis had to absent herself from the captain's table because of his 'offensive behaviour'.

The majority of the missionaries were unfamiliar with conditions at sea, and were quite unprepared to accept a lower standard of living. In contrast with many of the emigrants of the time, they travelled in comparative comfort. Ellis and his party complained that the food was insufficient and coarse, and that on more than one occasion sheep which had died of disease or starvation had been used as meat. The brethren Turner, Watkin and Woon and their wives had similar fare on board the whaling vessel, *Lloyds*. They complained that they had 'little more to eat than the common men before the mast',[3] a good indication that they were privileged nonetheless. Orsmond was very bitter because the wine was rationed. The captain informed him 'that the Directors particularly Mr Langton when forming a Covenant with him to take us out told him that we were very plain people, that we should not want above a glass or two of wine at the table. If we had been accustomed to live differently . . . they would give you more'.[4] If the directors ever made this statement it helps to affirm the class correlation of the missionaries. Orsmond expressed great indignation saying that 'the want of a little wine is a considerable loss'. As late as 1855, at a time when missionaries were less concerned with alcoholic beverages, John Thomas complained bitterly about the absence of such standard table fare as 'a little wine-buisket-cheese-spirit-raisins' and white sugar. 'True', he wrote to his friend Thomas Farmer, 'there was *one* bottle of ale — or Porter — but only one — brought to table for 4 persons and at time five persons partook of it'. In addition there was no proper steward and they had a 'cooped up cabin — jammed with other things'.[5]

It was customary for the missionaries to dine with the captain, and the relationship was not always a cordial one, especially when the captain did not conform to their own moral code. Bullen, Turner, Nisbet and Smee were shocked at the 'indecent if not immoral intercourse' between their captain and 'some of the females in the steerage'.[6] Reproof from the missionaries was regarded as presumption and bad form. On both his voyages out, Cargill was at enmity with the captains. He was told on his second voyage that 'to preach the necessity of coming to God through Christ, may be applicable to Feejeeans, or very bad people', but it was unnecessary on board his ship.[7] This captain also spent Saturday evening 'singing songs, stamping, hurraing'.

> Can the author of evil assist his votaries in giving vent to those feelings which are earthly, sensual and devilish? They continued this *amusement* until within a few minutes of 12 o'clock and then adjourned, to stamp on the deck over the beds of some of the more sedate passengers.[8]

Such experiences could be multiplied. Perhaps the most readable account of the voyage out was that of J. H. S. Royce. Royce mentioned the 'aversion of sailors to ministerial passengers'. He described the captain of the *Nimrod* as a man 'experienced and skilful in his profession, but as ungodly as one can well conceive, likes to kill time in shuffling a few cards, is pleased to hear his infant son lisp the name of the Devil, anticipates catching sharks on the Sabbath and was much surprised at the suggestion of divine service on that sacred day'. When they crossed the equator, however, nothing occurred amongst the crew 'by way of demand of their heathenish custom upon that occasion'. Though witty in his description of his fellow passengers, Royce possessed the typical lack of humour which characterized Evangelicals in his day. He would take no part in a performance of the *Lady of Lyons* which he considered a 'consummate piece of foolery', nor was he pleased with the other amusements. 'Scarce an evening passes in the saloon without cards, over which the most stupid and boisterous mirth is incessantly going forward.'[9]

In 1859 conditions of travel could still be as discomforting to the missionary as at the beginning of the century. Coming to the South Seas for the second time, Krause, with his young charges Baker and McFarlane, and their wives, complained of the trip. 'In sending Missionaries or friends from London to Sydney or any other part of Australia', wrote Krause to the directors, 'engage the Cabins on the portside, if possible avoid emigrant ships, and bachelor Captains, and provide a horse hair mattrass'.[10] He further complained that their wives could not leave the cabins without encountering half-naked stewards, waiters and midshipmen who 'performed their ablutions' and undressed in the space between the cabins. But that was not all: 'Our vessel is a perfect gambling shop, in the saloon, in our nondescript compartments, in the second class everywhere gambling'.

The evils of shipboard life were epitomized by the equatorial revels. It was in crossing the line that Satan, usually in the guise of the jovial Neptune, tested the earnestness of the assailants of his kingdom. In those days it was not easy for anyone to be a non-participant. Peter Turner records that when Mr and Mrs Neptune paid their visit on board the *Lloyds,* they locked themselves in their cabins, acting on the advice of their secretaries: 'When will our English sailors throw away their superstition and act like Christians'.[11] Watkin 'declined witnessing this relic of Heathenism'.[12] Not all 'crossings', however, were so easy to evade. When one band of Wesleyans came out in 1838 they were involved in 'disrespectful proceedings'. They were 'all but literally dragged from their Berths', and their wives (whose dignity perhaps was less sacrosanct) had several buckets of water thrown over them.[13] David Cargill, on his second voyage out to the islands, was certainly not amused when crossing the line.

About 7 o.c. when I was about to come down stairs from the deck, a bucket of water was thrown down from the mizen the greater part of which fell on my back. That the Captain and his officers knew nothing of such gross impudence I fully believe, and that the person who poured the water may have mistaken me for another individual is possible, though by no means probable. But such conduct is not much to be wondered at, when we reflect that several persons who sail with us in this vessel appear not to know how to value or treat a Minister of the Gospel.[14]

The Tahitian veteran, Henry Nott, knew best how to cope with 'Neptune and his ridiculous train'. 'Our new Brethren got a few buckets of water over them', he wrote, 'tho' they escaped the tar and the shaving by treating *Jack* with a little of what he is always fond of'.[15]

Those who came out in the mission ships, the *Camden,* the *John Williams,* and the *John Wesley,* were incomparably better off in so far as congenial company was concerned. But mission ships rarely came up to the standard of 'godliness' which had been set by the *Duff.* Even under the direction of the pious Captain Morgan, and the personal supervision of John Williams, there were bitter complaints by the missionaries on board the *Camden,* although Williams appears to have given them better fare than many sea captains.[16] Krause resented the 'insolent' and 'surly' treatment he received from Captain Williams of the *John Williams,* and complained of the 'disgraceful scenes' between the captain and the first mate, brought about by the captain's temper.[17] Williams also refused to allow the preserved meats, which were constantly bursting the tins, to be thrown overboard. This was after suspected typhus had already broken out on the ship.[18] Francis Wilson complained of the captain of the Wesleyan mission ship *Triton*: 'No one should be chosen who is not a *real Christian* and a *thoro' Methodist,* it does not matter what his nautical skill may be — No half and half man will do'.[19]

On the way out the missionaries preached when they could, and continued their studies. Often they had the company of an older missionary who was returning and sometimes there were also some islanders who had been exhibited before the religious public at Exeter Hall. Such companions greatly assisted in the acquisition of the language. Crossing the line was not an easy experience, but it was invariably an important one. From then on, the spiritual growth of the missionaries and their general development was to have new significance when in close contact with an alien culture, and forces of existence which they could only deem sinister.

The Evangelical missionaries were largely influenced in their work by the ideas which they brought with them, and by the nature of the work they came to do, to preach, teach and heal the sick. But there were environmental and circumstantial forces which played an important role in shaping the history of their missionary activity.

The dependence of the missionaries on home policy presented a problem of no small consequence. Distance, and the time taken to communicate with the directors or committees of the various societies, prevented the missionaries from receiving advice and assistance when it was most needed. Also, it was not easy for the home authorities to obtain a clear picture of affairs and conditions in the islands. Although full accounts were received from the field, these were often misinterpreted, and as all the matter for publication was carefully edited, a false picture was built up which careful study of the original documents would have dispelled. Popular missionary propaganda directed at obtaining funds and recruits drew upon the South Seas of the poets and romancers as much as upon the annals of the missionaries. The home authorities also made hasty decisions, and censured their agents on the basis of limited knowledge.

The founding directors of the Missionary Society had been methodical and thorough in their attempt to understand the environment to which the missionaries were being sent. Dr Haweis, the Reverend Samuel Greatheed and several others had lengthy interviews with sea captains and visitors who had been in the islands.[20] Greatheed, a scholarly and semi-invalid Congregational minister, took upon himself the onerous task of reading all the voyage literature and collating the material. Indeed, he probably surpassed Dr Hawkesworth in his extensive accounts of the islands and peoples contacted by 1800.* While Greatheed's researches were carried out in a scientific way, they were nevertheless limited. Some of his information was incorrect, and

*Much of Greatheed's Tahitian material was incorporated in the preliminary discourse to [James Wilson], *Voyage of the Duff*. His account of the Sandwich Islands (Hawaii) was afterwards sent to the American Board, but passed into private hands in Honolulu. The account of the Navigators Islands (Samoa and Tonga) should be with his private papers, if they are still extant. A later account of the Marquesas, written with the help of the missionary Crook, survives in his own handwriting. Other short papers were published in the periodical literature of the day.

there is a certain naivety about his 'Polynesian Grammar' based
on what he learned from Crook and his Marquesan companion,
'Temoteitei'.

Besides referring to such eminent visitors as Sir Joseph Banks
and Captain Bligh, the early directors appear to have had some
contact with Europeans who had actually lived in Tahiti. Their
knowledge of Tahitian religion was mostly gleaned from a manuscript account prepared by one of the *Bounty* mutineers, and at
least one vocabulary compiled by a mutineer passed into their
hands. Tahitians and other islanders who visited London on
shipboard familiarized the directors with some of the problems
involved. The Reverend William Francis Platt, for instance,
cared for several Polynesian youths between 1798 and 1820.[21]
Possibly the first generation of directors had a better knowledge
of the islands than those who succeeded them and who depended
for their information on mission reports designed especially for
the home churches. By the 1820s few of the old missionaries in
the field were known personally to the directors who did not
even know what they looked like. From about 1816, for a number
of years, the Society employed a miniaturist to record the features
of its agents.

When possible, the directors supplemented their information
by interviewing reliable authorities who had visited their mission
stations or the missionaries themselves. Returning missionaries
were subjected to the closest scrutiny. Their examination by the
mission board must have been even more gruelling than their
original interview for selection. In the early instances they were
virtually on trial. It was not easy to express their dilemmas and
difficulties in an adequate way when confronted by a body of
erudite clergy and business men with preconceived ideas and
prejudices. Cover, Crook and Shelley were little better than
'failures' while Bicknell, for all his zeal, was hardly the most
articulate representative of the missionaries. Bicknell's destitute
appearance must also have been an embarrassment. When Hayward visited England in 1819-20 to speak for the missionaries,
the rift between the directors and themselves was so great that
Hayward appeared a dissentient rather than a spokesman for
legitimate grievances. It was not until the missions had developed
their own momentum that returning missionaries such as Nott
and Williams suddenly found themselves public heroes and
began to exert a new personal influence.

Very few of the directors had any experience of the circumstances and environment in which the missionaries were placed.
Even William Ellis was unfamiliar with the state of Tahiti after

the accession of Pomare IV. His 'researches' were largely the researches of others, and yet he was regarded as being more of an authority on the South Seas than those who were actually engaged in the field.

The difficulties arising from an insufficient knowledge of conditions in the islands were numerous. Financial difficulties were perhaps the greatest cause of unrest and dissatisfaction. Invariably, the expenses incurred in New South Wales on the voyage out earned recriminations from the directors who did not appreciate the facts. The principal bone of contention in the islands was the question of salaries, and the belief of the directors that the missionaries could be self-supporting or live on the charity of the people. Largely because of the communication difficulties, the missionaries in the islands believed that they were both forgotten and neglected. The *Duff* had sailed to the islands with 'missionaries and provisions'. The provisions had not lasted for very long. At first Tahitian hospitality and natural fruitfulness created a false impression while wants were few. An early letter from the aged Mrs Eyre probably helped to lull the directors into a state of quiescence.

> This is our Winter, but little colder than your Summer. We have green peas and french beans that have been sowed since we came here, and likely to have fine Cabages to eat with our Pork. Our Hogs are very fine Meat and we have plenty of them. — Our Bread and our Drink grow on Trees. It is Cocoa nut, and we tap many bottles of them in a day. They are fine drink, and you would say so if you tasted them. Our Apples grow on Trees called Evee, if we had flower we could make nice Puddings and Pies, and they will also make Cyder. I was thinking my nose would be starved, but I hear there is some Snuff aboard, which pleases me — I am disappointed of my Snuff for there is none, pray send me some if you can, and some stone blew for the Linnen.[22]

When the *Betsey* called at the end of 1799 Mrs Eyre was less sanguine about conditions. She informed John Myers that she had been without wine or any other 'nourishing liquor' and she had difficulty in preventing the people from taking the clothes she had brought with her. Myers records giving her seven gallons of wine and the same of spirits which she had to conceal from the Tahitians.[23] Without fresh provisions conditions worsened. The missionaries persistently clung to the last vestiges of clothing, refusing to adopt native dress. They were reduced to rags and patches and put a high value on their clothing. Those who arrived in Sydney in February 1800 were in a wretched condition. Hassall reported to the directors: 'My Heart was sore pained to see these my D^r. Breth. almost Naked, and appearing like slaves, yet seemd. well satisfied with the dispensations of God'.[24]

The absence of footwear was possibly the greatest grievance, the missionaries having to itinerate barefoot around the mountain tracks and bush paths.

> Sometimes, when they had to cross great breadths of burning sands, they used to furnish themselves with bundles of foliage from the adjacent woods, and, laying down a green leaf at every step, they set the soles of their feet successively upon these cool, soft patches of carpeting, and thus escaped the blistering effects of treading upon a soil that resembled hot ashes concealing half-extinguished fires.[25]

When Bicknell arrived in England in 1809, he was little removed from beggary. Joseph Fox, an Evangelical philanthropist, said of him that he was 'reduced almost to a state of nakedness', and that 'he had not had a shoe on his foot for eight years, and his clothing was in the most tattered condition'. Fox told a pathetic story of the Tahitian 'Tapeoe' being sent back to Tahiti with a great quantity of clothing and footwear, while Bicknell had a very meagre supply for himself.[26] Orsmond recorded some of the difficulties of the older brethren.[27] He had seen the children of some families clad only in a 'roundabout' cut out of the mother's old garments, and the mother with hardly any clothing herself. Even the sheets were cut up into gowns for the children. Orange leaves were used instead of tea. In 1818 Threlkeld observed how the decline of the pork trade had affected the standard of living of the missionaries.

> The decrease of the demand for pork at the Colony will account for the unhappy appearance of the Miss^s Children whom we saw at our arrival running about the Sea shore without hats, shoes, or stockings, sometimes naked, boys and girls 6 or 7 years old who mixing together with the naked native children learn all those practices which stop the peace of a parent's breast . . .[28]

Conditions had not changed very greatly by 1820. Thus Platt commented on his condition after several years' labour on Moorea:

> I generally preached in a jacket made out of Mrs. Platt's old skirt, and my every day trowsers, through her good management and industry, were so patched that it would have been difficult for a stranger to tell which was the master patch or which the original piece.[29]

While the missionaries themselves deplored their destitute state, the fact that they were forced to live as the Tahitians did meant that they identified themselves more easily with the people. Nott and Davies in particular, who lived in native-style houses, secured the confidence of the chiefs and people which gave them untold advantages over their younger colleagues who complained of having to live temporarily in 'bird-cage' houses.

The first missionaries to arrive after the nominal conversion of Tahiti (1815) were disappointed not only by the actual state of the islands, but also by the treatment which they believed the older missionaries had received from the directors. Marsden had taken on himself the duty of furnishing the new arrivals with extra provisions, but when this was condemned by the directors as unnecessary extravagance, resentment burst into full flare. Williams informed his parents that there was a general shortage of breadfruit, taro and yams and the missionaries depended on the rice and flour (as well as tea, sugar and a little wine) which Marsden had sent them. At Barff's station on Huahine there was a famine:

> the people were obliged to eat the Gigantic Fearn — one meal of which would kill a Director — or Missionary either almost had it not been for the Rice and flour we had sent out about 3 weeks or a month — previous to the famine commenced the Bn. at Huahine would almost have been starved to death.[30]

Williams' vituperation against the directors was singularly bitter, and he argued for salaries, scoffing at the idea that missionaries in the islands could live 'of their own'.

> the kind hearted Directors — think because we are at a distance & not near any Colony — as other Missionaries they may treat us as they please . . . I only want what is necessary, decent and comfortable —and if the Directors will not allow it — but we must neglect our Missionary work and turn Merchants I think I shall soon see England again with a good number of my Brethren . . . The Directors have not a poor cowed down company to deal with now and they will find so very soon unless they materially alter their conduct towards us — The Great Mr. Platt . . . supposes we are so accustomed to the Native food — that we could live on it now — provided it were possible to live on native food — where are we to get it — We cannot buy a Pig under 2½ & 3 Fathoms of cloth . . . If we want Tarro or Yams we must give a fathom of Cloth for a few that will last about a week — if we want to feed our own Pigs — we have no Cocoa Nutts or food for them without buying it.

Threlkeld afterwards maintained that most of the younger missionaries would have left the mission had it not been for a suddenly awakened interest in their teaching exemplified in the 'conversion' of the people of Rurutu.[31]

In yet another matter Williams quarrelled with the policy of the directors. On his arrival in Tahiti he had completed the ironwork on the *Haweis*, a schooner built by most of the missionaries in collaboration with Pomare II of Tahiti. When the directors insisted that the missionaries should sell their shares in the vessel, Williams was particularly disturbed. To Williams a ship was not only an essential means of communication enabling the missionaries to secure their own supplies, but is was also a means by which they could become self-sufficient, teach the islanders to trade, and spread their work to other groups.

The idea was not a new one. At the commencement of the Tahitian mission, Captain Turnbull had written that it would be much to their advantage 'if the Society would allow them a small vessel . . . the expense of this would be small. . . . By the carriage of pork to Port Jackson, and bringing salt from the Sandwich Islands, it might almost clear its own expenses'.[32] At least two of the missionaries, Nott and Shelley, tried their hands at boat-building, and Shelley, who left the mission in 1806, afterwards sailed his ship to Port Jackson with a cargo of pork. In London he urged the need for a ship and Marsden also fully supported the view. On 26 October 1810 Shelley wrote to Hardcastle mentioning his own experience as supercargo on the *Elizabeth* as an argument in favour of a mission ship. 'To give you some idea of the profits arising from the trade permit me to observe that in a ten month's voyage . . . my share (which was but a small one) amounted to upwards of One Thousand Pounds'.[33] He also urged that a mission ship should be armed if the missionaries were to have adequate protection. During the absence of most of the missionaries in New South Wales, Nott had been involved in the building of a small craft in the Leewards and probably accompanied Pomare and the Leeward Island chiefs to the Tuamotus on a pearling expedition.[34]

The missionaries who had returned to Tahiti in 1812 informed the directors: 'We are about commencing the building of a vessel, as strenuously recommended to us by his Excellency Governor Macquarie, the Rev. M^r. Marsden etc'.[35] However the difficulty of the undertaking and the 'apprehension that a gainful commerce with the Colony could not be carried on' induced them to abandon the work, and the ill-fated *Haweis* was not completed until after the arrival of Williams in 1817. Meanwhile Marsden had purchased the *Active* on his own initiative and this vessel served the LMS stations in the islands and the CMS stations in New Zealand for a short period. Marsden was to charter other ships on behalf of the missions, and was involved in considerable financial difficulties as a result.

Despite the obdurate attitude of the directors, Williams was determined to act independently, and on a visit to Sydney in 1821 he purchased the *Endeavour*. Marsden was at first reluctant to co-operate because the scheme had not been sanctioned by the Society but, convinced of the need, he agreed to share the responsibility. The purchase was made with money Williams had inherited from his mother. The ostensible purpose of this ship was to introduce civilization (it sailed to Williams' station at Raiatea with a cargo of European clothing and tea-drinking equipment) and to engage in trade with New South Wales. Although Williams 'sold' the ship to the chiefs of the Leeward Islands, the directors censured him for his speculation. As in the case of the *Haweis* they failed to recognize the involvement of the island leaders, even though Tamatoa of Raiatea wrote to them that the ship would bring cloth to cover their nakedness and would also transport missionaries to other islands. It was not only the directors who opposed the venture, however; a tobacco duty introduced in New South Wales ended all prospects of a successful trade. The *Endeavour,* which had been rechristened *Te Matamua,* had to be sold. 'Satan knows well that this ship was the most fatal weapon ever formed against his interests in the great South Sea; and, therefore, as soon as he felt the effects of its first blow, he has wrested it out of our hands', Williams wrote angrily to the directors.[36] He continued his pleas, but to little avail.

Meanwhile Marsden continued to press for a ship to serve the three Societies.[37] He was probably the instigator of a plan propounded to the Wesleyan Society by its New South Wales district committee in May 1826. Orton suggested that a ship of 250 or 300 tons should be purchased in conjunction with 'one or both of the other Societies', and that a 'pious Captain' should be allowed the gratuitous use of the ship 'on condition of his paying an annual visit to the several stations, without charge'.[38] Such a scheme would 'exhibit to the Natives the solid benefits of trade and commerce, and thus incite them to habits of industry, and to appreciate the comforts of civilized life'. At the same time the Society would not compromise 'the great principle of our Connexion which forbids an intermeddling with trade, for all the mercantile business and emoluments would pertain to the Captain exclusively'. Marsden was said to 'approve' the project and it is certain that he had already put forward the name of Captain S. P. Henry who was approached to consider handling the 'annual conveyance' of supplies to the Wesleyan missions in New Zealand and Tonga.[39] However it was not until August 1832 that Henry presented the committee with a detailed scheme for an annual voyage to the islands. His tender was for £300 from the Wesleyans and £350 from the LMS. Although the Wesleyan committee appears to have endorsed the plan, no permanent arrangement was entered into, perhaps because already stories were being circulated concerning atrocities supposed to have been committed by Henry's Tongan crew at Eromanga.[40]

Although Henry and the other island captains helped to transport missionaries and native teachers throughout the 1820s and 1830s, most of this work for the LMS was taken over by John Williams who had refused to be dependent on secular arrangements.

Williams had constructed his own ship, using a great deal of ingenuity and conscripted labour. By using handmade tools, old iron, hibiscus cording and native matting, he seemed to outdo Robinson Crusoe himself, epitomizing in his achievement the principles of the gospel of self-help which he put before the islanders. The *Messenger of Peace,* or *Olive Branch* as it was sometimes known from its device, widened the scope of Williams' itinerant ministry and certainly extended LMS operations considerably. It was sold in 1833, shortly before Williams returned to England. At the mission stations, several trading schooners were also built under missionary supervision.

By taking action and initiative himself, Williams changed the whole conception of the South Seas mission, as the mission ship was to become the focal point for missionary endeavour in the islands. The story of the *Messenger of Peace* soon acquired legendary status and Williams became a popular hero during the remaining few years of his life. He was able to raise sufficient funds to purchase a brig of 200 tons, the *Camden,* whose master for many years was Captain J. C. Morgan, a pious Wesleyan who had been trading in the islands for a number of years.

The LMS was to name its subsequent ships after John Williams himself. The first bearing his name was purchased from collections made by children in the English churches and sailed in 1844. Missionary collections for the *John Williams* were inaugurated throughout the British Empire. The other missions soon acquired their own ships also. The Wesleyans had the *Triton* and afterwards the *John Wesley I.* They also used small schooners in their Fijian mission where small islands and rivers presented difficulties for regular itineration. In the 1850s both the *Glyde* and the *Dove* were employed, though Joseph

Waterhouse continued to 'risk his life' with Fijian canoes.[41] The 'yachting' ministry provided full-time work for at least one missionary. The Presbyterians in the New Hebrides depended on the *John Williams* until their own ship, the *Dayspring*, was launched in Nova Scotia in 1864. The American Board in Micronesia emulated the *John Williams* tradition with their *Morning Star*. The Melanesian mission also found a missionary vessel indispensable.

One major issue on which home policy was at variance with the needs of the missionaries was that of trade. The early missionaries at Tahiti had found it necessary to purchase hogs from the people by means of barter, salt the pork and send it to New South Wales. They continued to suffer many privations and found it difficult to support their families. The result of this was that most of them found a certain amount of trading necessary for their subsistence. They raised cattle in order to sell beef and milk to visiting ships, and some of them planted sugar. A fixed allowance was not paid until 1819, when it was resolved that each missionary should receive £30 for himself, £20 for his wife, and £5 for each child.[42] This annual allowance was to be payable in London as each missionary ordered. At first the annual allowance seemed adequate, but is was not long before it became insufficient. Most of the missionaries continued their trading activities in order to make ends meet. Some missionaries, like Darling at Punaauia, were fortunate in that the local chief saw that the people ministered to the missionary's wants. But this was not usually the case. Barter soon became a difficult means of purchasing foodstuffs, as the people came to demand money. Exorbitant prices were asked for local products. In addition, the fixed salary was not sufficient for the missionary to obtain all his overseas wants from London, or from New South Wales where prices were higher. In 1822 the Reverend Daniel Tyerman wrote privately to Burder: 'Should you hear any thing of the Little Commercial concerns of the Missionaries here, to their disadvantage — do not believe it. It is impossible for them to live upon the Salaries allowed them by the Society'.[43] However he disclosed that Hayward had been salting pork and 'enriching himself' instead of doing missionary work.[44] In 1831 Ellis publicly admitted that the missionary had been obliged to 'act more like a trader than he himself desired, or than he would otherwise have thought compatible with his office', but he believed that once civilization had been wholly achieved there would be no such need.[45]

The extent to which the missionaries became involved in trading soon became a scandal to the Tahitian mission. Of the missionaries before 1839, Charles Barff and Orsmond were the only ones who refrained absolutely from trading.[46] Orsmond, at one stage, had a sugar-cane fence for his own use, which he afterwards gave up. It was he who, in 1837, had informed the directors: 'We are a set of trading priests, our closets are neglected, and our cloth disgraced'.[47] Yet he was not willing to give up barter unless he could 'draw more deeply on the Society'. Pritchard, who was stationed at Papeete, acted as purveyor for the visiting ships on behalf of the other missionaries. They would send him their oxen, and he would purchase articles for the domestic use of the missionaries and for barter with the people. The directors charged Pritchard with 'trading to an unwarranted extent' and with 'great keenness in trade'.[48] The mission at Rarotonga was also considered 'a trading mission', even after the directors had expressly forbidden it, but it was never on the same scale as at Tahiti.[49]

The missionaries who arrived in the islands in 1838 and 1839 had no illusions about the trading habits of their predecessors. Stevens said that the Society was to blame in the first instance, and that it was only those missionaries who had been able to gather around them cattle and general stock who were able to manage satisfactorily.[50] Although they condemned mission trading, they found their salaries insufficient to support themselves.[51] The younger men urged that the salaries should be raised to at least £140 per annum. The directors took action, raised the salaries and remonstrated, but 'having some reason to fear that the practice [was] not altogether laid aside' decreed that any future instance of non-compliance with their wishes would involve the forfeiture of the Society's confidence. They felt that the practice, 'besides lowering the general tone and character of the mission', had brought them into 'invidious and degrading competition with their own people'.[52]

Even as late as 1855 the missionaries felt that the salary was inadequate for their needs. Nisbet reminded the directors that the Australasian Wesleyan Conference for 1855 allowed £140 for each married missionary and 12 guineas for each child in Tonga and Fiji,[53] while the LMS allowed £100 to each missionary in Samoa.* Although the directors granted a salary which they

---

*The Samoan missionaries were permitted to barter. In 1845 the Tahitian missionaries were allowed £120 but were forbidden to barter.

believed would supply the basic needs of the missionaries, they
do not appear to have grasped the real nature of conditions in
the islands, and perhaps they placed too much faith and too
little works in the dictum that the Lord would provide.

Until Arthur Tidman became Foreign Secretary of the LMS in
1841 the directors left the missionaries much to themselves in
conducting their stations, but they had a tendency to interfere
in matters of petty detail to an irritating degree.[54] In the early
years the problem of communication was a very real one, and
rumours often travelled home faster than fact. There was a
marked disposition to regard the missionary who wrote home
uncomplaining letters giving impressive figures as a successful
and faithful servant of the Society, whereas a missionary whose
reports attempted to give a full picture, frequently at the expense of his own success, was often regarded as a dissatisfied and
unbalanced person. Letters from the directors could be harsh
and cruel. Orsmond spoke some truth when he exclaimed, 'How
easy to sit in full board and deal out anathemas while coffee, tea
and cracknells feast the stomach'.[55]

Missionaries of the LMS and the American Board had greater
freedom in determining mission policy at their individual
stations than those at the WMMS. The LMS missionaries were
early divided on the score of authority. Officially, authority lay in
the directors, but as this authority was so far removed it was only
valid for general policy and as a court of appeal. Decisions involving the immediate problems of the missions had to be taken
in the field. The LMS agent in New South Wales was able to
exert some influence on mission policy, but he was really little
more than a business agent and a channel for communications.

At the beginning of the Tahitian mission the ordained
brethren had no more authority than the others, and decisions
were taken by a majority. One of the reasons behind the first
exodus from Tahiti was the failure to agree on this matter.
Examined by the directors in 1800, Cover said that the Society
had been 'disturbed' by the brethren Main, Oakes, Cock and
Gillam ('who was the worst of the whole'), and that both the
Puckeys and Smith had been influenced by them. Main had been
one of the ringleaders, and Cover accused him of having 'democratic principles' which he defined as 'want of due subordination
to the rules and orders of the Society', and maintaining that they
would 'have nothing done but by the whole body'.[56] Until
November 1806 one of the missionaries was elected 'President',

but this office was discontinued by a majority vote.[57] It was later urged that a director should be sent out to guide the affairs of the Society, but this was discouraged on the grounds that Pomare would resent anyone in this capacity, and that it would lower the present missionaries in the king's estimation. However it was also pointed out that if the directors felt that such a move was necessary, Nott was the logical person to be chosen as 'Head' of the mission, owing both to his knowledge of the people and his influence with Pomare.

After 1817 the independent nature of the missionaries, especially the newer ones, led to a reaction from the movement towards uniformity. A party spirit was not only created within the Windward mission, but it practically divided the Windward and Leeward missions into rival camps. In all questions where direction was absolutely necessary the lot was resorted to, as a scriptural means sacred to God. Even the four godly young women sent to New South Wales to become missionary wives were apportioned by lot! When the mission was divided in 1817 the separation was made by lot, and names were placed in a hat. But this method resulted in unpleasantness also. The names of the brethren connected with the printing press were not included, and some of the brethren resented being separated from their friends. Crook stated that he and his wife had come to 'a determination that it was rather our duty to separate ourselves from the society than to be stationed with persons with whom we could not unite'. Davies went so far as to read a paper on the evil of abiding by the decision previously reached by lot, and after some opposition, particularly from Nott, a new arrangement was made. It would also appear that, in this case, decision by lot would have run contrary to the wishes of the king, who did not wish to be separated from either Nott or Davies.[58] Davies mentioned the instance of Wesley and Whitefield disputing about election. Wesley, 'instead of making use of his reasoning powers and search[ing] the Scriptures in order to learn whether these things were so, had recourse to a lot, which, without a doubt was a rash act of sinful presumption'.[59] Not all the brethren were in favour of the lot system, but acquiesced because of the majority.

In 1818 the problem of authority was again raised in relation to the division of the mission. Threlkeld, Darling and Bourne strenuously opposed the decision to settle the number of persons for the Windward station by a majority of votes, and the placing of the names of the new brethren in a hat.[60] It had been suggested that as Threlkeld had received some medical training he should be expected to go to the Leeward islands, on the grounds that Crook, the other missionary with medical knowledge, had already been balloted for Tahiti. Threlkeld maintained that the Society had not sent him out as a doctor but as a missionary, and he was 'not going to submit to inconvenience because he happened to have a little medical knowledge'. Threlkeld, Bourne and Darling further declared that submitting to a majority was 'tyrannical'.

The breach was widened by a paper drawn up by Davies at the suggestion of Nott, which proposed a number of rules for the various stations to follow. These 'rules' were aimed at producing a 'unity of proceedings in respect of Missionary work in all the stations, particularly in respect of admittance to Baptism, the mode of administration, Church government and discipline'. These nine rules stressed the decision of the majority as binding, which had been the case since the commencement of the Tahitian mission. Davies thus recorded the reactions of some of the younger men:

> br. Threlkeld declared he was a free man, and would never consent to put the yoke of bondage on his neck, he would have no rules or regulations, nor would he ever submit to a *majority* nor could he think of ever joining himself to men that held such principles.[61]

Darling, Bourne and Platt shared this view, arguing that the Bible was their rule, and they would act 'notwithstanding "rules and majorities" everyone as he thought proper'. These men resolved to separate 'two and two' together in order to escape majorities. At this stage Crook adopted their principles, and maintained that 'everyone stands or falls to his own master'.[62]

As reports from the field and from the published journals of voyages were often conflicting and disturbing, the mission authorities in London felt it necessary to send impartial and disinterested observers to the field. The LMS sent the Reverend Daniel Tyerman and George Bennet as a deputation to the South Seas, Java, the East Indies and Madagascar (1821-29). These men were able to see for themselves some of the weak points of the missions, but their reports were written principally to boost the work of the missionaries, and little practical benefit — on a major policy level — seems to have been derived from this visitation. They did claim, however, that if they had delayed their arrival by six months the missionaries and directors 'would have been in such a state of open war as would have hazarded the present efficient existence of the Mission and have furnished abundant food to gratify the malevolent of all parties'.[63] They sympathized with most of the grievances of the missionaries, particularly the inadequacy of salaries. Their most notable achievement was the founding of the school on Moorea for the children of the missionaries. They assisted in revising the island legislation, and gave English names to most of the mission stations. They advised against the employment of artisan missionaries, whom they described as 'Clogs to Missionary operations',[64] and arbitrated between the older and younger missionaries. They believed that disunion in the mission was due to 'a firm, noble, independent spirit in the Younger Brethren' but also praised this spirit for counteracting hierarchical tendencies on the part of the older missionaries. However, they themselves were circumscribed by this spirit. Bennet informed Burder that they were loath to invoke the authority which the directors had given them:

> through the goodness of God to us it has not been requisite to proceed beyond advice and caution, and in one instance of affectionate admonition. . . . In these regions there is a feverish sensibility of and alarm at the slightest appearance of authority on the part of one brother towards another — or that of the Society towards the Mission. The spirit of independence and conscious sufficiency is certainly carried to its full extent among the Brethren & Sisters with perhaps two exceptions.[65]

The ineffectualness of the 'Deputation' was further highlighted by their own personal quarrels and disagreement over policy matters and the fact that Tyerman died on the way back to London.

The independent spirit was to remain a characteristic feature of the Tahitian mission. In 1828 Orsmond complained of what he termed the 'levelling system' and an 'injudicious use' of the terms 'We are independents'. He believed that the directors did not 'sufficiently consider the necessity of having a sort of head to the various Missions . . . We are dissenters, we are Independents, we have one master Christ and one rule the Bible sounds forth whenever remonstrance is made against any measure that appears inelligible'.[66] As late as 1840 Heath complained of the independent spirit in the Tahitian mission.

> The Tahitian Mission has suffered immensely, and lost its character, because each has been determined to have *his own* way. One will print off a book, another will remove to a fresh station etc. etc., without so much as consulting his brethren. Another will even concur in a vote at a committee meeting and then go and act contrary to it.[67]

The directors had given instructions that business should be conducted by the decision of majorities, and Heath said that the system had 'hitherto worked admirably and harmoniously' at Samoa. Davies, however, denied that the situation was so bad, and asked, 'did not the Directors know, that all the public affairs of the Mission were so conducted for more than 40 years past', and considered the charge of 'want of unanimity' to be a 'mystery'.[68] It is certainly true that in spite of this very vigorous independent spirit in the Society Islands missions, there was a considerable degree of unity on matters of major policy. Decisions *were* reached at quarterly meetings, and there was some degree of cohesion. Whatever individual missionaries might say in the heat of their ecclesiastical idealism, they realized that they could not push their independence too far without damaging the entire mission structure. Thus when Threlkeld changed the date of the Sabbath at Raiatea,* Hayward severely criticized him: 'It ought to be a matter of serious grief to every missionary here that such disunion should exist among them'.[69] When the directors finally wrote to him on the matter, Threlkeld excused himself on the grounds that the same alteration of the Sabbath had been intended by the Windward brethren. He further affirmed that it was always his endeavour 'to compromise, so far as [he] could with a clear conscience', and defended the 'purity of [his] motives', saying that he abhorred and detested 'the spirit of doing right for opposition's sake'.[70]

Other sources suggest that it was only the directors' letter which induced Threlkeld to have the Sabbath changed back,[71] but this illustration shows that the independent spirit was ultimately subject to the authority of the directors, and usually simply to the authority vested in the mission as a whole.

As each new mission was commenced by the LMS it became independent, subject only to the directors. New missions, worked mainly by a native agency, were subject directly to the parent mission, and authority was mainly vested in the missionaries sent as a 'deputation'. When the Marquesas mission was restaffed by Europeans in 1834, decisions concerning actual policy in the group were reached by the few missionaries themselves. Thus the date of the Sabbath was altered, although the Tahitian brethren had voted otherwise.

*Because Captain Wilson and the first missionaries had reached the Society Islands from the east they were a day out in their reckoning. The Raiatean government introduced the change on Friday 10 May 1822. With Threlkeld's connivance, it was almost certainly a political act of defiance against the new Tahitian government. The change was rescinded, and it was left to the French administration to effect the reform more than twenty years afterwards.

Interference, or more exact direction in policy, was much more marked after 1841 when Tidman became Secretary. As early as 1810 there had been complaints about the arbitrary management of the Society by the secretarial 'clique'. Joseph Fox complained of the assumption of power by the directors in 'constituting themselves a DISSENTING ECCLESIASTICAL COURT, from whence they might issue forth their bulls in strict analogy with those of the *degraded* and *dispersed* council of the Vatican'.[72] However there was considerable internal harmony until the secretaryship of Tidman. In 1847 an unpleasant popular controversy arose in which Dr Andrew Reed severely criticized the Tidman regime.[73] In their letters home most of the South Seas missionaries expressed their sympathy with Tidman, but it is difficult to know their real feelings. Thomson was the only missionary who openly criticized Tidman, and that was in a letter to Reed himself.[74] At the time of writing Thomson had separated from the other missionaries. He criticized the 'paramount influence' allowed to the Secretary in the sub-committees, and 'even at the Board', and attributed the fact that 'a clique ruled in the Mission House' to Tidman and his friends. 'The principles which now prevail in Blomfield St. need to be scrutinized. Ever since Mr. Tidman came into office, the correspondence here has been very unpleasant.' Thomson also asserted that the replies to some letters showed that their own letters had been read 'in a great hurry' and were 'often not understood'.

Tidman's policy is further reflected by a letter written by Davies at the same time.

> In former times our honoured Directors did not dictate to us as to our arrangements about the stations etc., but left it to ourselves as being better acquainted with local circumstances, and why it should be otherwise now we know not.[75]

The situation could not be easily accommodated. There was obviously a need for greater conformity to some sort of authority, but it was also obvious that it was the missionaries only who really understood the difficulties and exigencies of their situation. In the Samoan mission care was taken to avoid the dangers inherent in the system prevailing in the eastern islands, and when the missionaries differed, they were careful to ascertain whether they *agreed* to differ.[76]

With the Wesleyans there were similar difficulties concerning authority for action in the field. Although the Methodist system of church government did not allow for a great deal of independence at the various mission stations, there was a tendency for the mission field as a district to assert itself in a forcible way. The missionaries in the field were often highly critical of home policy, and distance and faulty communications were frequently responsible for misunderstandings. When Lawry followed the decision of the 'Colonial Committee for the South Sea Missions', and did not proceed with Leigh to New Zealand, he was censured by the general committee in London. Furthermore, he was transferred from Tonga to Tasmania. When he arrived in England in 1825 his interview with the committee was far from pleasant, and it was some days before he was acquitted of 'false doctrines, heresy and schism'.[77] Complications arose when new districts were created, and came into direct relationship with the general committee. When the New South Wales district meeting secured the approval of the New Zealand district meeting for the appointment of Weiss for Tonga, they were not aware that the islands had been formed into a separate district. In May 1827 they felt it necessary to enter the following statement in their minutes:

> The Committee will of course understand, that the relation in which we now stand to the Islands, is purely *executive* . . . our *official responsibility* will extend only to the due execution of the orders we receive from the Islands, and the safe custody of the goods sent out from London.[78]

The secretaries of the WMMS adopted a rather severe and paternalistic attitude to the secretaries of the various districts. They expressed their disapproval of the word 'Despatches' used by the Sydney committee to designate their business letters and reports.

Although the New South Wales district had virtually no authority in the island missions, the relationship was a much more significant one than that existing between the New South Wales auxiliary to the LMS and the LMS stations. Methodism had a large following in Australia, and it was ultimately the Australasian Conference which took over the entire responsibility for Wesleyan missions in the South Seas. Many of the Wesleyan missionaries were recommended to the New South Wales district meeting.

The problems of administration were also less complex in the Wesleyan missions. Whereas the LMS was an independent organization which had to form its own rules, the WMMS simply took the Church to the field. The Wesleyans followed the 'connexional' system, conducted class-meetings, leaders' meetings, quarterly meetings, and adopted most of the ecclesiastical machinery of the home church. In this way the chairman of the local district assumed the direction of local affairs. The system itself appeared to work sufficiently well in the islands, although many of the missionaries were criticized by their brethren for their ignorance of the correct system and procedures of Methodism.[79] In 1844 Hunt wrote of the success of love-feasts and class meetings. 'We find these means are as applicable to Feejee as to England. "Methodism for ever!!"' [80] The Methodist 'Rules of Society' and Wesley's service manuals were rigidly adhered to.[81]

The churches associated with the LMS were independent congregations, linked together through the missionaries who were all responsible to the Society. In the mission field the churches had a 'national' character about them, and consequently were less like the 'gathered' churches associated with English Congregationalism. A kind of association developed, which invariably adopted a Presbyterian complexion, and not infrequently the role of the missionary was definitely episcopal in character. The Wesleyan Methodist system was possibly better adapted for actual missionary endeavour, as lay agents were a necessary part of the scheme, and they reproduced the labours of the missionary to a great degree.

The Methodist system was fundamentally missionary in character, having evolved from an organization designed to stimulate spiritual revival *within* the English Church. Of course this system had natural drawbacks, owing to the very inadequate religious knowledge of most of the numerous lay agents, both local preachers and class leaders. The principal missionary disadvantage of the Wesleyan system was probably the rule that a minister could not stay indefinitely at one station. This had its disadvantages for the missionaries, in that they were possibly just beginning to make a little progress when required to move, but it must have been more disadvantageous to the people who tended to have proprietary rights over their teachers, and who would have to begin afresh to understand a new missionary. When, in 1850, the committee recommended the missionaries to make no unnecessary changes, it was decided to give up the itinerant system in the islands.[82] However this policy was not sustained and Royce wrote as late as 1860:

> I am inclined to think that our itinerating system is not the one to be carried out in Feejee, however admirably it may work at home, natives don't like fresh faces, and it takes some time to know the people and the work.[83]

He also added that the LMS missionaries had the better of them in this respect. Within the Methodist system of church government, there was no room for that spirit of independence which tended to disrupt the harmony of the Tahitian mission.

The Wesleyans took decisive action and appointed a general superintendent to visit their South Sea stations. The need for this post had been strengthened after a committee had been appointed to investigate the conduct of a missionary in New Zealand.[84] The Reverend John Waterhouse, who was appointed in 1838, arrived in Van Diemen's Land in 1839, made two important visits to the islands, but died in March 1842.[85] Lawry, the former missionary to Tonga, was appointed his successor. The appointment of a general superintendent who did not live in the islands, and yet who had so much influence in the mission, was a sore point with many of the missionaries, especially the younger colonial men. Thus Joseph Waterhouse wrote angrily in 1852:

> Mr. L. is of no use to us — The Gen. Super. should live in Feejee as one of us and not live comfortably at Auckland [and write lies]. We took Mr. L's book up very warmly and the seniors were obliged to interfere . . .[86]

In 1852 the Wesleyan Conference sent out the Reverend Robert Young on a deputation to Australia and Polynesia, in order to make preliminary arrangements for the colonial churches to be 'cast upon their own resources'.[87] Joseph Waterhouse welcomed the prospect of the missions being run from Australia, and wrote enthusiastically to his brother:

> I thank God for the prospect of an Australian Methodist Conference. The world requires it. I am more of a Methodist than ever; but I am for a Methodism startling *hell* itself by its aggressive movements . . .[88]

However, in another letter, he added:

> Remember — NO General Super. for us — With an Australian Conference there is no need of one and we don't want one. We should like a Missionary Secretary. . . . Don't let Mr. Boyce run this Mission for the sake of Australia.[89]

In another letter, Waterhouse wrote that Boyce had been very unpopular in Fiji and was so still.[90]

The missionaries were not very satisfied with Young's deputational visit. Waterhouse complained that they were spoken of 'disparagingly'. His brother Samuel's comment was brief: 'Young only paid a flying visit — He only called at two stations and we heard nothing of him until he had gone'.[91] Mutual satisfaction between the home authorities and the missionaries was thus a balance difficult to achieve.

The most delicate point of contact between the missionaries in the field and the home authorities was the observation of contracts made by the home Societies. Much unpleasantness was caused between LMS and Wesleyan missionaries because of a decision taken in London by the directors of the LMS and the Wesleyan committee. Both Societies agreed that the LMS should have the entire missionary charge of Samoa, whilst the Wesleyans should have entire charge of Fiji. This agreement was reached after John Williams had informed the directors that he had consulted the Wesleyan missionaries at Tonga, in company with Charles Barff, and that they had agreed to divide the field in this way. However the Tongan brethren did not bring the matter before their district meeting, and they had already entered the Samoan field before they received contrary word from London. The Wesleyan missionaries concerned in the first agreement with Williams did not consider it binding, because it was simply their opinion at the time that the spheres of the two Societies should be kept separate, and they did not have the sanction of the rest of the district to make a decision for the whole body. Moreover, the Tongan *lotu*, or Wesleyan Christianity, had already reached Samoa from Tongatapu and Niuatoputapu. The first misunderstanding led to others, and the two missions which had so much in common, and which had previously been on such good terms, became almost hostile competitors in Samoa. This was a case in which the LMS directors relied too much on the word of their missionaries in the field, and the Wesleyan committee took action without first obtaining the approval or advice of its agents. It should also be remembered that, whereas the LMS agents could not act without the authority of the directors, the Wesleyans in Tonga had more local authority, and strongly resisted the policy pursued by the committee. The whole affair was complicated by the Samoan-Tongan political situation, which ultimately decided the issue. Though the Wesleyan missionaries actually withdrew from Samoa in order to observe the London agreement, certain chiefs in Samoa and Tongan agents maintained a Wesleyan cause against all opposition and persuasive means. The Australasian Conference did not hesitate in sending a missionary to succour their cause, despite the London agreement and other contracts.

The policy of the home authorities depended on their knowledge of the conditions in the islands, and it was the limitations in this respect which most hampered good relationships between those at home and their agents in the field. Two of these limitations stand out. One was the tendency to regard the 'success' of mission work according to completely false standards, to see an Eden where the missionaries only saw one or two eyesores removed from the daily scene. 'I often wish', wrote Orsmond to the directors, 'that our joy on the shores of Tahiti were in some measure proportionate to yours on the platform in Exeter Hall',[92] and this was a sentiment which the other missionaries could share with him. The other limitation was the tendency to accept too readily the first impressions of new arrivals in the islands, who did not appreciate the changes already effected. The advice of the Tongan veteran, Thomas Adams, was fairly sound when he suggested that the correspondence of a missionary during his first year should be burnt.[93] It was exceptionally difficult for those at home to appreciate that change in the islands was a very gradual process.

6

A Set of Trading Priests

MANY OF THE early missionaries did not believe that the externals of civilization were necessary either to the improvement of the people or to the spreading of the gospel. They had been forced to suffer privations and hardships, and their standard of living was not a very high one. Principally through their contacts with New South Wales, many of them came to acquire cattle, horses, pigs and fowls, and they also cultivated gardens, some of which tended to become small plantations, but these were necessary for their subsistence. We have seen, too, that the first missionaries to Tahiti had to think more about clothing themselves than about clothing the poor heathen.

Because the older brethren had been forced to live poorly through necessity, many of them were reluctant to 'keep up' with their more progressive brethren. Henry Nott was content to live in a native-style house. John Davies perhaps gave greatest offence to his younger colleagues in this respect. Captain Grimes, who visited Tahiti in 1821, commented on the great difference between the manners of Davies and those of the other missionaries he met. Davies, he said, 'appears so much accustomed to the native habits, as to feel awkward in the company of Englishmen'.[1] Davies was much criticized by the other missionaries, particularly by those like Barff, Williams and Threlkeld who had not experienced the trials of the earlier years. Barff criticized Davies for his 'dress and a filthy habitation which was a great impediment to Civilization'.[2] Although the other missionaries respected Davies, they regarded his simple way of living as a betrayal of their cause. When his life style is compared with that of his brethren, it is less surprising that he was able to leave a small fortune to the son of Hephzibah Bicknell, his stepdaughter who kept house for him for a number of years.

Orsmond criticized Davies and some of the older missionaries for not stimulating the people's interest in the amenities of 'civilization', and for not bothering to alter the condition of the native houses.

> The person who ought to set a better example has an earthen floor; on the table you may see the teakettle, the frying pan, the tea-pot, one cup and saucer, one plate and an old tin pot to hold the milk.[3]

Even the Tahitian, he felt, had cleaner habits, for he changed the leaves from which he ate. Davies, however, regarded his own frugal existence as possessing some virtue. As late as 1845 he was criticizing the 'fine living' of younger men.

> To dine upon a piece of breadfruit, and a bit of fish or salt pork, and a drink of water from the brook as myself and Senior brethren had generally done was mean and vulgar, it would not do for a reformer or Gentleman missionary.[4]

We may conclude nevertheless that Davies was an exception to the general rule, on the evidence of the reactions of other missionaries who visited his station at Papara. Buzacott wrote in 1832:

> The old Gent was litterally a heap of dirt and rags, and his house in a most filthy state. It did not appear that his house or furniture had been cleaned for a long time. He had the appearance as if he had just returned from a long voyage, and we were the first to enter, the dirt and dust was so *patapata tui*. The good gent had dined; but he got a plenty of cold fish and breadfruit for us, of which we ate heartily being rather hungry from our long ride.[5]

The standard of living of the Leeward Island missionaries was noticeably higher than that of the Windward brethren. Williams and his colleagues believed that physical comfort was essential for the missionary and his family, and they were more keenly interested in the civilizing doctrines.

Closely bound up with the standard of living was the notion of social superiority, a tendency to snobbery, signs of which first appeared in the South Seas missions after the arrival of Pritchard and his brother-in-law Simpson. Although these men came from lowly backgrounds similar to those of the earlier missionaries, they had received longer periods of theological training than those still in the Tahitian mission, with the exception of Orsmond. They were much less willing to compromise with indigenous conditions, and posed as English gentlemen. The older missionaries expressed disgust when they heard of the recreations of their new colleagues, such as birdshooting and sailing. Pritchard and Simpson both took pride in their domestic establishments, and their standard of living was higher than that of most of their contemporaries. Indeed, much of the hostility to both these men was possibly engendered by their social pretensions. Mrs Simpson was very careful whom she received, on more than one occasion offending in this way the members of the older families who were obviously less refined,[6] and whose insular tastes, she believed, would have an inimical influence on her daughter, who received private tuition in music and French from a Frenchman living at Papeete.

Social distinction was yet more apparent after the arrival of the missionaries brought out from England by Williams in 1838. In earlier days college life had been all too often an intensive academic course following an even more intensive period of self-education combined with heavy manual work. Those who came out with Williams had had more opportunities to cultivate leisure, and the transformation from clerk to gentleman missionary was greatly assisted by the new prestige which missionaries were then enjoying in the public eye. Whilst, during his visit to England, Williams dallied with his dukes, the missionary recruit was conscious of his apprenticeship to the ranks of polite society. Williams himself was a popular figure rather than a social success. His contact at Chatsworth, for instance, was with Joseph Paxton, the celebrated gardener, rather than Devonshire himself though, as Paxton informed Williams at the height of his popularity in October 1837, 'the Duke sometimes asks if I have heard from the "nice boy" '.[7]

The older missionaries severely criticized the new missionaries for their 'modernism'. Orsmond, of course, was the most vituperative, but it is quite clear that there was a marked contrast between the life of the newcomers and that of the veterans of the mission. Orsmond remarked that the new missionaries found it irksome to live amongst the heathen, 'where there are no circles of polite Literature'.[8] He recorded with some little derision that they played at marbles, at swinging, at leap-frog, at boating and at horse riding. They slept late and ate voraciously. Surely they were going too far when they required their servants to *burn* and grind coffee on the Sabbath morning, 'that the more exquisite flavours might be enjoyed'. 'Why did the Directors not send them to the bowers of the Muses', he concluded, 'to dispute with doctors, to spin a mathematical garb for the Christian Church, and to split hair like syllogisms in defending Christian conduct'.[9] The older brethren who had nearly all become converts to teetotalism in the 1830s,[10] and had found the methods and propaganda of that movement a practical and effectual check to the drunkenness at their stations, also resented the moderate drinking of the younger men. Davies remarked that they did not co-operate with the temperance societies, and said that teetotalism might be 'consigned to Father Mathew and Co'. He wished that they would 'stay at home and enjoy their wine and their brandy without offending us and our mission'.[11]

Amongst the Wesleyan missionaries the standard of living

appears to have been a little lower than in the other missions. In Tonga, at least, this may have been due to the policy of one man, John Thomas. Like Nott and Davies, Thomas was content with a fairly humble dwelling. He maintained an influence unparalleled in any other mission, so that he could afford to voice his criticism. Thus, as late as December 1856, he gave his opinion about Vercoe having timber sent for his house at Mu'a:

> The day is gone by in these Islands when a Missionary will put up with *ground* floors with dry grass and mats upon it to walk on — your men nowadays — yes and their wives — are too *tender* — too delicate in their health to endure such a state of things and this country is only thinly wooded.[12]

Vercoe's dwelling, notwithstanding, was simply a 'good native house', and doors, windows and boards only were needed to make it complete.[13] Overall the Wesleyan missionaries seem to have placed less importance on domestic comforts. David Cargill was much criticized for bringing furniture to Tonga, a padded sofa being considered an unnecessary luxury.[14] His spirit-drinking habits were looked upon with critical disapproval. Although some of the Wesleyans kept domestic animals and planted gardens they relied principally on indigenous foods. Thus Cross (in 1841) had grown tired of salt pork, yams and arrowroot.

> Many a day I have had but little disposition to eat our food when a little bread and a glass of wine, or a glass of beer, or an egg or a little English meat would have been a luxury.[15]

Each generation of missionaries tended to demand a higher standard of living than the previous one, and older missionaries resented the improvements as unnecessary. Thus Platt of Raiatea was piqued at Charter because he employed European carpenters to make a better house than the Raiateans would have built.[16] However by the 1850s most of the missionaries in the South Seas were comfortably established. Although domestic servants could not always be obtained, in most instances the missionary's lady had several house-girls and boys at her beck and call.* The missionary housewife regarded herself as an ambassadress for the Christian women of Britain, and she took pains to cultivate the 'home of taste'. The table was well-stocked, and the guest at the mission station was possibly afforded the best hospitality which could be offered in the islands.

---

*In Samoa the unmarried women of the *aualuma*, who traditionally slept as a group in a house of their own, were moved where possible into the pastor's house — and probably into the environs at least of the European mission house. This gave a large supply of domestic labour.

The average Evangelical missionary was in the process of establishing himself more securely in the social class towards which his sympathies were directed. As a 'godly mechanic', or as a more privileged member of a mechanic-class family, he had claimed the privileges, adopted the conventions and imitated the manners of the greater middle class. In many ways the missionary career served as a qualifying certificate in this change of status. The emphasis on conformity to European social values was accentuated by the lonely condition of the missionaries isolated from their social group. It was the missionary's duty to preach to the islander, but the desire for congenial company and customary social intercourse induced him to relieve his Crusoe-like isolation by making Man Friday somebody acceptable to talk with. The missionary's wife must have found some social satisfaction in having tea parties with island royalty, dressed in gowns and bonnets, reclining on sofas, and being waited on by servants.

Besides accentuating this need for company, isolation developed many aspects of missionary character. Some men improved their intellectual capacities by research or literary pursuits. Others developed in a more individualistic way. Their rise in the social scale had been an independent struggle, much of their education had been acquired by personal efforts, and their conversions had been highly personal. Every man was his own priest and master of his own destiny. In this milieu two qualities became plainly discernible amongst some of the Evangelical missionaries. One might be described as a proclivity to trade, and the other as political opportunism. Those who were distinguished by these qualities tended to degenerate from the missionary ideal, but because their worldly interests reflected the economic and social ambitions of an important group of mission supporters they were readily accepted in these circles.

There must have been something about the personality of John Williams which captured the imagination of middle-class Englishmen. He was solid like John Bull, yet his voyages suggested an adventurous and daring folk hero. Williams was undoubtedly pious, but it is evident that there were more wordly strains in his nature. His interest in British commerce was also the interest of a trader, and Williams the navigator was very much a trader. As we have seen, many of the older LMS missionaries had been compelled to engage in some trading in order to keep themselves reasonably clothed and fed. This sort of trading, which had arisen from necessity, was not so necessary when salaries were raised. With Williams, however, trading acquired a virtue of its own. Commercial enterprise was as much a

civilizing agent as the gospel, and although he paid lip-service
to the doctrine that it was Christianity which produced the
desire for civilization, he was not unfamiliar with the nature
of cupidity.

Despite his limitations, Williams possessed a highly developed
sense of calling. Williams' interest in a missionary ship which
would pay for itself by engaging in trade does not seem beyond
the limits of the missionary vocation. However as early as 1823,
when Williams was required to sell his ship, the people of
Raiatea expressed their resentment at making sacrifices which
had come to nothing. According to Orsmond, the people 'called
him a liar and deceiver and said that because of him children
instead of being brought forth at home were brought forth on
the mountains while the parents were in search of arrow root
for the Ship'.[17]

> Not one of all the Islanders that I could find took his part or spoke
> in his favour. How dangerous to meddle with mercantile affairs to
> the utter neglect of ones more sacred duties.

It was in his later days that Williams more openly 'meddled
with mercantile affairs'. When he returned to the islands in the
Camden at the end of 1838 most of the new missionaries were
quickly disillusioned by his attitude. Both Royle and Charter
were unable to bring out all their luggage and supplies because
one-third of the vessel was occupied by goods belonging to John
Williams, junior, who was going to set up as a merchant at Apia.
Williams' high-handed manner in the direction of the ship made
him much disliked. The missionaries believed that he wished
them to be 'under the necessity of purchasing things from his
son John'.[18] The missionaries had no supplies of sugar and flour,
and on one occasion at Apia Williams and his family were eating
pancakes whilst the 'rest of the party' had to make do with
cold taro.

Both Simpson and Pritchard had similar trading tendencies.
Pritchard asserted that because he lived at the principal harbour
the other missionaries used him as their agent, especially in
selling their cattle to the ships. In defending himself against the
charge of 'great keenness in trade' he said that he had always
endeavoured to obtain things at the lowest rate possible, and
that most of the captains were 'a set of sharpers'. Furthermore,
he denied that he had any 'attachment' to trading.[19]

Pritchard's position calls for comment as he was the first of
a type of missionary resented by those in the islands who had to
earn their livelihood by trading. While the missionary was

neither a usurer nor a profiteer his influence was felt to be equally insidious; inevitably he undercut the commercial traders and frequently protected his customers from economic reality. Joseph Smith, a planter in Tahiti, believed that the bartering of the missionaries did not compromise their religious work but his comments suggest that Pritchard's business did detract from his effectiveness and that he should have ceased his vocation. In Smith's view, Pritchard's trading was the principal cause of the enmity of the Belgian trader Moerenhout, and hence of eventual French political interference.[20] The account given by Armitage in 1835 certainly confirms that Pritchard and Simpson had considerable business ties.

> They traded with the people in Arra root Oil and Hogs and Timber. The exchange was generaly Cloth, Ribonds, Hardware Slops and Muskets. With vessels the[y] bought and sold ships stores, Boats, Pearls and Shells. Mr. P. had bought a very extensive Shugar works on which he had upwards of 40 men. . . .[21]

Simpson also engaged in the sugar business, and defended his activities on the grounds of stimulating native industry and giving employment to an 'industrious white man'. As well he had acted on behalf of George Bicknell and Moerenhout on occasions 'without compensation'.[22] At a meeting of the missionaries at Tahiti after Williams' final return to the islands, Simpson is reported to have asked him if the directors considered sugar boiling equivalent to trading. 'The Rev John Williams said No, they do not. Mr Simpson will resign the School, but keep his sugar plantation.'[23]

The missionary trader, as a type, was less common amongst the Wesleyans. The missionaries in the islands were particularly sensitive on this point, as their colleagues at Hokianga in New Zealand in the early 1830s had engaged in timber speculation to the embarrassment of the Society, and their station had been labelled a 'Mercantile Establishment'.[24] However, while preaching missionaries were strictly forbidden to 'intermeddle' with trade, lay missionaries were not bound to any agreement. Binner, the Wesleyan school master at Levuka, did not regard it as inconsistent with his profession to engage in trading.

> With respect to my launching into business I don't think anything I do that way lessens my moral or other influences for good among this people, or among the white residents.[25]

It was his policy never to refuse to purchase native produce when it was brought to his door, and he believed that he was conferring a great benefit on the people, as many of the Fijians commenced attending the services 'in consequence of it'.

W. T. Pritchard suggests that some of the Wesleyan missionaries in Fiji not only purchased lands from settlers and Fijians 'in their own name or in the names of their children', in order to provide for their children, but often made such purchases 'avowedly for church purposes, with the unmistakable intention of keeping those lands for [their own] benefit'.[26] James Calvert was regarded as being the principal 'businessman' amongst the Wesleyans, though he apparently never sold for profit. Younger missionaries, anxious to absolve the mission of trading charges in the 1860s were clearly embarrassed by the commercial activities of some of the older men.

> The fact nevertheless remains that there have been two or three Missionaries, who, if they had taken to business instead of to Mission work, w^d probably have made large fortunes, so great has been their natural aptitude for buying in the cheapest market & selling in the dearest; & of these sinners Mr Calvert was perhaps the Chief. But the trading interests of those commercial shepherds have led them, not into buying & selling for their own gain, but for the use of the Mission in general. Thus, there is perhaps nothing under heaven wh. Mr Calvert w^d not buy, if he c^d get it at a reduced price; but at the same reduced price, he w^d sell it again to any Missionary who might be in want of it; or apply it to general Mission use, thereby effecting a saving in ye expenditure of y^e "Widder's Mites".[27]

While they deplored these commercial undertakings the other missionaries felt powerless to intervene.

Political opportunism was closely linked with the trading spirit. Indeed we find both qualities in George Pritchard. Because of his key position there were opportunities for Pritchard to become influential in the 'foreign politics' of Tahiti. He was constantly called upon to act as interpreter, and in his capacity as chaplain he acted as adviser to the native sovereign. To voyagers he often gave the appearance of having greater influence than he actually possessed. As a commercial agent for the other missionaries he was in constant contact with the visiting captains on purely business matters. Pritchard ultimately accepted a position as British consul, and resigned from the LMS. At first he had thought he could retain both offices, and justified this position on the grounds that Morrison of China had held a civil office.[28] Although, as consul, Pritchard was no longer an official representative of the LMS, he remained an active missionary and was regarded as being one of their number by most of his colleagues. Only Darling and Orsmond spoke openly against Pritchard's accepting the office of consul, and told their congregations that he had 'given up the sacred for a profane office'.[29] Most of the others favoured a consul who shared the same values, but few of them believed that the two offices could be united satisfactorily.

With the 'promotion' to consular status Pritchard became more completely absorbed into the greater middle class to which he had long aspired. It is typical of the man and his position that he dressed with much unnecessary flourish. Some of the missionaries were scathing in their remarks. 'Never was I so disgusted and so ashamed', wrote Orsmond, 'to see a poor missionary in the tinsel of gold bouncing about and swaggering with a long sword by his side'.[30] When he visited Papeete he observed that he did not call on consul Pritchard — 'He is now above us'. On the other hand many of the missionaries felt that Pritchard did them a service by being consul, and no doubt enjoyed the prestige which it seemed to give them as a body. Pritchard was by no means the most politically astute of the missionaries. His career was distinguished more by vigour than by natural ability, and his 'decay' as British consul in Samoa much more plainly reveals his limitations.[31]

Political opportunism was also a feature of the Wesleyan missionary. There was a tendency to apply Wesley's 'no politics' ruling to internal affairs while assuming a kind of moral responsibility for external political relations. The missionaries frequently behaved as if endowed with consular status and this no doubt helps to explain the hostility of W. T. Pritchard (son of the missionary, George Pritchard) who was appointed British consul in Fiji in 1857. Calvert and Joseph Waterhouse both assumed political importance through their influence with Cakobau. Calvert, who was hated by the European community, was regarded by them as 'the great political mover in Feejee'.[32] That Waterhouse appears to have had no qualms about acting as unofficial representative of the Fijian authorities is clear from his participation in the affair over the American indemnity in 1855. Williams, the U.S. consular agent, had claimed damages for the accidental burning of his house in 1849.

> What a pity that those who have no sympathy with the black races are sent to 'protect' American interests in Polynesia. But I question whether this gentleman's [i.e. the Captain] arbitrary conduct will not cost him his commission yet. My position as 'Attorney-General' for the poor befriendless native has thus prevented my attendance at the Annual District Meeting.[33]

It might be supposed, both from their interest in trade and their frequent readiness to accept consular or semi-official positions, that the missionaries were the voluntary promoters of their governments anxious for the extension of Anglo-Saxon rule. But this was not the general pattern. Most missionaries were opposed to annexation or colonization in the usual sense, though they came to favour 'protection' by either Britain or the United States. This need for 'protection' increased as it became much more difficult for the indigenous governments to control expatriate Europeans. At the same time it was felt that the presence of British or American authorities would prevent the islands from becoming French possessions and thus more exposed to Roman Catholic influence.

The very early missionaries and directors possibly saw the 'South Sea Mission' as an extension of the British *imperium*. Dr Haweis, at least, informed Henry Dundas, the Home Secretary, that the missionaries represented 'an English incipient Colony, and every Benefit resulting from the Civilization we hope to introduce must ultimately terminate in Britain'.[34] Latrobe of the Moravian Society even recommended that the missionaries should be designated colonists rather than missionaries.[35] There was also a general acceptance of the view that Tahiti lay within a sphere of British influence on the grounds both of discovery and continued contact. The friendship arrangements between the navigators and the Tahitian chiefs, symbolized by the British House at Matavai, served in lieu of the treaties of literate nations. After experiencing ill-treatment and abuse at the hands of the Tahitians on several occasions, the missionaries believed they could only succeed by increasing their numerical strength and forming their station into a regular garrison colony supervised by a president of their own body 'or Governor'.[36] Almost certainly they compared their position to that of the first Puritan settlers in North America.

A view that a garrison outpost of the colony of New South Wales should be set up at Tahiti to control the pork trade, however, met with opposition by the missionaries on the ground that the soldiers would be a corrupting influence.[37] If there were to be other colonists they must be godly citizens like themselves. Marsden's schemes for the CMS in New Zealand were in line with these beliefs, though in Lang's opinion many of the 'colonists' at the Bay of Islands were not fit associates for missionaries, being 'carpenters obtained at random from the Whalers & convict mechanics of the very worst character'.[38] Marsden's view of an 'English incipient Colony' anticipated full colonial status and Marsden had no qualms about associating his missionary endeavours with the British flag.

In Tahiti the idea of a 'godly colony' was largely abandoned following the 'conversion' of the entire population at the behest of Pomare II. The missionaries almost unanimously supported local autonomy, believing that the indigenous authorities should make their own laws and execute their own justice. In most cases they believed it would have been political interference to have done otherwise. As champions of the rights of indigenous governments the missionaries had little patience with visiting naval men (of whatever nation) who ignored the local regulations.

When the missionaries did advocate 'protection' by a maritime power, their intention appears to have been solely to prevent injustice: their choice of Britain as the protecting power was due as much to Britain's naval prestige as to their own patriotism. No island government could be relied on to withstand undue pressures of any kind after the death of Pomare II, and therefore some vague form of protection was sought as a means of recognizing the indigenous authority. Hitoti and the other Tahitian chiefs petitioned the Marquess of Londonderry for British protection in August 1822 and Pomare III petitioned George IV in October 1825.[39]

That missionaries encouraged unofficial use of the British flag is plain from advice given by Threlkeld to the chiefs and people of Rurutu when a ship belonging to the Tahitian government demanded tribute in the form of food supplies in 1822.

> My recommendation was to hoist the British flag, and place themselves under the protection of the British Government, as the only means by which they could preserve their freedom, little dreaming at that time that Great Britain would ever play falsely to King George's Islands. . . .[40]

Canning's reply in 1827 to Pomare's petition forbade the use of the flag and guaranteed only such protection as could be granted 'to a friendly Power at so remote a distance'.[41] Further petitions were made during the reign of Pomare IV.

Vigorous missionary support of a protectorate policy was more marked after the advent of French Roman Catholic missionaries in the Pacific. The Reverend Samuel Wilson of Samoa thus advised Malietoa Vai'inupō, then the highest-ranking chief of his group, to write to William IV 'to put the Samoan islands under the protection of the British flag and to solicit that a ship of war may occasionally touch here to acknowledge the native government'.[42]

In some instances American intervention and protection appear to have been regarded as a welcome alternative to British protection. Thus the visit of Captain Thomas ap Catesby Jones to Tahiti in 1826 proved the occasion for friendship treaties between the United States and Tahiti. In this affair the British consul (Charlton) and other British residents censured the missionaries for their involvement. Orsmond and Charles Wilson, the two who translated and explained the documents, were also criticized and condemned by Williams and the Leeward party. Most of the missionaries dissociated themselves and even Wilson allowed Orsmond to receive the full measure of blame, though at first he had defended his participation as 'an act of civility'.[43] The missionaries were as susceptible to public opinion as any other group and certainly did not wish to appear unpatriotic. In the Leewards, the influence of Williams with King Tamatoa of Raiatea restricted the American negotiations in that island to commercial matters. In Williams' view, Britain was the natural protecting power in the Society Islands.

In Fiji David Cargill earned the enmity of Captain Belcher of H.M.S. *Sulphur* by invoking the assistance of Captain Hudson of the U.S.S. *Peacock*. The missionaries translated the port regulations which Hudson drew up for the Rewa chiefs in their dealings with Europeans. Belcher was so angered by the proceedings that he openly abused Cargill: 'Captain Belcher threatened to tie me, take me on board of his vessel and to flog me'.[44] The Fijians who witnessed the performance are said to have called Belcher a *tamata lialia* (a foolish man) and a *tamata viavia turaga* (a man desirous of being a chief).

In Samoa in the 1870s both the LMS and Wesleyan missionaries were to support the idea of an American protectorate when that possibility seemed imminent.[45] In these affairs there were obviously no real imperial considerations. Anglo-Saxon protection was preferred to other arrangements and even an arrangement with Germany was preferable to one with France. In Tahiti there were several missionaries who preferred the possibility of French protection to that of none at all.

If the missionaries were not necessarily open advocates of British expansion, the islanders themselves viewed their mentors as agents of the governments of their countries. There was a widespread belief (no doubt based on their own indigenous experience) that all strangers sought land and property. Wherever missionaries settled, those ill-disposed towards them spread rumours that they had come to take the people's food supplies because they had none to eat in their homelands.[46] Even the missionary contributions were viewed as a form of tribute (see page 309). Pomare II, despot as he was, was greatly afraid that Europeans would overrun his country.

The first petitions to Britain were written under missionary influence and it is doubtful if the islanders themselves appreciated the need for recognition of their own governments. It was only when the French had actually intervened in their affairs that the Tahitians appeared to value possible British intervention, and even then their resistance was largely due to anti-French and anti-Catholic prejudice.

In other areas the islanders were also jealous of their independent position. Any missionary who appeared to support undue intervention by Britain or any other power was likely to lose the confidence of the local chiefs. The Wesleyan missionaries were probably less skilled in diplomacy than their LMS counterparts, as some of them 'lost face' in both Tonga and Fiji. As a rule, the Wesleyan displayed a more obvious patriotism than his LMS counterpart and had a greater tendency to wave the British flag.

In Tonga the missionaries were afraid that French intervention would follow the Tahitian pattern. John Thomas advised King George Tupou 'to apply to the English Government for protection — to offer themselves to be the friends — or subjects of the English'.[47] Thomas was evidently not careful to explain the nature of the treaty. The king believed he was merely entering into a friendship agreement with Britain whereas the British representatives viewed his overtures as an offer of cession to Queen Victoria. After this affair Thomas was viewed with suspicion and was forced to confess privately, 'I am thought to have used cunning in order to get the Friendly Islands for the British Government'.[48]

A similar incident took place in Fiji in 1855 during the visit of Captain Denham of H.M.S. *Herald*. On this occasion Calvert is said to have misled Cakobau, *'Tui Viti'*, into believing that he was seeking protection. Denham, on the other hand, understood he was receiving an offer of cession. The French priest at Ovalau, who recorded the affair, did not hesitate to label Calvert an agent of the British government.[49]

It is apparent that both Calvert and Joseph Waterhouse were anxious for British protection. Waterhouse exhibited all the zeal of a colonial's faith in Empire. His identification with British interests was symbolized by his flying the Union Jack from the masthead of his canoe, until Consul Pritchard sent an 'impudent half-caste boy' to order him to take it down. The flag had evidently been given to the missionaries by Sir Everard Home to give protection to their canoes but it was flown with a degree of national pride.[50] The other missionaries appear to have been indifferent to the question of annexation though Royce was, at base, another imperialist in the days of 'little England'. When negotiations between Britain and the Fijian chiefs appeared to break down in October 1859, Royce recorded in his journal: 'we are indifferent as to what compact is made, so that we are protected from French intrigue with its popish retinue'. However he had modelled himself on Sir Henry Havelock, a soldier of Empire, and when he became convinced that 'England means to have Feejee, whether or no', he believed he had contributed to this end.[51]

However, despite their ardent patriotism, the missionaries were motivated mainly by their own interests. Pritchard's own story of their apparent 'change of heart' at least suggests that they preferred some form of protectorate to direct annexation.

> When the question of cession was first mooted, the Wesleyan missionaries as a body heartily rejoiced at the prospect and cordially co-operated. But when I unwittingly stated that, in an interview with the late Duke of Newcastle, his Grace had asked me, 'What will the Wesleyan missionaries do when they see a bishop accompanying a governor, for the Church always goes where the State goes,' there was a sudden change. The cession was looked upon with suspicion — personal motives were imputed — and ultimately from cordial co-operation they passed to sullen opposition.[52]

It was, in fact, the missionaries who influenced Smythe, the visiting British representative, to recommend Britain's rejection of the offer.

If the missionary was largely indifferent to political imperialism, favouring autonomy with some form of naval protection, he was wholly committed to a concept of spiritual imperialism. The extension of Christ's kingdom was his avowed aim. Williams' demand for a ship had been made partly with a view to winning an empire of souls.

> A missionary was never designed by Jesus to get a congregation of a hundred or two Natives & sit down at his ease as contented as if every Sinner was converted while thousands around him are eating each others flesh & drinking each others blood with a savage delight living & dying without the knowledge of that gospel by which life & immortality are brought to light . . . for my own part I cannot content myself within the narrow limits of a Single reef & if means is

not afforded a continent to me would be infinitely preferable for there if you cannot ride you can walk but to these isolated Islands a Ship must carry you.[53]

In these frequently misquoted words he voiced sentiments which he must have heard expressed by his colleague Threlkeld who had wished to be sent to some large and populous Asian land.

The pattern of missionary work throughout the South Seas reflected the desire to reach new lands and peoples. In the wake of missionary expansion came the social attachments of Christianity. Williams and other missionaries had urged that they laid the foundations for civilization and commerce by pacifying the islands and engendering new wants in the island territories. In that the missionaries created spheres of British influence by introducing British institutions and concepts and a market for cotton cloth and other Western products, they assisted in stepping up the imperialistic process where other conditions were favourable. Had the British government been as anxious as the French to make use of the missionary work of its nationals, the islands of the eastern and central Pacific would almost certainly have come under one administration flying the flag of the United Kingdom.

7

The Enemy Within

RELIGIOUS EXPERIENCE, for the Westerner at least, is a highly personal matter, and the religious man, in difficult or trying circumstances, is easily the victim of intense introversion. The missionary was often alone. Frequently he was the only European resident, and apart from his wife and family, there were no kindred spirits with whom he could discuss his problems. Intellectually he was prone to frustration, for his wife did not always possess the qualities which made her an intellectual companion. Charlotte Yonge, perhaps unfairly, referred to the wife of Carey of Serampore as a 'dull, ignorant woman', saying that the missionary 'never manifested anything but warm affection and tenderness towards this very uncompanionable person, and perhaps, like most men of low station and unusual intellect, had no idea that more could be expected of a wife.' This was doubtless the position of many of the missionaries, although some of the missionary ladies were more talented and accomplished than their husbands.[1]

The Evangelical missionary constantly asked himself what increase he was showing for his talents. Always conscious of death and 'the brink of eternity', he lamented that there were many souls as yet unsaved by his labour. At the end of every year he reviewed his progress, always earnestly hoping that he would come out on the credit side of the great transaction of life.

Consciousness of time was not merely the result of the doctrine of stewardship, the belief that time, like property, was something which God had made available for man, and that a personal account had to be given for its use. It was also the result of strong contrast, contrast between the world of his youth and training and the exotic world of the present. There was always the feeling that the present would be cut off as dramatically as the past had been. There was a certain anxiousness to complete the missionary task and to return home. Something of the 'temporal' nature of their experience is captured by these reflections of Whewell, after labouring at Ha'apai for a year.

147

Such is the rapidity of the flight of days and months, and such the crowd of trivial circumstances cram'd in to every day, that at the end of these several portions of our "Fleeting Being" we stand stun'd and bewildered (as one waking up from some dream) afraid to think another day another month is gone, gone for ever and only recollecting the most prominent and striking feature of the dream — dream of real life — of this life, the Kataki' (endurance) of it, I do not know that we possess any superabundance of that all precious grace "Fua Kataki'" (patience). Yet in this place we find plenty of exercise for that grace.[2]

Soul-searching played an extremely important role in the daily lives of the missionaries. The Calvinist missionaries were careful to record their trials and blessings, and lamented their unworthiness. The Wesleyans were perhaps more prone to the most vigorous self-examination, and continually prayed for a renewal of their initial experiences. Very few of the LMS journals contain records of the heart-searchings and conflicts which troubled the missionaries, although Orsmond has left a fairly comprehensive record of his inner life. These are some entries from his journal:

11 August 1819: I fear lest I should incur divine displeasure.[3]
19 August 1819: [He gives a long prayer and utterances of spiritual desolation]
How long shall I wander in the dark, bear thy billows in my soul. When thou with rebukes dost correct man for iniquity thou makest his beauty to consume away as the moth. . . . Be propitious to me. Consign me not over to the power of darkness. Shew me thy bleeding heart, thy cheering smile, thy invincible grace. Surely my sins have separated between me and my God. . . . What is the cause of my distress. The ungodly all arround me sleep soundly sleep. They know nothing of these self loathings, these pangs of heart, these tears, these prayers. . . . Tell me my name is in the book of life. . . . I contemplate the plan of Redemption, admire the Goodness, Justice and love of God in all the features of the plan, but I am still destitute of an experiment[al] joy arising from these.
[More such entries follow including much religious verse.]

Orsmond found some sort of relief in describing his state of mind to the people. He records something of a conversation after dark with about thirty Tahitians.

> When I said that no one of them had a worse heart than myself, that I often had filthy dreams, that I was prone to base, sinful thoughts and that I stood guilty before God everyday, several of them said such things were new to them, that they had not heard a missionary say so much of himself and that perhaps I had been a very great sinner.[4]

Some, such as Thomas Slatyer, wrote of their spiritual experience in terms which bore the impress of the Evangelical Revival with its powerful love-to-Christ motif.[5] For others such as Isaac Henry, the soul-searching often assumed rather morbid proportions. Henry was himself a lay preacher, the son of the Reverend William Henry and later the father of the Tahitian scholar, Teuira Henry. His journal is in some ways a graphic record of his reclamation to the moral values of his parents by the discipline of Calvinist doctrines. In it he did not hesitate to specify his temptations. On one occasion he suspected a church member of attempting to seduce him, whilst in the cabin of a boat during heavy rain.

> I for some time remained unmoved, but pitied the woman for her folly, suddenly however the evil suggestions of Satan began to fly around me, and those wicked corruptions of my own nature which have been for some time, mercifully restrained by the divine aid began to grow, and if encouraged would have led me to commit a sin which painful experience in the past has led me to see grows insensibly upon a persons passions, and would eventually if practiced drown my poor soul in perdition. These reflections roused me to a sense of my duty and by the divine aid not from any strength of my own, I have been enabled to withstand this attack from the adversary. I write these things though ashamed of the depravity of my own heart, to show to myself or to any into whose hands these writings may eventually fall, that there is no dependance to be placed upon an arm of flesh.[6]

A real difference is discernible between the introversion of the Wesleyans and the Calvinist missionaries. If the Calvinist fell into the state of desolation, he accepted his early conversion, and when he had time for heart-searching, it was of a more intellectual nature: he weighed the pros and cons of his case, he measured his grace according to his works. The Wesleyan, however, demanded a renewal of his experience at frequent stages in order to give him the necessary stimulus. With a doctrinal emphasis on the importance of holiness, his introversion often became intense, and his reactions were, in consequence, much more emotional.

Orsmond found that there was too little time to devote to spiritual development. Although spiritually alone, he was far removed from the solitude which he craved.

> When at home I thought that a missionary had the finest opportunity for the cultivation of personal religion but now in the field I find it vastly different.[7]

Walter Lawry, whilst at Tonga, found that the reverse was the case:

> For my part, I feel the benefit of my solitude. It proves favourable to my growth in Grace, to my close application to study, and to my digesting many important subjects, which in the whirl of Society, I had attended to but superficially.[8]

Certainly the average missionary did find time for study, and however hard he worked during the days, the evenings were usually devoted to the family circle and to study. Much of the work which the missionary had to perform was of a research nature. He collected words for vocabularies, and translated the scriptures and various educational texts, as well as religious tracts.[9] Missionary wives frequently read to their husbands from the various histories and biographies which were sent out to them. Many of the missionaries felt that their spiritual life was threatened rather than assisted by the routine of missionary labour. Royce wrote:

> How easy it is for a man however holy to lose his piety in Feejee. I feel this; a number of things take your thoughts from your proper work; so many affairs upon which you are called to give advice, both Chiefs and white men, then your domestic affairs, constantly a number of things on your mind, in addition to all the heat, or the rain, the wind, or the mosquitoes and flies to annoy you; it is difficult to keep in a spiritual frame under such circumstances, retire to prayer and meditation, and a host of things crowd your mind, try to make a sermon and you have a number of calls — arrange for some engagement and ten to one if something does not cross you in the performance. Nothing can sustain one in Feejee but a sense of the Divine Presence, and a consciousness that we are not going a warfare at our own charge, the work is the Lords.[10]

As a Wesleyan's record of his inner life, Peter Turner's journal provides a typical example of recurrent spiritual problems and preoccupations over a long period.[11]

January 1831:	I felt that I had lost the blessing of sanctification during the voyage . . . I fear that I have sometimes given way to rebellious thoughts against the Government of the holy God.
May 1831:	[Ha'apai]: I do not feel so lively in spiritual matters as when at home, everything is new and am much tempted to omit private duties.
23 May 1831:	I am so dull, and stupid, and unthankful. Some unpleasant things have occurred — and have pained my mind. I fear my mind was unwatchful and I did not acquit myself manfully.
23 October 1831:	Have been attacked with temptation of a painful character, but have found relief by going to a throne of grace.
26 September 1832:	Still alive and possessed of the grace of God. I am longing for a clean heart.
4 July 1833:	I love solitude but a missionary must labour for the good of all.
25 December 1833:	[Tongatapu]: Have been tempted to be proud, but was enabled to resist the foul insinuations of the Arch-fiend.
25 April 1836:	[Savai'i]: My mind has been much subject to depression and foul temptations. Have been edified while reading Thornton on Prayer. I am much deficient in energy and perseverance in this duty.
17 September 1837:	I hardly deserve the name of missionary when contrasted with such men as H. Martyn and Brainard and Swartz.
14 May 1838:	I do not persevere in prayer as I should. . . . I have not any enjoyment in religion as formally. . . . My service is marred with sin.
31 January 1840:	[Ha'apai]: [I] meditated this evening upon my character and my state. I was convinced of my pollution; and my need for a deeper work. The entire sanctification of my soul.[12]

The pursuit of 'entire sanctification' was indeed the great work of the Wesleyan missionary. Its centrality is typified by the only piece of major didactic theology to appear from the Pacific mission field, John Hunt's *Letters on Entire Sanctification.*

Specific love to Jesus was also characteristic of the Wesleyan's inner life. Indeed, it had been one of the chief features of the Methodist Revival. We find expressions of this emotional approach which rank with the expressions of the great mystics. Such expressions are not only found in prayerful utterance, but they occur in a more impersonal way in much of the correspondence. Joseph Waterhouse wrote thus to his sister:

> Sometimes I feel a want of resignation to the Divine will:—but when I bow before the Mercy-seat and gaze upon *Jesus;* when the eye of my faith is firmly fixed upon the bleeding Saviour, my load falls off — my mourning is turned into joy — and the thought that there will be no melancholy in Heaven removed the sad feeling under which I labour.[13]

It was the continuance of the religious experience, the faith in their work, and their particular view of religion, which enabled the missionaries to adhere rigidly to their original views and opinions.

Not all the missionaries experienced that 'deeper work of the soul', and many left the field or offended their colleagues by some type of defection. Some were disillusioned. Some had had insufficient knowledge of the mission field. Some left because of personal danger, some because a false picture had been created by other missionaries, and others left because of disagreements in the field, persecution or scandal-mongering. Many left — especially the female missionaries — because of ill-health, nervous tension and climatic fatigue. Others left the missions after moral failings and backsliding.

Behind this failure and defection lies the problem of the search for stability, and the insecurity of the missionary in his strange environment. There were two classes of those who had moral lapses: those who rebelled against their previous religious convictions, and those who regretted their lapse and often gave service in other areas.

Various reasons have been assigned to the first defections. Of those who left Tahiti in 1798, the married brethren stated that they left because of the dangerous situation in which their wives and families were placed.[14] However the creation of a rather bitter party spirit was largely responsible for the division (see page 121), and apart from Clode, Cover, Hassall and William Henry, most of the brethren who left were not happy in the mission. Actually most of the single brethren who left had slept

with Tahitian women, although this was not discovered till they
were later found out in their affairs in New South Wales. Both
Oakes and Cock had liaisons with prostitutes in the colony, and
Oakes admitted that he had 'committed the like crime' at
Tahiti.[15] There had been rumours about Cock while he was still
at Tahiti. Main was living in adultery. He later professed repentance for his 'scandalous conduct' and desired to return to
Tahiti, but Marsden and Hassall opposed it because 'his bad
character was well known through all the Colony, and also
among the Natives of Otaheite'.[16] Main's subsequent conduct
convinced his more righteous brethren that he was an incor-
rigible backslider.[17] Smith was also regarded as an 'awful backslider' as he visited playhouses and added to the ignominy of the
party by being imprisoned for debt.[18] William Henry criticized
the directors for not allowing some of the single brethren to
marry before they left.[19]

Cock, Main and James Puckey all ruined their reputations by
drunkenness. After some years of valuable service with the CMS
in New Zealand, William Puckey and his wife both 'drank themselves to death'.[20] The Notts of Tahiti had a reputation for
'guzzling', and Mrs Nott, who was somewhat of a termagant, was
regarded as a disgrace to the mission. 'When intoxicated she is
absolutely mad and cares not what she does or says', wrote
Dr Ross in 1846.[21] When she died some months later, Ross wrote
that she had given no signs of repentance and he believed she
'drank herself to death'.[22]

In the later years, especially after the establishment of the
temperance movement, there was less danger of a missionary
drinking to excess. Thomas Jones and Alexander Simpson were
the only LMS missionaries who fell victims to intemperance (see
page 157). Some of the others like Orsmond and Rodgerson were
subject to occasional censure by their colleagues, but Orsmond at
least was a very moderate drinker, was one of the first missionaries to adopt temperance rules at his station, and regarded
himself as a 'teetotaller by conviction and pleasure'.[23]

Although the Church has been fairly uniform in its attitude
to sexual *mores,* the Puritan churches have always equated sin
more specifically with sex. Wesley, who might well have seen
more sinfulness in various aspects of social injustice, adopted
whole-heartedly the Puritan-precisionist attitude to sin. In his
view sexual laxity, like drunkenness and swearing, was a sign of
the deepest unregenerate state. Evangelicals, of whatever party,
were united in their severe denunciation and fear of anything
which savoured of different standards towards sex. The mis-

sionary who fell from grace not only offended God, but he betrayed his colleagues.

When Benjamin Broomhall found that heathens were not necessarily miserable in their unregenerate state and found himself desiring to accept the native way of life, he defied the Calvinist teachings of his chapel, denied the immortality of the soul and succumbed to the tempting offers of a Raiatean chieftainess.[24] When the Reverend Thomas Lewis was denied membership of the church in Tahiti, he refused to give up his friendship with a Tahitian woman, and preferred ostracism to Christian fellowship with his disapproving brethren.[25] George Vason of the first Tongan mission underwent a kind of conversion in reverse, for not only did he give up all the 'means of grace', but he adopted the way of life best adapted to gaining the confidence of his Tongan protectors. In taking several wives, and in adopting the dress and markings of the people, his defection was complete.[26] Of these three men, Lewis never rejected his Evangelical principles, and he was loyal to the one woman with whom he lived, who possibly instigated his murder. Dr Haweis lamented that Lewis had not been with Vanderkemp and Read who decided that, in such circumstances, a native wife was better than none at all.[27] It is also interesting that both Broomhall and Vason only adopted an unconventional way of life whilst in the islands. Removed from the scenes of their defections, they eventually showed signs of repentance. Nine years after his defection, when Broomhall appeared at Calcutta, he confessed himself to the Baptist missionaries there, and even spoke of rejoining the Tahitian mission, having abandoned his infidel principles.[28] Vason likewise underwent a second conversion, and ended his earthly career as the very respectable governor of Nottingham Gaol and a convert to Baptist principles.

Besides these early moral defections, very few of the LMS missionaries were found guilty of immorality. Moral charges were made against Thomas Heath of Samoa, but there is no evidence for them,[29] and his colleagues do not appear to have suspected him. Heath committed suicide in a fit of 'temporary insanity'.[30] He had not only been harassed by the peculiar difficulties of his station, but he had been nervously unsettled by the death of his wife, and of an English woman whom he had thought of marrying. It is possible, of course, that Heath's melancholia could have been caused by moral temptation.

In the case of Samuel Wilson, the son of Charles Wilson of Tahiti, the adoption of 'infidel' principles (like Broomhall he became a deist) was simultaneous with his moral lapse. Familiar with Polynesian ways since his childhood, and with some educational training in languages and theology (see page 77), he preferred to live on a more intimate level with the people, a proximity which possibly led him to sympathize more readily with native values and to crush the scruples which had been instilled into his conscience by mission teaching and the counsel of Dr Lang.

Carl Schmidt had a more unfortunate 'fall', if such it can be called. Like Heath, he was unmanned by the loss of his wife, and found solace in the company of a converted Samoan woman. It seems fairly clear that Schmidt never realized that his association with the woman was causing so much comment amongst the mission families and the native teachers.[31] After his dismissal from the LMS, he married the woman (as he appears originally to have intended), and accepted a responsible school-teaching position. However his good name had been marred, and he suffered from the prejudice that the motives for associating with an island woman were invariably base.

Here we have a real problem. Almost any missionary who was either single or widowed was likely to be subjected to the closest scrutiny by his colleagues and by the people. To the Polynesians, the virtue of chastity was something little understood. Even Christian converts who allowed, in theory, that it was possible to observe chastity till an early marriage, were intensely suspicious of persons of more mature years who were either unmarried or not living with a woman. The wife of a Marquesan chief undertook her own investigations to discern whether the Reverend John Harris was a whole man, when he failed to treat her as his wife, in accordance with the Polynesian notion of friendship.[32] The single brethren of Tahiti were suspected by the islanders of lying with the several married women or of lying together.[33] It was even a popular belief that the missionaries lay with their own daughters, as the natural means of producing their nubility.[34] When solicited by women the missionaries invariably resorted to the argument that their bodies were *tapu* or sacred, but this argument was only of use in unevangelized areas.[35] Loyalty to a living wife seems to have been accepted in most areas, although such fidelity was rarely found in the island communities.

The case of the Reverend John Davies is a pathetic commentary on the loneliness of a single missionary, on the prurience of the people, and on the petty-mindedness of some of the missionaries. Davies believed that to win the love and confidence of his people he must live as one of them. Though he lived in better quarters than they, he hoped that they would follow his example, and he was not averse to sharing his own room with natives of both sexes. It was not long before various stories were being circulated about him in both Tahitian and mission families. Davies defended himself, vigorously saying that 'European invention' was behind much of the 'vile business'.[36] Threlkeld, however, maintained that a Tahitian had seen Davies in 'criminal connection with a native woman', and that others 'acknowledged his throwing them on his bed and taking improper liberties with them'.[37] Examinations of witnesses were held; the old brethren at Tahiti tended to side with Davies, whilst Threlkeld and his colleagues appeared eager to have the charges confirmed. This unpleasantness lasted for several years. It seems quite clear that some of the missionaries had other grievances against Davies, and found a certain satisfaction in believing the rumours.[38] Crook spoke of Davies'

> usual method of fawning over the women, frequently having a great number at his lodging and keeping them till very late at night singing. Some that we considered loose girls took great liberties with him and one got clothing from him that had done no work for him of any consequence.[39]

The specific charge was that Crook's servant, Betty, had been 'shut up with him in his bedroom', while Orsmond and Crook tried to obtain admission. When the door was opened, Betty came out. When questioned she said that Davies had 'frequently taken liberties with her and once had fastened the door on her, laid her on the bed, laid down by her side, felt her breasts, and got up desiring her to let no one know what had passed'. Davies himself admitted the great improprieties of his behaviour, but he does not appear to have been guilty of Threlkeld's principal charge against him. Indeed, his position was very similar to that of the Reverend Samuel Dwight of Hawaii, who confessed to taking his school girls on his lap and fondling their breasts.[40]

Orsmond not only suspected Davies (and Simpson) of immoral conduct, but insinuated also that Pritchard had a 'lady of pleasure'.[41] Jones made similar charges against some of the other brethren, but these may largely be regarded as malicious slander. Crook refers to a document drawn up by Jones.

> It is to this effect. He is determined to be revenged on his enemies before he leaves the Island, he then proceeds. Darling keeps two in his printing office which he uses by turns. Crook called up Betty in the night to drive the cows out of the garden and used her as his wife. Crooks girls were tried at Mairipehe in their way to Papara.

As to myself, we never had a female about our house named Betty since we came to Tahiti,* nor did the cows ever break into our garden. The other matters are so vague that they may mean anything or nothing.[42]

Jones himself, disillusioned by the state of things at Tahiti, and frustrated in his career — he expected to be head of an academy in the islands — was addicted to drunkenness, profanity, and beating his wife. He imagined his wife was unfaithful, and treated her accordingly, although there appears to have been no foundation for his charges.[43] After his wife's death Jones' habits became a scandal to the mission, and he was forced to resign.

Only one other LMS missionary was dismissed for immorality, and that was the erstwhile 'highly useful' Alexander Simpson, whose reputation in his last days was spoilt by charges of drunkenness and adultery. Simpson, who was a family man, does not appear to have been popular with many of the missionaries, and his situation as headmaster of the South Sea Academy placed him in a difficult position. The moral charges against him were so many, and his position in the mission was so unsatisfactory, that the directors were forced to dismiss him.† His subsequent heavy drinking convinced the other missionaries of his guilt. Not having recourse to a proper trial, Simpson was in many ways the victim of slander, intrigue and jealousy. He may have had affairs with Tahitian women, but he denied them, and his wife supported him. It is unlikely that he was the 'monster of depravity' which some missionaries represented him. The pathetic thing was that a man who fell into temptation and subsequently repented was a marked man. His preaching became ineffectual, and he spent his days between suffering and remorse.

There were also Wesleyan missionaries in Tonga and Fiji who fell from grace, although none of them brought the mission into public obloquy, and none of them relinquished their religious principles. When Watkin was found guilty of a moral lapse, and had to leave the Tongan mission, even the authorities in New South Wales were reluctant to believe that the charges were true, and he was not prevented from becoming a leading Methodist minister in Australia and New Zealand. Watkin did not attempt

*The Betty previously mentioned was at Moorea.

†The evidence for Simpson's adultery, though cumulative, is not conclusive (see SSL for 1843). Too many of his accusers or traducers were interested parties, attempting to save the reputations of their families, reputations which were damaged by other evidence. The accusation that he had seduced or attempted the seduction of the daughters of the missionaries may well be regarded as the invention of sex-obsessed schoolgirls to explain some of their own indiscretions.

to conceal his lapse. He said that he had been 'accused of improper conduct which is alas too true and which caused [him]
immense misery but [he could] not but feel grieved with the
mode pursued by [his] accuser'.[44] 'I deserve to suffer. O that
religion may not suffer by my folly and wickedness.' If Watkin
was exonerated by the European missionaries, the affair had
social and political repercussions in Tonga. In the mouths of the
critics of the mission, the tale of the missionary's fall acquired
features of Rabelaisian drollery. Charles Simonet, Tāufa'āhau's
European offsider, narrated how Watkin had got his wife sent to
Ha'apai ostensibly so that she would be spared the horrors of the
war in the island but really because he wished to sleep with his
wife's maid.

> Some days after the departure of Mrs W. Mr. W. overslept himself,
> and the cook coming to ask him about breakfast was somewhat
> surprised to find that the holy man of God was not alone under his
> mosquito screen or curtain. Receiving no answer to his knocking and
> calling out, the cook entered the room and on looking through the
> mosquito netting was even more surprised to find the holy man of
> God and the dusky damsel fast asleep in each other's arms; and
> unencumbered with clothing. There was no longer any doubt as to the
> object of Mrs Watkin's departure, and the matter was too good a
> joke to be hushed up. The cook sent others into the room to have
> a peep at the holy man and the dusky demoiselle, and the amours of
> the Reverend gentleman became the topic of conversation and jest for
> the whole army.[45]

The Tongans emphasized that the missionary's relationship with
the girl was common knowledge and hinted that Watkin had
actually instigated the war against the heathen prior to his wife's
departure. Watkin's son became a highly respected and useful
missionary in Tonga. When he became head of the Free Church
in Tonga the story of his father's indiscretion was to be a
political weapon in the hands of the Wesleyan party.

In Fiji Thomas Jaggar left the mission under similar circumstances and was employed by the Church in New Zealand.[46] The
only other Wesleyan missionary to earn strict censure for moral
reasons was David Cargill, the talented pioneer missionary to
Lakeba. Cargill was a temperamental man, who easily irritated
some of his more coarse-grained colleagues like James Calvert.[47]
Whatever his personal defects, he was a man of considerable
imagination, talents and understanding.

As in other missions, characters were 'bandied about' long after
the decease of those concerned, and early heroes and idols were

later besmirched by less talented rivals. Thus Samuel Waterhouse wrote to his brother, Jabez:

> Did you ever hear that J. Bumby was not in N. Zealand what he was in England? That he used to sit with the Maoris round the fire smoking a dirty black pipe — that he was fond of brandy — that he felt very uncomfortable and quite out of place.[48]

It is in the children of the missionaries that we see more significant signs of a breakdown in the Evangelical moral fibre. Most of the missionaries had a particular brand of faith which enabled them to live apart from the environment in which they worked, having an inward vision of the moral world of more temperate climates. The children of missionaries, on the other hand, knew no other world than that of the islands, and even if they had seen other shores, their experience was really limited to contact with the islanders. They heard their speech, and understood their gestures; however carefully they were guarded, they seemed to have easy access to the native mind. The people, their nurses, and even casual acquaintances, would tell them things which their parents would never be told.

The mission children suffered considerably, for they could not be the children of both cultures and be happy. In accepting — largely through circumstances and ignorance — the morals of their island friends, they became estranged from their own proper social community. The temptations, inhibitions and opportunities for sexual experiment were more real for them than for children in other spheres. The moral records of some of the families of the most pious and industrious missionaries read like case-book examples of the degenerate family. In one family alone the eldest daughter was a nymphomaniac, most of the daughters had affairs with native boys while still at school, and most of the sons had had affairs with native women. Two of the children had also committed incest. Most of the members of this family were able to readjust themselves to the values of their parents, and attained a certain respectability in later life.[49] However, it needed an Evangelical conversion of the nature of their parents' experience to give them the strength to make the adjustment.

The story of the South Sea Academy is a record of the trials of the parents and teachers in the mission. The boys got themselves tattooed, were circumcised in the native fashion, and ran off to the hills; and the older ones fell into the sin of fornication.[50] The girls also found ways to offend the sensibilities of their elders, and some were also tattooed.[51] Orsmond, who was

the first Master of the Academy (largely against his better judgement), found his position extremely frustrating. Simpson, who
succeeded him, found the task equally difficult. He found that his
scholars were thoroughly familiar with native habits, and he
lamented that some of them were 'permitted to hear all kinds of
native Conversation, and to go abroad and return at their own
pleasure'.[52] Some of them came to school at the age of seven, not
being able to read words of one and two syllables. Some of the
older ones, about twelve years old, were permitted 'to roam
about in the bush with natives in search of cattle etc. during
the Annual Recess'. They then returned to school with 'depraved
and filthy minds'. Even Crook, who zealously guarded his large
family of daughters, was not able to guard them against the
effects of local rumour.[53]

The experience of the first missionaries was of considerable
value to those who came later, and it became the practice of the
LMS to send the mission children to schools in England endowed
for that purpose. Most of the children of the Wesleyan missionaries were also sent out of the islands to be educated,
generally to the Wesleyan boarding school in Auckland. However, whenever the children had remained too long in the islands
they presented a real problem.[54] One of the principal causes of
the disillusionment of later missionaries was the moral character
of the mission children and their families.

Most of those who left their missionary labours in the South
Seas were neither disillusioned nor dismissed for immorality. A
great many of them suffered from ill-health, and in the majority
of cases it was the ill-health of the wife. In the LMS service,
Blossom, Charter, Harbutt, Joseph, Mills, Pitman and Stevens
left because of their own ill-health. Bourne, Day, Hayward, Law,
Macdonald, Slatyer, James Smith and Sunderland all left because of the sickness of their wives. Many of the other missionaries who remained had ailing wives, and some died of illness
at their stations. Many of the missionaries who remained at their
stations were themselves in poor health. Missionary wives were
often as active as their husbands, especially when they taught
large classes of women, but there seemed to be a tendency
amongst many of them to succumb to every sickness. Dysentery
and nerves played frightful havoc. Amongst the Wesleyans,
Brooks, Daniel, Davis, Ford, Hazlewood, Hill, Hutchinson,
Millard, Spinney, Nathaniel Turner, Samuel Waterhouse, Wats-

ford and West, and their wives were some of those who left for reasons of health.

In some cases poor health was the direct result of failure to take proper personal precautions, as in the case of Crawford of Fiji. In other instances, as at the first station in Lakeba, the mission premises were situated in an unhealthy swamp region.[55] Diet must have played an important part also. However we should not ignore the incidence of hypochondria or allied mental states, which served to cloak the fears, frustrations, disappointments and failures of missionaries and their wives.

The first victim of mental ill-health in the islands was William Waters of Tahiti.[56] Completely unbalanced, he laboured under a peculiar infatuation for the Tahitian queen, refusing to be fed unless from her hands. At moments he could converse intelligently, but everyone grew tired of his simple-mindedness. Orsmond, whom some of his colleagues openly said was 'cracked',[57] was generally believed to suffer at times from the after-effects of continuous exposure to the sun.[58] Certainly his usually active mind suffered 'blackouts', and his writings occasionally betray a kind of melancholia. One curious case of mental ill-health was Joel Bate of Tonga. The missionaries at their district meeting in 1847 were 'clearly and unanimously' of the opinion that he was 'suffering and has long suffered from a disordered intellect'.[59]

> Those of the Missionaries wives who have had good opportunity of observing him have come to the conclusion that Mr. Bate is less mental than morally wrong, and in this opinion many of us concur, while others are unable to decide one way or the other; but all of us see and lament his indolence, pride, ignorance and indifference to the duties and objects of a christian Missionary.

Amongst the missionary wives both Mrs Slatyer and Mrs Gee became insane whilst in Samoa. Mrs Barff, the wife and mother of missionaries, suffered from 'hypochondriasis', or, as her son described it, 'that most distressing of all monomanias, viz. a religious one'.[60] Family affliction and political troubles had aggravated her condition. Hysterics were frequent in some households, especially where the women were directly confronted with unsavoury sights, such as were associated with cannibalism in Fiji. Joseph Waterhouse considered that his brother Samuel was too soft-hearted, and that he should have adopted the 'cold water cure' with his wife.[61]

Very few of the missionaries and their families continued unscathed by disease. The average missionary was constantly hindered in his work by domestic sickness. Even when not actually ill himself, he gave the appearance of general fatigue. What Consul Toup Nicholas said of the Society Islands missionaries in 1853 was true of most of them. 'Many of them look delicate and most of them fagged, as if their constitutions were crying out for more bracing air, and this I think would avail them much.'[62]

It was ill-health which was the canker within mission society, rather than the several cases of immorality. The effects of human frailty were sometimes quite considerable, but it was disease which took the greatest toll in zealous lives and which ate at the expenditure of the missionary societies.

Introversion, moral defection and ill-health played a significant part in the pattern of mission life and influence. These, however, were largely the concerns of individuals. Very many missionaries were able to bear their cross without stumbling. The inner life was tortuous for some; for others it was redeemed by a mystic vision. It was in his contact with other missionaries that the missionary revealed his character, and exposed his inner life to a considerable degree. In many of the groups mission stations were isolated and far apart, and depended on ships for contact with each other. At many of the more important stations, however, several missionaries and their families would be congregated, and at some stations there would be a teacher, an assistant or an artisan, besides the pastoral missionary. On some of the larger islands, such as Tahiti, or the islands of the Samoan group, the stations would be only a few hours travelling distance from each other, and communication would be far more frequent. Also, new missionaries would often spend up to a year at another missionary's station in order to learn the language and the working details of the mission. It was fairly common for at least two missionaries (as suggested in the apostolic injunction) to be stationed together.

These small European communities were shut off from the rest of the world. At many of the stations few other Europeans were seen. Interest in one another's family was often abnormally developed. The potential for a great intimacy was also the potential for great ill-feeling. A great deal of importance was assigned to fairly petty things. There was a tendency to develop unhealthy complexes, particularly persecution complexes. Certain personal characteristics were often developed which would otherwise have been kept in check. The 'broken reed' type of character had no chance of survival against the dominant personality, which in turn tended to become sadistic. When two ambitious characters were brought together there was a likelihood of their becoming fierce rivals, sacrificing many things in their fight to become foremost. Although great stress was placed on the maxim that they should all dwell at unity together, the missionaries were notorious for their failure to keep the Psalmist's advice.

The Tahitian mission was undoubtedly the worst offender in this respect, although none of the missions were entirely free from dissension. In the Tahitian mission, after the *Duff* missionaries had been joined by reinforcements, there was a greater range of denominationalism, education, age and temperament, and this division was not assisted by living together at close quarters. While a factional spirit developed early in the Tahitian mission there was a greater unity in the other missions, and those who did not fit in were promptly returned home with a certificate of incompetency. Orsmond of Tahiti, whose lengthy journals are a record of bitter feelings and the personal animosities of the missionaries, put his sentiments into verse:

> The natives hear and scoff
> The Devils gaze and smile
> To see Christian ministers in arms
> And Missionaries act like swarms
> Of Serpents swollen with guile.[63]

To review the various quarrels and personal animosities of the Tahitian missionaries would be tedious. The following extracts serve to illustrate both some of the internal difficulties of the mission, and the type of writing which the directors had to read and assess.

> Love never travelled 15 miles to cast cold water on the humble attempts of his younger brother, to turn away the minds of the people from him. Love never said to his enquiring brother do the best you can in the native language do not look to me among the people as the root of their own language. Love never had audacity enough to stand forward and tell people, friends all that you here these young Missionaries say comes from me. I wrote it with my own hand. . . . Love never said to a body of native chiefs. Oh these young teachers will do for you they are all dumb. . . . Love never held his head up the first time of meeting with a company saying Mind we are all on the same level. There is no one superior amongst us . . .[64]

In a paper entitled 'The Mission its own Bane', Orsmond denounced the 'little contracted, self-willed soul'.

> Those who cannot speak to each other but by the means of a note do sometimes meet to sign a public letter. . . . Yea some will surround

the Lord's table together who nevertheless will not speak to each other.

I have seen a Missionary order a native out of his house because he began to praise the Sermons and the knowledge of the Missionary where he resided![65]

When William Henry and Elijah Armitage were together at Papetoai, Moorea, they were frequently not on speaking terms. Henry, with his strong Church leanings, was horrified when Armitage committed the sacrilegious act of sitting on the communion table in the church during school hours.[66] Armitage accused Henry of trying to sabotage the cotton industry which he had come out to establish. Bitter notes passed between them, and both parties eventually appealed to the directors.

The matter which led William Woon to leave the Tongan mission seemed an equally petty affair. Newspapers had been sent to Woon from Sydney which he appropriated for his exclusive use. John Thomas contested Woon's rights, which led to angry words, and Woon resigned, joining the New Zealand mission.[67] However Woon had been out of harmony with the other missionaries since leaving England, and there was considerable dissatisfaction with him and discontent in the mission. 'I never met with so weak a Man', wrote Watkin, 'and as to his Ministerial qualifications they are out of the question. He trifles away his time. . . . Because I am severe upon his conduct he accuses me of sarcasm'.[68] At the District Meeting of 1832, Woon was admonished for 'having *prevaricated* on several occasions, also for not having *governed* his *family* according to the *doctrine of Christ*'.[69] He was placed in a difficult position as his wife was not a member of the Wesleyan society, and she neglected 'all the *ordinances* of *religion, social* and *public — English* and *native* to the grief of the Mission party and injury to the cause of God'. Thomas' attack on Woon was singularly bitter. Like Pratt of Savai'i, Thomas had nothing but contempt for a missionary who showed any signs of weakness.

There were women like Mrs Woon in the other missions. Mrs Scott of Tahiti was not a church member, but she was esteemed for her character. Mrs Nott, who came out as one of four godly young women, however, was a thorn in the side of the missionaries. A young woman of 'perfect curvature', according to Hayward, she employed 'her more superior Faculties to her own disgress and the griefe of others'.[70]

Her Tong is daily imployed in abusing her Husband in the most unjust and cruel manner and to slander others without the lest just cause. Her hands are imployed in endeavouring to blaiken in the Colony the Character of the most of us here. Her Feet of late are never directed to the place where prayer is wont to be made but daily she joines with those who are studious in their design to perplex and thwart us.

At one stage Nott was compelled to leave home for his own peace of mind.[71] The effect of such domestic unpleasantness must have been considerable as it was common talk amongst the Tahitians. After Nott's death Simpson referred to his widow as a 'messenger of Satan to buffet him', and 'a clog to her husband, and a bane to the Mission', and prophesied that she would be 'carried off by delirium tremens'.[72]

Some unfortunate affairs were caused indirectly by the directors. Often they would reveal information about some of their missionaries in the field to new missionaries about to join them. This was done with good intentions, but on the whole it was not wise. It was almost impossible for a new missionary to remain impartial, and he was rarely sufficiently discreet to withhold the information. Orsmond thus resented Simpson, because Dr Henderson had spoken to him about the directors' opinion of himself.[73] Similarly, Day was never able to obtain the confidence of his colleagues in Samoa, because Williams — 'on the authority of one to whom he was accustomed to look up with a degree of reverence as his spiritual father' — had introduced him to the Samoan missionaries as a 'litigious and overbearing character likely to prove a pest (if not a curse) to the Samoan Mission'.[74] A further cause of disharmony was the tendency of the mission families, always starved of news and company, to engage in gossip. A new missionary was very soon made acquainted with the 'true state of things', and which members of the mission families were 'really Christians' and which were not.

Mission feuds could be very bitter. That between Howe and Thomson regarding the position of pastor over the church at Papeete divided the mission and led to Thomson's dismissal. Thomson was hot-headed and stubborn; Howe was unbending and self-righteous. From the point of view of the directors Howe was in the right, but Thomson had quite a good case.[75] Similarly the feud between William Gill and Pitman at Rarotonga was singularly bitter. An observer found it difficult to believe that both men could really be devoted to the same cause. 'It is to me utterly inexplicable', wrote Royle of Aitutaki, 'how an enmity so deep and so complaisantly cherished should have obtained a place in hearts so long under the influence and operations of divine grace'.[76]

The islanders could not help witnessing the effects of controversies and feuds amongst their teachers. Williams had some
interesting remarks on this point, although his views of the other
missions appears a little rose-coloured.

> Whatever difference of opinion may arise among themselves they
> carefully avoid making the natives a party in those differences. This
> has been and still is the curse of the Tahitian Mission and I think
> Mr. Orsmond's conduct in this respect must be taken notice of and
> if he does not alter he must be removed. . . . It is ruining the
> Mission. The Tahitians would never have felt to the Missionaries as
> they now do had it not been for this impolitic this devilish practice.[77]

Perhaps the greatest cause of personal embitterment was the
different attitudes of a younger generation. It was usually not
easy for younger missionaries to adjust themselves to the direction which the mission was taking. On the other hand, the older
generation invariably resented the new ideas which the younger
brethren brought with them. It was also very easy for the
younger missionaries to underestimate the difficulties of the
situation. Not only did they have preconceived ideas about how
the mission should be organized, but they did not realize the
considerable changes which their predecessors had wrought.

There was another side to the closed community in which
diverse personalities were placed together. Some firm friendships
arose. Nott and Hayward of Tahiti were particularly intimate.
Crook and Davies were friends who ultimately fell out. Hunt
and Calvert of Fiji were friends from their days together at
Hoxton. Friendship or reserve was almost necessary, otherwise
familiarity tended to breed contempt. The growing mission
families were also a source of joy, despite the many causes for
sorrow. The pages of Orsmond's journals which describe the joys
of his domestic circle redeem his character from entire misan-
thropy.[78] Despite the emphasis on 'improvement', some of the
journals suggest a happy atmosphere within the family circle.
The average missionary regarded his 'home of taste' as a refuge
from all his other cares.

8

Enemies At Large

THE MISSIONARY CHARACTER in the islands was strongly influenced by the presence of other Europeans. In reading published missionary accounts, it is easy to assume that the missionaries, in particular cases, were the only white people on an island, when actually the presence of other Europeans was of considerable importance to them. In the majority of instances the lay community was indifferent to the missionaries. Others, however, actively opposed the work of missions, and made themselves as obnoxious as possible. In his sermon, *Puritan Missions in the Pacific,* the Reverend Samuel Damon told the story of the beachcomber who, when he was asked his name by an English missionary, replied: 'My name is Satan'. 'By no other name would the man ever be known. Alas, the name was fitly chosen. He was an adversary, and represented a class.'[1]

The spectacular lives of the rogues and criminals who set themselves up as adversaries present an illuminating and vivid contrast to the routine-dominated lives of the missionaries. Crook's adversary in the Marquesas was an 'Italian renegado', who led the islanders in 'furtherance of his abominable practices'.[2] Similar war-delighting vagabonds were found in Tonga. In Samoa the missionaries encountered men like the notorious Taluava'a, an escaped convict, who was regarded as a great warrior by the people. He blackened himself with charcoal, greased his body and went entirely naked. After a battle, he would besmear himself with the blood of his victims and ride in triumph to his village on a stage, surrounded by the heads of the slain 'in frightful array'.[3] Even as late as the 1850s there were settlers in some of the islands who lived more barbarously than the people, and who opposed the missions. Royce reports the savage practices of Burt of Kadavu. This man kept a number of Fijian women, one of whom ran to Royce for protection.

> Burt had marked her by cutting off one of her toes, and branding her private parts and arms, her body was one mass of scars with his stripes, and her ancles in a fearful state where she had been manacled. How can a missionary avoid coming in contact with such a brute.[4]

Most of the worst types lived separately, their strongest links being with the local residents. Nevertheless in mission eyes many of the secular communities of Europeans, despite the degree of social control within their groups, were as depraved as these individuals. In many instances, as at Tutuila,[5] the majority of these men moved to other islands when the missionaries appeared, not because they feared them, but because they knew that warships would be more likely to call at mission stations, and because in some instances the missionaries themselves represented law and order in a civil capacity.[6] The largest white community without a mission nexus was that of Levuka on the island of Ovalau, a settlement notorious in the mission annals for its drunkenness and debauchery. For the white community in Fiji in 1857 Royce had few good words to spare. They were 'a specimen of the devil's darlings, full of uncleanness, cursed children'.

> Their lives are drawn in flaming colours, lying, cursing, backbiting, fraud, murder, licentiousness, laziness, filth and foul deeds of the darkest dye fit only for some dark den in the bottomless pit.

He wrote of them 'fighting, cheating, lying, swearing, whoring, gambling and drinking in the superlative'.[7] He described Laucala as 'one out of the many watering places, or summer seat of Beelzebub'. Despite this fierce denunciation some of the missionaries appear to have been on friendly terms with several of the residents of these communities.[8]

Actually the missionaries had less to fear from the 'devil's darlings' than from some of the more respectable and articulate European residents. Native authority, and the influence of ships' captains, was generally opposed to the wild white men, especially wherever war had been outlawed. A great many Europeans of the runaway-sailor type willingly gave their services to the missionaries, partly because they realized that the missionaries were not likely to be turned away, and partly because they expected to benefit materially. Some were even converted and became assistant missionaries.[9] Others, such as Hagerstein of Tahiti and Singleton of Tonga, served as interpreters to the missions, but, useful as their services were, the missionaries were somewhat embarrassed by them, and the interpreters tended to use their position to their own advantage.

Yet another type of resident European anticipated the work of the missionaries. Some seamen and other shorebound individuals, motivated either by piety or humanity, influenced the native peoples to abandon customs contrary to accepted European ethical standards and even to adopt some of the tenets of the Decalogue. Morrison, the *Bounty* mutineer, records how the idea of the Sabbath was accepted in Tahiti years before the arrival of the first missionaries, and even the missionaries were to comment on the pharisaical nature of its observance.[10] In Samoa a beachcomber known as Salima Norval attached to the high chief Mauga at Pago Pago was instrumental in persuading that chief to abandon the old gods and is said to have translated part of the Church of England Prayer Book into Samoan.[11]

The influence of Norval, the arrival of drift-voyagers from eastern Polynesia including a Christian convert named Hura, and the arrival of Tongan Christians induced a demand for religious teachers in the Samoan group. Several of the beachcombers were quick to realize the profits to be derived from teaching a spurious Christianity. The leaders of this 'sailor religion' were known as Big Legged Jimmy, Tom Franklin and Indian John.[12] They taught that they themselves were sacred and that all food prohibitions (*sa*) were wrong. Polygamy was practised, converts were baptized, and sea shanties were sung at their services. A similar religion, afterwards known as the Siovili cult, was introduced by a Samoan sailor about the same time.* Though the 'sailor religion' fell into disrepute after the arrival of European missionaries, the Siovili cult provided the principal nativist challenge to Christianity in the Samoan islands.[13]

In those communities where the Europeans were on comparatively harmonious terms with the mission, the missionaries still kept themselves very much apart. They willingly employed any who appeared sympathetic with their cause, but they reprimanded any of their number who fraternized unduly with beachcombers and their like, and used their influence with chiefs and captains of ships to have all dubious persons removed. Caw, who had been received most ungraciously by the Tahitian missionaries, was censured for 'his intimacy with runaway seamen'.

> It has been found necessary to come to the resolution of denying to br. Caw the right of attending when any publick business of any kind is in agitation among us: for it has been found that he makes so improper use of it as even to carry the account of some of our proceedings to the seamen that are living about here . . .[14]

The most critical opponents of the missionaries were those of the semi-official and merchant type. Most of these men were of middle-class origin. Some were well-educated and highly intelli-

---

*The sailor's name is said to have been Joe Vili or Joe Gimlet and the services were imitative of Christian services which he had seen in Tahiti. It was believed that he had been influenced by the leaders of the *Mamaia* cult in Tahiti who opposed the missionaries.

gent, but they had different standards and values, and tended to despise anything which savoured of Evangelical enthusiasm. There were men amongst this class who maintained good relationships with some of the missionaries, but more often than not they would seize every opportunity to discredit missionary work. The Belgian, J. A. Moerenhout, merchant and consul at Papeete, was for some time on a fairly friendly footing with some of the missionaries. They deplored his deistic principles and were not very happy with his private life, but when he did not interfere with them they kept on polite terms. When he published an article which emphasized the adverse side of the mission and cast reflections on the missionaries, Moerenhout was regarded with much greater aversion.[15] His published journal did not mollify them, and when he openly sided with the Catholic interests he became their public enemy. The British vice-consul, Thomas A. Elley, also belongs to this category. He appears to have been friendly with William Henry, and told that missionary in 1827 that he was apprehensive that reports which he had already sent home would be considered too highly coloured and make him 'appear as if unfriendly to the Missionaries and their design'.[16] He gave as his excuse that at the time of writing 'a number of concurring circumstances of a perplexing, discouraging, and trying nature, excited in his breast most unpleasant feelings, and led him to give them too high a colouring'. However Henry's good opinion of Elley was not shared by many of the missionaries. Orsmond, of course, exceeded them all in his vituperation:

> Wicked, Letcherous, Debauched Mr. Elly has his bottom marked all over with the native tatoo, did all he could in company with Mr. Charlton [the British consul] to injure and displace Missionaries . . . he became like the Devil when sick, rather Monkish, borrowed money and other sorts of property of the Missionaries . . .[17]

Also amongst the 'infidels' were those missionaries who had left the mission, and the children of missionaries who reacted against the strict codes of their fathers. George Pritchard, the ex-consul from Tahiti, and his sons were bitterly criticized by the Samoan missionaries, especially when they engaged in the liquor trade.[18] George Platt's sons were a similar source of embarrassment at Raiatea.[19] Captains Henry and Ebrill of Tahiti engaged in the rum trade, and their depredations in the sandalwood islands were hardly in accordance with the gospel preached by William Henry.[20] Although Captain Henry openly assisted the LMS, many of his ventures, before he professed an Evangelical conversion in 1836, were carried out in contravention of the policies of the mission, and some even regarded the killing of John Williams at Eromanga as the direct consequence of the slaughter made by Henry's crew in earlier years (see page 118). W. T. Pritchard, British consul in Fiji (page 140), regarded himself as being pro-missionary, yet his policy conflicted considerably with that of the Wesleyan missionaries, and they were equally denunciatory of his actions.

With a third class of European the missionaries were less able to hold their own. They knew that they stood or fell by the reports of naval captains and distinguished visitors. It was a constant and often onerous duty for the missionary to defend himself and his colleagues against the insinuations or charges of those visitors whose reports tended to give one side of the picture only, or which cast doubts on the sincerity or accuracy of the regular reports of the missionaries. On the other hand, the missionaries were able to assess this criticism, and they often benefited by it. Criticism of the missionaries by contemporary visitors ranged from fierce denunciation to almost blind eulogy. Overall, the majority of the critics were convincedly pro-missionary, but their praise was not unmixed with censure.

Of particular interest in this context was the visit to Tahiti of Captain Otto von Kotzebue in the Russian vessel *Predpriatie* in 1824. Kotzebue appears to have been well received by the missionaries and Bennet informed Orsmond in March 1824 that he was 'a Gentlemanly-intelligent man but exceedingly less obliging than Captn. Dupery of the French Corvette or Captn. Lazaroff of the former Russian expedition'.[21] However with the publication of Kotzebue's *A New Voyage round the World in the years 1823, 24, 25, and 26* (London, 1830) the Russians suddenly became monsters of iniquity. In his marginal gloss to the LMS copy[22] Bennet wrote that if the Tahitian women remained virtuous 'it was not for want of all such temptations and tricks as this Captain and his people could employ', and he referred to 'the debauched and unprincipled and ———— crew of the Russian vessel'. Throughout the margins of the book Bennet reiterated 'False', 'What ignorance', 'What horrid lies', 'How diabolically untrue!' and 'Horribly false'. In several instances Kotzebue's observations were sufficiently close to the truth to be irritating, as in his assertions regarding Nott's authority or the character of Pomare II, and as the book was favourably received both on the Continent and in Britain a public reply was felt to be necessary. In 1831 William Ellis published *A Vindication of the South Sea Missions from the Misrepresentations of Otto von Kotzebue. . . .* Ellis was able to make use of his own knowledge of the islands, Bennet's criticisms, missonary correspondence and a number of favourable testimonies obtained from British, American and even Russian sources. Ellis also took occasion to criticize some statements made by Captain Beechey in his *Narrative of a Voyage to the Pacific and Beering's Straits* which had been 'noticed' by the reviewers. Hyper-critical visitors and reviewers probably did more harm to the interests of those they claimed to be protecting than they realized, for the refutations of their slanders tended to create an illusion amongst the English reading public that there was little room for improvement and that conditions in the islands were near-perfect.

It was in their contact with naval visitors that the missionaries were made most aware of their social position. The first missionaries, who were compelled to receive their honoured guests in comparative rags, made a sorry appearance which did not give a favourable impression to those already biassed against them.[23] In later years the missionaries made every effort to keep up appearances. Even if they had to go about their work in over-patched clothes, they kept a respectable dark suit packed away, to wear when they had to go on board ship or when they had to receive ships' officers on shore.[24] Often there were deeper barriers than appearances to overcome. Naval captains who shared other religious views, Catholic, Russian Orthodox (in the case of Kotzebue) and non-Evangelical Anglican, frequently would not give the missionaries their due, purely on sectarian grounds.

In most cases the missionaries and their visitors were on exceptionally good terms whilst together. Despite the few captains of standing who looked down on the missionaries, feelings of outward mutual respect usually prevailed. Many visitors who enjoyed hospitality from the missionaries were regarded as little better than traitors when they published their experiences and made unfortunate generalizations. Quite early the missionaries learned to be more guarded when speaking to visitors, and even recorded their suspicions of those who appeared most favourable to them. William Henry wrote of the visit of Captain Waldegrave to Tahiti in 1830:

> Captain W. himself informed us, that his officers on their arrival here were all strongly prejudiced against us, and were ready to take hold of and collect everything unfavourable respecting us, or to that effect; and that he and the Chaplain only were on our side or favourable to us. This being the case, and as we are not certain that the Captain's professions of friendship were sincere, and as we know that the Chaplain, although there is reason to believe is a truly pious good

man, (which, I think, there is reason to fear is not the case with the Captain, although he may be considered moral and religious) yet is rather a bigot, we ought not perhaps to be *sanguine* respecting the result of the visit . . .[25]

Usually when the visitors complained about the moral state of the stations the missionaries referred in their letters home to the personal immorality of their traducers.[26] Such charges could be conveniently made. On the other hand, 'blue laws' were notoriously unpopular with European seamen.

By the islanders naval captains were regarded as representing the countries from which they came; in the peoples' eyes English missionaries and English captains were equally the representatives of King George or Queen Victoria. The captains had property, and the missionaries always received property from the ships. The captains also had guns, and they were obviously more important chiefs than the missionaries in their own lands. The missionaries could denounce the behaviour of European residents, but it was not easy or altogether wise to speak out about ships' captains and other Europeans who to the islanders were obviously superior. The frequency of shipping contributed very considerably to the breakdown of the moral authority of the missionaries. The arrival of American temperance ships was usually regarded as a special thrust from Satan, as the seamen who were denied their grog on shipboard were usually the most abandoned on shore, and the captains of temperance ships frequently traded with spirits.[27] The confusion arising from a 'double morality' within the European community was a distressing feature of the culture contact. The missionaries constantly aimed at uniformity, when all the elements within their own society were various and divisional. Even the visit of the Quaker deputation to the South Seas missions illustrated this division, as the two visitors did not hesitate to travel on the Sabbath, to absent themselves from all formal worship (at that time it was compulsory at Tahiti), and to sit during hymns and prayer.[28]

The missionaries accepted preaching to visiting travellers and seamen as part of their general duties. At each of the mission stations, which were also frequent ports of call, churches were built which were known as Bethel chapels. The Hawaiian missionaries issued a newspaper entitled *The Friend, a Semi-Monthly Journal, devoted to Temperance, Seamen, Marine and General Intelligence,* which circulated widely in the islands.[29] This paper proved a more subtle means of spreading Evangelical doctrine since its pages contained much general information.

One of the attitudes which dominated Evangelical thinking in the South Seas, especially from the mid-1820s onwards, was that towards the Roman Catholic Church. The struggle against Catholicism was a peculiar one. In the islands it not only represented the more universal struggle within the Christian Church, but it became both a pastoral and a national issue. It also presented a conflict of conscience on the question of toleration.

Few Evangelicals doubted that the Papacy was the Anti-Christ referred to by the prophets. It was a belief dating back to Reformation times. Evangelicals undertook the war against Anti-Christ by disseminating the scriptures, particularly in Catholic countries.[30] But underlying the religious issues was a long history of national feeling. Cromwell had succeeded the great Elizabeth as English protagonist against the 'Catholic power', and the old national sentiments still lived. They were largely preserved in the literature of the period, especially in the novels of the Romantic school. In the novels of Marryat and Bulwer Lytton, for example, certain aspects of the Catholic Church had been exploited, particularly the horrors of the Inquisition and the evils of monasticism. Besides this sensational or Gothic material there was an even more insidious type of fiction which derived mainly from the Evangelical movement itself. Perhaps the greatest exponent of this school was the renowned Mrs Sherwood, friend of the missionary Henry Martyn, and author of such works as *The Nun* (1833) and *The Monks of Cimiés* (1834). Mrs Sherwood did not merely exploit Catholic 'evils' for the sake of deriving Gothic sensations of horror. She wrote deliberately as a Protestant propagandist, especially after the Catholic Emancipation Act of 1829. It should also be remembered that anti-Catholic feeling was almost as prevalent outside Evangelical circles.

Most of the Catholic missionaries who entered the South Seas were members of French orders, and the French priesthood was doubly obnoxious for 'patriotic' reasons. After the overthrow of the monarchy, instead of becoming a city of equality and fraternity, Paris had become the city of the goddess of Reason. After the rise of Napoleon, France had become the national enemy. After the restoration of the Bourbons, France was again viewed with suspicion as a Catholic power. It was not only Catholicism but 'the desolating encroachments of the French Antichrist'[31] which disturbed the Evangelical missionaries.

The feature most common to all the missionaries in their attitude to Catholicism was their ignorance of the doctrines and orders of the Roman Catholic Church. All priests were referred to as Jesuits, yet those in the South Seas belonged to two distinct orders. Even Jesson, who had been trained for the Catholic priesthood, exploited the popular hatred for Jesuits. 'Were I to judge from their dress', he wrote of the two priests at Papeete in 1842, 'I should say they belong to one of the orders of Mendicant Friars but I strongly suspect they are Jesuits in disguise. That they are contemplating some deeply laid project I feel tolerably confident'.[32] When confronted with statements of Catholic doctrine by the priests, the missionaries very often accused them of not giving a fair statement of their beliefs.[33] Their own conception of Catholicism, or Popery as they called it, was based on certain controversial doctrines, on pre-Reformation corruption in the Church, on Protestant martyrology and on highly-coloured anti-papal literature.

The missionaries watched the arrival of 'the Jesuits' with anxious eyes. In 1835 William Henry wrote that 'the grand enemy' was 'ready to pour in upon [their] field of labour like a flood, a host of popish Missionaries'.[34] Although the will of God was sovereign and could frustrate their designs, Henry feared that God might 'be about to chastise the people here and ourselves, by their instrumentality'. The missionaries were particularly upset when not all of the chiefs agreed with Queen Pomare's decision to forbid the establishment of a Catholic mission. Two of the principal chiefs 'wished to make a trial of the poisonous doctrines'.[35]

In view of the association of Evangelical Dissent with the general movement for religious and civil liberty, the question of toleration in the islands is particularly important. Most of the missionaries regarded tolerance as an essential feature of their beliefs. On the other hand, they were aware of the complications which would arise if there was a strong Catholic party in the islands, and regarded the priests as politically inimical to the state. Emotionally, most of them shared Hannah More's opinion that Mohammedanism or the Jewish religion were preferable to 'popery'.

In that Catholic mission policy was a challenge, the missionaries were justified in adopting means to distinguish between the two divisions of Christianity. Catholic policy, as formulated by the Propaganda at that time, was avowedly to convert those who had become Protestants rather than to win new converts.

Rumours of the designs of French Catholicism on the South Seas reached the islands some time before the actual arrival of missionaries belonging to the Picpus Fathers in the Hawaiian group (see page 26). At the beginning of 1827 the directors had received intelligence from France that a party of missionaries had already left for the islands; this news was passed on at the first opportunity, in a letter almost paranoid in its fear of 'popery', subversive political influence and expansionary commercial aims.[36] These rumours and the disturbances in Hawaii[37] early induced the LMS missionaries to alert their flocks.

At the advent of Catholicism in the South Seas there was considerable evidence of civil and moral breakdown in Tahitian society. Heresies had sprung up, intemperance had presented a major problem, and the influence of the missionaries was largely restricted to church members. The additional threat of a 'Romanist invasion' was openly regarded as a judgement on the people. In 1828 Orsmond stated that it was written in their District Minute Book that 'if the Jesuits are suffered to land' he and his colleagues would all leave.[38] In 1827 he had been requested to write a catechism exposing the 'Jesuits', but it was not published, and he enlarged it in 1829. This work contained 'the History, an account of the peculiar tenets, vile and desperate actions and fatal tendency of that body of people'.[39] Most of the information was derived from an article in the *Encyclopaedia Britannica* on the Jesuits. This catechism was not approved by all the brethren, as some thought that it was 'too plain and might be viewed as an unjust provocation'. Henry said that Orsmond had painted them as 'black as the Devil himself'.

When the first Catholic priests were expelled from Tahiti in December 1836 the missionaries believed themselves safe from the charge of intolerance, as the priests had broken the law that forbade foreigners to reside without obtaining the sanction of the queen. Despite this, it was inevitable that they could not depend on such legal provisos to exclude the priests from the island. It was a dangerous precedent to follow: indeed, the repercussions of that one episode were to lead to the intervention of the French and to provide the priests with a species of diplomatic immunity.

The toleration issue came to a head early in November 1838, when a meeting of the Tahitian assembly was held at Papara to establish a law by which the Catholic priests would be prevented from teaching their doctrines. This law forbade 'the propagation of any religious doctrines, or the celebration of any religious worship, opposed to that true gospel, of old propagated in Tahiti, by the missionaries from Britain: that is, these forty years past'.[40] The *Mamaia* sect,* which was regarded as a political

---

*The name *Mamaia* is said to mean 'fruit which has fallen before ripening' and was applied to a nativist millenarian movement in the Society Islands extant between 1826 and 1841, also known as the Peropheta or the Visionary Heresy, which had marked anti-missionary features.

faction, was specifically mentioned, but it had ceased to be a significant threat to the government of the island. The *Mamaia* were, however, regarded as 'a people prepared for the papists', as their practices were said to be very close to Catholic ones.[41] Mark Wilks, the apologist for the missionaries, was wrong when he asserted that they

> as a body, and probably as individuals, disapproved, on various grounds, of the act of the legislative assembly, and therefore could not have prepared the project; nor, had they desired its adoption, did they possess the means of procuring its enactment.[42]

The apologists justified the missionaries, just as the American missionaries in Hawaii had justified themselves,[43] by claiming that they were not really responsible for the civil laws of the country. In Tahiti, however, it was clearly in the power of the missionaries to have prevented this legislation. Darling, whose church had been disrupted earlier by the *Mamaia* sect, openly supported the law, on the grounds that 'every kingdom divided against itself is brought to desolation' (Luke xi, 17). Others were certainly uneasy about it and Rodgerson, the secretary, said that he had only given his consent as a temporary measure.[44] Orsmond urged that the missionaries should take no part in the matter. The law, however, did not prevent the priests from practising their own faith, although they were not to establish schools or churches.

Every attempt was made by the missionaries to 'expose' Catholicism. Towards the end of 1836 Davies had written that he was preparing an article 'concerning the Church of Rome, and its principal Errors', to print in the second issue of a periodical (*Te Teaaite Tahiti*) which he was publishing.[45] An early favourite translation into the island tongues was Foxe's *Book of Martyrs*. Lantern slide evenings were also given to illustrate the 'evils of popery'. The missions were not lacking in anti-Catholic extremists and only a leaven of more practical men prevented their measures from being effected. Thus the Samoan missionaries, in 1849, refused to accept *Footsteps of Popery* prepared by J. B. Stair. This work was 'with exception of little more than the last chapter, chiefly confined to the exhibition of the cruel persecutions and atrocious and murderous deeds of the papists, including statements respecting the political affairs of the French at Tahiti, and also respecting the Roman Catholic priests', some of which, the missionaries believed, could not be sustained.[46] They decided that their arguments should be scriptural rather than historical.

The Evangelical missionaries continually criticized Catholic mission policy. They regarded the emphasis on the importance of baptism, the neglect of Bible teaching and the policy of minimal interference as sops to heathenism. Repeatedly we find the missionaries lamenting the passive role of the Catholic priests in a society not converted to their word. Whereas the Evangelicals attempted to reform the society, whether heathen or nominally Christian, the Catholic priests appeared to be only interested in their own converts. Furthermore, the priests appeared to be more wary about applying pressure to their 'adherents', so that the Evangelicals repeatedly affirmed that the Catholic natives were little better, if not worse, than heathens. Something of this attitude is contained in an extract from a letter written by Joseph Waterhouse from Ovalau in 1851.

> Here the popish chameleon *allows* the eating of human flesh, indecent songs, and gross immorality: it burns the bible: and injures the property of the English missionaries: Is popery changed? Come to Feejee and see. It has fairly roused my Protestant blood. Let us hear no more about Popery being improved; Popery in Great Britain only yields to the Spirit of the Age, in Feejee it is darkness and blackness itself . . .[47]

To his brother Jabez he wrote, 'Popery raises its hideous head sanctioning the eating of human flesh, polygamy, adultery, and fornication!! There is nothing left for us but — to *pray*'.[48] It was also urged against the priests that they did little to encourage civilization. Samuel Waterhouse recorded in his diary that the promises of the 'Popish priest' bore 'fewer marks of civilization than those of any of the white residents in Feejee' and that his 'bare earthen floor' was 'destitute of a single mat'.[49]

The part played by the French priests at Tahiti,[50] their statement of grievances, and the backing of the consul, Moerenhout and the chiefs under his influence, rendered them particularly odious in Evangelical eyes. Throughout the other Evangelical mission stations in the South Seas considerable alarm was aroused at the movements of French priests and the French warships which so invariably escorted them or followed in their wake. Indeed, after the Tahiti affair, fear of Catholic and French intervention in the other island groups reached almost alarmist proportions.

In 1844 the chiefs of Manono in Samoa agreed among themselves to find and banish any chief or people who received Catholic priests. George Turner explained this by saying that the Samoans were 'in terror', and looked to them for counsel. He advised them 'to do nothing rashly — to beware of such forcible measures'.[51] Bullen added that he would have been sorry if the chiefs had adopted any measures 'which savour of persecution', and feared they might be used against themselves.[52] In these years the missionaries were much more willing for the chiefs to seek British protection.

A second major religio-political scare took place in the islands in 1852. After the Tongan war of that year, one of the French priests in those islands went to Tahiti to lodge a complaint against the Tongan king for depredations to mission property during the war.[53] Howe, at Papeete, was particularly indignant, because the priest was taken to Tahiti on board George Pritchard junior's schooner.[54] When the French warship, *La Moselle,* arrived on 12 November, a formal investigation was held, but Captain Belland acquitted the king of the charges against him, and the document claiming pecuniary compensation was not delivered. In the same year trouble was expected in Fiji.[55] In August Joseph Waterhouse wrote from Ovalau to his sister in Adelaide:

> The French are going to make another Tahiti affair of Feejee we fear. The priests expect two ships-of-war daily and then the natives are to be converted to the *Holy* Church. The priests do not tabu war or scarcely anything that is bad. What would Adelaide Papists say to this? They tell the most awful lies . . . I would sooner trust ten cannibals than one Papist. I came to Feejee with very little prejudice against the Papists, but their conduct makes me conclude them to be worse than any heathen I ever met with or read of. The Lord save us from Popery![56]

In 1854 the fear was still strong. Murray of Apia wrote that he had 'no reason to doubt' that the French had designs on Samoa, and that the 'popish priests, with the Bishop at their head' were their pioneers, 'as they were at Tahiti'. He believed that the French needed Samoa and Tonga 'to complete their chain across the Pacific'.[57]

In 1855 the French again intervened in the affairs of Tonga, and a convention was drawn up between King George Tupou and M. Du Bouzet, the French governor at Tahiti.[58] This convention declared Catholic religion to be 'free in all islands under the King of the Tonga islands', and guaranteed the priests the same privileges as those accorded to Protestants. Although this convention recognized the Tongan government as independent, the scare did not abate. Hysteria was again revived in 1858 when Vercoe of Ha'apai influenced the local high chief to prevent priests from landing. On behalf of himself, Whewell and Stephinson, Vercoe wrote:

> We do not shrink from the fact that we gave the advice to abide by Tonga law (and what nation is punished for abiding by its rules—though they be as foolish as those of Japan?) and keep them (the priests) on board till the King came. That advice was either good or bad. If bad, it was given conscientiously, we thinking it our imperative duty to throw every obstacle in the way of the coiling (slow but sure) of the deadly Boa around the emerald Isles of Oceania.[59]

However the Australian secretary did not approve of the action, feeling that 'the advice was wrong and under present circumstances impolitic'.[60] Although Vercoe was intensely anti-Catholic, he was more favourably impressed with his opponents than some of his brethren, saying that the priests were 'gentlemanly, well-bred men who have, evidently received a collegiate education', and he felt (to his shame) that they were 'better up with Ancient Church History and the Fathers' than himself. He felt that his opponents were better 'prayed down and lived down, than discussed down'.[61]

Perhaps no better idea of the influence of Evangelical instruction about Catholicism, and the overall attitude of the missionaries, could be obtained than from reading some verses which Joseph Waterhouse proudly asserted were the original composition of a blind Fijian boy aged about fourteen years.

On Popery

The articles of Popery are recapitulated:
Their religion is useless;
They hate the law of God;
They disbelieve it;
That which is prohibited they say is permissible;
Many things they nullify;
Their practices are abominable;
Their hearts are unenlightened.

They afflict mankind;
They frequently burn them with fire;
Awful deeds they perform;
Their road truly leads to Hell.
The religion of Jesus they hate,
They say 'let it be exterminated'.
Impossible: on account of the Lord:
Strong is the Almighty God:
His work still extends:
His miracles are *still* accomplished![62]

9

The Leisure Hour

AS PROPONENTS of middle-class virtues the missionaries have inevitably been associated with philistinism and prudery in art.
Certainly their Evangelical convictions bred an intolerance of all
that savoured of excess or idleness and their aesthetic appreciation was governed entirely by their moral point of view. The
Evangelicals, in the main, were the spiritual descendants of the
Puritans. However, the Puritans of the seventeenth century had
been dominated by their intellectual leaders who respected art,
even though there was an ascetic tendency to labour its inutility
and to decry the waste of time of polite entertainment. If the
Puritan intellect honoured art, the Puritan ethic, on the whole,
tended to undermine its dignity.

On the other hand, as the leaders of the Evangelical movement
tended to come from a lower rank of society, the small mercantile, tenant-farming and shopkeeping class, they held rigidly to
the idea of life as stewardship and were consequently natural
utilitarians, concerned with the 'economy of time'. Many of the
Evangelicals also believed that dramatic representation was bad,
not only for the traditional reasons, but because of the Platonic
notion that imitation is bad in itself. This view was held by
William Law, the Anglican mystic who greatly influenced John
Wesley.[1] John Wesley was less opposed to dramatic art as such
than Law, but stated that he could not see a serious tragedy
'with a clear conscience; at least not in an English theatre, the
sink of all profaneness and debauchery'.[2] The Evangelicals, however, became the irreconcilable opponents of dramatic art when
Samuel Foote and others satirized Whitefield and his followers.[3]

Two of the directors of the LMS, the Reverend George Burder
of Coventry and John Angell James of Birmingham, were
voluble on the subject. Both these men were extremely influential with the missionaries in the Pacific, and their sermons
were read widely.[4] Burder's most direct pronouncement on the
subject was a sermon entitled 'Lawful Amusements', preached
in 1805. His text, 'Be not conformed to this world', suggests that
he was a disciple of Law in the matter of recreation. Burder listed
four types of amusement which were unlawful: all such as are
evidently sinful, all such as the word of God condemns; those

amusements which, if not in themselves absolutely sinful, have a dangerous tendency to sin; those amusements which are not of good report; and those inconsistent with the spiritual nature of the Christian life. Mixed dancing was suspect because of its dangerous tendency. The playhouse was 'the very Exchange for Harlots' and 'the Flesh-market of the metropolis'. 'No doubt', he said 'the present prevailing system of *Nudism* had its origin in the Playhouse, and in the person of a prostitute or a player: but who could have supposed that such a mode of dress (or rather of *undress*) would ever have been adopted by virtuous women?'[5] These notions transported to the South Seas could not fail to lead the missionaries to see only evil in the dramatic representations of the Arioi Society,* the mixed dancing and the nudity.

James held similar views. He denounced the theatre as 'the corrupter of public morals' and the 'broad and flowery avenue to the bottomless pit'. Only the 'morals of the brothel' could be learnt at the theatre. In his work *The Christian Father's Present to his Children* he denounced killing flies, horse-racing, field sports of every kind, shooting, coursing, hunting and angling. The rejection of team games such as football and cricket was typical. Can it be wondered that the missionaries forbade the practices of boxing and wrestling and other native athletic games? All that James seems to have recommended for 'strengthening the body and improving the mind' was 'a country ramble amidst the beauties of nature'.[6] All the directors and missionaries may not have agreed with James in this respect but there was a strong tendency to regard field sports as a waste of time and as pastimes unbecoming to a Christian. Again the utilitarian viewpoint of the individual completely dwarfed any idea of social or community value.

Evangelical views on music were similar to those of the Puritans.[7] It was the dancing and dramatic art associated with music which was condemned. James pronounced against 'balls, routs and concerts'.[8] 'I look upon dancing among these [the humble] to be a practice fraught with immorality', he said. As during the Puritan Commonwealth, the poor were simply not trusted to behave themselves. Italian opera, which paradoxically enough had been introduced into England during the Commonwealth, was particularly offensive. As late as 1869 the *Christian Witness*, a Congregational periodical, supported George Steward's asser-

---

*The Arioi, called Arioi Society in the mission literature, was a group of Tahitian entertainers, connected with the cult of the god Oro, to whose members abortion or infanticide were obligatory.

tion that 'operas and theatres' were 'of the very essence of carnality' and argued that although the love of music was 'lawful' it was associated with 'what is absolutely unlawful'.[9]

The attitude of the Evangelical household to music, painting and poetry is perhaps best represented in one of those manuals of middle-class piety written by Sarah Ellis (see page 32). Music, according to Mrs Ellis in her *Daughters of England,* was 'universally regarded, both by the wise and good, not only as lawful, but desirable'. However, she continued, 'I will not say that music is a species of intoxication, but I do think that an inordinate love of it may be compared to intemperance, in the fact of its inciting the passions of the human mind so much more frequently to evil than to good'.[10] Mrs Ellis advocated moderation, and was always concerned with the right use of time.

The legitimate use or function of art was to glorify God. Poetry, of all the arts, could best serve this end, not only in the verse structure of religious hymns but also in its highest forms. The theme of the glorification of God had been ably handled by Milton in his great epics in which he sought to 'justify the ways of God to men'. Thus, even in the islands, poetry was the one art which the missionaries cultivated. Ellis, afterwards the friend of Southey and Coleridge, was the author of an unpublished epic based solely on native material.

The missionaries were conscious of the interest value of Polynesian history and culture. They recorded it merely to add to the sum of human knowledge[11] and they did good work in this field, but in art this material had to serve some higher end. In his epic, 'Mahine', Ellis no doubt sought to portray the evils of heathen society before conversion, and the beneficial effects of grace. God would be the more glorified by the more realistic portrayal of native superstition and ignorance and thus poetry perhaps gave a greater scope to the Evangelical artist than the other arts. It was removed from that physical imitation which damned the drama, and there was ample scope for reflection and didacticism.

Just as Milton effectively entered into the characters of his fallen angels, so Ellis was able to get into the characters of the heathen Polynesians. Thus the priest of the god Oro is made to speak.

> And from the temple's caverns deep and dark,
> Were heard the voices loud or low of gods
> And spirits mingling. Listening unto these
> I lay, till half the reign of night was past;
> When 'neath the power of sleep by Oro sent
> I sank unconscious . . .[12]

However if Ellis was justified in appropriating Polynesian material for his own ends, the islanders themselves, he believed, were not justified in preserving their own culture as it stood. It might be permissible for Ellis to write:

> Gay, youthful groups strayed o'er the flowery lawn,
> Weaving new garlands for their flowing hair,
> Or moving graceful to the plaintive flute,
> In artless dances mingled . . .
>
> O'er the wide beach beneath them, warrior bands
> Their martial sports pursued — cast the smooth stone,
> The light lance hurled, the sounding bowstring drew,
> Swift o'er the sands in eager contest ran,
> Or sought with manly strength the wrestler's prize.[13]

Yet, in actual experience, the 'manly' and 'graceful' pastimes were forbidden or discouraged.

Most of the LMS missionaries were less ambitious than Ellis. Their verse was modelled on the devotional poetry of Isaac Watts, Charles Wesley and John Newton or the pious lines which they read in the various religious periodicals. Other respectable models were Thomson, Hervey, Cowper and James Montgomery. Both Cowper, the friend of Samuel Greatheed, and Montgomery were admired as much for their subject matter as for their competence and were extremely popular in nonconformist circles. William Henry's appraisal of the verse of John Dunmore Lang clearly reveals the missionary criteria for poetry.

> I must not conclude without thanking you as an individual for the copy of your Book of Poems presented to our Library. They have afforded me much pleasure and edification. They are good poetry and purely Evangelical. The poem upon the Imaginary Creature the Coral Insect, is very ingenious and spiritual, but, in my opinion is not founded in truth. The old opinion that the Coral is a sea plant or production, is certainly correct.[14]

Henry evidently tried his hand at verse writing for in May 1822 he wrote 'Lines composed on the building of a Christian Church, in the District of Papetoai, Island of Eimeo, upon the ruins of the Royal Marae* in that District'.[15] The importance which he placed on edification can be gauged by the fact that his elucidatory footnotes far exceed his poem in length. Also, he confessed to the directors that he sent them his lines not 'from a

---

*The *marae* in Tahiti was a tiered stone structure used for public assembly and religious rites. These 'temple' sites made excellent church sites, particularly as there was no need to quarry new stones.

supposition of any excellence in their composition, but from a persuasion that their subject and the description they give of the Marae Rites and worship would be interesting'.

Just now a *human victim* fresh arrives
And the sage Priest plucks from it both its eyes,
And on his blood stain'd hand doth rudely place,
And them present before his Sovereign's face.

His royal mouth the sovereign opens wide,
The priest obsequious doth the morsel guide
Quite near his lips; then gently turning round,
Doth cast the eye balls on the sacred ground.

The lifeless victim lying near their side,
In platted leaves which did in carriage hide
It from the eye of man, the priests suspend
On sacred boughs, and thus the scene doth end.

Another poem written by the semi-literate Henry Bicknell at the height of the social and religious conversion of Tahiti is surprisingly articulate considering his limitations.

Instead of faces stained with red
And hands defiled with infant blood
To God they look, to him they cry
Their hands are stretched to the most high.

Instead of plays and necromance
Idolatry and Ignorance
Tis God they seek, they reach his word
They sing his praise and serve the Lord.[16]

Verse-writing was thus an art form which was both morally acceptable and a form of recreation for the missionaries. In their daily living it almost certainly served a cathartic role. Some of Orsmond's verses, for instance, allude to the imperfections of his colleagues. Others attempt to give words to his religious experience. The following verse must have been an attempt to give meaning to his missionary vocation in a moment of disillusionment.

Ah mournful thing to hear and tell
That sinners must for ever dwell
In Hell; in flames of fire
For ever live in quenchless flame
With those who lived to scorn the name
Of Jesus and his Lyre . . .

> Oh Jesus pierce my heart, and keep
> My feet among the chosen sheep
> And never let me tire
> Help me to sound this lyre till death
> And when I yield my fleeting breath
> Give me a new strung Lyre.[17]

During the deputational visit of Tyerman and Bennet (1821-29), versifying became fashionable in Evangelical circles both in the islands and in Sydney owing to the friendship between George Bennet and Montgomery, both of Sheffield. Even the unofficial 'laureate' of New South Wales, Barron Field, engaged in verse panegyrics for the deputation.[18] Bennet thanked Orsmond for a poetic welcome.

> The nature and importance of your very interesting, peculiar engagement you have well described in your paraphrase of the poet of nature and of the heart Thompson. Your *interesting effusion*, is to me highly grateful to receive, though the *subject* is not worthy of the poetry.[19]

Poetry was also an art form approved by the Wesleyans. Several of the earlier missionaries wrote verse, though none of it was published. Much of it related to commonplace experience. One lengthy poem in 79 quatrains described the wreck of a canoe in which the wife of the Reverend William Cross and twenty Tongans were drowned on the way to Vava'u.[20] John Hunt was perhaps the most talented versifier in the islands. His love poems to his wife may not be polished but they reveal a sensitivity not always found in the writings of some of his colleagues.[21]

Apart from Ellis, few of the LMS missionaries showed any interest in rendering island stories into verse. Orsmond and Wyatt Gill did in fact record traditional chants but more for their ethnological and linguistic value. Hunt, however, was keenly interested in the art forms of the Fijians and this gave him a new insight into the Fijian character. He tried to discover as much as he could about the nature of traditional Fijian poetry. In a letter written to the mission secretaries in 1842 he maintained that there were only two persons in the whole group who were 'favoured with the spirit of poetry', a man of Cikobia-i-Lau and a woman from Nairai. This 'spirit of poetry' was regarded as hereditary.

> The soul of the Poet is said to visit Bulu, that is the invisible world while he is asleep, and there they learn the song, and also how to put it to Music, that is, a dance is planned to correspond with it.[22]

These 'hereditary poets' were the chief asset of the people of Nairai and Cikobia who went to other parts of the group to feast, trade and teach their new songs. Hunt collected some of these traditional *mekes*. He thought they were not always intelligible. 'There is no necessity that it should be sense or rhyme or anything else, but divinely inspired. There is however some effort at rhyme and metre in these productions.' Hunt wrote an article on 'Feejeean Poetry' in the *Vewa Quarterly Letter* for December 1845. This contains the Fijian poem written 'on the death of Turukawa' in the Rakiraki dialect and the Bau dialect, together with a prose translation and 'an imitation in verse'.[23] Hunt's appreciation of the Fijian poem is the more remarkable considering the subtleties of the indigenous imagery. Joseph Waterhouse also collected specimens of Fijian verse but did not comment on their literary merit. The only other Wesleyan missionary to show as keen an interest in Fijian verse as Hunt was Jesse Carey. However, when he eventually came to write a poem based on traditional subject matter, he chose Longfellow as a model rather than a form more nearly parallel to the indigenous narrative verse. Out of his experience in Fiji grew his Hiawatha-like epic, *The Kings of the Reefs,* telling the story of Cakobau, 'Viti's last and greatest Ruler'.[24]

Drawing and painting were arts also favoured by Evangelicals, providing they served a utilitarian purpose or some religious and moral end. The directors of the Missionary Society early realized the propagandist uses of the graphic arts. Their commissioning of an eminent painter, Robert Smirke, to 'make a representation of the interview which took place with the Chiefs of the Island of Otaheite soon after the arrival of the Duff'[25] was a precedent followed throughout the nineteenth century. Smirke's *Cession of Matavai* was exhibited at the Royal Academy in 1799. Engravings of this (by Bartolozzi) and the ship *Duff* were sold for mission purposes. After April 1818 the LMS published a periodical entitled *Missionary Sketches* which featured woodcuts depicting mission life in various parts of the world. Other religious periodicals published the same and similar woodcuts. The didactic nature of these prints is fairly clear from their subjects and the way in which heathen and Christian subject matter is contrasted.

The art of portraiture was highly valued by the Evangelicals. The standard of the engraved portraits which appeared monthly in the *Methodist Magazine,* the *Gospel Magazine,* the *Evangelical Magazine* and the *New Evangelical Magazine* testifies to the appreciation of the portrait painter's skill. Mrs Ellis believed that 'above all, the art which preserves to us the features of the loved and lost, ought to be cultivated as a means of natural and enduring gratification'.[26] The portrait was also valued as an index to character and as a witness to the passing of time.

In 1837 missionary art reached its peak with the association of George Baxter the engraver with the Evangelical publishing house of John Snow, then publishers to the LMS. Baxter had perfected the art of oil colour printing and his work greatly appealed to John Williams. He was commissioned to illustrate *Missionary Enterprises*. His portraits of Williams and the Rarotongan chief Te Po were followed by a separate colour print of the *Camden* in 1838. The most famous prints were those designed to show Williams' reception at Tana and the murder of Williams and Harris at Eromanga. A further print of Williams appeared in Prout's account of his life. In 1845 two prints appeared in connexion with French 'aggression' at Tahiti: one of the French forces landing, featuring Queen Pomare and her family; and the other of George Pritchard. Other LMS subjects included portraits of the Samoan teacher Mamoe and his wife. Wesleyan mission subjects were also printed by Baxter, including the landing of the Reverend John Waterhouse in New Zealand and a portrait of the Fijian 'Princess Va-tah-ah'.

Of the first LMS missionaries only the Puckeys appear to have shown any aptitude for drawing,[27] although a number of those who arrived in the islands after 1815 had received instruction. Ellis, for instance, was given lessons by the engraver Joseph Strutt. A number of Williams' sketches were used by Baxter. Orsmond appears to have painted portraits of the Tahitian royal family during his residence at Afareaitu. Most missionary wives had sketchbooks and regarded drawing as an essential feature of education. Indeed it was emphasized in Evangelical manuals that drawing was a necessary accomplishment for the study of botany and all other natural history subjects. Many of the illustrations in missionary literature derived from original sketches by missionaries, especially those of stations, churches and religious gatherings.

Amongst the Wesleyans probably the most accomplished artist was Thomas Williams. In common with many Evangelicals he regarded his art primarily as a means to record scientific information. His careful observation and accurate delineation of Fijian ethnological subjects reveal his more universal talents.[28] It is perhaps no accident of heredity that his grandchildren should include the distinguished Australian artists Norman Lindsay, Sir Lionel Lindsay and Sir Daryl Lindsay.

It has been assumed that missionaries used the graphic arts to create a myth of the 'ignoble savage'.[29] Certainly the 'barbarization' of the classical type of figures in the Webber and other engravings reproduced in *Missionary Sketches* would suggest this. No doubt the editors of such a religious publication felt that the 'savagery' of the heathen should be more clearly defined. On the other hand, the missionaries themselves appear to have wanted no more than a realistic portrayal of island places and people. When Baxter prepared his print of the death of Williams the water-colour painting which he used displayed classical savages in heroic stance. The comments on the painting suggest that a greater degree of realism was required. In actual fact Baxter's Eromangans became even less realistic than the original drawing, for while the classical poses were abandoned the darker complexion was ignored. The Eromangans succeed in looking more like the Victorian conception of ancient Britons than Melanesians. The missionaries themselves were critical of Baxter's art and condemned his 1845 prints for their lack of realism, especially the study of Pomare and her husband which too closely resembled Queen Victoria and Prince Albert in dishabille.[30]

The missionary concern for realism and complete accuracy of detail is well illustrated by Henry's comments on two portraits of Pomare II.

> I am sorry the Portraits of Pomare that have been published do him such great injustice, representing him as mopish & stupid with his eyes half closed; and destitute of all nobleness or dignity of aspect, which was not the case. . . . He was longer visaged than either of the portraits represent him and his whiskers went down in a streak of about a quarter of an inch broad towards the chin, & then turned round the lower part of the cheek, then up until nearly opposite the upper lip, & then turned forward to it & joined the whisker on it.[31]

As with Oliver Cromwell, a portrait meant warts and all.

In the islands few indigenous art forms were to survive the impact of Christianity. Pagan motifs, many of an erotic kind, figured largely in dancing, miming and carving. In nearly every instance where missionaries were accused of proscribing the traditional art forms they replied by saying that the people themselves had taken the initiative.[32] But even if this were so it is not likely that the missionaries would have approved such things as the principal traditional dances. Although mixed dancing was frowned upon by many of the Evangelicals at home, with very little reason, the missionaries in the islands had the opportunity to see mixed dancing which *was* of a lascivious kind.[33] Ellis said that the least objectionable of the dances was the Tahitian *hura* which he described as being generally a pantomimic exhibition although the most decent consisted principally of dancing. However all these dances were associated with gods 'whose sanction patronized the debasing immoralities connected with them'.[34] When Queen Pomare encouraged the old dances and 'scenes' in 1830, one of them consisted of a number of women being enveloped in cloths, and then being unravelled by their male partners who spun them round like tops until they were naked.[35] The missionaries who had frowned on acting and mixed dancing at home were hardly likely to tolerate this type of conduct! Williams, in his journal for 1832, shows that many of the dances of the Samoans were of a licentious character, but the principal ones were conducted 'with decency'.[36] The missionary attitude was that, decent though some of them might be, dancing was a waste of time and tended to be conducive to sexual licence.

Burder had found very few lawful amusements for English Evangelicals to indulge in. In Tahiti the missionaries found very few lawful *heiva* for the people to indulge in. *Heiva vivo* (or flute playing) and *heiva ute* (singing) were proscribed because of their association with immoral dancing and tales of the gods. But other amusements were likewise proscribed: *heiva maona* (wrestling), *heiva moto* (boxing), kite-flying and archery. Ellis speaks of boxing and wrestling as 'barbarous sports'. Of course there were no Queensberry rules. Most of these games, however, were closely associated with religious ritual. The conclusion of Ellis was that 'when we consider the debasing tendency of many, and the inutility of others, we shall rejoice that much of the time . . . is passed in more rational and beneficial pursuits'.[37] Williams found similar games at Samoa but he was not aware that any of them 'were attended with religious ceremonies as formerly at Tahiti', and he possibly would not have proscribed them all.

It is difficult to ascertain just how the suppression took place. Bellingshausen suggested that the Tahitians themselves believed their practices to be inconsistent and so desisted;[38] but it seems rather that the missionaries decided on prohibition because they could not see how to 'reform' the games, and because they felt the Tahitians would not work at all if allowed to continue 'playing'. When FitzRoy arrived in 1835 he seemed to favour the policy adopted.

It was certainly better to suppress altogether, rather than only to restrain and alter their former licentious amusements, but it seemed to me that some kind of innocent recreation was much wanted by these light-hearted islanders.[39]

In their attitude to wood-carving the missionaries were uncompromising. The recurring sexual motifs were only too obvious, and viewed as evidence of moral depravity. That phallic emblems could have genealogical meaning or religious significance (as sources of *mana*) does not appear to have been considered. It is very likely that most missionaries shared the views of the Reverend Ralph Wardlaw whose sermon 'The Contemplation of Heathen Idolatry an Excitement to Missionary Zeal' was noticed in *Missionary Sketches* in October 1818.

> . . . what sort of deities must they be, of which images, so ridiculously fantastic, so monstrously uncouth, so frightfully distorted, as many of the heathen idols are, are considered by their worshippers as the appropriate and worthy representatives?[40]

Figure art offended the missionaries not only because of its idolatrous connexions but also because nature itself appeared to be outraged. Art must be realistic or a refinement of nature.

Only in the sphere of music was there any effective substitute for former custom. Of the LMS missionaries Crook, Ellis and Buzacott were decidedly musical. The early voyagers had recorded the love of the Tahitians for flute music. Thus Ellis took lessons in flute-playing which helped him in teaching singing to his converts.[41] Buzacott took a flute with him, but had to adopt another instrument which he could play whilst he led with his voice in the singing classes and family worship. He made his own bass viol.[42]

In 1826 Beechey was astonished that the *vivo* or reed pipe had been proscribed.[43] However this 'melodious little instrument' was the chief accompaniment to the proscribed dances, and was thus a temptation in itself. Possibly indigenous music was also proscribed because it seemed discordant to ears trained to harmonious choir work. Ellis complained of the 'discordant, deafening sounds' and he was appalled by the music of Hawaii.[44] But beyond all this was the conviction that the end of music was to glorify God, and its rightful use was to lead men in songs of praise.

Crook had a few Tahitian hymns printed for Davies in Sydney in 1815.[45] Ellis translated and composed hymns in the vernacular, while 204 of the 279 hymns in the Rarotongan hymn-book were composed by Buzacott.[44] So successful were the early attempts at

vernacular hymn writing and choral training that the singing of
himene became one of the leading features of missionary cul-
ture.⁴⁵ In the islands the same qualities of trained singing which
distinguished many Dissenting chapels in Britain were blended
with qualities of tone and an innate love of harmony which
have made the various choirs of the South Seas particularly
famous. It was in singing — both sacred and in a secular form
derived from the *himene* — that the islanders found the most
satisfactory compensation for the loss of the old arts.

It is doubtful if the missionary attitude towards fiction had
any profound effect on the lives of the South Sea islanders. However the fact that the majority of missionaries were prepared to
reject a goodly proportion of classic prose literature on grounds
other than moral shows that pagan literature was only likely to
survive by sheer strength of tradition.

The missionaries by no means under-rated the value of fiction.
Evangelical periodicals of the time were filled with pious tales
for the edification of young and old alike. Novels, however far
removed from probability and possibility, were approved if they
upheld the rewards of virtue and observed the conventions of
propriety. Moral intentions were not enough.

When missionaries resorted to fiction in the island languages
they usually chose the religious dialogue form (the Platonic
model as used by Hervey in *Theron and Aspasio*) or the
allegorical narrative as in Bunyan's *Pilgrim's Progress*. It is
significant that neither of these forms was very successful.
Amongst the islanders there was a general tendency to expect
literal truth in the written narrative. On learning that the
characters in a religious dialogue were fictional the disillusioned
reader would regard the book as a 'deceiver'.

Joseph Smith records several attempts to introduce fiction into
the Tahitian language during his residence in the islands, the
first of which was the publication of a monthly tract by the
mission press.

> Mr. Williams when in London translated several little publications
> into the Tahitian language, and some he composed himself upon
> subjects adapted to meet their taste and sent them out with embel-
> lishments; but their interest ceased with their novelty. Mr. Pritchard
> then circulated a spirited little dialogue between two individuals,
> natives professedly of the Islands, one of whom had just returned
> from a visit to England, and had much to relate of various import
> to his brother Tahitian. The book began in a way suspicious to the
> native eye, by Oomera enquiring of Taro, how many children he
> had? Such enquiry with that of other minute matters of domestic
> solicitude, being as inappropriate to the sympathies and foreign to

the habits of the Island as the 'good night' addressed to the first Pomare who in turn asked, 'What good is there in the night?' It was not in keeping with the native mind, and ominous of ill-success; as the Tahitian cannot reconcile fiction and truth. The book however became extensively read for a time; until the fatal stigma imagined against it of its fictitious character condemned it to disuse and oblivion. The enquiry became general — Who was Oomera and *who* was Taro? where did they live? and when informed, it was an allegory constructed as a vehicle for truth, they replied, it is a lying book. Even Pafai the most discerning among them gave it this character, in the face of all the explanation and justification which could be given, while the amused but annoyed writer lost fifty per cent in character.[48]

Pilgrim's Progress was translated into most Pacific tongues. Davies translated it into Tahitian, and Pitman made a translation of this into Rarotongan. It was also translated into Tongan and Fijian by the Wesleyans. One Tahitian is said to have regarded the book as a literal account of the religious life and went seeking earnestly for Apollyon to kill him. In most cases, however, the reaction was one of disillusionment and incomprehension. This is well illustrated by some extracts from the journal of Charter of Raiatea.

At our meeting today the people expressed their inability to understand what they had read in the Pilgrim's progress. They said 'it is a very dark book'. When we examined it we were able, at least some, to see its design to some extent. They thought it did not relate to any person but was entirely a 'parau faau', figurative account. That is a tale without foundation.

Titabu came to me and stated he felt very much ashamed yesterday because he could not understand the portion of the pilgrim upon which we conversed in the chapel. I told him he must not give way to shame, but persevere and he would understand it in time. He said 'we are not like christians.' I reminded him that a child did not become a man in a day.

This morning we conversed upon the subject of Christian's conflict with Apolian, and his passing the gloomy valley. Poor creatures they had no idea what Bunyan intends to convey, nor of the weapons he mentions. Some of them said we have looked it over and read it but do not understand its meaning. . . . They appear destitute of such doubts and fears, and probably it is not possible in their state of ignorance, so lately emerged from barbarism, to experience, to any great degree such emotions and conflicts. They cannot view sin in its true light, nor feel its burden.[49]

These extracts not only show the difficulties of the Raiateans in understanding the complex English allegory, but they also serve to illustrate the restricted outlook of the missionaries. Charter regarded the Raiateans as children in need of instruction. Possibly because he himself was so much involved in the inner struggle of Bunyan's world, he assumed that an understanding of the book came with a growth in inner experience.

The Bible alone replaced the traditional literature of the South Seas; in no other way did Western literature replace the humorous tales, the love epics, and the other ancient stories which had been both art and recreation to the island peoples. That some of these survived is only due to the initiative of a few more enlightened missionaries and the resilient nature of the stories themselves, for they dwelt in the mind and could not be destroyed by fire or axe, nor could they be effectively proscribed like games and dancing.

10

The Perishing Heathen Observed

Consider that with all the acknowledged variety in the
intellectual character and external circumstances of men,
HUMAN NATURE is universally the same; that it is found
in all the inveteracy of its enmity against God, and hatred
of truth and righteousness from the line to the pole. And
this — this in all the various dresses it wears, is the enemy
the missionary has to encounter and overcome. Human depravity is at the foundation of all the opposition made to
his efforts — and he is only successful in so far as he
obtains the victory over it.
  WILLIAM SWAN, *Letters on Missions*, pp. 100-01

THE EVANGELICAL MISSIONARY had little doubt that Satan, adversary of God and man, reigned as absolute sovereign over the
South Sea islanders. But if theological speculation provided
boundless scope for Satan, limited experience of mankind and
of alien cultures, together with a belief in the *natural depravity*
of man without God, tended to narrow the range of evil. Men
who believed that they were likely to be swamped and drowned
for going sailing on a Sabbath afternoon, or who went in fear
of being struck dead for some irreverence, hardly dared to believe
that God would suffer those things for which in the scriptures
he had destroyed cities and nations. However before any mission
contact had been made the islanders had gained a reputation for
licentious and evil ways.

Critics have often marvelled at the almost perverse way in
which the missionaries adopted a stern attitude towards the
islanders, and at the almost ruthless way in which they set about
to overturn the existing society. One can ascribe their policy to
a mere utilitarian attitude towards the economy of time, or a
puritanical distaste for 'unprofitable' amusement, or even a false
veneration for European forms and institutions. That these
motives existed cannot be denied. But the dominating influence
seems to have been their *aversion* to the manners and customs of
native society. This aversion was based on a belief, not only in
the natural depravity, but in the *utter depravity* of the South
Sea islanders.

What was it that convinced the missionaries of this utter de-

pravity? It is over-simplification to say that the missionaries were
revolted by nudity and polytheism. To answer this it is necessary
to examine many of the manners and customs prevailing in the
different groups. It is especially important in respect of Tahiti
as this island, consciously or otherwise, became the model of the
other South Sea missions.

In Tahiti infanticide was one of the practices which most
revolted the missionaries. It received particular mention in all
the published accounts.[1] Human sacrifice, which prevailed with
an alarming frequency during the early period of the mission,
also shocked the missionaries. They did not approve of the
promiscuity between the sexes, and saw only evil in a society
where a man permitted his wife to cohabit with other men. The
Arioi Society (see page 182), with its even looser code of behaviour, was regarded as the very organization of Satan. The
missionaries found the acceptance of homosexual behaviour particularly loathsome.[2] Pomare II, who was the mainstay of the
mission, and was referred to as the Reformer, continually
offended them in this respect. Furthermore the *mahu* or Tahitian
effeminate had an accepted place in society. So horrified were
the missionaries by homosexuality that when a converted *mahu*
expressed his wish to take a more active part in the Christian
services his offer was turned down.[3]

Orsmond, in his journals, gives frequent accounts of the various
immoralities, and his interest is only paralleled by his disgust
and a kind of loathing for the people. He gives details of sexual
games, secret night meetings, zooerasty and erotic conversation,
and maintains that no girl over seven years of age was a virgin.[4]
On one occasion Orsmond caught a man and a woman in the
'act of adultery' inside his pulpit. Although it had cost him
'prodigious toil' to make the pulpit, he felt it necessary to break
it to pieces.[5] These things, and more besides, convinced the missionaries that the dignity of the noble savage was an illusion.

The indigenous art forms and dances connected with sexual
promiscuity were regarded as further evidence of utter depravity
by the missionaries. Although cannibalism was not practised in
all the areas, the knowledge that some of the Polynesians
practised it was sufficient to establish it as a Polynesian trait in
the minds of the missionaries. Even Tonga and Samoa could
supply illustrations to support the doctrine. Human sacrifice had
been practised in Tonga, and the customs of war, as in Tahiti,
were unpleasant. In Tonga, where there was perhaps a more
restrictive moral code, the men gave considerable offence by
going naked.

The opening of the Fijian mission in 1835 gave still greater support to the belief in utter depravity. Cannibalism, widow-strangling and the killing of strangers were but a few of the offending customs. When speaking of the Fijians in 1818, Hugh Thomas, a 'navy agent' who had received much information from a sailor who had lived in Fiji, advocated them as a people for prospective evangelization. He finished his description of them by referring to their place in history.

> They are in one word the very *dregs of Mankind* or Human Nature, dead and buried under the primeval curse, and nothing of them alive but the *Brutal part,* yea far worse than the Brute-Savage quite unfit to live but far more unfit to die, and yet they are the Sons and Daughters of Adam, and destined to live for ever.[6]

In his famous *Pity Poor Fiji* James Watkin gave clear utterance to this doctrine. Some of the following extracts from a manuscript account entitled 'Rites and Customs of the Feejeeans' prepared by Joseph Waterhouse show the impression of the Fijian character as received by a new missionary.[7] Although based on the genuine observations of missionaries, this account is emotionally written and gives a distorted picture of Fijian customs by selecting the worst cases of cannibalism during local wars.

> Go to Feejee and behold the training of the *infant,* his lips rubbed with human flesh in order that a taste for such food may be excited and early acquired . . . In Feejee kings order the limbs of refractory chiefs to be cut off, cooked, and eaten in the presence of the living trunk.

In referring to the seizing of strangers, he writes:

> Some of them could not wait till they were cooked, but came and pulled off the poor fellows' ears and eat them. They afterwards cut off their arms placing a bowl under to catch the blood. If any of the blood fell on the ground, they fell down and licked it up most greedily. They ate the poor fellows' arms in their presence, and then their legs, and then cut pieces off their bodies. Many of the poor fellows lived during this part of the operation.

One of the American missionaries in the Marquesas, the Reverend Richard Armstrong, expressed the views of his colleagues in a paper entitled 'A Sketch of Marquesian Character' published in *The Hawaiian Spectator* for 1838. One of his principal aims was to present 'a specimen of what man is without God, without the Bible, the Savior, the Sanctifier, the Sabbath and all the blessings of pure Christianity'.

In point of morals, the Marquesians must be classed with the lowest
of our species. Nothing we have ever beheld in the shape of human
depravity in other parts of the world will compare for a moment with
their shameful and shameless iniquities. The blackest ink that ever
stained paper is none too dark to describe them.[8]

In listing their vices he was almost disappointed to learn from
his informants that there was no evidence for sodomy ever having 'had an existence among them as it has on neighbouring
groups of islands; they themselves deny that it has', but in other
respects he believed their morals answered to the description of
gentile morality given by St Paul. The intolerance and initial
disgust of the missionary is clearly revealed in the paper, which
ends with the argument

Can such beings, without a change as great, and requiring as much
power as a resurrection from the dead, ever dwell in a holy heaven,
with a holy God? Will any one but an infidel or an ignoramus
cherish, for a moment, the thought that they can? Can any one, then,
but an infidel or frozen-hearted misanthrope, be indifferent to
sending them the light which came down from above?

In the same periodical an extract from the journal of the master
of a merchant vessel describing the Marquesans at Porter's Bay
contrasts markedly with the missionary effusion.

Nor can civilization in my opinion make them either better or
happier. They are like children of one family dwelling in unity and
peace, generous to an extreme; they would divide what they got in
trade, and share it with all around them. . . . if there be a terrestrial
Paradise, or happiness in this mundane sphere, it is there.[9]

The missionary commentator could only scoff, arguing that tigers
'in fact, and tigers in human form, are sometimes well disposed'
and that happiness is a relative state as 'the merriment of a slave
in chains, or a maniac in his mental estrangement'. Finally he
insinuates the degraded morality of any man who 'born and educated in civilized and Christian lands, can plunge with a relish
into the same pit under the impression that it is Paradise, and
strip himself to the *malo*, and become tataued, and lie on the
earth, and, as a foreigner at Porter's Bay remarked concerning a
fellow foreigner, "learn in three months to eat lice very fluently"'.

Convinced of the *utter depravity* of the South Sea islanders,
the missionaries were reinforced in their initial missionary
enthusiasm. Thus when he first saw a baked man Moore
exclaimed:

Are these the descendants from him who was created in the Image of God? have these being souls? Are they really accountable beings? is there any hope for them? My heart replied. O yes! This is man without the Gospel, "A beast in body, A demon in mind," but there is still hope . . . My commission extends even to these, for they are still out of Hell, although at its very jaws.[10]

This conviction also led the missionaries to conclude that there was a progressive degradation of the natural man, and that once man ceased to believe in one God he became worse, as St Paul suggested in his Epistle to the Romans. This concept was to have far-reaching effects, because it encouraged a state of war between two cultures, in which Jehovah sought to overthrow Satan who thus assumed Manichaean proportions. The war of Christian against 'devolo' (the devil) was a war against absolute evil, and therefore knew little compromise. The pattern of Evangelical missionary activity became the story of Elijah and the priests of Baal, and although the missionaries rarely took the risk of asking for a miracle they were considerably assisted in waging their war by the people putting their gods and Jehovah to the test. As their own gods were usually tried first and succeeded less, Jehovah was invariably the victor in these crude metaphysical experiments.

Besides the theological belief that the South Sea islander typified the natural man given over to a reprobate mind, there was another view of man which is sometimes less easy to isolate. This was the racial view. It was not always easy for the missionary to forget that he was white. Many of the old arguments which had been used to justify slavery were still valid theologically. Because Noah cursed Ham for discovering him naked, all Ham's descendants, who were the dark races, were subject to that curse. The Reverend John Inglis, who went to the New Hebrides in 1852, enlarged on this theme in his *Bible Illustrations from the New Hebrides*. It is perhaps significant that Inglis regarded the Polynesians as the descendants of Shem and therefore not subject to the curse.

> Now in the New Hebrides we see this curse lying in all its crushing weight. The Papuans, the poor descendants of Ham, are lying in the lowest state of degradation, trodden down by the iron heel of every oppressor. . . . the whole of the Malay race, descendants of Shem, in the South Seas, had abandoned heathenism, had embraced Christianity, and had the Bible translated for them into the six principal dialects of their language, while the whole, or nearly the whole, of the Papuan race, the children of Ham, were still lying in heathen darkness.[11]

He then proceeded to show that the descendants of Ham were destined to be the servants of the descendants of Shem until the Europeans (as descendants of Japheth) should replace them.

> But especially has God enlarged us, and given us the heritage of Shem, by making us the representatives of His visible Church, to dispense its blessings to the heathen; and these poor Gibeonites are willing to become hewers of wood and drawers of water to us for the house of the Lord. Yes, "Canaan shall be his servant".

Thus, despite the fact that the Evangelical missionary societies were foremost in the ranks of those who sought to end the slave trade, a view persisted that the darker races were of inferior ethnic stock and somewhat less than brothers, although brotherhood could be obtained through a common faith in redemption through Christ. Certain traits and popular racial prejudices were kept alive by the missionaries themselves, some simply due to colour consciousness, but others due to the various arguments which asserted the superiority of the white races. It was all too easy for a well-educated young Wesleyan missionary in the 1860s to refer to the European settlers in Fiji as 'astute enterprising Jacobs, who, here as elsewhere must in yᵉ end supplant these poor foolish Esaus, who seem incapable of rising above yᵉ level of a mess of pottage'.[12]

Often such views were kept alive by the initial aversion induced by coming into contact with a people whose ways were different and whose technical culture was inferior. When Mary Fletcher, the daughter, wife and sister of missionaries, arrived in Fiji in 1853 she recorded her feelings thus:

> Felt exceedingly disgusted and annoyed with the half-naked people around me, whose ideas of pleasant smells were very different to mine; their bodies, or, rather parts of their bodies, are well smeared with coconut-oil, scented with sandal wood.[13]

The missionary women took much longer to adjust to the new environment than the men, and some were never able to overcome their aversion. Peter Turner praised Mrs Lyth for her sociable and kind attitude to the people, and said that she was 'not like some whom [he had] seen who cannot bear the native to sit with them on the same form'.[14]

The male missionaries also expressed disgust at the appearance and manners of the people. George Turner regarded the covering worn by the men of Tana as being highly indecent, as it accentuated the parts concealed.

I make no apology for telling you these things in plain terms. You know what use to make of them. If it is revolting to *read* this description, how much more so it is to be hourly surrounded by the reality.[15]

Joseph Waterhouse, though he prided himself on his colonial *savoir faire*, informed his brother Jabez: 'At first sight the Feejeeans disgust you: even the Christians are all but naked, some of them'.[16] Thomas Baker was equally disgusted by the Fijians:

They wish to walk in and out one's house at their pleasure. I had to take a tall, dirty Chief by the arm today and walk him out of my bedroom . . . All this man had to hide his nakedness was 3 inches width of native cloth.[17]

On another occasion he was sleeping at Waninito. This was not a very pleasant experience as 'the Chief, dirty fellow' woke him several times by 'thumping' Baker's head with 'his dirty black feet'.[18] Baker, of course, finally came to a grisly end when he mortally offended one of these 'dirty fellows' by retrieving his precious comb from the sacred head of an inland chief. This natural disgust was hard to overcome and must have helped to perpetuate the old racial view.

It is not easy to determine how much this racial view contributed to their attitudes to intermarriage. Very few missionaries in the South Seas took native wives, and most of them appear to have regarded intermarriage with little favour. The only LMS missionaries who went through forms of marriage with island women between 1799 and 1810 did so without the general approval of the brethren. The Tahitian brethren argued mainly on the lines that the women were not only unconverted but still attached to a social system which allowed them freedoms not permitted in the Christian code. This was certainly the view supported by the directors who gave specific instructions to the missionaries on the *Royal Admiral.*

Avoid to the utmost every temptation of the native Women. Let no brother live separately from all the rest, and if any one sleeps alone, let it be in a house that is prohibited to the Women. We doubt whether any of them would regard the obligations of the Marriage state without effectual conversion, and therefore, if sought for as a remedy it might prove the worst of evils.[19]

However the subject was frequently discussed. Bicknell went so far as to say that 'the Natives in some respects would make better Wives than European women, as they can travel thro' the Rivers and live on the productions of the Island better'.[20] The Reverend

Thomas Lewis and Henry Nott both appear to have gone
through some form of marriage.[21] What became of Nott's wife
has not been recorded, but as the rest of the brethren disapproved the union was possibly regarded as an indiscretion
and annulled by common consent, and no doubt conveniently
forgotten when four 'godly young women' arrived by special
shipment.

It is certainly in the period after the nominal conversion of
Tahiti that we find the racial view more prevalent. Perhaps this
was due to the greater number of missionary wives in the field,
who may not have been so willing to receive their 'coloured
sisters' on terms of equality. Although in this later period several
affairs took place involving both missionaries and native girls
in the LMS and the WMMS, the only persons connected with
either mission who were married to native women were two
'assistant missionaries'.[22] Both these men had married prior to
accepting missionary responsibilities. Even in the Hawaiian mission, where the personnel was so much larger, only one marriage
took place between a missionary and a Hawaiian.[23] This marriage
was precipitated by the lonely condition of the Reverend Samuel
Dwight, who caught one of his pupils, Anna Mahoe, in bed with
a Hawaiian boy. His rather unexpected reaction to this was to
marry Anna Mahoe himself, though he earned the censure of
the mission. Even amongst second-generation missionary families,
intermarriage was exceptional, though more frequent in third-
generation families which had remained in the islands and which
had little active connection with the missions.

An interesting feature of those liaisons and marriages which
did take place between members of missionary families and
islanders is that the islanders were usually of high rank. Benjamin Broomhall's partner was a high chiefess of Raiatea. Nott's
'wife' was a high chiefess, apparently a close relative of Pomare
II. Adam Darling, son of a missionary, married a member of the
high chiefly family at Punaauia, his father's station. Rowland
Barff's wife, however, was his mother's maid.

The relationship between the missionaries and their island
servants had its effect on the general attitude of the missionaries
towards the people. The native youths and girls lived in the
family in the manner of English domestics. They cooked, waited
at table and acted as nurses to the children. Many of the native
preachers began as domestics and were treated with that familiarity which developed during the days of service. This domestic
relationship was to some degree extended to the people as a
whole. Even the impatience of the missionary's lady with her

When John Barff returned from his schooling in England in 1839 his father urged him 'to beware of the hateful Idea that "anything will do for Black Dick"', which had been a 'sore evil' to the Tahitian mission.[34]

The young missionaries who came out in 1838 and 1839 appear to have given offence both to the Tahitians and the older missionaries by their attitude to the people. Orsmond records how they exclaimed, 'What filthy creatures these natives are', even though the natives bathed five times to the missionaries' once![35] Davies complained that they treated the Tahitians with a 'haughty reserve' which the people regarded as contempt.[36]

The methods of instruction used by the missionaries were those used in teaching children. The conception of the islanders as children has always been present in mission thought. In lamenting the absence of initiative missionaries do not realize that this is largely due to their paternalistic attitude; that it is inconsistent to regard their charges as 'children' or as 'poor brown dick', and yet expect them to show initiative. Brown dick was the weaker brother, and the missionary remained his keeper.

Examples of racial arrogance and colour consciousness can be found in the records of the other missions. W. T. Pritchard records an instance in which the self-interest of Binner of Ovalau was affected by the duplicity of Tui Levuka. 'You are a bad man', he cried. 'When an English man-of-war comes to Levuka, I shall make the Captain tie you to the mainmast, and flog you till your blood runs on the deck'.[37] This is perhaps no more than an angry statement, but it is in some ways typical of the overbearing attitude often adopted by the missionaries who were convinced of their own superiority, and who were annoyed by opposition in any form. This attitude is illustrated most forcefully by the account given by Royce of his attempt to convert an important Fijian chief, Cagilevu. It reads not unlike a police interview. Royce and his accomplices got Cagilevu in a room and for two and a half hours they

> tried him at all points of the compass, but without success — he is a sharp, shrewd fellow, as full of guile and the venom of asps as the devil can possibly wish him to be . . . the man was like a bomb tower, every shot fired, though it hit the mark, yet it rounded off: at last we got it out of him, I don't want to lotu, and there we had to leave him, till the Lord deal with him either in judgment, or mercy.[38]

Although the missionaries were often easily irritated by seeming stupidity or 'childishness', most of them regarded the various

island peoples as being capable of the same intellectual development as themselves. Even the West Indian planter Gyles asserted
that 'in point of Intellect' the Tahitians were 'not inferior to
Englishmen'.[39] Royce regarded the Fijians as an 'intelligent
people', but he felt that the missionaries would not make very
rapid progress owing to the 'limited conceptions' of the Fijians.[40]

Despite the belief that the native races possessed the limitations
of the children of Ham, the missionaries did believe that Christianity could transform their lives to such an extent that they
would be trained to look and act like themselves, even if the
people did not actually think like them. The missionaries inculcated emulation rather than self-expression. The European
missionary was to be the 'example', and the people were to
imitate him. The emphasis placed on conformity was very
marked.

The belief in the utter depravity of the South Sea islanders
held by the missionaries depended very largely on a particular
conception of history. In the period before 1860 the theologian
did not have to encounter the doubts aroused by evolutionary
theory. The leading ethnologists of the early nineteenth century
were advocates for the unity of man. Prichard maintained that
the primitive stock of men were Negroes. Blumenbach regarded
the 'five varieties of man' as having degenerated from some ideal
perfect type.[41] Consequently the theologians did not hesitate to
ascribe the origin of the entire human race to the miraculous
creation of Adam and Eve and the repeopling of the world after
the deluge by the Japhetic, Semitic and Hamitic races. It was
because of this belief in the direct association between the antediluvian world and the modern races of mankind that the missionaries actually collected traditions which they regarded as
garbled versions of the original historical events, and what remained of the mythological systems were regarded as accretions
picked up during the centuries of exile from the cradle of the
race.

Ellis records a tradition of the creation of Adam and Eve, and
although he was inclined to doubt the genuine origin of this
tradition, he believed that if it could be proved it would be the
'most remarkable and valuable oral tradition of the origin of the
human race yet known'. He also recorded traditions of the deluge
which he regarded as 'the most decisive evidence of the authenticity of revelation'.[42] S. M. McFarlane of Lifu records a tradition
'substantially the same as the Scripture account of the flood' in
which an old man named Nol (= Noah) made a canoe inland
from the coast. Other stories 'identified' were those of the tower

of Babel and Joseph and his brethren.[43] When told a Fijian legend about a great flood, David Hazlewood regarded it as a tradition of the universal deluge, and his reaction illustrates this historic view admirably:

> What a poor account it has sunk into. Instead of being a record of the greatest display of almighty power, and Divine wrath, in punishing a guilty world, the devil has turned it into a pretty affair of his own, to lead men to fear and worship him.[44]

Most of the missionaries believed that the native mythology was a distortion of that 'ancient, primitive, patriarchal religion', which, in the belief of John Dunmore Lang, was 'doubtless taught by Noah and his sons to their immediate posterity, but which was so speedily forgotten or debased by the great majority of the tribes of men'.[45] Bishop Russell developed this view most fully in his account of Polynesia:

> It requires no ingenuity to discover in the religious usages of the Polynesians such a resemblance to those of the other Asiatic nations as to afford the greatest probability that they sprung from the same source. In the practices everywhere prevailing, we perceive traces of that original faith which, though given to man by a divine agency, has perpetuated itself through a channel so corrupted as to have lost the sublime import and the purer ceremonies by means of which it first addressed itself to the acceptation of the descendants of Noah.[46]

Russell compared the ancient forms of worship amongst the Polynesians with those forms adopted by the Israelites when they embraced idolatry. He discerned similarities in the form of the temples and also suggested that human sacrifices and infanticide were abuses of a sacred institution. He denied the Malthusian explanation for infanticide and regarded it as a perversion of the Levitical law. He gave similar explanations for human sacrifice and other customs, and finally concluded:

> Their traditional recollections, not less than their superstitions, identify them with nations who have acted a more prominent part in the theatre of the globe, though climate food, and peculiar habits have in some degree obscured the resemblance.

It was this belief in the perversion of history rather than in originality which led the missionaries to regard most of the tales as nonsense and as 'wicked lies' rather than as the attempts of these people to explain the world in which they lived. It is true that many of the missionaries who examined the cultural systems more minutely came to have an admiration for the ingenuity and natural virtues of many of these tales, and valued them for their own sake, but there was always present a belief that the stories were traps, manufactured by the devil for ensnaring the people to his vicious service.

In attempting to convince the Marquesans that it was Jehovah and not Tiki who was responsible for creating the world, and hence their own islands, George Stallworthy displayed considerable impatience. 'This benighted and sin-stricken people seem to be wholly insensible to any discrepancy between the book of nature and their own absurd and wicked legends.'[47] He was even more vexed when they could not be persuaded that Jehovah did not have a mother.

Although the missionaries shared the belief in the progressive degeneration of natural religion, in their discussions on sacred objects with the islanders there seems to have been a great variety of approach. Some missionaries displayed a much more sympathetic and less iconoclastic spirit, and others were so filled with zeal that they did not hesitate to offend the supporters of the traditional system. Usually when the latter was the case the missionary felt that he had much to gain by his 'sacrilege', for by his act he hoped to prove that the gods or spirits were impotent to act against him.

In Polynesia the power of the *tapu* system was one of the most powerful forces which prevented any degree of success in mission work. The examples set by certain chiefs, particularly in the Society Islands and Tonga, in defying the system in the most public way must have had great influence in ending it.[48] In the Marquesas it was the *tapu* system more than any other single cause which frustrated the mission, and the whole progress of the missionaries depended on the chief Iotete of Vaitahu, who was afraid to break any of the *tapu*. Very often missionaries of another generation have lamented the breakdown of the *tapu* system because it gave at least a certain cohesion to society on questions of morality. However, as the early missionaries repeatedly affirmed, the facets of native life were so inextricably interwoven that all stood or fell together.

In order to combat utter depravity and the 'religion of false gods' the missionaries had to launch a full-scale attack which meant not only war to the death with priestcraft and immorality, the particular things with which they were concerned as religious teachers, but also serious encroachments on the power of the chiefs and prevailing notions of order and allegiance.

This policy was realized very early in the Tahitian mission. The Arioi Society (see page 182), which was so prominent a feature of Tahitian society, was regarded as a legitimate object of attack. In writing about his own views on mission policy in 1799, William Henry maintained: 'I deem it necessary that the Consequence and Influence of the Arioi Society be Counteracted, or indeed distroyed, before any real permanent good (humanly spaking) can be done there . . .'.[49]

Yet in their dealings with the people in the matter of their traditional religion the early missionaries showed some courtesy. During a tour of Moorea in 1813 one of them recorded a conversation between himself and some people in a house devoted to the god Oro. The man permitted him to handle the image, although they themselves were afraid to do so.

> Turning to the men with the god in my hands, I said, look here, is it not great foolishness to trust this, to worship this: What power has he? What can he do? He has no power now to deliver himself out of my hands. Do you think I am afraid of him? No, I bid him defiance, and all his company in the *po*, and I could now break him, tear him to pieces, and tread him in the Dirt under my feet — but I shall not do so, why? because I fear him? No, no, I fear him not, but I respect the people of this country, therefore I will put him in again without any injury . . .[50]

At times one reads of less compromising attitudes. Thus Joseph Waterhouse, in his Fijian Journal for August 1851, mentioned a wayside stone which, he was informed, was a god, and which none of the Fijians would dare touch.

> An unsculptured stone, a female god: . . . No wonder they have *hearts of stone* when they worship *gods of stone!* In taking my leave of her Majesty I filled the Natives with alarm and dismay by raising my foot and giving the god a hearty kick.[51]

One of the main reasons for interference with native beliefs before the people showed any inclinations to adhere to the new faith was not the assertion of one set of values over another on the grounds of superiority and truth, but the missionaries' sincere belief that the pagan ceremonies were an offence in the eyes of God. Hence the first ground to be won was a conformity to the Decalogue, irrespective of conversions or belief. Thus the *tapu* observance of the Sabbath was always the first effect of mission penetration, as it was an offence for anyone to work on the Sabbath. Sometimes the observance of the Sabbath even preceded the coming of the missionaries, but it was always one of the first things which they secured.

When the Marquesan mission was recommenced in 1834

Darling and his colleagues discovered the people engaged in an elaborate ceremony connected with Iotete's daughter. 'We have thought it most prudent', said Darling, 'not to interfere with the present ceremonies as they appear to be of a harmless nature . . .'.[52] Any interference would have been on the grounds of offence to God. This statement reads like toleration of 'harmless' customs, but other comments show that Darling regarded it as 'frivolity', and naturally expected that any converts they should make to Christianity would no longer practise such customs.

David Darling, who was familiar with Tahitian culture and had been in close contact with the *Mamaia* movement in Tahiti (see page 176), was extremely interested in Marquesan lore. Whilst at Vaitahu he took pains to search out an old priest in order to familiarize himself with the local beliefs. Though genuinely interested, he was too ready to dismiss these beliefs as 'nonsense'. The Marquesan account of the creation he regarded as being 'nothing but a confused heap of names without any meaning or sense'.[53] When the people persisted in affirming their belief in some miraculous legends he called them an 'ignorant self-conceited people'. Such an attitude was fairly general in the pre-1860 period and there were few exceptions.

The missionaries had to find out more about the religious systems of the South Sea people as a legitimate part of their work. The Tahitian brethren very early found that the Tahitian system was not as closely allied to 'natural religion' as Morrison's manuscript and Dr Haweis' abstract from it had led them to think.[54] However most of the missionaries who came out in succeeding years had a greater fund of information to draw upon. The missionaries were also influenced in their approach by the scriptural accounts of idolatry, and they were only too ready to apply the 'appropriate' passage to the context of the South Seas.

It was inevitable also that some of the missionaries possessed the type of mind which induced them to carry out systematic research into the island cultures, about which so little was then known. William Ellis was one of the first to publish such material in his *Polynesian Researches*. John Davies took a scientific interest in Polynesian linguistics, and his comparative studies formed the basis of other reseach in that subject.

The stimulus to research of a scientific nature usually came from outside the mission field. It was because of Samuel Greatheed's keen interest that the missionary W. P. Crook supplied him with information concerning the peoples, customs and natural history of the Marquesas, which formed the basis of a three-volume manuscript account of that group.[55] Similarly, the investigations of Dr Lang of Sydney stimulated the interest of some of the missionaries in Tahiti. In 1834 Lang published his *View of the Origin and Migrations of the Polynesian Nation* which postulated the theory that the Polynesians belonged to the same 'race' as the American Indians. Before he wrote this work Lang had corresponded with some of the missionaries, particularly Davies, William Henry and Orsmond. It is quite probable that Orsmond might not have become the foremost authority on Tahitian traditions had it not been for Lang. On 1 January 1824 Orsmond wrote in his journal that 'the two renowned priests' of Moorea sat down and gave him 'several specimens of their original mode of praying'.[56] After describing this he made the following comment: 'I now saw the nature of the services performed for Tahitian gods and who would have supposed it to be the eldest sister of Popish ignorance'.[57] This was hardly the remark of a man who was well versed in Tahitian lore. It does show, however, that Orsmond was taking a particular interest in the old customs. Lang, who was preparing his book, wrote to Orsmond in the ensuing years, and doubtless asked for information to support his theories. Whatever may have transpired, Orsmond wrote to Lang at the beginning of 1828 casually announcing that 'the Mythology shall be forthcoming'.[58] In 1833 Samuel Wilson wrote to Lang from Tahiti saying that Orsmond had 'been long employed in Researches into the institutions etc. of these islands', and asked Lang if he also should devote some time to 'that department of study', and whether it would be of 'service to the cause of religion and the cause of man'.[59] Lang's reply was almost certainly in the affirmative, for during his brief missionary career in Samoa Wilson acquired a considerable fund of information about Polynesian mythology.

It has often been supposed that when missionaries became interested in the folklore and traditions of the islands this interest was an indication of something different from the usual Evangelical approach. It was either a sign that the missionary had come under the influence of new humanistic feelings as a result of his contact with a reasonably advanced, but alien culture, or an indication of a more humane and sympathetic personality than that of the average missionary. It could also be an indication of an attempt to escape from the reality of failure, or loneliness, or even lack of faith. For instance Thomas Williams of Fiji has been claimed as a 'born anthropologist',[60] a missionary whose anthropological interests saved him from falling prey to spiritual disillusionment, though in that respect it would seem that the feelings which Williams expressed were no more intense than those of other missionaries in their periods of depression. It is true, of course, that Williams developed a natural sympathy for the Fijian character.

> Fijians are greatly wronged by being supposed to be a set of rough untutored brutes. They can feel as keenly, weep as sincerely, love as truly and laugh as heartily as any European. White men who call them brutes, devils and such-like find on better acquaintance that they have an elaborate system of etiquette, and that among themselves none but the very lowest are ill-behaved.[61]

However, this favourable testimony does not contradict Williams' earlier assumption that Fijians were 'without natural affection'. When the missionaries referred to the islanders as being 'without natural affection' they alluded to such customs as cannibalism, wife-strangling and the burial alive of the aged. They regarded these practices as crimes against nature, even when they recognized the high value attached to them in the indigenous culture. Most of the missionaries saw from the beginning that there were finer shades of feeling. Usually, however, when they spoke out in defence of the people they referred particularly to their own circle of converts. There is comparatively little evidence to indicate that the views of the missonaries were, or could have been, modified in any way by contact. In fact, the evidence seems to suggest that the missionaries tended to become more firmly convinced of the doctrine of natural depravity, that men without a knowledge of the laws of Jehovah were incapable of achieving salvation and were worthy of death.

Orsmond's interest in Polynesian customs and traditions represents an interesting parallel with Thomas Williams. Perhaps more than all his brethren, Orsmond was revolted by the character and manners of the Polynesians. Although he collected traditions and anthropological information he used all his strength to combat the worship of the old gods and the perpetuation of heathen customs. In Orsmond's journals we have not only a record of his rooted antipathy to the culture about which he was so knowledgeable but also a revulsion at everything associated with the former way of life of these peoples. Orsmond, like Williams of Fiji, genuinely believed that all the human virtues could be found amongst the people, but for him too they were 'without natural affection'. It was an Evangelical 'love to souls' which made him persevere, not sympathy for their culture.

Indeed, when an Evangelical missionary became more than scientifically interested and showed definite signs of having a sympathetic interest we must begin to question his doctrinal position. Evangelical religion in the early nineteenth century made no allowance for any system other than the Jewish and Christian revelations. No theologian had postulated such modern doctrine as that of progressive revelation, and such comparative mythology as existed was associated only with the schools of rationalistic or latitudinarian thought. Thomas Kendall of the CMS in New Zealand can serve as an illustration of this. As with other members of his own mission and those of the LMS, Kendall's theology was Calvinistic. We cannot but conclude that his interest in Maori culture led him into what would be termed 'a dangerous Antinomian position'. Kendall fell into mental conflict, his mind and training accepting the Evangelical teaching whilst his curiosity and passions were powerfully attracted towards the way of life which he had come to change. 'It is true I have carried my measures of conciliation and social intercourse with the natives to a criminal excess,' he wrote, 'and I have not done those things which I ought to have done . . .'.[62] Although suspended from the CMS, Kendall continued to regard himself as a missionary and continued his investigations. The peculiar degree to which he was involved personally is made clear by his own admission:

> There is also another inconvenience attached to the study of the ideas of the New Zealanders which has almost overpowered and overwhelmed me, and which I ought to mention, namely, that as they in all respects draw their spiritual and metaphysical notions from the study of Nature, they are of course frequently obtained from very impure sources.[63]

But even Kendall, who admitted succumbing to the 'vile passions' of the Maoris, regarded his own conduct as sinful and continued to think in the same theological terms.

> I must nevertheless speak the truth, trusting that such a deviation will not be imputed to any other motive than an earnest desire to represent and expose the mysterious system of the natives with all its horrors, to point out the secret lurking place of the subtle deceiver of mankind, and not to write so much with a view of exciting the wonder as the compassion of the Christian world . . .[64]

On the other hand when men such as Benjamin Broomhall and Samuel Wilson became particularly involved in the Polynesian way of life they rejected their Calvinist doctrines and embraced more latitudinarian theologies, systems more tolerant of the dreams and fancies of the Polynesian people. They realized that the importance given to sex in the Polynesian traditions and way of life could never be reconciled with the Christianity which they had come to teach.

When the Evangelical missionary investigated the mythology, traditions and customs of the islanders his aim was twofold. He sought to learn more about the peoples amongst whom he was living, mainly so that he would be better equipped to overthrow the 'system of false gods'. He also hoped that his work would add to man's knowledge of the world. If the knowledge gained by such men as Orsmond, Williams and Kendall did not modify their doctrinal view of man, at least it helped them and their colleagues to appreciate the intellectual and artistic talents of the islanders, and it set a worthy example for their successors.

PART THREE

The Missionary as a Social Force

It is a Bible Society; for to translate, and print, and circulate the Scriptures, is its first labour. It is a Tract Society; for the circulation of short addresses to the understanding, heart, and conscience, is one of its principal operations. It is a Sunday-school Society; for wherever it establishes itself, it sets up these useful institutions. It is an auxiliary to the British and Foreign School Society, by extending education over the face of the whole earth. It is a Home Missionary Society; for wherever it fixes itself, it sends out its agents into its own neighbourhood to preach the gospel. . . . It is a Peace Society; for its very message is an echo of the angel's song. . . . It is an anti-slavery Society; for it diffuses that religion which teaches the principles of justice and universal benevolence. It is a Civilization Society, and a Mechanics' Institute; for it is introducing all the common arts of life in the dreary wilds of barbarism.

JOHN ANGELL JAMES, Sermon, Poultry Chapel 1828,
Works, vol. II, pp. 165-66.

11

Converts and Revivalists

THE WAY IN WHICH missionaries were received into the island societies varied according to place and time, although the variants were relatively few. The old myth that the white men were returning ancestors or gods was quite widespread, although in some groups the people were already disillusioned when the missionaries arrived. Nevertheless there was much to perpetuate this belief. Fair skin was regarded as a sign of high birth throughout Polynesia and some of the western islands, and in some communities youths in chiefs' families were protected from the sun. Naturally the superior skills of the white men also suggested divinity or chieftainship. Even the arrival of the missionaries was sometimes fraught with mystery. The Tahitians reported an earth tremor at the time of the arrival of the *Duff*, and a very high tide which left 'prodigious heaps of fish' behind. One old chief recalled the event in 1827. 'I felt the trembling of the earth when the Duff first came. We were all frightened but now I think it was the struggle of the false Gods.'[1]

In many of the groups the missionaries gave the impression that they were gods, or at least the vehicles into which gods entered. This was largely due to the conceptions of priestcraft and chieftainship in the various societies. In some groups, however, much of the contact between the people and visiting white men had been disastrous. Also the people soon realized that the white men fell into different categories and had different values. When not converted to Christianity, they regarded Jehovah as the particular god of the white people, existing independently of all their own deities and unrelated to the creation of their own lands and peoples. Traces of this belief can be illustrated from several groups. For instance Samuel Waterhouse reported the following interview with an influential Fijian chief:

"Why should I worship Jehovah, as he was not my Father's God. . . ."
"True, He was not your Father's God, in the sense that your father worshipped Him — but Jehovah was truly your father's God — Who else made him — who else decreed his death, and who else but Jehovah will judge him."
"Look — Jehovah is not — cannot be our God — For you and we are

217

different — He is the white man's God — but he is not the black man's God — if He were our God we also would have white skins."[2]

In those island communities where there was a long period of trial preaching and contact before the generality of the people accepted Christianity, either by instant political decision or some form of group reaction, the missionaries encountered stubborn resistance from all sections of the community. This was especially true in Tahiti before the conversion of Pomare II, in Tongatapu even after the conversion of the Tupou family, in the Marquesas for most of the nineteenth century, and in Fiji and other parts of Melanesia. The priests of the old religions maintained their positions as long as they could, though frequently exposed to the scepticism and ridicule of the missionaries. They either asserted the truth of their own beliefs or, as was more frequently the case, acknowledged the validity of the beliefs of the missionaries for other Europeans. The American missionaries in the Marquesas were surprised at the vehemence with which the Marquesans defended their 'superstitious creed' as though they possessed 'all the learning of the schools'.[3]

> More than once have we been interrupted in the midst of an attempt at preaching in their language by such expressions as the following — *tevava*: kikino to oukou Atua: motaki matou, tiatohu to matou Atua [It is false: your God is bad: we are good, and our gods are true]; and these expressions were accompanied with a profusion of sneers, grimaces and other marks of contempt and ill-humor quite as significant, and more insulting than words.

It was general in many of the Polynesian islands to express contempt by exposing the buttocks and farting. This was done frequently in Tahiti even after 'conversion'.

In Tahiti and the neighbouring islands the missionaries were finally accepted as the priests of the king, having his protection, and consequently to be feared and respected. If they gave prestige to a local community it was largely due to their property, and the fact that they were visited by ships. In less sophisticated groups, however, they were regarded more as chiefs in their own right, not very far inferior to the kings, George and William, and Queen Victoria, whom they were always mentioning. This was often reinforced by the personal appearance of the missionary. If he was a big, corpulent man he was usually reckoned a great chief in his own country. The fact, also, that these men were religious teachers strengthened rather than weakened this belief in their chiefly status, because of the priestly function exercised by many of the chiefs in their own communities. Thus missionaries often had the protection or assistance of a supernatural power credited to them by the indigenous people, of which they were not always conscious.

On the other hand, the missionaries were accepted only on the basis of their property or the protection of a chief. If they were regarded as chiefs, it was as chiefs of another land, and, where Christianity had been adopted, of another god. In fact it was more usual for the missionary to be regarded as an alien than as an accepted member of the society in which he worked. Although usually protected by the laws of hospitality, he was often in a position where his actions could be misunderstood, to his embarrassment or at the risk of his personal safety.

There were groups in which the missionaries had to overcome the widely held belief, often founded on fact, that missionaries (no less than their irreligious countrymen) were the bringers of disease. This was the principal cause of the failure of the first mission to Tonga, and the belief which was then prevalent was still active when the Wesleyans recommenced the mission, and proved a serious handicap to their progress on Tongatapu.[4] In the New Hebrides this belief was also widely held, and many native teachers were sacrificed accordingly.

Thus the range of acceptance varied considerably. In their role as religious teachers, the missionaries not infrequently possessed an authority derived not so much from what they preached and taught as from their role as the priests of the chief, or as chiefs in their own right. On the other hand, as white persons they were regarded as aliens, and only those, like the mission children, who were actually born in the islands were accepted fully into the native societies. This point is doubly illustrated in a letter written by Pomare II to Captain S. P. Henry in which the Tahitian king referred disparagingly to the latest missionary arrivals.[5] In their role as chiefs the missionaries were supported by the activities of British and American naval power, which played a considerable part in effecting the social reforms and peace which missionaries advocated but could not always secure.

The Evangelical missionaries were not backward in assuming the role of 'big white chiefs' where circumstances were favourable. When they adopted attitudes of dependence it was usually only before one supreme chief or king. They had nothing but scorn for the Catholic priest who assumed the mantle of servility and went through the obsequious rites of homage. Pratt wrote in 1846 that the two priests in Samoa carried their 'voluntary humility' to great lengths. 'If chiefs are gathered together in a house, they stoop down while passing them like the most abject menials and sit on the very threshhold of the house.'[6] The Wesleyans perhaps exceeded the other missionaries in their assumption of chiefly status. Erskine was a little discouraged by what he saw at Tongatapu in 1849.

> I am, indeed, bound in justice to remark, that, in respect to their treatment of the people here and at Vavau, the gentlemen of this mission do not compare favourably with those of the London Society in the Samoan Islands. A more dictatorial spirit towards the chiefs and people seemed to show itself, and one of the missionaries in my presence sharply reproved Vuke, a man of high rank in his own country, for presuming to speak to him in a standing posture, a breach of discipline for which, if reprehensible, I was probably answerable, having encouraged the chief on all occasions to put himself on an equal footing with myself and the other officers. The missionaries seemed also to live much more apart from the natives than in Samoa, where free access is allowed to them at all times.[7]

Against this picture of the missionary shutting himself up like a sacred king, and issuing ultimatums like a patriarchal law-giver, we must also place the picture of the missionary literally 'despised and rejected' by the people. Henry Nott in his old age, no longer protected by the powerful Pomare II, was all but persecuted by the people at his station.[8] In the final analysis the missionary's place in native society was determined by the degree of sophistication attained by the people and by his own personal effectiveness.

It would possibly be true to say that the missionary was not fully accepted into native society until the people had been 'converted', or in other words until the entire religious basis of society had been changed. Until this change took place the missionary was a powerful alien and a rival priest. There were two types of conversion experienced by the islanders. There was the experience of heart-acceptance or faith, and there was the outward profession necessitated by a national change of religion. Even this nominal profession, or renunciation of the old gods, was a major break with the past, and it gave the missionaries considerable advantages, especially as there was an element of novelty in the situation. The people invariably displayed an eagerness to learn, not only to please their chiefs but because of their own great curiosity. However this was only part of the pattern. Old superstitions persisted, and it was only the heartfelt conversion in which the missionaries found satisfaction.

As elsewhere, the reasons for conversion were not always

wholly spiritual ones. An examination of accounts of these conversions demonstrates that they were either dramatic emotional
experiences, as at revivals, or that they were due to particular
events, such as the influence of another person by example,
persuasion, or even nagging; the fear of disease or death, and
the belief that Christianity provides either immunity or eternal
life, and also the desire to be united with deceased loved ones;
vows taken on the sick bed, or in dangerous circumstances where
recovery or rescue could be regarded as an intervention of divine
providence; fear of God's wrath as gathered from mission teaching, especially in regard to carnal living, and perhaps also a
simple belief in the story of the crucifixion iself, which might be
regarded as a 'spiritual' means of conversion.*

Actually the spirituality of the reasons for conversion was not
regarded as of supreme importance by the missionaries. Most had
themselves been led to change their lives by similar influences.
What mattered in this conversion experience was that the convert became serious in his religious duties, attended all the
'means of grace and instruction', adopted the practice of regular
prayer, and eventually showed by his changed way of life that he
was, in all likelihood, a regenerate soul.

But despite the similarities to English revival experience, the
differences were far greater. These differences were mainly due to
the strangeness of many of the Christian doctrines to the native
mind, and also to the difficulties of the missionaries in determining how thoroughly, or how accurately, these doctrines were
understood. It is quite clear that they did not always know. They
quite early realized that lip-service could be given to some
doctrines, when the person was quite incapable of explaining
them.

Missionaries were frequently surprised by the nature of the
questions which they were asked. George Turner records several
of the questions asked by students at Malua:

"If we feel sleepy at prayer, should we open our eyes?"
"How tall was Zaccheus; how many feet do you suppose?"
"What is the meaning of cymbal? Is it an animal, or what?"
"Did Isaiah live before Christ, or after him?"[9]

Charter records some native 'howlers' which are even more
revealing:

After a week's consideration our deacons and those who attend the

---

*This paragraph is based on an examination of over sixty accounts of
conversion and religious experience written by or taken down from
islanders and comparison with similar accounts by Europeans.

Monday class expressed it as their opinion that the 'Joseph' who begged the body of Jesus was the same Joseph who was sold into Egypt, i.e. the son of Jacob.

Mark vi. 9. This means Missionaries should not have two coats, and they ought to give their property to the people.[10]

But if the missionaries were a little puzzled by the knowledge of their heart-converts, they had fewer illusions about the many nominal adherents, especially in those islands where the 'conversion' had been on a national level. The pre-church Christianity of Tahiti, for instance, was merely an expression of the will of Pomare II, based on the religious habits (not the beliefs) of the English missionaries. It was perhaps less easy for the missionaries to distinguish those nominal converts whose reasons for adherence were other than political. In Samoa, for instance, support of a particular church was often closely linked with social prestige. Nevertheless an Evangelical missionary could usually pick out his 'Christians' from the rest, by means of various tests (see page 305). In some instances, however, nominal adherents were accepted as genuine until they betrayed their true feelings. The chief of Moala in Fiji, who had been a political convert, called himself a Christian for many years. He chaired the annual missionary meetings and his speeches were even printed in *Missionary Notices*. However he horrified the missionaries by exclaiming on his death bed, 'This lotu is a lie! Paint my face, & perform upon me "yᵉ custom of yᵉ dead," that I may follow my fathers'.[11]

The missionaries knew that they held their place in the community only through their acceptance by this same community reformed as a church. Where no church could be formed, as at the Marquesas, the missionary was very much a displaced person in society. Although it was the chiefs who were the arbiters, who decided whether the missionaries remained or not, little could be done unless they also sanctioned the establishment of a nominally Christian society. Once this was achieved the chiefs were often more of a handicap than an asset to the missionaries. Chiefs who were only nominal converts were inclined to interfere in what the missionaries regarded as their own particular province. In the secular world the co-operation of the chiefs was often the only way to effect social reforms, but in spiritual matters it was through the church members rather than the secular authorities that the real changes were made. Only by creating fellow-Christians was the missionary able to make a place for himself.

Something of the missionary's place in the new society is revealed in Hardie's report on the Sapapali'i station in 1840. The church members had obtained 'a decided influence over the people'. Almost every matter of importance was 'more or less referred to their decision'.[12] The church members were the surest guarantee to the missionary's investment.

The missionaries often found it hard to understand why the islanders were not in abject misery in the first stages of conversion, when they were made aware of their past iniquities. Ellis remarked that there was 'no individual among them, whose past life had not been polluted by deeds which even natural conscience told them were wrong, and consequently, no arguments were necessary to convince any one that he was guilty before God'.[13] However the missionaries were surprised at the lack of emotion at conversion.

> Under declarations of the nature and dreadful consequences of sin, aggravated as theirs had been, the denunciation of the penalties of the law of God, and even under the awakenings of their own consciences to a conviction of sin, we seldom perceived that deep and acute distress of mind, which in circumstances of a similar kind we should have expected.

The apprehension of the doctrine of the cross had not been attended very often by 'that sudden relief, and that exstatic joy, which is often manifested in other parts of the world, by individuals in corresponding circumstances'. Ellis did not believe the emotions of the islanders to be as acute as those of 'civilized' people. Also, 'the varied representations of the punishment and sufferings of the wicked, and the corresponding views of heaven, as the state of the greatest blessedness, being to them partial and new, the impressions were probably vague and indistinct; while with us, from long familiarity, they are at once vivid and powerful'. The missionaries did all they could to change this rather indifferent attitude to one of real experience. They wished their converts really to feel their guilt. This was the aim of both civil and ecclesiastical discipline. Mothers guilty of infanticide were frequently reminded of the fact.[14]

We have seen how the reality of the experience of conversion filled the missionaries with a holy zeal and a desire to make reparation for their past. The missionaries, by endeavouring to instil a sense of guilt into their converts, were often able to achieve the same effects. That very often a superficial zeal was imparted without a conviction of sin is evidenced by Williams when he described the religion of the Raiateans as 'a blazing form scarcely a spark of the power of godliness'.[15]

However where this missionary policy was successful the measure of sin determined the measure of reparation, and we find some of the best native teachers were formerly the most licentious and abandoned of the natives. There appears to have been a large proportion of Arioi Society members who, on transferring their allegiance, became some of the best native teachers in the Society Islands. Ellis gave the following testimony: 'With few exceptions, they have been distinguished by ardour of zeal, and steady adherence to the religion of the Bible. Many of them have been its most regular and laborious teachers in our schools, and the most efficient and successful native Missionaries'.[16] He then proceeded to explain this zeal in the light of the doctrine of reparation.

> Among this class, also, as might naturally be expected, have been experienced the most distressing apprehensions of the consequences of sin, and the greatest compunction of mind on account of it. Many of them immediately changed their names, and others would be happy to obliterate every mark of that fraternity, the badges of which they once considered an honourable distinction. I have heard several wish they could remove from their bodies the marks tataued upon them, but these figures remain too deeply fixed to be obliterated, and perpetually remind them of what they once were.

Perhaps the most famous convert from the Arioi Society was the indefatigable Auna of Huahine who had been the principal Arioi of Raiatea.[17] He fought in the front line for the 'Christian' party at the decisive battle of 1815, was influential at court, was made a deacon, and was successively missionary to Hawaii and Maiaoiti. His life deserves as much attention as that of many of the European missionaries. Other such converts were Manu of Punaauia, Pati'i of Moorea and Taua of Huahine. The valued Maretu of Rarotonga bore the burden of remorse for past cannibalism.[18]

In relation to this it appears that the first generation of converts was productive of more zeal than the second, a feature which had been common to other missions.[19] By instilling a sense of guilt the missionaries were able to establish the church for one generation, but the faith was not of that positive kind which made the young desire religion. There was not such an obvious need for the atonement by a generation which had grown up untainted by infanticide, human sacrifice or cannibalism and whose chief sin might be said to be concupiscence. The islanders could see the wrongfulness of destroying infant life when the gods who demanded it were non-existent, but they were not so repelled by the sins of the flesh. Williams recorded the remorse of Christian mothers for their guilt of infanticide but he found it difficult to understand their tolerance of an adulteress. The missionaries were confused by the general lack of guilt feelings in their converts, aware that even the fear of breaking a *tapu* was fear of some physical penalty. They therefore placed considerable emphasis on preaching 'the wrath to come'. Mrs Crook records that her first class of Tahitian women were 'greatly afraid of the fire'.[20]

The native teachers also, realizing the tendency of their brethren to 'live in sin', endeavoured to create a fear of hell. They regarded themselves as 'brands plucked out of the burning'.[21] Maretu, one of the better-known teachers, preached on one occasion from Isaiah i, 28, 'They that forsake the Lord shall be consumed'. One of the islanders who had already developed a 'sense of exceeding sinfulness' and who feared 'his exposure to the wrath of God' was so impressed by this sermon that he could not sleep and went to Maretu the next morning. 'He talked to me', he said, 'and directed me to the way of mercy, which greatly relieved me of my heavy burden . . .'.[22] Queen Kapeolani of Hawaii who had been converted by Taua of Huahine was heard to utter the following distressing soliloquy:

> O the punishments of wicked men! They will cry for water; O yes; they will cry for water; but there will be no water, none at all, not even a drop for their tongues.[23]

Puna, the missionary to Rurutu, exhorted: 'Should you not listen to that word you will die, and you will bear the wrath of God, and you will be led by the Evil Spirit, you have now cast away, into the fire of hell . . .'.[24] Many more examples could be quoted. One which suggests the doctrine of reparation operating among the Tahitians is this exhortation by King Tamatoa:

> Remember there were many drowned who helped to build the Ark: do you take care lest you die in your own sins, after sending the Gospel to others; lest you become at last fuel for the fire, as the scaffolding that we use about our houses does. If we are not true believers, God will not regard us. We shall go to the fire of hell.[25]

Of course this 'fear of hell' did not always have its effect. In 1839 when some of the youth of Tahaa were told they were going in the road to everlasting death they replied, 'We know it, but it is very pleasant to live in sin'.[26]

The Wesleyans also emphasized the threat of hell. A young Fijian who recovered from a near-fatal illness at Rewa confessed to the Reverend William Cross.

Before this death which came upon me, I did not think much of the
fire of hell but now I have seen it I thought I was to be cast into it,
but one said to me: 'Go back for a time.'[27]

Cross spoke of those who were committed Christians, 'some
through the fear of hell and the hope of getting to heaven,
others from a sense of duty and from love to God'.[28] Hellfire was
emphasized particularly in Fiji as the missionaries and Tongan
teachers were disturbed by the easy way in which death was
accepted in Fijian society. When a Fijian informed Hazlewood
in 1849 that there was a teacher at Tiliva 'who taught two things,
that there is one God, and a hell of fire' he was no doubt reflecting the principal content of much preliminary teaching.[29]
A demonstrative display of guilt and shame for past sins was
almost obligatory in the Fijian mission, considering the natural
loathing of the missionaries for many of the traditional practices. Thus the conversion of the young chief Buli i Taulaubua
proved a spectacular affair. After the missionary left the chapel
he 'was deeply convinced of sin' and 'roared out and struggled
so that he could not be held'.[30] The missionary read, talked and
prayed with him for several hours. Some days afterwards he
fainted in the missionary's house. Later, at midnight, he went
to the house of a chiefly friend who was still a heathen. He
'roared and woke up the chief and his wife, and fell down and
kicked and tore the fence and fainted'. After being revived he
attempted to talk his friend into 'lotuing'.

Methodism had evolved, or rather perfected, a technique which
in some measure counteracted the Laodicean tendencies associated with the 'parish' type church. This was revivalism, which
played an important role in the ecclesiastical history of the South
Seas. Although it was inseparably linked with the Wesleyan
missions, it became a feature of the missions of the LMS. It
never developed to any great extent in Tahiti and the groups to
eastward, although examples can be cited, but it developed in a
typically Methodist fashion in the LMS missions in Samoa,
particularly on the island of Tutuila. Evangelical religion, by its
very nature, contained a fair measure of enthusiasm or holy zeal.
The revival was more than a mere manifestation of holy zeal.
It was held to be the pentecostal visitation of the Holy Spirit; it
was a form of religious crowd hysteria. Revivals have occurred
throughout the history of the Christian Church. Some theologians
have maintained that they are essential to true Christianity,
whilst a great many Christians have frowned upon them as

exhibitions of emotionalism. However they may be interpreted, revivals can be explained in part by the accustomed laws of behaviour.*

Although Methodism perfected the technique of revivalism, some of the first revivals in the history of Christian missions occurred under the preaching of Calvinist missionaries, the most notable examples being those amongst the American Indians in response to the preaching of David Brainerd.[31] In the South Seas the Calvinist missionaries tended to be wary of any movement which savoured too much of enthusiasm. To the Calvinist the visitation of grace was always a much more rare and individual act than it was to the Wesleyan. The Calvinist was more often visited with grace on the lonely road to Damascus. The Wesleyan received it in a more communal, less intimate way, whilst rubbing shoulders with his neighbours. In Samoa the LMS missionaries tended to be apologetic when referring to the mass movement. They presented the evidence for the world to draw conclusions. The Wesleyan revivals were readily accepted. They did not have to cater for the rationalistic Dissenting tradition of the Calvinists. As Methodists, purely and entirely, they accepted revivalism as an essential feature of their religion.

It must not be imagined, however, that there were no critics of the phenomenon of revivalism within Evangelical circles at home. The Reverend William Brown, a doctor of medicine and a missionary secretary, did not fully accept the explanations of the revivals in the Pacific. Of the 'Awakening' on Tutuila, which Lundie described in his *Missionary Life in Samoa,* he had this to say:

> Of such scenes, we confess, we are exceedingly jealous; but it would be rash to express any unfavourable opinion of them. Amidst something that was human, there might be also something that was divine; but how much there might be of the one or the other, we presume not to judge.[32]

He was more critical of the Wesleyan revivals.

> In judging of what are commonly called revivals of religion, we apprehend that great caution is necessary, more than is commonly shewn both by those who doubt or reject them. We are not prepared to pronounce an opinion in regard to the religious movement in the Friendly Islands . . . , but yet we cannot help feeling great jealousy of it. Even supposing it to be, to some extent, a work of divine grace,

*Religious revivals have been analysed by social historians and psychologists. In most instances revivals take their character from the personality of the revivalist who is frequently emotionally unstable. The relationship between religious hysteria and the sex instinct has also been demonstrated.

we fear that the missionaries greatly over-estimated their success, and that they spoke much too confidently both as to the numbers converted, and as to the nature and truth of their religious experience. The work appears to have essentially resembled those movements which have not infrequently taken place among the Methodists both in England and America, and which they are accustomed to speak of as the work of God, though much of it is probably nothing more than the excitement of the imagination and the passions acting on numbers by means of sympathy, without being followed by any change of heart and life.[33]

It was even more significant when such criticism came from the Wesleyans themselves. Walter Lawry, as we have seen (page 91), was quite a competent revivalist. However he was a keen observer, and regarded the glowing reports from the field with some degree of cynicism, possibly the more so because he was familiar with the native responses. When Lawry visited the Tongan district in 1847 he showed that he was quite out of sympathy with the revivalists. Peter Turner complained of Lawry's 'bitterness' towards him, and of his innuendos about the revival at Vava'u in 1846.

He complained of what he called unholy excitement — getting up a revival — long meetings extravigences, and all the objections which are generally brot. by those who hate or disapprove of any uncommon religious movement in any place.[34]

Much has to be taken into account in examining the revivals in Polynesia. We should expect to find features inherent in the various island societies which would be conducive to mass movements in religion of a demonstrative nature. Most of the island communities were small and well-integrated. The emphasis was on conformity rather than on individual choice. If the order of the day was enthusiastic conversion, then all were expected to conform. Religion in the islands was regarded very much as a public thing, whereas European religion usually emphasized the role of private devotion. Furthermore most Polynesians were familiar with religious experience of a demonstrative nature. Possession by supernatural agencies was widely attested, and some of the externals of possession bore a close resemblance to the physical manifestations of revivalism. It was also asserted from the beginning of the nineteenth century that the Polynesian religions emphasized the need for sacrifice for sin, and certainly this much is true, that there was a religious notion prevalent in the islands that gods or ancestors could be placated by sacrifice. Not only were offerings of first fruits made, but in some instances a human sacrifice was demanded. The missionaries asserted that the doctrine of the atonement fitted into this scheme of things, and their converts appreciated the idea of a willing sacrifice by the god himself through love to his people. A gifted preacher was able to 'melt the heart' by means of preaching this doctrine of the cross.

In some of the island groups reactions from Evangelical Christianity took place which resembled the revivals in that they were characterized by spirit possession. Reactions appear to have been more marked in the Society Islands and Hawaii than in any of the other areas. The reactionaries were usually those who had been punished by civil law, or put out of the church for moral offences, and they invariably resorted to traditional practices as an assertion of their hostility. The *Mamaia* heresy in Tahiti and the *Hulumanu* movement in Hawaii, besides the later Hauhau movement amongst the Maoris in New Zealand, were more subtle and organized forms of this reaction.* It may be significant that these movements arose not only in areas where Calvinist doctrine was imparted, but where the church bore a more exclusive character.

It was difficult for the Polynesians to understand the more mystical experience which the missionaries claimed to have themselves, and naturally they brought their own concepts of the 'spirit world' to their assistance. Usually the chronology of the scriptures was beyond the comprehension of the islanders, and it is probable that they accepted scriptural accounts of miracles in a more immediate and contemporary sense. Quite possibly the intuitive demands of the *Mamaia* prophet Teao were as real to him as any of the visionary experiences about which he had read in the scriptures, and he was noted for his great reading.[35] Whereas the missionaries had endeavoured to foster a type of religious experience which was pietistic in nature, their converts sought for more visionary and mystical experiences. Hunt mentioned how revival experience was often of a visionary nature,[36] and Peter Turner made the same observation. During the first revival at Vava'u he remarked that some of the people wanted to tell him about the views they had of heaven and Christ while in a state of unconsciousness. The missionaries discouraged such accounts 'as tending to lead their weak minds astray'.[37] But the people claimed visions of heaven when quite uninfluenced by revivalism. Charter of Raiatea records the case of Terematai who

---

*The Siovili cult in Samoa (see above p. 169), although it may have derived in part from the *Mamaia* heresy, must be viewed in a different light as it developed simultaneously with Christianity in Samoa.

had been almost insensible for two or three days. When she came to herself she said:

> ['] I have been to heaven. I saw Mr and Mrs Williams and a number of Raiateans there and I wished to remain but God sent me back to exhort my family that they may be saved. ['] She was in a very happy state of mind and appeared wholly absorbed in spiritual subjects.[38]

The greatest incentive to revivals came from the individual missionary preachers. The chief 'means' in the process of 'baptism by fire' was the prayer-meeting, as long hours at prayer usually effected the desired state. Peter Turner even conducted prayer-meetings throughout the night.

Although it was never actually acknowledged, revivalism had become an established theological science. An observant minister, given the psychological requirements, could educate himself to be a successful revivalist. The number of 'text-books' on the subject written by experienced revivalists is significant. These ranged from Gillies' *Historical Collections* (first published in 1754 but republished by Horatius Bonar of Kelso in 1845 and also serialized in the *Methodist Magazine*) and the writings of Jonathan Edwards and John Wesley to the nineteenth century works of the great American revivalists Edward Payson, William Buell Sprague and Charles Grandison Finney, all of which were widely read by the missionaries. Finney's *Revivals of Religion* was a classic of its kind and ran through numerous editions, the first of which was published in New York in 1835. Finney had some direct influence on the South Seas as his disciple, Titus Coan of Hilo, was the revivalist of Hawaii.[39] Several of the missionaries record their indebtedness to Finney, notably L. H. Gulick of Micronesia, John Jones of Mare, R. B. Lyth of Fiji and the revivalist Peter Turner.[40]

It has been shown that a revivalist always precedes a revival, and sometimes the individual history of the revivalist is significant (see page 227). It seems reasonable to assume that those who had themselves experienced dramatic conversions were less likely to be disciplined in their psychological attitudes. Sufficient evidence of a psychologically impelling nature might be deduced from the doctrine of reparation to account for the approach taken by the revivalist (see page 49).

Archibald Wright Murray was an extraordinarily interesting figure. His zeal seemed limitless. Brought up for a time by his grandmother, who was a niece of the explorer Mungo Park,[41] Murray was early familiar with the adventures of his illustrious relative, and doubtless wished to emulate him. As we have seen,

Murray had spent part of his young manhood in the intensely Evangelical atmosphere of Kelso. In this town he had been familiar with the circle of Mrs Lundie Duncan, the author of *The History of Revivals*.[42]

Murray fostered intense religious application amongst his flock in Samoa. Long periods of prayer were encouraged. It is also significant that, although the revival broke out in different places at the same time, there were young men present who had attended Murray's sermon on the previous Sabbath. Murray appears to have selected a band of disciples whom he trained in rigorous revival discipline. One young Samoan named Lazereti lived with the Murrays. Murray said that he 'hardly ever knew an individual whose prayers were so characterized by fervour, contrition and earnestness'.[43] 'He is altogether a very exemplary character, and has been, I believe, to a considerable extent instrumental, in bringing about the great awakening in our family.' It was the awakening in 'the family' that preceded the general revival.

Murray claimed that another young Samoan was 'seized with deep concern', whilst at the village of Nu'u'uli, at the same time that the movement began at Pago Pago, about a mile away.

> He was quite ignorant of what was going on here, having left this early on the morning of the day when the awakening began; — this was on *Monday*. He had been present at the *Sabbath* services. He describes himself as having been greatly surprised when he came here and found so many similarly effected with himself.[44]

Surely it was Murray's Sabbath sermons which ignited the revival which had been in preparation for some time. The prevalence of disease and the high death rate undoubtedly gave the revivalist's appeals more meaning to the people.

One of the first fruits of the Tutuila mission was the young chief, Pomale. When Pomale and others went as missionaries to the New Hebrides at the time of the revival Murray wrote of the painful parting with those to whom his 'bowels yearned'. There may also be some psychological significance in the fact that the 'lightest and giddiest' were the ones to be most affected amongst the people generally.[45] The element of 'compulsion' which Murray observed, and assigned to a divine cause, may well have been a compulsion of a more sociological nature.

It is of particular interest that revivals occurred throughout Evangelical Polynesia. They were just as widely spread as nativist heresy movements, and some features were common to both. The principal revivals in Polynesia occurred between 1830 and

1850. A revival began at Vava'u in the Tongan group in July
1834, spreading to Ha'apai and Tongatapu, and lasting till 1835.
In September 1835 a revival was reported in the Society Islands,
but it seems to have been no more than a swelling of church
congregations by legal means, coinciding with the decline of the
Mamaia sect and the beginnings of the temperance movement.
In 1834 Buzacott reported a 'spirit of religious excitement' at
Rarotonga.[46] The 'Great Revival' of Hawaii took place in 1838
and 1839. In November 1839 a revival took place on Tutuila
which lasted till 1842. The missionaries supposed a connexion
with the Scottish revivals at Jedburgh, Kelso, Perth and Dundee
at the same time. In 1845 a revival took place at Viwa and Ono
in the Fijian group, and in the following year another took
place at Vava'u. In 1851 there was one at Rarotonga that was
attended by a minimum of physical excitement. Krause reported
another in 1860.[47]

The revivals in the South Seas all followed similar patterns.
Even many of the Society Island churches manifested revivalistic
features more usually associated with Wesleyan missions. As
early as February 1820 William Henry and Platt wrote from
Moorea that at the communion service on the first Sabbath in
January there had been 'few dry eyes' amongst the forty-three
church members. 'Some wept aloud, and some were so agitated
that they could scarcely get the cup to their mouths. Yea, we had
literally to assist some lest it should be spilt through their
trembling.'[48] However, most of the LMS missionaries in the
eastern groups had a little too much austerity and a little too
much cynicism to be good revivalists. Orsmond suggests that if he
had been less cynical he could have organized a revival.

> If high sounding expressions of grief and pain for sin, and high toned
> declarations of experience be needful as a proof of sincere love to
> God we have them not as yet. It is however a thing perfectly within
> our reach. There is no form of expression that is applicable to
> Christian experience that I could not put into the mouth of the
> people, but I prefer to witness the work of God, the Holy Ghost
> develope itself etc.[49]

The period of revival began at Utui, Vava'u, on 25 July 1834,
under the ministry of Peter Turner. It was characteristic of such
movements that the first manifestation was reported at a nearby
out-station, as if to draw attention away from the revivalist himself. Isaiah Vovole, the Tongan local preacher, preached from
Luke xix, 41-42. 'As he preached he was much affected and the
Holy Spirit came down upon him and on the people — he wept

and the people wept.'[50] That Turner was able to stimulate a revival is not surprising when we examine his journal. For months beforehand he records his longings and strivings for a revival.

2 October 1832	Still I am longing to see a glorious revival among this people, when the word shall be attended with greater displays of saving power.
17 June 1833	We are too formal, too dead. The natives do not pray for a revival as they should; Poor things they have not seen an outpouring of the Holy Spirit.
1 September 1833	I hope the revival is not far distant.[51]

On 27 June 1834 Joel Bulu was 'powerfully wrought upon' at a love-feast or testimony meeting. He 'wept aloud and fell exhausted to the floor'. Whilst in this swoon the Tongan preacher thought that 'a great light shone about him'. This was the prelude to the revival, and it shows the direction of all the preaching and teaching. Turner explained to the people that such emotional demonstrations were what he had seen in England, and that this was what they had all been praying for. In the chapels the people became as 'dead persons'. They 'swooned away by complete exhaustion of body and the overwhelming manifestation of saving power'.[52] Scores were carried out of the various chapels. Schools had to be suspended. On 29 July 1834 Turner wrote jubilantly that 'more than 1000 souls' had been saved within the preceding five days.

The fire of the great revival spread rapidly. James Watkin, then at Lifuka, greeted the news with enthusiasm.

> The account corresponds with some we have of ancient methodism and of the American revivals. O that the fire may come southward in all its plenitude and power . . . We are expecting the descent of the Holy Spirit.[53]

The revival began suddenly, and all the mission party were affected besides the people. All were in tears, 'men, strong and bold men became as little children, they could not pray for groans and sobs'. Prayer meetings were held, and very few were unaffected. Watkin found difficulty in persuading the people to leave the chapel at night. On the Sabbath it was impossible to preach, so prayer meetings were held. Similar scenes took place at the out-stations. Watkin found difficulty in writing up his journal. 'I am too much exhausted', he wrote, adding at the same time, 'O Jesus ride on'.

Chiefs are not ashamed to be seen weeping for their sins. We are not without noise but we have no confusion . . . the blind and lame and some who are far from well crawl to the chapel that they may receive the blessing of forgiveness and a new nature.[54]

For weeks no business could be attended to.

In the case of Ha'apai the influence of King George Tupou cannot be ignored. Moreover he sent messengers from Vava'u where he had participated in the revival himself.[55] From Watkin's vivid description of the revival, and his own admission, it appears that he felt that the 'latter day glory' was at hand.

The revival at Tutuila began almost simultaneously at three places near and including Pago Pago.[56] Much prayer had preceded the emotional manifestations at each place. At Pago the revival actually commenced in Murray's house during evening prayers, and the place became 'a very Bochim'. Murray's description suggests the emotionally charged atmosphere of the time:

> A cloud seemed as if it was hovering over us, charged with blessings, which seemed daily to thicken, while some few first drops here and there descending, till it actually burst and came down upon us, with a largeness and fullness, which equally surprised and delighted us; and, blessed be God, our cloud is not yet exhausted, but continues from day to day, to descend upon us 'like rain upon the mown grass and as showers that water the earth'.[57]

In June 1840 the awakening seemed to be at its peak. At Leone, on 8 June, it seemed to Murray that 'the Spirit descended like a rushing mighty wind and filled the place'.[58] Thomas Slatyer arrived at Tutuila in the midst of the revival, and was at Leone when it broke out there in full force. On 28 June he wrote,

> I have not seen more feeling amongst the men, — the preacher himself too tho' of a decidedly phlegmatic temperament was almost prevented from proceeding through the fullness of his heart . . .[59]

On 31 August 1840, after a period of 'retrogression', revivalism was again excited at Leone. Some were 'taken out in violent convulsions as when the awakening first began — some were carried out less convulsed or not at all but overcome with feeling and some rushed out as quickly as they could to give vent to their feelings'.[60] During some services the missionary was forced to wait for over a quarter of an hour before he could make himself heard.[61]

The revival at Tutuila also spread to Harbutt's district on Upolu. Harbutt was highly sceptical of the faintings, hysterics and violent weeping, but he was satisfied by the sentiments expressed by those affected. However he did not know whether it was 'really the work of God or whether having heard of the work in Tutuila they consider it necessary to imitate'.[62]

Descriptions of the Fijian revivals display even more violent features of emotionalism. Watsford gave an account of the revival at Viwa in a letter to the secretaries.

> The joy of those who were pardoned was as great as their distress had been. They danced and shouted aloud for joy. One man was so happy and danced at such a rate, that we thought it well to hold him, and spoke to four or five men to do so; but he shook them off with the greatest ease, and went dancing away, and shouting, 'My heart is on fire, and my soul is burning.'[63]

At the conclusion of a similar account Hunt remarked that when the congregation chanted the *Te Deum,* and came to such passages as 'Thou art the King of Glory O Christ', some of them would clap their hands and shout for joy.[64] But Hunt was aware of the other phenomena which accompanied these revivals.

> Some had remarkable dreams, and others what almost amounted to visions, indeed the excitement was exceeding great, and some strange, useless and dangerous things could not but take place. It always was so in revivals.[65]

About the same time Peter Turner was working for another revival at Vava'u.[66] He held lengthy prayer meetings, and felt at the end of 1844 that the atmosphere was similar to the commencement of the previous revival. However it did not commence until 21 January 1845. On the evening of that day the chiefs of Neiafu and the head teachers of the stations in the circuit were in Turner's study taking tea together. They were all affected.

> God did indeed baptize us with the holy light and with fire. One proposed that we should take the lights and proceed to the Chapel forth with that others might catch the divine influence.

The meeting grew. Some of the women followed Turner back from the chapel to the study, and 'God blessed them in an uncommon manner'. The meeting continued till daybreak. The native drum was then struck, and the people assembled in the chapel for prayer. All cried out 'for mercy'. The meeting lasted for two hours and was followed by an infant school feast. This was followed by another prayer meeting. The fervour of revival was Turner's supreme joy! 'I am now in my element and in this work would I live and die.' During the revival physical gymnastics were even more prevalent than during the first revival. Turner wrote that the 'effects on some were very strange — Their bodies were greatly affected, some swooned away — while others were almost frantic — and violent'. No one could doubt that 1 March was a 'glorious day'.

> In the prayer-meeting in the evening the young men were so power-fully wrought upon as to make it almost impossible to keep them within bounds. They tore up the fence round the pulpit in their agony of mind. They seemed quite unconscious of what they were doing.

Indeed, throughout the revival no work was done, prayer meetings were almost continuous and the people became 'quite exhausted and almost spent out'. For several months all the meetings were scenes of much weeping and demonstration.

Thus it may be seen that revivals were largely organized religious movements, and depended on a revivalist. Where they occurred in the South Seas the missionary was invariably a revivalist preacher, who, like Jonathan Edwards, Whitefield or Wesley, or his own contemporaries Sprague and Finney, could instruct, discipline and stimulate a given audience into a revival fervour. These missionaries had either studied the writings of the great revivalists and emulated their preaching styles and their type of sermon, or they had actually participated in revivals themselves. Religious revivals were also very well suited to a church which was coterminous with the community. For a people who had taken the first step together, by making a *public* profession of faith, it was appropriate to have the opportunity of being converted together.

12

Teachers and Healers

EARLY MISSION WORK consisted mainly in collecting groups of people together and preaching to them, in having conversation with them in public meetings, and in giving them some form of catechetical instruction, so that they would know the form even if they were unable to feel the spiritual experience of religious worship. Apart from occasional journeys, tours lasting from a few days to over a month, the missionary's life was restricted by routine, of which the regularity was seldom broken. All the missionaries had secular teaching duties during the week and also taught in the Sabbath schools. One morning each week was usually devoted to medical or dispensary work. The LMS missionaries usually held Monday church meetings, mid-week services and Friday 'conversational' meetings, besides several services on the Sabbath. The Wesleyans held love-feasts and class meetings during week nights, and several Sabbath services. The short terms of residence of many of the Evangelical missionaries, in contrast to those of Catholic missionaries, affected the proficiency of teaching, translating and preaching; and, consequently, the actual effective work of the missions was largely that of those men who gave longest service.

Lesson, the French voyager, attempted to denigrate the educational work of missionaries.[1] He argued that the South Sea islander had more knowledge of poetry, cosmogony and religion, more dexterity in gymnastics and more skill than the peasants of France had ever had. The missionaries, however, were not concerned with non-Christian civilizations. They saw nothing of the presence of God in the pagan systems, and they tended to associate the externals of worship of the islanders with the 'superstitions of Popery'. They believed that the 'means of instruction' were necessary to enable the people to read the Bible for themselves. Study of the Bible inevitably led to the study of other subjects, such as geography and history. Training in the 'three Rs' was also another means to civilization. Primary education had played an important part in the home missionary labours of the Evangelicals, and week day schools, besides Sabbath schools, were sponsored by the various Evangelical churches. Because of this interest the Evangelicals were in the forefront of educational method, and the various theories of the leading educationalists were usually first put into practice in the Evangelical schools. The monitorial system first developed by Joseph Lancaster and Dr Andrew Bell, and promoted by the British and Foreign School Society and the National School Society respectively, was introduced into the islands very shortly after this system had first been promulgated.

Bell's mutual instruction or Madras system of education, evolved in 1789, encouraged pupils to do as much as possible for themselves, under the teacher's direction.[2] Lancaster's similar system involved mutual instruction by children trained as monitors, under the teacher's supervision. His system, like the Sabbath schools of Robert Raikes and the ragged schools of Rowland Hill, was designed particularly for poor children.[3] One of his early pupils was the Tahitian, 'Tapeoe', who returned to the islands with Bicknell in 1810.[4]

In the Society Islands the works of both Bell and Lancaster appear to have been used, although in published reports only the Lancastrian system was mentioned, no doubt out of courtesy to the Dissenting churches, who patronized that system in connexion with the British and Foreign School Society. Besides relying on monitors, the Lancastrian system also depended on means such as slates, globes, alphabet wheels, and other aids which the missionaries were sometimes at a loss to procure. As a result this system could sometimes be only partially adopted, although substitute means were often found.

The first missionaries may not have been very well educated, but they could read their Bibles and spell well enough to convey meaning. They had acquired the rudiments of Sabbath school education and would have qualified as Sabbath school teachers in England. The directors regarded them as being fully capable. 'There is one branch of duty', they wrote to those missionaries who arrived in Sydney from Tahiti in 1798, '. . . the discharge of which we hope most of you are qualified, and which is equally incumbent on the preacher and on the lay brother; we refer to the education and religious instruction of the children both of convicts and the poor colonists and of as many of the native heathens as you can procure and attend to'.[5] Cover, Henry, Harris, Hassall, Crook, Davies, Youl, Shelley and Eyre all at some time taught in schools in New South Wales.

The first mission school in the islands was that conducted by John Davies at Matavai in Tahiti. Davies, who had graduated from the circulating schools of Madam Bevan to be a teacher in the service of Thomas Charles of Bala, was trained to old methods. However, he took upon himself the credit for having introduced at least one of the new teaching aids on his own initiative.

> Writing in sand I had partly in use, before I ever heard of Bell or Lancaster or their plans. I had heard of the Bengalese writing on the ground, and many years ago . . . at Matavai, I used to amuse the late King Pomare in writing with him on the sandy beach, under the shade of a tree.[6]

In his report for April 1808 Davies said that he had a daily attendance averaging between fifteen and twenty-four. On Sabbath evenings about thirty attended catechism exercises. Several persons had been reading 'for some time', and would have made good progress in writing, but at that time there was no paper for them to practise on. However most of his pupils could spell 'pretty well'. His pupils were mostly boys between the ages of twelve and eighteen.[7] Most of these youths had been mission servants, and it was from them that the first converts were drawn, before Christianity was adopted as the national religion by Pomare II.

Although the school had to be abandoned when most of the missionaries withdrew to New South Wales, many of Davies' pupils were able to pass on some of their knowledge. When Davies resumed his school teaching in 1812 he introduced the system of mutual instruction and writing on the sand. In the ensuing years he lamented that he could not follow the whole of the plan 'for want of slates, proper lessons, the irregularity of attendance'.[8] Davies' knowledge of the Lancastrian system was doubtless somewhat limited, although he would have learned about its practical application from W. P. Crook, who was at that time his bosom friend. Crook had introduced the system into his academy at Sydney.

In 1820 Gyles reported to the directors that some of the missionaries continued to instruct in the 'old way', although Crook pursued 'Bell's system'.[9] In 1821 Barff of Huahine reported that they followed the Lancastrian plans as nearly as they could.[10] However, as they had an 'abundance of teachers', they had no need to adopt some of Lancaster's recommendations. On the other hand, Platt wrote in 1822 from Moorea that they wished to make an attempt 'on the Lancastrian or British system', but they had no means. They contrived to teach the people to read and spell 'in the old way' which, in part, was to write on the sand. He required an alphabet wheel and slates. 'The adults must continue to be taught on the old plan, as they could not be brought to the system.'[11] In 1824 Orsmond wrote that he wished they had lessons prepared and adapted to the 'Foreign and British school's' mode of instruction.[12]

The directors sought for some uniformity in the means of instruction, and accordingly required their missionaries to conduct their schools on the plan of the British and Foreign School Society. Orsmond replied that such was to be desired, but that none of the missionaries 'perfectly comprehended the plan'. He suggested that a teaching assistant should be sent out.[13] Davies took occasion to remind the directors that the plan had been 'partly adopted' in many of the schools for upwards of fourteen years.[14]

Possibly the most indefatigable educationalist in the first thirty years of missionary activity was W. P. Crook. Most of his experience had been obtained in New South Wales where he and his wife established the first boarding school in Australia at Parramatta and undertook to teach the children 'to read, speak, and write the English Tongue with accuracy and propriety, Bookkeeping, Geometry, Trigonometry, and Mensuration, practically applied in Navigation, Surveying, Gauging, &c.'[15] Crook also undertook 'to store their minds with a general knowledge of Geography, History and Astronomy making every part of Education as pleasing as possible'. In 1811 his school, which had been moved to Sydney, was remodelled on the Lancastrian plan. His homely philosophy of education was thus outlined:

> Education is to mankind what culture is to vegetables, if this is neglected the Garden is overrun with noxious weeds; if that is forgotten the manners of men degenerate into vice and profaneness. As far, therefore, as the reasonable creature excels the vegetable, so far does education surpass agriculture. Shall a man, therefore, attend with the utmost diligence to the improvement of his ground, and neglect this far more important concern, the instruction of his offspring?[16]

Despite his ideals he had declined taking charge of the Orphan School

> because it seemed impossible as matters then were to rectify the dreadful abuses of that institution: the far greater part of the female orphans when they left the school turning out prostitutes and many there is just ground to conclude were little better while in the school.[17]

In the islands he had less choice regarding his pupils.

In 1824 he had, at his station of Bogue Town on Tahiti, an adult school for women comprising four classes, two of which were taught by his daughters Mary and Hannah. There was also a men's school of five classes, and a children's school. His daughters took five classes of girls and he took the boys, assisted by his son and another missionary youth.[18]

In 1829 Orsmond was still bewailing the fact that little assistance was being given to promote the cherished plan. He requested the Society to send them supplies of slates and pencils, with books on their system, and 'to print a large supply of their reading papers which have been translated by J.M.O.', and several other elementary books. He further praised 'the suitableness and expediency of the British system of education among these people'.[19] Just how accurate Orsmond's assessment of the educational position at this time was it is not easy to say, and it certainly did not apply to every missionary.

> All of us have been wickedly slothful in the schools $1\frac{1}{2}$ hours in each day seems almost more than some can spare . . . The present general mode of adult teaching is highly injudicious . . . The youths are growing up like organ pipes, they make signs but they do not generally know how to put 2 letters together . . . The foreign and British mode of teaching should be extensively used and introduced into all the Islands of these Seas.[20]

Orsmond, although perhaps not justified in abusing his colleagues thus, was deeply concerned with the educational problem because of his own position as tutor to the missionaries' children.

It was not easy to get the young Tahitians to attend school, and youths were always running off to join the 'wild young men' in the mountains. Even the more promising scholars preferred the wreath of faded leaves, the badge of the *tutae auri,* to the laurels of scholarship. In the mountain forest, away from the discipline of the stations, sexual license and intemperance carried no moral stigma. Besides, it might be all right for Orsmond and his kind to punish their own sons, but no islander would endure such an indignity. In cases of severe discipline punishment was consigned to the judges. When some of Crook's scholars tattooed themselves, he 'prevailed' on the judges not to send them to labour on the road 'with those who will not fail to make them worse', but to bring them to the school and punish them with a dozen lashes with a cat-o'-nine tails. The punishment was inflicted by the teachers, some of whom were judges.[21] The missionaries usually resorted to some form of confinement for ordinary class misdemeanours. When compulsory education was introduced the chiefs exercised a greater degree of disciplinary power. Orsmond was not very happy with the system.

Chiefs and others make laws to enforce the attendance on schools, the[y] make stocks into which to put the feet of delinquents, i.e. those who do not learn and who will not attend worship yet all is ineffectual.[22]

Infant schools were first introduced in the South Seas following their success in South Africa. Buzacott wrote in 1833 that he was much interested in Dr Philip's account of their progress in Africa, and wished that they could adopt something of the kind.[23] John Williams felt the need for more efficient training of the very young, and regretted that none of the missionaries who went out in 1838 knew anything of the system. At Capetown he was 'very anxious to procure a nice youth about 14 years of age who has just been received by the Infant School Committee as a Master'.[24] He was, however, dissuaded from engaging him by Dr Philip. Williams maintained that training in the infant school system was preferable to training received in a theological college. At the time of Williams' visit to the Cape three of the sons of James Buchanan, one of the founders of the English infant school system, were engaged in infant school teaching.[25] One of the sons, Ebenezer, responded to Williams' appeal and was engaged for five years 'to introduce the system into all our stations'.[26] His experience in teaching both European and native children and his familiarity with his father's teaching methods were of great benefit to the mission.

On the voyage to the islands Buchanan instructed the Royles in the system, so that when they arrived at Rarotonga they were able to assist Buzacott in establishing an infant school.[27] Buchanan began a very intensive programme at Falealili, in Samoa, where he conducted five schools each day. He gave his teaching instruction in English in the afternoons for two months. He was also employed in making 'arithmeticians' and lesson boards for the use of the schools. During his first year twelve schools were established on Upolu and about twelve on Savai'i.[28] He continued his duties of training infant school teachers and opening schools in Samoa until 1841 when he removed to Tahiti.

The infant school system had preceded Buchanan to Tahiti about 1839, when it was introduced by George Pritchard at Papeete.[29] When Buchanan arrived in 1841 he was expected to replace Johnston, the only other teacher in the mission, who had to go to New South Wales. Johnston had conducted a boys' boarding school at Papara since 1839, and Buchanan was not particularly suited to the kind of work involved. However he continued to foster interest in infant schools, despite the cool reception accorded him by older missionaries such as Davies.

Such schools, patterned closely on the English model, were introduced at Papara and at Orsmond's station at Teahupo.[30] Teaching in the infant schools was work particularly suited to the
adult daughters of the missionaries. A knowledge of Tahitian
was necessary, as the rhymes were recited in the vernacular, and
English was also taught. Isabella and Mary Orsmond conducted
a school with more than fifty children attending.[31] Darling's
daughter also used the system at Punaauia.

Buchanan's career is of particular interest as it shows the difficulties facing an educationalist when confronted by island conditions. The boarding school at Papara was for the sons of chiefs
and 'youths of talent and piety'. It was also open to mixed-blood
boys whose parents wished to send them. English was given
special study.[32] Johnston had considerable difficulty in managing
this school, especially in regard to discipline, and Buchanan had
to face the same difficulties. The thing which most appalled
Buchanan was the apparent obscenity of much of the conversation and gestures of the Tahitian youth. Because of his background and his limited understanding of the Polynesian way of
life, Buchanan could not but fail to understand the full extent
of the moral problem involved. Perhaps of all the missionaries,
only Orsmond realized that the Polynesians could be made to
conform to another set of standards in public for a time, but
that they would still accept the old pattern of behaviour as normal. Buchanan dealt with the problem as if it was something
which could be suppressed by schoolroom discipline. For a time
he believed that he had effectually 'banished obscene gestures
and much of filthy conversation' from the school and playground.
However the number of his scholars was greatly increased by the
law requiring parents to send children to school.[33] He complained that the children and young people attended the public
trials where 'cases of the most disgusting nature and impure
tendency' were examined, and attributed the behaviour of the
new boys to witnessing these trials.[34]

Buchanan next moved to Papeete, where he conducted a
'flourishing Infant and day school', but he regretted that there
were no eligible young men to train as teachers. In August 1844
he returned to Samoa, and trained twelve young men in the
Normal School at Saluafata in a course of reading, writing, arithmetic, astronomy, scripture and natural history.[35] He made
counting frames, blackboards and maps and other aids to teaching. Whilst Mills was in England, Buchanan conducted a Normal
School, a boarding school, and an infant and day school at Apia,
where he was assisted by Pritchard, who was then British consul

in Samoa. Pritchard, of course, was thoroughly acquainted with the infant school system.[36] After 1848 Buchanan's position was not a very satisfactory one. The missionaries who conducted the institution at Malua for giving theological training to Samoan teachers tended to be rather jealous of his separate institution. Others complained that the teachers Buchanan had trained would not obey orders. Petty charges were brought against him, his institution was no longer considered necessary, and he was left without a station or occupation. Although it was intended that he should join the staff at Malua, he decided to leave the mission and return to England. With Buchanan's departure, educational work in the LMS missions once again came under the more exclusive control of the ordained missionaries.

By the time the Wesleyan missionaries took a specialized interest in the means of instruction, the systems of Bell and Lancaster had in many ways been replaced by those of other educationalists, particularly that of David Stow of Glasgow. Stow's school system combined monitorial methods with the object teaching of Pestalozzi, while considerable emphasis was placed on the Bible and 'moral training'. Stow did not believe in prizes and corporal punishment but stimulated or rebuked pupils 'by sympathy of numbers' or the public opinion of the school. As we have already seen, the Wesleyan teachers were sent to Stow's 'normal seminary' at Glasgow in order to be trained by him (see page 86). After this policy was adopted in 1839 it was not long before the Glasgow system was introduced into all the distant fields of Methodism. When Amos returned to England from Sierra Leone in 1845 the WMMS sent him at their own expense, to Stow's Training Institution, after which he was appointed as superintendent of the mission schools in the Friendly Islands. He was expected to 'teach the Glasgow System to the Native Teachers and Children in these Islands', and 'to take charge of the Educational Department'. He was also to teach English to the trained teachers and 'perhaps a few children'.[37] Amos was allowed the same salary and privileges as a regular missionary, but the teachers could only be selected by the other missionaries. At the other Tongan stations, attempts were made to introduce the system. In May 1851 Peter Turner of Vava'u wrote in his journal that he was reading Stow's *Training System,* and was quite discouraged 'as we seem to come so far short'. 'We cannot carry out the System', he wrote, 'for want of better school houses, an open school or a playground'.[38]

When the Reverend Robert Young arrived on his deputational visit to Tonga in 1853, he seemed to be satisfied with the state of education.[39] Not fewer than 8,000 could read the scriptures 'with more or less ability', and about 5,000 could write. Writing was taught on slates in the schools. Arithmetic, geography, and 'some other branches of learning' were also taught. The principal disadvantage was that the teachers received no salary. Amos appealed for an educational grant from the Society, because the men repeatedly said that they could not teach so many schools, and work for their families besides.

The Glasgow system was also introduced into Fiji by the appointment of two qualified teachers of the system, or 'training masters' as they were known. These two men, Binner and Collis, appear to have been fairly successful. Collis was stationed at Lakeba, and had already made considerable progress when Young arrived. At that time he was instructing about 400 scholars under 'a modification of the Glasgow system'. The subjects included scripture knowledge, reading, writing, spelling, arithmetic, geography and singing, 'with some hints of Natural History'.[40] Similar methods were used in teaching a class of young men composed of teachers and trainees. Young reported favourably of the experiment, and was pleased to find so many who already possessed 'a considerable amount of New Testament knowledge'. Several could read well, and a few could write a good and legible hand, and work sums in simple addition. In 1854 Collis reported that the system was being adopted by the native teachers.[41] Binner conducted his school on the same plan at Levuka, Ovalau. Although the Wesleyans placed much more importance on primary education than they did on secondary education, their schools do not appear to have reached the standard of those at Calvinist stations. However there was definitely a marked improvement following the appointment of the 'training masters'.

Most of the missionaries appreciated the value of giving their converts a basic secular education. Not only did it help the people to read the Bible and understand much of what they read, but it also helped to promote 'civilization'. Nevertheless, the greater emphasis was on the means of religious instruction. Religious instruction was given mostly by the catechetical method. Catechisms had been drawn up and translated very early in the history of the Tahitian mission.[42]

Although the missionaries drew up their own catechisms, they also made use of several standard Evangelical ones. Those of Dr Isaac Watts were popular. Ayliffe's *Catechism on Divine Revelation* and the Westminster Assembly's Shorter Catechism were more standard ones. *Milk for Babes* was a catechism in verse, intended as an introduction to the Assembly's Catechism.[43]

There were also non-scriptural catechisms on geography, grammar and rhetoric. The first Tahitian catechism was sent to England to be printed in 1806. No copies of this survive, but the Catechism printed at Sydney about 1815 consists of 118 questions and answers.[44] Amongst the Wesleyans, James Watkin was an assiduous writer of expository tracts. According to him a short catechism which he had written in 1832 described 'in a vivid or at least novel manner some of the prevailing evils and their consequences'.[45] He gave as examples:

> Who are they who love war? The true sons of the Devil.
> Who are they that seek war? Wild beasts thirsting for blood.
> Who are they who have more wives than 1? Thieves from other men, Sinners against God, and in the high way to destruction.

The catechetical method of instruction had been popular in the early Sabbath schools, and it had been the principal means of instruction in Evangelical homes. Its main disadvantage in the islands was that the people quickly learnt their catechisms, understanding them even less than European children. Often they learnt their lessons by rote without learning to read. When Stevens arrived in Tahiti in 1839 he was appalled that the old system had survived so long. He spoke of remodelling the instruction of children, and hoped that the 'uninteresting and injurious practice of repeating by rote some of the most abstruse doctrinal and experimental chapters in the Scriptures' would be superseded by the 'more useful and rational efforts of teaching the children to read and understand'.[46] If the 'reforming' missionaries of the late 1830s were mistaken in their approach to other problems, their attitude to religious instruction was possibly a wiser one than that of the older brethren.[47]

One of the other chief means of instruction was the dissemination of vernacular literature. In most stations spelling books, catechisms and abstracts of scripture facts were distributed before the missionaries were able to translate the separate books of the Bible. This was a matter of necessity rather than policy. The missionaries felt that actual translations from the scriptures should be as perfect as possible, and therefore they could not be too premature in publishing the Bible.[48] Most of the books which were printed for the people in the vernacular were of a religious character.

The limited range of this literature raised the question of giving some instruction in English. In 1820 it was announced from Tahiti that Hayward was about to 'attempt the introduction of English, by the British system of Education: this will

15 Coral lime chapel with curved thatched roof at
Raiatea; possibly built on rubble from a *marae*.

16 Interior of the Tongan-built chapel at
Lifuka, Ha'apai

17 Rev. George Pratt
translator and authority on
Samoan custom

18 Elijah Armitage
artisan missionary on
Moorea and Rarotonga

19 Rev. Alexander Simpson
missionary on Moorea and a principal of the South Sea Academy

open sources of instruction, which never can be opened to them by their own'.[49] Tyerman and Bennet, however, effectively quashed the experiment, informing the directors in 1823 that they even doubted the *'desirableness'* of such a measure and that they were surprised that any missionary should advocate such a scheme.[50] The Wesleyans also regarded instruction in English as being 'utopian' though they lamented the scarcity of 'mental food'. Samuel Waterhouse wrote in 1853 that their Maori converts in New Zealand only possessed five books: the New Testament, the Psalms, the Prayer Book, a catechism and Robinson Crusoe. 'Is not every thinking people a reading people', he urged.[51]

The missionaries early realized the importance of pictures to convey ideas, and this overcame many of the difficulties of teaching. John Williams wrote in 1821:

> For a serpent their present Idea is a *sea eel,* and for a trumpet a *Conch shell!* Many beautiful passages in Scripture relative to pastoral affairs are utterly lost to them, for want of a mode of conveying Ideas which pictures alone can afford.[52]

Visual aids were a necessary part of every teacher's equipment. Lantern slides, when they were introduced, became a very popular means of instruction.

The Friday evening conversational meetings held at most of the LMS stations were concerned mainly with religious instruction. It is significant that when the new Christians became more sophisticated in their religion these meetings were discouraged. In Tahiti they very frequently developed into political discussion groups, or at least the discussion tended to become secular. In Samoa such meetings were designed more for the promotion of morals. However, Pratt of Matautu, Savai'i, was for a long time suspicious that the 'Friday' was exerting a pernicious influence on the minds of many, by leading them to look with satisfaction on their conduct.[53] He disbanded the meeting and substituted a Bible class. His example was followed by Hardie and Macdonald, all being convinced that 'it tended to obliterate the line of demarcation which should separate the church from the world'.

The view of the missionaries towards education was that it should assist people to read and understand the Bible. Most of them also believed that a religious education not only produced a Christian man, but that it opened all the doorways to civilization. Moreover education was something for which every missionary had a profound respect. To teach all, but especially the young, was one of his principal duties.

The missionaries to the islands were also cognisant of their duty to heal the sick. The word was plain.

> And Jesus went about all the cities and villages, teaching in their synagogues, and preaching the gospel of the Kingdom and healing every sickness and every disease among the people.
> As ye go, preach . . . heal the sick.
> Heal the sick . . . and say unto them, the kingdom of God is come nigh unto you.

However, the strict Calvinists among the first missionaries denied the motive of philanthropy as such and in its place exalted the motive of the glorification of God. In as much as an action was philanthropic it was because it was in obedience to the decree of God. God was glorified by carrying out his commands and by doing good works in his name. However, the conception which the first missionaries had of their vocation did not specifically include ministry to the sick. It was the heathen souls which were in danger of perishing, not the bodies.

When Dr Haweis outlined the advantages which Tahiti possessed as a missionary base, his glowing picture of the island paradise suggests that he had little thought about the ravages of existing disease and the worse ravages of disease yet to be introduced. If he was aware that 'every guilty creature feels the necessity of atonement' he was not aware that the Tahitians were in equal need of sound medical attention.[54]

The attitude taken to disease was a typical projection of Calvinist thought. Disease was an agency of the providence of God, a judgement on the sins of the people and the necessary consequence of their immoral state. Turnbull, in his account of Tahiti in 1803, expresses the prevailing attitude:

> The wickedness is enough to call down the immediate judgement of heaven; and let me not be thought too presumptuous, if I assert that the hand of God is visibly amongst them. Unless their manners change, I pronounce that they will not long remain in the number of nations. The *sword of disease* is no less effectual than the waters of a deluge.[55]

The way to heal this disease was not to apply physical remedies but first to heal the spiritual state of the people, to effect salvation.

But if the missionaries saw disease as a judgement on the people, they regarded the curing of disease as a special means of introducing the Christian gospel. By the analogy of the diseased soul they urged the need for 'the divine physician'. Sickness also could be used to illustrate the nearness of death and the displeasure of God. If many of those cured believed that their cure was due solely to Jehovah-Jesus having greater efficacious powers than their own deities or spirits, the missionaries saw no harm in allowing this belief.

Despite their grim view of the providential role of sickness, the Evangelicals were keenly interested in the advance of medical science. Dr Edward Jenner had no more enthusiastic disciple than Rowland Hill, whose *Cow-Pox Inoculation vindicated, and recommended from Matters of Fact* was published in 1806. Hill claimed to have inoculated nearly five thousand persons with his own hand. The reviewer in the *Evangelical Magazine* was at pains to justify acceptance of the medical advance.

> If Divine Providence has graciously afforded an easy means of preventing a loathsome and fatal disorder, it must be our duty thankfully to accept of such a provision in favour of the rising generation, and of future generations yet unborn.[56]

The magazine provided news of vaccination experiments in its column on 'religious intelligence'.

The inclusion of a surgeon on the *Duff* was thus in accordance with the views of the Missionary Society. Although Dr Gilham did not stay in Tahiti but returned on the home voyage, he had been able to pass on some useful rudimentary knowledge. Whilst on the *Duff* he had given 'lectures upon a prepared skeleton of the human body, and instructed them in the use of medicines'.[57] At least two of the missionaries acquired enough medical knowledge and experience to be regarded as surgeons. Clode, for instance, had not been long resident when he set a boy's broken arm, which he attempted to reset five days later after a second break due to native ignorance. Broomhall helped Clode in doing the work originally assigned to Gilham, and seems to have been in charge of the surgical instruments. He had some knowledge of medicine, and attended the young chief Temarii when he was suffering from the fatal effects of a gunpowder explosion. However both men were quite unable to do anything for Hodges when his leg was crushed by a log.[58]

Soon after their arrival in Tahiti the missionaries established a medical centre where they cared for the sick and attempted to treat venereal and other diseases, but the Tahitians were prejudiced in favour of their own treatments and regarded most of the ailments as punishments meted out by offended gods. Some diseases were attributed to England and the English God. 'You tell us of salvation, and behold we are dying', they cried.

The missionaries, quite clearly, cared more for regenerated souls than revitalized bodies. It was because of the stress on regeneration that the natives confused the miraculous powers of Christ with the unsuccessful medical aid administered by the missionaries, and this inability to understand the spiritual significance of 'being born again' is evident in their mockery. The Tahitians would say to a deformed person: 'Go you hump-back, to the preacher, and he will set you straight'; or to a cripple, 'Take your lame leg to the white man, he will cure it'.[59]

The medical ministry of Clode and Broomhall was short-lived. After the excommunication of Broomhall in July 1800 (see page 154) there was no 'surgeon' until the arrival in 1801 of Elder, whose 'practice' had been thrust upon him during the voyage out on the *Royal Admiral*. The ship's surgeon, Samuel Turner, was the son of an Independent minister and had been assistant surgeon at Haslar Hospital, near Gosport, where he came under the ministry of Bogue. He had previously sailed on the second voyage of the *Duff*. It is said that his knowledge in medicine and surgery was 'very considerably advanced' and that he had benefited considerably from 'many useful improvements' then revolutionizing medicine.[60] On the voyage Turner contracted a fever raging amongst the convicts and died shortly afterwards. Elder had been assisting him and probably learnt quite a lot in a short space of time. Certainly he applied himself to medical work in Tahiti even more enthusiastically than Clode and Broomhall. It is possible that, in his own conception of Christianity, he was primarily concerned with the physical suffering of the 'perishing heathen'. He did not get on well with his colleagues who complained of his general 'Spirit and Disposition', and considered that he was wanting in grace.[61]

Elder left the islands in 1809. Shortly before this he had been superseded as surgeon by the Reverend Gregory Warner, whose medical training had been similar to that of Turner and who was specially charged to attend to those suffering from venereal disease and other introduced maladies.[62] When he also left, the missionaries were thrown on their own resources.

While no official doctor was sent to the islands several of the missionaries were given special training. Threlkeld's experience at St Bartholomew's Hospital in London[63] was matched by Crook's initiative in learning for himself in Sydney.

I spoke to Wm. Redfern Esq. of the medical department at this station who attended my family. That Gentleman with a frankness and affability peculiar to him offered me every assistance in endeavouring to gain a little medical knowledge. I now attend the general Hospital daily, and visit the patients with my kind Tutor from who I obtain lessons in Materia Medica and Anatomy and receive many valuable hints of information. After the dissection which is shortly to take place M[r]. Redfern intends to deliver lectures on Anatomy with the subject before him solely for my benefit and that of M[r]. Henry Cowper son of our worthy Clergyman at this station who is M[r]. Redfern's apprentice.[64]

Redfern was to have his own niche in Tahitian history as the surgeon who attended the dying Pomare II. Other surgeons in the colony took an interest in the missionaries. William Bland, the notable emancipist, who was Henry's son-in-law, became proficient in the treatment of filariasis through attending the children of the mission families. He passed on his knowledge to both LMS and Wesleyan missionaries.[65]

After the national conversion, the missionaries were sought after for medical aid. The LMS had furnished them with medical books and instruments, and also a liberal supply of medicines for their own use. However little thought had been taken for the medical needs of the islanders and the missionaries had to beg for such supplies from benevolent persons at home. Ellis remarked *en passant* that perhaps it would not be considered 'a just appropriation of the Society's funds to expend them in providing medicine for those among whom its agents labour', and mentioned the misery which could be relieved by cheap medicine.[66] Tyerman and Bennet record how the missionaries distributed medicine when they felt it was needed, one labour which was permissible on the Sabbath.[67]

Aaron Buzacott was very conscious of the medical duties of a missionary, and lamented that *all* the missionaries could not pass through 'a brief and wise course of medical instruction'.[68] At his Avarua station a number of patients presented themselves at his surgery for examination and treatment at six o'clock every morning, and at the same hour in the evening. He also experimented in medicines and tackled difficult diseases such as filariasis. Perhaps more than others he placed considerable emphasis on this part of his work. He would have agreed with Ellis that the time was well spent.

> It is perfectly compatible with the higher duties of our station — the care of their spiritual maladies. We have only to regret that we have not possessed better qualifications, and more ample means for its efficient discharge.[69]

In their policy of adopting in full the social machinery of Evangelical religion, the missionaries introduced the institution of the Benevolent Asylum. The directors of the LMS reported in 1822 that

> many of the people having formerly died, through neglect, in the seasons of sickness and infirmity, especially aged persons, a house was appropriated, at the instance of Messrs. Bicknell and Tessier, in each of the three districts immediately contiguous to the Station; as a receptacle for such persons, where they should receive proper attention: and the Natives united with the Brethren in a subscription for the support of these benevolent asylums.[70]

In 1824 Mrs Crook and her eldest daughter established a Female Benevolent Society at Bogue Town, which they superintended. The report observed that 'many sick, diseased, and infirm persons have been visited and relieved — several of them from distant settlements, who have returned home cured. A similar Society has been since formed among the men'.[71] Benevolent societies were established at the other stations.

By 1830 the missionaries had come to regard the medical and humanitarian side of their mission as one of their most important labours. Huahine, for instance, was divided into ten parts with a view to the operation of a Sick Visiting Society which was established there. A leading man was appointed to each division, with several persons, both male and female, as his assistants. 'Beside the relief afforded, individuals are appointed to read the Scriptures and pray with the sick person.'[72]

Nevertheless the idea that disease was intimately connected with divine judgement was still strongly held, as can be seen by Pitman's attitude to the fever which raged in Rarotonga. 'Those of two or three districts, in particular, which had ever manifested much opposition to the advancement of godliness, and caused considerable trouble ever since the introduction of Christianity, have been nearly all cut off.'[73] He added that the people 'seem to be generally convinced that it is judgment of the Almighty, in consequence of their guilt'. Such conclusions were rarely discouraged. No doubt some of the 'troublers' would have survived if they had received the benefit of Pitman's supply of medicine. Similarly in Tahiti, when the followers of the *Mamaia* cult refused to be inoculated against smallpox and were annihilated by the disease in 1841, the missionaries regarded it as a just judgement on the 'visionary heretics'. Darling said they had 'ridiculed and even blasphemed the idea of vaccination' and that it was 'astonishing the manner in which the providence of God by this disease [had] sought out and cut off this class of foolish persons'. Eliza Pritchard regarded it as the outpouring of the 'vengeance of God'.[74]

Medical work became increasingly important on LMS stations though it never assumed a dominant role while the old Calvinist views prevailed. Medical missionaries as such were not appointed, and one or two missionaries in a group became known for their abilities as physicians. Unfortunately missionaries did not keep records of their failures, though occasionally when deaths took place they declared that they would not have occurred if the patients had carried out their exact instructions.

Apart from those missionaries who were fully trained medical men, such as Dr Lyth, the Wesleyans appear to have had even less specialized knowledge than their colleagues in other societies. However Calvert, we are informed, 'put himself under the instruction of a well-qualified man, who had the good sense not to attempt to teach him too much', and he also accompanied a medical student friend to a hospital 'where he got some general outlines of anatomical knowledge in the dissecting-room, and some valuable practical principles of surgery in the operating theatre'.[75] Most remedies were culled from one of the standard 'doctor's books'. In January 1841 Cross wrote from Viwa that he was in the 'habit of making up medicines according to prescriptions in Graham's Domestic Medicine'.[76] In 1857 the position was much the same. Lee wrote from Hihifo, Tonga, that he required a large pot of mercurial ointment and some beeswax.

> I have no lance or surgical instruments, and here I must be a Doctor whether I know or not I must prescribe for them. This compels me to study Graham and another book I have on the principles of medicine but I am yet a very poor physician I cannot do without my book.[77]

At least one of the Wesleyans appeared to put less faith in his own skills than in native remedies. Hill of Tonga observed that many Tongans suffered from 'neuralgia' similar to his own. He had his head shaved and 'yielded to the importunities of the natives and tried Tonga medicine'.[78]

One of the keenest Wesleyan advocates for medical work was the Reverend Thomas West, who wrote that his colleagues 'considered the art of healing the body, or alleviating the sufferings of the dying, as second only to that of saving the soul'.[79] His claim that medical science and the elementary principles of surgery were studied by them 'next to the Bible itself' would represent his own experience at least. Though he scorned the traditional Tongan 'doctors' he recognized that in some cases, such as setting limbs, they were particularly skilful.

In 1855, Dr W. H. Harvey, Professor of Botany at Trinity College, Dublin, visited Tonga and Fiji. From Tonga he wrote to a friend in London suggesting the establishment of a Polynesian Medical Aid Society.

> I find that the Missionaries here, and at the other Stations, are in the habit of distributing, at an almost nominal charge, large quantities of medicines; which medicines are entirely provided by these devoted men out of their slender pittance.[80]

Harvey's letter, published in the *Wesleyan Missionary Notices* in 1856, led to the establishment of the Protestant Missions Medical Aid Society under the presidency of the Earl of Shaftesbury, which made available simple surgical instruments and a large supply of medicine for gratuitous distribution. The Tongan missionaries were full of praise for the new society as it enabled them to 'compete' more successfully with the Marist missionaries.[81]

If humanitarian concern for suffering frequently manifested itself, the missionaries rarely failed to connect the healing art with their religious values. Hunt of Fiji believed that the provision of medical aid achieved three things. It gave the Fijians an opportunity to see the difference between the attitude of Christians and heathens towards the sick, it gave them confidence in 'English medicine' when otherwise they would allow the patient to die, and it would lead them to believe that it was 'the true God that makes medicine effectual'.[82] Hunt later had doubts concerning encouraging sick persons to become religious and suggested that too many 'converts' made in this way afterwards abandoned their beliefs.[83] Certainly in Fiji, and amongst the Maoris too, it was a common belief among many of the early converts that the adoption of Christianity would prolong life indefinitely. However in most of the groups medicine played a prominent part in winning adherents, even if only in convincing them that Jehovah was more powerful than their own gods or spirits. One of the most illustrious converts to accept Christianity mainly for medical reasons was Malietoa Vai'inupō of Samoa who owed his recovery from a severe infection to a lancet wielded by a native teacher.[84] Healing was a missionary duty which brought its own reward and effectively undermined faith in traditional remedies and sanctions.

13

Getting the Word Across

ALL THE Evangelical missionaries accepted preaching as one of the principal means of conversion, but for this end, and indeed for all other purely religious purposes, a knowledge of the vernacular was necessary. The first directors of the LMS believed that there would be little difficulty involved in learning Tahitian. This was largely due to the fact that Dr Haweis had supplied the missionaries of the *Duff* with a vocabulary drawn up by the *Bounty* mutineers (see page 96). This vocabulary was hopelessly inadequate, and it would seem that a considerable time passed before the missionaries realized that the grammatical and idiomatic differences between English and Tahitian were so marked. Nor were they assisted with the 'gift of tongues' to overcome these difficulties. Certainly they had the aid of interpreters, but these interpreters gave very loose translations, and even their integrity was questionable. James Puckey asserted that the 'sole cause' of the missionaries leaving Tahiti in 1798 was Peter Hagerstein, who misrepresented things to the Tahitians and was their 'secret enemy'.[1]

Perhaps in no other mission did the missionaries take such a considerable time to acquire anything like a proficiency in the vernacular as in the Tahitian mission. Broomhall, Jefferson and Nott appear to have been the only *Duff* missionaries to have made much progress in the first ten years, and of these, only Nott remained in the mission.[2] Elder, writing in 1802, spoke of Jefferson as an authority. 'Mr. Jefferson says that it is a copious language, and not a barren one. He says it is sufficient to teach any Doctrine taught in the Bible.'[3]

Davies, who arrived in 1801, soon came to share the linguistic honours with Nott. He developed quite a scholarly interest in philology, and being Welsh had the natural advantage of being bilingual. After the defection of Broomhall and the death of Jefferson, and until 1817, Nott and Davies were the only missionaries to have obtained anything like a mastery of the Tahitian language, although others were able to preach and to make some conversation. Preaching in the language was often the mere reading or recitation of a sermon which had been

255

written by someone else, and very often the same sermon was used. Tessier died in the service without ever mastering the simple elements of the language, his missionary labour consisting mainly in the transcription method of teaching.[4]

Orsmond asserted that when he arrived in 1817 Nott was the only missionary at Tahiti who could preach to the people intelligibly. Orsmond had acquired some knowledge of Tahitian on the voyage out, and made sufficient progress to be able to make himself understood. At a meeting shortly after his arrival he states that one missionary spoke as follows:—

> Oh brethren, you must now try to preach. Here is one new Missionary who can already converse with the natives, perhaps others are coming, and what will be said if you do not try to preach.[5]

Orsmond further asserted that the people could not understand them when they did preach.

> He who had come to preach came in and read the verse which on Saturday night had been translated for him, in my presence, by Mr. Nott, made a short oration, said farewell, turned on his heel and departed . . .[6]

The older missionaries were not as unintelligible as Orsmond insinuated, although it is doubtful whether many of them spoke Tahitian fluently. Henry Bicknell took the first opportunity to refute the charge:

> I wish I knew the Language better but I have been preaching to the natives these fifteen years and were never told till now of late that I did not understand the language.[7]

Orsmond, however, was the first missionary to reside permanently in the islands who had received a regular academic training. Doubtless he had a better understanding of grammatical principles than the others, and he would have been more conscious of incorrectly phrased speech.

After 1817, owing largely to the pioneering work of the older brethren, the missionaries made much greater progress in learning the language, and it no longer constituted the real difficulty which it had been for so many years. In 1820 Gyles reported to the directors that all the missionaries were able to preach in Tahitian except Hayward and Tessier, and that each missionary had a native to consult with on all occasions as an instructor. Nott, Davies, Henry, Bicknell, Wilson, Crook, Orsmond, Williams, Ellis and Barff were all reasonably advanced. Darling, Threlkeld, Bourne and Platt were not so proficient.[8]

Before the compilation of dictionaries the missionaries were more prone to use words incorrectly. Stories of wrongly used or wrongly pronounced words in missionary sermons are legion, and not a few missionaries have had the disturbing experience of unwittingly turning a hallowed sentiment into a gross obscenity, or a highly comical image.* This danger was particularly real in the early years of any mission. However when the older missionaries criticized the younger ones for being 'too forward'[9] in addressing the people the younger men regarded this caution as a measure of jealousy, and not as an attempt to prevent them from falling into gross errors of speech.

Through the efforts of the missionaries the Tahitian language become a written one, and much time was spent in settling questions of phonetics and orthography. The missionaries who went out on the *Royal Admiral* were urged to 'attend to the Rules for expressing the Sounds' of the Tahitian language, which had been 'digested' for their use.[10] They were to transmit copies of what they translated to the directors 'with observations upon its Construction', together with further word lists. The pioneer work done by Nott and others in this field was considerable. Most missionaries began by drawing up vocabularies. In 1820 Crook had one in hand, and William Henry and Orsmond had each begun a Tahitian grammar, though Henry destroyed his 'from vexation and in a kind of pet' when he found that his spelling was inconsistent with that used by Nott, Pomare and Crook.[11]

Translation of the scriptures was a part of every missionary's accepted duty, and began quite early in the Society Islands.[12] Gradually the work fell more and more to the translators with the greatest output, although in the initial stages of the work each missionary attempted one or two books. The missionaries went through each other's translations and usually took copies. Sometimes it happened that duplication occurred. Orsmond translated Ruth, Nahum, Peter's Epistles, Hebrews and Habakkuk, only to find that Nott had also translated them.[13] Fresh translations were continually being made as the missionaries learnt more about the language, and manuscript translations, especially of extracts, were in circulation.

Henry Nott was the principal translator, but he was assisted by Crook and Davies. Considerable assistance was also given by Pomare II. Crook records how Pomare would write down the verses on his slate and correct the language. He would furnish

---

*The Wesleyan missionary who informed his congregation that 'the time of woman was now come' had less reason to be embarrassed than some of his colleagues.

the missionaries with words that they had not heard before, give them examples, and tell them where it was proper or improper to use them.[14] Davies would give Pomare the manuscript and he would mark every place where he thought the language was faulty.[15] Translating in conjunction with the king must have had its disadvantages, as Crook tells how Nott had to avert his eyes to avoid seeing the attentions of the king to a favourite *mahu* (transexual).[16]

In 1821 Thomas Jones was sent out by the directors for the express purpose of supervising the translation work. Like Davies, Jones was a bilingual Welshman, and had devoted his time at Llanfyllin and Gosport particularly to language studies. A few months after his arrival he had already collected some hundreds of words. He regarded the language as being 'in some points very precise, in some, very redundant, and in some, very defective'.[17] At the end of the following year he had compiled the draft of a Tahitian-English dictionary containing above 5,000 words. Jones' attempts to systematize the language were cut short by his resignation from the mission. After Jones left, Nott again asserted his position as the principal authority on the Tahitian language. Events determined that a 'mechanic missionary', rather than a man who had received academic training, should be regarded as the most competent linguist.

On 18 December 1835 Nott completed his revision of the scriptures for the press. He had been employed longest on the task and had done most of the translation. However, it should not be forgotten that Nott also revised the work of others for the complete translation, and others had translated separate parts of the Bible which he did not use. Williams was not very pleased with Nott's sense of justice.

> It is much to be regretted that Mr. Nott is coming back. He will be of no use here and might have rendered lasting good to the Mission by translating and writing books in England. . . . He has done great injustice to his brethren by representing himself as the sole translator and they feel it[,] especially to good old Mr. Davies.[18]

Orsmond's criticism was much more stringent than that of Williams, but it should not be ignored. In his lengthy paper entitled 'Queries for Directors' he asked eleven pertinent questions.[19] Most of these were reflections on the ability of Nott as a translator. In thirty years he had not formed a vocabulary of his own. He felt that the translation must suffer because Nott had performed it 'for the most part away from all natives', whilst being daily goaded by domestic broils, or else ill in bed. He complained that it had not been investigated by a select committee, and that only parts of it were sent round to the other missionaries, 'the mass having never been seen by any eye save that of the individual translator'. More important, Orsmond lamented the fact that Nott wrote in language which the average Tahitian did not use. Not only was there a paucity of words, some being used to convey meanings which the people never thought of, but the language already differed from when the missionaries first arrived. Orsmond believed the Bible was in danger of becoming a sealed book, saying that already it was being called a 'dark Foreign language'. Nott was also criticized for forming his own vocabulary from the Pomare translation, hence giving the words meanings which had not always been attached to them. Two years later Orsmond was complaining that the 'host of foreign words' in the translation was 'as dark as the wilds of America'.[20] In the main Orsmond's criticism was valid, although one must take into account a kind of professional jealousy, the refusal to believe that an untrained bricklayer was capable of such an achievement.

> Though there may be fidelity to the great leading doctrines of Christianity yet what sort of a Translation might we expect from him who cannot speak his own language grammatically, who has never learned his own grammar, much less the Tongue, the original tongue[s] in which the Bible was written.[21]

It is not easy to assess Nott's place as a linguist without a thorough knowledge of Tahitian. On the other hand the meaning of many words has possibly been fixed by the work of the early missionaries, so that it is almost impossible, even for the comparative philologist, to know the full qualities of the vernacular spoken in the Society Islands at the beginning of the nineteenth century. As early as 1823 Orsmond had made the following relevant criticism, at the same time acknowledging Nott's competence as a linguist:

> He however labours under this inconvenience that he leans almost implicitly to a Native's ipse dixit, instead of aiming to possess the resources within himself. A native you know can conceive of nothing with regard to the word of God but through the medium of representation. If this falls short that is defective. Not to say that natives from mere indolence will often give a yes to a profound absurdity.[22]

Orsmond himself believed in obtaining his knowledge from 'purer' sources. He said that he 'dug' all his information from the 'stores of the old Priest[s], Prophets, Public Speakers, with whom alone are the beauties and delicacies of the language'.[23] In this respect, at least, one feels that Orsmond was competent to speak.

Notwithstanding this criticism, Nott had acquired a familiarity with the language of everyday living which gave a certain value to his translation. Davies praised the actual rendering as being 'very excellent', saying that Nott 'excelled in being dramatic, which is a more rare attainment than many are aware of'.[24] Simpson remarked that although Nott had received much assistance, it was 'his mind that cast them into that classic form in which they appear'.[25] Nott appears to have had a wide knowledge of Polynesian idiom and, whatever mistakes he made, his translation was used as the basis of Bible translations in some of the other groups.[26]

It was obvious from the great number of technical errors that the Tahitian Bible would have to be revised.[27] This task was given to Orsmond.[28] In 1844, when Orsmond's connexion with the LMS ceased, the task was given to Howe and Joseph. Davies regarded them both as not being 'competent to the work'. Although the typographical errors were very numerous, he was 'not aware of a single instance where a point of Doctrine, or a moral precept' was affected.[29] The revision process was complicated by the fact that Nott had used Boothroyd's edition of the Bible, and the Bible Society required conformity to the Authorized Version. Davies protested because of Howe's imperfect knowledge of the language. Although Joseph's knowledge was better, he was a 'heedless young man', who was 'in the habit of using words that did not convey to the people the meaning he intended'. Furthermore, Henry, Wilson, Simpson, Orsmond, Darling and Davies himself had not been consulted on the matter.[30]

The new edition gave less satisfaction. Although the typographical errors had been corrected and the omissions from Boothroyd's version had been supplied, Davies felt that unnecessary changes had been made and that there had been 'meddling with things not well understood'.[31] In listing these, he mentioned that 'where no erroneous ideas were conveyed by the words formerly used', the words in their place conveyed 'positive errors'. Thus, with a modifying word omitted, the sense of Luke ii, 7-12, was changed to suggest 'a pig's sty for the place and a pig's trough for a manger'! There was every justification, he felt, for the Catholics to call it a 'monkey Bible'.

Similar difficulties arose in connexion with the translation of the Rarotongan Bible. Most of the translation work was done by Pitman and Buzacott, but like Nott, Pitman was charged with 'monopolizing the Scriptures'.[32] Matters were further confused by Williams, who altered the Rarotongan New Testament to be in conformity with Nott's translation. In 1847 Pitman resigned from 'all future labour in translating, correcting or revising the Scriptures', so that the work of translating the whole of the Old Testament devolved on Buzacott.[33] The Rarotongan translation was evidently a work of greater scholarship than the Tahitian. Pitman was a fine Hebrew scholar, and he had the advantage of being able to draw on the idioms and theological terminology used by Nott, Barff, and Baldwin of Hawaii.

The translation of the Bible into Samoan was the result of a greater division of labour, and there was possibly greater critical revision than in the other missions. Separate books were issued, as in the other missions, until a complete New Testament was printed in 1849. The Old Testament was completed in 1855, and the whole was then revised and printed in 1860. It was Pratt who was ultimately claimed as the principal translator, but the 'experimental' translation was carried on by most of the missionaries. Many of the Samoan missionaries also attempted translations into the various Melanesian tongues of the westward islands.

Translation work was an exacting task, and the missionary translator had little leisure time. Joseph Johnston, in describing a scene of domestic bliss at the Papara station in Tahiti, thus describes the visiting missionary:

> Whilst I am writing thus Mr. Heath is sitting in my parlour translating one of David's Psalms into Samoan. He has before him the Hebrew Psalter and the English and Tahitian versions. Mrs. Johnston is preparing dinner, and little Eliza Mary is in the verandah calling out to the horse that is feeding a few yards from the door.[34]

William Day, whose classical knowledge earned him the nickname of 'the professor', regarded Heath as an assiduous translator, but not a 'close' one.[35] He believed that the most accurate translators were Turner and Pratt. Heath had very definite views about the acquisition of language. In surveying all the Evangelical stations in the Pacific in 1842 he stated that 'all the languages want more careful studying and comparing and measures taken for the progressive improvement of translations and the extension of literature among the people'.[36] He complained that one Tahitian word was made to answer to 'some half score in the original' (for example, *faaora*, to save, etc.; *maitai*, good, etc.); Heath's principal criticism was an important one:

In this translation also, as well as the New Zealand, Tonga and others, due care has not been used in the adoption of *theological* terms. Thus *faaroo* (in Tahitian and the corresponding word in several other dialects) made to translate [pisteuō], to believe, whereas it sometimes answers for [akouō], to hear, give attention etc., and sometimes to [peithō], to obey. In the Hawaiian and Samoan other terms have been adopted for [pisteuō], but there also, it may be, other words of this class want revising.

Heath was least satisfied with the translations made by the Wesleyans. They had 'decidedly the far greater number of faults'. They had 'so much anglicized the idioms, and introduced so many broken English words,* that to one who knows anything of pure Polynesian, the effect on the eye and ear is tormenting'.

The linguistic difficulties of the pioneer Wesleyan missionaries to Tonga had been considerable, and not having any intimate connexion with the Tahitian mission, the Tongan brethren had also to become pioneers in this field. For many years they had no other textbook than the vocabulary and grammar appended to Mariner's *Tonga Islands*. It is quite evident that Thomas and Hutchinson had great difficulty in mastering the language, and it was only Thomas who persevered and finally achieved success. When the elder brethren were critical of the linguistic abilities of Wellard, the Reverend Joseph Orton was not backward in reminding Thomas of his own slow progress.

> With every feeling of respect to some of the Brethren now labouring in your District had these cases been disposed of at the termination of a period *much greater* than *3 months;* the mission would have lost some of the most valuable Missionaries now employed in the Friendly Islands who laboured for a considerable time under the most distressing discouragements as to their ever obtaining a competency to teach in the native language etc.[37]

Thomas attained his linguistic efficiency by dogged hard work. His day commenced at 4 a.m. and he seldom retired before 10 or 11 in the evening. In 1832 William Cross commented that Thomas pronounced the language badly but that this was a 'small fault' as he was more at home in Tongan than in English. By 1844 Thomas had translated Genesis, Matthew, John, and most of the Epistles, the second catechism, and 'several other pieces'.[38] Some of the missionaries acquired the language very quickly. West mingled a great deal with the Tongan children and received daily lessons from the chief judge of Vava'u, so that by

*I.e. English words spelt as Polynesians would pronounce them.

the end of three weeks he claimed that he was able to compose a short sermon and conduct part of the service. Rabone published a *Vocabulary of the Tonga Language* in 1846 and West published a grammar in 1865 which was the first since Mariner's *Tonga Islands* had been published. Bible translation was considerably behind translation work in the other groups.

The Fijian translators appear to have been more talented. Cargill was responsible for the adoption of the orthographical conventions used in writing the Fijian language.[39] He began the translation of the New Testament and commenced a grammar and dictionary of the language spoken in the Lau group. He took an academic interest in the work and wrote an essay on the language. Hunt did not altogether approve of Cargill's methods, saying that he 'found it easy to translate; but he translated carelessly and used a kind of Anglo-Fijian idiom'.[40] Various elementary books were translated into the dialects of Lakeba, Rewa, Bau and Somosomo, but it was decided that the New Testament should be translated into the Bau dialect. Lyth and Hunt were appointed the principal translators. When Hunt began his translation work he had part of a translation by Cross and Cargill's translation in the Lakeba dialect. However he stated that he did not intend 'to call any man master', but to think for himself.

> I know it is the way of opposition, but I think it is the right way for me. I leave others to do as they please. My plan is this: 1. To read over the chapter for translating in the Greek Testament, and examine particularly any word of which I have any doubt as to its meaning. I read Bloomfield's Notes and Campbell's translation and any other books that I have to assist me to ascertain the meaning of the text. 2. After having mastered the chapters as I think, I commence translating and I use as my standards for the text the Greek and the English translations and for the translation not any man exclusively, but myself, all the Natives I can have access to, and the translations that have been already made.[41]

Hunt was a careful translator, and had systematic rules for writing.

> A translation should if possible make the sense of the original as plain to those who read his translation as the original was for those for whose use it was written. When we can be literal and do this, let us be literal, but when we are so literal as not to give the sense of the original, we are so far from being good translators that we are no translators at all. At the same time I think we should not use too great freedom, or use too much circumlocution. The first thing I think in a translator should be to give the sense, and the second to

give it in a form as much like the original as possible. By giving the sense I do not mean that he should explain the meaning of the words in the original. What I mean is that he must use such words and in such a form as when explained will bring out the meaning of the original.[42]

As in the other missions, one missionary dominated the translation of the scriptures. The New Testament appeared in 1847, and Hunt was asked to undertake the work of translating the Old Testament. The various local grammars were early superseded by David Hazlewood's *Grammar and Dictionary of the Fijian Language,* which was completed in 1850, and which became a standard of its kind.

Another remarkable linguist was Hiram Bingham of Micronesia. After six months' residence at Abaiang he was preaching publicly to the Gilbertese. His main mission work was destined to be connected with the language, and his Bible and Dictionary have been accepted standards.

In Polynesia the acquisition of one language usually enabled a missionary to make better progress in another. Thus Darling, who had learnt to speak Tahitian comparatively fluently, was able to acquire Marquesan in a very short time, whereas his younger colleagues, Stallworthy and Rodgerson, had great difficulty in mastering the language. When Darling finally left them they were merely reading sermons which he had written. Nor does it seem that they made very rapid progress after he left, and their backwardness in this respect may well have been a decisive factor in their abandoning the mission. According to the Reverend Richard Armstrong, the American missionaries were able to preach to the people of Nukuhiva after a residence of five weeks because of their scanty knowledge of Hawaiian, while their Hawaiian assistants could converse freely after a few days. Armstrong also testifies that Orsmond was able to communicate in Marquesan 'with considerable freedom' towards the end of his eight-day residence with the missionaries in February 1834.[43] The short time that Ellis spent in the Society Islands gave him sufficient knowledge to acquire Hawaiian fairly rapidly, and both these tongues were useful to him in Madagascar. However this experience was not always the case. Wyatt Gill asserted that a sermon in Tahitian would be 'perfectly unintelligible to a Rarotongan or Mangaian congregation', and Krause did not find it so easy to adapt himself to the Rarotongan dialect after his missionary experience in Tahaa.[44]

Missionaries tended to have specialized vocabularies, and very often they were able to grasp sufficient detail of the language to be able to speak correctly, but they were still ignorant of much of the idiom, and many aspects of the language were not known to them. Often they realized their limitations at the expense of their dignity. Orsmond complained that there was a monotony about most of the missionaries' sermons.

> There is so much sameness in the words in common use, so much lameness in the construction of sentences, such a share of English Tahitian, so great a portion of lifeless monotony, and so great an absence of native oratorical vivacity that it is no wonder sermons become uninteresting. He who exhibits a greater variety than is usual is said to study the old customs too much,* while the natives are at the same time rejoicing in what they have heard. In the choice of words and phrases there certainly [is] great need of chastity and prudence, yet there is no getting either at feelings, or judgement but through the avenues which words in constant use open to the preacher.[45]

The Tahitians, so Orsmond said, had a proverb that the man who continued to bring out the same song (*pehe*) without variety would not be listened to.[46]

Apart from the limitations of the language, the missionaries had to be careful that they did not use words which gave offence. On the other hand missionaries could often be 'insulting', whereas native pastors would have been discredited for the same thing. Heath recorded the example of a Samoan chief who ceased to attend chapel because the preachers introduced the subject of 'the fire' appertaining to the miseries of hell.

> I ought to tell you that allusions to such matters, or even to death, before Chiefs, are contrary to Samoan etiquette. From *us* the chiefs will hear anything, but our native teachers are sometimes reminded of this old custom.[47]

Although preaching to the heathen was a regular missionary pursuit, it is questionable whether much success could be attributed to this means. Converts were rarely gained by preaching, except under revival conditions. Thomas Williams of Fiji was quite aware of this.

> I preached more than 20 sermons, and delivered a greater number of addresses. These were chiefly to persons already Christians; not that I judge it useless to preach to the heathen, or neglect to conduct open-air out-of door services for their benefit; but I think sermons alone are not calculated to do the thorough heathen much good, because of their inability to comprehend the import of many even

*An early comment on Orsmond's growing interest in Polynesian culture.

of the commonest terms that occur therein. I think they might hear sermons alone for 40 years and be no wiser at the end . . .[48]

This was certainly the experience of the Marquesas mission, 1834-1841, when preaching was the principal method used. The natives regularly attended open-air services for weeks on end without comprehending what the meetings were about.

In most areas the written word had a much more far-reaching effect than the spoken word. There was a kind of magic appeal about the printed book: it came first to each island as a sacred object which spoke to them. The book was one object of 'civilization' which retained its appeal when the enthusiasm for missionary ways had subsided. It has frequently been argued that the popularity of the 'means of instruction' and the desire to be literate were due to the widespread belief that literacy provided immediate access to European goods.[49] The *mana* of the Europeans and their gods could be acquired by mastering the letters which were written on paper or by learning by heart the talismanic sentences of the Bible. Certainly on most mission fields there was a period of intensive interest in reading and writing which gave the missionaries a false sense of the effectiveness of their 'means of conversion'.

From the secular point of view, one of the greatest achievements of Evangelical missionaries in the South Seas was the standardization of the various island tongues and the creation of a vernacular literature. Whereas Evangelical doctrine was destructive to the old culture, the preservation of the language was a modifying force.

14

The Gospel of Civilization

DURING THE eighteenth century the exponents of missions had
been concerned with the theoretical problem of whether natural
religion should be taught before revealed religion, particularly
the doctrine of the atonement.* Certainly, divines such as Edmund Law, Bishop of Carlisle, and the nonconformist Nathaniel
Lardner, believed that barbarians had to be made rational before
they could become civilized. This was accepted by the reviewers
as well as by large sections of the clergy. 'At the commencement
of modern Missions', observed Harris, 'the opinion very generally
prevailed among the friends of Missions themselves, that in barbarous lands, civilization must pioneer the way for Christianity,
but on this *important condition,* that the Christian Missionary
himself should be the pioneer'.[1]

Largely because of the apparent failure of missions conducted
on the principle of 'civilization first',[2] the Evangelical clergy at
home increasingly urged the direct preaching of the doctrine of
the cross as the only means of converting the heathen, whilst the
missionaries themselves placed complete faith in the power of
this doctrine *alone* to change the hearts of the heathen. It is this
essentially Evangelical doctrine which thwarted the philosophical
approach to the missionary enterprise, and it was the faith in this
doctrine which was in many ways responsible for some of the
errors and misconceptions of missionary policy. The 'social doctrine of the cross', if we may so describe its corollary, was the
belief that the preaching of Christ crucified, *ipso facto,* would
effect the transformation of primitive society to civilized society;
the belief that social progress was inextricably bound up with
the message of the atonement.

Preaching the doctrine of the cross had been an early feature
of the Protestant missionary tradition.[3] That the missionaries

---

*Natural religion was understood to be knowledge of God obtainable by
human reason alone without the aid of revelation. Dr John Love, an
LMS director raised in the Presbyterian Moderate tradition, wrote his
*Addresses to the People of Otaheite, designed to assist the Labour of
Missionaries, and other Instructors of the Ignorant* (London, 1796) with the
claims of the natural religion advocates in mind. His textbook was never
used.

should preach Christ crucified was the theme of many of the early sermons.[4] One of the most famous London Missionary Society annual sermons, entitled 'The Attraction of the Cross', was preached by John Angell James at Surrey Chapel, 12 May 1819. The chief instrument of conversion was the doctrine of the cross:

> If then you would arrest the savage of the desert; if you would detain him from the chase; if you would rivet him to the spot, and hold him in the power of a spell that is altogether new to him, do not begin with cold abstraction of moral duties, or theological truths; but tell him of Christ crucified, and you shall see his once vacant countenance enlivened by the feelings of a new and deep interest.[5]

The doctrine, as an exhibition of unparalleled love, 'melts and captivates the heart'. Like Haweis, James believed that native peoples had deduced the need for an atonement from 'the light of nature'.[6] He scorned the idea of the philosophical approach.

> O, had the cannibal inhabitants of Taheite been persuaded to renounce their wretched superstition and cruel customs, by any efforts of a purely rational nature; had the apostles of philosophy been the instruments of their conversion . . . how would the world have rung with the praise of all-sufficient reason.[7]

In examining the same question, William Ellis ascertained that the missionaries in Tahiti had preached the doctrine of the cross or the atonement as the sinner's justification before God from the beginning.

> The doctrine of Divine benevolence, thus displayed, was altogether new to the Tahitians; nothing analagous to it had ever entered into any part of their mythology. Its impression on their minds was at this time proportionate.[8]

Ellis himself echoed the words of James: 'the attractions of the Cross move and melt the human heart'. He records the story of the Tahitian scholar who was so overcome by the message of John iii, 16 that he burst into tears in the presence of Henry Nott.[9] John Williams was also conscious of the message of this sermon. In 1834 he told James in person: 'According to the ability which God has given me, I *have* preached the doctrine of salvation by faith in a crucified Redeemer'.[10]

In Evangelical mission policy it was taken for granted that civilization was necessary. The prevailing attitude was that the natives would be either civilized or destroyed.[11] The missionaries had an extraordinary faith in the power of the Evangelical gospel to affect men's minds so that they would promptly assume the social system of northern Europe and the doctrine of the cross was the magic key to civilization. As James observed, 'Religion is strictly and essentially a civilizing process'.[12]

The idea that the role of the missionary was to introduce civilization together with the doctrine of the cross thus developed into a principle of missionary enterprise. By 1836 this procedure had received official approval. In that year a committee of the House of Commons was selected

> to consider what measures ought to be adopted with regard to the native inhabitants of countries where British Settlements are made, and to the neighbouring Tribes, in order to secure to them the due observance of justice, and the protection of their rights; to promote the spread of civilization among them, and to lead them to the peaceful and voluntary reception of the Christian Religion.

Various missionaries were called before the committee to give evidence. William Ellis, then Secretary of the LMS, appeared on 6, 8 and 11 June, and John Williams on 29 July. The evidence was widely published in 1837 in a work entitled *Christianity the means of Civilization* and was soon followed by other works on Christianity and colonization (see page 102). However the conclusions reached had long been the practising beliefs of the LMS and these views were shared by most Evangelical missionaries. The opinion of Ellis was decided. 'True civilization and Christianity are inseparable; the former has never been found but as a fruit of the latter. An inferior kind of civilization may precede Christianity and prevail without it to a limited extent.'[13] Ellis expanded this doctrine. 'In proportion as individuals receiving Christianity yield themselves to its influence, just in that proportion they must be civilized. No man can become a Christian, in the true sense of the term, however savage he may have been before, without becoming a civilized man.'[14]

The thesis of men such as James and Ellis was that Christianity supplied a motive, and that those led to Christ were led to the 'better life' in every respect. 'It is a fact, which I received from Mr Nott', said James in 1826, 'that by no efforts whatever could they induce the natives to learn to read, before their conversion to Christianity . . . the grace of God, when it took possession of their hearts, planted in their nature all the germs of civilization'.[15] This was the social doctrine of the cross. The mistake was that the new civilization had to be an artificial one instead of one based on the traditional pattern of native life.

The original LMS mission to Tahiti has often been regarded

as an experiment in civilization to precede Christianity, but this was not the case. This assumption was based largely on the nature of the occupations of the original mechanic missionaries, and the fact that their selection was considerably influenced by their trade or profession.[16] However these men were sent to preach the gospel before all else. Certainly they employed themselves in those trades, such as carpentry and smithy work, necessary for their own purposes, which were of use in training the Tahitians, but it was not the principal part of their vocation. Indeed, after the first exodus in 1798 the missionaries affirmed that the evangelization system had failed. When the directors asked the Reverend J. F. Cover whether he had any reason to think that good had been done to any of the natives, he replied: 'No. They must be civilized first'.[17] At this time William Henry also held a similar view.

The supposed failure of the Tahitian mission was perhaps the reason why Marsden commenced his mission for the CMS in New Zealand on the civilization plan. Although Marsden also placed great emphasis on catechetical work, he expected Christianization to follow civilization. Even Lawry, who commenced the Wesleyan mission to Tonga in 1822, largely under the guidance of Marsden, was not uninfluenced by the civilization school, and had several mechanics to assist him. The Wesleyans, however, placed less importance on civilization as a means than any other society. Although some of the Wesleyan missionaries did acquire property, it was certainly not approved of by their Society; except for the schoolmasters, who were not bound by the rules, the Wesleyans were divorced from all secular affairs. Amongst the other missionaries there were some who shared this ideal, but there were also those who indulged in secular pursuits. John Williams, of like mind to Marsden, was a great advocate of civilization, though for him civilization and evangelization were more or less synonymous. In placing less emphasis on the role of 'civilization', the Wesleyans were largely influenced by the Conference rulings governing their own activities, but the failure of Thomas Coke's mission, on the civilization plan, to the Foulahs of Africa was an accepted precedent. Nevertheless, Wesleyan missionaries did not lose sight of the fact that Christianity was a means of civilizing the native peoples, which seemed to be an end much desired by other sections of the community.

Before the nominal conversion of Tahiti the importance of 'civilization' was considerably emphasized. 'You must first make them men before you make them Christians . . .', was the opinion of the Reverend Dr Mason of New York. 'You must teach them

to live in fixed habitations, to associate in villages, to cultivate
the soil.'[18] Most of the English Evangelicals, however, felt that
the civilization of the heathen was not absolutely necessary before their conversion, arguing that the human mind was not, in
any country, 'below the reach of discipline and religious instruction'.[19] Notwithstanding this, in 1812 the directors of the LMS
criticized the missionaries for not paying sufficient attention to
their civilizing duties: 'In reviewing your proceedings for some
years past . . . we feel disappointed at the small degree of
Improvement made among the natives in respect of Industry
and civilization'.[20] This criticism was based on considerable
ignorance of the delicate position in which the missionaries
were placed.

The first systematic attempt at 'civilization' came with the
appointment of Gyles the 'agriculturist' in 1817. His four years'
contract stipulated that it was his duty to

> communicate gratuitously, to all persons who, with the approbation
> of the general body of the Missionaries shall be desirous to learn the
> art of rearing and cultivating the Sugar Cane, Coffee and Cotton
> Trees, and any other of the products of the Country, and of curing
> such products, and generally to teach according to the best of his
> skill, whatever may tend to the promotion of agriculture or other
> useful application of the Soil or natural products of the Country.[21]

This first attempt was a failure. Far from communicating his
knowledge 'gratuitously', Gyles found that his Tahitian labourers
kept stopping work to demand payment.[22] Most of them left
because he would not give them cloth before it was due, and he
was obliged to get seamen to turn the sugar mill. The missionaries seem to have been suspicious of Gyles' intentions, and
spread the rumour that he intended to distil spirituous liquors.
When Gyles resigned, Marsden urged the missionaries to 'push
on'. However by that time they were beginning to change their
views. 'A Tahitian would not give his breadfruit trees to be cut
down, for any improvement in agriculture you could suggest',
wrote Platt; 'I myself am inclined to think that nothing can be
offered as a sufficient compensation for the breadfruit'.[23]

In 1821 the two 'artisans', Armitage and Blossom, were sent
out to continue the civilizing plan in Tahiti. The work of Armitage, connected with the spinning of cotton, was not an absolute
failure, but his progress was considerably hampered by the non-
co-operative policy of the other missionaries. Most of the older
missionaries tended to regard the 'civilization' work as not being
essential. The hours at the cotton factory at Moorea frequently

conflicted with school and service times at the mission station.[24] Opposition came from many quarters, and the British vice-consul told the people that the manufactory could be injurious to them.[25] Even Tyerman and Bennet, who favoured civilization schemes, were opposed to the appointment of artisans and believed that only ordained missionaries should be sent to the islands.[26]

The theorists, however, were again emphasizing the duty to civilize, and their ideas were heeded by the younger missionaries in the islands. Douglas of Cavers in his *Hints on Missions* (1822) criticized the first missionaries for not making 'the moderate exertions requisite to procure the comforts of life for themselves and those around them'.[27] Similarly John Angell James preached in favour of industry.

> We must find out the best means of employing them; we must give them something to do; we must devise what will best suit them as staple articles of production; *we must multiply their artificial wants;* by education we must elevate their minds; by the arts we must refine their manners, and multiply their comforts; by stimulating their industry, we must keep them from indolence, and mischief, and vice.[28]

The creation of artificial wants was regarded as a progressive step in every way. The missionaries genuinely believed that the entire social system of the Anglo-Saxons would make the islanders *happier.* They did not regard it as a problem of adjustment but merely as a simple change from ignorance to the 'civilized way'. This is exemplified in their attitude to the minor problem of diet.

> It is not to be imagined that a civilized people, whose habits, through cultivation of mind, and consequent personal delicacy, shall be proportionately raised above *mere animal nature,* could, under any circumstances, *remain satisfied* to subsist on breadfruit and plantains, with occasional relishes of hogs' flesh.[29]

The argument which had most appeal was that 'civilization' was the most effectual way of combating the natural indolence of the islanders. Little industry was necessary for subsistence, and in the indigenous social system much time was spent in social ritual. The policy of the missionaries invariably decreased the amount of social ritual and so increased inactivity. The solution of providing manual employment was ill-suited to climatic and economic conditions and little was achieved.

Christians throughout the centuries have maintained that idleness is conducive to viciousness. It was the cry of St Chrysostom in Constantinople before it was the cry of William Ellis in

Huahine. And idleness in '*la nouvelle Cythère*' was that wasting idleness of the lotus-eaters. As Ellis observed:

> Much of their time, however, is passed in sleep, and unless urgent engagements forbid, all classes without hesitation resign themselves to slumber during the sultry hours of the middle of the day. A strong healthy man feels it no disgrace to lie stretched on his mat from morning till evening, scarcely rising, except to eat, unless some amusement, or other call, urgently require it.[30]

Ellis had a conscience which told him that such waste of time was a disgrace in his own way of life. A people who could spend whole days without working must surely be condemned when they came to give an account of their stewardship. The situation had to be remedied, and so civilization, which theoretically — and practically, so they said — grew out of their teaching, was encouraged as a means of countering idleness. Ellis made a subtle distinction between civilization being essential and being necessary to the Christian converts. It was not essential but 'necessary to their consistent profession of Christianity' to provide an outward sign of perseverance in industrious living.[31]

'Civilization' was much more than the teaching of useful skills. It was the imposition of a completely new way of life, conforming closely to the manners and taste of Evangelical middle-class society. The missionaries believed that civilization could be introduced simultaneously with instruction in the Christian religion. When new missions were commenced an attempt was made to bring the people into villages. Gradually the missionaries came to see that this system was not really suited to the domestic economy of the islands, for it collapsed whenever the influence of the missionaries was at an ebb. However, when missionary influence was strong the people were encouraged to build cottages, from limestone (coral) blocks, equipped with sofas, tables and chairs, dwellings patterned on the 'home of taste' of the proud mechanic. Even when the people took their most active interest in these cottages, they preferred to sleep in the traditional houses. In one generation they had usually fallen into ruin, or were used for purposes not intended by the missionaries.[32]

The chiefs were usually the first to be initiated into the mysteries of domestic civilization. In this respect the Leeward Islands mission was far ahead of the Tahitian mission. In 1821 Williams wrote:

> The Chiefs are getting cups and saucers and wish to become Europeans and enjoy the comforts of life. Surely this ought to disgrace that abandoned Pomare who lives in the most despicable manner of

any one Native in all the Whole of the Islands, this was what the Deputation expressed their greatest surprise at, the dirty filthy manner in which he lives.[33]

Hugh Cuming the naturalist visited Huahine in 1828 and was surprised at the civilized state of the chiefs. The young ex-king of the island possessed two dozen well-made chairs of Tahitian wood, tables, two sofas, a number of pictures and looking-glasses on the walls, a plank floor, and glass windows. 'Such order and magnificence I had not witness'd before in any of the Islands and to add to my surprise his Ex-Majesty ask'd us to take a glass of Wine or some spirits.'[34] The young chief was dressed in 'a light Duck, Frock and Trowsers, and a white shirt made fast at the neck with a piece of Black Ribbon'. Cuming thought it was all in very good taste.

The place of clothing in the civilizing scheme is an interesting one, as much blame has been attached to the missionaries for clothing the islanders unnecessarily, and helping to spread disease and ill-health. It is usual to regard Mother Hubbards for the women as an essential feature of Evangelical Christianity. European clothing was regarded by the missionaries as the mark of civilization, but they fully realized the discomfort of much clothing. It was not unusual for missionaries to argue that too much clothing was not healthy, or to advocate a more indigenous form of costume. Indeed, the full-length cotton loincloth, still worn in the South Seas, was usually preferred as the sensible working dress for the men, and as a substitute for grass or bark cloth girdles. It was the women who suffered most in having to conceal their breasts. Shirts for the men were encouraged at most of the mission stations for ordinary wear.

The first missionaries to Tahiti did not hesitate to commend the coverings worn by the people. In answer to questions put to him by the directors in 1819 Hayward replied: 'No alteration has taken place in the dress of those who wear the native cloth, which is by no means indecent'.[35] Nevertheless, the desire to teach new crafts, to promote industry and to give some degree of regularity to the desires of the people induced the missionaries to encourage 'dressing up', especially for church services. The women were expected to wear full-length dresses, and the men were considered more suitably attired when wearing cotton coats. In fact, the standard for church clothing was set by the first persons to be baptized. Barff recalled that the men wore the *maro* and the women wore a wrapper 'not reaching to their knees'.

We requested the men to get a tiputa, a wrapper reaching to the middle of the leg, and the women to get a hu tipono, a wrapper reaching down to the foot. In the above new dress the first 14 were baptized in 1819 . . . more than 1000 were all in the old costume except oiling the body all over on the Sabbath; but from that day they all adopted the dress of the 14 at least on the Sabbath day, and have continued to improve in clothing from that time to the present.[36]

When Pomare's wife and her sister, Pomare Vahine, were baptized in September 1820 they were each dressed in 'an elegant Tahitian dress' while the royal children were baptized in white frocks provided by Mrs Crook. The baby, less than three months old, also wore a scarlet silk hat for the occasion.[37] Indeed, Mrs Crook, as royal midwife, had put the child into clothes immediately after birth.

Mrs Crook was probably responsible for introducing the art of bonnet-making, as in March 1821 she was giving lessons to the royal women 'in sewing a bonnet'.

We have lately found means to supply ourselves with bonnets, by taking the inner bark of the purau and splitting platting and sewing it as straw is used with us at home. As we wish the people to be employed we have recommended the same to them. They seem inclined to follow our advice. Many are platting the purau bark and attempting to sew bonnets, they come to our house one day in the week for instruction in this work.[38]

The adoption of European clothing, particularly in the first instances of contact, was often a process uncontrolled by missionary influence, and due more to the desire to wear the strange garments and gain a certain prestige thereby. Hence the many burlesque descriptions of incongruous dress in the narratives of visiting travellers. We read more frequently of missionaries lamenting the inordinate desire for European clothing than complaining about immodest dress.[39]

William Gill's description of the clothing worn by Christian Rarotongans perhaps comes nearest to the popular conception of clothing worn at the South Seas mission stations, but it should be remembered that the climatic conditions of the Cook Islands are more temperate than in some of the other groups. One must also take into account the fact that missionaries wrote for the church people at home, who did not understand island conditions.

Their dress consists of light English and American cotton material, made up in loose European style: the women having a native cloth wrapper, as inner garment, over which is worn a long flowing robe; they have no shoes, but a bonnet of *finely wrought plait,* and neatly trimmed with foreign ribbon, is considered essential to complete their dress. The men wear shirt, trousers, waistcoat, and coat; most of them have strong rush hats, for common use, and finer ones for occasional service, and about 1 in every 20 completes his full dress by putting on stockings and shoes.[40]

Gill regarded this dress as 'appropriate to their climate and habits', and in this sense it was 'civilized, decent, and respectable'. Stallworthy of the Marquesas and Samoa stated very fully the reasonably enlightened views of most of the missionaries in the matter of dress.

> If you cloth[e] your convert fully for company and public worship, he will retain no more than decency requires in his dwelling, and in sun and rain he will pursue his daily avocation in the same scanty dress. And frequent change from dress to undress undermines his constitution.[41]

Undue emphasis on clothing was mostly the whim of individual missionaries, no doubt the more repressed and inhibited. There was, however, a definite pressure from the 'religious public' to clothe the poor heathen, and one wonders how much the development of the art of photography in the 1850s influenced the clothes-consciousness of missionaries.

The standard of 'civilization' at the mission stations varied. From 1797 till about 1817 the missionaries had to rely on limited resources. However after the advent of Williams and his colleagues the standard of 'civilization' of the LMS stations rose considerably, with coral lime dwellings and chapels being built by the native converts as well as by the missionaries. Indeed, it was regarded as a test of sincerity in their religious profession for church members to adopt the new mode of living. Just how rigorously this was carried out can be seen from an entry in Orsmond's journal:

> Today agreeably to a law the church established last church meeting I have with a book and pencil been to every house south of the place of worship and have noted down under the name of each member what has been done. The condition of the house and its furniture and it is resolved that if they do not from this time forth begin to hurl paganism in all its abominable shapes from our City such person shall not be a member of the church. The house must [be] plastered in and out, have doors and windows, bed rooms with doors and shutters, and a garden encircling the house.[42]

In the 1830s it was growing apparent that the standards demanded by the European missionaries were not entirely suited to the people. The change of mission policy is noted by Simpson of Moorea:

> Many new houses have also been built during the past year. Not plastered houses. We do not approve of them unless great cleanliness [is] observed inside, which is not generally the case in Tahitian houses. The house most approved of by us are those thatched in the usual manner but [wattled] all round with slight bamboos to the wind and thereby prevent noxious vapours.[43]

Similarly in 1832 Williams judged the native-style dwellings in Samoa better suited to the climate than the introduced coral lime and Stallworthy was equally satisfied with the Samoan house in 1857:

> It is not easy for the natives to introduce a kind of house superior for their accommodation in this climate to Samoan houses. A well built, and carefully managed Samoan house is comfortable, neat and even beautiful. The large majority of houses are not well built, nor tidily kept. The change desirable among the people is not so much a new kind of dwelling, but the general adoption of the better kind of native dwelling, and more attention to its internal arrangement and keeping. Boarded houses which answered so well at Tahiti do not suit here as the ants soon destroy them.

He felt that stone walls, and doors which shut out the cooling winds, would be an 'intolerable grievance'.[44]

The missionaries themselves usually dwelt in substantial houses built on European lines, and the chapels were usually built of coral lime. The Wesleyans in Tonga, Fiji and Samoa were very often content with Europeanized native dwellings, but some built good weatherboard houses. The mission teachers, who were permitted to trade, could well afford to build very comfortable European dwellings. Wesleyan mission chapels never reached the European standards attained at LMS stations, largely due to the retention of native-type buildings. Amos wrote in 1857 that all the chapels in Tonga were erected without nails, 'being tied together with cocoanut fibre plaited into synet'.[45] It was not until the late 1850s that boarded chapels were becoming uniform in Tonga. Vercoe wrote angrily in 1858 that he had 'long been tired of pigeries and stables — and such our chapels must be while they remain without doors'.[46]

When Hiram Bingham went to Abaiang in 1857 he took with him sufficient lumber to erect a one-storey house, twenty-four by sixteen feet, but it was not expected that the people should adopt the same style of house. The Hawaiian teachers also built timber cabins.

Most of the missionaries were convinced that social change would have to be gradual. The earlier missionaries and theorists had held firmly to the social doctrine of the cross; they believed that Christianity was the touchstone for a revolution in manners, and that civilization followed rapidly after the preaching of the atonement. The comparatively slow progress, viewed after fifty years of contact, tended to prove otherwise. In 1854 Mills wrote from Sydney that all the early efforts to collect the various villages of a Samoan district into one settlement had failed. He had reached the conclusion that it was 'really difficult to change the social habits of a people, even when they receive the Gospel'.[47] Stallworthy was even more emphatic. Civilization which was equated with 'good houses, good bedding, and good clothing,' would very likely 'be fatal, on a large scale to health and life'.

> The philanthropist who seeks to change the lodgings and dress of the people without regarding these things, may furnish them with shrouds instead of clothing, and with tombs instead of substantial dwellings.[48]

Such a policy might change the tastes and habits of a few, but it placed those few in 'serious peril'.

Although during the first two decades of missionary contact 'civilization' was imposed rather drastically on the islanders, especially in the Society Islands, the missionaries early became aware that their own conception of civilization was not necessarily the best one for the islands. Indeed, in the matter of clothing, except for a few extremists, most of the missionaries had a more liberal outlook than has usually been imagined. Despite the pressure from the advocates of 'civilization' at home, most of the Evangelical missionaries to the South Seas gave prior importance to their religious duties, and were fully aware of the dangers of recreating the heathen in the image of themselves.

However there were some who became disillusioned when the social doctrine of the cross was belied by the experience of several decades. They looked for the explanation in terms of their racial view of man and anticipated those ideas of social Darwinism which became popular towards the end of the century. The failure of Fijians to achieve civilization through the acceptance of Christianity, for instance, confirmed their inherent prejudices.

> They seem to be utterly incapable of social & political improvement. That they are capable of a *moral* improvement is an established fact; & therefore they can be made fit for Heaven: but they cannot be made fit for Earth. It is useless to say that such as they *are,* our forefathers *were.* They are made of different stuff. . . . They live in a different mind-world, out of wh. it seems utterly impossible to bring

20 Rev. Nathaniel Turner
pioneer Methodist missionary in
New Zealand and Tonga

21 Rev. John Hunt
Wesleyan theologian and
translator in Fiji

22 Rev. John Thomas
first chairman of the Wesleyan Friendly Islands
district, authority on Tongan history and culture

23 Mission chapel at Apia, Upolu, with the graves
of Williams, Barnden and Harris

24 Mission premises at Avarua, Rarotonga, reflecting
mid-Victorian missionary ascendancy

them. They oppose a dull apathy to all social & political improvement: their houses are no better than they were in yᵉ old heathen
times: their gardens are tilled in yᵉ same primitive style: their canoes
are in no one point, improved: their habits are as filthy as ever: in
short they show themselves (with very, very few exceptions — few &
far between) to be utterly incapable of better things: & therefore do
I feel assured that they must perish from off yᵉ face of yᵉ earth. For
national advancement is a *law of God,* who has sent man upon yᵉ
Earth to replenish & subdue it; & if any people oppose thereto,
Either a stubborn will, or a sluggish indolence, they must accept yᵉ
inevitable consequence — national destruction.[49]

15

Advisers in Affairs of State

AMONGST ENGLISH Evangelicals there was a considerable range of difference concerning the nature of political freedom. On some major issues they were openly divided. Wilberforce and many of the Anglican Evangelicals who took a decided view on the question of slavery were quite antipathetic to the claims of the industrial workers. Most of the Evangelicals also stressed the value of education in teaching the duty of subordination to Christian government. Wesleyan Methodism tended to have a soporific effect on the people instead of stirring them up to take political action. The Reverend Jabez Bunting, for many years the guiding spirit of the WMMS and of Wesleyan Methodism in general, was a thorough-going Tory.[1] Occasionally a 'Methodist' preacher was found amongst the Radicals, but he was usually a renegade.[2] Methodism's major contribution to political and social reform was the adaptation of its system and methods to the more radical movements.[3] The Wesleyans, however, were champions of religious liberty, and also, like most Evangelicals of the nineteenth century, they had an emotional hatred of slavery.

It was from the tradition of Dissent that the principal impetus to the cause of 'liberty' received its strength. Dissenters had a much greater political awareness. They had been forced to fight for most of the religious privileges which they enjoyed, and which had made the lot of the various Connexionalists so much easier.[4] During the first quarter of the century sentiments were fostered amongst Dissenters which became known as 'Christian Patriotism', and which, to a large extent, influenced the Evangelicals in their attitude to state affairs. The Protestant Society for the Protection of Religious Liberty was formed and the *Patriot* newspaper was revitalized. It was restricted mainly to the nonconformist public, but was nonetheless an influential paper. Many of the LMS missionaries subscribed to it, and some contributed to it.

Despite the pressure for parliamentary reform and religious or denominational equality, the Evangelicals mostly adhered to a constitutional platform. Not only was the parliamentary system upheld as an almost sacred institution, but the House of Hanover was regarded with pious veneration, despite the mental disorder of one king and the morals of his sons. This veneration increased considerably after the accession of Victoria.

Insofar as the missionaries had a united political view, it was that every man had a right to worship as he chose, and that government should be in the interest of the greatest number. This central core of belief in religious and civil liberty found many forms of expression, from an almost Jacobinical attitude to despotism to a conservative revulsion from anything which seemed to threaten the peace of society and the sacred institution of parliament.

It has been suggested that the missionary found some compensation for his position in the fact that he was denied the opportunity of attaining public influence in England, and that the missionary career served as an outlet for the talents and intellectual energy of an ambitious labourer or artisan.[5] The latter statement is undoubtedly true, but it would be false to assume that the missionary went to Africa or the South Seas because he was denied political rights at home, and one could question if there would have been fewer missionaries if the position of Dissenters had been on a level with that of the Anglicans, both politically and socially.

The missionary had his political views and they naturally influenced him, but it must always be kept in mind that he was honour bound not to take any *active* part in politics. Wesley's dictum of 'No politics' was matched by a ruling of the LMS (see Appendices I and II). The missionary's political role was determined solely by his circumstances and environment. The very nature of the forms of government prevailing in the different island groups, in all of which religion played a predominant role and was considered an inseparable feature meant that religious change entailed a reform of government. Naturally the missionaries were expected to contribute to this rethinking process.

The political influence of the South Seas missionaries has frequently been examined,[6] but the actual dilemma of the missionaries has not always been clearly stated. The question of the relationship between Caesar and Christ has been the occasion for much dispute throughout the history of Christianity, so that, independently of the nature of native governments, there were many potential problems. The principle that missionaries should not interfere with native governments was always maintained by Evangelical missionaries. It was the policy of directors and committees, and a maxim taught to missionary candidates. The missionaries, however, regarded their role as *advisers* very seriously, and in this capacity exercised considerable and far-reaching influence in island politics.

The first missionaries to Tahiti were under the protection of the chief Pomare I, and his son Tunuiaeiteatua (the nominal king), who had obtained the ascendancy in Tahitian politics. The high chiefs of Tahiti and the neighbouring islands exercised despotic power over their people. Although the missionaries realized that they owed the preservation of their property and persons to this power, they did not believe in any form of tyrannical oppression; and, if they did not preach active rebellion, they did not think it inconsistent with their profession to proclaim the virtues of the British system, which limited the authority of the monarch.

Although the direction of the French Revolution had effectively stemmed the republican movement in England, many of the leading Evangelicals had been associated with such principles. William Carey, the leading missionary of the new era, had been censured by Andrew Fuller for not drinking the King's health.[7] Haldane had voiced equally revolutionary opinions, although he afterwards modified his position, and Dr Bogue had republican sympathies, though he kept out of controversy. We have noted, too, that there were a number of missionaries (both clerical and lay) who paraded their sympathy with the French revolutionary régime when the *Duff* was taken as a French prize. Indeed, many of the leading nonconformist divines were identified with radical political views through their writings on behalf of civil and religious liberty. It is little wonder then that the first missionaries to Tahiti talked to the people about the virtues of the rule of law and parliamentary institutions.

In 1808 a political revolution took place in Tahiti which overthrew the despotic government of Pomare II. The immediate cause of this uprising was the commission of a number of atrocities by Pomare in June 1807.[8] However James Elder, writing of the event in 1824, asserted that the missionaries had their share in stimulating opposition to the despotism.

> The conversations of the Missionaries on Civil Government, hastened the Revolution, and *was* the *cause* of *their* forming the present Government in existence at the Society Islands . . . When the free and equitable Government of England was made known to them, they quickly perceived all its advantages, and panted for one as nearly as possible to resemble it. The Chiefs were well aware of the Tendency of our Conversation, and address to produce rebellion.[9]

Elder's statement must be regarded in a polemical context, as he was attempting to refute the claim that the state of things in

Tahiti in 1824 was directly attributable to the preaching of his former colleagues. However a statement by Davies in the Public Journal for 1808 partly confirms Elder's claim that the missionaries made their sentiments known. It was believed in May 1808 that Pomare was likely to die, and the missionaries expected that there would be a restoration of the old government, '*Heau Manahune* or government of the people'. 'We think the people universally know, we do not approve of the arbitrary and oppressive proceedings of their chiefs.'[10] As far as the missionaries were concerned, chiefly government, whether by one paramount chief or by a number of independent chiefs, was tyrannical. However, with one ruler they had a better opportunity of introducing constitutional reform.

When Pomare finally returned to Moorea it was on condition that he conformed to the new order. Elder went so far as to say that Pomare accepted Christianity because his people regarded such a profession as a virtual acceptance of an enlightened government. On the other hand, the account given by the official mission historians suggests that it was the king's conversion which brought about the change, and they regarded the 'glorious Revolution' as nothing more than an insurrection against Pomare's rule. For the historians, the battle of Feipi in 1815 was the significant event. Orsmond regarded Pomare's acceptance of Christianity as being merely the ratification of a contract. Before he went to Tahiti the missionaries said to him:

> Now Pomare we have followed your father and you many years, have fallen and risen, have rested, and taken flight with you, and we have not yet effected that for which we came . . . You are now going to Tahiti to wage war, and if you get your government again, order that all must be Christians and burn their idols.[11]

Pomare's agreement with the missionaries not only secured for him the position of virtual 'head of the church', but assisted him in re-establishing his despotism.

The missionaries, however, had exerted political influence in other ways very soon after their arrival. The first change which they demanded was a reformation of the country's morals. On 11 November 1797 they had a meeting, in order to adopt rules to suppress infanticide, sodomy and human sacrifices.[12] There was disagreement at this meeting, as some were in favour of telling the people that if they did not give up these customs they would do nothing for them, and not allow them to come near their dwelling. A deputation was finally sent to Tunuiaeiteatua (Pomare II) and the other chiefs to inform them that if they would give up these customs the missionaries would serve them in anything that lay in their power. Although little was then secured, they continued their campaign against these practices. But if to urge for suppression was legitimate, any concern with punishment came under the category of interference with politics. Hence in February 1803 they wondered whether they should apply to the chiefess Itia to have a man removed from the district who had murdered another on account of theft.

> Some thought that we could not act in the path of duty as Christians and missionaries, unless we did inform Edeea of the heinousness of the man's crime and request his removal from the district. Others again thought it had nothing to do with our Christian and missionary character to interfere in the business in so publick a manner. It belonged to the civil government of the Island, which we were not to intermeddle with: and tho' it was murder in our eyes, it was not so in the eyes of this government.[13]

The majority decided against any interference.

Wherever entire communities in the South Seas adopted Christianity, there arose a need for replacing the old religious regulations for governing society. Laws adapted to Christian society were felt to be absolutely necessary for the better governance of the people. In the formulation of law codes the missionaries acted in the capacity of legal advisers. Although they were responsible for the wording of the codes, these documents were submitted to the chiefs and people for approval, in the manner that constitutions are usually submitted at public meetings. It is quite apparent that the chiefs desired to have some guide in civil affairs, as they could not invoke the threats of the old system, and they were constantly being told by the missionaries that their punishments and commands were unjust.

However the actual formulation of law codes was the result of home policy. As early as November 1815 Matthew Wilks proposed to George Burder that the mission should promote the formulation of laws. The precedent for introducing simple law codes had been established in the Calvinist missions amongst the Indians of North America. However Wilks was most directly influenced by the code of laws drawn up by the Reverend John Campbell, and agreed to by the people of Griqua town in South Africa.[14] Wilks further suggested that a deputation of missionaries should go and

> call a meeting of all the chiefs and others[,] present them for their consideration — but not to interfere at all, or act except called *by all parties* — or they might send to a few of the leading chief[s] to meet and consult on what shd. be read to them, and then all the chiefs

together to deliberate — that might bring in all the Society Islands
under the same regulations — I think you ought to draw up something of the kind — send it to the brethren, and leave it to their
discretion how to act, that is whether to present it or not.[15]

Nott and Davies carried on a correspondence with the king
on the matter. It is probable that the missionaries received legal
advice from Edward Eagar, an emancipist lawyer in Sydney, at
that time a strong supporter of all things Evangelical.* At a
meeting in January 1818 Nott stated that progress had been
made. It is significant that the missionaries who had recently
arrived questioned the propriety of the matter.[16] At a meeting in
May 1818 Nott was requested to produce the laws which had
been 'violently opposed at a former meeting'.[17] These were read
and approved. Nott and Davies were appointed to confer with
the king on the matter, and Nott was to *translate* them into
Tahitian.

Pomare at first showed considerable reluctance to act on the
advice of the missionaries. He hankered after his former despotic
powers, and yet he could also see that the missionaries, and
general contact with Europeans, had so influenced the people
and chiefs that he could do nothing without popular consent. He
was an astute politician and compromised to his own advantage.
It was not until after his death that the Tahitian government
could be brought to resemble more closely 'the free and equit-
able Government of England'.

The Tahitian code, containing eighteen articles, was publicly
'approved' on 12 May 1819.[18] Although it demanded strict observance of the Sabbath, most of its clauses related to the normal
requirements of criminal law. In most respects it did not impinge
very greatly on the arbitrary will of the king. A similar code,
containing twenty-five articles, was adopted for Raiatea, Tahaa,
Borabora and Maupiti on 12 May 1820. The missionaries Threlkeld and Williams, who designed it, introduced the measure of
trial by jury as a deliberate means of checking the power of the
chiefs,[19] and it is clear that the Tahitian missionaries would
have liked to have been able to induce Pomare to limit his own
powers. In May 1822 a further code of thirty articles, worked out
after a careful review of the Tahitian code, was adopted at
Huahine.

When Tyerman and Bennet arrived in the Society Islands

---

*Eagar was a Wesleyan local preacher. If he did not have a hand in the
1819 code, he probably assisted with the Leeward Islands codes. Lawry
stated that the laws were originally drawn up in Sydney, *Missionary
Notices*, NS IX, p. 154; Lawry, 1851, p. 82.

they observed that the laws of Tahiti had 'almost become a dead Letter'.[20] This is not surprising considering that Pomare appeared to override them himself. Mrs Crook observed that he was the first person to break the laws which he himself had established when he had two political prisoners executed despite the ruling of the judges.[21]

Both members of the deputation appear to have taken an active part in reformulating the laws, and informed the directors that they had 'assisted' in the 'forming and improving' of all the codes except that of Raiatea.[22] On 10 April 1823 an amended version of the Raiatean code was adopted at Borabora and on 2 May 1823 a revised code was adopted at Huahine.* The deputation further appears to have organized the 'first Tahitian parliament' or general assembly convened to revise the Tahitian code in February 1824, when it was extended to include forty clauses. The missionaries were in a particularly influential position as they were the virtual guardians of the young king Pomare III.

The involvement of the missionaries in the affairs of the Tahitian State did not pass without comment in Dissenting circles in Britain. Thus the Reverend John Arundel was assailed in writing by one indignant 'subscriber to missions' regarding the coronation of Pomare III, presided over by Henry Nott in 1824 'when our Missionary so *grossly abandoned the principle of Protestant Dissent* and confirmed that alliance between Church and State which we profess to deprecate, and our opposition to which subjects us to daily injuries and insults'.[22] Not content to denounce the '*treachery* or *folly* of the "Archbishop of Tahiti"' and the '*farce*' of the coronation, he called for a vote of censure on Nott's conduct at the next board meeting.

The revised code of Tahiti came much nearer to the missionaries' ideal, and approximated more closely to the codes of the Leeward Islands. Some of the new laws concerned rights of land usage. Crook wrote thus in November 1825:

> The law that is now printed and is in the hands of the chiefs, tends gradually to civilize the people: As it ascertains more clearly the right

---

*The revised laws of Huahine had been brought to Tahiti in February 1823 for Pomare Vahine to read and approve in her capacity as Teritaria, Queen of Huahine. Crook observed that the 'law concerning the protection of private property was reluctantly submitted to but that immediately following relating to the revenue was so manifestly advantageous that she consented to the whole'. Crook copied out the laws of Huahine 'by desire of the people' of Papeete who wished to have a similar code 'as our present laws leave them open to the most arbitrary abuse'. Crook, 20-21 February 1823 — SSJ, no. 63.

of private property, and protects them from the unjust ravages of the chiefs. The natural consequences however are numerous litigations and disputes amongst the various claimants of the land . . . We have taught them the nature of arbitration and have prevailed on some of our church members to settle their matters in that way . . .[24]

The code of Huahine was further revised in 1826 and extended to include fifty articles. The process of revision was more or less an annual event, and new laws were added as the necessity arose.[25]

A form of the Raiatean code was adopted at Rarotonga on 19 September 1827. Much time had been spent in conversation with the principal chiefs as to the 'propriety of which laws it would be best to introduce'.[26] One of the main difficulties concerned land rights. Pitman expressed his wish to avoid having anything to do with the political concerns of the people, and maintained that when the laws were finished he would do no more than give his advice when asked. Law codes similar to the first three codes were adopted in all the islands where the LMS had teachers. Platt records taking part in a meeting at Rimatara in 1827 when four new laws were adopted by the people. These laws concerned land usage, and Platt found it difficult to understand two of the 'statutes' because of his ignorance of native custom.[27]

The guidance given by the LMS missionaries is in strict contrast to the policy followed by the American missionaries in Hawaii, who considered that

> to write out any thing like a system of government and a corresponding code of laws, make the ideas plain and familiar to the chiefs and people, and help them to carry the whole into practice, would have been a task hopelessly formidable, and an intermedling with political affairs, plainly inconsistent with explicit instructions.[28]

The adoption of the Ten Commandments as the basis of the laws of Hawaii was a measure with definite theocratic implications. In 1827 more definite laws were adopted, and in 1829 these laws were extended to resident foreigners. When at Tahuata in the Marquesas, Darling felt it necessary to read the Ten Commandments to the people, 'that they might know the Laws of God'.[29] At that stage, however, he was not in a position to see that they were adopted.

The Wesleyans followed the procedure of the Tahitian missionaries and urged the formation of a Christian law code. Already Tongan converts had been introduced to the rigid discipline of the Ten Commandments and Wesley's Rules of

Society which had been adapted to forbid tattooing but which as yet did not extend to the community at large.[30] The first formal law code in the Tongan group was adopted at Vava'u on 10 March 1839.[31] This code was presented publicly to the chiefs and people, and each regulation was approved singly. Thomas remarked that the system was not a novel one.

> The code of laws is not altogether new, the spirit of most of them having been acted upon for some time past; but a few hundred copies have just now been struck off; and the King has given them the royal sanction.[32]

These laws contained the essence of a criminal code, but they also reflected the supreme power of the king, and regulated Christian duties. It was some years before a more comprehensive and sophisticated code was adopted. At the annual meeting of the Tongan missionaries in 1847, presided over by Lawry, it was recommended that the king should obtain the 'opinion and advice of the highest English legal authority in New Zealand'.[32] The advice received from this authority, the Chief Justice, Sir William Martin, was that the king could do no better than adopt a code similar to that of Huahine published in Ellis' *Polynesian Researches,* with the necessary alterations and modifications. A translation of the Huahine laws was prepared and placed in the hands of the king and chiefs, and various alterations and additions were made. The missionaries also suggested several important alterations.

> We were very careful to impress them with the conviction, that these laws must be adopted and promulgated as their own, and not as the laws of the Missionaries. This was accordingly done; and, when the code was finally completed, and made law, by public and regal authority, the Missionaries found in it much that was contrary to their own views. It was, however, a great advance upon the brief and imperfect code already in operation, and would, no doubt, prepare the way for something better still.[34]

The resulting code of forty-three articles was a marked advance on the earlier one. The more theocratic element was excluded, and specific punishments were recommended.[35] Pritchard, the British consul at Samoa, appears to have influenced the chiefs to unite with the king in drawing up the new code.[36] Peter Turner remarked in November 1849 that the king and chiefs were becoming jealous of the missionaries 'interfering with what they think their prerogatives.'

> We have been recommending to them a better code of laws, but o no things must remain as they are and we are thought evil of for our

wishing to elevate them in the scale [of] civilization; and we have but little hopes of seeing them much better.[37]

As the law codes helped to support traditional authority, there was little opposition from the chiefs. It was also characteristic of these codes that they were regarded as the arbitrary rule of a supreme high chief, and as being consonant only with his rule. When there was opposition from chiefs it was usually rooted in opposition to Christian morality.

In Samoa, and also in Fiji, where chiefly authority was restricted to comparatively small districts, and where even paramountcies rarely extended over all the districts of an island, there was a virtual absence of any authority which might enforce a law code. In the smaller islands and groups, national circumstances and the considerable influence of European contact had enabled one high chief to establish a 'permanent-type' authority unknown in traditional culture. This had not eventuated in Samoa, although the missionaries, especially Williams, had at first thought that Malietoa was the equivalent of the other island kings. The missionaries regarded all attempts at Samoan unification by themselves and other interested parties to be in vain.[38] They found that even in each district there were chiefs and heads of families who were not 'converted', and who were not 'willing to abide by the laws of God'. However, in Samoa traditional 'law' survived the effects of contact and from the point of view of civil order there was less need for laws. The missionary felt his duty was more obviously the amelioration of methods of punishment.

Tutuila and Manu'a were the only islands in the Samoan group where the missionaries made any progress in introducing a law code. There opportunities were greater than in other parts because of the comparative smallness of the islands, the apparent political unity, and the strength of religious pressure.

Both Slatyer and Murray were considering the question in 1841. In October 1841 Slatyer explained to the chiefs 'a court of Justice in England and shewed them the firmness of English Judges'.[39] In November he talked with Murray about the 'propriety of advising the Chiefs to have a code of simple laws drawn up and written'.

> We definitely fixed on 3 only, on which to give them our advice at present — as new laws can be added according as circumstances require — On Adultery — Theft and fighting — we were particular in explaining to them the footing on which we stood as only *advising* — and they *conscious of their standing* replied to our statements — saying very good you have stated your advice — leave it with us —

we will assemble our body of Chiefs and consult whether these things
be agreeable to us — and we will tell you the result saying also as for
themselves they felt the need of such arrangements and were quite
agreeable to it.[40]

The first Tutuila law code was drawn up under the guidance
of Murray, and consisted of a number of written laws 'respecting
murder and theft, and adultery, and fornication; and clandestine
marriages, and lost property and fruit gathered without the
owner's consent, and assisting those who act wickedly'.[41]
Although it was officially adopted, this written code was considered a failure by the missionaries. In July 1853 Powell wrote
that the code was ineffectual because it did not affect the law-
givers. He considered the real weakness to lie in the fact that
each chief had so much authority in his own local sphere, and
the other chiefs did not have sufficient power to see that the
code was observed outside their own spheres. Furthermore, the
individual chiefs resented the 'interference by missionaries' in
their local concerns.[42] However during 1851 Powell and Murray
had visited Manu'a, and Murray had been successful in 'getting
a written code of laws ostensibly adopted by the whole island'.[43]

Powell endeavoured to frame a more definite code for Tutuila
in 1854. He attempted to persuade the people, by means of a
sermon, that their 'path of duty was plain, *not as politicians,* but
as *Christians* and *Christian teachers'*, to propose new measures.[44]
A code of nineteen laws was framed, based on Murray's earlier
code. Although some of the most influential chiefs were in
favour of its adoption, it was vetoed by several of them who
'asserted that the former code was maintained and enforced'.
Nothing more could be done. However even in Fiji, where there
was no overall unified government, it was still possible for
missionary-inspired law codes to operate in areas dominated by
powerful chiefs. Thus, in Lakeba, as the result of an influential
chief's visit to Tonga, a brief code of laws was introduced before
the end of October 1862.[45]

Besides the law codes, the missionaries were instrumental in
persuading the chiefs to institute port regulations. In this they
received considerable co-operation from visiting ships' captains,
who occasionally took the initiative in the matter.[46] The missionaries were frequently abused for the moral support which
they gave to the chiefs in enforcing these regulations. In cases
where action was taken against offending captains, especially in
the first days of missionary activity, the culpable parties quite
often regarded it as a kind of bad joke that 'black men should
make laws'. For instance Captain Potten of the *Westmoreland,*

known to the natives as 'the savage beast'— he was reputed to hoist naked females to the yardarm — must have been peculiarly incensed when subjected to Raiatean justice.[47] European settlers were also irked at mission-sponsored restrictions. Even in 1859 Platt reported similar sentiments being voiced at Raiatea.

> These Americans have no idea of being subject to a coloured government: Are disaffected to the laws, on which they always wish to trample, or set them at defiance, because they are only blackfellows laws.[48]

The existence of a theocratic element in the island states was more readily accepted, because of the close interrelation of religious and civil affairs under the old order, but it would be misleading to regard the 'missionary kingdoms' as theocracies. Theocracy necessarily implies rule by either the clergy, or by the saints or church members. The island states were primarily chiefly in government, and it was the chiefs in their secular role who had the ultimate authority. It was largely the theocratic bias in the law codes which was responsible for spreading the idea that theocracies had been established. William Ellis was not quite correct when he compared the influence of a missionary with that of an active clergyman in England.[49] The missionary's influence was more far-reaching than that of a parochial clergyman, and more comparable to the influence of Christian leaders during periods of the Church's ascendancy. The real nature of missionary influence might be gathered from the following narrative. On one occasion the judges of Moorea made a by-law concerning price-fixing which William Henry, the resident missionary, considered unjust.

> On these things coming to my knowledge I was much surprised, grieved and vexed. Surprised that they should take such a step without consulting me, as they had been in the habit of consulting me in everything of any importance; and grieved and vexed that they should establish so unjust and opressive a law.[50]

Henry's anger increased when several women (including one of his own servants) were committed to prison. When the morning of the trial arrived he went to the place of judgement.

> As soon as the judges had assembled and taken their seats, I arose and addressed them and the court at considerable length, pointing out the unlawfulness, injustice, and wickedness of such proceedings, and exhorted them to repent and to desist from judging the women . . . I endeavoured to aggravate their guilt by the consideration that the women were members of the Church, and the greater part of the judges themselves members also.

Henry persuaded the judges to release the women, and letters arrived from Tahiti ordering them not to judge the women.

Henry was censured by the directors for his interference in this matter, and wrote a lengthy defence of his actions.

> My opinion is that Judges, Noblemen, and Kings too who imploy Chaplains and put themselves under spiritual guides, should be sharply and faithfully reproved by these guides when they deserve to be so delt with.

He qualified his action still further by saying that all concerned were under his direct pastoral care.

> There is scarcely one of the Judges and Chiefs I reproved, but were members of the Church over which I am Pastor, and the very few who were not, had been baptized and were my hearers, and I therefore ask whether I had not a right to reprove them and that sharply when they deserved it? Not one of them ever told me that I had no right to reprove them; such an idea never entered into their heads.

Nevertheless Henry agreed with the propriety of not publishing his account, as the world was ready to make 'false judgements'.[51]

Although this was a case of the exertion of influence in civil matters, it was a type of influence which might take place in any Christian community, though in a less dramatic way. It was actual interference in political situations which was expressly forbidden to the missionaries, and such interference rarely took place. On the other hand, the influence of private conversations may have been far-reaching, and almost certainly sermons which carried political overtones were chosen.

Very often the missionary was unaware of the extent of his influence. Slatyer of Tutuila spoke to the chief Olo about the crime of the native teacher Isaia who had committed adultery. He urged Olo 'as one holding high civil authority to be firm in showing his disapprobation and abhorance of the crime'.

> I refused (though strongly requested by him) to specify any punishment — said it was entirely their business to determine the penalty as to nature and extent — all I said was it ought to be heavy — He said they would not flinch. . . . His remarks led me to suppose I had a much greater influence over the people than I had been accustomed to think I had.[52]

Most of the missionaries did not hestitate to influence civil affairs when they thought that their influence had a justifiable moral end. Orsmond went so far as to require certain standards of civilization from his church members (see page 276), and had a church law established to secure this end.

> While the people see they can obtain their wishes because the teacher is lenient they use every measure to deceive but I will now be prompt and will have uniformity both in carnal things as well as spiritual things.[53]

Orsmond was speaking about church members. Chiefs did not always appreciate the distinction.

If the missionaries influenced the making of laws, they were sometimes guilty of a certain social injustice by adhering too closely to their platform of non-intervention in civil affairs. This is seen very clearly in their attitude to punishment. Not infrequently they had to intervene, in order to dissuade the chiefs from using rather barbarous methods. On the other hand, they did not always make it their business to know the real conditions of 'justice'. For them the purpose of punishment was to induce shame; for the judges and chiefs the old maxim of an eye for an eye still prevailed, and there was a tendency to obey the letter rather than the spirit of the law. Some of the charges laid against Thomas of Tonga by the Chevalier Dillon were based on harsh treatment meted out by the judges and chiefs.[54] Armitage was surprised at the indifference of the missionaries at Rarotonga.[55] Some men who had committed adultery received a whipping near where he was working. Not only were they whipped, but they also had to give up their property. The offenders were tied to a long pole, the drums beat, and then the judges came to administer the flogging. Some had whips and others had rope ends. Armitage watched six judges each giving each offender sixteen lashes, and Makea told him that sometimes more than ten persons flogged one individual. He asked the missionary why each person had received more than ninety lashes, and was told that the law was for forty only. Shocked by this Armitage appealed: 'Have missionaries any business to make laws for the State?' Perhaps it would have been more fruitful to ask if the missionary did not have a duty to see that the law was rightly understood, and to see that it was administered adequately.

There is considerable foundation for the belief that consciousness of the duty of the Christian missionary to remain aloof from political interference was in itself the root of much political difficulty. When a missionary acted simply as an adviser, chaplain-fashion, his influence was often a corrective in island politics. As a mediator, he was able to prevent bloodshed or acts of barbarous cruelty. In island politics the 'aloofness' of the missionaries often meant that the native legislation departed from the spirit of the teaching of the missionaries, and they themselves were usually blamed for such legislation. However in cases where international politics were involved missionaries came close to converting non-participation into passive resistance, obstructionism, and a policy of non-co-operation which had far-reaching political implications. This is made very plain by the attitude adopted by the dominant section of the LMS missionaries in Tahiti at the time of the establishment of the French Protectorate.

The missionaries had a very good case for resenting the direction of affairs after the ultimatums of Du Petit-Thouars. The grievances and agitation which had brought about French intervention were viewed as quite insufficient justification for such drastic political interference. The chiefs who sought protection were regarded as dupes to Moerenhout's cunning, or as traitors to their sovereign. The missionaries were also imbued with a fiercely nationalist spirit, and saw in French policy the unseen hand of the Catholic Propaganda. Disappointment and uneasiness were to be expected.

The behaviour of certain members of the Tahitian mission after 1842 is highly questionable, for though they took no political action as such, their demeanour was calculated to frustrate and offend the French authorities. The missionaries cannot altogether be blamed for this as to a certain degree they were misled by the nature of the religious-cum-political agitation emanating from Exeter Hall and the Mission House. This propaganda and pressure was itself stimulated by a good deal of misinformation derived from faulty knowledge of the real state of Tahiti, and from biased accounts sent home from the field. It seems quite clear that the shooting of McKean at Matavai in June 1844 was accidental, and the missionaries on the spot did not suggest otherwise, yet Thomas Heath, who had not been present on the occasion, wrote in an article expressly written for publication that it appeared 'without doubt, that poor McKean was *designedly* shot by the French, tho it is not known that it was by the order of their commander'.[56] Indeed, some of the missionaries appeared to welcome every unfortunate incident which they could bring against the French.

It is surprising that some of the missionaries were tolerated to the extent they were by Governor Bruat, and perhaps only his knowledge that the British Government had promised to maintain the right of the British Protestant missionaries 'to enjoy entire and unrestricted freedom in the exercise of their religious functions' prevented him from taking more stringent measures.[57]

Thomson was always complaining of having the inconvenience of obtaining passports to visit the Tahitian camp at Papenoo, yet this very camp was hostile to the French, and by visiting it and by only celebrating the ordinances there Thomson was equally guilty of encouraging the 'Patriots' to hold out against the French. Until Britain acknowledged the Protectorate, the missionaries, as Tahitian citizens as well as British nationals, were in the unhappy position of having to accept the French Protectorate simply as a *de facto* government, and most of them did this whilst openly sympathizing with the Tahitian resistance. Heath described the camps as 'well-managed, and full of praying men — men of the Parliamentary-army-stamp in the struggle against Charles I'.[58] Orsmond's connexion with the LMS was terminated on the grounds of collaboration with the French, yet his policy seems to have been in the best interests of peace. When Britain recognized the Protectorate the more militant missionaries still refused to co-operate, hoping that the continued resistance of the Tahitians would induce the French to withdraw. They earned the displeasure of Captain Hamond for expressing doubts respecting the durability of the Protectorate, and for introducing a subject 'so foreign to the exercise of their religious functions' in a letter to Governor Bruat.[59] Hamond advised them to persuade the Tahitians to submit to the French. 'This we could not do; partly from the temper of Pomare and her people, and partly from the efforts of their friends in Europe . . .'[60] Davies, who exerted all his influence to induce the people to remain quiet, and who showed a 'strong inclination to apologize for the French', was regarded as almost as much a traitor as Orsmond.

The Tahitians were mainly responsible for their own stubborn resistance to the Protectorate, but it cannot be denied that they were considerably encouraged to resist, even after Britain had acknowledged the Protectorate, by the proceedings and attitudes of the missionaries who then, more than at any other time, voiced the doctrine that missionaries had no part in politics.

The Evangelical missionaries, whether they were Dissenters with a radical bias or conservative Methodists, found that the world of island politics was quite distinct from anything they had previously known. Most of them believed in a doctrine of liberty, 'England's boast' as Hunt called it,[61] and openly preached against any absolute measures which they deemed to be anti-Christian. Their influence in island politics tended to be indirect and ecclesiastical, in a theocratic sense, rather than political. They were never agitators like some of their brethren in other parts. The great political issues of the world at large had no place in the missionary endeavour. The Reverend John Waterhouse wrote in 1841:

> But what a stir! Popery, Puseyism, Chartism, Socialism, and all the varieties of Republicanism, etc! But the armies of Emmanuel are in the field; the struggle may be severe; but 'truth is mighty, and must prevail.' Now, I must look to my own work among the Heathen. Lord, help me![62]

Missionaries in the South Seas were early confronted with local wars and with the problems arising from them. Warfare had a definite place in most island societies, and prestige went with military prowess. War was one of the evils which the missionaries declared they had come to overthrow. Even the most sophisticated island peoples merited the style of 'savages' for the atrocities which they committed in their wars. Burning of dwellings, indiscriminate slaughter, impaling of infants on pikes and even cannibalism were common to many of the groups. European arms helped considerably to overthrow the existing balance of power, and early missionaries (in Tahiti) were occasionally forced to exchange muskets for their protection and for their subsistence.

Missionaries were rarely able to prevent war, although they denounced warfare in their sermons. Nevertheless they reduced the range of traditional type wars. One of the many associations which arose out of British Evangelicalism was the Peace Society, which aimed at the 'adjustment of international disputes, and . . . the promotion of universal peace, without resort to arms'.[63] The influence of this society was quite extensive, but if pacifism was the ideal, most Evangelicals believed that there were 'righteous wars'. Despite the efforts of missionaries to prevent war, it was left to the colonial governments of the latter half of the century to enforce the peace.

The missionaries came to distinguish three types of war, pagan, religious and political. Pagan wars were, for the most part, political. They took place where Christianity was not established, or where the Christian cause was very small. In these wars the missionaries desired their converts to take no part. However they felt they had to permit them to fight in wars of self-defence. Only in Fiji was pacifism encouraged to almost disastrous lengths. By forbidding their converts to follow their chiefs in any campaigns, the Wesleyans not only encouraged disloyalty, but placed their followers in a highly compromised situation.[64] It is little wonder that when the Christians were themselves threatened and were obliged to take part in a defensive war they were refused assistance by their logical 'protectors'. The missionaries also discovered that by adopting pacifism the people were encouraging bloodshed. During the Bua War from 1849 to 1852 the missionaries gave up their policy of forbidding their converts to engage in war, and instead urged them to do all in their power to effect humane settlements.[65]

Pagan wars were mostly regarded as a direct visitation of providence, in the same manner as famines and hurricanes. Thus the missionaries at Tahiti wrote in 1800:

> We hear great preparations are making, whether for war or peace is to be determined in a short time by some heathenish divination. If it should prove for war, those who are eager for blood seem determined to glut themselves. We rejoice that the Lord of Hosts is the God of the heathen as well as the captain of the armies of Israel; and while the potsherds of the earth are dashing themselves to pieces one against the other, they are but fulfilling his determinate counsels and foreknowledge.[66]

The wars which the missionaries recognized as religious were fought by parties which took sides on the question of the new religion and the old culture. In these wars the missionaries saw a miniature war of light against darkness, and they were not slow to tell their flock of Jehovah, the God of battles. There was also a tendency to see religious issues as the object of wars which were equally political. However the missionaries did not regard these wars as a necessity. It would be more correct to say that the wars themselves were inevitable wherever pockets of pagan resistance remained. In most of the groups these partly religious wars occurred before the final establishment of Christianity.

The tradition in parts of Tonga that some of the missionaries were war-mongers no doubt arose from a spirit of militant righteousness. It is also possible that many Tongans believed themselves justified in giving physical expression to the anti-pagan views of the missionaries. Certainly in the months immediately before the war of 1837, the texts of the missionary sermons and the lessons contained in the bellicose passages from Isaiah and the Psalms printed in the schoolbooks could all be interpreted by the Christian soldiers of Tonga as a mandate to slay and disfigure the enemy, even to the smashing-in of his teeth.[67] The following account must also be shorn of polemic overtones, but even when this is done it is difficult to exonerate the missionary for allowing his image to be tarnished.

After the sack and massacre of Huli [Hule, 25 January 1837] the bodies of some of the dead were taken inside the Wesleyan Mission premises and stacked up there for inspection by the missionaries. The missionaries asked why the corpses were brought into their yard, and the natives replied by asking 'was it not by your instructions that we made war upon the heathen?' 'We have brought the corpses here that you may know how obedient we have been.' The missionary said 'We do not wish the corpses to be brought here', and asked the natives to remove them; when the natives again asked 'Was it our wish to kill our relatives and friends?' 'Was it not at your advice, and suggestion, and instigation that we did so?' Then they removed the corpses. The missionary who instigated them most to massacre, and ill-treat the heathen was the Rev. James Watkin . . .[68]

In some areas the issues were complicated by the advent of Roman Catholic priests, who usually sought the protection of a pagan chief. In the Tongan war of 1852 it appears that the Wesleyans gave their full support to King George Tupou in his attempt to put down minority resistance to his government. In this war the chiefs of Houma and Pea armed themselves, because they did not wish to submit to 'the general laws of the land'. They argued that the king wished to force them to become Christians. The offensive seems to have been taken by the 'rebels', but for them there was little alternative. The missionaries acted as mediators, but they could achieve little. West offered to accompany a messenger to Houma 'to employ what influence a Missionary might have on such an occasion'. Throughout the war the missionaries 'felt it to be their duty to visit regularly the few fortified towns, as well as the stockades and camps thrown up around Bea, for preaching and other spiritual purposes'.[69] However they never went alone, and were provided with a guard of armed men by the king.

The political wars of the nominally Christian islands were the most disturbing. It was natural that pagans should war amongst themselves; it was inevitable that Satan should make his last stand against the forces of righteousness; but only human perversity and inattention to the gospel could explain the wars of Christian countries. Political wars raged principally in Tahiti and the other Society Islands and in Samoa. In these political wars the situation of the missionary was often painfully delicate. In the disturbances of 1831-32 the missionaries of the Leewards tended to be ranged on the opposite side from that of the missionaries on Tahiti. According to the chief Utami and one of Tati's sons, Williams of Raiatea made powder for the war and gave sheet lead from the bottom of a sugar mill for bullets. They asserted that there would have been less trouble if he had been neutral. Utami regarded Williams as the *tamu* or root of the war — 'Had he staid at his post all would have been right'.[70] Certainly Williams desired the defeat of Tapoa because of his support of the powerful *Mamaia* sect, or 'fanatics' as he called them.[71] On the other hand, Orsmond did all he could to prevent the chiefs of Taiarapu from taking up arms against the Queen, and was rewarded by having his station pillaged. In his own account Orsmond tells how he took a piece of melon to Taviri, the native governor and leader of the disaffected party, and held it by one end, desiring the chief to hold the other, and break it into two pieces. He reports himself as saying: 'Now let us eat for the last time together. In eternity tell God that the gospel you would not hear, but that before you entered destruction your teacher and you mingled our tears over a large piece of melon'.[72] This device was only temporarily effective, but reflects Orsmond's pacific policy.

In the later wars in the Leeward Islands the missionaries were continually acting as mediators, but they found it very difficult to prevent fighting taking place. Even in these political wars one side was usually more pro-missionary than the other. The war of Tahitian resistance might be included amongst the political wars. The missionaries had access to the camps of the 'patriots', and regarded the Tahitians as being on the side of 'civil and religious liberty'.[73] Most of them were sympathetic with the movement of resistance. Davies was the only missionary who expressed definite pacifist views. 'I do confess that my views of Christians engaging in war are not far from those of the Society of Friends.'[74] He criticized his brethren for deserting their stations, and lamented the charge that the Christian missionary, 'the man of peace had been swallowed up in the hostile politician'.

During the Samoan wars the missionaries did not restrict their pastoral activities to one side, and they had free access into most of the camps. At some stations church members were excluded for joining the 'war party'.[75] Stallworthy deprived a teacher of his office for going to war in 1848, but he did not consider 'the mere fact' of his church members and candidates going to war 'a call for the exercise of discipline'.[76] He feared, however, that they would be 'exposed to many evil influences'. Barbara Isabella Buchanan records how difficult it was for those residing at her father's mission station.

> The people inevitably had relations in both of the belligerent parties, and their Christianity was severely tested when they firmly ignored

taunts and rejected the temptation to avenge the death of these relatives as they would have done in pre-missionary days. This was specially hard when passing war parties, in addition to their jeers, exhibited the heads of those they had slain.[77]

In preaching against war the missionaries naturally became involved in island politics. In teaching that the 'conquered' party had equal human rights with the 'victorious' party they were introducing entirely new conceptions of justice and government. Although they considered that 'righteous wars' were included in God's plan for the nations, the missionaries believed that their essential task was that of 'messengers of peace'.

16

The Churches Consolidate

IN THE PATTERN of missionary activity in the South Seas two cross-currents of missionary influence can be discerned as moulding the shape of the new society. One of these currents, the more dramatic, was of a negative kind. It swept away many of the old features of the traditional society, robbing the old gods of their power and the people of many of their pleasures. But against this was a more positive current which in large measure helped to preserve much of the old culture. This was the form of Christianity itself, the movement towards formation of churches and associations of churches.

In some of the groups (Tahiti and the Society Islands, Tonga, and some of the other Polynesian islands) Christianity was established as the national religion under benevolent despotisms. In other groups where the power of one chief was not predominant large numbers professed the new creed due to the influence of powerful chiefs, as in Samoa. Even in Fiji and the Melanesian islands the power of local chiefs cannot be ignored. Certainly, persecution of individual Christians did take place in many of the groups, but where it was more pronounced, as in Fiji or Tongatapu, we find that the persecuted minorities were headed by Christian chiefs, who were allied to more powerful Christian chiefs.

Thus it was that in the areas fully evangelized before 1860 we find that the communities affected by Christianity were generally the whole population of an island, or all those in allegiance to a particular chief or group of chiefs. Instead of being minorities who had to refashion their corporate life within social contexts radically unaffected by the change, each entire community took the decisions which otherwise would have been taken by individuals. Because of this community development, the essential fabric of native society remained unchanged, and consequently we do not find independent, more democratic, institutions growing up beside the old traditional forms, as has occurred in other mission fields. Naturally, the church which grew up in one of these chiefly communities approximated more to the 'parish' type than to the 'gathered' type.

Most of the Evangelical missionaries were more familiar with
the concept of the 'gathered' church. The majority of the LMS
missionaries were Dissenters, and were so imbued with this concept that they used the term 'chapel' rather than 'church'. Thus
we find William Henry, a Churchman who had been associated
with the Countess of Huntingdon's Connexion, resenting his
octagonal church building at Moorea being referred to as a
chapel, instead of a church, by the other missionaries.[1] In the
'gathered' churches membership was always strictly regulated,
and was usually by profession of faith and the consent of the
other members. In the 'parish' type churches membership was
usually controlled by the minister of the church, and the baptized were usually admitted to membership automatically.

In the islands the Methodist system was possibly more adapted
to the situation, as all converts could become 'members of society'
whether they belonged to the inner circle or not, whereas in the
churches formed by the LMS missionaries the distinction between
the elect (or church members) and adherents was much more
marked. The first missionaries to Tahiti, possibly owing to the
influence of Calvinistic Methodism, had published a catechism
in Tahitian which implied that all who were baptized might be
admitted to communion. Thus it was that in the period immediately after the mass 'conversion' of the people due to Pomare's
influence no baptisms were permitted, although numerous nominal adherents could be found. This was further complicated by
the fact that Pomare, who had declared himself to be on the side
of Christianity in such a public way, was not regarded as a fit
subject for membership for moral reasons. The directors took
the view that there should be little delay in baptism, and resolved
'that every person making a deliberate and credible profession
of believing in the Lord Jesus Christ, as the Saviour of sinners,
ought speedily to be baptized'.[2] They also resolved that the passage in the Tahitian catechism relating to the subject of baptism
should 'be made to conform' to these instructions, contained in
the Secretary's letter of 1 September 1818.

After the first baptism, it was left to the individual missionaries of each station to decide for themselves on the question of
membership. Most of the missionaries drew a marked distinction
between the qualifications of candidates for baptism and candidates for church membership. Naturally, the Evangelical missionary was not satisfied with a mere profession of belief, and demanded a second conversion, which he believed to be the work
of grace. Because a community movement was so deeply involved
with the desire for membership, it was not easy for the mission-

aries to cope with the situation. It meant, very often, that they accepted people into the church, only to exclude them again. This suspension and excommunication became marked features of church life. Some missionaries endeavoured to restrict membership as much as possible, but the majority, no doubt for a variety of reasons, including their own missionary reputation and the difficulty of discriminating between the converts, were content to accept those who appeared to be consistent in their professions of faith. Bourne was criticized by Buzacott for having baptized numerous persons at Rarotonga whom Buzacott felt were devoid of godliness.[3] The LMS missionaries made similar criticisms of the Wesleyans.

Orsmond stated his position as follows:

> I do not baptize them because I believe them to be really converted to the Lord Jesus Christ, but because they have avowedly cast away their vile practices of stealing, adultery, cursing, and are learning with diligence the word of eternal life . . . on this subject I pleaded when I first entered the Islands and though it was then scorned it has at length come to the same thing.[4]

Of candidates for church membership he said:

> I see the same people from years end to years end, not a new face, I know their dwellings, habits, and have them in daily tuition; I can say nothing against the external deportment, they attend punctually all meetings, yet when they come to solicit the privilege of church fellowship there is a vagueness and certain something in the conversation that leaves the case doubtful as to the propriety of refusing the person's request.[5]

No doubt most of the missionaries would have agreed with George Pritchard, who affirmed in 1826 'that nine-tenths, of those who were in Church fellowship [were] strangers to the power of vital Godliness'.[6]

The 'reforming' missionaries who came to Tahiti in 1838 and the years following attempted to apply the principles of the 'gathered' church more rigidly to the Tahitian churches. McKean was particularly critical of the different standards of communion which had been adopted in Tahiti.

> It must be remembered, however, that a principle part of the former missionaries have either imbibed their views of church fellowship from an indifferent source at home, or having no experience of such matters ere they came forth, have found their views on this topic from their experience here. For example when it has been expressed as a matter of surprise to one missionary that he could dispense the

ordinance of the supper to such people, — it has been answered that
the great bulk of Church members were almost as good as those of
the Church of England of which he himself had been a member.[7]

McKean reduced the number of his church members from 97 to
28,[8] but he was sadly disillusioned by them. The older brethren,
who preferred to work in larger numbers, felt that fewer mistakes were made in being less restrictive. The remodelling of the
churches was not a success. As far as the missionaries were concerned, the flaws in the church systems which emerged in the
islands were those which Dissenters usually claimed to be the
flaws in established churches.

When forming the churches under their care the missionaries
attempted to make them resemble those with which they were
familiar at home. Amongst the missionaries who shared a Congregational background the *Church Members' Guide*, by John
Angell James, was very popular. Pritchard translated this work
into Tahitian, and it was retranslated into Rarotongan by the
native teacher Okotai.[9] Even some of the church buildings were
closely modelled on English chapels. The church at Moorea was
built in the tradition of the Methodist octagonal chapels built
during the Evangelical Revival, and was inspired by Surrey
chapel. This building had certain local features and blended
quite well with the local architecture. On the other hand, Buzacott of Rarotonga did not seem to be concerned with retaining
any of the native features, and wanted a building which had
'buttresses, Gothic windows, Tower and vestry'.[10] However a
great many of the church buildings were native-style structures,
combining features of the traditional art with the few essential
features of a Christian place of worship. Native-style churches
were perhaps more predominant in the Wesleyan missions,
where some of them really did achieve an indigenous variant of
the 'beauty of holiness'. Royce thus described a chapel at Ono in
the Lau islands, constructed of *vesi* timbers:

> thatched in Tongan fashion, and matted throughout with fine sail
> mats: the rafters 7 feet up from the wall plates were covered and
> spangled with sinnet work, and between the rafters, the ridge pole
> and several other of the large timbers entirely covered with sinnet;
> a pulpit and neat communion rail were arranged with taste and
> displayed considerable ingenuity; from the border of the thatch all
> round streamers of the white courie shell dangled most gracefully.[11]

It is fair comment on the formation of churches in all the islands
that the missionaries often had to remove from the church build-

ings emblems and designs of a sexual nature which they deemed ugly and obscene, but which the people regarded as part of the basic pattern of life, and not inconsistent with the glory of God. Often in the interior design of the church buildings the native craftsmen excelled themselves, thus preserving some of their culture which the missionaries were destroying in other ways.

As an institution in the life of the islanders the church had a disciplinary function. In endeavouring to 'sort the sheep from the goats', the Evangelical missionaries used every means to test the faith of the people. Thus, often certain things were required of members as a kind of outward sign, although these require-ments were not essential to the Christian system. As the principles of the Decalogue were usually enforced by the civil law, the godly community needed to be distinguished by conformity to yet stricter standards. In the Society Islands tattooing was not forbidden by civil law, except when the codes were first intro-duced, and consequently it was forbidden only to church mem-bers. Candidates for baptism were also required to show that they were earnest in their wish to become Christians by conforming to these outward signs (for Rarotonga, see Appendix III). Smoking was another issue used to separate the godly from the rest of the community. It was believed that by these means the church would more readily approximate to the gathered company of believers. This policy was not simply the result of arbitrary whims, as the things forbidden were regarded as being unbecom-ing practices for a Christian.

The missionaries of the LMS and the WMMS were not con-sistent in their attitude to smoking. In Tahiti Jones and Darling were both continuous smokers, whilst Platt threatened his mem-bers with excommunication for smoking on the Sabbath.[12] Lee of Tonga, who was a non-smoker, made scornful reference to the 'fumish Fijian Brethren', and criticized some of his Tongan brethren for relaxing the laws that local preachers should not smoke. He said that the prohibition was 'admirable as a test of principle'. Lee praised Thomas for his condemnation of smoking as a 'silly, nasty, dirty custom productive of much evil as well as an uncleanly and unwholesome self-indulgence'.[13] The policy advocated by Lee, Adams and others was that unless the preachers 'smoked for some purpose — and glorified God by it, it was wrong'. Lee allowed the preachers to act according to their conscience, 'but soon found that they made it not a matter of conscience but being unrestrained by any positive rule — many of them would take each a man with him when going to his appointment to follow with a firestick so that they might smoke when they pleased: Some of them went into the pulpit with a cigar behind their ears: so much for Tongan conscience and Tongan sense of propriety'. Lee was able to persuade the majority of local preachers in his particular circuit to give up the habit. If they were unable to do so they were expected to resign. Several local preachers and leaders were lost in this way. The test of principle was a prominent feature of Evangelical church life in the islands.

In Samoa and Rarotonga the LMS missionaries were more united in their crusade against smoking. In 1848 the Cook Island missionaries passed a resolution to the effect that they resolved 'to oppose by all moral means the use of tobacco, by the natives of these islands believing it to be most detrimental to the physical and social interests of man'. In the same years two students from the training institution at Rarotonga were dismissed 'for not being willing to give up the use of Tobacco'.[14] When Powell visited Manu'a in 1851 he found that all the members were addicted to smoking, and consequently founded an 'anti-Tobacco association'.[15] A similar association was commenced at Tutuila. On Savai'i smoking was only forbidden to teachers. According to Pratt, when a teacher wished to leave the mission he would make his pipe 'a kind of devil's colors', an outward sign that he had 'gone over to the enemy'.[16]

There was a strong tendency for the Evangelical missionaries to tell their converts that smoking was morally wrong or sinful, instead of arguing that it was a 'useless and wasteful indulgence'. In doing this, as Bishop Patteson later remarked, they produced a 'confusion of the moral sense'. It was difficult to respond naturally to an 'arbitrary prohibition of a practice which, as a matter of fact, is a common practice with thousands of excellent Christians'.[17]

Another test of principle was abstention from alcoholic beverages. As in the case of smoking, there was division amongst the missionaries on the question of abstinence. It was not until after the advent of the temperance movement, so active in the 1830s, that teetotalism became a distinguishing feature of Evangelicals in British countries and in America, and even then there were those who regarded total abstinence as an unnecessary measure. In 1841 Dr Ross advised the directors of the LMS that all their missionaries should belong to temperance societies, and that teetotallers should be preferred. Each missionary should be asked 'Do you smoke? Do you drink brandy or gin or rum?'[18] It is interesting that some 'teetotallers' did not regard the moderate drinking of wines and ales, when taken at meals or medicinally, as being contrary to their pledge. In 1840 John Hunt of Fiji examined himself, and came to the determination 'to give up those needless self indulgences, which [he had] not yet fully abandoned, such as drinking wine or spirits, or smoking tobacco, except any of them may be needed as medicine'.[19]

Naturally, in establishing 'a steady people', the missionaries excommunicated their church members for drunkenness. The temperance movement, however, was a means used to influence the entire community, not only the church members. Very few mission stations were unaffected by the spirit trade carried on by visiting ships and resident 'grog' sellers. It is a revealing commentary on the missionaries that, although they attempted to protect their members and adherents from 'the drinking Devil', they were slow to take public action and took their initiative from the more universal movement. Although the missionaries were worried about the problems arising from heavy drinking by the people, it was not until they received temperance literature from their pastors at home and from some American missionaries that they decided what action to take.

When a deputation of American missionaries visited Tahiti in 1832, they particularly urged 'the doctrine of total abstinence from *ardent spirits*'. The reaction of the Tahitian missionaries shows that, at that time, teetotalism was exceptional.

> They were all disposed to plead for the *temperate use*. When we urged that at best it was unnecessary, some disputed and said they doubted not but we used strong ale or some other substitute, and when assured that we used nothing but water, they scarcely knew whether to believe us or not. We next urged that even if they did not drink to excess and if their health was not injured by it, their reputation was, for we had heard many reports that intemperance existed among them, founded no doubt on the fact they were moderate drinkers. We dwelt principally, however, on the consideration that the tide of intemperance which all acknowledge is desolating the land, could not be stayed while the people can plead the example of their teachers. The brethren received our remarks with kindness . . . and agreed to read some reports of the American Temperance Society and other temperance documents . . . Before we left the islands, we were pleased to know that the leaven we had cast into the mass was operating. Mr. Pritchard had resolved to purchase no more brandy for his brethren . . . Mr. Armitage has resolved never more to taste spirits except as a medicine. Mr. Simpson (Principal of the South Sea Academy) is almost ripe for the same decision. Mr. Orsmond had adopted it some time ago.[20]

From then onwards temperance societies, with an emphasis on total abstinence, were founded in those islands where there had been a thriving spirits trade. In Tahiti liquor laws were adopted, but Nott claimed that the Temperance Society had a greater effect than any laws could have.[21] So popular did the idea become that in Samoa societies were established to combat the influence of kava drinking and smoking.[22] The Wesleyans also deprecated kava drinking in Tonga, Watkin viewing it as 'pernicious to the body as well as the mind', but it was difficult to make it a test of membership.[23] However proscription of kava was for a time introduced at the Wesleyan stations in Fiji. Joseph Waterhouse wrote in November 1862:

> I have called in the aid of Teetotalism as a Missionary Auxiliary. In addition to ardent spirits the yagona or Kava root, is the curse of Fiji. For twelve years I have preached moderation, but in vain. With the Fijian of the present day it is all or none — stupefaction, or sense. What opium is to China that kava is to Fiji, and at last I have lifted up the standard of total abstinence.[24]

Abstinence became a matter of principle, and the character of the Evangelical missionary tended to become more restricted, whilst the native churches became even more exclusive.

Although establishing a steady people appeared to be the principal work of the island churches, the missionaries very early stressed the obligations of church membership, not least of which was the duty of extending the work of the church. In the islands the financial obligations of church membership were mostly directed towards missionary enterprise, and for this purpose auxiliary missionary societies were formed to which yearly contributions were made. These contributions were paid in kind. Arrowroot, coconut oil, cotton and mats were the more general articles of contribution, although more perishable articles were often sold and the money contributed.

As the missionaries themselves were supported by the home societies, the contributions went, or were supposed to go, directly to the parent missionary societies where they were added to the general funds. Contributions were often far from voluntary in the accepted sense of the word. It became not only a duty to the Church to give, but a social obligation also. The word of the chief was often a substitute for the voice of conscience. Visitors to the islands regarded the system of contribution as a form of taxation rather than as 'spontaneous giving'. In some of the groups, particularly in Samoa, very liberal giving was induced by a competitive spirit, one community not wishing to be outdone by another. This competitive spirit also extended to families. In 1860 Pratt of Savai'i introduced the plan of writing down all contributions, with the result that 'the whole herd of sixpenny and dime contributors vanished'. One chief was compelled to sell one of two horses in order to maintain his prestige. 'Accordingly like gentlemen's plate at home the horse is melted into cash and all are satisfied and your funds increased', wrote Pratt to the directors.[25]

In Tonga, apart from the free-will offerings which, according to Whewell, were in many cases not very freely given, the remainder was raised in obedience to the king's command. The men had to bring a bucket of coconut oil annually. Whewell was not a little critical of the system: 'Taxes in support of religion are disliked by Englishmen, enlightened and civilized, from this you may judge that to a people like the Tonga people this oil making for the Church is unpopular'.[26]

The history of contributions was not a smooth one. Very often the missionaries found that the people were reluctant to contribute, which was especially the case when a powerful chief was disaffected in some way, or had doubts about the affair. Doubts and suspicions in the minds of the chiefs and people were not uncommon. Sometimes these were due to misunderstandings with the local missionaries; and sometimes Europeans who were unsympathetic with mission work implied that the missionaries derived some personal profit from the collections. What Crook said of the people generally was particularly true in regard to the question of contributions: 'When they dip into money matters, they make the grossest mistakes, and sometimes unchristian reflections on us'.[27]

Discontent first came to a head in the Society Islands at the May meetings at Moorea in 1827, and the result was that Henry, the missionary at Papetoai, decided to leave the island. The accusations were as follows:

> You Missionaries told us to make a ship for the King [the *Haweis*] and that you have taken to yourselves. You then told us to buy one for the king, we did so, and that you have taken for yourselves. You then said Tamatoa must have one for himself. He purchased it and gave all the property off his Island, that you have taken for yourselves. We have been collecting oil for the Society these many years and all that you have taken for yourselves, this little money you have given into our hands [i.e. to the Treasurer] and now you want it back again. We will not give it . . .[28]

Of these charges we are mainly concerned with the belief of the people that the missionaries appropriated all the money of the Society. In this particular instance the coconut oil had been sold for cash, and the missionaries regretted not having received a bank bill.[29] Long before this occasion, however, the people, and also Pomare II, had resented the fact that the contributions from each separate auxiliary were not acknowledged separately. In May 1828 Barff wrote from Raiatea:

> It is of much importance to write short letters to the natives acknowledging the reception of their little subscriptions. Such a letter in the first place stops the mouths of mischievous men, who reside on the islands.[30]

The subscription issue was also one of the principal 'grievances' which the *Mamaia* sect held against the missionaries. Darling affirms that the *Mamaia* leaders were endeavouring to convince the church people that they were purchasing the salvation of their souls with the oil which they subscribed.[31] In 1830 Platt wrote from Borabora:

> You have heard of the Prophets of Tahiti and of the Visionaries of Maupiti, but perhaps you are not aware that one half of their disaffection and spleen is against the subscriptions to the Society and the selling books and their teaching and practice are entirely against the Society — and all they have against us is our being agents of the Society and consequently embezzlers of People's property, and not a few of the simple have been beguiled by them.[32]

Some of the missionaries feared that the society would be dissolved at the May meeting in 1829, owing to the persistent belief in the charge of misappropriation. However, when it was put to the vote whether each governor should receive the contributions or a person under the eye of the missionary at each station, the latter proposal was carried.[33]

Similar charges were made by enemies to the missions throughout the period, and similar suspicions were aroused. Charter of Raiatea did, for instance, retain the native contributions to meet his expenses, and asked the directors to lay the amount to his account.[34] He also complained of the failure at headquarters to acknowledge the native subscription separately, and said that his position was made worse because of the efforts of certain foreigners to persuade the people that the missionaries misappropriated the contributions. The same problem was experienced in Samoa. As late as 1856 we find Pratt writing to ask that the contributions should be separately acknowledged, instead of

with those from the whole of Polynesia, in order to clear the
individual missionaries from the insinuations of the Roman
Catholic priests that they had kept the money.[35]

The problem which faced these young churches was much the
same in all the missions, and it was natural that some of the
missionaries realized that contributions, especially in cash, could
well be spent in the field for the advancement of the churches
and to cover local needs. That this was not apparent at an earlier
date is surprising. However the contributions were given largely
on the assumption that they would help to free the peoples of
Africa and India from the yoke of idolatry, and as a sort of
tribute to the great chiefs in London.

In Tonga, where the Wesleyans had a well-established church
in 1860, the problem was becoming very real, and was ultimately
to lead to big changes in policy. Vercoe of Ha'apai lamented the
unfairness of the contribution system as it stood in 1858, and
what was more, he was conscious that the people were aware of it.

> Our chiefs and many of our people are quite sufficient arithmeticians
> to know the value of 30 tons of oil at £30 per ton. They know that,
> for *four years,* they have far more than covered all their Haabai
> Circuit expences.

On the other hand the people of Tongatapu and Vava'u had
given far less in contribution to the Society, and yet they received
the same benefits. Vercoe took a firm stand:

> That this little group, with some 4,000 people, should send away
> £1,000 per annum, whilst her chapels are mere sheds and her native
> ministers and local preachers are in rags, is, I confess, a matter of
> which in the future we shall be ashamed.[36]

Perhaps the most interesting commentary on the contribution
system was the disaffection of the teachers of Tutuila in 1851,
and their demand for salaries. Their principal ground of complaint was that the missionaries were paid and they were not
paid. They further complained that the missionaries had not
given them sufficient property. Their leading question was,
'where . . . were the contributions of oil which were received
year after year?'.[37] Powell, who was highly indignant at their
conduct, told them that if the churches had anything to give
them, it should be distinct from the contributions for the heathen.

> 'Are missionaries everything then?' asked Vaiofaga in a rage. 'Are we
> birds to fly hither and thither and live on the bush? If that be the
> case, let Britain support the Missionaries and leave the contributions
> of the church here to support the teachers.'

The teachers further argued that the missionaries were paid to support them as well as themselves. The immediate result of this protest was that the teachers went on strike, and most of them were dismissed.

Notwithstanding this case, there were those who felt that the local churches should support their teachers. Doubtless the Tutuila affair impressed them with the need for such a system. In April 1852 it was entered in the committee minutes that the missionaries had 'long been convinced' that their native teachers in Samoa 'might and ought to be supported' by the villages in which they worked.[38] In many places this had already been the case 'to a considerable extent'. An annual and strictly voluntary subscription was to be made in every village 'of native and other property for the support of its teacher', commencing in January 1853. The brethren also felt that it was desirable to obtain the co-operation of their colleagues in the Society and Cook Islands. In 1855 George Turner reported that the increasing contributions for the support of the native teachers did not detract from the usual ones to the Society.[39]

In Tahiti several of the native pastors refused to accept government pay. Napario, the pastor at Papaoa, was the last to resist the French in this matter. He was compelled to resign his office, and consequently he went to Raiatea where he was put in charge of the station at Opoa. However the people of his station were obliged to contribute to his support.[40] At Maupiti the entire May subscription was devoted to the maintenance of Hiomai, another ordained Tahitian pastor who had left Tahiti.[41]

Thus it was not until the 1850s that missionary contributions were being used more directly for the support of the island churches. It was also a period in which the missionaries became more aware that one of their principal tasks was to make the island churches self-supporting.

To what extent did the institution of the church bridge the gulf between the island cultures and European culture, and to what extent was the church, as an institution, affected by the island cultures? From the point of view of Evangelical Christianity the church was an institution adapted to the work of adjusting spiritual values to a hostile world. Thus, from the Christian viewpoint there was no question of reconciliation to the world in a spiritual sense, and the bridge had to be crossed regardless of culture. In other words Christianity, as a religious way of life, stood outside both cultures. The problems lay mainly in the interpretation of the Christian gospel.

In most of the islands the Christian religion was eventually adjusted to the existing structure of society, although not always without some civil reform. Perhaps the most difficult problem for the missionaries in this adjustment process was the role of the chiefs in the religious life of the community. In Tahiti, where Christianity had been established after a political revolution, the king became virtually head of the church, even to the extent of appointing teachers. Thus the first missionaries from Moorea who went to the Australs had to receive the approval of Pomare II. No religious changes could be introduced without the consent of the king, who still retained those powers which had regulated the observance of the old religion. In 1834 Davies attempted to refute the insinuation that the Queen of Tahiti was actually 'head of the Church', and show that the Tahitian churches were 'voluntary societies' in accordance with Congregational principles.[42] However the ideal of the missionaries was often far removed from the actuality, and although the missionaries believed that they had established voluntary societies, they were also aware of the influence of the chiefs in church matters. The laws enforcing church attendance at Tahiti shortly afterwards united the ecclesiastical and civil authorities much more closely, and the chiefs regained an arbitrary influence in church matters which the missionaries had been discouraging. Though some of the missionaries welcomed the opportunity to preach to crowded congregations again, most of them recorded their disapproval of compulsory worship. How much their attitude was one of compromise to British Evangelical opinion it is difficult to determine. Simpson, although he disapproved of 'compulsory religion', gave his approval to some resolutions passed at his own station by the principal chiefs and judges which required compulsory attendance at the schools as well as the chapels.

> Believing as [I] do that the principles of Nonconformity as generally understood by Congregationalists, are the principles of the bible, and that perfect religious freedom is the birth-right of every son and daughter of Adam I should pause ere I gave my sanction to any Measure which would deprive them of that boon. This I conceive is not done in the preceeding resolutions. They impose no restraint on the conscience nor tests but those of good citizenship, and no infr[inge]ment but such as are congenial with the Law of the land, and calculated to promote the common weal.[43]

It was in the period after 1834 that Tahiti came nearest to being a theocracy, in that ecclesiastical authority was assumed on a national basis. However the power was in the hands of the lay rulers, and this was not necessarily to the best interests of the church. New missionaries who arrived during this period were appalled by the state of religious life, and thought it would be far better to disband all the churches. Stevens wrote in 1839 that 'the whole churches according to the most pious and candid Missionaries are radically corrupt and that it would be far better if they were entirely dissolved'.[44] 'We are Chief-ridden, law ridden, and form ridden', wrote Orsmond in his typical angry style in 1836.

> You may were you now in Tahiti see cripples, blind and bedridden persons crawling on all fours to schools and to hearing of the gospel. Some who cannot walk shuffling along on their bottoms the hands behind and the heels before with a sort of skid tied fast to the thighs on which to sit, sliding ludicrously but most painfully along over the stones and thro. the mud to the Chapel.[45]

Something of the nature of this chiefly influence might be gauged from the prevalence of the superstition that the churches were the sacred property of the queen and chiefs, because of the rule that the chapels should be built on the ruins of the old *marae*. At first the missionaries had regarded this as a symbol of the overthrowing of Satan's kingdom,[46] but they began to wonder when, on occasion, the chapels were subjected to the arbitrary rulings of the chiefs. Indeed, sometimes the royal party would camp in a chapel when *en route* round the island.[47]

Although when under the French protectorate government Tahitian pastors were appointed by the chiefs and paid by the state, many of the missionaries protested that such state interference was contrary to all they stood for, some of them openly acknowledged that the system under the native government had been very similar.[48] The chiefly church was a very flourishing institution when the chief was sufficiently interested in promoting Christianity and was a zealous Christian himself. Thus the Wesleyans in Tonga had every reason to rejoice when their protégé, who became king of the three groups, was one of their foremost local preachers, and even something of a revivalist. However, even the chiefly church in Tonga had its drawbacks. If the influence of the chief was beneficial in establishing the church as an essential feature of community life, this influence often undermined the effectiveness of the preaching of the Tongan pastors. Thus George Lee, writing from Tongatapu in 1857, observed:

It will be sometime before natives are completely from under the influence of their Chiefs so as to preach as fearlessly as the English Minister who feels he is the Messenger of God, and a subject also of Queen Victoria *and as great a chief himself as any of them*. Indeed the great men of Tonga will bear that from the 'Faifekau' which a native teacher would be terrified to say.[49]

The chiefly church depended on the chiefs for its establishment in the community, and was governed, as it were, by their temporal decisions. The question of church membership, however, was necessarily the department of the pastor or of the other members. In the churches associated with the LMS every attempt had been made to show that office in the church was not synonymous with office in the state, and although chiefs were appointed as deacons, the first men appointed to that office, and most of the others, were not chiefs of the first order. A great number of the Society Islands chiefs never became church members, and not a few of the royal family were publicly excommunicated.

Some missionaries endeavoured to democratize the role of the church as completely as they could. Thus in Raiatea Threlkeld and Williams curtailed the temporal influence of the chiefs in spiritual matters as much as possible. They insisted that the native missionaries were sent by the church.

We are sorry to say that the choice of native teachers and the sending of them would not have been in the hands of the Church had Pomare gained his aim in subjecting these Islands to himself; it has always been his practice to govern in the Church and it still remains in the hands of the chiefs at Tahiti, a measure we must conscientiously disapprove as contrary to primitive Christianity, and as such are counted by those chiefs, myself especially, as enemies to Caesar.[50]

In chiefly communities it was also quite natural that the power of the pastor should be pitted against that of the chief. There were possibly signs of this before 1860, but it was more pronounced in the later period. Where it did occur, we usually find that the pastor was from another group. In some of the islands not a few of the native teachers set themselves up as petty kings (see page 321 below).

It was not easy for many of the missionaries to accept the limitations of the chiefly church. Their democratic social views were often offended by concepts which they regarded as feudal and archaic. They were not always pleased with the way in which the chiefs were treated with ceremonial respect and homage. There were many concepts of behaviour which they found difficult to understand, but which were part of the character of the

peoples. They had been forced to reconsider many of the issues
for which they believed Christianity had but one law, such as
the question of marriage.

Rethinking in the light of the indigenous culture was a necessary part of the adaptation process. After the establishment of
Christianity in some of the groups the idea prevailed that the
native marriages were invalid, and that wives could be cast off
and a new one taken and married according to Christian rites.
Hunt of Fiji came to the conclusion that such persons were
under the obligation of marrying one of their former wives.
What was more, he recognized the native marriage as a legitimate
one. He believed that when the man became a Christian it was
his duty to keep only one wife and to provide for the rest and
for their families; and although he regarded the previous union
as sufficiently valid, he thought it a good plan to have a church
marriage to make it a religious contract as well as a personal
and civil one.[51]

It is not easy to define the Christian character of the new
churches which emerged. Certainly there were individual converts who satisfied the requirements of the missionaries, and who
were as sincere Evangelical Christians as themselves. But the
pattern of the churches derived as much from the traditional
nature of the communities as from the personal qualities of the
individuals who made up each church. It is difficult also to discern just how much the religious values inculcated by preaching
and reading the scriptures were received on the level of the old
religions. It might be satisfactorily assumed that the distinction
between nominal and converted Christians in the islands was
far greater than in European Protestant communities, for
although the islanders probably had a greater degree of formal
knowledge, they had not accepted the concept of personal and
voluntary action in religious matters. The converted native
Evangelical, however, took a more definite step in this direction.

The reaction of the missionaries to the native churches was
often one of great disappointment. The picture which Orsmond
drew of the Tahitian church towards the end of his career was
not a favourable one.

> Sleep, not lively interest, seems to fill our chapels at the times of
> divine service.
> The feelings of Godly sorrow for sin — the love of all Holy Conversa-
> tion, — the hatred of the soul to those who love and make lies, —
> the love of the brethren . . . glorifying in the Cross of Christ, and
> the whole round of feelings that characterize the true guileless

disciple of Jesus, and aspirations of souls after God, are not to be found on our coasts.[52]

In this outburst it must be remembered that Orsmond was deliberately endeavouring to show that the opposite kind of picture which Williams and others had popularized was false. The new brethren who arrived in the Society Islands after 1838 wrote reports which were just as damning — if not more so — than those of Orsmond.[53]

Missionaries in other missions were equally despairing of the state of the church. Whewell of Tonga's letters in the late 1850s give a picture which contrasts greatly with that drawn by the revivalists.

> The Tonga character and 'gaahi Aga' (manners) is a source of continual trial and endurance to the missionary. They are naturally proud indolent forgetful dirty and ungrateful and I may add deceitful.

One might compare criticism of the *fa'aSamoa* or Samoan way of life. Whewell proceeds to show that their Christianity was largely a matter imposed upon them by the government.

> As Christianity has taught the government to relax this influence and respect the rights of conscience — giving to the people a power of choice — they have settled down into a state of great indifference of spiritual religion and mental and moral improvement . . . They disregard the proprieties of common decorum in the rituals of Christianity, and in the house of God they yawn and sleep and spit, and talk and laugh all the time of worship.[54]

Whewell's letters were full of similar criticism, and he painted a picture no gloomier than some of the Tahitian missionaries. He condemned the social state of the people, lamenting their 'filthy premises and wretched houses', and said that one half of the young women were working to atone for fornication. In another letter Whewell went so far as to say that the people were better off in their heathen state so far as industry, hygiene and morality were concerned.[55] The families of church members were baptized heathens, and the churches were made up of the aged and the maimed. Whewell was very early admonished for his gloomy reports, and after 1857 he conformed to the usual type of missionary letter, giving only the brighter side.

The angry or disillusioned missionary compared the church in the islands to the European churches with which he was familiar. He did not always appreciate the great changes which his earlier brethren had wrought, and he had invariably been

led astray by the general, though nominal, profession of Christianity in most of the groups, which had raised his hopes before
he reached the islands. It is when we find a reluctant though
honest acceptance of the character of the new churches that we
can discern some progress in Evangelical enterprise, for only by
understanding the situation and people in an honest way was the
missionary able to adapt himself, not only to the people themselves, but also to the Christian church in the islands. This
comes out most clearly in a letter written by Thomson of Tahiti
to the Reverend C. B. Andrews of Molokai in December 1845
and published in the Hawaiian *Friend*.[56] In this letter Thomson
spoke of the bitter disappointment he had received on landing
at Tahiti, when 'one scheme of usefulness after another, planned
during a long voyage' proved to be 'airy castles'.

> Oh! how withering to the fresh love of the young missionary, the
> heartless coldness which met him at every step. How different indeed
> from the picture drawn by a Williams.

Thomson suspected that such feelings were common to most
missionaries on entering the field. He said that his imagination
had been dazzled by reading the works of Ellis and Williams, and
maintained that the fault lay not so much with the actual state
of things as with himself. He said that he was more able to adjust
himself to the state of things at Tahiti after he had returned
from the Marquesas. He then found that the scene at Tahiti
appeared differently, due to a change within himself.

> When I entered upon the duties of a church I felt surrounded by
> innumerable difficulties; I was not satisfied with what I found, and
> yet taken one by one I could find little to which I could object.
> I saw that the apparent tone of piety was low. I tried to raise it.
> This led to a full examination of their christian profession and
> national character. I compared the Tahitian churches with the report
> of missionary stations in other parts of Polynesia, in India, East and
> West, in Madagascar, in Africa, and come to the conclusion that the
> character of a Tahitian church is only the character of every church
> formed of unconverted heathens. Their conversion has elevated their
> character, improved their nature, not altered it. Many evil passions
> have been subdued; some remain, but religion does not make perfect
> on earth.

Thomson's conclusion was a valuable admission:

> The churches of the apostolic days exhibited after the departure of
> the apostles the influence of old habits and prejudices. Every church
> partakes more or less of the previous character of its converts . . .

The Tahitian church is indolent, ignorant and fettered by narrow prejudices unbecoming them, but part of their former nature is gradually disappearing. There is much which I cannot approve, still I cannot condemn for there is much which I admire, and a spark of fire is as real fire as that in a furnace, and a spark of grace is grace though in the midst of corruption, and our Saviour will never quench the smoking flax or break the bruised reed.

This attitude, which it took later missionaries a considerable time to appreciate, helps to explain why the older missionaries like Henry and Nott not only tolerated but almost venerated Pomare II, whom the younger missionaries of the Leeward Islands detested and abhorred, and why Thomas and Peter Turner gave great praise to the Tongan teachers, for whom many of the younger brethren, such as Dyson, had little sympathy. The adjustment process was slow, and each generation of missionaries, vigorously critical of the last, seemed to begin afresh. The native churches, however, now an integral feature of the community life, developed as a natural growth, and it was the missionary who had to become adjusted in order to improve.

One of the most important features of the consolidation of the island churches was the training of a native agency. The LMS very early employed teachers, and in 1820 native missionaries were sent to other groups.* This policy of sending unordained missionaries to commence new stations was also adopted by the Presbyterian missionaries in the New Hebrides. The Americans had ordained Hawaiians working in the Marquesas and Micronesia. The Wesleyans very quickly raised a great army of local preachers and class-leaders, and quite early appointed 'Native Assistant Missionaries' who were given the designation 'Reverend'.

The work of the native missionaries was twofold. Those whom the LMS called 'pioneers' were expected to use their influence to break down the traditional religious systems. The instructions given by John Williams to some of the first teachers to go to the Cook Islands in 1823 are of interest, as the 'evils' of Polynesian life are put in categories.

All their lesser evil customs you will endeavour to cast down, going in a State of Nudity or nearly so, cutting and scratching themselves in seasons of grief — tatooing their bodies. Eating raw fish, their lewd dances etc. but the greater Evils will require your first attacks and then the smaller.[57]

*A list of the LMS native missionaries and ordained Hawaiian, Tongan and Fijian missionaries is given in Appendix V.

Besides this work of a negative character, the native missionaries were expected to adopt similar procedures to the European missionaries. Those who were merely 'pioneers' were usually replaced by teachers with more qualifications to carry out this work. Hugh Cuming gives an interesting picture of the native missionary at work in 1828 at Rurutu. He found that 'every frivolous amusement of the most minute description such as dancing and Music have vanished even the wearing Flowers in the Hair is no longer practised'. He regarded Puna, the native missionary, as the best educated islander he had met. After the morning meal, the 'Sexton' of the church struck three or four blows on a metallic stone and everyone at the mission settlement came to prayers, after which Puna and 'all those capable of cultivating ground' marched to their gardens.[58] Houses similar to those at Huahine had been introduced, and all ate together without distinction in the 'Banqueting House'. Besides preaching sermons from 'skeletons' prepared for them, the native missionaries gave catechetical instruction and commenced schools.

Although the missionaries gave the highest praise to the native agency in their more public pronouncements, the prevailing opinion in all the missions seems to have been one of dissatisfaction with the system, or at least a disturbed recognition of its limitations. The missionaries possibly wrote more about this question than any other, as they naturally conceived that the island churches should and would be ultimately the responsibility of the people.

It was quite early realized that native teachers and missionaries should receive some specialized training, and the publication of *Hints on Missions* by James Douglas strengthened this conviction. However attempts at systematized training came much later in the field than all the other progressive measures, and a great host of missionaries and teachers were employed who had only a rudimentary knowledge of Christianity, and some few of the LMS agents were not even church members.

Even when the native teachers were adequate in a purely technical sense they often disappointed the missionaries owing to what might be termed cultural characteristics. Some of these characteristics just had to be accepted by the missionaries, who ultimately became convinced that even Christianity could not change them. The *fa'aSamoa* or 'Samoan way', to take one example, which disturbed the missionaries of this period, was still characteristic of Samoan pastors in New Guinea and the Gilbert Islands throughout the present century.[59] The Samoan teacher took a certain course of action because it was 'the Samoan way', whereas the European missionary would have determined his action according to his 'inner lights'. Also the continued influence of Polynesian sexual *mores* was disturbing to the missionaries, who were shocked at the attitude adopted by many of their teachers to sexual lapses. Some of the most celebrated native missionaries were ultimately disgraced for having committed adultery. The Raiatean, Paumoana of Aitutaki, and the Reverend Benjamin Latuselu of Tonga and Samoa were two offenders in this respect.

Another characteristic of the native teachers who went to other groups was their assertion of superiority over the peoples to whom they ministered. This was particularly true of the Society Islands teachers in the Tuamotus and Australs, of the Tongans in Fiji, and of the Samoans in all the lands to which they went. In 1828 Hugh Cuming observed that the teachers on Tubuai 'wish'd the people to consider them above their Chiefs'.[60] They would cause the people to be punished 'for very trifling offences such as for singing a song'. According to Watsford, the teachers at Ono were equally tyrannical.

> They thought too much of themselves and wished to ride over the people, and had we not been led to take the step we did when I was left here I believe our cause here would have been ruined. One of the teachers was a Tonga Chief and he wished to rule the land as well as preach the Gospel.[61]

When writing of native teachers in 1835, Pitman of Rarotonga said how difficult it was to convince islanders of the difference existing between church and state.[62] When he had first arrived at Rarotonga in 1827 he had found the people living in fear of the teachers.[63] In 1839 C. G. Stevens of Tahiti visited some of the outstations on his way to New Zealand, and remarked that the native teachers 'had not escaped the common failure of Natives elevated to Teachers — that of becoming both Mercenary and despotic'.[64] Very often differences would arise between two native teachers and the people of the island or station would divide themselves into two parties. Also, the first teachers to an island were very often received into the chiefly families by marriage. When these men were superseded it was very difficult for the younger men to introduce more progressive methods than those hitherto used.

The missionaries early realized that the majority of native teachers were inadequately trained for their work, and that even the more sophisticated teachers misunderstood the significance of much Christian doctrine. Charles Wilson wrote in 1829 that the teachers were 'all very deficient' and 'only babes in knowledge and experience'.

> It is true many of the natives have tolerable consistent views of the way of salvation releaved in the gospel through a Mediator; but all I have met with even the best, are deplorably ignorant of the scope and sense of the Scriptures, they have in their hands, generally putting a fanciful interpretation upon them, indeed we have reason to fear that they teach things not contained in the Word of God, so that all must be convinced of the necessity and propriety of using means for remedying so great an evil.[65]

Although training methods greatly improved in the ensuing years, the same type of criticism of the native agency was as valid in 1860 as in 1820. Pratt of Savai'i, who had as full an understanding of the Samoan character as any of his colleagues, wrote in 1856 that he had been 'staggered' by a trifling circumstance in the conduct of a teacher whom he hoped to ordain to pastoral status.

> After the service was concluded and I was about leaving the chapel I saw him (the teacher) throwing down what bread was left over from the ordinance and they (the church members) still seated, scrambling for it as a lot of boys would for marbles.[66]

Pratt, like Joseph Waterhouse of Fiji, felt that the whole object of mission work was to raise up an effective native agency, on the assumption that the generality of the people could only understand Christianity in their own terms, and in the language of their own experience. Pratt remarked in 1859 that many of the Samoan teachers excelled as preachers, and that the Samoans were 'getting to prefer them to a white preacher'.

> Often the white preacher gives a white sermon — brim full of good theology, but in its effects, pretty much like trying to fill a small mouthed bottle by pouring water into it from a bucket.[67]

Yet these same teachers were often 'very confused in their chronology'. Pratt had even been asked by a graduate of Malua if Joseph the husband of Mary, the mother of Jesus, was the same as the Joseph who was sold into Egypt.

Most of the concern for the native teachers related to their high rate of moral defection. In 1839 Pitman and Buzacott lamented the 'unholy lives and glaring crimes of *too* many who have here to fore been engaged as native Teachers', and the 'irreparable mischief' they had done.[68] For instance out of four Tahitian teachers placed over the church at Aitutaki only one had been free from the sin of adultery, whilst the current teacher was in 'a state of imbecility'. Pratt of Savai'i believed in the maxim that little should be said about any of the native converts until after their death.[69]

Yet despite these limitations some of the indigenous missionaries were men of extraordinary calibre and dedication. For instance one of the Rarotongan teachers, Ta'unga, possessed a remarkable understanding of Christianity as taught by the missionaries.[70] His perseverance under the most difficult conditions in New Caledonia in the 1840s exemplify both his faith and his heroic qualities. That his own people later credited him with miraculous powers is indicative of the great respect in which he was held. A great many native teachers gave their lives in islands where Europeans were not prepared to land. Some were killed and others fell victim to various diseases. Their contribution to the spread of missionary work was a major one.

Pritchard was the first missionary to devote his attention to training native teachers in the Society Islands. In the same year, 1829, Orsmond also began a training course. Up to this time the native agency was simply regarded as a means to 'clear away the rubbish' as the missionaries termed it. This was still regarded as the principal function of the native missionary throughout the period. In 1859 Pratt readily agreed with Bishop Selwyn that the native teachers were 'better adapted for pulling down heathen systems, and reproving sin than for building up converts in the faith'.[71] The instructions given by Williams to the Raiatean teachers in 1823 (see page 319), partly explain the radical changes which took place in many of the islands and illustrate the emphasis placed on 'clearing away the rubbish'.

The missionary course given by Pritchard at Papeete was based on the course which he had received himself at Gosport. Bogue's lectures, which Orsmond had translated into Tahitian, were used by him. In 1831 Pritchard reported that each student was taught reading, writing and arithmetic, and took with him to his station in manuscript 'a course of lectures in Jewish Antiquities, a course on the Scriptures, and a course of Missionary lectures'. They were also accustomed to 'write the heads and particulars of all the sermons they heard'.[72] In 1833 the sole remaining student at Pritchard's institution, an Hawaiian, returned to his own group.[73] During the ensuing years the main reason for not reviving the institution was the shortage of eligible young men. However in June 1842 it was resolved to establish a seminary for training native pastors at Afareaitu, Moorea, under the superintendence of Howe. The course was to be not less than four years, and the students were to be given 'a sound philosophical and Theological' training, together with instruction in English.[74] In 1844, when Howe departed for England, the institution was conducted by John Barff, but it was soon afterwards closed. After his return to Tahiti in 1848 Howe re-established the theological seminary at Papeete. At the same time, Thomson, who refused to recognize Howe's pastorate at Papeete, took in a number of students also.[75] Matters were further complicated in 1851, when the protectorate government granted permission to Orsmond to train students for the ministry, independently of the LMS.[76] These men were then ordained and officially recognized as ministers of the national church. In 1852 Howe's connexion with the Tahitian church was dissolved, and his institution was closed. John Barff established another institution for the Society Islands in 1857 at Tahaa. The principal texts studied at these institutions were Bogue's *Outlines of Theology*, Anderson's *School Geography*, and Chamber's *Introduction to the Sciences*.

Events in the training of native teachers had taken a more even course in the other groups. In 1832 Buzacott commenced the education of Rarotongan teachers, and Bogue's lectures were also used.[77] The English practice of copying out the lectures was likewise adopted. However a proper institution was not established till 1839.[78] Pitman declined superintending the institution because he preferred the old system of each missionary instructing one or two teachers. In September 1839 Buzacott wrote that he had two students at the institution at Avarua. Apart from their theological studies they were expected to devote four hours daily to mechanical and agricultural pursuits, and one of their first projects was to prepare wood for the construction of sofas.[79]

Perhaps the most significant event in the training of the native agency was the establishment of the 'Samoan Mission Seminary' or Malua Institute on Upolu in 1844. Until the establishment of this institution Samoan teachers were given a three month course of 'theological and General Instruction of which the leading feature [was] a historical view of Human Redemption on the plan of President Edwards'.[80] This course was conducted by Day, who afterwards became a tutor with Hardie and Turner at Malua. By the 1840s most of the 'pioneering' work in other groups was being undertaken by the Samoan and Cook Islands missions. The Malua Institute not only became a seminary for Samoan teachers but for potential teachers from the various Melanesian islands to westward. There were two courses of four years each. The first was a course in general education, similar to that given in other mission schools. The second was for those who were accepted as teachers.[81] Something of the nature of this course might be gathered from the report of the annual examination of the teachers' class in 1847. The students were examined in 'Scripture Exposition, in portions selected from the Gospel of Matthew and the Epistle to the Hebrews . . . Scripture History selected from the facts from the giving the law on Sinai to the reign of Saul inclusive; also in various doctrines selected from the course of lectures on Systematic Theology; and in Pastoral Theology on the work of the Christian Ministry'. In this examination 'considerable prominence was given to the doctrines of Protestantism as opposed to Popery'. Arithmetic, geography, astronomy and 'some branches of Natural Philosophy viz. the elements of Pneumatics, Optics and Acoustics' were also included in the course.[82]

The training of the Wesleyan native agency was never as efficient, in the earlier years, as the training provided by the LMS. Buzacott went as far as to say that the only qualification of the Wesleyan teachers in Samoa in 1835 was that they could read the 'B-A, ba'.[83] Pratt was equally uncomplimentary on their abilities in 1841.

> They are preaching this week — at the night dances next week, and about a month after they may again be appointed Teachers. . . . Their preaching (which I have often heard) is a mere jumble of Old Testament History in which they make Abraham, Joshua and Dagon actors in the same story; or they talk about the laws of God and the necessity of a moral life in order to salvation.[84]

The LMS missionaries also maintained that the Tongan teachers were mainly responsible for creating the party spirit in Samoa. According to Macdonald of Savai'i, the Reverend Benjamin Latuselu preached 'through the length and breadth of the land that "it is the will of God that Samoa should be divided into two parties" '.[85] Nisbet maintained that the Tongan teachers wished to keep a hold on Samoa 'on account of the good things of this life they obtain thereby'.[86]

However some of the Wesleyans had no illusions about many of their teachers. Whewell wrote of the ignorance of the 'Assistant Missionaries' in 1856.

> What can they know . . . See their literature. Mr Thomas' hymns — a translation of our I and II catechisms — one also on Geography — an unfinished Bible and the 'Morning Service'. This would be something to an english man but a Tonga-man's cast of mind and calibre of intellect and range of observation are as different as the

same natural object appears viewed through different ends of a telescope.[87]

When the Reverend John Waterhouse visited Tonga and Fiji in 1841 he advocated the need for the better training of native teachers. At the Fiji district meeting it was proposed to establish an institution 'to be called the Feejee Islands Wesleyan Academy for the training of Native Assistant Missionaries'. This institution was to be established at Lakeba under the superintendence of Hunt, who was to instruct them in 'the great principles of Wesleyan Theology, as embodied in our standard works[,] also in the English language[,] Geography, writing and other branches of useful knowledge'.[88] Hunt never fulfilled his role, and the training institution was commenced under the charge of Francis Wilson.

Joseph Waterhouse was perhaps one of the greatest advocates for an efficient well-trained indigenous ministry. He wrote that when he first came to Fiji he enquired where the institution was which his father had started. He found it amongst the things which 'had been', principally owing to a remark made by one of the Australian secretaries to the effect: 'We want no colleges'.[89] Waterhouse wrote angrily that unless a special missionary was set aside for this purpose they were in danger of promulgating a 'mongrel' Christianity. 'I could tell you tales of Native Teachers that would fill you with alarm and cause you to object to their employment altogether.' The 'District Teachers' Training Institution' at Mataisuva, Rewa Bay, was not commenced till 1852, when the Reverend John Polglase was appointed principal. Waterhouse continued to advocate the importance of a native ministry. His reasons were set forth very clearly in a paper which he sent to the General Secretary after he had left Fiji in 1873.[90]

It was in training up a native agency, and in extending the churches through these men, that the missionaries both established their work and enabled the church to take more of its character from the indigenous society. The native teachers could understand the exigencies of local situations; where the missionary was often confused, they could realize the difficulties involved. They could understand idiomatic speech, which was difficult for the European, and use it to their advantage. Although the teachers had satisfied the missionaries that they had experienced heart conversion, their faith was generally tempered by influences which the missionaries themselves tended to discountenance. They considered traditional prejudices, local political feeling, and traditional standards of morality. In consolidating the church they helped to break down the barriers of distrust, and they were free from the mental revulsion which was often discernible in the European missionary. The native teachers and missionaries, whatever their defects as Evangelical Christians, were at least free from many of the defects of their mentors.

Epilogue

The Mid-Victorian Image

THE DOCTRINAL POSITION of Evangelical missionaries had been much more clearly defined at the beginning of the modern missionary era in 1797 than in 1860. Apart from the Wesleyans, who did not arrive permanently in the islands until 1826, the missionaries confessed to a belief in moderate Calvinism, often to extreme Calvinism. The emphasis was on soul-saving, and in consequence there was a greater range of method. In the first decades one could find missionaries who lived physically much closer to the islanders. It was an age of itineration, perseverance and many trials. It was a kind of group Robinson Crusoe existence in which, as in the story, Crusoe was very much concerned with his own soul. It was a time of isolation. Indeed years passed by before the mandates of the great men of the Mission House reached this new variety of missionary, who had chosen to live away from the countries of the civilized world. The early years were years of experiment and of discovery. Great opportunities for mental expansion were in the reach of men who had been bound in the social fetters of their homelands.

Yet it is a curious though perhaps not a surprising thing that the early missionaries and their successors were largely dependent on their own social origins. In seeking for a new security, they inevitably returned to the values and standards which European, particularly British middle-class, opinion had impressed on the social life of the time. Edward Irving had postulated a St Francis of Assissi type of missionary, one without scrip and without purse, as the model to be followed; but it was in vain.

The formulation of new theories of colonization and of civilization, the pursuit of wealth, and the belief in the manifest destiny of the 'British Israel', all tended to influence the course of missionary activity. Economic development, which was rapidly turning the godly mechanic into a solid middle-class citizen in England or the colonies, had an indirect effect on the missionaries, who were largely drawn from the mechanic class. The missionary attained, by a kind of 'professional means', that rank in the social scale which his industrious brother achieved by economic means. Occasionally, as we have seen, the missionary was not beyond using economic means himself.

The missionary before 1860 belonged intrinsically to an age of faith, an age which had seen the triumph of the values and ideals inherent in the Evangelical Revival. It was an age in which orthodox Reformation theology reigned supreme, as yet undisturbed by the findings of science. It was an age in which the Evangelical polemic was more concerned with Puseyism and Newmanism than with Neology and other latitudinarian doctrines. The missionary was not an isolated religious flying from some metropolitan Babylon. He came to the islands rather as an ambassador from a chosen people whom God had raised up to be supreme in civilization.

Although by 1860 missionary activity had become an accepted feature of society, and the idea of a man devoting his life to the peoples of non-Christian countries had ceased to appear novel and strange, men could still remember the time when missionary enthusiasm was generally regarded as being something extraordinary. As a consequence the view prevailed that the 'latter days' referred to in the scriptures were commencing in reality. In pulpits throughout England and the colonies, and also the United States, preachers pointed to the work of missionaries as a sure sign that the prophecies were being fulfilled. It was in this context of millennial dawn that the missionary saw himself as a man of destiny. The importance which he placed on his office was very considerable, and at times appeared little short of megalomania. The missionaries who had sailed in the *Duff* in 1796 believed that their charge was the most important since the days of the apostles. Their successors were imbued with the same belief. They were men who were conscious that they were making history. Their role was absolutely clear to them, as if the pillar of cloud was ever before them, and as if God was dividing the waters for their triumphal entry into the promised land. The missionary view of history was a simple one. As an instrument of providence, the missionary was helping to effect God's plan for the world. In his difficulties the missionary could call on God for supernatural assistance. He would also have to withstand the temptations and interference of the devil, but in the end he could be assured of an eternal reward.

Because he was so conscious of his vocation, the average missionary was often given to self-dramatization. Hardships and privations were overdrawn, perils and dangers were frequently exaggerated, and stories of the interposition of providence were tirelessly narrated. On the other hand, the missionary was thus equipped with the appropriate frame of mind to face real hardships, to face real dangers, and to take considerable risks. Although many stories of missionary endeavour contain much that is exaggerated, it is only fair to remember that some missionaries, at times, proved themselves real heroes by any standards.

Conscious of himself as a man of destiny, the missionary emulated the great figures of the past whom he admired. He also believed implicitly that he had a mission to effect social change. It was said that man was born free, but that everywhere he was in chains. The missionary believed that man would remain in chains wherever Evangelical Christianity did not prevail. He voiced the doctrine of utter depravity, that man without God was given over to a reprobate mind, and was at enmity with God.

It was the first duty of the missionary to save souls, but wherever he went he brought havoc to the existing social systems. In the period before 1860 the missionary's principal concern in the South Seas was with the overthrowing of the old idolatries and heathen systems and the formation of churches. In the period after 1860 the role of the Evangelical missionary became more diverse. His role as a crusader for social justice became much more marked. The concern for social justice came naturally within the framework of missionary thought. Those who had agitated for the abolition of slavery naturally resented all forms of racial intimidation. The missionaries first appeared as champions of the rights and liberties of the South Sea islanders against the occasional cruelties of sea captains or European residents. They also protested against the depredations of various captains and crews engaged in the sandalwood trade.[1] However it was not until the 1860s that the missionaries appeared as the champions of their island parishioners in any definite and influential way, when they organized opposition to the recruiting of island labour.[2]

Although there were certain doctrinal and denominational differences amongst the Evangelical missionaries, there was a doctrinal and denominational unity which led to the development of similar attitudes, methods and patterns of contact in the islands of the South Seas. The Calvinist missionaries placed a stronger emphasis on 'civilizing' schemes than did the Wesleyans. The Calvinists also appeared to have a more definite interest in secular affairs. The Wesleyans tended to be more conservative in these matters, just as in the education of missionary candidates, they moved in line with public opinion, rather than in advance of it. They were slower in developing the methods and means of their more politically-minded brethren. But they did adopt them, and in the end there were few obvious contrasts between Calvinist and Wesleyan mission stations, except on the level of personal efficiency.

Binding Calvinist and Wesleyan together in the pursuit of their vocation was the great theme of the Evangelical Revival, the salvation of souls, and the need for a personal faith in the atonement of Christ. John Hunt perhaps came nearest to expressing the core of missionary theology in his time:

> It was one of the lessons our Lord taught his disciples that few should be saved. Even the preaching of the Gospel is the savour of death unto death to some, but we preach it to all because it is the savour of life unto life unto others. I would go on to the same plan with respect to all other means we may use for the good of man and the glory of God.[3]

This was the belief common to the Evangelical missionaries, which they introduced into the islands. In the mouths of the native teachers it found blunt expression. 'I make known to them that don't *lotu* the fire of hell', wrote the Fijian Noa, 'and to them that *lotu* the love of our Lord Jesus Christ, and his anger also'.[4] The pioneer missionary in the South Seas was a theologian before all his other interests, and his theology was something by which he lived, a type of faith which knew little about compromise and cultural tolerance.

Notwithstanding the vigour and zeal of the Evangelical missionaries, and their own belief that their methods were the most effective, they nowhere raised up a nation of believers or a new Israel amongst the South Sea islanders. The church of gathered Christians had to remain a small minority, separated from amongst the indifferent and unheeding portion of the community. It seems to have surprised these modern apostles that the people they came to instruct could be just as unconcerned about their salvation as so many, perhaps the greater part, of their fellow countrymen. They had thought that a 'simple faith' would have appealed to peoples whom they believed to be less sophisticated than themselves. Everywhere in the islands the facts belied the idealistic conceptions still held by the orators of Exeter Hall, and often half-believed by the missionaries themselves. It was true that idolatry had been put down, that polygamy and homosexuality were no longer openly practised, and that infanticide, cannibalism and the burial alive of the aged were practices which the missionaries had effectively eradicated, but the faith of the Evangelical Revival was still but a dim light in the conceptions of the islanders. There *were* revivals of religion, but these revivals were part of the Methodist machinery, and must be viewed as such, rather than as outward signs of an inward and spiritual grace. There *was* a church in the islands, but it was a smaller one than that envisaged by the speakers of Exeter Hall.

A different stage of development had been reached in each of the groups. In the Marquesas little headway had been made by 1860. In the Society Islands and Tonga the missionaries saw much which disturbed their minds, and which they tended to keep to themselves, rather than destroy the illusions of those supporting them. In Fiji there was still a certain pioneering excitement — the same can be said of the whole of Melanesia in that period — and consequently there was less room for cynicism and more outlets for creative energy. In the Cook Islands and Samoa the missionaries had more reason to be satisfied, but they were aware that it was their prestige alone which — at that time — ensured the dignity of the Church. They realized that the indigenous church could be developed only gradually, that it was not something which sprang up spontaneously after the sowing of the Christian gospel.

But it was one characteristic of the Evangelical missionary that he was essentially an optimist. All his thinking depended on the maxim that 'all things work together for good to them that love God'. John Barff wrote in 1857:

> You will rejoice in the report of the voyage of the John Williams to the West. Our American brethren are also succeeding in Micronesia and the Marquesas. As also the Wesleyans at the Figis. Are we about another onward move in Polynesia. I trust we are, and that the spirit is granting us one of those seasons of progress with which he makes the hearts of his people glad.[5]

In 1860 missionary doings were on the tongues of all sorts and conditions of men. Williams, Livingstone and many others had been given a place in the national history. The missionary vocation, like the various trades, had been given a *respectabilit* of national recognition. The missionary, whether in the South Seas, Africa, or the East, was by 1860 regarded not simply as a religious eccentric with misplaced zeal, but as a representative of Victorian English values.

Appendices

I *Printed questions to missionary candidates*

1 Questions to be answered by missionary candidates. LMS form dated 1820.

1 Are you in communion with any Christian Church; with what church — and how long have you been so?

2 Are your sentiments in favour of *Infant Baptism?*

3 State your age, place of birth, and whether your parents are living: if living, has your application their approbation — are they in any degree dependent on you for support?

4 What advantages of education, or subsequent improvement, have you enjoyed; and in what manner have you been employed up to the present time?

5 What has been the general state of your health since your infancy; and is your constitution such as to be likely to endure a change of climate, and the various hardships of the Missionary calling?

6 Have your habits of life been such as to prepare you for such hardships?

7 Your views of the doctrines of the gospel, and the grounds of your hope that you are called by grace to an experimental and saving knowledge of them; and your motives of offering yourself to the Missionary Society, will be fully stated by you hereafter in a distinct paper.

8 Have you been used to engage in any services for the promotion of religion — the instruction of the young and the ignorant — the spiritual benefit of the sick — the relief of the poor; and have you been active and constant in such engagements?

9 How long have you had the desire of becoming a Missionary to the Heathen, and what were the circumstances which first excited such desire? Has that desire been steady or changeable?

10 Has that desire led you to special, frequent, and fervent acts of devotion; and are there any providential circumstances which induce you to conclude that your wishes are consistent with the Divine will concerning you?

11 Have you communicated your desire to any Minister, or other Christian friends; and do they encourage you in it?

12 As you must be aware that a wish to engage in Missionary-work is in many instances founded on false principles; have you deliberately and solemnly examined your own motives and ends; and do they approve themselves to your conscience, as in the sight of God?

13 State your views of the obligations which the calling of a Missionary includes.

14 Have you seriously weighed the privations, hardships, and dangers to which a Missionary must be exposed; and are you willing to make such sacrifices?

15 In offering to become a Missionary to the heathen, do you intend to devote your whole time and talents to the service, so that you will consider it unlawful to withdraw from its proper duties, in order to pursue the worldly advantages which the station to which you may go may present to you?

16 Do your principles lead you to yield all due respect and subjection to the civil authorities instituted in the country to which you may go, and to consider it to be your duty to abstain from all interference in the political concerns of such country?

17 In the event of your proposal being accepted, do you promise to cultivate the spiritual, humble, self-denying, and devoted dispositions so befitting a Christian Missionary, to be diligent in the preparatory studies to which you may be directed; to conform to the regulations of the Society relating to their students; to leave the appointment of your future station, and the time of entering upon it, and other circumstances, to the discretion of the Directors?

18 Are you married, or are you under any engagement relating to marriage; and should it be judged to send you to your station in the single state, are you ready to comply with the wishes of the Directors?

19 Do you propose your answers to these inquiries, as the ground of your application to the Missionary Society, to be received as one of its Missionaries?

2 Questions to be answered by missionary candidates. LMS form used from 1836.

1 As it is indispensably necessary, that he who undertakes to teach Christianity to the Heathen should himself be a real Christian, you are desired to state what are the grounds on which you have been led to conclude you are such, together with any memorable circumstances connected with your first religious impressions, and the period of their commencement.

2 What are your views of the principal and distinguishing doctrines of the Gospel?

3 What is your judgment of Christian Baptism? Have you thoroughly investigated the question respecting the Baptism of Infants, and is your mind established as to the Divine authority of Infant Baptism?

4 Of what Christian Church, or Society, are you a member? How long have you been such; and to what Minister or Ministers can you refer, for information respecting your religious character?

5 Have you been accustomed to engage in any social or public religious services — in prayer-meetings — in the instruction of the young — in visiting the sick — in the distribution of tracts, or in any other effort for the spiritual good of others? — and if so, state the particulars.

6 Where were you born? What is your age? Are your parents living? Do they depend on you, in whole or in part, for their support? Do they know of your wish to become a Missionary, and do they approve of it?

7 What has been your occupation? Are you so employed at present as to be able to obtain a comfortable maintenance? Have you a reasonable prospect of the same support in future? Does the desire of improving your worldly circumstances enter into the motives of this application?

8 What advantages of education have you enjoyed, and what books have you read?

9 What has been the general state of your health from your infancy? What is it at present? If your health be good, is it such as is likely to continue, especially if you should go to a sultry climate? Have you seriously considered the hardships and dangers to which a Missionary may be exposed? Are you willing to subject yourself to them; and do you judge your constitution is able to support them? — (Before your offer

can be finally accepted, the opinion of some medical person on this point will be required.)

10 How long have you entertained the desire of becoming a Missionary? What first led you to form that desire? Has that desire been constant or fluctuating? Has it led you to any particular exercises of mind? — if so, state them.

11 Have you felt a decided preference to the work of a Missionary abroad above that of a Minister at home? and do you think you should continue so to feel, were an equal opportunity of becoming a Minister to present itself? — if so, state the reasons of this preference.

12 As there is too much reason to fear that some persons have become Missionaries under the influence of improper principles, you are desired seriously and sincerely to state what are the MOTIVES by which you are actuated in offering yourself as a Missionary to the Heathen.

13 What in your judgment, are the *Qualifications* necessary to form a good Missionary of Jesus Christ?

14 What do you apprehend are the proper *Duties* of a Christian Missionary? and what do you conceive to be the peculiar temptations to which he is exposed?

15 Have you communicated your desire to any Minister or Ministers, or other Christian Friend; and do they encourage or discourage you in this application?

16 Are you married? If not, are you under any engagement relating to marriage; or have you made proposals of marriage to anyone; or are you willing to go out *unmarried,* should circumstances render it desirable?

17 As your personal expenses, for Clothes, Washing, &c., may, while residing at College, amount to from 20 to 30 pounds per annum, can you, from your own resources, or that of your friends, meet that sum, or any part of it?

3 Questions for Wesleyan missionary candidates, dated 30 April 1822. For commentary and additional regulations see William Peirce, *The Ecclesiastical Principles and Polity of the Wesleyan Methodists,* 3rd ed., (London, 1873), pp. 721-53.

1 From what circuit is the candidate recommended?

2 What is his age?

3 How long has he acted as a local preacher?

4 What is his occupation or profession? and is he acquainted with any other art?

5 Is he of robust or slender habit of body?

6 Has he enjoyed uninterrupted health; and if not, what is the disorder to which he is most liable?

7 Has he been given to reading, and what books?

8 Does he appear well acquainted with the Scriptures?

9 Does he know English grammar?

10 Does he write a good hand?

11 What other language or languages, besides his native tongue, is he acquainted with; and what science, or sciences?

12 Does he prefer missionary labour to any other, feeling deeply for the state of the heathen, and being earnestly desirous of enlarging the kingdom of Christ?

13 Is he willing to go to any part of the world where his labours may be likely, under God's blessing, to be most useful?

14 Is he willing to remain abroad as long as the committee may think proper?

15 Does he offer himself to the committee to go out as a married, or as a single man?

16 If as a married man, can the person to whom he is engaged be recommended for her piety, prudence, general fitness for the wife of a missionary, and her zeal in the cause of Christ?

17 Have the parents of the young woman given their consent?

II *Printed instructions to Wesleyan missionaries*

Abridgement of the printed *Instructions to the Wesleyan Missionaries,* dated 20 February 1825.

I. We recommend to you, in *the first place and above all things,* to pay due attention to your personal piety; which, by prayer, self-denial, holy diligence, and active faith in Him who loved you and gave himself for you, must be kept in a lively, vigorous, and growing state. . . . Amidst all your reading, studies, journeyings, preaching, and other labours, let the prosperity of your own souls in the Divine life be carefully cultivated; and then a spirit of piety will dispose you to the proper performance of your ministerial duties; and, by a holy re-action, such a discharge of duty will increase your personal religion.

II. We wish to impress on your minds the absolute necessity of using every means of mental improvement with an express view to your great work as Christian Ministers. You are furnished with useful books, the works of men of distinguished learning and piety . . . we press upon you the absolute necessity of studying Christian Divinity, the doctrines of salvation by the cross of Christ. . . . You are to disseminate the knowledge of Christianity, in order to the salvation of men; let the Bible then be YOUR BOOK; and let all other books be read only in order to obtain a better acquaintance with the Holy Scriptures, and a greater facility in explaining, illustrating, and applying their important contents. We particularly recommend to you to read and digest the writings of WESLEY and FLETCHER, and the useful commentaries with which you are furnished . . . recollect every day, that whilst you endeavour by reading, meditation, and conversation, to increase your stock of useful knowledge, it is necessary for you to acquire a proportionate increase of holy fervour.

III. We exhort you, Brethren, to unity of affection, which will not fail to produce unity of action. . . .

IV. Remember always, dear Brethren, that you are by choice and on conviction WESLEYAN-METHODIST PREACHERS; and, therefore, it is expected and required of you, to act in all things in a way consistent with that character. . . . *You have promised to preach, in the most explicit terms, the doctrines held* as scriptural, and therefore sacred, in the Connexion to which you belong. . . . You have engaged also to pay a conscientious regard to our discipline. . . . We also particularly press upon your constant attention and observance MR. WESLEY'S Twelve Rules of a Helper.

V. We cannot omit, without neglecting our duty, to warn you against meddling with political parties, or secular disputes. . . . It is, however, a part of your duty as Ministers, to enforce, by precept and example, a cheerful obedience to lawful authority. You know that the venerable WESLEY was always distinguished by his love to his country, by his conscientious loyalty, and by his attachment to the illustrious family which has so long filled the throne of Great Britain.

VI. You will, on a foreign station, find yourselves in circumstances very different from those in which you are at home, with regard to those who are in authority under our gracious Sovereign. . . . On your arrival at your stations, you will be instructed what steps to take in order to obtain the protection of the local Governments. . . .

VII. [Refers to the West-India Colonies; these ten directions were to be considered 'as strictly obligatory on all others as far as they are applied to the circumstances of their respective stations'. They include]

3 It is enforced upon you, that you continue no person as a member of your Societies, whose 'conversion is not as becometh the Gospel of Christ.' That any member of Society who may relapse into his former habits, and become a polygamist, or an adulterer; who shall be idle and disorderly; . . . who shall steal, or be in any other way immoral or irreligious, shall be put away, after due admonition, and proper attempts to reclaim him from the 'error of his way.'

4 Before you receive any person into Society, you shall be satisfied of his desire to become acquainted with the Religion of CHRIST, and to obey it; . . . no person is to be admitted into Society, without being placed first on trial, for such time as shall be sufficient to prove whether his conduct has been reformed, and that he has wholly renounced all these vices to which he may have been before addicted.

8 As many of the negroes live in a state of polygamy, or in a promiscuous intercourse of the sexes, your particular exertions are to be directed to the discountenancing and correcting of those vices, by pointing out their evil, both in public and in private, and by maintaining the strictest discipline in the Societies. No man, living in a state of polygamy, is to be admitted a member, or even on trial, who will not consent to live with one woman as his wife, to whom you shall join him in matrimony, or ascertain that this rite has been performed by some other Minister; and the same rule is to be applied, in the same manner, to a woman proposing to become a member of Society. No female, living in a state of concubinage with any person, is to be admitted into Society so long as she continues in that sin.

9 The Committee caution you against engaging in any of the civil disputes or local politics of the Colony to which you may be appointed, either verbally, or by correspondence with any persons at home, or in the Colonies . . .

VIII. It is *peremptorily required* of every Missionary in our Connexion to keep a Journal, and to send home frequently such copious abstracts of it as may give a full and particular account of his labours, success, and prospects. He is also required to give such details of a religious kind as may be generally interesting to the friends of Missions at home; particularly, accounts of conversions. Only, we recommend to you, not to allow yourselves, under the influence of religious joy, to give any *high colouring* of facts; but always write such accounts as you would not object to see return in print to the place where the facts reported may have occurred.

IX. It is a positive rule amongst the Wesleyan Methodists, that no Travelling Preacher shall 'follow trade.' You are to consider this rule as binding upon you, and all Foreign Missionaries in our Connexion. We wish you to be at the remotest distance from all temptation to a secular or mercenary temper. . . .

[Further directions, taken from the Annual Circulars were published as *Miscellaneous Regulations: being an Appendix to the General Instructions of the Wesleyan Missionary Committee. For the Private use of the Missionaries* (London, 1832). They were arranged under the following heads: Adjustment of Funds, Regulations; Artizans; Assistant Missionaries; Book-Room Regulations; Catechizing; Chairmen of Districts to examine Missionaries on Trial; Chapel Building, &c.; Children; Correspondence; District Minutes; Drawing Bills; Effects of deceased Missionaries; Financial Regulations; Foreign Missionary Societies; Journeys; Leaders' Meetings; Letters, Modes of sending; Marriage and Baptism; Missionaries taken out on Foreign Stations; Natives sent to England; Periodical Works; Preachers' Fund; Printing Books; Quarterage; Return of Missionaries; Return of Suspended and Resigned Missionaries; School Allowance; Schools, Reports of; Solitary Stations; Stationing of Preachers; Terms of Service; Unattached Stations.]

III *Missionary teaching: sermons and questions for candidates*

Skeleton Sermon (LMS)

Heb. 11, 6: 'But without faith *it is* impossible to please *him:* for he that cometh to God must believe that he is, and *that* he is a rewarder of them that diligently seek him.'

   I A profitless faith is
      1 one that is born in man.
      2 one that dwells in a heart full of sin.
      3 one that knows not God as its author.
      4 one that has not strength to conquer the flesh.

   II A faith that is pleasing to God.
      1 We must not suppose that faith reconciles God to man or man to God.
      2 A faith coupled with beautifully shining conduct.
      3 A faith that glorifies all God's great truths/attributes.
      4 A faith that purifies the heart and guards the mouth.
      5 A faith that is bestowed by the power of the Holy Ghost.
      6 A faith that believes God and trusts his Son Jesus.

   III A faith that is followed by a great reward.
      1 It is pleasing before God.
      2 It brings great comfort into the heart.
      3 It leads us to see that sin is pardoned.
      4 An endless rest above the skies is its end.

   IV The improvement to all of us.
      1 Faith and knowledge should go together.
      2 Alas for all enemies of Jesus who have the faith of Devils.
      3 Let us all pray that the Good spirit would increase our faith in God.
      4 The man of God must wait till he obtain the end of his faith.

      Translated from the Tahitian by J. M. Orsmond, 23 September 1827.

Skeleton Sermon (WMMS)

John 3, 3: 'Jesus answered and said unto him, Verily, verily I say unto thee, Except a man be born again, he cannot see the kingdom of God.'

I The Nature, II The need of this change. In the first place I removed certain errors which I fear some of them have fallen into on this subject. I commenced with the fact that a person who is born again is a child of God, and they all think they are such. I therefore showed

  1 That renouncing the gods and practices of heathenism is not being born again, though this is necessary to it.

  2 Being baptized is not being born again, though baptism is a sign of it, and if rightly used may be a means of it.

  3 That meeting in Class is not being born again, though an important means of grace.

  4 Nor is repentance the new birth, though many are much affected by it and much changed by it.

  5 Those who are born again truly repent of all sin, so as to abandon all sin. They truly believe in Christ so as to obtain the forgiveness of sin, and it is a consciousness of their acceptance with God given them by the witness of the Spirit which produces in them love to God in return and this is the principle of the new nature which is called being born again. This change is a change of soul, a change of the whole soul, and a change from sin to holiness. It is a spiritual change, a change of the whole spirit, and a holy change seen and known by its fruits.

II We must have this change

  1 In order to enjoy the blessings of God in this world.

  2 In order to enter heaven.

  It will avail nothing to be able to say at the bar of God, I have renounced idolatry, theft, adultery, fornication, murder, etc. I have met in class, been baptized, have cried for my sins, read the Bible, heard preaching etc. Unless these means have led to a change of heart and mind; 'Except a man be born again he cannot see the Kingdom of God.'

John Hunt, 11 January 1842, Private Journal II, pp. 36-37.

Skeleton Sermon (WMMS)

Heb. 11, 24-26: 'By faith Moses, when he was come to years, refused to be called the son of Pharoah's daughter; choosing rather to suffer affliction with the people of God, than to enjoy the pleasures of sin for a season; Esteeming the reproach of Christ greater riches than the treasures in Egypt: for he had respect unto the recompence of the reward.'

I What Moses refused. Three things which men in general seek after.

  1 Honour. He refused to be called the son of Pharoah's daughter.

  2 Pleasure. He refused to enjoy the pleasures of sin for a season.

  3 Riches. He esteemed the reproach of Christ greater riches than the treasures of Egypt.

II What Moses Chose. To be united to God's people.

  1 He chose this though his people were in bondage. He *chose* it he did not endure it.

  2 He considered this his honour, his pleasure, his riches. He esteemed the reproach of Christ greater riches than the treasures in Egypt.

III The cause of such a choice and such a conduct. Faith. By this faith he saw —
1 The invisible God.
2 The invisible world, the recompence of the reward.
3 The blessedness of being united to the people of God, because by that means we are connected with Christ here and with heaven hereafter.

Conclusion
1 What do you refuse.
2 What do you choose.
3 Why do you choose the one and refuse the other.

John Hunt, 13 November 1843, Private Journal II, pp. 177-78.

Hunt's private journal contains the outlines of a number of sermons preached by him. Two interesting but lengthy sermons, which reflect on Fijian life, are those on Matthew 16, 24 (pp. 39-42) and the parable of the rich man and Lazarus (pp. 100-102). The latter gives a description of hell. See also pp. 27-28, 29-32, 46-47, 49-51, 52-53, 67-68, 68-72, 72-82, 129-135, 170-71, 183-84. There are also notebooks containing skeleton sermons by Hunt, Peter Turner, and others.

Questions to propose to Candidates for Baptism
LMS: Rarotonga

1 Is it agreeable to you to live with one wife?
2 Have you children? Are you willing to have them neatly attired, to attend with punctuality the Ord[inances] of Religion — schools etc?
3 Are you willing to erect a comfortable house — attend to cleanliness within and without?
4 Are you desirous of being taught to read — and attending to the word of God — also to instruction in your bubu [bible] every morning?
5 To renounce your former practices and regard them of Christianity?
6 Why do you desire baptism? Here explain its nature, design and requirements.

Pitman, Journal, III, (looseleaf).

Questions proposed to Candidates for Church Membership
LMS: Anaa, Tuamotus

1 Do you really and ardently desire to be united as one body, and to live as brethren before God, and the world?
2 Are you willing to take the Scriptures as your guide as to doctrine and practice?
3 Is it your determination to seek the destruction of all vice, and cultivate peace wherever you live?
4 Do you believe that Jesus is God and do you trust his blood as the only ground of acceptance with Jehovah?
5 Is it your belief that Jesus Christ, not the Chiefs, nor the King, is head of the Church on earth, and that the gospel is the rule for your practice?

Orsmond, 8 May 1839 [Anaa, 21 March 1839] — SSL

LMS: Samoa

Q: What is the meaning of this ordinance?
A: It is the command of Christ to his disciples, and is symbolic only.
Q: What advantages may be derived from it?

A: It will be of advantage only to those who rely on Jesus Christ [illustration given].

Q: Is there salvation in this ordinance?

A: Oh no! That is only to be found in the blood of Christ.

Q: What is the meaning of the bread and the wine used in the ordinance?

A: They are the symbols of the body and blood of Christ, and not his real body and blood.

Q: Who are the proper persons to partake of the ordinance?

A: True believers.

Q: What ought to be the conduct observed by them?

A: A constant submission to the requirements and will of God, and strict propriety in their conduct towards all men.

Q: What are your thoughts respecting yourself; I mean respecting yourself *now*, and what you *once* were?

A: When I think of my past sins my heart is pained, but I rejoice that Christ has taken them away, and it is my prayer to Christ that he would take away all my sins and cleanse me in his blood.

Q: What think you, is it right in *you* to desire this ordinance?

A: I hope it is, for I feel different to what I once was. If I truly repent and trust in Christ, it will be well for me; I desire and hope I do. The last two questions caused much hesitation and feeling.

> Harbutt, 1 July 1841, *Extracts from the Correspondence of Rev. W. Harbutt, Missionary in the South Seas, to a Friend in England* (Bradford, n.d.), pp. 12-13.

IV Particulars of Evangelical missionaries, 1797-1860

This list includes all official missionaries, both lay and ordained, sent to the Pacific Islands before 1860, as well as several helpers recruited by the missionaries themselves. It does not include the children of missionaries who frequently taught and preached unless they were ordained or given the status of assistant missionary. Denominational or occupational status at time of joining is usually followed by description or place of education. Biographical detail covering mission service and later marriages is not given beyond 1860.

I London Missionary Society

ARMITAGE Elijah (1780-   ), b. Manchester; Congregational cotton manufacturer; artisan missionary on Tahiti 1821-23, Moorea 1823-33, Rarotonga 1833-35, Moorea 1835; m. Nancy (1791-   ).

BAKER William (1834-1905) b. Keynsham, Somerset; Congregational city missionary; 'English' education, ordained, on Lifu 1859-61; m (-   ).

BARFF Charles (1792-1866) b. South Cave, Yorkshire; Calvinistic Methodist farmer, bricklayer and plasterer; Homerton, ordained, on Moorea 1817-18, Huahine 1818-64, Tahaa 1860; m. Sarah Swain (1792-   ), Calvinistic Methodist.

BARFF John (1820-60) b. Raiatea; Congregational missionary's son; South Sea Academy, Silcoates School, and Turvey; assistant afterwards ordained, on Huahine 1839-43, Moorea 1844-47, Tahiti 1847-52, Borabora 1852-53, Tahaa 1857-60; m. Amelia Banes (1824-1906) b. Hackney, London.

BARNDEN George (1811-38) b. Portsea; Congregationalist; Turvey, ordained, on Tutuila 1836-38; unm.

BICKNELL Henry (1766-1820) b. Dorset; Countess of Huntingdon's Connexion house carpenter, sawyer, and wheelwright; 'mechanic' missionary on Tahiti 1797-1808, Moorea 1810-18, Tahiti 1818-20; m. Mary Ann Bradley (-1826) b. Sherborne, Dorset.

BLOSSOM Thomas (1777-1855) b. Swanland near Hull; Congregational carpenter, turner and wheelwright; village schools; artisan missionary on Tahiti 1821-23, Moorea 1823-44; m. Sarah Radly (1796-1842) Congregationalist.

BOURNE Robert (1794-1871) b London; Calvinistic Methodist printer; ordained, on Moorea 1818, Tahiti 1818-22, Tahaa 1822-27; m. Ann (1793-).

BOWELL Daniel (1774-99) b. Ipswich, Suffolk; shopkeeper; 'mechanic' missionary on Tongatapu, 1797-99; unm.

BROOMHALL Benjamin (1776-1809) b. Birmingham; Congregational buckle and harness maker; 'mechanic' missionary on Tahiti 1797-1800, left 1801; unm.

BUCHANAN Ebenezer (1812-97) b. Haddington, Scotland; Congregational apprentice to armourer and brazier; Lancastrian school; schoolmaster on Upolu 1844-49, Tahiti 1842-44, Upolu 1844-49; m. Jane Cowan (1815-1901).

BUCHANAN John (1765-) b. London; Presbyterian tailor; 'mechanic' missionary on Tongatapu 1797-1800, unm.

BULLEN, Thomas (1812-48) b. Clonakilty, Ireland; Congregationalist; medical education and Hackney; ordained, on Upolu 1841-43, Tutuila 1843-48; m. Hephzibah George (-) b. Salisbury; Baptist.

BUZACOTT Aaron (1800-64) b. South Molton, Devon; Congregational farm labourer; Hoxton Academy and Hoxton Mission College; ordained, on Tahiti 1827-28, Rarotonga 1828-46, 1852-57; m. Sarah Verney Hitchcock (1802-77) b. South Molton; cornfactor and maltster's daughter.

CAW William (-1820) Congregational shipwright, carpenter, boatbuilder; 'mechanic' missionary on Tahiti 1804-08; resided there 1808-20; unm.

CHARTER George (1811-98) b. Melbourn, Cambridge; Congregational farmer's son; Turvey, ordained, on Tahaa 1839, Raiatea 1839-53; m. Martha Unwin (-) b. Melbourn; Congregationalist.

CHISHOLM Alexander (1814-62) b. Turriff, Aberdeenshire; Presbyterian upbringing; Congregational clerk in counting house; Blackburn (Lancashire), ordained, on Savai'i 1843-46, Tahiti 1847-52, Raiatea 1852-60; m. Elizabeth Davies (1822-) b. Oswestry, Shropshire; Congregationalist.

CLODE Samuel High (1761-1799) b. London; whitesmith and gardener; 'uneducated', 'mechanic' missionary on Tahiti 1797-98; unm.

COCK John (1773-) b. Penzance, Cornwall; Congregational ship's carpenter; 'mechanic' missionary on Tongatapu 1797-1800; unm.

COOPER James (1768-1846) b. Edinburgh; shoemaker; 'mechanic' missionary on Tongatapu 1797-1800.

CORRIE Rosanna (-) b. Newport, Isle of Wight; Congregational school teacher, helper on Rarotonga 1843-46.

COVER James Fleet (1762-1834) b. London; school teacher; ordained, on Tahiti 1797-98; m. Mary (1759-).

CREAGH Stephen Mark (1826-1902) b. Plymouth; Church of England upbringing; Congregational painter and stationer; Western College (Plymouth), ordained, on Mare 1854-57, Upolu 1857-58, Mare 1858-86; m. (I) Susan Anna Peek (-1855) b. Plymouth; Congregationalist; m. (II) Sarah Ann Buzacott (1829-1915) b. Rarotonga; Congregational missionary's daughter.

CROOK William Pascoe (1775-1846) b. Dartmouth, Devonshire; Calvinistic Methodist gentleman's servant; 'mechanic' missionary on Tahuata 1797-98, Nukuhiva 1798-99, Moorea 1816-18, Tahiti 1818-30; m. Hannah Dare (1777-1837) Calvinistic Methodist.

DARLING David (1790-1867) Congregational carpenter, ordained, on Moorea 1817-19, Tahiti 1819-34, Tahuata 1834-35, Tahiti 1835-59; m. Rebecca Woolston (1788-1858) b. Northamptonshire; Calvinistic Methodist.

DAVIES John (1772-1855) b. Pontrobert, Montgomeryshire; Welsh Calvinistic Methodist apprentice to grocer, then teacher; 'mechanic' missionary on Tahiti 1801-08, Huahine 1808-09, Moorea 1811-18, Huahine 1818-20, Tahiti 1820-55; m. (I) Sophia Browning (-1812) Calvinistic Methodist; m. (II) Mary Ann Bicknell (-1826) missionary's widow (q.v.).

DAY William (1794-1864) b. Lichfield, Staffordshire; Congregational minister; Wymondley; on Upolu 1838-45; m. Barbara Stewart (1801-86).

DRUMMOND George (1808-93) b. Cumnock, Scotland; Congregational (snuff) box maker; Theological Academy (Glasgow), Turvey and Ongar; ordained, on Savai'i 1841-46, Upolu 1846-58, 1860-72; m. (I) Agnes Drummond (-1855) b. Glasgow; Congregationalist; m. (II) Catherine Ann Ogilvie (1822-1905) b. North Shields; Congregationalist.

ELDER James (1772-1836) b. Scotland; Presbyterian (Secession Church) builder and stonemason; medical education, ordained, on Tahiti 1801-08, Huahine 1808-09; m. Mary Smith (1788-1861) free settler's daughter in N.S.W.

ELLA Samuel (1823-99) b. London; Congregational printer, afterwards ordained, on Upolu 1848-62; m. Eliza Catharine Black (-1898) b. Ireland; Congregationalist.

ELLIS William (1794-1872) b. Wisbeach, Cambridgeshire; Unitarian upbringing; Congregational candle manufacturer, then gardener; Gosport and Homerton; ordained, on Moorea 1817-18, Huahine 1818-22, Oahu 1823-24; m. Mary Mercy Moor (1793-1835) b. London; Congregationalist.

EYRE John (1768-1854) b. London; Calvinistic Methodist blockmaker; ordained, on Tahiti 1797-1808, Huahine 1808-09; m. Elizabeth (1733-1812).

GAULTON Samuel (-1799) b. Poole, Dorset; assistant to cook on *Duff;* 'mechanic' missionary on Tongatapu 1797-99; unm.

GEE Henry (1833-1901) b. Woburn, Bedfordshire; Congregational grocer's assistant; 'good English' education and Bedford; ordained, on Savai'i 1860-61, Upolu 1861-64; m. Mary Burr (-   ) b. Bedford; Wesleyan afterwards Congregationalist.

GIBBONS Henry (-1864) b. Islington, London; sailor belonging to mission church, helper on Tutuila 1837-64; m. Samoan (?)

GILHAM John Allan (1774-   ) b. Horndean, Hampshire; Calvinistic Methodist surgeon; medical education; on Tahiti March-August 1797; unm.

GILL George (1820-80) b. Tiverton, Devon; Church of England upbringing; Congregational attorney's clerk; Hackney; ordained, on Mangaia 1845-57, Rarotonga 1857-60; m. Sarah Trego (1818-98); Congregationalist.

GILL William (1813-78) b. Totnes, Devon; Church of England upbringing; Congregationalist; Turvey; ordained, on Rarotonga 1839-52; m. Elizabeth Lansborough Halliday (1811-79).

GILL William Wyatt (1828-96) b. Bristol; Congregational student for ministry; University of London, Highbury and New Colleges; ordained, on Mangaia 1852-72; m. Mary Layman Harrison (1830-83) b. London; Church of England.

GYLES John (-1827) sugar planter in West Indies; agricultural missionary on Tahiti 1818, Moorea 1818-19; m. Maria Slyth (-).

HARBUTT William (1809-66) b. Newcastle-on-Tyne; Congregational clerk; 'commercial' education and Airedale College, ordained, on Upolu 1840-49, 1853-58; m. Mary Jane Dixon (1813-85) Congregational shipowner's daughter.

HARDIE Charles (1802-80) b. Newburgh, Scotland; Congregational whaler; Turvey and Homerton, ordained, on Savai'i 1836-44, Upolu 1844-54; m. Jane Hitchcock (1813-94) b. South Molton, Devon; Congregationalist.

HARPER Samuel (1770-99) b. Manchester; cotton manufacturer; 'mechanic' missionary on Tongatapu 1797-99; unm.

HARRIS John (1757-1819) b. Reading; Calvinistic Methodist cooper; 'mechanic' missionary afterwards ordained, on Tahuata 1797, Tahiti 1797-1800; unm.

HASSALL Rowland (1768-1820) b. Coventry; Congregational weaver; 'mechanic' missionary on Tahiti 1797-98; m. Elizabeth Hancox (1766-1834) b. Coventry; Congregationalist.

HAYWARD James (1769-1850) b. Tisbury, Wiltshire; Calvinistic Methodist teacher, London Itinerant Society; 'mechanic' missionary on Tahiti 1801-08, Moorea 1808-09; Huahine and Moorea 1809-18; Tahiti 1821-22; m. (I) Sarah Christie (-1812) b. London; Calvinistic Methodist; m. (II) Mary Hewlitt née Wilshire (1770-1854); Church of England widow.

HEATH Thomas (1797-1848) b. Bramshall Staffordshire; Congregational legal clerk; Hackney, ordained, on Manono 1836-42, Tana 1842, Manono 1845-48; m. Eliza (-1838).

HENRY William (1770-1859) b. Sligo, Ireland; Countess of Huntingdon's Connexion carpenter and joiner; 'mechanic' missionary on Tahiti 1797-98, 1800-08, Huahine 1808-09, Moorea 1811-27, Tahiti 1827-31, Moorea 1831-32, Tahiti 1832-42, resident on Moorea 1844-48; m. (I) Sarah Maben (1774-1812) b. Dublin; m. (II) Ann Shepherd (1797-1882) b. Ryde, N.S.W.; Church of England free settler's daughter.

HODGES Peter (1797-) b. Woolwich, Kent; blacksmith; 'mechanic' missionary on Tahiti 1797-98; m. Mary (-).

HOWE William (1798-1863) b. Ireland; infant-school teacher afterwards Congregational minister in Manchester, on Moorea 1839-44, Tahiti 1847-63; m. —— (c.1795-1882).

HUNKIN Matthew (1815-88) member of mission church; helper resident on Tutuila; Manu'a 1841-49; m. Samoan (?).

JEFFERSON John Clark (1760-1807) b. Cornwall; actor, schoolteacher, then Congregational minister, on Tahiti 1797-1807; unm.

JESSON John Thomas (1806-57) b. Littlewood Green, Warwickshire; Roman Catholic seminarian afterwards Congregational minister; Downside Benedictine College (Bath), Highbury, on Tahiti 1842-44; m. Mary (1800-89).

JOHNSTON Joseph (1814-92) b. Stamford, Lincolnshire; Congregational schoolteacher afterwards ordained; Stamford Grammar School, on Tahiti 1839-49; m. Harriett Platt (1822-) b. Moorea; missionary's daughter.

JONES John (1829-1908) b. Leigh Sinton, Worcestershire; Congregational shoemaker; Cotton End Academy, ordained, on Mare 1854-87; m. Sarah Herbert (1822-97) b. Worcester; Church of England.

JONES Thomas (1790-) b. Llwynadda, Cardiganshire; Congregational ostler's-boy; Llanfyllin Academy and Gosport, ordained, on Tahiti 1821-26; m. Cox (-1825) widow.

JOSEPH Thomas (1816-63) b. Llanybri near Caermarthen; Congregational student; Caermarthen Grammar School and Presbyterian College (Caermarthen), ordained, on Tahiti 1839-44; m. Catherine Evans (1814-82) b. Caermarthen; Congregationalist.

KELSO Seth (1748-   ) b. Manchester; cotton weaver; 'mechanic' missionary afterwards ordained, on Tongatapu 1797-1800; unm.

KRAUSE Ernest Rudolph William (1812-73) b. Torau, Prussia; student for ministry in Prussian church; Torau Gymnasium, Institute of Berlin Missionary Society and University of Berlin, ordained, on Atiu 1842-43, Tahaa 1843-51, Borabora 1851-55, Rarotonga 1859-67; m. (I) Mina Carolina Ernestina Henrietta Banes (1824-55) b. Hackney, London; m. (II) Scharnberger (-1879).

LAW William (1877-1907) b. Rawmarsh near Rotherham, Yorkshire; Congregational roll turner (ironworks); Rotherham and Bedford, ordained, on Upolu 1852-54; m. Sarah Hawley (-   ) b. Masbrough, Yorkshire; Congregationalist.

LEWIS Thomas (1765-99) b. Caermarthen; minister in Countess of Huntingdon's Connexion; Cheshunt; on Tahiti 1797-98; m. Tahitian (?).

LIND William Alexander (1828-   ) b. London; Wesleyan afterwards Congregational copper plate engraver; Hackney, ordained, on Tahiti 1852, Rurutu 1852-55; m. Jane Tritton (-   ).

LOXTON James (1809-34) b. London; Congregationalist; Highbury, ordained, on Raiatea 1834; m. Emily Nutter (1809-89) b. London; Congregationalist.

LUNDIE George Archibald (-1841) b. Scotland; Presbyterian minister's son; helper resident on Tutuila 1840-41; unm.

MACDONALD Alexander (1813-88) b. Perth, Scotland; Presbyterian then Congregational ship's surgeon on whaler; apprentice in drugshop and Turvey, ordained, on Rarotonga 1836-37, Savai'i 1837-50; m. Selina Blomfield (-   ) Congregational minister's daughter.

McFARLANE Samuel (1837-1911) b. Johnstone, Scotland; Congregational railway mechanic; Bedford, ordained, on Lifu 1859-71, afterwards New Guinea; m. Elizabeth Ursula Joyce (1837-1913) b. Bedford; Congregational missionary's sister.

McKEAN Thomas Smith (1807-44) b. Garlieston, Wigonshire; Congregational minister; Glasgow Theological Academy 1834-38 and University of Glasgow, on Tahiti 1842-44; m. Jane Gordon (1806-72) b. Elgin, Scotland; Congregationalist.

MAIN Edward (1772-   ) tailor, then soldier in Royal Artillery; 'mechanic' missionary on Tahiti 1797-98; unm.

MILLS William (1811-76) b. Arbroath, Scotland; Congregational blacksmith; Glasgow Theological Academy, ordained, on Upolu 1836-46, 1848-54; m. Lillias McClymont (1810-61) b. Wigton; Presbyterian (Relief Church) governess.

MITCHELL James (-1827) 'mechanic' missionary, resigned Sydney 1800; unm.

MOORE Joseph (1816-93) b. Fareham, Hampshire; Congregational schoolteacher; Cheshunt, ordained, on Tahiti 1843-44; m. Mary Pinnick (1815-97) b. Fareham; Congregationalist.

MURRAY Archibald Wright (1811-92) b. Jedburgh, Roxburghshire; Relief Secession afterwards Church of Scotland grocer's assistant; Turvey and Homerton, ordained, on Tutuila 1836-   , Manono, Upolu 1854-61; m. Ruth Cobden (1814-82) b. Chichester, Sussex; Congregationalist.

NISBET Henry (1818-76) b. Laurieston, Glasgow; Presbyterian (Relief Church) clerk in hardware store; 'English' education, Relief Divinity Hall (Paisley) and Cheshunt, ordained, on Tana 1842-43, Upolu, 1843-50,

Savai'i 1850-59, Upolu 1859-   ; m. Sarah Crook (1811-68) b. Sydney, N.S.W.; Congregational missionary's daughter.

NOBBS George Hunn (1799-1884) b. Ireland; preacher on Pitcairn, helper on Mangareva 1834; m. Sarah Christian (1810-99), b. Pitcairn.

NOBBS Isaac (1772-   ) b. Wymondham, Norfolk; hatter; 'mechanic' missionary on Tongatapu 1797; unm.

NOTT Henry (1774-1844) b. Birmingham; Congregational bricklayer; 'mechanic' missionary on Tahiti 1797-1808, Moorea 1808-18, Huahine 1818-19, Tahiti 1819-44; m. Ann Charlotte H. Turner (-1846) b. London; Calvinistic Methodist.

OAKES Francis (1770-1844) b. Coventry; Congregational shoemaker; 'mechanic' missionary on Tahiti 1797-98; unm.

ORSMOND John Muggridge (1788-1859) b. Portsea, Hampshire; Congregational carpenter; Gosport 1813-16, ordained, on Moorea 1817-18, Huahine 1818, Raiatea 1818-20, Borabora 1820-24, Moorea 1824-31, Tahiti 1831-56; m. (I) Mary L. Brine (-1819); m. (II) Isabella Nelson (1795-1854) b. Liverpool, N.S.W.; Church of England teacher-farmer's daughter.

PITMAN Charles (1796-1884) b. Portsmouth; Congregational clerk, afterwards superintendent of timberyard; day school and Gosport, ordained, on Tahiti 1825-26, Raiatea 1826-27, Tahaa 1827, Rarotonga 1827-54; m. Elizabeth Nelson Corrie (-1880) b. Newport, Isle of Wight.

PLATT George (1789-1865) b. Arnfield (Manchester); Congregational cotton manufacturer; 'uncultivated', ordained, on Moorea 1817-24, Borabora 1824-35, Savai'i 1835-36, Raiatea 1836-65; m. Judith (1788-1854).

POWELL Thomas (1817-87) b. Cookham Dean, Berkshire; Church of England upbringing; Congregational grocer's assistant; Hackney, ordained, on Tutuila 1845, Savai'i 1845-48, Aneityum 1848-49, Tutuila 1849-83; m. Jane Emma Harrison (1822-90) Congregationalist.

PRATT George (1817-94) b. Portsea, Hampshire; Church of England upbringing; Congregational apprentice to druggist; 'public school' and Turvey, ordained, on Savai'i 1839-61, continued in Samoa; m. (I) Mary Parsons Hobbs (1815-44) Congregationalist; m. (II) Elizabeth Bicknell (1827-1906) b. Tahiti; Congregational missionary's relative.

PRITCHARD George (1796-1883) b. Birmingham; Church of England upbringing; Congregational brassfounder; 'deficient' education then Stafford and Gosport, ordained, on Tahiti 1824-37, resided on Tahiti 1837-41, 1843-44, and on Upolu 1845-56; m. Eliza Aillen (-1871) Congregationalist.

PUCKEY James (1771-1803) b. Fowey, Cornwall; Congregational carpenter and joiner; 'mechanic' missionary on Tahiti 1797-98; unm.

PUCKEY William (1776-1827) b. Fowey; Congregational carpenter; 'mechanic' missionary on Tahiti 1797-98; unm., afterwards with C.M.S. in New Zealand.

READ William (-   ) 'mechanic' missionary, resigned Tahiti 1801, unm., afterwards in Ceylon.

RODGERSON John (1803-47) b. Workington, Cumberland; Congregational shipbuilder; 'no reading habit' in early life, then Turvey, ordained, on Tahiti 1834, Tahuata 1834-37, Tahiti 1837-39; Borabora 1839-47; m. Ellen Haslam (-   ) b. Liverpool; Congregationalist.

ROYLE Henry (1807-78) b. Manchester; Congregational factory worker, then town missionary; 'few advantages' and Manchester Mechanics Institute, ordained, on Rarotonga 1839, Aitutaki 1839-76; m. Sarah Griffiths (-1877) Congregationalist.

SCHMIDT Carl William (-1864) b. Germany; Reformed minister and missionary to Aborigines, Moreton Bay District, N.S.W. 1838-44; Universities of Halle and Berlin; on Savai'i 1848-57, resident on Upolu 1857-64; m. (-1855).

SCOTT William (-1815) b. Scotland; Presbyterian; 'mechanic' missionary on Tahiti 1801-08, Moorea 1808-09, Huahine 1809, Moorea 1811-15; m. Ann Bradley (-1836) Church of England and colonist's daughter, not communicant.

SHELLEY William (1774-1815) b. Hanley (Green), Staffordshire; Congregational cabinetmaker, 'mechanic' missionary on Tongatapu 1797-1800, Tahiti 1801-06; m. Elizabeth Bean (1782-1878) Church of England free settler's daughter, N.S.W.

SHEPHERD Isaac (1800-77) b. Ryde, N.S.W., Church of England; helper on Tahiti 1818, Moorea 1818-19; unm.

SHEPHERD James (1796-1882) b. Ryde; Church of England; helper on Moorea 1816; unm.; afterwards with C.M.S. in New Zealand.

SIMPSON Alexander (1801-66) b. Dundee, Scotland; Congregational naval , employee; Gosport and Hoxton Mission College; ordained, on Tahiti 1827-29; Moorea 1829-50, resident on Moorea 1850-66; m. Sarah Aillen (c. 1800-77) b. Alton, Hampshire; Congregationalist.

SLATYER Thomas (1816-54) b. Olney, Buckinghamshire; Congregational schoolteacher; 'commercial' education, Turvey and Western College, ordained, on Tutuila 1840-42, Upolu 1843-45; m. Amelia Goulding Anstie (-   ) b. Exeter; Baptist minister's daughter.

SMEE Alfred (1815-47) b. Crayford, Kent; Congregational printer and compositor; 'English' education, mission printer on Tahiti 1841-47; m. M. Elizabeth Credland (1805-90) b. Croydon, Surrey; Congregationalist.

SMITH James (1803-   ) b. Aberdeen, Scotland; Congregationalist; Hoxton Mission College, ordained, on Raiatea 1831, Huahine 1831-32, Tahaa 1833; m. (-   ).

SMITH William (1775-1824) b. London; linen draper; 'mechanic' missionary on Tahiti 1797-98; unm.

SPENCER George (1823-   ) b. Taunton, Somerset; Congregational bookseller, stationer and binder; 'commercial' education and Hackney, ordained, on Tahiti 1852-53; m. Emily Sheard (-   ) b. Oxford; Congregationalist.

STAIR John Betteridge (1815-98) b. Warminster, Wiltshire; Congregational bookseller and stationer; 'commercial' education; printer afterwards ordained, on Upolu 1838-45; m. Emily Maria Rolls (-   ) b. Basingstoke, Hampshire; Congregationalist.

STALLWORTHY George (1809-59) b. Preston Bissett near Buckingham; Congregational apprentice; Homerton, ordained, on Tahiti 1834, Tahuata 1834-41, Tahiti 1841-44, Upolu 1844-59; m. (I) Charlotte Wilson (1817-45) b. Moorea; missionary's daughter; m. (II) Mary Ann Darling (1819-72) b. Moorea; missionary's daughter.

STEARNS A. W. (-   ) b. Boston, U.S.A.; member of mission church, helper resident on Upolu   -1858.

STEVENS Charles Green (1810-   ) b. Walsall, Warwickshire; Congregational foreman in hatter's shop; Homerton, ordained, on Tahiti 1839-40; m. Deborah Blomfield (-   ) b. Denton, Norfolk; Congregational minister's daughter.

STONIER [Miss] (-   ) Congregational schoolteacher, helper on Tahiti 1857-[63].

SUNDERLAND James Povey (1821-89) b. Sheffield; printer and binder, then Congregational minister; Airedale College; on Upolu 1845-51, Tutuila 1851-54, Mare 1854-55; m. Mary Elizabeth Mann (-   ) b. Stockport; Congregational accountant's daughter.

TESSIER Samuel (-1820) 'mechanic' missionary on Tahiti 1801-08, Huahine 1808-09, Moorea 1813-18, Tahiti 1818-20; unm.

THOMSON Robert (1816-51) b. Dumfries, Scotland; Presbyterian (United Secession) joiner and architect's assistant; Turvey, ordained, on Tahuata 1839-41, Tahiti 1841-50; m. Louisa Norton Barff (1822-) b. Huahine; missionary's daughter.

THRELKELD Lancelot Edward (1788-1859) b. Exeter, Devonshire; Calvinistic Methodist actor; educated as druggist's apprentice, ordained, on Moorea 1817-18, Huahine 1818, Raiatea 1818-24, afterwards missionary to Aborigines at Lake Macquarie, N.S.W.; m. Martha Goss (1794-1824) b. Hatherleigh, Devonshire; Calvinistic Methodist.

TURNER George (1818-91) b. Irvine, Ayrshire; Presbyterian (Relief Church) clerk to stationer-woollen merchants; Glasgow University, Relief Divinity Hall (Paisley) and Cheshunt, ordained, on Upolu 1841-42, Tana 1842-43, Upolu 1843-82; m. Mary Anne Dunn (1817-72) b. Glasgow; Presbyterian (Relief Church) minister's daughter.

VASON (VEESON) George (1772-1838) b. Nottingham; bricklayer; 'mechanic' missionary on Tongatapu 1797- ; unm.; resident there -1801.

WARNER Gregory (-) Countess of Huntingdon's Connexion surgeon; ordained, on Tahiti 1807-08, Huahine 1808-09; unm., afterwards at Macao.

WATERS William (-) b. London; 'mechanic' missionary on Tahiti 1801-04; unm.

WILKINSON James (1769-) b. Manchester; Calvinistic Methodist carpenter and tool manufacturer; 'mechanic' missionary on Tongatapu 1797-1800; unm.

WILLIAMS John (1796-1839) b. Tottenham High Cross; Calvinistic Methodist apprentice to furnishing ironmonger; ordained, on Moorea 1817-18, Huahine 1818, Raiatea 1818-27, Rarotonga 1827-28, Raiatea 1828-31, Rarotonga 1832-33, Upolu 1838-39; m. Mary Chawner (-1852) b. London; Calvinistic Methodist.

WILSON Charles (1770-1857) b. Tongh, Aberdeen; Presbyterian apprentice to baker; 'mechanic' missionary on Tahiti 1801-08, Moorea 1808-09, Huahine 1809, Moorea 1812-17, Tahiti 1817-42, resident on Tahiti 1842-44 and Upolu 1844-57; m. (I) Charlotte Burnett (-1818) b. London; Calvinistic Methodist; m. (II) Margaret Jacques née Philips (1783-1848) Church of England widow of Sydney gaoler.

WILSON Samuel (1811-? 1844/45) b. Sydney; Presbyterian missionary's son; Caledonian College (Sydney); ordained assistant missionary, on Tahiti 1834-35, Savai'i 1835-36, Upolu 1836-39; unm.

YOUL John (1773-1827) b. London; Calvinistic Methodist itinerant preacher, ordained, on Tahiti 1801-07; unm.

II Wesleyan Methodist Missionary Society and Australasian Wesleyan Methodist Missionary Society

ADAMS Thomas (1821-85) b. Lidcot, Cornwall; farmer; private school and Richmond Theological Institution 1845, ordained, on Tongatapu 1847, Vava'u 1848-53, Tongatapu 1853-54, Vava'u 1857-60, Tongatapu 1860- ; m. Maria French (-1860) b. Taunton, Somerset; tanner's daughter.

AMOS Richard (1821-1870) b. Bulkington near Birmingham; brassfounder; Stow's Training Institution (Glasgow); schoolteacher afterwards ordained, on Tongatapu 1847- , Vava'u 1856-57, Tongatapu 1857-59; m. Elizabeth Capewell (1819-72) b. Birmingham, schoolteacher.

BAIRD Charles J. (-   ), in Fiji 1859-61; unm.

BAKER Thomas (1832-67) b. Playden, Sussex; boot and shoemaker; ordained, in Fiji 1859-67; m. Harriet Moon (-1878).

BAMBRIDGE Thomas (1801-79) ticket-of-leave carpenter; artisan on Tongatapu 1826-   ; unm., resident on Tahiti from 1832.

BATE Joel (1821-   ) b. Bideford; on Tongatapu 1846-47; unm.

BINNER John (-1863) b. Leeds; schoolteacher in Fiji 1852-63; m. Leslie Crawford (-   ) b. Ireland.

BROOKS William Allen (-   ) ordained, on Vava'u 1836-40; m. Mary Ann Outridge (1810-41) b. (?) Hobart, Van Diemen's Land.

CALVERT James (1813-92) b. Torquay, Yorkshire; printer, bookbinder and bookseller; Hoxton Theological Institution 1837, ordained, in Fiji 1838-55; m. Mary Fowler (1814-82) b. Aston Clinton, Buckinghamshire; baker's daughter.

CAREY Jesse (1832-1914) b. Loxton, Somerset; Church of England upbringing; clerk, then schoolteacher in Australia; National and British and Foreign schools, ordained, in Fiji 1859-74; m. Lydia Lawford (1839-   ).

CARGILL David (1809-43) b. Brechin, Forfar, Scotland; banker's son; King's College, Aberdeen University, ordained, on Tongatapu 1834-35, Fiji 1835-40, Vava'u 1843; m. (I) Margaret Smith (1809-40) b. Aberdeen; Presbyterian sea captain's daughter; m. (II) Augusta Bicknell (-   ).

COLLIS William (-   ) schoolteacher in Fiji 1852-   ; m. (-   ).

CRAWFORD John (1828-58) b. (?) Ireland, in Fiji 1857-58; m. (-   ).

CROSS William (1797-1842) b. Cirencester, Gloucestershire, Church of England upbringing, ordained, on Tongatapu 1827-35, Fiji 1835-42; m. (I) Elizabeth (-1832); m. (II) Augusta Margaret Smith (1817-47) b. Paramatta, N.S.W.; builder's daughter.

DANIEL George (1823-96) b. Bristol; printer; private school, ordained, on Tongatapu 1847-52, Vava'u 1853-56; m. Caroline Elizabeth Burge (1821-1905) b. Bristol; doctor's daughter.

DAVIS Walter James (1824-1904) b. Shoreditch, London; printer afterwards ordained, on Vava'u 1847-53; Tongatapu 1853-55, Ha'apai 1855-57, 1861-67; m. Jemima Jane Newman (1819-80) b. Shoreditch, London.

DYSON Martin (1830-1910) b. Wash, Yorkshire; draper; ordained, in Ha'apai 1857, Upolu 1857-65; m. Sarah Ann Fielding (1836-1921) b. Manchester; immigrants' home manager's daughter.

FLETCHER William (1829-81) b. Granada, West Indies; minister's son; schoolteacher; Kingswood and Taunton schools, University of London, ordained, in Fiji 1857-64, afterwards Rotuma; m Wallis (-1924) missionary's daughter.

FORD James (1819-87) b. Gloucester, in Fiji 1847-49; m. (-   ).

FORDHAM John Smith (1828-1904) b. Sheffield; Church of England upbringing; medical training and Richmond Theological Institution 1852, ordained, in Fiji 1854-62; m. (-   ).

HAZLEWOOD David (1820-55) b. Fakenham, Norfolk; gardener and farm servant; ordained, in Fiji 1844-50, 1851-53; m. (I) Jane McIntyre (-1849) quartermaster's daughter, N.S.W.; m. (II) Sarah Webster (1819-   ) b. Frome, Somerset; dyer's daughter, teacher.

HILL William (1832-99) b. Kennington, Kent; Church of England upbringing; farmer's son and grocer's assistant; on Vava'u 1859-60, Tongatapu 1860; m. Cecilia Kezia Gibbs (1840-63) b. Jersey, Channel Islands.

HOBBS John (1800-83) b. St. Peter's Thanet; builder; ordained, in New Zealand 1823-27, 1827-33, Tongatapu 1833-35, Vava'u 1835-36, Ha'apai

1836-38; m. Jane Broggref (1799-1888) b. Ramsgate, Kent; actuary's daughter.

HUNT John (1812-48) b. Hykeham Moor near Lincoln; farm worker; Hoxton Theological Institution 1836, ordained, in Fiji 1838-48; m. Hannah Summers (-).

HUTCHINSON John (1792-1866) b. Scarborough, Yorkshire; ordained, on Tongatapu 1826-28; m. Mary Oakes (1810-80) b. Parramatta, N.S.W.; chief constable and former missionary's daughter.

JAGGAR Thomas James (1814-82) printer; Kingswood school; ordained, in Fiji 1838-48; m. (-).

KEVERN George (1817-75) b. Devonport, Devon; printer; 'common English' education, ordained; on Vava'u 1840-45, afterwards in Calais; m. (-).

LANGHAM Frederick (1833-1903) b. Launceston, Van Diemen's Land; builder's son, schoolteacher; ordained, in Fiji 1858-94; m. Ann Elizabeth Knight (1883-1902) b. London; grocer's daughter.

LAWRY Walter (1793-1859) b. Rutheren near Bodmin, Cornwall; farmer; ordained, on Tongatapu 1822-23, afterwards Superintendent of Missions; m. Mary Cover Hassall (1799-1825) b. Parramatta, N.S.W.; storekeeper and former missionary's daughter.

LEE George (1829-79) b. Tullamore, Ireland; farmer; ordained, on Tongatapu 1857-60, Vava'u 1860-69; m. Elizabeth Matthews (1832-99) b. Penzance, Cornwall; mason's daughter.

LILLY George (1803-67) b. Roscommon, Ireland; carpenter; artisan on Tongatapu 1822-25; unm.

LYTH Richard Burdsall (1810-87) b. York; grocer's son and surgeon; Church of England Grammar School (York) and University of London, ordained, in Ha'apai 1838-39, Fiji 1839-54; m. Mary Anne Hardy (-) goldsmith's daughter.

MALVERN John (1818-1901) b. Tewkesbury; English, French and Latin education; ordained, in Fiji 1847-58; m. (-).

MARTIN Edward P. (-) b. France; resident in Fiji from 1849, printer, 1856-63.

MILLARD John Gane (1827-97) in Fiji 1850; m. (-).

MILLER George R. H. (1806-54) ship's surgeon resident on Tongatapu 1832-41, assistant missionary afterwards ordained, on Tongatapu 1841-53; m. (I) Mary Ann Lou'akau (-1847) b. Tonga; m. (II) Mrs Susannah Miller (1813-69) widow.

MOORE William (1821-93) b. Parramatta, N.S.W.; tanner and currier then missionary in Moreton Bay District; ordained, in Fiji 1850-61; m. Mary Ann Ducker (1826-) b. (?) Richmond, N.S.W.

POLGLASE John (1823-60) b. St. Breage, Cornwall; Richmond Theological Institution 1850; ordained, in Fiji 1852-60; m. Mary Fletcher (-) b. (?) West Indies; missionary's daughter.

RABONE Stephen (1811-72) b. Burn Tree, Staffordshire; nailmaker ordained, on Vava'u 1836, Tongatapu 1837- , Ha'apai 1839-47, Vava'u 1847-50; m. Eliza Thomas (1811-68) b. Clent, Staffordshire; blacksmith's daughter.

ROYCE James Stephen Hambrook (1829-1907) b. (?) Dover; draper; Richmond Theological Institution, ordained, in Fiji 1856-61; m. Elizabeth Jenkins Berry (-) b. Boughton, Kent.

SHAW Joseph Taylor (1826-94) b. Halifax, Yorkshire; schoolteacher; on Tongatapu 1859-60; m. Anna Riley (1827-1909) b. Oldham, Lancashire; grocer's daughter.

SPINNEY John (1813-40) ordained, on Vava'u 1836-38), Ha'apai 1838-39, Fiji 1839; m.   (-   ).

STEPHINSON William George Richards (1829-90) b. Sunderland, Durham; painter's son; ordained, in Ha'apai 1858-61; m. Emma Swanton (1836-1904) farmer's daughter.

THOMAS John (1796-1881) b. Clent, Staffordshire; Church of England upbringing; blacksmith, ordained, on Tongatapu 1826-30, Ha'apai 1830-31, Tongatapu 1856-59; m. Sarah Hartshorne (1792-1867).

TINDALL Charles (-   ) blacksmith, artisan on Tongatapu 1822-27; unm.

TUCKER Charles (1808-81) b. Horton, Glamorganshire, Wales; farmer; ordained, on Tongatapu 1833, Ha'apai 1833-37, Tongatapu 1837-41; m. Jane Hall (1806-75) b. Bristol; glazier's daughter.

TURNER Nathaniel (1793-1864) b. Wynbunbury, Cheshire; Church of England upbringing; farmer's son; ordained, in New Zealand 1823-27, Tongatapu 1827-31; m. Anne Sargent, b. Ipstones, Etruria, Staffordshire; farmer's daughter.

TURNER Peter (1802-73) b. Manchester; cotton afterwards silk weaver; ordained, in Ha'apai 1831-32, Vava'u 1832-35, Samoa 1835-39, Ha'apai 1839-42, Vava'u 1842-43, Tongatapu 1843, Vava'u 1843-47, Ha'apai 1847-48, Tongatapu 1848-49, Vava'u 1849-55; m. Mary Smallwood (-1885) b. Macclesfield, Cheshire.

VERCOE John (1827-1904) b. Pendavey, Cornwall; farmer; Richmond Theological Institution, ordained, on Vava'u 1854, Tongatapu 1855-58, Ha'apai 1858-60; m. Jane McBean (1829-1910) b. London; tea merchant's daughter.

WATERHOUSE Joseph (1828-81) b. Halifax; minister's son; Kingswood school, ordained, in Fiji 1850-57, 59-64; m. Elizabeth Watson (1828-1909) shipbuilder's daughter.

WATERHOUSE Samuel (1830-1918) b. Halifax; minister's son, ordained, in Fiji 1853-57; m. Esther Day Wilson (1829-56) b. (?) Hobart, Van Diemen's Land.

WATKIN James (1803-86) b. Manchester; soldier's son; ordained, on Tongatapu 1831, Ha'apai 1832-35, Tongatapu 1835-37, Vava'u 1837, afterwards New Zealand; m. Hannah Entwisle (1807-1900) b. Manchester, niece of Rev. Joseph Entwisle.

WATSFORD John (1820-1907) b. Parramatta, N.S.W.; coachman's son; King's School (Parramatta), ordained, in Fiji 1844-49, 1852-53; m. Elizabeth Jones (-1908).

WEBB William (1812-52) b. Botolph, Buckinghamshire; carpenter and joiner; national school and Hoxton Theological Institution 1837; ordained, in Ha'apai 1841-   , Tongatapu   -1852; m. Maria Powell (1811-71) b. Harrow-on-the-Hill; boot and shoemaker's daughter.

WEISS John Von Mangerhoussen (1799-1872) b. Liverpool, England; super-intendent of government boats (Sydney); Royal Naval College; assistant missionary on Tongatapu 1827-28; m. Elizabeth Wilshire Hewlitt (-   ) missionary's step-daughter.

WELLARD Thomas (1803-89) b. Bromley, Kent; builder; assistant mis-sionary on Tongatapu 1836; m. Mary Ann Calvert (-1877) b. Leeds; gunmaker's daughter.

WEST Thomas (1824-90) b. Glasgow; bookseller's son; ordained, on Vava'u 1846-   , Tongatapu 1850-   , Ha'apai 1853-55; m. Mary Orr (-1869).

WHEWELL John (1825-86) b. Glassop, Derbyshire; civil engineer; ordained, in Ha'apai 1855-58, Tongatapu 1858-60, Vava'u 1860, Tongatapu 1861-65; m. Sarah Russell (1833-1914) b. Cork, Ireland; architect's daughter.

WHITTLEY William (-   ), in Fiji 1860-61; m. H. (1830-60).

WILLIAMS Thomas (1815-91) b. Horncastle, Lincolnshire; builder's clerk and draughtsman; ordained, in Fiji 1840-53; m. Mary Cottingham (-   ) farmer's daughter.

WILSON Francis A. (1812-46) b. Bickerton, Yorkshire; farmer's son; Hoxton Theological Institution 1837; ordained, on Vava'u 1840-46; m. (I) Sarah Snow (1813-40) linendraper's daughter; m. (II) Sarah Hull (-   ) governess.

WILSON Matthew (1808-76) b. Bradford, Yorkshire; ordained, in Samoa 1836-39, Ha'apai 1838, Vava'u 1839, Tongatapu 1840, Ha'apai 1845-54; m. Maria Smith (1808-90) b. Bradford; cordwinder's daughter.

WILSON William (1828-96) b. Dumfries, Scotland; Presbyterian upbringing; Richmond Theological Institution 1850, ordained, in Fiji 1854-59; m. Jane McOwan (-1859) minister's daughter.

WOON William (1803-58) b. Truro, Cornwall; printer; on Tongatapu 1831-34, afterwards in New Zealand; m. Jane Garland (1804-59) b. Marazion, Cornwall.

WRIGHT Thomas (-   ) ticket-of-leave servant; agriculturist on Tongatapu 1822-[29]; unm.

III Presbyterian Mission

ARCHIBALD Isaac A. (-   ) b. Nova Scotia; Presbyterian (Nova Scotia) schoolteacher; lay catechiest on Tutuila 1847-48, Aneityum, 1848; m. ?

COPELAND Joseph (183 -1908) b. Scotland; Reformed Presbyterian; Theological Hall; ordained, on Tana 1858-   , then Aneityum; unm., afterwards m. Elizabeth, widow of S. F. Johnston (q.v.).

GEDDIE John (1815-72) b. Banff, Scotland; Congregational upbringing; Pictou Grammar School, Pictou Academy (Presbyterian Church of Nova Scotia) and Dalhousie University; ordained, on Tutuila 1847-48, Aneityum 1848-57; m. Charlotte Leonora MacDonald (1822-1916) b. Antigonish, Nova Scotia; surgeon's daughter.

GORDON George Nichol (1822-61) b. Cascumpec, Prince Edward Island; United Presbyterian (Nova Scotia) farmer; Free Church College (Halifax); ordained, on Eromanga 1857-61; m. Ellen Catherine Powell (1833-61) b. Bow, Essex, England; builder's daughter.

INGLIS John (1819-91) b. Scotland; Reformed Presbyterian tradesman; University of Glasgow and Theological Hall; ordained, on Aneityum 1852-   ; m. Jessie McClymont (1821-85) b. Corriefeckloch, Scotland; Reformed Presbyterian farmer's daughter.

JOHNSTON Samuel Fulton (1830-61) b. Middle Stewiacke, Nova Scotia; United Presbyterian (Nova Scotia) schoolteacher; West River Seminary, Princeton College and Pennsylvania Medical College; ordained, on Tana 1860-61; m. Elizabeth O'Brien (-1876) b. Noel, Nova Scotia; United Presbyterian.

MATHESON John William (1832-62) b. Roger's Hill, Pictou, Nova Scotia; United Presbyterian (Nova Scotia) farmer's son; Pennsylvania Medical College; ordained, on Tana 1858-62; m. Mary Geddie Johnston (1837-62) b. Pictou, Nova Scotia; United Presbyterian merchant's daughter and missionary's niece.

PATON John Gibson (1824-1907) b. Kirkmahoe, Scotland; Reformed Presbyterian stocking manufacturer's son; free normal seminary (Glasgow), Theological Hall and University of Glasgow; ordained, on Tana 1858-62; m. Mary Ann Robson (-1859) b. Coldstream.

IV Gossner's Missionary Society

HONES Julius (-   ) b. Germany; ordained, on Borabora 1851-52, Rurutu 1852.

KRAUSE Ernest Rudolph William. See under L.M.S.

MOHN Leopold (-   ) b. Germany; ordained, on Borabora 1851-52, Rurutu 1852.

SCHMIDT Carl William. See under L.M.S.

V American Board of Commissioners for Foreign Missions and Hawaiian Missionary Society

ALEXANDER William Patterson (1805-84) b. Paris, Kentucky; Presbyterian; Princeton 1831; ordained, on Nukuhiva 1833, afterwards in Hawaii; m. Mary Ann McKinney (1810-88) b. Wilmington, Delaware.

ARMSTRONG Richard (1805-60) b. Turbotville, Pennsylvania; Dick College 1827 and Princeton 1831; ordained, on Nukuhiva 1833, afterwards in Hawaii; m. Clarissa Chapman (1805-91) b. Russell, Massachusetts.

BICKNELL James (1829-92) b. Tahiti; Congregational carpenter and missionary's relative; South Sea Academy; 'mechanic' missionary afterwards ordained, on Fatuhiva 1853-55, Hivaoa 1855-57, 1858-61; unm., afterwards in Hawaii.

BINGHAM Hiram (Junior) (1831-1906) b. Honolulu; Congregational missionary's son and schoolteacher; Williston Academy, Easthampton and Yale; ordained, on Abaiang 1857-64; m. Minerva Clarissa Brewster (1834-1903) b. Northampton.

DOANE Edward T. (-1890) Illinois College 1848 and Union Theological Seminary 1852, ordained, on Ponape 1855-57, Ebon 1857-90; m. Sarah Wilbur (-1862).

GULICK Luther Halsey (1828-91) b. Honolulu; surgeon; New York College of Physicians and Surgeons and Union Seminary; ordained, on Ponape 1852-62; m. Louisa Lewis (1830-94) b. New York City; dry goods merchant's daughter.

PARKER Benjamin Wyman (1803-77) b. Reading, Massachusetts; Amherst College 1829 and Andover 1832; ordained, on Nukuhiva 1833, afterwards in Hawaii; m. Mary Elizabeth Barker (1805-1907) b. Branford, Connecticut.

PIERSON George (-1895) surgeon and missionary to Choctaw Indians; Illinois College 1848 and Andover 1851; on Kusaie 1855-57, Ebon 1857-60; m. Nancy Shaw (-1892).

ROBERTS Ephraim P. (-1893) Williams College 1854 and Bangor 1857, ordained, on Ponape 1858-61; m. Myra H. Farrington (-   ) b. Holden, Massachusetts.

SNOW Benjamin C. (-1880) Congregational minister; Bowdoin 1846 and Bangor 1849, on Kusaie 1852-78; m. Lydia V. Buck (-1887).

STURGES Albert A. (-1887) Wabash College (Indiana) 1848 and New Haven 1851, ordained, on Ponape 1852-84; m. Susan M. Thompson (-1893).

V *Particulars of South Sea Islander Missionaries, 1820-60*

1 Principal Agents of the LMS, 1820-60.

The following list does not claim to be complete. Apart from Minutes of Committee meetings, and Davies's *History of the Tahitian Mission,* names and particulars have been derived from the journals of the voyages to the outstations, and from incidental references. Ordained pastors in Tahiti and Samoa and teachers who laboured exclusively in their own groups or islands are not listed. This includes teachers such as Ko Iro of Ngatangiia in Rarotonga, whose labours belonged to the category of pioneering. Those Cook Islanders who went to other islands in their own group have been included. Unless otherwise specified, most of the teachers listed were married men. A plus sign indicates that the teacher remained after the last date given.

AHURIRO, Papetoai, Moorea: Raivavae, 1822-[25/29].
AHURIRO (died before 1851), Papeete, Tahiti: Rurutu, 1822-24.
AIRIMA, Huahine: Tupuaemanu, 1822-[34].
AKAEA, Mangaia: Aneityum, 1852-53. Dismissed.
AKATANGI, Arorangi, Rarotonga: Eromanga, 1852- , Lifu 1857-60.
    Dismissed for immorality.
AMOSA, Samoa: Aneityum, 1852-57, Niue 1857- .
ANANIA (-1848), Averua, Rarotonga: Manu'a (Tau), 1839- , (Olosega),
    1842-46, Tamarua, Mangaia, 1847-48.
APAISA, Samoa: Aneityum, 1845- .
APELA [ABELA] (-1843), Leone, Tutuila: Futuna, 1841-43. Died by
    violence.
APERAU, Ngatangiia, Rarotonga: Samoa, 1858- .
APOLO, Tutuila, Samoa: Tana, 1841- .
APOLO,   : Aneityum, 1842-[45].
APOLO, Samoa: Lifu, 1854-60, Uvea, 1860- .
APOLO, Aitutaki: Manihiki, 1849-[59] +.
ARU, Papetoai, Moorea: Marquesas, 1826-28.
ARUE, Raiatea, unm.: Sapapali'i, Savai'i, 1830-[36].
ARUI,   : Tupuaemanu [1850].
ATAMOE,   : Marquesas, 1829.
ATAMU [ADAMU], Manono: Tana [1840], Aniwa, 1840-45 [Tana, 1845].
AUNA (-1835), Huahine: Hawaii, 1822- , Tupuaemanu, 1825-35.
AVAEINO, Tahaa: Mitiaro [1823].
BA[R]NABA, Rarotonga: Aitutaki, 1839. Dismissed.
BORABORA [PORAPORA, BOLAPOLA], Borabora: Vava'u, 1822- ,
    Tongatapu. Died before 1830.
BOTI, Huahine, unm.: Savai'i 1830- , Upolu, 1834-36. Dismissed for
    immorality.
BURE'IAU, Rarotonga: Samoa (Samata), [1840].
DAVIDA (1793-1849), Tahaa: Mangaia, 1823-49.
DAVIDA, Tubuai: Tubuai [1830, 1842].
ELIA, Samoa: Eromanga, 1854-57, Aneityum, 1857-58. Niue, 1859- .
FAAI, Papetoai, Moorea: Marquesas (Tahuata), 1831-[35]. Dismissed for
    adultery.
FAARAVA, [Borabora]: Rimatara, 1823-[29].
FAAROAU [FAAROAVAU]: Marquesas (Uapou), 1826-[27]. Died before
    1830.
FAARUEA (1786-   ), Raiatea: Mangaia, 1829-[38].

FAARUEA[ARUE] (-1846), Moorea, unm.: Fiji (Lakeba), 1830-32, (Oneata), 1832-46.

FAATIA [FAATEA], Papeete, Tahiti: Marquesas (Fatuhiva), 1831-   , Tubuai, [1835]-36. Dismissed for adultery.

FAINOU [FAINAU], Papeete, Tahiti: Rurutu, 1822-[25/29].

FALEESE (1826-   ), Tutuila, unm.: Tana, 1841-42, Aniwa, 1842-   .

FALETA, Huahine: Hawaii [1825].

FANA, Tiarei, Tahiti [Native of Hivaoa], unm.: Tahuata, 1831-32.

FARAIRE,   : Mauke, [1830, 1838].

FARANI,   : Tongareva, 1859-   .

FARAVA (1789-   ), Borabora: Rimatara, 1823-[38].

FAREBUA [FAREPUA], Borabora: Maupiti, 1822-[24].

FARE ORE, Huahine: Marquesas (Vaitahu), 1825-   .

FAVELU, Samoa: [Western Polynesia], 1846-   .

FETIU [FITIU, FITITIIU], Borabora: Atiu, 1831-42.

FILI (-1852) [FILA?], Samoa: Mare, [1846]-52. [Efate, 1848].

FRIDAY (1791-   ), Borabora: Mauke [1831], [Raivavae, before 1835], Mangaia [1835] -c.1840. Adultery?

FUATAIESE, Sapapali'i, Samoa: Aneityum, 1841, Tana, 1842-   .

NGATIKA[RO], Arorangi, Rarotonga, unm.?: Tongareva, 1854-   .

NGATIKILI, Rarotonga: Samoa [1841].

NGATIMOARI, Rarotonga: Pukapuka, 1857-   .

HAAMA INO [HAAMA INE], Papetoai, Moorea: Marquesas (Tahuata), 1826-28.

HAAPUNIA [HAAPUNEA], Matavai, Tahiti: Tubuai, 1822-30. Adultery?

HAARI [HARANEA?],   : Atiu [1831].

HAAVI (-1853), Tahaa: Mangaia [1823], Mauke, 1823-53.

HAPE, Papara, Tahiti, unm.: Tongatapu, 1826-28, Rapa, 1831-[46]. **Died before 1851.**

HATAI [ATAI, FUATAI] (-1846), Moorea, unm.: Fiji (Lakeba), 1830-32, (Oneata), 1832-46.

HIOMAI, Tahiti, ordained: Maupiti, 1854-   .

HITIMAHANA, Papeete, Tahiti: Tubuai, 1830-[before 1836].

HITIMAHANA, ordained: Rurutu, 1857-   .

HOROINUU (-1833), Papetoai, Moorea: Raivavae, 1822-[31/32].

HOSEA, Samoa: [Western Polynesia], 1859-   .

HOTA, Papara, Tahiti: Rapa: [1825], 1826-35. Bigamy?

HUMI,   Anaa [before 1830].

IOANE, Samoa: Tana [1845, 1846].

IOANE, Rarotonga: Samoa,   -1858, Mare, 1858-   .

IOANE, Aitutaki: Upolu, 1857-   [Matautu near Apia].

IONA, Falefa, Samoa: Tana [1840], Aniwa, 1840, Tana, 1845, [Lifu, 1845?]. Returned 1846.

IONE [IOANE?] (-1849),   : Efate, 1848.

IONE,   : Efate, 1852-54.

ISAAKA, Samoa: Lifu, 1854 (1857?)-   .

ISAIA, Samoa: Tokelaus [1858], [Western Polynesia], 1859-   .

ITIO, Avarua, Rarotonga: Mauke, 1845-52, 1854-   .

JAKOBA [IACOPO], Samoa, unm.: Rotuma, 1840-45, Mare, 1845-46. Returned.

JOSIA, Samoa: Mare, 1847-48. Returned.

JOSIA, Samoa: [Western Polynesia], 1859-   .

JOSIA, Ngatangiia, Rarotonga, unm.: Tongareva, 1854-   . Adultery?

KAIAAU, Oneroa, Mangaia: Tongareva, 1858-   .

KAKORUA [KAKARUA, KOKURUA], Rarotonga: Lifu, 1855-57, Uvea, 1857- .

KALEPA, Samoa: Niue, 1852- .

KAPAO, Rarotonga: Tana, 1842- . Consumptive.

KAUI (-1850), : Tana, 1848-50.

KA'TUKE, Arorangi, Rarotonga: Ivirua, Mangaia, 1844- .

KAVERIRI [KAVIRIRI] (-1853) , Mangaia: Ivirua, Mangaia [1851], Efate, 1853. Died by violence.

KUKU, Ngatangiia, Rarotonga: Tana [1849], Aneityum, 1849- .

LALOLANGI, Samoa (not church member): Tana, 1839-41. Returned.

LASALO (-1842), Tufulele, Samoa, unm.: Eromanga, 1840-41, Isle of Pines, 1841-42. Died by violence.

LEALAMANU[A] (-1848), Samoa: Efate [1847]-48.

LEFAU, Samoa: Aniwa, 1845- .

LEIATAUA, Falefe, Manono: Rotuma, 1839-45.

LUKA, Aitutaki, Pukapuka, 1857- . Dismissed for adultery.

MAHAMENA [MAHAMENE], Raiatea: Rurutu, 1821-30. Returned.

MAHANA, Papara, Tahiti: Rapa, 1826-[36].

MAILEI? Samoa: [Western Polynesia], 1854- .

MAKA [John Turner Cummins] (-1875?), Averua, Rarotonga: Mare, [1848]-58, Apia, Samoa, 1858-61. Appointed Tokelaus, 1861.

MAKEA (-1860), Aitutaki: Aniwa, 1859-60.

MANAO, Tahiti: Anaa, 1827-37.

MARAE ORE, Taiarapu, Tahiti, unm.: Marquesas (Vaitahu, Tahuata), 1825-26.

MARAMA, Rarotonga: Manono, 1841- .

MARATAI, Borabora: Atiu, 1823-31. Dismissed for adultery.

MAREKO (-1850), : Tana, -1850.

MARETU (c. 1802-80), Ngatangiia, Rarotonga: Mangaia, 1839-41, Manihiki, 1854-55, Ngatangiia, 1855- .

MAROKAA, Arorangi, Rarotonga: Atiu, 1856-57. Returned.

MARU[N]GATANGA, Mangaia: Tana, 1845- .

MATAIO (-c. 1842), Averua, Rarotonga: New Caledonia 1841[-42].

MATAITAI, Raiatea: Aitutaki, 1823-[38]. Rarotonga.

MATATIA (-1855), Ngatangiia, Rarotonga: Savai'i, 1839-41, 1842-45, (Malua), 1845-52, Rarotonga, 1852-55.

MATTATORE [MATAORE], Huahine: [Marquesas], Hawaii 1822- .

MEARIKI, Arorangi, Rarotonga: Eromanga, 1853- , Aneityum, 1857, Mare, 1858- .

MEREU, : Anaa, c. 1827- . Dismissed for immorality.

MIKA, Samoa : Mare [1848]-58.

MOEA [MOIA] (-1854), Huahine [native of Raiatea]: Marquesas [1828], Savai'i, 1830-34, Falelatai, Upolu, 1834-42.

MOOREA, Papeete, Tahiti [native of Anaa]: Anaa, 1821-[before 1830]. Returned.

MOSE, Saleimoa, Samoa: Tana. 1839-[41]. Dismissed for immorality.

MOSE, Samoa : Efate, 1845-[48].

MOSE, Samoa : Niue, 1852-[54].

MUNAMUNA : Aneityum, [1848].

NARII, Huahine : Marquesas (Tahuata), 1825-26.

NARII, Huahine : Tupuaemanu. Chosen Pastor, 1856.

NEHEMIA, Avarua, Rarotonga [native of Rurutu?]: Manu'a, 1839-[54].

NENE, Papara, Tahiti: Rapa [1825], 1826-[31]. Died before 1851.

NIKI, Ngatangiia, Rarotonga: Tongareva, 1857-59. Returned.

NOA, Manono, Samoa, unm.: Isle of Pines, 1840-42, New Caledonia, 1842-45. Returned.

NOOTU (-1860), Arorangi, Rarotonga: Uvea, 1857-   [Mare, 1858-60?], Lifu [1860].

OBEDA, Aitutaki: Manu'a (Olosega), 1857-   .

OKOTAI, Avarua, Rarotonga: Atiu, 1841-45, Samoa [1846]-58, Pukapuka, 1858-   .

OO[O], Borabora, unm.: Rimatara, 1823-   . Died before 1826.

OPETAIO [OBEDAIO] (-1853), Arorangi, Rarotonga, unm.: Aneityum, 1848-49, Tana, 1849-53.

PAGISA [PANGISA], Pago Pago, Tutuila, unm.: New Caledonia, [1840].

PAKIAO [PAKAIO],   : Samoa, 1841-44, [Aitutaki, 1844-   ].

PAKU, Rarotonga [native of Mangaia?]: Mitiaro, 1845-48. Dismissed.

PALALA [PARARA], Huahine: Samoa,   -[1844]. Died before 1855.

PAUO, Papara, Tahiti: Rapa, 1826-[31].

PA'O[O], Aitutaki: Mulifanua, Samoa, 1837-   [Mare], 1841, Lifu, 1842-[58] [Mare, 1849].

PAPATAI [PAPETAI], Rarotonga: New Caledonia [1846]. Returned. Tahiti, 1846-[47]+.

PAPEHIA [PAPEIHA], Raiatea: Aitutaki [1823], Rarotonga, 1823-   , Atiu, 1836-37.

PAREPOU [PALEPO], Mangaia, unm.: Aneityum, 1848-   , Mare, 1852-53. Dismissed for immorality.

PATII (-c. 1854), Papetoai, Moorea: Raivavae, 1831-[40].

PAULA, Samoa: Niue, 1854-59. Returned.

PAULO, Samoa: Niue, 1849-[59].

PAULO, Samoa: [Western Polynesia], 1854-   .

PAUMOANA, Raiatea: Aitutaki, 1825-33. Dismissed for adultery.

PELEASARA[BELE(HE)AZARA], (-1853), Aitutaki: Aneityum, 1849-52, Tana, 1852-53.

PENIAMINU [PENIAMINA], [native of Niue]: Niue, 1846-[48]+.

PETELU [PETERO]   : Tana, 1845, [Aneityum, 1846].

PIKIKAA (-1853), Avarua, Rarotonga: Efate, 1853. Died by violence.

PITA (-1870), Tutuila: Tana, 1845 [Aneityum, 1846-52], Tana, 1852-53, Aneityum, 1853-59. Returned.

PITIU? Borabora: [1834].

POAKI [POAHI?], Rarotonga: [Western Polynesia] 1853-54. Returned. Dismissed.

POITO (-1857), Mangaia: Mare, 1853-57.

POMALE (-1840/41), Tutuila: Tana, 1840-40/41.

POTI[POTO], Samoa: Aneityum, 1845-   .

PUNA (c. 1788-c. 1831), Raiatea (Borabora?): Rurutu 1821-30.

RAEKURA?, Rarotonga: [Western Polynesia], 1859-   .

RAKI, Aitutaki: Savai'i, 1830-34, Upolu, 1834-36, Tutuila, 1836-40. Dismissed for immorality.

RANGI (-1842), Rarotonga: Isle of Pines, 1841-42. Died by violence.

RANGIA [RANGIIA], Mangaia: Tana, 1845-   .

RATAI (-1847), Averua, Rarotonga: Efate, 1846-47.

RAURAA, Mangaia: Mitiaro, 1848-54, Mangaia, 1857-59. Dismissed.

REVAE[REVA E], Borabora: Maupiti, 1822-   .

RU, Aitutaki: Futuna, 1859-   , Atiu, 1870-78.

RUATAI, Tahiti: Tuamotus (Makatea), 1829-[31].

RUPE, Aitutaki: Tamarua, Mangaia, 1841-   , Atiu, 1844-   , Arorangi, Rarotonga, 1847-48, Atiu, 1849-56, Arorangi, 1857-61, Atiu, 1861-   .

SADARAKA (formerly called MAMAE), Oneroa, Mangaia: Tamarua, Mangaia, 1848-[57]+.
SAILUSE, Samoa   : Efate, [1848]-   .
SAKAIO [SAKAIA], Samoa: Aneityum, [1852]-57, Niue, 1857-[58]+.
SAKARIA [ZAKARIA], Rarotonga: Lifu, 1842-45. Returned. Dismissed for immorality.
SALAMIA [SALAMEA] (-1840/41), Sagana, Upolu: Tana, 1839-40/41.
SAMUELA, Matavai, Tahiti: Tubuai, 1822-30. Returned.
SAMUELA (-1843), Falealili, Upolu: Futuna, 1841-43. Died by violence.
SAMUELA,   : Niue, [1857]-[59]+.
SARIA, Samoa: Mare,   -1859. Returned.
SAU, Sanapu, Manono: Rotuma, 1839-[40].
SEPANIA [SEFANIA] (-c. 1849), Samoa: Efate 1847-c. 1849.
SEPETAIA [SEPETAIO] (-1860), Samoa: Lifu, [1857]-60.
SETEFANO, Samoa: Efate, 1845-53. Returned.
SIMEONA, [Samoa]: Aneityum, 1842-[48], 1853-   .
SIMI, Samoa: Tana.
SIMONA (-c.1849), Samoa: Efate, 1846-c. 1849.
SIMONA [SIMIONA], Samoa: Aneityum, 1853-[58].
SIPI (-c.1847), Tutuila: Efate, 1845-c.1847. Died by violence.
SOLIA, Samoa: Mare, 1846-52, Tika, 1852-59. Returned.
SUALO,   : [Western Polynesia], 1854-   .
TAALILI?,   : Efate, [1845]-   .
TAAMORE [TAMORE],   , unm.: Tupuaemanu, 1836-   . Died before 1855.
TA AMOTU, Huahine: Hawaii [1825].
TAATU ORI [TAATA ORI], Raiatea: Savai'i, 1830-[36].
TAAVILI, Samoa: Efate, 1845-[48].
TAERO ITI, Raiatea: Maupiti [1839].
TAEVAO [TAEVAE], Arorangi, Rarotonga: Eromanga, 1857-   , Mare [1861].
TAFETA [DAVIDA], Papara, Tahiti, unm.: Tongatapu, 1826-27.
TANGI-PO [TAGIPO] (-c.1846), Samoa: Tana, [1845]-c.1846. Died by violence?
TAHARAA [JACERO], Papara, Tahiti, unm.: Fiji (Lakeba), 1830-32, (Oneata), 1832-   .
TAIHAERE [TAI] (c.1796-   ), Borabora: Aitutaki, [1830], Sapapali'i, Samoa, 1830-   , Solosolo,   -1840. Dismissed for immorality.
TAIRI [TAILI] (-1847), Rarotonga: Mangaia, Efate, 1846-47.
TAILI, Rarotonga   : Manihiki [1859].
TAIRI, Ngatangiia, Rarotonga: Manihiki, 1849-[59]+.
TAITI, Atiu: Manihiki, 1858-   .
TAIVAO?, Rarotonga: Eromanga, Mare, 1858-[59]+.
TAMARUA, Ngatangiia, Rarotonga: Ngatangiia, 1856-58, Tongareva, 1858-59, Matavera, 1859-   .
TAMUA (-1860/61),   : Aitutaki, 1848-52, Arorangi, 1852-56, Atiu, 1856-60/61.
TANAO [TANIAO],   : Mare, 1858-   .
TANGI[I]A (-1846), Avarua, Rarotonga: Mangaia, 1845-46.
TANIELA [DANIELA] (-1842), Mulifanua, Upolu: Eromanga, 1840-41, Isle of Pines 1841-42. Died by violence.
TANIELA [DANIELA], Tutuila: Isle of Pines, 1840-42. Returned.
TANIELA (-1844), Pago Pago, Tutuila: Mare, 1841-44.
TANIELA, Falealili, Samoa: New Caledonia, 1841, [Isle of Pines, 1842].

TANIELA, Samoa: Lifu [1854]-[59]+.

TAOITI, Oneroa, Mangaia: Tongareva, 1854-[59]+.

TARIPOU, Rarotonga: Aneityum,   -1849, Mare, 1849-   .

TATAIO, Sapapali'i, Savai'i: Mare, 1841-48. Returned. [Western Polynesia]. 1854-   .

TATAU [TATAI], Rarotonga: Tahiti [printing], 1854-   .

TAUA, Huahine,   : Hawaii 1823-[55]+.

TAUA[A],Tahaa: Mangaia [1823], Mitiaro, 1823-42. Returned.

TAAVINE [TAVINI], Papeete, Tahiti: Marquesas (Fatuhiva), 1831-   .

TAUNGA (1818-98), Ngatangiia, Rarotonga: New Caledonia, 1842-45, Mare, 1845-56, Samoa, 1847, Manu'a, 1849-52, 185 -   .

TAURI (-1854),   : Efate, 1852-54.

TAUTE?, Huahine: Samoa. Died before 1855.

TAUTE, Borabora: Vava'u, 1822-[1830]+. Apostate; later joined Wesleyans.

TAVITA (-1843), Sapapali'i, Savai'i: Aneityum, 1841-43.

TEAHU [TEEHU?], Papetoai, Moorea: Marquesas (Uapou) 1826-   .

TEAIA, Ngatangiia, Rarotonga: Atiu, 1848-52, Titikaveka, Rarotonga, 1852-[59]+.

TEAMARA [TEAMARU], Arorangi, Rarotonga: Efate, 1858-61.

TEAOA, Avarua, Rarotonga: Avarua, 1853-[59]+, chaplain to 'Hervey Islanders', Tahiti, 1854-   .

TEANAROA, Mangaia: Manu'a, 1835-   .

TEARIKI, Ngatangiia: Mangaia, 1859-   .

TEAUTOA (-1859), Arorangi: Efate, 1858-59.

TEAVA, Rarotonga: Manono, 1832-36, Falealili, Upolu, 1836-38, Leone, Tutuila, 1838-52. Returned [1857].

TEAVAE [TEAVAI], Ngatangiia, Rarotonga: Mare, 1853-59. [Sydney, 1859-   ].

TEHAU, Tahiti   : Tuamotus (Takaroa), c.1830-37. Dismissed.

TEHEI (c.1784-   ), Borabora: Atiu, 1823-36, [Rarotonga, 1836-38]. Returned. Maupiti, 1839-[45].

TEKORI, Ngatangiia, Rarotonga: Safune, Samoa, 1842-44, 1844-46. Dismissed.

TEPAIRU, Tahaa, unm.: Mangaia, 1823-   .

TERAA, Papeete, Tahiti: Anaa 1821-[before 1830]. Dismissed for immorality.

TEREAVORI [TEREAUORE], Rarotonga?: Upolu,   -1836. Returned.

TEREMU, Tahaa: Mauke, 1823-   .

TEUKI [TEUHI?], Avarua, Rarotonga: Mitiaro, 1856-[59].

TEURA (-1844), Rarotonga: New Caledonia, 1843-44.

TEURUA, Ngatangiia, Rarotonga, ordained: Rimatara, 1856-   .

TIAVAIRAU, Tiarei, Tahiti: Marquesas (Tahuata), 1831-32.

TIBERIO [RIO], Raiatea: Rarotonga, 1823-   .

TIERE, Tahaa, unm.: Mangaia [1824]. Died before 1826.

TILU?,   : Atiu   -[1838].

TINOREI [TINONEI?],   Manihiki [1858, 1859].

TOHI, Papetoai, Moorea: Raivavae, 1822-[29/32]. Returned.

TOMA, Samoa: Lifu [1854]-60. Returned.

TOMA, Oneroa, Mangaia: Efate, 1858-[59]+.

TUATAI[A],   : Mauke, 1852-[54].

TUAVA, Aitutaki: Samoa, 1830-   . Died before 1836.

TUI,   : Mare, [1846], Lifu, 1848-[58]+.

TUKA[A], Mangaia: Eromanga, 1857-   .

TUKU, Arorangi, Rarotonga: Mitiaro, 1854-[56].

TUKUAU, Rarotonga: Samoa, 1842-   .

TUMATAIABU [TUTAIEPO] (-1850/51), Rarotonga: Aneityum, 1846-47, Tana, 1847-50/51.

TUPOU, Samoa: Efate [1848].
TUTANE, Rarotonga: Samoa, 1842-   .
TUTAU, Rarotonga: Eromanga 1853-   , Mare,   -1857, Lifu, 1857-[58].
TUTE (-1858), Huahine: Hawaii, 1826-58.
TUTIU, Borabora: Atiu, 1824-   .
UEA, Mangaia: Manu'a, 1835, Solosolo, 1836-   .
UMIA, Raiatea: Savai'i, 1830-[37]+.
UPA [OUPA] (c. 1794-   ), Borabora: Atiu, 1824-[49]+.
UPOKUMANU (-1853),   : Tana 1845-[Aneityum, 1846], Tana, 1847-49. Returned, Tana, 1852-53.
UTU, Huahine: Tupuaemanu, 1822-[25]. Died before 1855.
VA'A (-1857), Aitutaki: Eromanga, 1852-[53]+.
VAARU [VAALU, VARU] (-1854), Mangaia: Efate, 1853-54.
VAHAPATA, Raiatea: Aitutaki, 1823-   .
VAIOFANGA [VAIAFAGA], Tutuila, Tana, 1840-[41].
VAHINE-INO, Raiatea: Rarotonga [1823], Aitutaki, 1830-[38]+. Adultery?
VASA (-c.1846),   : Aniwa, 1845-   , [Tana, c.1846]. Died by violence.
ZORABABELA, Borabora: Vava'u, 1822-   . Died before 1830.

2 Wesleyan Native Assistant Missionaries (NAM)

This list only includes those Tongans and Fijians who were ordained as pastors. It represents a very small proportion of the total number of teachers and local preachers serving as 'native missionaries' in these groups. In a few instances dates may refer to circuit appointments which were not taken up.

'AHONGALU Barnabas (-1881), Vava'u: teacher Samoa 1835-51, 1856 +, ord. 1858.
BAONGO Mark: Vava'u 1858, Niuafo'ou 1859 +.
BUIDOLI Benjamin: Bau 1857, Viwa 1858-60, Rewa 1860 +, ord. 1860.
BULU Joel (-1877), Vava'u: teacher, Lakeba, Rewa, Viwa, Nadi, Ono, 1850, ord. 1852. Lakeba 1853, Nadi 1858, Bua 1859, Taveuni 1860 +.
CATAKI Nathan: Ono, Moce etc. (Lakeba circuit) 1854 +.
FAUBULA John, son of Tui Nayau, Lakeba: teacher Ha'apai [1839], Vava'u 1856, Tongatapu 1857, Ha'apai 1859 +.
FIFITA Naphtali: Tongatapu 1859+.
FOTOFILI Aaron: Bua 1859, Bau, Viwa and Ovalau.
KATA David: Ha'apai 1856, Vava'u 1859.
KETECA Joel (-c.1875): Kabara (Lakeba) 1855.
KIENGA Jeremiah (c.1813-1855/6?): Ono (Lakeba) 1854.
LAGI Wesley (-1853), Vava'u: teacher Viwa [1844]; Viwa and Bau 1852-53.
LANGI Elias [Ilaiase, Eliesa], Vava'u: chief teacher Niuafo'ou [1834], Uvea 1848+; Niuafo'ou 1856, Ha'apai 1859+.
LATU John: teacher Lakeba [1848]; Uvea 1852, Niuafo'ou 1853, Ha'apai 1857, Vava'u 1859+.
LATUSELU Benjamin, Vava'u: teacher Feletoa [1833], Samoa 1835-45; ord. 1847, Niuatoputapu 1847, Samoa 1848-52, Vava'u 1853, Tongatapu 1856. Dismissed for adultery.
MAIMAFAINOA Moses: teacher Lakeba [1848]; Cicia, Kabara etc. (Lakeba) 1855+.

MASUKA Cornelius: Bau 1857+, ord. 1860.
MATAYENANIU [MATAININIU] Joshua: Viwa and Bau 1852, supernumerary 1853+.
MOHULAMU John: Tongatapu 1860+.
RAWAIDRANU Isaac: Bau 1857+, Koro; ord. 1860.
TAKELO Eliezer (-1886): Rotuma 1854-57, Bua.
TUILAGI Solomon: Ovalau 1856+.
VAVE Matthias: Vanua Balavu, Moala etc. (Lakeba) 1856+.
VEA Paul (-1865), Vava'u: teacher Viwa [1844]; Kadavu (Viwa and Bau circuit) 1852+, Rewa and Ovalau 1855, Kadavu 1859+.
VI Peter: bapt. Nuku'alofa 1829, teacher Ha'apai 1856, Vava'u 1857, Ha'apai 1859+.

3 Ministers and Teachers of the Hawaiian Evangelical Association
AUMAI D. P.: Abaiang, 1858-   . Returned 1868.
KAAIKAULA B. (-1859): Ponape, 1852-59.
KAIWI I[saia] W., ordained 1857: Fatuhiva, 1853-57, Hivaoa, 1857-60, Fatuhiva, 1860-   .
KAIWI Levi: Hivaoa, 1858-59, Tahuata, 1859-   [Vaitahu, 1860].
KAMAKAHIKI S.: Ponape, 1855-57. Licensed preacher, Maui.
KANOA J. W. (-1896): Kusaie, 1855-57, Abaiang, 1857-65, Butaritari, 1865+.
KAPOHAKU Paulo (-1869): Hivaoa, 1858-61. Became blind.
KAUKAU A., ordained: Hivaoa, 1857-   .
KAUWEALOHA Samuel, ordained: Fatuhiva, 1853-55, Hivaoa, 1855+.
KEKELA James, ordained: Fatuhiva, 1853-55, Hivaoa, 1855-58, 1859+.
KUAIHELANI Lota, ordained 1858: Fatuhiva, 1853-57, 1858+.
MAHOE J. H. (1831-91), ordained 1860: [Abaiang, 1857] Tarawa, 1858-   , Abaiang, 1860-70.

Notes

ABBREVIATIONS

ABCFM	American Board of Commissioners for Foreign Missions
ADB	*Australian Dictionary of Biography*
AL	LMS, Australia Letters
AWMS	Australasian Wesleyan Methodist Missionary Society
CCWM	Congregational Council for World Mission (formerly LMS)
CMS	Church Missionary Society
CP	LMS, Candidates' Papers
CQ	LMS, Candidates' References and Examination Papers (Questionnaires)
DNZB	*Dictionary of New Zealand Biography*
EM	*Evangelical Magazine and Missionary Chronicle*
JPH	*The Journal of Pacific History*
JPS	*Journal of the Polynesian Society*
JSO	*Journal de la Société des Océanistes*
LMS	London Missionary Society
ML	Mitchell Library, Sydney
MMS	Methodist Missionary Society (London) — formerly WMMS
MOM	Methodist Overseas Missions (Sydney)
NLA	National Library of Australia (Canberra)
NSW	New South Wales
Pac. Hist.	Department of Pacific and Southeast Asian History, Australian National University, Canberra
PRH	Papers of Rowland Hassall
R-O'R	Ropiteau-O'Reilly collection, Paris
SMH	*Sydney Morning Herald*
SSJ	LMS, South Seas Journals
SSL	LMS, South Seas Letters
SSM	South Sea Missions (Mitchell Library)
WC	Waterhouse Correspondence
WMM	*Wesleyan Methodist Magazine*
WMMS	Wesleyan Methodist Missionary Society

365

PREFACE

1 Damon, 1866 and 1869.
2 Gunson, 1954.
3 Neill, 1966.
4 M. Warren, 1967, pp. 39 ff.
5 John Davies, 19 December 1829, in SSL.
6 For example, Lovett, 1899, vol. I, p. 311.

PROLOGUE

1 See Corney, 1913-19.
2 J. Williams, 5 October 1838—SSL: Prout, 1843, p. 520.
3 See, for instance, the wording in *Voyage to the Pacific Ocean* (2nd edn, London, 1785), vol. II, p. 77; and Bishop Russell's comments in Russell (3rd edn, 1845), pp. 99-100.
4 See H. R. Haweis, 1896, vol. II, pp. 198-200; J. Davies, The History of the Tahitian Mission (LMS archives), chapter 1; Lovett, 1899, vol. I, pp. 117-9.
5 S. Marsden, Funeral Sermon, pp. 40-41—ML.
6 Marsden to Joseph Butterworth, 22 December 1817, WMMS, Records of Wesleyan Mission to New South Wales.
7 See Prout, 1843, pp. 438-40.
8 Selwyn to Nihill, 22 November 1853—SSL.
9 Murray and Sunderland, 9 July 1852—SSJ, no. 146; Nisbet (Secretary), 22 July 1852—SSL.

1 A SET OF TINKERS

1 Jorgensen, 1811, p. 15.
2 J. M. Orsmond, July 1829 — SSL.
3 This verse is taken from 'The Home of Taste'. The 'home of taste' was also described in other poems such as 'Saturday' and 'The Summer House'.
4 For the teetotal movement in the context of Pacific missions see Gunson, 1966.
5 Bebb, 1935, p. 97.
6 Henry Brooke, *The History of Henry, Earl of Moreland* (Manchester, 1812), p. 35.
7 See White, 1877, p. 5.
8 See P. M. Waterhouse, Papers — ML.
9 See Carnachan, n.d. [1855], pp. 49, 51.
10 Henry to W. P. Crook, 23 January 1828, quoted *SMH*, 23 February 1835.
11 E.g. Bedggood (wheelwright), Cowell (twine-spinner), Edmonds (stone-mason), Fairburn (carpenter), Hamlin (flax-dresser), Kemp (smith), etc.
12 Bennet's *Life of Bogue*, quoted in John Morison, 1844, p. 198.
13 22 September 1798, quoted in Lovett, 1899, vol. I, p. 28.
14 Haweis, 1795, p. 173.
15 Melvill Horne to S. Greatheed, 17 June 1796 — Nan Kivell Collection (NK 2619), NLA.
16 Z. Macaulay to Joseph Hardcastle, 10 February 1800 — Nan Kivell Collection (NK 7099), NLA.
17 The LMS missionaries Henry, Shelley, Orsmond, Stevens and Macdonald had brothers-in-law attached to the CMS in New Zealand; William Puckey was a member of the LMS before he joined the CMS.
18 J. Elder to directors, May 1801 — SSJ no. 11.
19 See *EM*, IV (1796), p. 385.
20 *SMH*, 23 February 1835.

21 Fox, 1810, pp. 80-1.
22 For this view, held by Crook's descendants, see Lockley, n.d.
23 See Crook, 11 November 1820 — SSJ, no. 54.
24 The Welsh Calvinistic Methodists have maintained their distinct and separate identity.
25 Threlkeld's 'candidates' papers' are contained in SSM, 11.
26 For an account of the Armitage family see Robinson, 1954, pp. 52-4.
27 Professor John Couch Adams discovered the planet Neptune, and William Grylls Adams became Professor of Natural Philosophy and Astronomy at King's College, London.
28 W. P. Burgess, 27 May 1843, Candidates' Papers (Adams), box 2 — WMMS.
29 Others from Australia were Hazlewood, Moore, Millard and Thomas Baker.
30 Jos. Waterhouse to Jabez Waterhouse, 21 July 1852, Correspondence from Jos. Waterhouse — ML.
31 Buzacott, 12 February 1852 — SSL.
32 One of these, Martha, was the mother of George Clarke, junior, afterwards a missionary, a Congregational minister and Chancellor of the University of Tasmania. Several other missionaries had interesting clerical connexions. John Vercoe was a nephew of Walter Lawry. Jane Hall, the wife of Charles Tucker, was a member of a very old Wesleyan family in Bristol, and Dr Richard Burdsall Lyth was the grandson of Richard Burdsall, a famous local preacher of York. One of Lyth's brothers later conducted a Methodist mission in Germany.

2 DOUBLY CALLED

1 Knox, 1950, pp. 495-6.
2 LMS, *Four Sermons . . . 1796*, Sermon 2, pp. 66-7.
3 LMS, *Sermons . . . 1795*, p. 139. See also *ibid.*, p. 115.
4 For example, George Pritchard, 1844, p. 201.
5 Harris, 1842, p. 467.
6 L. Tyerman, *The Life of the Rev. George Whitefield*, 2 vols. (London, 1877), vol. II, p. 506.
7 Ellis, 1831a, vol. II, pp. 429-31.
8 See James Montgomery, 1831, vol. I, p. 27; Morison, 1844, p. 429.
9 This was also true of the directors of the LMS; see Morison, pp. 14 (Eyre), 139 (Shrubsole), 270-1 (Burder), 302 (Hill), 365 (Roby), 377 (Lambert), 411 (John Townsend), 429-30 (Williams), 463-5 (Knight), 500-1 (Mends) and 529-30 (Kingsbury).
10 Williams, July 1816 — CP; Prout, 1843, p. 15.
11 For Johannes Theodorus Vanderkemp, LMS missionary to South Africa, 1798-1811, see A. D. Martin, *Doctor Vanderkemp* (London, n.d.).
12 Powell, 18 November 1842 — CQ; Chisholm, 3 July 1840 — CQ.
13 Macfarlane (later also McFarlane), 9 July 1856 — CQ.
14 See CP for Charter, Nisbet and Turner.
15 Moore, 30 May 1838 — CP.
16 Lind, 4 July 1848 — CQ.
17 Law, 22 May 1849 — CQ.
18 Wilson, 1797 — CP.
19 Barff, 1816 — CP.
20 Darling, 1816 — CP.
21 Pitman, 1820 — CP.
22 See Johnstone, 22 December 1837 — CQ.
23 Spencer, 28 January 1851 — CQ; see also Creagh, 23 November 1852 — CQ.
24 Peter Turner, A brief account of myself — ML.

25 Hunt, Private Journal, vol. I, pp. 1-2 — ML.

26 *Ibid*, vol. I, p. 15.

27 See Birtwhistle, 1954, pp. 168-85.

28 Hunt, 15 April 1844, private journal, vol. II, pp. 206-7.

29 Lyth, 12 November 1839, journal, vol. I, pp. 407-11 — ML.

30 Watsford, 1900, pp. 14-16.

31 See J. Carey, Materials for my biography, p. 9 — ML.

32 T. Baker, Diary, pp. 3-6 — MOM.

33 T. Baker, 2 September 1850, Diary, p. 10.

34 Matt. xxviii, 18-20; Mark xvi, 15; Luke xxiv, 46-9; John xx, 21, 22; Acts i, 8-10.

35 *EM*, vol. I (1793), pp. 252-3; vol. II (1794), p. 33.

36 Hancox to Hassall, 6 March 1800 — PRH, vol. I, p. 35.

37 Burder to Hassall, 9 December 1800 — PRH, vol. I, p. 37.

38 For example, Richard Davis of the CMS; Threlkeld of the LMS; Lawry of the WMMS.

39 Yonge, 1874b, contains popular accounts of these missionaries as do most pious missionary collections of the Victorian era.

40 S. M. Creagh was influenced by reading the life of Martyn; see 23 November 1852 — CP.

41 Birrell, 1861, p. 244.

42 See the relevant CP.

43 Birrell, *op cit.*, p. 54; Sunderland and Buzacott, 1866, p. 5.

44 Campbell, 1842, pp. 217-43.

45 See particularly Stevens, 10 June 1839; Johnston, 16 September 1839 — SSL.

46 Platt, 12 April 1840 — SSL, see also Orsmond, 10 October 1839 — SSL.

47 See relevant CP.

48 A typical piece of verse written after the visit of Dr Winter and Richard Knill to Penzance is printed in the *Evangelical Magazine* for December 1820.

49 Hunt, Private Journal, vol. I, p. 4.

50 Law, 1851 — CP.

51 Howe, 19 July 1838 — CP.

52 For example, C. Wilson, 1797 — CP.

53 See *DNZB*.

54 Lawry, 19 July 1818, Diary, p. 14 — ML.

55 Lawry, 2 February 1820, Papers — ML.

56 Law, 22 May 1849 — CQ (5).

3 A SMATTERING OF MANY THINGS

1 J. Puckey, 1796 — CP.

2 See Wilkinson, 23 April 1796 — CP; Robinson, 1954, pp. 136-8.

3 Rule No 2, quoted Lovett, 1899, vol. I, p. 43.

4 King, 1899, p. 25.

5 Memorandum, 30 January 1801, read before the Committee in London on 19 April 1802, quoted in J. B. Marsden, n.d., p. 38.

6 For Davies' qualifications, see pp. 238-9, see also P. Lesson, 1839, vol. II, p. 54; Wheeler, 1842, p. 326.

7 Lovett gives the Report in full, vol. I, p. 67-72.

8 Darling, 4 July 1816 — CP.

9 Barnden, 2 February 1834 — CP.

10 See Bogue and Bennett, 1808-12, vol. I, pp. 530-1.

11 For the attitude towards the study of Latin see *ibid.*, vol. III, p. 271; and of classics, *ibid.*, vol. IV, p. 300.

12 Minutes of the Committee of Examination, 15 May 1815, pp. 376-7 — LMS. There is a transcribed set of these lectures at New College, London.

13 Bogue was a moderate Calvinist.

14 'Each lecture, after having been taken down from the tutor's lips, was read a second time.' Choules and Smith, 1842, vol. I, p. 554.

15 This was the policy of the directors: 'Our desire is to communicate to them a sound judgment and comprehensive acquaintance with the principles of divine revelation, rather than to give them the talents for criticism, or perplex them with unedifying controversies . . .'. Quoted in Lovett, 1899, vol. I, p. 70.

16 James, 1860-64, vol. XVII, pp. 131-2; see also Birrell, 1861, pp. 35-7.

17 Walter Lawry, who visited the Seminary in 1817, thought that the students were 'very polite', but his comments suggest that he thought them below standard in piety and zeal (see Lawry, December 1817, Papers — ML).

18 See Pitman, 16 June 1819 — CP.

19 See L. E. Thelkeld, 'Reminiscences', *Christian Herald*, I, p. 330.

20 John Eimeo Ellis, 1873, p. 22.

21 Chalmers, 3 March 1820 — CP, Pritchard.

22 Chalmers, 26 August 1820 — CP, Pritchard.

23 For a detailed account of the course at Llanfyllin see *EM*, XXIX, p. 293; XXX, p. 277.

24 Jones, 10 January 1821 — CP.

25 See *Missionary Register* 1818, p. 281; 1820, p. 428, etc.

26 For the syllabus at Hoxton Academy see *EM*, XXVIII, p. 339; XXIX, p. 340. Aaron Buzacott, founder of a training institute in Rarotonga, was trained at both Hoxton Academy and Hoxton Mission College: See Buzacott — CP, and Sunderland and Buzacott, 1866, p. 11.

   Alexander Simpson, afterwards tutor of the South Sea Academy, completed his four-year course under Henderson: see Simpson, 16 August 1843 — SSL.

27 James, 1860-64, vol. II, p. 80.

28 For an account of Turvey see H. G. Tibbutt, 'The Dissenting Academies of Bedfordshire — Part 1', *Bedfordshire Magazine*, V (1957), pp. 321-3.

29 R. Steel, A. W. Murray of Samoa . . . , p. 42 — ML.

30 Cecil, 16 June, 26 June 1832 — CP, Rodgerson.

31 Jack, 29 August 1832 — CP, Rodgerson.

32 Thomson, 30 November 1836 — CQ (8).

33 Deas, 26 September 1836 — CP, Thomson.

34 Thomson, 18 December 1837 — CP. Besides those mentioned, others who passed through Turvey were Barnden, Macdonald, Charter, William Gill, Drummond and John Barff.

35 See particularly Irene Parker, 1914 and J. W. Ashley Smith, 1954.

36 For the history of the academy see Ashley Smith, pp. 193-8.

37 See *EM*, XXVII, p. 382; XXVIII, p. 339.

38 His students included Ellis, Barff, Stallworthy, Hardie and Murray. For one of his perceptive assessments see Pye Smith, 23 October 1837 — CP, Stevens.

39 The Reverend Thomas Lewis of the *Duff* received his training for the ministry at Cheshunt.

40 For example, H. Nisbet and G. Turner. See also J. Moore, 1842 — CP.

41 Rev. Messrs Jukes and Alliott. For Bedford see H. G. Tibbutt, 'The Dissenting Academies of Bedfordshire — Part II', *Bedfordshire Magazine*, VI (1957), pp. 8-10: for Cotton End, see *ibid.*, pp. 84-6.

42 Legge took in other missionary students, e.g. W. A. Lind.

43 Jefferson, 21 September 1838 — CP, Bullen. For more detail of the course

see G. Gill, 23 November 1842 — CP; 18 November 1842 — CQ (8) ; Powell, 1842 — CP.

[44] For an outline of the course see *EM*, XXIX, p. 116.

[45] Mills, 6 June 1835 — CP.

[46] Howe, 1838 — CP; 20 August 1838 — CQ.

[47] See, for example, *EM*, XXX, p. 404; John William Adamson, *English Education 1789-1902* (Cambridge, 1930), pp. 38-9.

[48] Mills, 28 January 1833 — CP.

[49] For the similar case of Henry Royle, see Royle, 11 October 1837 — CQ (8).

[50] For a comprehensive course see George Patterson, [1864], pp. 49-93, but contrast J. G. Paton, 1902.

[51] The education of W. P. Alexander, missionary to the Marquesas, was typical. See Mary C. Alexander, 1934, pp. 21-30.

[52] Samuel Wilson, John Barff and James Bicknell.

[53] Second annual report, quoted in *South-Asian Register* (Sydney), December 1828.

[54] *ibid.* The report for 1831 (see SSL) suggests further parallels with Gosport. Boys in their third year read in Hebrew, Greek and Latin, and were also examined in arithmetic, 'evidence of Christianity', rhetoric, mental philosophy, logic, ichthyology, astronomy and the use of globes.

[55] S. Wilson, 4 August 1826 — SSL; Lang, 5 October 1827 — AL.

[56] He had been a pupil there, 1822-24, before going to the South Sea Academy.

[57] Crook, 25 May 1831 — AL.

[58] S. Wilson, 31 January 1834; MacGarvie, 8 November 1832 — SSL.

[59] See S. Wilson, 4 April 1835, Lang Papers, vol. XV — ML.

[60] J. Barff, 2 May 1838 — CQ (8) .

[61] Pritchard, 31 October 1840 — SSL.

[62] C. Barff, 9 June 1841 — SSL.

[63] Howe, 9 March 1842 — SSL.

[64] August Toplady, himself a follower of Whitefield, poured scorn on the more humble followers of Wesley. See *WMM* (1834) , p. 827.

[65] See *WMM* (1834) , pp. 338-9, 861-2.

[66] See [Hastling, Willis and Workman], 1898; F. C. Pritchard, *Methodist Secondary Education* (London, 1949) .

[67] Quoted in G. Stringer Rowe, 1885, p. 31.

[68] WMMS, Sydney, District Despatch Book 1826-36, pp. 20-23 — ML.

[69] Watsford, 1900, p. 32.

[70] J. Orton, 28 July 1839, Journal 1832-41, p. 301 — ML.

[71] See P. Turner, A brief account — ML.

[72] *ibid.*, 2 October 1827.

[73] P. Turner, 1858, Books read 1832-73 — ML.

[74] Lawry, 28 November 1815, Papers — ML.

[75] See Lawry, 30 April, 19 July 1818, Diary . . . — ML.

[76] I.e., the writings of Wesley, Fletcher, etc.

[77] WMMS, Sydney, District Despatch Book 1826-36 — ML.

[78] Cargill, 3/4 December 1832, 3/11 January 1833, Journal 1832-38 — ML.

[79] *WMM* (1835), p. 41. The writer appears to have been a returned missionary from India.

[80] For examples of the arguments used by advocates of the scheme, see *WMM* (1834), pp. 338 ff, 820 ff.

[81] For details of the proposed course see *WMM* (1834), pp. 676-8.

[82] A skeleton outline of his course can be found in his *Letter to a Junior Methodist Preacher, concerning the general Course and Prosecution of his*

Studies in Christian Theology. This small work not only served as a prospectus for the institution, but it was influential in guiding the reading of all those preachers and missionaries who had not been able to attend the institution. Peter Turner, for instance, wrote in 1840 that he was organizing his theological reading by following the plan suggested by Dr Hannah (P. Turner, Books read 1832-73 — ML).

83 *WMM* (1836), pp. 682-3.

84 Calvert, 7 April 1845, MS vol. no. 2, Biographical: South Seas, Box 2 — MMS.

85 Hannah, 1853, p. 65.

86 See Report of the Wesleyan Theological Institution, 1834-35 in *WMM* (1836), pp. 207 ff.

87 Hunt, 27 May 1835, Biographical: South Seas, Box 5 — MMS.

88 Hunt, diary, quoted in Rowe, [1860], p. 48. Francis Wilson was another graduate of Hoxton. On his way out to the islands he was concerned because he could not get at his books and continue with his 'Institution studies'. However he did a little Greek and Latin to 'keep up the knowledge' that he had gained (F. Wilson, 11 February 1840, WMMS, Correspondence and Documents — ML).

89 Bush, 1886, pp. 28-73.

90 See W. G. Taylor, 1920, p. 60.

91 Carey, Materials for my biography, pp. 6-11 — ML.

92 See Watsford, 1900, pp. 12-14; T. Baker, Diary, pp. 21, 39, 45a — MOM.

93 WMMS, Missionary Candidates 1844-[56], p. 86 — MMS.

94 For a more complete account of the Methodist interest in education and Stow's system see F. C. Pritchard, *The Story of Westminster College 1851-1951* (London, 1951), pp. 1-19; Fraser, 1868, pp. 168 ff.

4 APPRENTICED TO THE MEANS OF GRACE

1 Threlkeld, 8 November 1815 — SSM, item 11.

2 See Thomas Hassall to Rowland Hassall, 1 May 1818 — PRH, I, p. 197.

3 Clayton, 24 January 1834 — CP, Barnden. David Darling wrote that he spent most of his evenings visiting the sick, teaching adults and collecting for the Bible Society (Darling, 4 July 1816 — CP). Mills, whilst pursuing his medical studies, visited the district poor (Mills, 6 June 1835 — CP).

4 Buzacott, 1825 — CP. See also Buzacott, n.d. — SSM, item 106.

5 W. Scott, 9 February 1838 — CP, Harbutt.

6 See, for instance, Slatyer, 29 September 1836 — CQ.

7 Gee, 3 April 1856 — CP.

8 See Pratt's letters for 1860 — SSL.

9 See, for instance, Royle, 11 October 1837 — CQ; Drummond, 23 May 1837 — CQ.

10 Testimonial, 4 June 1832 — CP, Murray.

11 Jesson, 7 September 1840 — CP.

12 Sunderland, 8 November 1843 — CQ.

13 See Schmidt to Lang, 12 April 1844, Lang Papers, XX — ML; Journal of W. Schmidt during a journey to Toorbal . . . 28 December 1842 to 6 January 1843, Lang Papers, XX — ML.

14 For his record of these days of apprenticeship see James Paton, n.d., p. 13. For a more detailed account see John G. Paton, 1902, pp. 53-82.

15 Rowe, 1885, p. 5.

16 Lawry, 29 October 1816, Papers — ML. Similarly enthusiastic accounts are found in *ibid.*, 17 January 1816; 20 January 1817.

17 See P. Turner, A brief account — ML. For the case of John Watsford,

whose later success as a revivalist missionary must be attributed in part to his preaching and revivalist experience in New South Wales, see Watsford, 1900, pp. 21 ff.

18 See Orton to Thomas, 25 April 1837, WMMS, Sydney District Letter Book — ML.

19 Orton, 31 May 1837, WMMS, Sydney District Letter Book — ML.

20 Waterhouse to Mary Ann Padman, 14 October 1850 — WC.

21 Calvert, 22 July 1852, WMMS, Letters from Feejee . . . , VI — ML.

22 WMMS, Minutes of the Committee of Discipline, 4 July 1845 — MMS.

23 See relevant CP.

24 Rowe, 1885, p. 7.

25 Pratt, 22 June 1861 — SSL.

26 Murray to Ella, 27 March 1859, Ella Correspondence, II — ML.

27 Hunt, 4 January 1820 — CP, Pitman.

28 J. D. Morell, *The Philosophy of Religion* (London, 1849).

29 The full account is given in SSM, item 103, pp. 627-34.

30 For example, *Sermons*, 1795, p. 119.

31 Bogue, Missionary Lectures, pp. 55-6 — LMS.

32 Barker, 15 November 1818 — LMS, Africa Letters.

33 Henry Adams, 1947, p. 128.

34 Jorgensen, 1811, pp. 98-101.

35 Jefferson, 25 July 1804 — SSJ, no. 22.

36 See Orsmond, 6 October 1820 — SSJ, no. 55.

37 See Harris, Burder, etc., 24 June 1825 — CP, Buzacott; Henderson, 12 June 1851 — CP, W. W. Gill; Cecil, 20 June 1833 — CP, Hardie; Roby, 25 November 1815 — CP, Platt; James, 21 February, 3 March, 17 April 1824 — CP, Pritchard.

38 Law, 3 April 1851 — CP. Slatyer, 6 August 1836 — CP.

39 This was certainly why Lancelot Threlkeld suggested himself as a pioneer missionary to the Afghans and the Tartars (see Threlkeld, 27 September 1815 — CP).

40 James, 29 April 1824 — CP, Pritchard. See also letter from James, 3 March 1824.

41 Knill, 5 August 1818, quoted *EM*, XXVII, p. 73. Others who were sent to the South Seas because they were not considered robust enough for other fields include George Gill, Lind and Thomas Slatyer. See Darling, 26 October 1842 — CP, G. Gill; Darling, 1851 — CP, Lind; Darling, December 1836 — CP, Slatyer; Conquest, 22 August 1837 — CP, Slatyer.

42 Both Thomas and Hutchinson were regarded as inadequate leaders of the Tongan mission by the Sydney committee. See 25 August 1828, WMMS, Sydney District Despatch Book, p. 111 — ML.

43 October 1836, WMMS, Tonga District Minutes — ML.

44 *Ibid.*, 23 March 1841.

45 Davis, 9 August 1856, AWMS, Tonga — Missionaries' Letters — MOM.

46 Amos to Rabone, 13 October 1856, Letters to Rabone — ML.

47 See *Wesleyan Missionary Notices* (1858), pp. 77-80.

48 Samuel Waterhouse to Jabez Waterhouse, 31 January 1853, Correspondence from S. Waterhouse — ML.

49 Joseph Mullens, A Brief History of the South Sea Mission established and maintained by the London Missionary Society (1878), p. 45 — LMS.

50 See below for Heath's comments. See also Orsmond, 1829 — SSJ, no. 97.

51 Quoted Campbell, 1843, pp. 91-2.

52 The entrenched nature of these views might be gauged by the hostile reaction to the Reverend Edward Irving's famous sermon, 'Messiah's

Instructions to the First Missionaries' (13 May 1824) and the controversy it aroused. See Irving, 1825. The Rev. William Orme, foreign secretary of the LMS, published a refutation; see his obituary, *Sydney Gazette*, 7 December 1830.

[53] See for example, Bannister, 1838, and Howitt, 1838.

[54] Heath, 26 February 1842 — SSL.

[55] Williams, 1832 — SSJ, no. 101.

[56] William Swan (1791-1866) was a missionary in Siberia working among the Buriats.

[57] Murray and Mills, 7 February 1844 — SSL.

5 INNOCENTS ABROAD

[1] Quoted in Rowe, 1885, p. 11.

[2] See J. E. Ellis, 1873, p. 31.

[3] P. Turner, Journal, I, p. 16 — ML.

[4] Orsmond, 20 October 1816 — SSJ, no. 39. Others, however, who responded to the 'hospitality' of a captain were afterwards defamed as 'the wine-bibbing missionaries' by him (Harbutt, 25 March 1844 — SSL).

[5] J. Thomas to Thomas Farmer, 18 October 1855, Biographical Papers, Box 3 (Calvert) — MMS.

[6] Bullen, etc., 11 February 1841 — AL.

[7] Cargill, 10 July 1842, Journal — Fiji Museum.

[8] *ibid.*, 17 July 1842.

[9] Royce, 7, 21 and 26 December 1855, 8 January 1856. Journal — MOM.

[10] Krause, 8 March 1859 — SSL.

[11] P. Turner, Journal, vol. I, p. 16 — ML.

[12] Watkin, 30 September 1830, Journal — ML.

[13] Orton, 9 April 1838, Letter Book 1836-42 — ML.

[14] Cargill, 14 June 1842, Journal — Fiji Museum.

[15] Nott, 10 September 1827 — SSL.

[16] See Williams, 26 March 1839 — SSL.

[17] Krause, 8 December 1859 — SSL.

[18] G. Turner, 14 March 1860 — SSL.

[19] F. Wilson, 11 February 1840, WMMS, Correspondence and Documents — ML.

[20] For reports of these interviews see LMS South Seas Odds, Box 2; and *Minutes of the Missionary Society* for 1795-6.

[21] Morison, 1844, vol. II, pp. 299-302.

[22] Mrs Eyre to Dr Haweis, Home Letters to 1799, Home Extra, Box 1 — LMS.

[23] John Myers, 1817, p. 172. The garbled names and dates of this account are probably the result of faulty memory rather than fabrication — Mrs Eyre appears as Mrs Hare.

[24] R. Hassall, 22 April 1800, Bonwick Transcripts, Box I, no. 29 — ML. Captain Fanning's description of Crook dressed in the *maro* in the Marquesas also highlights the condition of the missionaries. See Fanning, 1924, pp. 89 ff.

[25] J. Montgomery, 1831, vol. I, p. 137.

[26] Fox, 1810, pp. 74, 79.

[27] Orsmond, 'A Friendly Hint to Missionaries', 26 March 1828 — SSJ, no. 92.

[28] Threlkeld, 29 September 1818 — SSL.

[29] Platt, 7 November 1820 — SSL.

[30] Williams to his parents, 4 September 1819, South Seas Personal Box 2 — LMS.

[31] Threlkeld, Memoranda, pp. 16-17 — Archives of NSW 1123. See also Reminiscences, *Christian Herald*, vol. I, p. 92.

[32] Turnbull, 1805, vol. III, p. 22.

[33] Shelley, 26 October 1810, Bonwick Transcripts, Box I, no. 75 — ML.

[34] See Gunson 1969a, p. 73.

[35] 21 October 1812, quoted *Missionary Register*, 1813, p. 33. See also Prout, 1843, p. 53.

[36] Quoted Prout, p. 194.

[37] For Marsden's earlier efforts in England to found a joint missionary trading venture based on New South Wales, see J. Hardcastle to W. Wilberforce, 28 January 1812 and W. Wilberforce to J. Hardcastle, 26 February 1814 — Nan Kivell Collection (NK 7100), NLA. See also letters from S. W. Tracy (NK 2629); W. Hall (NK 2631).

[38] J. Orton, District Despatch Book 1826-36, p. 7 — ML A1716-1.

[39] See Orton to Capt. Henry, 26 May 1826,, District Letter Book, No. 3, pp. 1-2 — ML A1716-2.

[40] Certainly in 1839 Orton attributed the murder of Williams to the alleged atrocities of Captain Henry in 1827-28. See his Journal 1832-39, vol. I, p. 328 — ML A1714.

[41] J. Waterhouse, 25 October 1856, Correspondence — MOM, item 100.

[42] Marsden, Papers, vol. V, p. 68 — ML.

[43] Tyerman to Burder, 13 November 1822, Deputation Papers, Home Odds, Box 10 — LMS.

[44] Tyerman, 31 March 1823, *ibid.*

[45] William Ellis, 1831b, p. 66.

[46] John Barff, 29 August 1846 — SSL.

[47] Orsmond, 25 December 1837, quoted in Lovett, 1899, vol. I, p. 311.

[48] See Pritchard, 31 January, 1834 — SSL.

[49] For documentation on this point see the correspondence of the Rarotongan missionaries in 1847 — SSL.

[50] Stevens, 10 June 1839 — SSL.

[51] See, for instance, Joseph, 13 December 1839 — SSL: Howe, 12 October 1840 — SSL.

[52] Miller, 1847, pp. 149-54. See also J. Barff, 29 August 1846 — SSL.

[53] Nisbet, 15 October 1855 — SSL.

[54] William Henry, for example, was censured for his choice of a name for his son and felt obliged to defend his choice. See Henry, 26 January 1828 — SSL.

[55] Orsmond, 8 October 1820 — SSJ, no. 55.

[56] 'The examination of Mr. Cover', 12 September 1800 — SSL.

[57] Youl, Bicknell, etc., 3 November 1806 — SSJ, no. 29.

[58] For this episode see Crook, 24 and 25 February, 11 March and 29 April 1817 — SSJ., no. 40.

[59] Davies, 21 February 1817 — SSJ, no. 44.

[60] Davies, 15 January 1818 — SSJ. no. 50.

[61] *ibid.*, 15 January 1818.

[62] *ibid.*, 11 and 13 February 1818.

[63] Report from Borabora, 13 March 1823, Deputation Papers, Home Odds, Box 10 — LMS.

[64] Tyerman and Bennet, 3 October 1823, *ibid.*

[65] Bennet, 29 September 1823, *ibid.*

[66] Orsmond, 'The Mission its own Bane', 26 March 1828 — SSJ, no. 92.

[67] Heath, 17 December 1840 — SSL.

68 Davies, 31 December 1842 — SSL.
69 Hayward to Rev. R. Hill, 16 August 1822 — SSL.
70 Threlkeld, 10 February 1824 — SSL.
71 E.g. Bourne, 31 March 1824 — SSL. Sixteen documents connected with this affair are contained in LMS, Home Letters, box 10.
72 Fox, 1810, p. 131.
73 See *The Case of the London Missionary Society; Where Lies the Truth?; The Marrow of the Controversy;* and *A Peep at the Controversy* (London, 1847).
74 Thomson to Reed, 30 March 1850 — SSL.
75 Davies' letter is enclosed with Thomson's letter to Reed.
76 E.g. Murray and Powell agreed to differ on the question of baptism: Powell, 1 September 1851 — SSL.
77 Lawry, Diary, pp. 125, 146 — ML.
78 WMMS, Sydney District Despatch Book, p. 57 — ML.
79 See Calvert to Hoole, 16 July 1843 (Cross), WMMS, Letters from Feejee, III — ML; Orton to Thomas, 18 November 1833 (Cargill), 3 October 1834 (Hobbs), Orton, Letter Book 1822-36 — ML.
80 Hunt, 30 August 1844, WMMS, Letters from Feejee, IV — ML.
81 See WMMS, Tonga District, Minutes, 23 March 1841 — ML.
82 See Adams to his parents, 6 June 1850, Letters 1850-53.
83 Royce, 25 May 1860, Journal — MOM.
84 See John Waterhouse, Diary to July 1838, p. 31 — Waterhouse family.
85 For John Waterhouse's journal see *Wesleyan Missionary Notices* N.S. I (1841), pp. 489-512, II (1844), pp. 453-75, 485-512; see also Orton, Letter Book 1836-42, p. 487 — ML.
86 Joseph Waterhouse, 21 July 1852, Correspondence from Jos. Waterhouse — ML. See also Jos. Waterhouse to T. and M. Padman, 14 October 1850 — WC.
87 R. Young, 1855, p. 2.
88 Quoted in *ibid.*, p. 337.
89 Joseph to Jabez Waterhouse, 24 July 1854, P.S. 15 August 1854, Correspondence from Jos. Waterhouse — ML.
90 *ibid.*, 20 September 1856.
91 Samuel to Jabez Waterhouse, 25 December 1853, P.S. 24 January 1854, Correspondence from S. Waterhouse — ML.
92 Orsmond, 8 May 1839 — SSL.
93 Adams, 16 October 1858, Letters to S. Rabone — ML.

6 A SET OF TRADING PRIESTS

1 Grimes, Journal, 1821, p. 9 — SSJ, no. 57.
2 C. Barff, 2 July 1822 — SSL.
3 Orsmond, 10 November 1828 — SSJ, no. 92
4 Davies, 2 October 1845 — SSL.
5 Buzacott, Tahitian Journal, p. 3 — SSM, 225.
6 See Sarah Simpson, 26 July 1843 — SSL.
7 J. Paxton to Williams, Chatsworth, 23 October 1837, South Seas Personal, Box 2 — LMS.
8 Orsmond, 22 November 1840 — SSL.
9 Orsmond, 16 January 1841 — SSL.
10 See Gunson, 1966, and pages 307-8 above.
11 Davies, 2 October 1845 — SSL.
12 Thomas, 4 December 1856, AWMS, Tonga: Missionaries' Letters — MOM.

13 Vercoe, 9 February 1857, AWMS, Tonga: Missionaries' Letters — MOM.

14 See Orton to Thomas, 30 November 1833, WMMS, Sydney District Letter Book, pp. 160-2 — ML.

15 Cross, 11 June 1841, Extracts from Letters and Diary, p. 76 — MOM.

16 See Platt, 8 July 1841 — SSL.

17 Orsmond, 14 October 1823 — SSJ, no. 69.

18 Peter Turner, 17 January 1839, Journal, V — ML. See also Charter, 1 March 1839 — SSL. See also Orsmond, Memorandum 1839 — SSJ, no. 118.

19 See Pritchard, 31 January 1834 — SSL.

20 [J. H. Smith], 'Sentimental Reminiscences' (transcript) — Bishop Museum Library, Honolulu, 'Ross MS'.

21 Armitage, 25 March 1835 — SSL.

22 See Pritchard, 16 April 1834 — SSL.

23 Orsmond, Memorandum 1839 — SSJ, no. 118.

24 Orton, 13 February 1834, Letter Book 1822-36 — ML A1718-1.

25 Binner, 13 October 1859, AWMS, Fiji: Letters 1855-1903 — MOM.

26 W. T. Pritchard, 1866, p. 245.

27 L. Fison, Journal, Letters, Memos etc., pp. 134-5 — Pac. Hist. M120.

28 G. Pritchard, 11 March 1836 — SSL.

29 Williams, 16 May 1839 — SSL.

30 Orsmond, 21 November 1837 — SSJ, no. 118.

31 See Mills, 12 October 1852 — SSL; Hardie, 11 June 1853 — SSL.

32 S. Waterhouse to J. B. Waterhouse, 19 June 1855, Correspondence 1852-1855 — ML.

33 Joseph Waterhouse, 13 November 1855, quoted in *Missionary Notices*, 3rd ser., III (1856), p. 128.

34 Haweis to Dundas, 22 July 1796, Copy, Haweis Papers, IV — ML. See generally Gunson, 1965.

35 Latrobe to Haweis, Monday noon, n.d. [1791], Haweis Papers, V — ML.

36 See W. Henry to S. Pinder, 29 August 1799 — SSL; Second Examination of Mr Cover, 15 September 1800 — LMS, Home Office Papers, Extra box 1.

37 Missionary Society, printed circular dated London, 1 August 1802.

38 See J. D. Lang, 'fragment' on [Henry] Williams, Lang Papers — NLA.

39 Pomare III to George IV, 5 October 1825, Copy — SSL. See also Hitoti to the Marquis of Londonderry, 22 August 1822 (FO 58/14).

40 L. E. Threlkeld, 'Reminiscences', *Christian Herald*, I, p. 187.

41 See G. Canning to Pomare, Chief of the Island of Tahiti, 3 March 1827, Copy — SSL.

42 S. Wilson, 9 April 1837 — SSL.

43 C. Wilson, 4 December 1826 — SSL. The 'agreement on maritime regulations' was signed by Jones, Pomare, Tati, Utami, Rora and Vairaatoa, and witnessed by Orsmond and Wilson.

44 D. Cargill, entries for May-June 1840, Journal 1832-38 — ML. Belcher was in no humour to be diplomatic, having been seriously grounded. See his *Narrative*, 1843, vol. II, pp. 38-9.

45 See Ellison, 1938, pp. 53-5, and SSL (Samoa file) for 1876.

46 For example, Harbutt to Mr. F., 20 August 1841, Harbutt, n.d., p. 3.

47 J. Thomas, 11 November 1849, Journal — WMMS. See also W. Lawry, 1850, p. 62.

48 J. Thomas (above cited). See also P. Turner, 11 June 1850, *WMM*, 1851, p. 71.

49 See in particular M. Favier to J. B. Williams, 27 September 1855, Despatches from U.S. Consuls in Lauthala 1844-1890, II — National Archives, Washington.

50 See J. Binner, 31 December 1860, AWMS, Fiji: Letters 1855-1903 — MOM.
51 J. H. S. Royce, entries for October-November 1859 and *passim*, Journal — MOM.
52 W. T. Pritchard, 1866, pp. 216-7.
53 J. Williams, 30 September 1823 — SSL.

7 THE ENEMY WITHIN

1 See Yonge, 1874b, p. 97.
2 Whewell, 4 August 1856, AWMS, Tonga: Missionaries' Letters — MOM.
3 Orsmond — SSJ, no 53. For other examples of his (frequently despairing) self-examination see also Orsmond — SSJ no. 55; SSJ no. 64; SSJ no. 77.
4 Orsmond, 17 December 1824 — SSJ no. 77.
5 See, for example, Slatyer, 4 October 1841, Journal — ML.
6 I. S. Henry, Journal, pp. 40-1 — ML.
7 Orsmond, 6 March 1825 — SSJ, no. 77.
8 Lawry, 12 January 1823, Diary, p. 102 — ML.
9 Tyerman found in the Society Islands 'a Degree of Mental Cultivation, an extent of intelligence, a prudence in the management of their affairs, and a devotedness to their work, that would do credit to the Missionaries of any Country', Tyerman to Burder, 13 November 1822, Deputation Papers, Home Odds, Box 10 — LMS.
10 Royce, 19 February 1860, Journal — MOM. Another who found his work in Fiji 'not so conducive to piety as one would suppose' was Joseph Waterhouse. See Joseph Waterhouse, 22 October 1854, Correspondence from Jos. Waterhouse — ML.
11 See also the journals of Lyth and Hunt.
12 P. Turner, Journal, I, p. 42; IV; VI — ML.
13 Joseph Waterhouse to Mary Ann Padman, 18 March 1848 — WC.
14 See *Missionary Transactions*, I (1804), p. 72.
15 W. Henry to S. Pinder, 29 August 1799 — SSL. Shelley, 30 April 1800 — SSJ, no. 8.
16 Elder and Youl, 22 January 1801 — SSJ, no. 9.
17 See Crook, 31 January 1831 — AL.
18 Elder and Youl, 28 November 1800 — SSJ, no. 9.
19 Henry to S. Pinder, 29 August 1799 — SSL.
20 See Marsden, 9 November 1827 — AL.
21 Ross, 27 May 1846 — AL.
22 Ross, 25 November 1846 — AL.
23 Orsmond to Rev. T. Cuzens, 1849, Orsmond Papers, vol. 2 — ML A2606. Marsden was 'much hurt at Mr. Orsmond taking so much wine', 15 May 1818 — AL.
24 See Jefferson, 24 July 1800 — SSJ, no. 7.
25 For Lewis' defence of his marriage see Haweis, Supplement, pp. 179-82 — ML.
26 Vason's own account first appeared as *An Authentic Narrative of Four Years' Residence at Tongataboo* (London, 1810), edited by S. Piggott. See also Orange, 1840.
27 Haweis, Autobiography, vol. II, p. 107 — ML.
28 See Broomhall to Harris and Hassall, 27 July 1810 — PRH, I, pp. 317-19.
29 These charges were recorded by the Marist priests — *Annales de la Société de Marie*, I, p. 132.
30 See Macdonald, 16 May 1848 — SSL; Mills, 18 August 1848 — SSL.
31 Full details of this case are given by Turner, 20 March 1857 — SSL. See also unsigned letter to Lang, 27 May 1862, Lang Papers, XV — ML.

[32] [W. P. Crook and Samuel Greatheed] Account of the Marquesas Islands (c. 1800), pp. 147 ff — ML.

[33] Davies and Youl, 24 March 1806 — SSJ, no. 27.

[34] Orsmond to T. Cuzens, 1849, Orsmond Papers vol. 2 — ML.

[35] See Williams, 25 October 1832 — SSJ, no. 101.

[36] Davies, 19 March 1819 — SSL.

[37] Threlkeld, August 1819 — SSL.

[38] Some of these grievances are listed by Davies, 24 February 1821 — SSL.

[39] Crook, 11 September 1821 — SSL. On another occasion Mrs Ellis and Mrs Crook went to visit him and were 'shocked at the indelicacy and indecency of his appearance'.

[40] See Bradford Smith, 1956, p. 315.

[41] Orsmond to T. Cuzens, Orsmond Papers 2, p. 24 — ML.

[42] Crook, 2 April 1827 — SSJ, no. 85.

[43] See Crook, 14 December 1825 — SSJ, no 80. Wilson, Pritchard and Darling, 20 November 1826 — SSL.

[44] Watkin, 17 April 1837, Journal — ML.

[45] Anonymous MS History of Tonga, formerly owned by Hettie Moulton — copy, Pac. Hist.

[46] Details of this case are given in WMMS, Feejee District: Minutes and Reports,1848, Appendix A — ML.

[47] It was believed by the missionaries that he committed suicide by overdosing himself with laudanum and alcohol. Calvert to Rev. E. Hoole, 16 July 1843, WMMS, Letters from Feejee, III — ML.

[48] Samuel Waterhouse to Jabez Waterhouse, 6 November 1852, Correspondence from S. Waterhouse — ML.

[49] See Gunson 1970.

[50] Orsmond, 24 July 1829, 28 August 1829 — SSJ, no. 97; Buzacott, 30 July 1832, Journal — SSM, item 39. See also Platt, 16 January 1849 — SSL.

[51] Orsmond, 19 August 1829 — SSJ, no. 97; Crook, 25 May 1831 — AL.

[52] Simpson, 18 May 1833 — SSL.

[53] See Mary Crook to Thomas Hassall, 23 September [1823], Hassall Correspondence, II, pp. 643-5 — ML.

[54] Samuel Waterhouse to Jabez Waterhouse, 31 January 1853, Correspondence from S. Waterhouse — ML.

[55] See Seemann, 1862, pp. 16 (Lakeba), 224 (Bua).

[56] See Jefferson, 8 December 1802 — SSJ, no. 13; 7 September 1804 — SSJ, no. 22.

[57] For example, Heath, 7 December 1844 — SSL.

[58] Howe, 21 June 1842 — SSL; Platt, 2 February 1841 — SSL.

[59] Minutes of Friendly Islands District Meeting, 1847, WMMS, Synod Minutes — MMS.

[60] J. Barff, 4 November 1852, 21 July 1853 — SSL.

[61] Joseph Waterhouse to Jabez Waterhouse, 24 July 1854, Correspondence from Jos. Waterhouse — ML.

[62] Toup Nicolas, 31 March 1853 — SSL.

[63] Orsmond, 8 March 1829 — SSL.

[64] Orsmond, 14 October 1824 — SSJ, no. 75. Cf. Orsmond, 8 October 1826 — SSJ, no. 81.

[65] Orsmond, 26 March 1828 — SSJ, no. 92.

[66] See Armitage, November 1826, pp. 45-6 — SSL.

[67] See Orton to Woon, 13 March 1834, WMMS, Sydney, District Letter Book, pp. 184-8 — ML.

[68] Watkin, 22 December 1830, Journal — ML.

69 Thomas, 10 December 1833, WMMS, In-Letters: Australia and the South Seas, box 14 — ML.

70 Hayward to R. Hassall, February 1813 — PRH, II, pp. 50-1.

71 See Crook, 24 January 1828 — SSL.

72 Simpson, 16 August 1844 — SSL.

73 Orsmond, 'A Friendly Hint to Missionaries', 1828 — SSJ, no. 92.

74 Day, 15 February 1845 — SSL: also 23 February 1841 — SSL.

75 See SSL for Tahiti, 1847-51.

76 Royle, 15 December 1849 — SSL.

77 Williams, 16 May 1839 — SSL.

78 See Orsmond, 8 May 1839 — SSL. For another account of missionary domesticity, see Crook, 4 May 1829 — SSJ, no. 95.

8 ENEMIES AT LARGE

1 Damon, 1866, p. 21.

2 Fanning, 1924, p. 91.

3 See John Williams, 27 October 1832 — SSJ, no. 101; also his *Missionary Enterprises*, 1837, pp. 463-4.

4 Royce, 23 August 1859, Journal — MOM.

5 See Murray, 1876, pp. 34-8.

6 For example, Henry was a J.P. at Tahiti; Chisholm was acting consul at Raiatea.

7 Royce, 3 and 19 May 1857, Journal — MOM.

8 For example, there are several complimentary references to the family of David Whippy in Wesleyan letters.

9 Examples are Hunkin and Gibbons at Tutuila and Martin in Fiji.

10 Morrison, 1935, p. 84; W. Ellis, 1831 a, vol. II, pp. 407-8 and *passim*.

11 Murray, 1876, p. 33.

12 For Indian John's later career see Calvert, 'Missions', pp. 37-8, Biographical: South Seas, Box 4 — MMS.

13 See Freeman, 1959.

14 Jefferson, 22 October 1804 — SSJ, no. 22.

15 See Darling, 4 January 1833 — SSL; Orsmond, 14 January 1833 — SSJ, no. 100.

16 Henry, 4 September 1827 — SSL.

17 Orsmond, July 1829 — SSL.

18 E.g. Hardie, 11 June 1853 — SSL.

19 Charter, 18 August 1846, 18 September 1846, 1 June 1847 — SSL.

20 See Armitage, November 1826, p. 50 — SSL.

21 Bennet to Orsmond, 30 March 1824, Deputation Papers, Home Odds, Box 10 — LMS.

22 In the LMS collection, School of Oriental and African Studies Library, University of London.

23 For instance, Jorgensen, 1811, p. 22.

24 See Platt's account of himself, for example, (p. 114).

25 Henry, 14 June 1830 — SSL.

26 For example, Orsmond's diatribe on Captain Beechey, 22 April 1832 — SSJ, no. 100.

27 See Wheeler, 1842, p. 316.

28 Henry, 7 October 1835 — SSL.

29 Originally published as *Temperance Advocate and Seamen's Friend*.

30 The opposition which the British and Foreign Bible Society met with from the Catholic Church because of this activity, such as the imprisonment of George Borrow in Spain, only increased the hostility of the Evangelicals.

See George Borrow, *The Bible in Spain* (first pub. 1843), chapters 38 and 39.

31 Lundie, 1846, p. 280.

32 Jesson, 22 March 1842 — SSL.

33 See Pratt, 24 January 1846 — SSL.

34 Henry, 7 October 1835 — SSL.

35 Wilson, 30 March 1836 — SSL.

36 For the text of this letter, dated 9 February 1827, see Gunson, 1974, vol. II, pp. 229-33.

37 For the ABCFM version see Dibble, 1843, ch. XI; for the Catholic version see J-B. Piolet, 1902, vol. IV.

38 Orsmond, 'Friendly Hints to the Directors', No. 23 — SSJ, no. 92.

39 Orsmond, 4 August 1829, 3 November 1829 — SSJ, no. 97.

40 Wilks, 1844, p. 86.

41 See Darling, 18 January 1842 — SSL. For the detailed history of the *Mamaia* see Gunson, 1962.

42 Wilks, 1844, p. 86.

43 Dibble, 1843, pp. 386-7.

44 Rodgerson, 9 November 1838 — SSL.

45 Davies, 2 November 1836 — SSL.

46 Stallworthy (Secretary), 20 June 1849 — SSL.

47 Joseph Waterhouse to G. M. Waterhouse and T. Padman, 12 December 1851 — WC.

48 Joseph Waterhouse to Jabez Waterhouse, 4 November 1851, Correspondence from J. Waterhouse — ML.

49 Samuel Waterhouse, Copy of Diary, Correspondence from S. Waterhouse — ML.

50 The most popular account of the role of priests available to missionaries was Wilks, 1844.

51 G. Turner, 3 July 1844 — SSL.

52 Bullen, 6 August 1844 — SSL.

53 See West, 1865, pp. 329-30.

54 Howe, 16 November 1852 — SSL.

55 For an account of the situation in Fiji see the chapter 'Wesleyan Methodists and Roman Catholics' in Henderson, 1931a, pp. 204-29.

56 Joseph Waterhouse to T. Padman, 30 August 1852 — WC.

57 Murray, 28 June 1854 — SSL.

58 The articles of the convention are given by West, 1865, pp. 388-9.

59 Vercoe, etc., 13 August 1858, AWMS, Tonga: Missionaries' Letters — MOM. See also Adams, 18 October 1858, AWMS, Tonga: Missionaries' Letters— MOM.

60 Eggleston to Thomas, 1 October 1858, AWMS, Letterbook: Friendly Islands 1856-58 — MOM.

61 Vercoe, July 1857, AWMS, Tonga: Missionaries' Letters — MOM.

62 Joseph Waterhouse, 27 November 1853, WMMS, Letters from Feejee, VI. Calvert writing in 1852 mentioned that the priests were much annoyed with a rhyme 'composed by a native blind youth, which they attribute to the Missionaries'. *Missionary Notices*, N.S. XI (May 1853), p. 66.

9 THE LEISURE HOUR

1 Quoted in Eric W. Baker, *A Herald of the Evangelical Revival. A critical inquiry into the relation of William Law to John Wesley and the beginnings of Methodism* (London, 1948), p. 97.

2 *ibid.*

3 See Samuel Foote, *The Dramatic Works,* 4 vols. (London, 1788), vol. II (The Minor); L. Tyerman, *The Life of the Rev. George Whitefield,* 2 vols. (London, 1877), vol. II, pp. 425, 427, 434, 438-9; T. B. Shepherd, *Methodism and the Literature of the Eighteenth Century* (London, 1940) pp. 187 ff.

4 Burder's sermons were possibly those most frequently read. See, for instance, 'Journal of the Missionaries put ashore from the 'Hibernia' on an islet in the Fiji Group in 1809-10', *The Journal of William Lockerby,* Hakluyt Society, Series 2, vol. LII (London, 1922), pp. 117-60.

5 Burder, 1805, pp. 5-6.

6 Youth Warned, quoted in *The Plagiary 'Warned': A Vindication of the Drama, the Stage, and Public Morals, from the plagiarisms and compilations of the Rev. John Angell James . . . in A Letter to the Author* (London, 1824), pp. 10, 19, 44; 20, 13; 15.

7 See P. A. Scholes, *The Puritans and Music* (London, 1934), p. 78.

8 *The Plagiary Warned,* p. 14.

9 *Christian Witness and Congregational Magazine,* 1869, pp. 152-53.

10 Mrs [Sarah] Ellis, *The Daughters of England: Their Position in Society, Character and Responsibilities* (London, n.d.), pp. 107, 109.

11 William Ellis was the first to publish in this field with his *Polynesian Researches.* Other missionaries, particularly Orsmond and Barff of the LMS and John Thomas of Tonga, made substantial collections of Polynesian folklore and history. W. W. Gill's later publications about Mangaia were widely acclaimed by his scientific contemporaries.

12 John Eimeo Ellis, 1873, p. 209.

13 *ibid.,* p. 207.

14 Henry to Lang, 10 January 1828, Lang Papers, XV — ML.

15 Henry, 21 May 1822 — SSL.

16 Bicknell, 31 July 1819 — SSL.

17 Orsmond, 5 October 1827 — SSJ, no. 91.

18 See Barron Field, *Geographical Memoirs on New South Wales* (London, 1825), pp. 499-500.

19 Bennet to Orsmond, 30 March 1824, Deputation Papers — Home Odds, Box 10 — LMS.

20 Miscellaneous papers, Biographical: South Seas, Box 5 (John Hunt) — MMS.

21 See Biographical: South Seas, Box 5 — MMS.

22 Hunt, Letter No. 5 [1842], WMMS, Letters from Feejee, III — ML.

23 See also Hunt, Letter No. 3, 30 March 1846, WMMS, Letters from Feejee, V; R. B. Lyth, Tongan and Feejeean Reminiscences, vol. I, pp. 69-73 — ML B549.

24 See Carey, 1891.

25 LMS, *Minutes of the Missionary Society,* 23 July 1798.

26 Mrs Ellis, *The Daughters of England* (London, n.d.), p. 125.

27 James Puckey knew something of architecture and drawing — see relevant CP. For William Puckey's sketches of canoes, breadfruit, etc. see William Puckey Papers — Turnbull Library, Wellington.

28 Many of Williams' original sketches are contained in his Sketch Book and other papers in the Mitchell Library. Some are reproduced in Henderson, 1931b.

29 See Bernard Smith, 1960, pp. 243 ff.

30 According to Orsmond, Pomare herself scoffed at the portraits, see Orsmond to T. Cuzens — 1849, Orsmond Papers, Vol. II — ML A2606.

31 Henry, 21 May 1822 — SSL.

32 Cf. William Ellis 1831a, vol. I, p. 220 on the abandonment of games with bows and arrows, spears etc.

33 S. W. Powell, a critic of the missionaries, who resided in Tahiti this century confessed that the Tahitian 'hula hula' (*hura*) was an immoral dance 'by Christian standards of morality'. 'The missionaries banned nearly all the peoples' sports and entertainments, but there was an excuse for their objection to the *hula hula* . . . The tourists see a corrupt version of it, but you must live in a country district to see the real thing.' *A South Sea Diary* (Harmondsworth, 1945), pp. 41-3.

34 Ellis, 1831a, vol. I, pp. 215; 217.

35 Moerenhout, 1837, vol. I, p. 315, n.l.

36 Williams, Description of the Navigator Islands, appendix to Journal 1832 — SSJ, no. 101.

37 Ellis, 1831 a, vol. I, p. 208. See also pp. 209-10, 219; 229.

38 Debenham, 1945, vol. II, p. 279.

39 Fitz-Roy, 1839, vol. II, p. 324.

40 *Missionary Sketches*, No. 111 (London,1818).

41 John Eimeo Ellis, 1873, p. 22.

42 Sunderland and Buzacott, 1866, p. 273.

43 Beechey, 1831, vol. I, p. 286.

44 J. E. Ellis, 1873, vol. I, p. 193.

45 W. P. Crook to Marsden, 29 June 1815, Marsden Papers, V, pp. 39-40 — ML.

46 Sunderland and Buzacott, 1866, p. 273.

47 The detailed nature of musical instruction is well illustrated in the introduction to the Gilbertese Hymn Book, *Te Boki N Anene Ma B'ana* . . .

48 [Joseph Smith], 'Sentimental Reminiscences' (Ross MS), TS from original — B.P. Bishop Museum Library, Honolulu.

49 Charter, Journal, 17, 18 and 20 November 1848 — ML. CCWM Papers.

10 THE PERISHING HEATHEN OBSERVED

1 Ellis wrote an article on infanticide for *The Amulet* (1832), pp. 70-82.

2 The missionaries also reported bestiality with dogs and pigs. Paete, uncle of Pomare II, was found in an act of fellatio with his attendant. G. R. Taylor, *Sex in History* (London, 1953), classifies fear of homosexuality as a feature of patristic societies. In his analysis the missionaries would be representative of patristic society, whereas the Tahitians were dominantly matristic.

3 See Davies, 12 January 1818 — SSJ, no. 50.

4 Orsmond, 9 March 1827 — SSJ, no. 87; see also Charter, 21 April 1848 — SSL.

5 Orsmond, 7 June 1838 — SSJ, no. 118.

6 Hugh Thomas, 18 June 1818 — SSL.

7 Joseph Waterhouse, 4 April 1850 — WC.

8 *The Hawaiian Spectator* (Honolulu, 1838), I, no. 1, p. 11.

9 *ibid*, I, no. 1, p. 87.

10 Moore, [28 January 1850], 1 September 1850, WMMS, Letters from Feejee, VI — ML.

11 Inglis, 1890, pp. 10-11.

12 Lorimer Fison, 7 January 1868, Journal . . . , p. 90 — Pac. Hist.

13 Mary Polglase, 21 October 1853, Diary . . . 1850-59 — MOM.

14 P. Turner, 28 May 1853, Journal — ML.

15 G. Turner, 1843, p. 4 — SSJ, no. 134.

16 Joseph Waterhouse to Jabez Waterhouse, 13 November 1850, Correspondence from Joseph Waterhouse — ML.
17 At Wairiki, a new station. Baker, 25 July 1860, Diary — MOM.
18 *ibid.*, 1 September 1861.
19 [S. Greatheed] Instructions to the Missionaries . . . , South Seas Odds, Box 2 — LMS.
20 Bicknell, 25 December 1806 — SSL.
21 For evidence of Nott's marriage see Davies, 22 July 1809 — SSJ, no. 33, p. 44 (*Missionary Transactions*, III, p. 337); Marsden, 25 October 1810 — AL; Thomas Haweis quoted in Hugh Reginald Haweis, 1896, vol. II, p. 286.
22 Miller (WMMS) and Hunkin (LMS).
23 See Bradford Smith, 1956, p. 315.
24 Mrs Elizabeth Chisholm, Biographical Notes, p. 19 — LMS.
25 Binner, 3 October 1860, AWMS, Correspondence: Fiji — MOM.
26 Pitman, 12 September 1827, Journal, I, pp. 42-3 — ML.
27 Hayward, 'Observations', 1819 — SSL.
28 Elder quoted in Youl, Bicknell, etc., 18 October 1806 — SSJ, no. 30. The early Wesleyan missionaries at Hokianga in New Zealand frequently struck Maori youths who provoked them, a source of great discontent to their parents and undoubtedly one of the contributing factors in the withdrawal of native support.
29 Youl, Bicknell, etc., 28 October 1806 — SSJ, no, 30. See also Davies, 27 January 1818 — SSJ, no. 50.
30 Orsmond, 8 April 1832 — SSJ, no. 100
31 Orsmond, 'A Friendly Hint to Missionaries', 1828 — SSJ. no. 92.
32 See Orsmond, 31 July 1829 — SSJ, no. 97.
33 Nott, 28 July 1829, 11 May 1835 — SSL; also quoted by Orsmond, 8 May 1839 — SSL.
34 Charles Barff, 3 September 1839 — SSL. Williams also used the phrase 'brown Jacketed gentry', 21 October 1830 — SSL.
35 Orsmond, 16 January 1841 — SSL.
36 Davies, 27 December 1841 — SSL.
37 W. T. Pritchard, 1866, p. 262.
38 Royce, 6 December 1859, Journal, p. 166 — MOM.
39 Gyles, July 1820 — SSL.
40 Royce, 1 September 1856, 24 November 1857, Journal, pp. 39, 84 — MOM.
41 See James Hunt, 1865, vol. I, p. 4.
42 Ellis, 1831a, vol. I, pp. 110-11, 386-94.
43 Samuel McFarlane, 1873, pp. 19 ff. See also Thomas Williams and James Calvert, 1870, p. 212; Basil Thomson, 1908, pp. 17, 137.
44 Hazlewood, Somosomo, 6 May 1846, WMMS, Letters from Feejee, V — ML.
45 John Dunmore Lang, 1834, p. 198.
46 Russell, 1842, pp. 378-85.
47 Stallworthy, 3 March 1839, 19 April 1839 — SSJ, no. 120.
48 Tāufa'āhau broke the *tapu* in Tongatapu; Pomare II ate sacred turtle in Tahiti.
49 Henry to S. Pinder, 29 August 1799 — SSL.
50 Davies, 14 April 1813, Journal. Also quoted in *EM*, XXII (1814), p. 499.
51 Joseph Waterhouse, 31 August 1851, Correspondence from J. Waterhouse — ML. Another version is quoted by Henderson, 1931a, pp. 278-9.
52 Darling, 23 October 1834 — SSJ, no. 105.
53 Darling, 11 June 1835, 4 July 1835 — SSJ, no. 106.
54 Morrison in his Journal and Dr Haweis in some articles in the *Evangelical Magazine* stated that the Tahitians possessed a concept of the Trinity.

[55] Part of this work, Account of the Marquesas, is in the Mitchell Library. The Vocabulary is in the LMS archives in London.

[56] One of these priests was Pati'i. The other was possibly Tamera of Tahiti.

[57] Orsmond, 1 January 1824 — SSJ, no. 74

[58] Orsmond to Lang, 1 January 1828, Lang Papers, XV — ML.

[59] Wilson to Lang, 4 April 1833, Lang Papers, XV, pp. 7-8 — ML.

[60] This claim is made by Henderson. Henderson, 1931b, vol. I, p. xxxvii.

[61] T. Williams, 1850, quoted in *ibid.*, vol. I, p. xl.

[62] Kendall to Rev. John Butler, 1822, quoted in John Rawson Elder, 1934, pp. 191-3. Since the above was written Mrs Judith Binney has published her biography of Kendall, *The Legacy of Guilt* (Auckland, 1968).

[63] Kendall to Francis Hall, 1 January 1823, quoted in Elder, 1934, p. 197. Polynesian cosmogony attached particular importance to the generative functions. See particularly E. S. Craighill Handy, 1927, pp. 143-9; J. F. Stimson, *Songs and Tales of the Sea-Kings* (Salem, 1957), pp. 218-20.

[64] Quoted in Elder, 1934, p. 198; see also Elder, 1932, pp. 347, 415.

11 CONVERTS AND REVIVALISTS

[1] Orsmond, 31 October 1827 — SSJ, no. 92. See Henry, 1928, pp. 4, 9, 430.

[2] Samuel Waterhouse, copy of diary, Correspondence from S. Waterhouse — ML.

[3] *Hawaiian Spectator,* I (Honolulu, 1838) no. 1, p. 10.

[4] It was believed by the Tongans that the missionaries caused death by their prayers: see Lawry, 30 June 1823, Diary, pp. 120-1 — ML; WMMS *Missionary Notices*, no. 257, p. 462.

[5] Pa (i.e. Pomare II) to S. P. Henry, June 1820; Pa to G. Bicknell, 19 June 1820, in Orsmond, Letters from Tahitians — ML.

[6] Pratt, 24 January 1846 — SSL.

[7] Erskine, 1853, p. 131

[8] See Nott, 11 November 1834 — SSL; Pitman, 27 August 1835, Journal, III — ML.

[9] George Turner, 1861, pp. 138-9.

[10] Charter, Journal (end pages) — ML, CCWM Papers.

[11] Lorimer Fison, 26 March 1867, Journal — Pac. Hist. M120.

[12] Hardie, 3 April 1840 — SSL.

[13] Ellis, 1831 a, vol. III, p. 67.

[14] John Williams, 1837, pp. 559-60; Ellis, 1831 a, vol. II, p. 329.

[15] Williams, quoted in Lovett, 1899, vol. I, p. 273.

[16] Ellis, 1831 a, vol. II, p. 170.

[17] Particulars of Auna's life may be gleaned from Ellis and Montgomery and the *Missionary Register* for 1838, pp. 479-80. For the original of his journal see SSJ, no. 62.

[18] George Pritchard, 1844, pp. 13-14, 84, 124. A number of Maretu's vernacular writings survive.

[19] See Brown, 1854, vol. I, pp. 130-1.

[20] Mrs Crook, September 1819, Journal — ML.

[21] James Montgomery, 1831, vol. I, pp. 95, 191.

[22] George Pritchard, 1844, p. 84.

[23] Quoted in *ibid.*, pp. 20-1.

[24] James Montgomery, 1831, vol. I, p. 505; George Pritchard, 1844, p. 37, also pp. 77-8, 225.

[25] *Missionary Register* 1820, p. 318.

[26] Johnston, 16 September 1839 — SSL.

27 Cross, [18 September 1839], 30 September 1839, Extracts from Letters and Diary — MOM.
28 *ibid.*, June 1841.
29 Hazlewood, 20 May 1849, Diary — MOM.
30 *ibid.*, 13 May 1849.
31 See Gillies, 1845, p. 474.
32 Brown, 1854, vol. II, p. 232.
33 *ibid.*, I, p. 530n.
34 P. Turner, 22 December 1847, Journal, X — ML.
35 See Gunson, 1962, p. 216.
36 Hunt, Private Journal, II, p. 289 — ML.
37 P. Turner, Journal, II, p. 79 — ML.
38 Charter, Journal (end pages) — ML, CCWM Papers.
39 See Arthur T. Pierson, 1895, p. 43; Daws, 1961, pp. 20-34.
40 See J. Jones, Notes of Autobiography — ML; Lyth, Journal, I, p. 721 — ML; P. Turner, Books read — ML.
41 Steel, A. W. Murray of Samoa, p. 30 — ML.
42 See Duncan, 1853, pp. 171-2; Lundie, 1846, p. 106.
43 Murray, 24 November 1839 — SSJ, no. 122.
44 Murray, 18 February 1840 — SSJ, no. 124.
45 Murray, 23 July 1840 — SSJ, no. 128.
46 Buzacott, 1 July 1834 — SSL.
47 Pitman, 23 July 1851, 23 August 1851, 18 November 1851 — SSL; Krause, 7 September 1860 — SSL.
48 Quarterly Report, 14 February 1820 — SSL.
49 Orsmond, 13 November 1823 — SSJ, no. 71
50 P. Turner, 23 July 1834, Journal, II, pp. 68-9 — ML.
51 P. Turner, Journal, I, II.
52 A very full account is given by Cargill, 28 July 1834, Journal — ML.
53 Watkin, 9 August 1834, Journal — ML.
54 *ibid.*, 11 August 1834.
55 For the King's 'justification' see Cargill, 31 July 1834, Journal [Vava'u] — ML.
56 See Murray, 1876, pp. 122 ff.
57 Murray, 20 March 1840 — SSJ, no. 122.
58 Murray, 7 June 1840 — SSJ, no. 124.
59 Slatyer, 28 June 1840, Journal — ML.
60 *ibid.*, 31 August 1840.
61 *ibid.*, 25 October 1840.
62 Harbutt, 29 January 1841 — SSL.
63 Watsford, 1 May 1846, WMMS, Letters from Feejee, V — ML.
64 Hunt, Private Journal, II, p. 288 — ML.
65 *ibid.*, II, p. 289.
66 P. Turner, Journal, vol. IX *passim* — ML.

12 TEACHERS AND HEALERS

1 Lesson, 1839, vol. I, p. 427.
2 See Bell's *Experiment in Education made at the Male Asylum at Madras* (1797) and *The Madras School, or Elements of Tuition* (1808).
3 Lancaster, *Improvements in Education* (1803); *EM* (1806), pp. 361-2, (1812), p. 73.
4 See Fox, 1810, p. 14.
5 Joseph Hardcastle and John Eyre to missionaries, 21 October 1799 — PRH, I, pp. 21 ff.

6 Davies, Report, 1827 — SSL.

7 See Davies, May 1808 — SSJ, no. 33.

8 Davies, Report, 1827 — SSL; see also *Missionary Register* 1814, p. 33.

9 Gyles, 1820 — SSL.

10 Barff, 7 June 1821 — SSL.

11 Platt, 26 June 1822 — SSL.

12 Orsmond, 27 January 1824 — SSJ, no. 74.

13 Orsmond, 8 June 1826 — SSL.

14 Davies, Report, 1827 — SSL.

15 *Sydney Gazette*, 19 August 1804.

16 *Sydney Gazette*, 22 May 1808.

17 Crook, 18 June 1813 — AL.

18 Crook, 5 January 1824 — SSJ, no. 73.

19 Orsmond, May 1829 — SSJ, no. 97.

20 Orsmond, 'Friendly Hints to the Directors', 1828 — SSJ, no. 92.

21 Crook, 5 January 1824 — SSJ, no. 73.

22 Orsmond, 26 September 1837 — SSL. Pomare sent a circular letter to all the governors on the subject of education. *Missionary Register* 1820, p. 315.

23 Buzacott, June 1833 — SSL.

24 Williams, 18 July 1838 — SSL.

25 On James Buchanan's experience and system see Barbara Isabella Buchanan, 1923.

26 Williams, 18 July 1838 — SSL.

27 Williams, 16 May 1839 — SSL.

28 Buchanan, 14 May 1839, 2 April 1850 — SSL.

29 Howe, 27 August 1839 — SSL.

30 Buchanan, 2 April 1850 — SSL. See also Orsmond, 16 August 1842 — SSL.

31 See Buchanan, 3 December 1842 — SSL.

32 See Rodgerson, 16 March 1839 — SSL.

33 Buchanan, 3 December 1842 — SSL.

34 See Buchanan, 29 August 1842 — SSL; also 3 December 1842.

35 Buchanan, 18 October 1847, 2 April 1830 — SSL.

36 George Pritchard gave some details of the system at work in the islands in *The Missionary's Reward,* p. 128.

37 See Amos to Lawry, 18 July 1847, Letters to Rabone — ML.

38 P. Turner, 4 May 1851, Journal, X — ML.

39 Robert Young, 1855, p. 241.

40 *ibid.*, p. 286.

41 Collis, 4 October 1854, WMMS, Letters from Feejee, VII — ML.

42 See a specimen prepared by Dr Haweis, Letters 1757-1820, IV — ML.

43 See review in *EM* XII (July 1804), p. 326.

44 *Te mata no te parau — na te Atua* (The first of the books of God), 16 pp.

45 Watkin, 1 December 1832, Journal — ML.

46 Stevens, 25 July 1839 — SSL.

47 For typically bitter comments about the neglect of catechising by the later missionaries see Davies, 31 December 1845 — SSL.

48 See Lovett, 1899, vol. I, p. 203 for discussion on this point.

49 *Missionary Register* 1821, p. 80; see also Hayward's Observations (1819) — SSL.

50 See, for instance, Bennet, 29 September 1823, Deputation Papers, Home Odds, Box 10 — LMS.

51 Samuel Waterhouse, 31 January 1853, Correspondence from S. Waterhouse — ML.

52 Williams, 8 June 1821 — SSL.

53 Pratt, 10 February 1841 — SSL.

54 *Sermons* 1795, p. 119.

55 Turnbull, 1805, vol. III, pp. 78, 105.

56 *EM* (1806), p. 276.

57 [Wilson], 1799, p. 49.

58 These events are recorded in *Missionary Transactions* and retold by Brown, 1854, Mortimer, 1838, and other early writers.

59 James Montgomery, 1831, vol. I, p. 118.

60 Turner, *EM* (1801), pp. 89-97.

61 For his suspension from church membership see Davies, 18 October 1806 — SSJ, no. 30. For a favourable opinion see Turnbull, 1805, vol. II, p. 75. See also vol. I, pp. 190, 230.

62 Directors to S. Marsden, 23 September 1805, Home Office Extra, Box 1 — LMS.

63 See Minutes of the Committee of Examination of the Missionary Society, London, 1799-1816, p. 364 — LMS. In addition, Threlkeld was well acquainted with the use of drugs, having been apprenticed to an apothecary in his youth.

64 Crook, 29 June 1815, Marsden Papers, V, pp. 39-40 — ML. For Crook's medical work in Tahiti, see Lesson 1839, vol. II, pp. 55 and 27, 212-13, 218; *Missionary Register* (1824), p. 80; and *Brief Sketch of the Life and Labours of the Late Rev. W. P. Crook*, pp. 8-9.

65 See in particular W. Henry to T. Hassall, 7 February 1827, Hassall Correspondence, II, p. 804 — ML; R. B. Lyth, 21 June 1837, Journal — ML B533. For Bland's connexion with the Henry family see Gunson, 1970.

66 Ellis, 1831a, vol. III, p. 45.

67 James Montgomery, 1831, vol. I, p. 146.

68 Sunderland and Buzacott, 1866, pp. 98-112.

69 Ellis, 1831a, vol. III, p. 44.

70 CMS *Missionary Register* 1822, p. 354.

71 CMS *Missionary Register* 1827, p. 130. See also 1828 issue, p. 131.

72 CMS *Missionary Register* 1831, p. 90.

73 *ibid.*, pp. 513-4.

74 Darling, 18 January 1842 — SSL; E. Pritchard, 13 February 1842 — SSL.

75 Rowe, 1893, p. 16.

76 Cross, 20 January 1841, Extracts from Letters and Diary — MOM.

77 Lee, 6 August 1857, AWMS, Fiji: Sundry Correspondence — MOM, item 166.

78 Hill, 27 October 1860, AWMS, Fiji: Sundry Correspondence — MOM, item 166.

79 West, 1865, p. 175.

80 W. H. Harvey to N. B. Ward, 29 July 1855, *Wesleyan Missionary Notices*, 3rd ser. III, pp. 24-8; West, 1865, pp. 178-81. For Harvey's visit to Tonga see Pacific Manuscripts Bureau microfilm 29.

81 See Adams, 3 February 1859, AWMS, Tonga: Missionaries Letters 1852-1879 — MOM, item 170.

82 Hunt, April 1840, Private Journal, I, p. 106 — MOM, item 133.

83 *ibid.*, II, p. 159.

84 Chas. Barff, 'Account of Buzacott's labour', p. 8, South Seas Personal, Box 1 — LMS.

13 GETTING THE WORD ACROSS

1 J. Puckey, 1 September 1799 — AL. Cf. Lawry, 1 January 1823, Diary, p. 101 — MOM, item 134.

[2] J. Puckey, 1 September 1799 — AL. However, Cover believed that William Puckey, Nott and Broomhall were the most proficient. See also Davies, 25 July 1802 — SSL.

[3] Elder to Waugh, 28 July 1802 — SSL.

[4] See Crook, 29 June 1813 — AL.

[5] Quoted Orsmond to Rev. T. Cuzens, pp. 4-5, Orsmond Papers — ML.

[6] Orsmond caricatured the average service in his journal, 8 October 1826 — SSJ, no. 81.

[7] Bicknell, 5 July 1817 — SSL.

[8] Gyles, 1820 — SSL.

[9] See Hayward, 1819 — SSL.

[10] [S. Greatheed], Instructions to the Missionaries . . . , South Seas Odds, Box 2 — LMS.

[11] Henry, 21 May 1822 — SSL.

[12] For the history of Bible translation in the Pacific, see Archibald Wright Murray, 1888 and Lingenfelter, 1967. For a fairly complete list of translations and other works printed in the Society Islands, see Harding and Kroepelien, 1950.

[13] Orsmond, 24 September 1823 — SSJ, no. 68.

[14] Crook, 27 and 28 July 1817 — SSJ, no. 46.

[15] Davies, 31 March 1818 — SSJ, no. 50.

[16] Crook, 6 February 1821 — SSJ, no. 54.

[17] Jones, 6 April 1822 — SSL.

[18] Williams, 16 May 1839 — SSL.

[19] Orsmond, 16 December 1839 — SSJ, no. 118.

[20] See Orsmond, 6 September, 12 October 1841 — SSL.

[21] Orsmond, 16 December 1839 — SSJ, no. 118. Orsmond stated that when he arrived he began to teach Nott the conjugation of English, and that when he asked Nott for a sentence containing every part of speech in Tahitian, he could not give it.

[22] Orsmond, 24 September 1823 — SSJ, no. 68.

[23] Orsmond, 14 January 1824 — SSJ, no. 74.

[24] Davies, 29 March 1839 — SSL.

[25] Simpson, 16 August 1844 — SSL.

[26] Nott's translation has been esteemed by many generations of missionaries. 'The remarkable Tahitian bible of Nott is the masterpiece of the Tahitian language — everybody agrees with it. It is a real pleasure to speak and to preach at Paofai in that language.' Charles Vernier to T. Green, 20 September 1944 — LMS.

[27] Davies attributed the misprints to Nott's infirmities, 29 March 1839 — SSL.

[28] Joseph (Secretary), 30 September 1843 — SSL.

[29] Davies, 2 October 1845 — SSL.

[30] Davies, 23 November 1846 — SSL.

[31] Davies, 30 March 1849 — SSL.

[32] See Pitman, 14 June 1846 — SSL.

[33] See W. Gill, 28 February 1847 — SSL.

[34] Johnston, 5 June 1846 — AL.

[35] Day, 11 January 1849 — AL.

[36] Heath, 26 February 1842 — SSL.

[37] Orton to Thomas, 25 April 1837, WMMS, Sydney District Letter Book, p. 409 — ML.

[38] Cross, 25 December 1832; Hazlewood, 25 July 1844, Diary — MOM, item 132.

39 See Henderson, 1931a, pp. 187-8. John Hobbs, then in charge of the press at Tonga, was actually responsible for choosing the letters used — Spooner, 1955, p. 23.

40 Hunt, February 1846, quoted in Henderson, 1931a, p. 196 no. 6.

41 Hunt, Private Journal, p. 92 — ML.

42 *ibid.*, p. 114. See also Henderson, 1931a, p. 196, for a further statement.

43 R. Armstrong, 'Have all the Polynesian Tribes a Common Origin?', *Hawaiian Spectator,* I (Honolulu, 1838), no. 3, p. 289.

44 See W. W. Gill, 26 August 1859 — SSL.

45 Orsmond, 29 November 1826 — SSJ, no. 83.

46 *ibid.*, 13 December 1826.

47 Heath, 30 March 1840 — SSL.

48 T. Williams, January 1847, quoted in Henderson, 1931b, p. 386.

49 See Gunson, 1962, p. 240; Parsonson, 1967.

14 THE GOSPEL OF CIVILIZATION

1 Harris, 1842, p. 361. This missionary ideal was closely associated with the Moravians and influenced the missionary societies, including the LMS, the CMS and the various German missions, founded during the later period of the Evangelical Revival.

2 For examples of the failure of attempts to teach the principles of natural religion by the Moravians in Greenland, under Thomas Coke's plan for the Foulahs of Western Africa, the Quaker Missions and John Kicherer of the LMS in Africa, see Harris, 1842, pp. 369 ff.; Coates, Beecham and Ellis, 1837, pp. 124, 125, 129, 187-97, 338; S. Bannister, 1838, p. 177; James, [1819], p. 30. The last exponent of preparatory civilization was probably Samuel Marsden in New Zealand, though he did not altogether abandon the idea of preaching and teaching. J. D. Lang, sceptical of the 'civilizing scheme', took delight in exposing the weaknesses of Marsden's New Zealand mission. See Lang, 1834, pp. 241 ff; also *New Zealand in 1839* (London, 1839).

3 For examples, in the work of David Brainerd and the Moravians, see James, [1819], p. 30; Ellis, 1831a, vol. II, p. 179; Brown, 1854, vol. I, p. 436.

4 Sermon 1, *Sermons* 1795, pp. 8, 18; Sermons 3 and 4, *Four Sermons,* 1798, pp. 114, 161; Sermons 1 and 4, *Four Sermons,* 1799, p. 97.

5 James, [1819], p. 17.

6 See 'Memoir', *Sermons* 1795, p. 171.

7 James, [1819], p. 30.

8 See Ellis, 1831a, vol. II, pp. 179-81.

9 *ibid.*, pp. 187-8.

10 Prout, 1843, p. 411.

11 See Harris, 1842, pp. 362-6.

12 James, [1819], p. 12.

13 Coates, Beecham and Ellis, 1837, p. 171.

14 *ibid.*, p. 174.

15 'Missionary Prospects', in James, 1860-64, vol. II, p. 84.

16 See Report of Committee of Examination, 8 February 1796 — LMS.

17 'The Examination of Mr Cover', 12 September 1800 — SSL.

18 Quoted *EM*, XV (1807), pp. 12-16. Similar opinions are quoted by John Dumore Lang, 1834, p. 241.

19 *EM,* XV, pp. 12-16.

20 See Davies, 8 September 1813 — SSL.

21 Gyles's contract, 3 April 1817 — SSL.

22 See SSJ, no. 51.

23 Platt, 11 May 1821 — SSL.

24 See Armitage, November 1826, pp. 15-17 — SSL.

25 See Armitage, 8 September 1827 — SSL.

26 See their report, dated 3 October 1823, Deputation Papers, Home Odds, Box 10 — LMS.

27 Quoted in Campbell, 1843, p. 82.

28 James, 1860-64, vol. II, p. 84.

29 Montgomery, 1831, vol. I, p. 295.

30 Ellis, 1831a, vol. I, p. 130.

31 *ibid.*, vol. II, p. 338.

32 See Moerenhout, 1837, vol. I, pp. 247, 221; Tilley, 1861, pp. 346-7.

33 Williams, 24 November 1821 — SSL.

34 Hugh Cuming, Journal of a Voyage from Valparaiso to the Society and the Adjacent Islands performed in the Schooner Discoverer . . . in the years 1827 and 1828, pp. 84-6 — ML.

35 Hayward, 'Observations', 1819 — SSL.

36 Barff, 26 September 1865, Folder 9 — LMS, Miscellaneous Folders.

37 Mrs Crook, Journal, p. 99 — ML MSS604.

38 *ibid.*, pp. 121-2. For bonnet-making also see Darling and Bourne, 16 May 1821 — SSL; Johnston, 16 September 1839 — SSL.

39 For example, Whewell, 4 August 1856, AWMS, Tonga: Missionaries' Letters — MOM.

40 For example, William Gill, 1856, vol. II, p. 96. See also Robert Young, 1855, p. 269, for one of the most revealing commentaries on the place of clothing in the 'civilization' of the South Seas.

41 Stallworthy, 4 December 1854 — SSL.

42 Orsmond, 4 December 1823 — SSJ, no. 71. See also Ellis, 1831a, vol. II, p. 346.

43 Simpson, 18 May 1833 — SSL.

44 Stallworthy, 15 August 1857 and 4 December 1854 — SSL.

45 Amos, 19 February 1857, AWMS, Tonga: Missionaries' Letters — MOM, item 170.

46 Vercoe, 22 July 1858, AWMS, Tonga: Missionaries' Letters — MOM.

47 Mills, 20 November 1854 — SSL.

48 Stallworthy, 4 December 1854 — SSL.

49 Lorimer Fison, 26 March 1867, Journal, Letters, Memos etc — Pac. Hist. M120.

15 ADVISERS IN AFFAIRS OF STATE

1 See particularly E. R. Taylor, 1935, pp. 115-33.

2 For an account of John Waterhouse's intervention in the 'Pitman's Strike' of 1810 see John Waterhouse, Diary to July 1838, p. 9 — Waterhouse family. Waterhouse also mentions going in peril of his life in the Huddersfield Circuit owing to the marked hostility of the Luddites, who were provoked by the 'known loyalty of Methodist Preachers'.

3 For this aspect of Methodism see Wearmouth, 1948.

4 For an indication of the political activities and consciousness of the Dissenters see the pages of the *Evangelical Magazine;* and the works of Rev. Robert Hall: *Christianity consistent with a love of Freedom* (London, 1791); *Apology for the Freedom of the Press, and for General Liberty* (London, 1793).

5 Wolfram Kistner in his monograph, *The anti-slavery agitation against the Transvaal Republic 1852-1868* (Groningen, [1948]), p. 21, suggests that the

missionary career offered considerable political power to men who had been excluded from the possibility of attaining public influence in Great Britain without compromising their religious principles.

6 See Martin, 1924; Koskinen, 1953; Lātūkefu, 1974.

7 See S. Pearce Carey, *William Carey* (London, 1924), p. 6.

8 See particularly Adams, 1947, pp. 149, 153.

9 Elder, 10 March 1824 — AL.

10 Davies, 2 May 1808 — SSJ, no. 31.

11 Quoted in Orsmond to T. Cuzens, 1849, Orsmond Papers — ML.

12 Hassall, 11 November 1797 — SSJ, no. 2.

13 Jefferson, 16 February 1803 — SSJ, no. 13.

14 The code was given in full in John Campbell, *Travels in South Africa, undertaken at the request of the Missionary Society* (London, 1815), pp. 254-5.

15 'Mr. Wilks' observations on the public letter to Eimeo', November 1815 — LMS, Home Letters, box 3.

16 See Davies, 15 January 1818 — SSJ. no. 50.

17 *ibid.,* 14 May 1818.

18 Ellis, 1831a, vol. III, p. 136. This code is given in full with French translation in Bouge, 1952.

19 Threlkeld, Memoranda Selected . . . 1838, p. 18 — ML.

20 Tyerman and Bennet, 3 October 1823, Deputation Papers, Home Odds, Box 10 — LMS.

21 Mrs Crook, 25 October 1819, Journal — ML.

22 Tyerman and Bennet, 11 February 1824, Deputation Papers, Home Odds, Box 10 — LMS. On amendments accepted elsewhere see Montgomery, 1831, vol. II, pp. 19, 34; Ellis, 1831a, vol. III, p. 178; C. Barff, Translation of the Laws established at Huahine and Maiaoiti 1823 — R-O'R.

23 J. Read to Arundel, 12 September 1827, Home Office Extra, Box 2 — LMS.

24 Crook, 21 November 1825 — SSJ, no. 80. Cf. Crook, 27 February 1823 — SSJ, no. 63.

25 For the laws under Pomare IV see one of the volumes marked 'Polynesia. Tahiti. Miscellaneous' in Sir Geo. Grey's Collection, South African Library, Cape Town.

26 Pitman, 19 September and 28 July 1827, Journal, I — ML.

27 Platt, 11 May 1827, 8 May 1828 — SSJ, no. 93.

28 Dibble, 1843, pp. 209, 237-8.

29 Darling, 16 November 1834 — SSJ, no. 105.

30 For a discussion of the vernacular texts containing these rules see H. G. Cummins, 1975.

31 This code is given in full, *Missionary Notices,* new series I, pp. 282-5.

32 Thomas, 10 March 1839, quoted *Missionary Notices,* new series I, p. 350.

33 West, 1865, p. 212.

34 *ibid.,* pp. 212-3.

35 A copy of this code is given in Robert Young, 1855, as an appendix.

36 P. Turner, 1 November 1849, Journal, X — ML.

37 *ibid.,* 28 November 1849. See also *Missionary Notices,* new series IX, p. 71.

38 See George Turner, 1861, pp. 291-2.

39 Slatyer, 15 October 1841, Journal — ML.

40 *ibid.,* 15 November 1841.

41 Murray, 21 January 1852 — SSL.

42 Powell, 14 July 1853 — SSL.

43 Powell, 1 September 1851 — SSL. Murray, 21 January 1852 — SSL. Murray said it was the Tutuila Code but some laws had not been adopted.

[44] Powell, 12 July 1854 — SSL.

[45] J. Calvert to G. S. Rowe, Ovalau, 31 October 1862, Biographical Papers: South Seas, Box 3 — MMS.

[46] For example, port regulations were adopted at Tutuila on the recommendation of Captain Bethune.

[47] See Threlkeld, Memoranda, pp. 18-20 — ML.

[48] Platt, 13 September 1859 — SSL.

[49] Ellis, 1831b, p. 76.

[50] Henry to Burder, 3 February 1825 — SSL.

[51] Henry to Burder, 26 January 1828 — SSL.

[52] Slatyer, 1 March 1841, Journal — ML.

[53] Orsmond, 4 December 1823 — SSJ, no. 71.

[54] See WMMS, Tonga District: Minutes, 23 March 1841 — ML.

[55] Armitage, 25 March 1835 — SSL.

[56] Heath to Mark Wilks, 7 December 1844 — SSL. Cf. Davies, 24 December 1844 — SSL.

[57] See Hamond to the Missionaries, 6 May 1846 — SSL.

[58] Heath, 25 December 1844 — SSL.

[59] Hamond to the Missionaries, 6 May 1846 — SSL.

[60] Heath, May 1846 — SSL.

[61] Hunt, 15 May 1844, *Missionary Notices,* III, p. 134.

[62] John Waterhouse, [1842], pp. 13-14.

[63] See Campbell, 1842, p. 48.

[64] For discussion on this point see 'The Breakdown of Pacifism' in G. C. Henderson, 1931a, pp. 242-60.

[65] See *ibid.,* p. 246.

[66] 20 August 1800, quoted in Adams, 1947, p. 143.

[67] See Cummins, 1975, pp. 110 ff. The missionaries were censured by the committee in London for their part in the wars against paganism and were quick to substitute texts of peace in the schoolbooks.

[68] Anonymous MS History of Tonga — copy, Pac. Hist.

[69] See West, 1865, pp. 303-41, 325, 327.

[70] See Orsmond, 13 December 1832 — SSJ, no. 100.

[71] Williams, 27 September 1832 — SSL.

[72] Orsmond, 17 January 1833 — SSJ, no. 100.

[73] See Thomson, 18 May 1845 — SSL.

[74] Davies, 3 July 1848 — SSL.

[75] See Drummond, 14 May 1851 — SSL.

[76] Stallworthy, 15 August 1848 — SSL.

[77] Buchanan, 1923, p. 76.

16 THE CHURCHES CONSOLIDATE

[1] Henry, 3 February 1825 — SSL.

[2] Resolutions [1819], Marsden Papers, V, p. 67 — ML.

[3] Buzacott, June 1833 — SSL.

[4] Orsmond, 24 December 1820 — SSJ, no. 55.

[5] Orsmond, 24 September 1823 — SSJ, no. 68. See also Appendix III.

[6] Pritchard, 19 October 1826 — SSL.

[7] McKean, 3 September 1843 — SSL.

[8] Simpson, 16 August 1844 — SSL. The first figure is for 1839.

[9] Buzacott to Ellis, 1 July 1840 — SSM, item 63.

[10] Buzacott, 16 January 1854 — SSL.

[11] Royce, 18 July 1860, Journal — MOM.

12 See Orsmond, 'Friendly Hints to the Directors', 1828 — SSJ, no. 92; Orsmond, 5 October 1836 — SSL.
13 Lee, 16 May 1862, AWMS, Tonga: Missionaries' Letters — MOM.
14 W. Gill (Secretary), 31 December 1848 — SSL.
15 Powell, 1 September 1851 — SSL.
16 Pratt, 10 June 1851 — SSL.
17 J. C. Patteson to S. McFarlane, not sent, in Yonge, 1874a, vol. II, pp. 591-2.
18 Ross, 2 November 1841 — AL.
19 Hunt, 17 July 1840, Private Journal, I, p. 137 — ML.
20 Journal of the American missionaries at Tahiti, 1832, quoted in Alexander, 1934, p. 105.
21 Nott, quoted in *Missionary Register* 1835, p. 210.
22 See Powell, 1 September 1851 — SSL.
23 Watkin, 22 April 1833, Journal, p. 110 — ML.
24 Joseph Waterhouse, 25 November 1862, quoted in AWMS, *Wesleyan Missionary Notices,* p. 362.
25 Pratt, 19 September 1860 — SSL.
26 Whewell, 4 August 1856, AWMS, Tonga: Missionaries' Letters — MOM.
27 Crook, 10 May 1827 — SSJ, no. 85.
28 Orsmond, 20 May 1827 — SSJ, no. 87; see also Henry, 26 January 1828 — SSL.
29 The charge of misappropriation was also voiced at Tahaa at the May Meeting in 1826, Bourne, 16 May 1826 — SSL.
30 Barff, 26 May 1828 — SSL.
31 Darling, 18 March 1829 — SSL.
32 Platt, 15 November 1830 — SSL.
33 See Crook, 4 March and 15 May 1829 — SSJ, no. 95.
34 Charter, 11 April 1843 — SSL.
35 Pratt, 27 November 1856 — SSL.
36 Vercoe, 22 July 1858, AWMS, Tonga: Missionaries' Letters — MOM.
37 Powell, 1 September 1851 — SSL.
38 Murray (Secretary), 7 April 1852 — SSL.
39 G. Turner, 28 September 1855 — SSL.
40 Chisholm, 20 April 1855 — SSL.
41 Krause, 2 January 1854 — SSL.
42 Davies, 'Some Remarks', 18 July 1834 — SSL.
43 Simpson, 14 August 1836 — SSL.
44 Stevens, 10 June 1839 — SSL.
45 Orsmond, 5 October 1836 — SSL.
46 See Henry, 21 May 1822 — SSL; Howe, 28 October 1840 — SSL.
47 Orsmond, 29 May 1839, Journal 1840-48, p. 15 — ML. See also Orsmond, 22 June 1839 — SSL.
48 For example, Darling, 1 November 1853 — SSL.
49 Lee, 14 December 1857, AWMS, Fiji: Sundry Correspondence — MOM.
50 Threlkeld, 8 July 1822 — SSL.
51 Hunt, 'On Marriage', Private Journal, II, pp. 83-96 — ML.
52 Orsmond to Rev. T. Cuzens, 1849, Orsmond Papers — ML.
53 See particularly Stevens, 10 June 1839; Joseph, 22 September 1840 — SSL.
54 Whewell, 4 August 1856, AWMS, Tonga: Missionaries' Letters — MOM.
55 *ibid.,* 24 December 1856.
56 Thomson, quoted in *The Friend* III, p. 177.
57 Williams, 6 July 1823 — SSL.
58 Cuming, Journal, pp. 107, 110 — ML.
59 See Goodall, 1954, pp. 378-9.

60 Cuming, Journal, p. 118.
61 Watsford, 21 July 1847, WMMS, Letters from Feejee, V — ML.
62 Pitman, 21 July 1835 — SSL.
63 Pitman, 22 May 1827, 12 September 1827, Journal — ML.
64 Stevens, 19 December 1839 — SSL.
65 C. Wilson, 29 July 1829 — SSL.
66 Pratt, 30 April 1856 — SSL.
67 Pratt, 31 December 1859 — SSL.
68 Pitman and Buzacott, 25 May 1839 — SSL.
69 Pratt, 30 April 1856 — SSL.
70 See in particular Crocombe, 1968, pp. 6-7 and *passim*.
71 Pratt, 31 December 1859 — SSL.
72 Pritchard, 3 June 1831 — SSL.
73 Pritchard, 23 May 1833 — SSL.
74 Howe, 21 June 1842 — SSL. For Howe's course see Howe, 13 March 1844 — SSL.
75 See Howe, 27 March 1850 — SSL.
76 Howe, 27 March 1851 — SSL.
77 Sunderland and Buzacott, 1866, pp. 132, 134.
78 Williams, 26 March 1839 — SSL.
79 Pitman and Buzacott, 25 May 1839 — SSL.
80 Harbutt (Secretary), 29 November 1842 — SSL.
81 See Erskine, 1853, p. 83.
82 Heath, Buchanan and Sunderland, 30 September 1847 — SSL.
83 Buzacott, 21 November 1835 — SSL.
84 Pratt, 6 September 1841 — SSL.
85 Macdonald, 13 September 1843 — SSL.
86 Nisbet, 15 October 1855 — SSL.
87 Whewell, 4 August 1856, AWMS, Tonga: Missionaries' Letters — MOM.
88 WMMS, Feejee District: Minutes, 1841 — ML; Colwell, 1914, p. 424. A similar resolution was adopted by the Tonga District Meeting, 25 March 1841, WMMS, Tonga District: Minutes — ML.
89 Joseph Waterhouse, n.d., AWMS, Correspondence of Rev. J. Waterhouse — MOM.
90 *ibid.*, 24 February 1873. See also AWMS, *Wesleyan Missionary Notices*, April 1873, pp. 88-94.

EPILOGUE

1 See George McLean to Murray, 27 December 1845 — SSL.
2 For protests before 1860 see G. Gill, 30 November 1846 — SSL; Buchanan, 1923, p. 77 (29 January 1848); Nisbet (Secretary), 29 November 1847 — SSL.
3 Hunt, Private Journal, II, pp. 160-1 — ML.
4 Quoted in WMMS *Missionary Notices*, IV (1846), pp. 66-7.
5 J. Barff, 30 September 1857 — SSL.

Calendar of Ms Sources

THE MOST IMPORTANT sources are undoubtedly the writings, especially the private papers, of the missionaries themselves. The majority of such documents are in manuscript collections, and together they represent a formidable body of knowledge on island life and mission affairs. Missionaries kept journals, wrote letters and memoirs, pursued literary and ethnological studies and even conducted research in the natural sciences. Some missionaries wrote so much that they had to compile indexes to their own papers.

The principal manuscript sources which I have used fall into two main categories; documents relating to the London Missionary Society missions and those relating to the Wesleyan missions. Of the LMS material kept in the archives of the Council for World Mission presently held in the Library of the School of Oriental and African Studies, University of London, I have found the letters of the missionaries to the directors to be the most representative source. The journals of the LMS missionaries form an important supplement to these, and contain much detailed information which is nowhere else recorded. I have listed the journals separately in a calendar of manuscript sources (below), not only to indicate the variety of these documents but also to reveal their limited authorship. This might be gauged by comparing the list of missionaries with the list of authors recorded in the calendar. Whereas the letters give a fairly complete picture of the personalities and experiences of all the missionaries, the journals reflect the lives of a limited number only. The journals of J. M. Orsmond, for instance, give a detailed picture of island and missionary life as seen by a man with definite prejudices, who was not afraid to commit his views, often unwelcome to the directors, to writing. On the other hand, many of the missionaries did not send their journals to the directors, only making occasional extracts. Fortunately some of these more private journals are still held by descendants or form part of the collection in the Mitchell Library, Sydney. Of the other official LMS manuscripts the Candidates' Papers have been invaluable. These fall into two main divisions; letters of recommendation, testimonials, medical and academic reports, and other personal papers and a more regular series of printed questions with answers written by the candidates. These official LMS documents are available on microfilm, at the National Library of Australia, Canberra.

Besides this microfilmed material I have used the large collections of LMS material in the Mitchell Library. The principal collections are the Haweis Papers, many of which were reports sent home by early missionaries and retained in the family after the death of the Reverend Thomas Haweis, 'father' of the South Sea mission; a book of letters entitled South Sea Missions mostly relating to the missionaries Threlkeld, Barff and Buzacott, once in the possession of the Reverend Joseph King; the Hassall Papers and the Papers of Rowland Hassall, which are large letterbooks containing many letters written from the missionaries to New South Wales; and the Papers of J. D. Lang and of Samuel Marsden. The journals of Pitman and some additional journals of Orsmond are also important sources.

The Wesleyan source material is much more dispersed than the LMS material. Because the Australasian Conference took over the Wesleyan missions in the South Seas in 1855, a considerable body of material can be found in the archives of the Methodist Overseas Missions now housed in the Mitchell Library. Many of the official documents relating to the period before

1855 have been given by the Methodist Missionary Society in London to the Mitchell Library, whilst the same library has bought other official material which had been in private hands. The Mitchell Library also has photostat copies of mission papers in London. There are further documents in the Wesleyan archives in Fiji which were not available for my use when the thesis was being written. This material is mostly post-1855 and much of it is duplicated in the reports sent to London. The Mitchell Library possibly possesses a greater number of Wesleyan private diaries than any other institution, and those of Thomas Williams, Richard Lyth and Peter Turner are very comprehensive. I have also been fortunate in having access to a number of papers relating to the Waterhouse family.

In 1958, I was able to work in London on some biographical missionary studies. This gave me the opportunity of reading more widely in the mission archives. The Minutes of the Committee of Examination, South Sea Odds, Personal and Deputation Papers, all since microfilmed, provided further detail. In the Muniments Room of the Wesleyan Methodist Missionary Society I was able to read the papers of the important missionaries Thomas, Hunt and Calvert, and various candidates' papers. Further material was obtained in the library of the late Bjarne Kroepelien in Oslo in 1959. In more recent years I have also been able to draw on other papers from the Haweis collection, mostly in the Nan Kivell holdings of the National Library of Australia. To this has been added material acquired by other Australian libraries or made available to me by descendants of missionaries. Although a considerable amount of this new material has been incorporated in this book, its main use has been to confirm and supplement my earlier findings. The new detail is also of considerable value in expanding our knowledge of various missions and individual missionaries.

Many other missionary manuscripts must still be in private hands. Already the Pacific Manuscripts Bureau, established at the Australian National University in 1968, has acquired microfilms of such material, including the papers of Dr Henry Nisbet of Samoa, located in Canada, and further papers of John Williams. While much of this material does not add greatly to our general understanding, it helps considerably in completing the biographical backgrounds of individual missionaries, the greatest of whom merit full studies. The papers of the more observant or scholarly missionaries are also likely to be of considerable ethnological value.

ADAMS Thomas, Letters 1850-53, copy of original MS, Pac. Hist.
ANON, Extracts from A Private Journal on board H.M.S. Dauntless, January 1822, TS, formerly R.-O'R.
ANON, History of Tonga, formerly owned by Hettie Moulton, TS, Pac. Hist.
ANON, Journal of the Missionaries at Otaheite, 1796-1797, ML, Haweis Supplement, pp. 425-622 (see Haweis).
AUNA (translation by William Ellis), Journal of Voyage to Hawaii May-July 1822, SSJ, no. 62.
AUSTRALASIAN WESLEYAN METHODIST MISSIONARY SOCIETY, Correspondence — Fiji — Rewa, Rotuma, Ovalau, Bau and Miscellaneous, 1855-1879, MOM, item 98.
—— Correspondence of Rev. J. E. Moulton, Rev. J. B. Watkin and Rev. J. Calvert, MOM, item 99.
—— Correspondence of Rev. J. Waterhouse, 1855-1878, MOM, item 100.
—— Fiji — Letters 1855-1903, MOM, item 165.

—— Sundry Correspondence; Minutes, etc. 1855-1912 [mostly Tongan material], MOM, item 166.

—— Letterbook — England 1856-1859 [mostly Eggleston to Hoole], MOM, item 29.

—— Letterbook — Feejee Islands, June 1856 — August 1859, MOM, item 32.

—— Letterbook — Friendly Islands, 1856-1858, MOM, item 30.

—— Minute Book of the Missionary Committee of, appointed at the Conference of 1855, (1855-Dec. 1860), ML, A2808.

—— Mission District Minutes, 1855-1857, 1858-1860, MOM, items 5, 6.

—— Official Letters, London, 1842-1879, MOM, item 97.

—— Tonga: Missionaries' Letters, 1852-1879, MOM, item 170.

BAKER Thomas, Baker Relics (envelope containing documents, photographs, etc.), MOM.

—— Diary (Journal extracts begin 1850), TS, MOM, item 128 (iv).

BALDWIN Dwight, Account of Visit to Society Islands, 1836, SSL, Box 10, VIII A.

BARFF Charles, Account of Buzacott's Labour, LMS, South Seas Personal, Box 1.

—— Account of Voyage to Austral Islands and Anaa, May-June 1846, SSL, Box 19, II E.

—— A Brief Memoir of Mahine, ML, Supreme Court Papers 24, item 83A.

—— A Memoir of Auna translated from a Memoir of him printed in Tahitian 1837, ML, Supreme Court Papers 24, item 106.

—— Journal and Report 1838-1839. (Bound with Memoir of Auna).

—— Journal (extracts) 1819-1820, 1822, 1835, 1837, 1842, 1844-1845, SSJ.

—— Papers, LMS, Miscellaneous Folders No. 9.

—— Translation of the Laws established at Huahine and Maiaoiti 1825, TS, R-O'R.

—— Visit to Samoa in the Dunnottar Castle . . . 1836, SSJ, no. 112.

—— Visit to the Australs, November 1858, SSL.

—— See also under Buzacott and John Williams.

BARFF John, A Brief Statement regarding the Tahitian and Society Islands Missions, July, 1855, SSL.

BELCHER Edward, Private Journals. Remarks. H.M. Ship Blossom on Discovery during the years 1825, 6, 7, Capt. F. W. Beechey, Comdr, from original in Alexander Turnbull Library, Wellington, Pac. Hist. M51.

BICKNELL Henry and HENRY William, Journal, Eimeo . . . 1805, SSJ, no. 24.

BICKNELL Henry and WILSON Charles, Journal . . . Tahiti 1805-1806, SSJ, nos. 25, 28.

BICKNELL Henry and YOUL John, Journal 1803, 1804, SSJ, Nos. 17, 19.

BINGHAM Hiram, Junior, Correspondence 1856-1879, Letters to ABCFM, Harvard College Library.

BLOSSOM Thomas, Life of Mr T. Blossom (c. 1847) copy of MS copy, Hull Reference Library, Pac. Hist.

BOGUE David, Lectures transcribed by J. Lowndes, 9 vols., New College, London.

—— Missionary Lectures . . . transcribed by Robert Moffat 1817, LMS.

BONWICK James, Missionary Transcripts, 1780-1841, 6 vols., ML, BT 49-BT54.

BOURNE Robert and WILLIAMS John, Journal of a Voyage . . . performed by Messrs. Williams and Bourne, in the Schooner Endeavour . . . in the months of July and August 1823, SSJ, no. 67.

BUCHANAN J., KELSO S. and WILKINSON, Tonga Journal 1797-1800, SSJ, no. 4.

BUZACOTT Aaron, Journal to Sydney 1842, ML, SSM, item 74, pp. 349-415.
— Samoan Journal 1836, incomplete, ML, SSM, item 98, pp. 533-602.
— Tahitian Journal, July 1832-August 1832, ML, SSM, item 39, pp. 223-230.
— The Power of Divine Grace as exemplified in the Life and peaceful death of Makea a Chief of Rarotonga, through the blessing of God on Missionary exertions, Rarotonga 1839, SSL, Box 12, VD.
— Visit to Atiu, Mitiaro, Mauke and Mangaia, July-August 1845, SSL.
— Visit to Penrhyn Islands, 1858, SSL.
— Voyage from Rarotonga to Sydney, March-July 1842, SSJ, no. 133.
— Voyage to Navigator's Islands, May 1836-March 1837, SSJ, no. 113.

BUZACOTT Aaron and BARFF Charles, Journal of Voyage to the Out-stations [Hervey Islands and Samoa] in 1834 in the Uliatea, SSJ, no. 104.

BUZACOTT Sarah, Journal Feb. 1830-Sept. 1832, ML, SSM, item 35, pp. 177-214.
— Missionary Reminiscences (Penrhyn Islands and history of the Makea family) 1857, ML, A384.

CALVERT James, Papers, MMS, Biographical: South Seas Boxes 1-4.

CAREY Jesse, Materials for my biography, 1832-1859, (1910), 2 vols., ML, B439.

CARGILL David, Journal 1832-1838, ML, A1817, 1839-1840, ML A1818, 1842-1843, Fiji Museum 5085/37, now in Central Archives of Fiji.

CHARTER George, Journal April 1838-Sept. 1856, LMS, Sydney.
— Journal 1840, SSJ, no. 125.

CHISHOLM Alexander, Visit to the Australs, Sept.-Oct. 1857, SSL.

CHISHOLM Elizabeth, Biographical Notes by Mrs Alexander Chisholm, also TS, LMS.

COLLIS W. Letters . . . 1855-1876, TS, MOM, item 128 (iii).

COLLOCOTT E. E. V., Collection of Tongan Manuscripts, 1845-1929 (15 items including History of 19th Century in Tonga by J. Havili, 3 vols.; Account of beginnings of Christianity in Tonga by Peter Vi; Notes on History and Customs by J. Havea), ML, Parcel 48 (basement).

CREAGH Annie C., A Short Record of the Life and Missionary Work of the Rev. Stephen Mark Creagh and Mrs Creagh in the Loyalty Islands from 1853 to 1901, TS, original in possession of Mrs Dorothy Maynard, Sydney.

CROOK Hannah (Mrs), Journal of . . . from Sept. 1st 1819 to August 1826, ML, MSS 604.

CROOK William Pascoe, Journal . . . 1797 giving experiences at Tongatabu and on voyage to Christiana on ship Duff, ML, Haweis Papers, pp. 603-622.
— Journal, 1816-1817, 1821-1829, SSJ.
— Papers, ML, Ac 6. See also under Greatheed.

CROSS William, Extracts from Letters and Diary, 1838-1842, TS, MOM, item 134; ML, B 686.

CUMING Hugh, Journal of a Voyage from Valparaiso to the Society and the Adjacent Islands performed in the Schooner Discoverer . . . in the years 1827 and 1828, ML, A 1336.

DARLING David, Journal of Voyage to the Outstations, Oct. 1836-January 1837, SSL.
— Marquesan Journal 1834-1835, SSJ, nos. 105-106.

DAVIES John, The History of the Tahitian Mission . . . , LMS, South Seas Odds, Box 6.

—— Journal of a Tour of Morea or Eimeo, commencing April 14th and ending April 20th 1815 with Diary Extracts, March-July 1813, TS, R-O'R.

—— Some Remarks upon the late Misrepresentations of the moral or Religious Change in the South Sea Islands, 1834, SSL, Box 9, VD.

—— Tahitian Journal 1807-1810, 1813-1814, 1816-1818, 1820-1821, 1825-1826, 1845-1846, SSJ.

DAVIES John and YOUL John, Journal and Correspondence with James Elder 1806, SSJ, no. 27.

DAY William, Domestic Correspondence, papers etc., original and transcription by Phillip K. Cowie, Launceston Public Library, Tasmania.

DYSON Martin, Journal 1858-1908, ML, A 2579-A 2582.

—— Papers 1858-1908, ML, A 2583- A 2584.

ELDER James, Journal 1801, also TS, SSJ, no. 11.

—— Journal 1806, Proceedings, SSJ, no. 50.

ELDER James and YOUL John, Journal, 1805, SSJ, no. 25 (ii).

—— Journal, Rio to Port Jackson 1800-1801, SSJ, no. 9.

—— Journal, Port Jackson to Tahiti, 1801, TS, SSJ, no. 11.

ELLA Samuel, Ancient Samoan Government, (1895), ML, A 229.

—— Journal 1847-1851, ML, B 248.

—— Letterbook 1849-1875, ML, A 200.

ELLIS William, Correspondence with missionaries 1832-38, LMS, Home Personal, Box 5.

—— Journal 1817, SSJ, no. 49.

—— Journal, Oahu 1823-1824, SSJ, nos. 65, 72.

FISON Lorimer, Journal, Letters, Memos etc. Pac. Hist. M 120.

FORDHAM John Smith, Memoir of the Rev. John Polglase, Missionary to Fiji (1861), MMS, Biographical: South Seas, Box 6.

GEDDIE John, Diary 1848-1857, original in possession of Mrs J. McLennan, Melbourne, Pac. Hist. M 161.

GILL George and STALLWORTHY G., Journal of Voyage of Deputation in the John Williams to the New Hebrides, Loyalty Islands, Niue, and Fakoaofe, Tokelau Group 1858, SSJ, no. 150.

GILL William, Journal Mangaia 1841, SSL, Box 14, IV D.

GILL William Wyatt, Papers, LMS, South Seas Personal, Box 1.

[GREATHEED Samuel], Account of Marquesas Islands [by W. P. Crook c. 1800], ML, C 111.

GRIMES [John] (Brig Hope), Journal of Voyage from Port Jackson to England, via New Zealand and the Society Islands . . . 1821, SSJ, no. 57.

GYLES John, Journal 1818-1819, SSJ, no. 51.

HANKEY Frederick B., A Journal of the Cruizes and Remarkable Events occurring on board H.M.S. Collingwood, 1844-1846, ML, A 430-1.

HARBUTT William, Papers, LMS, South Seas Personal, Box 1.

HARBUTT W. and DRUMMOND G., Journal of Voyage from Apia in the John Williams, Deputation to New Hebrides, Loyalty Islands and Niue . . . 1857, SSJ, no. 149.

HARDIE Charles, Diary 1835-37, South Sea Missions, etc., ML, A 368.

—— The Eleventh Missionary Voyage to the N. Hebrides and N. Caledonia groups, and Savage Island 1854, SSJ, no. 148.

—— Journal around Savaii . . . 1837, SSJ, no. 116.

HARPER Samuel, A Missionary Journal by Harper, Farmer and Cotton Manufacturer, ML, Haweis Supplement, pp. 295-334.

HASSALL CORRESPONDENCE, vols. 2-4, ML, A 1677-2–A 1677-4.

HASSALL Rowland, Journal 1796-1799, SSJ, no. 2.

—— Journal 1800, LMS, Australia Journals, no. 1.

—— Papers, 2 vols. ML, A 859-A 860.

HAVEA Jotame, Narrative, free translation by Martin Dyson, TS (1868), MOM, item 128 (ii).

HAWEIS Thomas, Autobiography 1735-1796, 1796-1820, ML, B 1176-1177.

—— Fragments of a Diary, ML, B 1178.

—— Journal on board the Duff, Blackwall to Portsmouth, 1796, SSJ, no. 1.

—— Letters 1757-1820, ML, A 3023; Letters to . . . , ML, A 3024.

—— Papers, ML, A 1963; Family Papers, ML, MSS 1961/2.

—— Supplement (Collection of papers relating to early missions to the South Seas 1795-1802), ML, A 1965.

HAYWARD James, Observations on the State of the South Sea Mission . . . 1819, SSL, Box 3, I B.

HAYWARD James and NOTT Henry, Journal 1805, SSJ, no. 25(1).

HAYWARD J., NOTT H., SCOTT W., WILSON C., Journal 1808-1809, SSJ, no. 34(1).

HAZLEWOOD David, Diary, 1841-1844, 1846-1850, also TS, 3 vols., ML, B 568-B 570; MOM, item 132.

—— Diary 1844-1889, MJ, A 2494.

HEATH Thomas, On certain defects and desiderata in the Polynesian Missions of the London Society . . . 1842, SSL, Box 15 VA.

—— Substance of T. Heath's Journal of Visits to several of the South Sea Islands on his return from Sydney to Samoa 1840, SSJ, no. 129.

—— Voyage to Rotumah, New Hebrides, and New Caledonia in the Camden 1840, SSJ, no. 129.

HENDERSON G. C., The History of Government in Fiji, 1760-1875, 2 vols., TS.

HENRY Isaac Shepherd, A Journal containing the religious experience and particular occurances in the life of Isaac S. Henry 1854, ML.

HENRY Teuira, Notes on Tahiti and Hawaii, etc., M.L., A 2611.

HENRY William, Early Days on Tahiti, SSJ, no. 5.

HENRY William and DAVIES John, A Journal of a Tour round both the Islands of Huahine Preaching the Gospel and instructing the Natives, with Observations and remarks on the face of the country 1809, TS, R-O'R.

HOBBS John, Journal 1833-1838; Letters to and from c.1833-1837, from originals in Trinity College Library, Auckland, Pac. Hist. M143, M145.

HOUSE William, Transactions on Board the Armed Colonial Brig Norfolk at Otaheita 1801 and 1802, ML, C 229.

HOWE William, A statement, shewing the present position of the Missionaries of the London Missionary Society in Tahiti 1852, SSL, Box 24, XVIII D.

HUNKIN Matthew, A Journal of a Voyage from Pagopago to Savage Island and back 1840, SSJ, no. 127.

HUNT John, Papers, MMS, Biographical: South Seas, Box 5.

—— Private Journal 1839-1841, ML, A 369, also TS, ML, A 3349; MOM, item 133. 1842-1848, TS, ML, A 3350; MOM, item 135.

HYACINTH, H.M.S., Journal of a Voyage on board . . . 1833, ML, A 429.

INGLIS John and GEDDIE John, Account of New Hebrides Mission, SSL, Box 25, VIII A.

JAGGAR T. J., Journal 1838-1843, 2 vols., Methodist Archives, Epworth House, Suva.

JEFFERSON John, Tahitian Journal 1799-1806, SSJ.

JEFFERSON John and SCOTT William, Journal 1803, SSJ, no. 16.

—— Journal of Journey round Otaheite 1802, TS (incomplete), R-O'R.

JOHNSTON Joseph, Account of Tahiti and Personal Recollections of the Tahitian Mission; Journal 1838-1841 (incomplete), originals in possession of Mrs A. H. Savage, Cottesloe, Western Australia.

JONES John, Notes of Autobiography (1907), ML.

LANG John Dunmore, Papers: Vol. 15, Missions 1826-1877 (includes MS history and correspondence), ML, A 2235. Vol. 6, ML, A 2226; Vol. 20, German Mission Moreton Bay 1837-1867, ML, A 2240.

LAWRY Walter, Diary 1818-1825, TS, ML, A 1973; MOM, item 134.

—— Letters from, 1818-1825 Extracts from Journal, 1825, ML, Uncat. MSS, set 197, item I.

—— Papers 1815-1825, ML, A 402.

LAWRY Mary C. (Mrs), Journal 1822 and 1824, ML, B 860.

LEIGH Samuel, Letters from 1819-1824, ML, Uncat. MSS, set 197, item I.

LEWIS Thomas, Journal, ML, Haweis Supplement, pp. 137-172, 179-182.

LONDON MISSIONARY SOCIETY, Australia Journals, 1800-42 (listed separately), LMS.

—— Australia Letters 1797- , Boxes 1-5 (1797-1868), LMS.

—— Board Minutes 1795- .

—— Candidates' References and Examination Papers, LMS.

—— Correspondence 1795-1837, NLA, Nan Kivell collection, items 2605-42.

—— Documents relating to the Ship Duff 1795-1796, NLA, Petherick MSS 71, Box 2 (item 3).

—— Duff documents, LMS, South Seas Odds, Boxes 2-3.

—— Home Odds (includes Tyerman and Bennet papers), LMS.

—— Home Office Letters 1795- , LMS.

—— Home Personal (includes William Ellis correspondence), LMS.

—— Letters from English Missionaries at Tahiti, 1797-1887, R-O'R.

—— Loyalty Islands Mission, Minute Book 22 June 1857 — 14 November 1877, South Seas Odds, Box 12.

—— Minutes of the Committee of Examination of the Missionary Society 1799- , LMS.

—— Minutes of the Hervey Islands Mission 1845-1874, LMS, South Seas Odds, Box 12.

—— Miscellaneous folders, LMS.

—— New South Wales Auxiliary Minute Book 1853- , LMS, Sydney.

—— Niue Island Church Book 1857- , LMS, South Seas Odds, Box 5.

—— Reports of Committee of Examination, 1796 (Loose sheets), LMS.

—— South Seas Journals 1796- (most listed separately), LMS.

—— South Seas Letters 1796- , 28 boxes, 1796-1860, LMS.

—— South Seas Odds, 16 boxes, LMS.

—— South Seas Personal, 4 boxes, LMS.

—— Tahitian Affairs 1844-1860, Letters and Minutes annotated by Teuira Henry, LMS, South Seas Odds, Box 6.

—— Western Outgoing Letters, South Seas and West Indies 1823-35; South Seas 1835- , LMS.

LYTH Richard Burdsall, Day books 1847-1848, ML, B 535.

—— Journal, vols. 1-4 (1836-1850), ML, B 533-B 536.

—— Letterbooks 1836-37; 1840-41; 1850-53; 1852-55 and Miscellaneous Papers, MMS, Biographical; South Seas Odds, Box 6.

—— Letters to and from 1836-1854, ML, A 836.

—— Lyth Index, ML, B 559.

—— Scrap Book, ML, B 543.

—— Tongan and Feejeean Reminiscences, 2 vols., ML, B 549.

McFARLANE Samuel, Journal 1859-1869, ML, A 833.

McKEAN T. S. Account of the Tahitian Mission, SSL, Box 16, III C.

MARETU. The Autobiography of . . . one of the Early converts to Christianity at Rarotonga and a Teacher of the Gospel in that Island and in Mangaia and Manihiki Islands (c.1821-c.1880), from original in Alexander Turnbull Library, Wellington, Pac. Hist. M.64.

MARSDEN Samuel, Copies of Letters to 1810-1833, relating to the Mission in the Society Islands, transcript from Hocken Collection, Dunedin; ML, A 404.

—— Funeral Sermon for Mr Shelley — 1815, MS copy, ML.

—— Papers, Vol. 4, Letters from LMS 1802-1836, ML, A 1995; vol. 5, Letters from South Sea Missionaries 1810-1836, ML, A 1996.

MEDWAY John, Charge delivered on the occasion of the ordination of George Charter as a missionary to the South Seas 1838, ML, C 701.

MILLS William and Lillias, Letters 1838-52, originals and TS, LMS, South Seas Personal, Box 1.

MORGAN Robert Clark, Camden Journal 1842-1843, ML, A 377.

—— Diary 1829-1831, 1835, 1838-1841, 1844-1852, ML, A 376, B 277, B 278, B 279-1, A 378, B 279-2, A 379, B 280, B 281.

—— Duke of York Journal 1836-1838, ML, A 270.

—— An Extract of a Voyage from Sydney to Sydney again in the Brig Camden 1838-1839, LMS, Australia Journals, no. 3.

—— First Voyage of 1st John Williams 1844-1847, ML, A 373.

—— Journal Entries 1840-1842, LMS, Australia Journals, nos. 4, 5.

—— A Private Journal of a Voyage from England to the South Seas in the Brig Camden 1838-1842, ML, A 572.

—— Second Voyage 1847-1850, 1856-1857, ML, A 374.

—— Third Voyage 1851-1855, ML, A 375.

MULLENS Joseph, A Brief History of the South Sea Mission established and maintained by the London Missionary Society (1878), LMS.

MURRAY, A. W., Journal Extracts 1839, SSL, Box 13, VA.

—— Journal Extracts 1839-1842, SSJ, nos. 122, 124, 128.

—— Voyage from Tutuila to Sydney in the Camden visiting the Loyalty Islands, New Hebrides and New Caledonia 1841, SSJ, no. 130.

MURRAY A. W. and HARDIE Charles, Journal of Voyage 1849, SSL, Box 23, III D.

MURRAY A. W. and SUNDERLAND J. P., Voyage of Deputation from Apia to New Hebrides in the John Williams 1852, SSJ, no. 146.

MURRAY A. W. and TURNER G., Journal of Deputation to New Hebrides and New Caledonia 1845, SSJ, no. 140.

ORSMOND John Muggeridge, The Arioi; War in Tahiti, ML, A 2608.

—— General Report and Account of Society Islands Missions 1830, SSL, Box 7, VI A.

—— General Report 1832, SSL, Box 8, V.

—— General Report 1837, SSL, Box 11, II B.

—— Journal 1816-1817, 1819-1829, 1832-1833, 1837, 1839, SSJ (29 items); 1839, SSL, Box 12, II B; 1840-1848, ML, A 2605 (incomplete).

—— Journal of Voyage to Rurutu, Rimatara and Chain Islands 1839, SSL, Box 12, II A.

—— Letter to Rev. T. Cuzens 1849, 'the Old Orsmond MS,' TS, R-O'R. (page missing from original in ML).

—— Letters from Tahitians 1816-1826, ML, A 2607; 1820-1825, Tahitian II Book (10 Jan. 1826), Kroepelien collection, Royal University Library, Oslo.

—— Miscellaneous Papers, ML, A 2610.

—— Notes on the Mission (includes 'Old Orsmond MS'; Reception of the Gospel: Justification . . . of his attitude towards the French), ML, A 2606.

—— Part of Tahitian Dictionary, ML, A 2609.

ORTON Joseph, Journal 1832-1841, 2 vols., ML, A 1714, A 1715.

—— Letter Book 2 [No. 1 Letter Book 1822-1836], ML, A 1718-1.

—— Letter Book 1836-1842 [No. 4 Letter Book], ML, A 1719.

—— Papers (Journal and notebooks), MMS, Biographical: South Seas, Box 6.

PAPEHIA, Narrative. See J. Williams.

PITMAN Charles, Journal, 1827-1842, 6 vols., ML, A 370-A 372.

—— Letters containing Journal Extracts 1830-1835, SSJ, nos. 99, 103, 108.

PLATT George, Journal 1850, SSJ, no. 145.

—— Journal of Voyage to Outstations [1827] with Reports 1826-1829, SSJ, no. 93.

—— Voyage to the Hervey Islands 1829-1830, SSJ, no. 98.

—— Voyage(s) to the Harvey and Samoa groups, 1835-1836, 1837, SSJ, nos. 110, 114.

PLATT George and KRAUSE E. R. W., Visit to the Australs and Anaa 1845, SSL, Box 18, IV C.

POLGLASE Mary, Diary 1850-1859, TS, MOM, item 128(i).

POWELL Thomas, Journal 851, SSL, Box 24, V C.

PRITCHARD George, Letters etc., Kroepelien collection, Royal University Library, Oslo.

—— Visit to Moorea, Tubuai, Marquesas, in the Olive Branch 1835, SSJ, no. 109.

PRITCHARD George and SIMPSON Alexander, Voyage to Austral and Marquesas Islands 1829, SSJ, no. 96.

PUCKEY William, Journal (March-September 1796); A Journal consisting of a few Remarks, of a Voyage from Portsmouth to the Society Islands in the Great South Sea (Sept. 1796-August 1797) including an account of Tahiti, written June 1797. Copy from original in Alexander Turnbull Library, Wellington; also Pac. Hist. M50.

RABONE Stephen, Journal, 2 vols., ML.

—— Letters to 1856-   , (from Adams and Amos), ML, Uncat. MSS, set 197, item II.

RANSOME Henry, Log of the barque Elizabeth Capt. Edward Deanes 17 April 1831-6 June 1834, 2 vols. ML, A 1481.

REYNOLDS John, Extracts from the Diary of, 1794-1800, TS, LMS.

ROBY William, Lectures on Theology . . . transcribed by Robert Moffat 1817, LMS.

RODGERSON John, Extracts from Journal of a Visit to the Outstations connected with the Windward Mission 1838, SSJ, no. 119.

—— Journal 1839, SSJ, no. 121.

ROYCE, J .H. S., Journal (prefaced, Sydney, 1862), TS, MOM, item 135 A.

S—— W. G., A Record of Missionaries etc. sent out by the Wesleyan Missionary Society from 1769 to 1865, . . . compiled for, and respectfully presented to the General Secretaries, by a Missionary, MMS.

SCHMIDT, C. W. E., Diary 1849-1850, LMS, SSJ, no. 144.

SHEAHAN, G. M., Marquesan Source Material, 2 vols. ML, A 3507.

SHELLEY William, Journal 1800-1801, SSJ, nos. 8, 12.

SIMPSON Alexander, Journal of a Voyage on board the Missionary Brig Camden 1841-1842, SSJ, no. 132.

SLATYER Thomas, Journal of the Proceedings at the Mission Station, Leone, Tutuila, Saluafata or Lufilufe 1840-1845, ML, A 1770.

—— Journal of a Voyage in the Camden from Samoa, among the New Hebrides 1842, ML, A 1770.

SLEIGH James, Papers, LMS, South Seas Odds, Box 1.

[SMITH Joseph], Sentimental Reminiscences, TS and original, formerly called 'Ross MS', Bishop Museum Library, Honolulu.

SOUTH SEA MISSIONS (Letters from LMS missionaries, 1800-   ), ML, A 381.

STAIR John Bettridge, Early Samoan Voyages and Settlements (1895), ML, A 229.

STALLWORTHY George and RODGERSON J., Marquesan Journal 1836, 1837-1839, SSJ, nos. 111, 117, 120.

STEEL Robert, A. W. Murray of Samoa and Mission Pioneering in Polynesia (c.1893), TS, ML.

STEVENS Charles Green, Statement for the Directors on the Political Educational and Religious aspects of Tahiti, 1841, SSL Box 14, II A.

SUNDERLAND J. P., and MURRAY A. W., Journal of Voyage from Apia to New Hebrides and New Caledonia, 1853-1854, SSJ, no. 147.

TAUNGA (trans. by Rev. A. Buzacott), Journal, New Caledonia, 1842, SSJ, no. 135.

THOMAS John, Diary and Letter Book, 1825-1835, ML, A 1959.

—— History of the Friendly Islands (1879), ML, A 1961.

—— Letters of Rev. John Thomas and his wife to parents and friends, 1834-1850, and letters received by them, 1836-1844, ML, A 1960.

—— Papers 1821-75, MMS, Biographical: South Seas, Boxes 7-12.

THOMSON Robert, History of Tahiti, LMS.

—— The Marquesas. Their Discovery and Early History, 1841, SSJ, no. 151.

THRELKELD Lancelot Edward, Journal, 1824-1825, LMS, Australia Journals, no. 2.

—— Memoranda Selected from Twenty Four Years of Missionary Engagements in the South Sea Islands and Australia, 1838, ML, Supreme Court Papers, 27 — Miscellaneous 2.

—— Papers (include Declaration of Mr Bourne and self respecting the Independence of the Leeward or Society Islands, February 1846 etc.) Camden College Library, Sydney.

—— Threlkeld Papers, ML, A 382.

TURNER George, Diary 1837-40, LMS, South Seas Personal, Box 1.

—— Eromanga, notebook signed 13 November 1885, *loc. cit.*

—— Fifty-five years Mission work in Samoa, *loc. cit.*

—— Journal, New Hebrides, with account of flight to Upolu, Samoa 1842-1843, SSJ, no. 134.

—— Report of the Westward Voyage 1859, SSJ, no. 151.

TURNER George and NISBET Henry, Voyage from Upolu to New Hebrides, New Caledonia and Savage Island 1848, SSJ, no. 145.

TURNER Peter, Books read 1832-1873, ML, B 322.

—— A brief account of myself, from my birth to the time when I became a Wesleyan missionary in 1829. Autobiography, ML, B 323.

—— Journal 1830-1855, 11 vols., ML, B 301-B 310.

—— Missionary Papers 1831-1838,ML, A 1506.

—— Sermons 1830-1867, 2 vols. ML, B 317, B 318.

TYERMAN Daniel and BENNET George, Deputation Papers, 1821-1828, LMS, Home Odds, Box 10.

WARNER Gregory, Journal Tahiti 1807-1808, SSJ, no. 32.

WATERHOUSE CORRESPONDENCE. TS copies of original letters from Revs. John, Joseph and Samuel Waterhouse to members of the Waterhouse family, 1840-1876. Originals in possession of Mrs Elma Andrews of Auckland and Dr C. M. Churchward, Sydney.

WATERHOUSE FAMILY, Notes by C. A. M. Hawkins, Sydney.

WATERHOUSE FAMILY PAPERS, ML Uncat. MSS, set 192, item 2.

WATERHOUSE Jabez Bunting, Letters to and from, ML, Uncat. MSS, set 192, item 2.

WATERHOUSE John, Diary to July 1838, TS, original held by Mrs Elma Andrews, Auckland.

—— Letters to 1814-1858, ML, Uncat. MSS, set 192, item 2.

WATERHOUSE Joseph, Correspondence from 1849-1862, ML, Uncat. MSS, set 192, item 2.

WATERHOUSE P. M., Papers, ML, Uncat. MSS, set 192, item 3.

WATERHOUSE Samuel, Correspondence from 1852-1855, ML, Uncat. MSS, set 192, item 2.

WATKIN James, Journal 1830-1839, ML, A 834.

—— Papers, 1832-1855, ML, A 1540.

WESLEYAN METHODIST MISSIONARY SOCIETY, Candidates Papers, 2 boxes. (Box 2, 1832-1857), MMS.

—— Correspondence and Documents relating to the Wesleyan Mission Ship 'Triton', ML, A 421.

—— [Further Candidates' Papers] c. 1839-1850, 8 vols. MMS.

—— In-Letters: Australia and the South Seas, 1818-1836, Photostat copies, ML, A 2827-A 2829, A 2852-A 2839.

—— In-Letters: Fiji, 1836-1854, Photostat copies, ML, A 2860.

—— Letter Book 1822-1855, ML, A 342.

—— Letters from Feejee, 1835-1857, 7 vols. ML, A 2809-A 2815.

—— Log of the John Wesley 1852-1860, 9 vols., ML, A 411- A 419.

—— Minutes of the Committee of Discipline, 1845-1864, MMS.

—— Minutes of . . . the Preachers of the London District for the Examination of Missionary Candidates, 1829-1841, MMS.

—— Missionary Candidates, 1844-[1856], vol., MMS.

—— Records of Wesleyan Mission to New South Wales, 1817-1826, 2 vols. ML, Uncat. MSS, set 197, item 1.

—— Records of Wesleyan Mission to Tonga, 1826-1832, 2 vols. ML, Uncat. MSS., set 197, item I.

—— Synod Minutes (Australia, New Zealand, Tasmania; Fiji, Tonga), MMS.

—— FEEJEE DISTRICT, Minutes and Reports 1835-1852, ML, A 2816.

—— Feejee District, SYDNEY, District Despatch Book, 1826-1856, ML, A 1716-1.

—— SYDNEY, District Letter Book, vol. 3, Island and Miscellaneous, ML, A 1716-2.

—— TONGA DISTRICT, Minutes 1827-1849, ML, B 668.

WILLIAMS John, Account of Visit to Rurutu and Rimatara 1829, SSL, Box 7, I.

—— Journal . . . Papeiha's Narrative 1821-1825, SSJ, no. 59.

—— Journal 1832 (incomplete), SSJ, no. 99a.

—— Journal 1839, SSJ, no. 123.

—— Narrative of a Voyage performed in the Missionary Schooner 'Olive Branch' 1832-1835, SSJ, no. 125.

—— Papers, LMS, South Seas Personal, Box 2.

—— [Statement] Brief Account of his achievements while preparing his Narrative, ML, Aw 41.

WILLIAMS John and BARFF Charles, Journal of a Voyage undertaken chiefly for the Purpose of introducing Christianity among the Feegees and Saamoas 1830, ML, A 403. There is another narrative, an obvious copy, in either Barff's hand or that of one of his children, ML, A 1636. Also TS, SSJ, no. 98a.

WILLIAMS Thomas, Index Rerum (1862), ML, B 499.

—— Journal of the Voyage of the 'Triton' 1839-1840, ML.

—— Letters to 1832-1839, 4 vols., ML, A 852-855.

—— Letters to his father 1839-1843, ML, B 460.

—— Miscellaneous Notes chiefly concerning Feejee and Feejeeans, 1843-1852, 3 vols., ML, B 496-A 498.

—— Mission Work in Fiji, also a copy entitled A short account of the translation of the Bible into the Fijian language, ML, B 459 and B 461.

—— Ordination Charge, ML, B 458.

—— Sketch Book, Rough sketches of places, persons and things, for the most part Feejeean, ML, B 579.

—— See also Whittell Papers, I, pp. 24-81, A 2782.

WILSON Samuel, Papers, ML, A 383.

WILSON William F., The Rev. Charles Wilson of Tahiti (1770-1857). With Notes about his ancestors in Scotland, and descendants in Tahiti, Sydney, Samoa, Fanning Island, Honolulu, England and Canada (192), TS extracts, LMS, South Seas Personal, Box 1.

YOUL John, BICKNELL Henry, and others, Tahitian Journal 1806, SSJ, no. 29.

Select Bibliography of Published Sources

(1) *Periodicals and newspapers with religious affiliations*

The Amulet; or Christian and Literary Remembrancer (ed. S. C. Hall), monthly, London 1826-36.

[Australasian Wesleyan Methodist Missionary Society] *Report*, annual, Sydney 1857+.

—— *The Wesleyan Missionary Notices relating to the Missions under the direction of the Australasian Wesleyan Methodist Conference*, quarterly, Sydney 1857-66.

[British and Foreign Bible Society] *Monthly Extracts from the Correspondence of the British and Foreign Bible Society*, London 1817-58; *Monthly Reporter*, 1858+.

The Children's Missionary Magazine . . . , London 1838.

The Christian Keepsake and Missionary Annual (ed. W. Ellis), London 1835-38.

[Church Missionary Society] *The Missionary Register . . .* , London 1813-55.

The Colonist; or Weekly Journal of Politics, Commerce, Agriculture, Literature, Science, and Religion, for the Colony of New South Wales, Sydney 1835-40.

[Congregational Churches] *The Christian Witness and Church Members Magazine* (ed. J .Campbell), London first series 1844-64.

—— Congregational Year Book, London 1846+.

—— *The London Christian Instructor; or Congregational Magazine*, monthly, London first series 1818-24; *The Congregational Magazine*, new series 1825-36, new series 1837-45; *The Biblical Review and Congregational Magazine* 1846-50.

[Congregational Churches in Australia] *The Southern Spectator; a magazine of religious, philanthropic, social and general literature* (ed. R. Fletcher), Melbourne 1857-59.

The Evangelical Magazine and Missionary Chronicle, monthly, London first series 1793-1822; new series 1823-58; new/third series 1859+.

The Friend, a Semi-Monthly Journal, devoted to Temperance, Seamen, Marine and General Intelligence, Honolulu 1843+.

Goleuad Gwynedd . . . neu'n hytrach Goleuad Cymru, Caerlleon 1818; *Goleuad Cymru* 1820-30.

Hawaiian Spectator, quarterly, Honolulu 1838-39.

[London Missionary Society] *Abstracts of Reports*, annual.

—— *Four Sermons*, annual, London 1797-1820, and *Sermons* 1795.

—— *Juvenile Missionary Magazine*, monthly, London first series 1844-66.

—— *Minutes of the Missionary Society*, monthly, London 1795-[?].

—— *The Missionary Magazine and Chronicle*, monthly, London first series 1836-59, new series 1860-66.

—— *Missionary Sketches*, occasional then quarterly, London 1818-68.

—— *Report of the Directors to the Members of the Missionary Society*, annual, London 1795-1815; *Report of the Missionary Society* 1815+.

—— *Transactions of the Missionary Society*, occasional, London 1804-17, quarterly from 1813; *Quarterly Chronicle of Transactions of the London Missionary Society*, new series 1821-33.

Missionary Magazine, monthly, Edinburgh 1796-[1812].

The Missionary Repository for Youth, and Sunday School Missionary Magazine, London 1839-50.

The New Evangelical Magazine, and Theological Review London 1815-[20].

The Patriot, weekly, London 1832-52.

[Presbyterian Church in New South Wales] *The Christian Herald, and Record of Missionary and Religious Intelligence, etc.* Sydney 1853-55.

—— *The Voice in the Wilderness,* Sydney 1846-52.

[Presbyterian Church in Victoria] *Australian Messenger and Presbyterian Record,* Melbourne 1857-61.

The Samoan Reporter, half-yearly, Leulumoega first series 1845-62.

[Société de Marie] *Annales des Missions de la Société de Marie,* Lyon 1856-60.

The South-Asian Register, quarterly, Sydney 1827-28.

[Wesleyan Methodist Church, Sydney District] *The Australian Magazine; or Compendium of Religious, Literary, and Miscellaneous Intelligence* (ed. B. Carvosso, W. Lawry and R. Mansfield), monthly, Sydney 1821-22.

—— *The Christian Advocate and Wesleyan Record* (ed. W. Hessel and W. A. Quick), monthly, Sydney 1858-61.

—— *The Gleaner* (ed. W. B. Boyce), weekly, Sydney 1847-48; *The Christian Standard,* 1848.

[Wesleyan Methodist Church, Victoria District] *The Wesleyan Chronicle* . . . monthly, Melbourne first series 1857-60.

[Wesleyan Methodist Conference] *The Christian Miscellany and Family Visiter,* London first series 1846-55, second series 1856-76+.

—— *The Methodist Magazine,* monthly, 1798-1821; *The Wesleyan-Methodist Magazine,* third series 1822-44; fourth series 1845-54, fifth series 1855-76+.

—— *Minutes of Conference,* annual.

—— *The Watchman,* weekly, London first series 1835-48, new series 1849-62+.

[Wesleyan Methodist Missionary Society] *Missionary Notices,* monthly, London first series 1816-38, *The Wesleyan Missionary Notices* new series 1839-53, third series 1854-68+.

—— *Papers relative to the Wesleyan Missions, and to the state of heathen countries,* quarterly, London 1820-70.

—— *Report,* annual, London 1818+.

—— *The Wesleyan Juvenile Offering: A Miscellany of Missionary Information for young persons,* monthly, London first series 1844-66.

(2) Books, articles, and theses

ADAMS, Henry, 1947, *Tahiti: Memoirs of Arii Taimai e Marama of Eimeo, etc: Memoirs of Marau Taaroa, last Queen of Tahiti,* ed. with an Introduction by Robert E. Spiller, New York.

ALEXANDER Mary C., 1934. *William Patterson Alexander in Kentucky, The Marquesas, Hawaii, compiled by a granddaughter,* Honolulu.

ANON, *Brief Sketch of the Life and Labours of the late Rev. W. P. Crook, chiefly gathered from his own Writings, and with occasional Extracts from several Publications,* n.p., n.d.

ANON, *Exposé de l'état actual des Missions Evangéliques chez les Peuples infidèles,* Geneva, 1821.

ANON, *History of the Otaheitean Islands from their First Discovery to the Present Time. To which is added an Account of a Mission to the Pacific Ocean, in the years 1796, 97, 98,* Edinburgh, 1800.

ANON, *Missionary Records: Tahiti and Society Islands,* London, n.d.

ANON, *A New Year's Day in the Island of Raiatea, one of the Leeward Society Islands. A Narrative of Facts,* Dublin, 1830.

ANON, *Polynesia: or Christianity in the Islands of the South Sea,* Dublin, 1828.

ANON, *Progress of the Gospel in Polynesia, Southern Group: Georgian, Society, Harvey Islands,* Edinburgh, 1832.

BANNISTER S., 1838. *British Colonization and Coloured Tribes,* London.

BARTLETT C. S., 1880. *Historical Sketch of the American Board in the Sandwich Islands Micronesia, and Marquesas,* Boston.

BARTLEY Nehemiah, 1896. *Australian Pioneers and Reminiscences,* Brisbane, [Robert Bourne].

BAYS Peter, 1831. *A Narrative of the Wreck of the Minerva whaler of Port Jackson, New South Wales . . . ,* Cambridge.

BEAGLEHOLE Ernest, 1957. *Social Change in the South Pacific, Rarotonga and Aitutaki,* London.

BEALE Thomas, 1839 and 1973. *The Natural History of The Sperm Whale . . . to which is added, a Sketch of a South-Sea Whaling Voyage . . . ,* London.

BEBB E. D., 1935. *Nonconformity and Social and Economic Life 1660-1800,* London.

BEECHEY, F. W., 1831. *Narrative of a Voyage to the Pacific and Beering's Strait, to co-operate with the Polar Expeditions: performed in H.M.'s ship Blossom . . . in the years 1825, 26, 27, 28,* 2 vols., London.

BELCHER Edward, 1843. *Narrative of a Voyage round the World, performed in H.M.S. Sulphur, during the years 1836-1842 . . . ,* 2 vols., London.

BENNETT Frederick Debell, 1840. *Narrative of a Whaling Voyage Round the Globe (in the Tuscan) from the year 1833 to 1836 . . . ,* 2 vols., London.

BENNETT James, 1827. *Memoirs of the Life of the Rev. David Bogue . . . ,* London.

BINGHAM Hiram (Junior), 1897. *Story of the Morning Stars . . . ,* Boston.

BINNEY Judith, 1968. *The Legacy of Guilt: A Life of Thomas Kendall,* Auckland.

BIRRELL C. M., 1861. *The Life of the Rev. Richard Knill, of St. Petersburgh. With a review of his character, by the late Rev. John Angell James,* London.

BIRTWHISTLE Allen, 1954. *In His Armour: The Life of John Hunt of Fiji,* London.

BLISS Theodora Crosby, 1906. *Micronesia. Fifty Years in the Island World,* Boston.

BOGUE David and BENNETT James, 1808-12. *The History of Dissenters from the Revolution to the Year 1808,* 4 vols., London. Also second edition by James Bennett, 2 vols., London, 1835.

BONWICK James, 1870. *Curious Facts of Old Colonial Days,* London.

BOUGE L-J., 1952. "Première Legislation Tahitienne. Le Code Pomaré de 1819. Historique et Traduction", *Journal de la Société des Océanistes,* VIII, Paris, pp. 5-26.

BROWN William, 1854. *The History of the Propagation of Christianity among the Heathen since the Reformation,* third edition, 'brought down to a Recent Date', 3 vols., London.

BRUNEL G. (Mme), 1931. *John Williams: Sa Vie et son Oeuvre, 1796-1839,* 2 vols., Cahors.

BUCHANAN Barbara Isabella, 1923. *Buchanan Family Records. James Buchanan and his Descendants,* Capetown.

BULU Joel, see Rowe.

BURDER George, 1805. *Lawful Amusements, A Sermon* . . . , London.

BURTON John Wear, n.d. *The Call of the Pacific,* London.

— 1930. *The Pacific Islands. A Missionary Survey,* London.

— 1949. *Modern Missions in the South Pacific,* London.

BURTON J. W. and DEANE Wallace, 1936. *A Hundred Years in Fiji,* London.

BUSH Joseph (ed.), 1886. *W. O. Simpson, Methodist Minister and Missionary,* London, [Richmond College].

BUZACOTT Aaron, see Sunderland, J. P.

CALVERT James, 1848. *Copy of a Letter addressed to the Rev. Dr. Hannah . . . on the occasion of the death of the Rev. John Hunt . . . ,* Vewa.

— 1855. *Events in Feejee: Narrated in Recent Letters from Several Wesleyan Missionaries,* London. Also second edition (1856) with additions by the Rev. James Calvert and Professor Harvey.

CAMPBELL John, 1840a. *Maritime Discovery and Christian Missions,* London.

— (ed.) 1840b. *The Missionary's Farewell: Valedictory Services of the Rev. John Williams, with his Parting Dedicatory Address, to which is added, an Account of his Voyage to the South Seas, and of his Mournful Death at Erromanga,* London.

— 1843. *The Martyr of Erromanga: or The Philosophy of Missions, illustrated from the Labours, Death and Character of the late Rev. John Williams,* London, 3rd edn.

CAREY Jesse, 1891. *The Kings of the Reefs. A Poem,* Melbourne.

CARGILL David, 1842. *Refutation of Chevalier Dillon's Slanderous attack on the Wesleyan Missionaries in the Friendly Islands in a letter to the Society.*

— 1855. *Memoirs of Mrs. Margaret Cargill, wife of the Rev. David Cargill, A.M., Wesleyan Missionary. Including Notices of the Progress of Christianity in Tonga and Feejee,* 2nd edition, London.

CARNACHAN, Mary A. A., [1955]. *The Spreading Tree: The Story of an Enterprise and a Family,* Auckland, n.d., [Henry and Orsmond].

CARNE John, 1833-34. *Lives of Eminent Missionaries,* 2 vols., London.

CAVE Alfred, 1898. *The Founding of Hackney College,* London.

CHOULES John O. and SMITH Thomas, 1842. *The Origin and History of Missions Compiled and Arranged from Authentic Documents,* 6th edn, 2 vols., Boston.

COATES D., BEECHAM John and ELLIS William, 1837. *Christianity the Means of Civilization: shown in the Evidence given before a Committee of the House of Commons on Aborigines . . . ,* London.

COLWELL James (ed.), 1914. *A Century in the Pacific,* Sydney.

CORNEY Bolton Glanvill (ed.), 1913, 1914, 1919. *The Quest and Occupation of Tahiti by Emissaries of Spain during the years 1772-1776, told in despatches and other contemporary documents: translated into English and compiled, with notes and an introduction,* 3 vols., London, Hakluyt Society.

COULTER John, 1845. *Adventures in the Pacific: with observations on the natural productions, manners and customs of the natives of the various islands; together with remarks on the Missionaries, British and Other Residents,* Dublin.

COUSINS George, 1895. *The Story of the South Seas,* London.

CREIGHTON Louise (Mrs), n.d. *Missions: Their Rise and Development,* London.

CROCOMBE R. G. and Marjorie, 1968. *The Works of Ta'unga,* Canberra.

CULLEN A. H., 1916. *Blazing the Trail: Some LMS Pioneers of 1816,* London.

CUMMINS H. G., 1975. 'Missionary Politicians', *JPH,* X, pp. 105-12.

DARWIN Charles, 1839. *Journal of Researches into the Geology and Natural History of the Various Countries visited by H.M.S. Beagle, under the command of Captain Fitzroy, R.N., from 1832 to 1836,* London.

DAMON Samuel C., 1866. *Puritan Missions in the Pacific: A Discourse delivered at Fort Street Church, on the Anniversary of the Hawaiian Evangelical Association . . . 1866,* Honolulu. Another edition edited and with preface by Hiram Bingham, 1869.

DAVIDSON James W., 1942. European Penetration of the South Pacific 1779-1842, Ph.D. thesis, Cambridge.

—— 1975. *Peter Dillon of Vanikoro: Chevalier of the South Seas,* ed. O. H. K. Spate, Melbourne.

DAVIES John, 1827. *Hanes Mordaith y Parch . . . Rapa, Raivavae, a Tupuai etc.* Llanfair-Caer-Einion.

—— 1851. *Tahitian and English Dictionary,* Tahiti.

—— see Newbury.

DAVIS Elizabeth, 1857. *The Autobiography of Elizabeth Davis, a Balaclava Nurse, daughter of Dafydd Cadwaladyr,* ed. Jane Williams, 2 vols., London, [John Davies].

DAWS Alan Gavan, 1961. 'Evangelism in Hawaii: Titus Coan and the Great Revival of 1837', *Sixty-ninth Annual Report of the Hawaiian Historical Society,* Honolulu, pp. 20-34.

DEBENHAM Frank (ed.), 1945. *The Voyage of Captain Bellingshausen to the Antarctic Seas 1819-1821, translated from the Russian . . . ,* 2 vols., London, Hakluyt Society.

DELESSERT Eugene, 1848. *Voyages dans les Deux Océans, Atlantique et Pacifique 1844-1847 . . . ,* Paris.

DENING, Greg. (ed.), 1974. *The Marquesan Journal of Edward Robarts 1797-1824,* Canberra.

DERRICK R. A., 1946. *A History of Fiji,* Suva.

D'EWES J., 1857. *China, Australia and the Pacific Islands, in the Years 1853-56,* London.

DIBBLE Sheldon, 1843. *A History of the Sandwich Islands,* Lahainaluna.

DIMOND Sidney G., 1926. *The Psychology of the Methodist Revival . . . ,* Oxford.

—— 1932. *The Psychology of Methodism,* London.

DOUGLAS James, 1822. *Hints on Missions,* Edinburgh.

DUMONT D'URVILLE J., 1834. *Voyage Pittoresque autour du Monde,* 2 vols., Paris.

DUNCAN Lundie (Mrs), 1853. *Memoir of Mrs Mary Lundie Duncan . . . ,* Edinburgh.

DUNN Thomas C., [1856]. *A Refutation of the Charges against the Wesleyan Missionaries in the Feejee Islands . . . ,* London.

EASON W. J. E., 1951. *A Short History of Rotuma,* Suva.

EDWARDS O. M. (ed.), 1905. *Gwaith John Davies* [in 'The Peoples' Series], Llanuwchllyn.

ELDER John Rawson (ed.), 1932. *The Letters and Journals of Samuel Marsden 1765-1838,* Dunedin.

—— 1934. *Marsden's Lieutenants,* Dunedin.

ELLIOT-BINNS L. E., 1953. *The Early Evangelicals,* London.

—— 1956. *Religion in the Victorian Era,* London.

ELLIS James J., n.d. *John Williams, the Martyr Missionary of Polynesia,* Kilmarnock.

ELLIS John Eimeo, 1873. *Life of William Ellis, Missionary to the South Seas and to Madagascar, by his son* . . . , London.

ELLIS William, 1831a. *Polynesian Researches during a residence of nearly eight years in the Society and Sandwich Islands,* 2nd edn, 4 vols., London.

—— 1831b. *Vindication of the South Sea Missions from the Misrepresentations of Otto Von Kotzbue,* London.

—— 1832. 'Infanticide in the Islands of the Pacific', *The Amulet,* London, pp. 70-82.

—— 1838. *Memoir of Mary Mercy Ellis,* London.

—— 1844. *History of the London Missionary Society,* Vol. I, London.

ELLISON Joseph W., 1938. *Opening and Penetration of Foreign Influence in Samoa to 1880,* Oregon.

ELWES Robert, 1854. *A Sketcher's Tour round the World,* London.

ERSKINE John Elphinstone, 1853. *Journal of a Cruise Among the Islands of the Western Pacific, including the Feejees and others inhabited by the Polynesian Negro Races, in H.M.S. Havannah,* London.

FANNING Edmund, 1924. *Voyages and Discoveries in the South Seas 1792-1852,* Salem.

FARMER Sarah S., 1855. *Tonga and the Friendly Islands: with a Sketch of their Mission History. Written for Young People.* London.

FERGUSON R., 1839. *Affecting Intelligence from the South Sea Islands. A Letter addressed to the Directors and Friends of Bible and Missionary Institutions in Great Britain and America,* London.

FINDLAY George G. and Mary Grace, 1913. *Wesley's World Parish: A Sketch of the Hundred Years' Work of the Wesleyan Methodist Missionary Society,* London.

FINDLAY G. G. and HOLDSWORTH W. W., 1921. *The History of the Wesleyan Methodist Missionary Society,* 5 vols., London.

FINNEY Charles Grandison, 1910. *Revivals of Religion: Lectures,* London.

FISHER John, 1952. *The Midmost Waters,* London.

FITZ-ROY Robert, 1839. *Narrative of the Surveying Voyages of H.M. Ships Adventure and Beagle, between the years 1826 and 1836* . . . , 3 vols., London [vol. 2, Proceedings of the Second Expedition, 1832-1836].

FLETCHER Joseph Horner, 1892. *Sermons, Addresses and Essays,* Sydney.

FOX Joseph, 1810. *An Appeal to the Members of the LMS . . . with remarks on certain proceedings relative to the Otaheitan and Jewish missions,* London.

FRASER William, 1868. *Memoir of the Life of David Stow; Founder of the Training System of Education,* London.

FREEMAN J. D., 1959. 'The Joe Gimlet or Siovili Cult: An episode in the Religious History of Early Samoa' in Freeman J. D. and Geddes W. R. (eds.), *Anthropology in the South Seas,* New Plymouth, pp. 185-200.

GILL William, 1856. *Gems from the Coral Islands; or, incidents of contrast between Savage and Christian Life of the South Sea Islanders,* vol. I, *Western Polynesia,* vol. II, *Eastern Polynesia,* London.

—— 1880. *Selections from the Autobiography of . . . Being chiefly a record of his life as a missionary in the South Sea Islands,* London.

GILL William Wyatt, 1876. *Life in the Southern Isles; or Scenes and Incidents in the South Pacific and New Guinea,* London.

—— 1876. *Myths and Songs from the South Pacific,* London.

—— 1880. *Historical Sketches of Savage Life in Polynesia with illustrative clan songs*, Wellington.

—— 1885. *Jottings from the Pacific*, London.

GILLIES John, 1845. *Historical Collections relating to Remarkable Periods of the Success of the Gospel, published originally in 1754 . . .* , Kelso.

GILSON Richard P. 1952. Administration of the Cook Islands (Rarotonga), M.Sc. (Economics) thesis, London.

—— 1970. *Samoa 1830 to 1900: The Politics of a Multi-Cultural Community*, Melbourne.

GOODALL Norman, 1954. *A History of the London Missionary Society*, Oxford.

GRAHAM J. A., 1898. *The Missionary Expansion of the Reformed Churches*, Edinburgh.

GRATTAN, F. J. H., 1948. *An Introduction to Samoan Custom*, Apia.

GREGORY William, n.d. *A Visible Display of Divine Providence: or the Journal of a Captured Missionary, designated to the Southern Pacific Ocean, in the Second Voyage of the Ship Duff . . .* ,London.

GRIFFIN John, 1827. *Memoirs of Capt. James Wilson . . . Second American edition with an Appendix, exhibiting the glorious results of the South Sea Mission*, Portland.

GRIFFITH G. Penar, *Hanes Bywgraffiadol o Genadon Cymreig, Wledydd Paganaidd, etc.* [Biographical History of Welsh Missionaries to Heathen Countries, etc.], Cardiff, 1897 [Davies, Jones, Joseph].

GRIFFITHS Rhys Lewis, 1955. *Y Bara Gwell John Davies, Tahiti 1772-1855*, London.

GUNSON W. N., 1954. The Missionary Vocation as conceived by the early missionaries of the L.M.S. in the South Seas, and the extent to which this conception was modified by their experiences in Polynesia, 1797-1839, M.A. thesis, Melbourne.

—— 1960. Evangelical Missionaries in the South Seas, 1797-1860, Ph.D. thesis, Australian National University.

—— 1961. 'The Nundah Missionaries', *Journal of the Royal Historical Society of Queensland*, VI, pp. 511-38.

—— 1962. 'An Account of the Mamaia or Visionary Heresy of Tahiti, 1826-1841', *JPS*, LXXI, pp. 209-43.

—— 1965a. 'Co-operation Without Paradox: A Reply to Dr. Strauss', *Historical Studies, Australia and New Zealand* XI, pp. 513-34.

—— 1965b. 'Missionary Interest in British Expansion in the South Pacific in the Nineteenth Century', *The Journal of Religious History*, III, pp. 296-313.

—— 1966. 'On the Incidence of Alcoholism and Intemperance in Early Pacific Missionaries', *JPH*, I, pp. 43-62.

—— 1969a. 'Pomare II of Tahiti and Polynesian Imperialism', *JPH*, IV, pp. 65-82.

—— 1969b. 'The Theology of Imperialism and the Missionary History of the Pacific', *The Journal of Religious History*, V, pp. 255-65.

—— 1970. 'The Deviations of a Missionary Family: the Henrys of Tahiti', in J. W. Davidson and Deryck Scarr (eds), *Pacific Islands Portraits*, Canberra, pp. 31-54.

—— 1972. 'John Williams and his ship: the bourgeois aspirations of a missionary family', in D. P. Crook (ed.), *Questioning the Past: A Selection of Papers in History and Government*, Brisbane, pp. 73-95.

—— (ed.) 1974a. *Australian Reminiscences & Papers of L. E. Threlkeld Missionary to the Aborigines 1824-1859*, 2 vols, Canberra.

—— 1974b. 'Victorian Christianity in the South Seas: a Survey', _The Journal of Religious History_, VIII, pp. 183-97.

HAM John, 1846. _A Biographical Sketch of the Life and Labours of the late Rev. William Pascoe Crook. Extracted from a Funeral Sermon_, Melbourne [LMS copy with MS. additions].

HANNAH, John, 1853. _A Letter to a Junior Methodist Preacher, concerning the General Course and Prosecution of his Studies in Christian Theology_, London.

HANDY E. S. Craighill, 1927. _Polynesian Religion_, Bernice P. Bishop Museum Bulletin 34, Honolulu.

HARBUTT W., n.d. _Extracts from the Correspondence of Rev. W. Harbutt, Missionary in the South Seas, to a Friend in England_, Bradford.

HARDING George L. and KROEPELIEN Bjarne, 1950. _The Tahitian Imprints of the London Missionary Society 1810-1834_, Oslo.

HARRIS John, 1842. _The Great Commission: or, The Christian Church constituted and charged to convey the Gospel to the World_, London.

HARRISON G. Elsie, 1935. _Methodist Good Companions_, London [Thomas Adams].

HASSALL, n.d. _The Genealogy of the Hassall Family from the Year 1794_, [Sydney]

[HASTLING A. H. L., WILLIS W. Addington, and WORKMAN W. P.] 1898. _The History of Kingswood School . . . By Three Old Boys_, London.

HAWEIS Hugh Reginald, 1896. _Travel and Talk 1885-1895_, 2 vols., London, [vol. II, pp. 190-331, original correspondence].

HAWEIS, T., 1795. 'A Memoir . . .' in _Sermons Preached in London, at the Formation of the Missionary Society . . . 1795_, London.

HAYES Ernest H., 1922. _Williamu, Mariner Missionary, The Story of John Williams_, London.

HAZLEWOOD David, 1872. _A Fijian and English and An English and Fijian Dictionary . . . brief hints on Native Customs, Proverbs, The Native Names of Natural Productions and Notices of the Islands of Fiji, and a Grammar of the Language, with examples of Native Idioms . . . ,_ ed. James Calvert, London.

HENDERSON G. C., 1931a. _Fiji and the Fijians 1835-1856_, Sydney.

—— (ed.) 1931b. _The Journal of Thomas Williams, Missionary in Fiji, 1840-1853_, 2 vols., Sydney.

HENRY Teuira, 1928. _Ancient Tahiti. Based on Material Recorded by J. M. Orsmond._ B. P. Bishop Museum Bulletin 48, Honolulu.

HILL S. S., 1856. _Travels in the Sandwich and Society Islands_, London.

HOLMES F. Morell, 1881. _Exeter Hall and its Associations_, London.

HORNE C. Silvester, 1908. _The Story of the L.M.S., with an Appendix . . . to the year 1904_, London.

HORNE Melvill, 1794. _Letters on Missions: Addressed to the Protestant Ministers of the British Churches_, Bristol.

HOUGHTON Walter E., 1957. _The Victorian Frame of Mind 1830-1870_, New Haven.

HOWITT William, 1838. _Civilization and Christianity: A popular history of the treatment of the Natives by the Europeans in all their colonies_, London.

HUNT James, 1865. 'On the Negro's Place in Nature', _Memoirs Read before the Anthropological Society of London 1863-4_, I, pp. 1-71.

HUNT John, 1846. _Memoir of the Rev. W. Cross, Wesleyan Missionary to the Friendly and Feejee Islands, with a short notice of the early history of the missions_, London.

—— 1853. *Entire Sanctification: Its Nature, The Way of its attainment, and Motives for its Pursuit. In Letters to a Friend,* London.

INGLIS John, 1890. *Bible Illustrations from the New Hebrides,* London.

—— 1887. *In the New Hebrides: Reminiscences of Missionary Life and Work, especially in the island of Aneityum from 1850 till 1877,* London.

IRVING Edward, 1825. *For Missionaries after the Apostolical School, a Series of Orations. In Four Parts,* London.

—— 1865. *Miscellanies from the Collected Writings,* London.

JAMES John Angell, [1819]. *The Attraction of the Cross. A Sermon,* London.

—— 1860-1864. *Works,* ed. T. S. James, 17 vols., London.

JEWETT Frances Gulick, 1895. *Luther Halsey Gulick, Missionary in Hawaii, Micronesia, Japan and China,* London.

[JONES John D.], 1861. *Life and Adventure in the South Pacific By a Roving Printer* [1849-54], London.

JORE Léonce, 1939. *George Pritchard, L'Adversaire de la France à Tahiti, (1796-1883),* Paris.

—— 1944. *Un Belge au Service de la France dans l'Océan Pacifique, Notice Historique et Biographique concernant J. A. Moerenhout,* Paris.

JORGENSEN Jorgen, 1811. *State of Christianity in the island of Otaheite and A Defence of the Pure Precepts of the Gospel, Against Modern Anti-christs, with Reasons for the Ill Success which attends Christian Missionaries in their Attempts to Convert the Heathens. By a Foreign Traveller,* London.

JOURNAL AND PROCEEDINGS OF THE AUSTRALASIAN METHODIST HISTORICAL SOCIETY, 1952. Ed. by Rev. F. H. McGowan, Sydney.

KING Joseph, 1899. *Christianity in Polynesia. A Study and a Defence,* Sydney.

—— 1895. *Ten Decades. The Australian Centenary Story of the LMS,* London.

KISTNER Wolfram, [1948]. *The anti-slavery agitation against the Transvaal Republic 1852-1868,* Groningen.

KNOX R. A., 1950. *Enthusiasm: a chapter in the History of Religion, with special reference to the XVII and XVIII centuries,* Oxford.

KOSKINEN Aarne A., 1953.*Missionary Influence as a Political Factor in the Pacific Islands,* Helsinki.

—— 1957. 'On the South Sea Islanders' View of Christianity', *Studia Missiologica Fennica* (Helsinki), I, pp. 7-16.

KOTZEBUE Otto von, 1830. *A new Voyage round the world, in the years 1823, 24, 25, and 26,* 2 vols., London. Another edition appeared as *Second Voyage 1823-26,* edited by M. Albert-Montemont, in *Bibliothèque Universelle des Voyages,* vol. 17.

LANG Andrew, 1899. 'Are Savage Gods borrowed from Missionaries?' *The Nineteenth Century,* no. 263, pp. 132-144.

LANG John Dunmore, 1834. *View of the Origin and Migrations of the Polynesian Nation; demonstrating their ancient discovery and progressive settlement of the Continent of America,* London. Also second edition, *Origin and Migrations,* etc., 'greatly extended and improved', Sydney, 1877.

LATOURETTE K. S., 1949. *A History of the Expansion of Christianity,* vol. 4, *The Great Century 1800-1914;* vol. 5, *The Great Century in the Americas, Australasia and Africa . . . 1800-1914,* London.

LĀTŪKEFU Sione, 1974. *Church and State in Tonga: The Wesleyan Methodist Missionaries and Political Development, 1822-1875,* Canberra.

LAWRY Walter, 1850. *Friendly and Feejee Islands: A Missionary Visit to*

Various Stations in the South Seas, in the year MDCCCXLVII, etc., ed. by the Rev. Elijah Hoole, London.

—— 1851. *A Second Missionary Visit to the Friendly and Feejee Islands*, London.

LESSON P., 1839. *Voyage autour du Monde . . . sur la Corvette la Coquille*, 2 vols. Paris.

LINGENFELTER Richard E., 1967. *Presses of the Pacific Islands 1817-1867*, Los Angeles.

LOCKERBY William, 1925. *The Journal of, Sandalwood Trader in the Fijian Islands during the years 1808-1809 . . .*, ed. by Sir Everard im Thurn and Leonard C. Wharton, London. [Hakluyt Society].

LOCKLEY G. Lindsay, n.d. An Estimate of the Contribution made in New South Wales by Missionaries of the LMS arriving there between 1798 and 1825, M.A. thesis, Sydney.

LONDON MISSIONARY SOCIETY, 1843. *Exposé des Faits qui ont accompagné l'aggression des français contre l'île de Tahiti.*

—— 1847. *A Reply to the Animadversions of the Rev. Dr. Reed, in his Appeal to the Constituents of the LMS by the Directors of the Society*, London.

LOVE John, 1796. *Addresses to the People of Otaheite, designed to assist the Labour of Missionaries, and other Instructors of the Ignorant, to which is prefixed A Short Address to the Members and Friends of the Missionary Society in London*, London.

LOVETT Richard, 1899. *The History of the London Missionary Society 1795-1895*, 2 vols., London.

[LUCETT E.], 1851. *Rovings in the Pacific, from 1837 to 1849; with a Glance at California, by a Merchant long resident at Tahiti*, 2 vols., London.

LUNDIE George Archibald, 1846. *Missionary Life in Samoa, as exhibited in the journals of the late George Archibald Lundie, during the Revival in Tutuila in 1840-1841, edited by his mother . . .*, Edinburgh.

LUOMALA Katharine, 1947. 'Missionary Contributions to Polynesian Anthropology', in B. P. Bishop Museum Bulletin 193, Honolulu, pp. 5-31.

McFARLANE Samuel, 1873. *The Story of the Lifu Mission*, London.

MARCHAND Léon, 1911. *L'évangélisation des indigènes par les indigènes dans les Iles centrales du Pacifique (de Tahiti à la Nouvelle Calédonie)*, Montauban.

MARLOWE John, 1956. *The Puritan Tradition in English Life*, London.

MARSDEN J. B., n.d. *Memoirs of the Life and Labours of the Rev. Samuel Marsden . . .*, London.

MARSDEN Samuel, 1835. *A Letter . . . to Mr. William Crook; accompanied with a few observations, published in the 'Sydney Herald', by one of Mr. Crook's Missionary Colleagues to the Society Islands*, Sydney.

MARSHALL Thomas William M., 1863. *Christian Missions: Their Agents and their Results*, 2 vols., London.

MARTIN K. L. P., 1924. *Missionaries and Annexation in the Pacific*, London.

MATHESON Jessy J., 1843. *A Memoir of Greville Ewing, Minister of the Gospel, Glasgow, by his Daughter*, London.

MATHEWS Basil, 1915. *John Williams the Shipbuilder*, London.

MAUDE H. E., 1968. *Of Islands and Men: Studies in Pacific History*, Melbourne.

MELVILLE Herman, 1847. *Omoo. A Narrative of Adventures in the South Seas*, London.

MILLER Joseph A., 1847. *Memoir of the Rev. Thomas S. McKean, M.A. Missionary at Tahiti . . . with Introduction by the Rev. Arthur Tidman . . .*, London.

MILLER R. S., 1975. *Misi Gete: John Geddie, Pioneer Missionary to the New Hebrides*, Launceston.

MINNS George B., n.d. *A complete list of the Wesleyan Methodist Missionaries who have served in Tonga*, n.p., [processed 1933].

MOERENHOUT J. A., 1837. *Voyages aux Iles Du Grand Océan*, 2 vols., Paris.

MOISTER William, 1871. *A History of Wesleyan Missions, in all Parts of the World, from their commencement to the present time . . .*, London.

—— 1885. *Missionary Worthies being brief Memorial Sketches of Ministers sent forth by the Wesleyan Missionary Society who have died in the work from the beginning*, London.

MONTGOMERY Helen Barrett, 1906. *Christus Redemptor: An Outline Study of the Island World of the Pacific*, New York.

MONTGOMERY James (ed.), 1831. *Journal of Voyages and Travels by the Rev. Daniel Tyerman and George Bennet, Esq., deputed from the London Missionary Society to visit their various stations in the South Sea Islands, Australia, China, India, Madagascar, and South Africa, between the years 1821 and 1829, compiled from original documents*, 2 vols., London; also one-volume edition, 1840.

MORISON John, 1844. *The Fathers and Founders of the London Missionary Society. A Jubilee Memorial, including a Sketch of the Origin and Progress of the Institution*, London.

MORRISON James, 1935. *The Journal of . . . Boatswain's Mate of the Bounty describing the Mutiny and Subsequent Misfortunes of the Mutineers together with an account of the Island of Tahiti*, with an Introduction by Owen Rutter, London.

MORTIMER T. Favell Lee (Mrs), 1838. *The Night of Toil, or A Familiar Account of the Labours of the First Missionaries in the South Sea Islands . . .*, London.

MURRAY Archibald Wright, 1853. *The Claims of Western Polynesia on the Friends of Christian Missions in the Australian Colonies*, Sydney.

—— 1863. *Missions in Western Polynesia, Being Historical Sketches of these Missions, from their commencement in 1839 to the present time*, London.

—— 1874. *Wonders in the Western Isles*, London.

—— 1876. *Forty Years' Mission Work in Polynesia and New Guinea, from 1835 to 1875*, London.

—— 1880.'Memoir of Mrs. Mills', *Illustrated Words of Grace*, Sydney.

—— 1885. *The Martyrs of Polynesia; Memorials of Missionaries, Native Evangelists, and Native Converts, who have died by the Hand of Violence, from 1799 to 1871*, London.

—— 1887. *Eminent Workers. Some Distinguished Workers for Christ*, London.

—— 1888. *The Bible in the Pacific*, London.

MYERS John, 1817. *The Life, Voyages and Travels of Myers Detailing hr Adventures being Four Voyages Round the World . . .*, n.p.

NEILL Stephen, 1966. *Colonialism and Christian Missions*, London.

NEWBURY C. W., 1956. The Administration of French Oceania, 1842-1906, Ph.D. thesis, Australian National University.

—— (ed.) 1961. *The History of the Tahitian Mission 1799-1830 written by John Davies . . .*, Cambridge, [Hakluyt Society].

NORTHCOTT Cecil, 1939. *John Williams Sails On,* London.

OLIVER James, 1848. *Wreck of the Glide, with Recollections of the Fijiis, and of Wallis Island,* New York and London.

OLMSTED Francis Allyn, 1841. *Incidents of a Whaling Voyage, to which are added Observations on the Scenery, Manners and Customs, and Missionary Stations, of the Sandwich and Society Islands . . . ,* New York.

ORANGE James, 1840. *Life of the late George Vason of Nottingham, One of the Troop of Missionaries first sent to the South Sea Islands by the London Missionary Society in the Ship DUFF . . . 1796. With a Preliminary Essay on the South Sea Islands,* London.

ORCHARD R. K., 'David Bogue, Founder Strategist', *LMS Chronicle,* September 1945, pp. 129-31.

ORLEBAR J., 1833. *A Midshipman's Journal, on Board H.M.S. Seringapatam, During the year 1830; containing Brief observations on Pitcairn's Island and Other Islands in the South Seas,* London.

ORME William, 1825. *An Expostulatory Letter to the Rev. Edward Irving, A.M. occasioned by his Orations for Missionaries after the Apostolical School,* London.

—— 1827. *A Defence of the Missions in the South Sea and Sandwich Islands against the misrepresentations contained in a late number of the Quarterly Review in a letter to the editor of that Journal,* London.

OWENS J. M. R., 1974. *Prophets in the Wilderness: The Wesleyan Mission to New Zealand 1819-27,* Auckland.

PARKER Irene, 1914. *Dissenting Academies in England: Their Rise and Progress and their Place among the Educational Systems of the Country,* Cambridge.

PARSONSON G. S., 1967. 'The Literate Revolution in Polynesia', *JPH,* II, pp. 39-57.

PATON James (ed.), n.d. *The Story of John G. Paton, His Work Among South Sea Cannibals,* London.

PATON John G., 1902. *An Autobiography,* London.

PATTERSON George, [1864]. *Memoirs of the Rev. S. F. Johnston, the Rev. J. W. Matheson, and Mrs. Mary Johnston Matheson, Missionaries on Tanna . . . ,* Philadelphia.

PAULDING Hiram, 1970. *Journal of a Cruise of the United States Schooner Dolphin among the Islands of the Pacific Ocean . . . ,* ed. with new introduction by A. Grove Day, London.

[PEMBROKE George Robert Charles Herbert (Earl of) and KINGSLEY George Henry], 1911. *South Sea Bubbles,* London.

PERKINS Edward T., 1854. *Na Motu: or, Reef-Rovings in the South Seas. A Narrative of Adventures at the Hawaiian, Georgian and Society Islands,* N.Y.

PFEIFFER Ida, 1852. *A Woman's Journey Round the World, from Vienna to Brazil, Chili, Tahiti, China, Hindostan, Persia and Asia Minor . . . ,* London.

PHILLIPS Charles, 1890, *Samoa, Past and Present. A Narrative of Missionary Work in the South Seas,* London.

PICKEN Andrew, 1830. *Travels and Researches of Eminent English Missionaries . . . ,* London.

PIERSON Arthur T., 1895. *The Miracles of Missions or The Modern Marvels in the History of Missionary Enterprise,* Second Series, N.Y.

PIERSON Delavan L. (ed.), 1906. *The Pacific Islanders from Savages to Saints: chapters from the life stories of famous missionaries and native converts,* New York & London.

PIGGOTT, S., 1815. *An Authentic Narrative of Four Years Residence at Tongataboo, One of the Friendly Islands, by Geo. V - - -, who together with 28 other Missionaries was sent there by the London Society in the Ship Duff . . . in 1796, and survived them all; and lived as one of the Natives for two Years . . .* , London.

PIOLET J. B., 1902. *Les Missions Catholiques Françaises au XIXe Siècle,* vol. 4, Paris.

PITMAN Emma Raymond (Mrs), 1882. *Central Africa, Japan and Fiji: A Story of Missionary Enterprise, Trials and Triumphs,* London.

—— 1880. *Heroines of the Mission Field,* London.

PRITCHARD George, 1844. *The Missionary's Reward; or, the Success of the Gospel in the Pacific, with an introduction by the Rev. John Angell James,* London.

PRITCHARD W. T., 1866. *Polynesian Reminiscences; or, Life in the South Pacific Islands . . . ,* London.

—— 1865. 'Viti, and its Inhabitants'; 'Notes on Certain Anthropological Matters respecting the South Sea Islanders', *Memoirs Read before the Anthropological Society of London 1863-4,* vol. I, pp. 195-209; 322-26.

PROUT Ebenezer, 1843. *Memoirs of the Life of the Rev. John Williams, Missionary to Polynesia,* London.

RAMSDEN Eric, 1936. *Marsden and the Missions,* Sydney.

REED Andrew and Charles (ed.), 1866. *Memoirs of the Life and Philanthropic Labours of Andrew Reed, D.D., with Selections from his Journals,* London.

REYNOLDS J. S., 1953. *The Evangelicals at Oxford 1755-1871. A Record of an Unchronicled Movement,* Oxford.

RIGG Charles W., 1863. *A Digest of the Laws and Regulations of the Australasian Wesleyan Connexion,* Sydney.

RIVETT Collinridge, 1956, *The Fabulous Woolpack Story,* Parramatta, [James Elder].

ROBERTSON H. A., 1902. *Erromanga: The Martyr Isle,* London.

ROBINSON W. Gordon, 1954. *William Roby (1766-1830) and the Revival of Independency in the North,* London.

ROWE G. Stringer, [1860]. *The Life of John Hunt, missionary to the cannibals in Fiji,* London.

—— 1871 (ed.), *Joel Bulu: The Autobiography of a Native Minister in the South Seas. Translated by a Missionary,* London.

—— 1882. *Memoir of Mary Calvert,* London.

—— 1885. *A Pioneer: A Memoir of the Rev. John Thomas, Missionary to the Friendly Islands,* London.

—— 1893. *James Calvert of Fiji,* London.

RUSSELL M., 1845. *Polynesia: or, an Historical Account of the Principal Islands in the South Sea, including New Zealand . . . ,* 3rd edn., Edinburgh.

SCHERZER Carl Von, 1861-3. *Narrative of the Circumnavigation of the Globe by the Austrian Frigate Novaro . . . in the years 1857, 1858, and 1859,* 3 vols., London.

SEEMANN Berthold, 1862. *Viti: An Account of a Government Mission to the Vitian or Fijian Islands in the years 1860-61,* Cambridge.

SHEVILL Ian, 1949. *Pacific Conquest: The history of 150 years of missionary progress in the South Pacific,* Sydney.

SHOBERL Frederic (ed.), 1828. *Present State of Christianity, and of the Missionary Establishments for its Propagation in all parts of the World,* London.

SIBREE James (ed. for LMS), 1923. *A Register of Missionaries, Deputations . . . From 1796 to 1923*, London.

SMITH Bernard, 1960. *European Vision and the South Pacific 1768-1850*, Oxford.

SMITH Bradford, 1956. *Yankees in Paradise: The New England Impact on Hawaii*, New York.

SMITH J. W. Ashley, 1954. *The Birth of Modern Education: The Contribution of the Dissenting Academies 1660-1800*, London.

SMITH Thomas, see Choules.

SMITH William, 1813. *Journal of a voyage in the missionary ship Duff to the Pacific Ocean in the years 1796-1802*, N.Y.

SMYTHE W. J. (Mrs), 1864. *Ten Months in the Fiji Islands . . . with an Introduction and Appendix by Colonel W. J. Smythe . . .* , London.

SPOONER T. G. M., 1955. *Brother John. The Life of the Rev. John Hobbs*, Auckland.

SPRAGUE William Buell, 1833. *Lectures on Revivals of Religion, . . .* Glasgow.

STAIR John Bettridge, 1897. *Old Samoa; or, Flotsam and Jetsam from the Pacific Ocean . . .* , London.

Statistics of Protestant Missionary Societies 1861, London, 1863.

STEEL Robert, 1880. *The New Hebrides and Christian Missions*, London.

STEWART C. S., 1832. *A Visit to the South Seas, in the U.S. ship Vincennes, During the years 1829 and 1830 . . . ed. and abridged by William Ellis*, London.

STOCK Eugene, 1899. *The History of the Church Missionary Society. Its environment, its men and its work*, 3 vols., London.

STRACHAN Alexander, 1870. *The Life of the Rev. Samuel Leigh, Missionary to the Settlers and Savages of Australia and New Zealand: with a History of the Origin and Progress of the Missions in those Colonies*, London.

STRONG William E., 1910. *The Story of the American Board. An Account of the First Hundred Years of the American Board of Commissioners for Foreign Missions*, Boston.

SUNDERLAND J. P., 1882. *Memorial Sermon, preached . . . for Mrs. Henry, who died at the Glebe . . .* , Sydney.

— and BUZACOTT A. (ed.), 1866. *Mission Life in the Islands of the Pacific. Being a Narrative of the Life and Labours of the Rev. Aaron Buzacott, Missionary of Rarotonga . . .* , London.

SWAN William, 1830. *Letters on Missions. With an Introductory Preface by William Orme*, London.

TA'UNGA, See Crocombe.

TAYLOR E. R., 1935. *Methodism and Politics 1791-1851*, Cambridge.

TAYLOR William George, 1920. *The Life Story of an Australian Evangelist . . .* , London.

TELFORD John, [1906]. *A Short History of Wesleyan Methodist Foreign Missions*, London.

THOMPSON A. T., 1935. *Australia and the Bible. A brief outline of the work of the British and Foreign Bible Society in Australia 1807-1934*, London.

THOMSON Basil, 1908. *The Fijians. A Study of the Decay of Custom*, London.

THRELKELD L. E., 'Reminiscences', in *The Voice in the Wilderness* (Feb.-Nov. 1852) and *The Christian Herald . . .* , (Feb. 1853-1855).

—— 1835. 'Traits of the Aborigines of New South Wales', *The Christian Keepsake and Missionary Annual*, pp. 301-6.

—— See Gunson.

TIBBUTT H. G., 1957. 'The Dissenting Academies of Bedfordshire', *Bedfordshire Magazine*, V, pp. 321-3, VI, pp. 8-10, 84-6.

TILLEY Henry Arthur, 1861. *Japan, the Amoor, and the Pacific. A Voyage of Circumnavigation in the Imperial Russian Corvette 'Rynda', in 1858-1860*, London.

TIPPETT A. R., 1954. *Cakobau Papers*, Suva.

—— 1971. *People Movements in Southern Polynesia: Studies in the Dynamics of Church-planting and Growth in Tahiti, New Zealand, Tonga, and Samoa*, Chicago.

—— n.d. *The Christian (Fiji 1835-67)*, [Auckland].

TOPLADY Augustus, 1794. *Works*, 6 vols., London.

TROOD Thomas, 1912. *Island Reminiscences: A graphic, detailed Romance of a Life spent in the South Sea Islands*, Sydney.

TURNBULL John, 1805. *A Voyage Round the World in the years 1800, 1801, 1802, 1803, and 1804; in which the Author visited the principal Islands in the Pacific Ocean, and the English Settlements of Port Jackson and Norfolk Island*, 3 vols., London.

TURNER George, 1861. *Nineteen Years in Polynesia: Missionary Life, Travels and Researches in the islands of the Pacific*, London.

—— 1884. *Samoa, A Hundred Years Ago and Long Before, together with Notes on the Cults and Customs of Twenty Three other islands in the Pacific . . .* , London.

TURNER J. G., 1872. *The Pioneer Missionary: Life of the Rev. Nathaniel Turner, Missionary in New Zealand, Tonga and Australia*, Melbourne.

TYERMAN D. and BENNET G., see Montgomery.

THE UNIVERSAL NAVIGATOR, AND MODERN TOURIST . . . , London, 1805 [contains accounts of first and second voyages of the *Duff* and 'proceedings of the missionaries'].

VAN DEN BERG Johannes, 1956. *Constrained by Jesus' Love: An Inquiry into the Motives of the Missionary Awakening in Great Britain in the Period between 1698 and 1815*, Kampen.

VERNIER Ch., 1934. *Tahitiens D'Autrefois: Tahitiens D'Aujourd'hui*, Paris.

VERNON R., [1892]. *James Calvert; or, From Dark to Dawn in Fiji*, London, n.d.

VINCENDON-DUMOULIN M. M. and DESGRAZ C., 1844. *Iles Taiti Esquisse Historique et Géographique . . .* , 2 vols., Paris.

WALDEGRAVE W., 1834. 'Extracts from a Private Journal kept on board H.M.S. Seringapatem, in the Pacific, 1830', *Journal of the Royal Geographical Society of London*, III, pp. 168-96.

—— 1836. 'Notices of Tahiti and Eimeo', *The Christian Keepsake and Missionary Annual*, pp. 73-9.

WALLIS Mary Davis (Mrs), 1851. *Life in Feejee: or Five Years Among the Cannibals*, Boston.

WALPOLE Frederick, 1849. *Four Years in the Pacific in H.M.S. 'Collingwood' from 1844-1848*, 2 vols., London.

WARD John M., 1948. *British Policy in the South Pacific 1786-1893*, Sydney.

WARNECK Gustav, 1906. *Outline of a History of Protestant Missions from the Reformation to the Present Time . . .* , London.

WARNER Wellman J., 1930. *The Wesleyan Movement in the Industrial Revolution*, London.

WARREN Jane S., 1860. *The Morning Star: History of the Children's Missionary Vessel, and of the Marquesan and Micronesian Missions,* Boston.

WARREN Max, 1965. *The Missionary Movement from Britain in Modern History,* London.

—— 1967. *Social History and Christian Mission,* London.

WATERHOUSE —, 1937. *A Brief Account of the Life and Activities of Rev. John Waterhouse more particularly from the time of his arrival in Van Dieman's Land until his death,* Sydney.

WATERHOUSE John, [1842]. *Journal of a Second Voyage from Hobart-Town, Van-Dieman's Land, to the Polynesian Islands, commenced Wednesday, October 28th, 1840,* n.p.

WATERHOUSE Joseph, 1866. *The King and People of Fiji: containing a Life of Thakombau . . . previous to the Great Religious Reformation in 1854,* London.

WATSFORD John, 1900. *Glorious Gospel Triumphs as seen in My Life and Work in Fiji and Australasia,* London.

WATSON Charles H., 1926. *Cannibals and Head-Hunters: Victories of the Gospel in the South Seas,* Washington.

—— 1931. *Adventures in the South Seas,* Washington.

WEARMOUTH Robert F., 1937. *Methodism and the Working-Class Movements of England 1800-1850,* London.

—— 1945. *Methodism and the Common People of the Eighteenth Century,* London.

—— 1948. *Some Working Class Movements of the Nineteenth Century,* London.

—— 1954. *Methodism and the Struggle of the Working Classes 1850-1900,* Leicester.

WEST Thomas, 1860. *Hafoka: A Missionary Tale of the South Sea Islands,* London.

—— 1865. *Ten Years in South-Central Polynesia: Being Reminiscences of a Personal Mission to the Friendly Islands and their Dependencies,* London.

WHEELER Daniel, 1842. *Memoirs of the Life and Gospel Labours of the late Daniel Wheeler, a Minister of the Society of Friends,* London.

WHITE M. S. (Mrs), 1877. *Memoir of Mrs. Jane Tucker, wife of the Rev. Charles Tucker, Some time Missionary to Haabai and Tonga . . . ,* London.

WILKES Charles, 1845. *Narrative of the United States Exploring Expedition. During the years 1838, 1839, 1840, 1841, 1842 . . . ,* 5 vols., Philadelphia.

WILKS Mark, 1844. *Tahiti: A review of the origin, character and progress of French Roman Catholic efforts for the destruction of English Protestant missions in the South Seas . . . ,* London.

WILLIAMS Charles, 1828. *The Missionary Gazetteer; comprising a Geographical and Statistical Account of the Various Stations of the Church, London, Moravian, Wesleyan, Baptist, and American Missionary Societies . . . with their Progress in Evangelization and Civilization,* London.

WILLIAMS John, 1835. 'Missionary Perils', *The Christian Keepsake and Missionary Annual,* pp. 275-84.

—— 1837. *A Narrative of Missionary Enterprises in the South Sea Islands,* London.

WILLIAMS Samuel Tamatoa, 1847. *An Appeal to British Christians, and public generally, on behalf of the Queen of Tahiti and her outraged subjects . . . 1844,* London.

WILLIAMS Thomas and CALVERT James, 1870. *Fiji and the Fijians:*

Missionary Labours among the Cannibals, ed. by George Stringer Rowe, 3rd edn, London.

WILLIAMSON Alex., 1885. *Missionary Heroes in the islands of the Pacific,* Edinburgh.

WILLIAMSON Robert W., 1937. *Religion and Social Organization in Central Polynesia,* ed. by Ralph Piddington, Cambridge.

[WILSON James], 1799. *A Missionary Voyage to the Southern Pacific Ocean, performed in the years 1796, 1797, 1798, in the Ship Duff, commanded by Capt. James Wilson compiled from Journals of the Officers and the Missionaries . . . with a Preliminary Discourse,* London.

WOOD A. Harold, 1975. *Overseas Missions of the Australian Methodist Church, Volume I, Tonga and Samoa,* Melbourne.

WOOD Arthur Skevington, 1957. *Thomas Haweis 1734-1820,* London.

WORSLEY Peter, 1957. *The Trumpet Shall Sound. A Study of 'Cargo' Cults in Melanesia,* London.

WRIGHT Louis B. and FRY Mary Isabel, 1935. 'Puritanism in the South Seas', *The Atlantic Monthly,* CLV pp. 89-99.

—— 1936. *Puritans in the South Seas,* New York.

YONGE Charlotte Mary, 1874a. *Life of John Coleridge Patteson, Missionary Bishop of the Melanesian Islands,* 2 vols., London.

—— 1874b. *Pioneers and Founders, or Recent Workers in the Mission Field,* London.

YOUNG Robert, 1855. *The Southern World: Journal of a Deputation from the Wesleyan Conference to Australia and Polynesia, including Notices of a Visit to the Gold Fields,* London. Also 1858 edition.

YOUNG W. Allen, 1922. *Christianity and Civilization in the South Pacific. The influence of missionaries upon European expansion in the Pacific during the Nineteenth Century,* London.

Index

An asterisk following a personal name indicates a separate biographical entry in either Appendix IV or V. The names in these lists and the endnotes have not been indexed unless also mentioned in the text.